Wayne County, Nebraska, Newspaper Abstracts 1876-1899

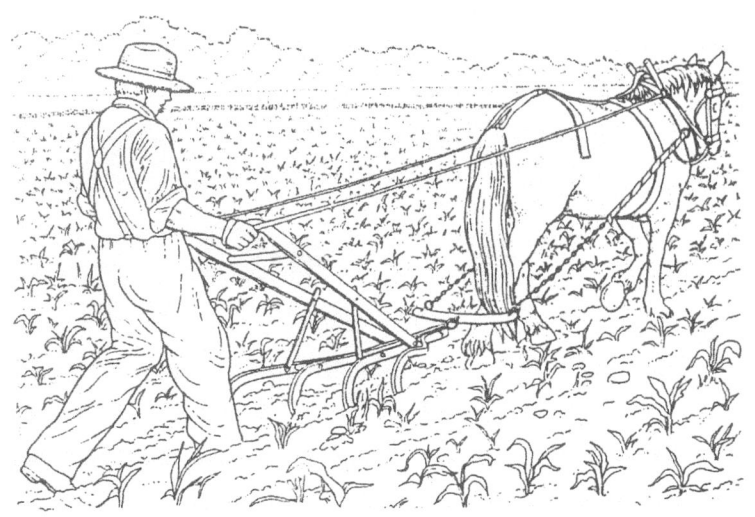

Compiled by
Marueen M. Lee

HERITAGE BOOKS
2008

HERITAGE BOOKS
AN IMPRINT OF HERITAGE BOOKS, INC.

Books, CDs, and more—Worldwide

For our listing of thousands of titles see our website at
www.HeritageBooks.com

Published 2008 by
HERITAGE BOOKS, INC.
Publishing Division
100 Railroad Ave. #104
Westminster, Maryland 21157

Copyright © 2008 Maureen M. Lee

Other books by the author:

Potter County, Pennsylvania Potpourri, Volume 1, The Years 1880-1884
Township Tidings, from Potter County, Pennsylvania, Volume 1, 1880-1884

All rights reserved. No part of this book may be reproduced or transmitted in any form or by any means, electronic or mechanical, including photocopying, recording or by any information storage and retrieval system without written permission from the author, except for the inclusion of brief quotations in a review.

International Standard Book Numbers
Paperbound: 978-0-7884-1175-5
Clothbound: 978-0-7884-7100-0

TABLE OF CONTENTS

Introduction	v
List of Newspapers	vi
Wayne County Review Abstracts	1
Logan Valley Herald Abstracts	8
Wayne Herald–Tribune Abstracts	56
The Wayne Herald Abstracts	121
The Wayne Journal Abstracts	153
The Wayne Republican Abstracts	154
Index	509

Introduction

Wayne County, located in northeast Nebraska, was first settled by the white man in May 1869, when a group of farmers, mostly from Illinois, established their homesteads in the eastern part of the county. Not long after, in the spring of 1870, a German settlement was established in the southwestern portion of the county, at what is now the area in and around Hoskins.

Wayne County was officially organized in 1870, the town of La Porte serving as the county seat. When the railroad bypassed La Porte in favor of Wayne (then called Brookdale) four miles west and two miles north, many of La Porte's residents and merchants soon followed, and Wayne became the county seat in 1884.

The qualities of the early white settlers to Wayne County ran parallel to those of other immigrants; they possessed a strong desire to provide a better life for their families, an industrious work ethic, and the selfless willingness to help their neighbors and friends. They placed their fate in God's hands, believing that through hard work and faith they could, if not greatly prosper, at least improve the conditions in which they lived.

From these early days over a century ago, when the miles of endless, treeless prairie seemed hypnotic, to the present fertile, cultivated and growing county of Wayne, the attitudes of the descendants of the early settlers, and those who have adopted Wayne County as their home, have remained unchanged.

Wayne County, Nebraska, Newspaper Abstracts, 1876-1899 has been compiled to provide a glimpse into the earliest history of the white man's settlement in Wayne County.

Using available microfilmed newspapers, this compilation contains, among other things, birth, marriage and death notices, suicides, homicides, crimes, information relating to the early merchants and businesses, election results, tax-payer lists, soldier lists, school honor rolls, church and society information, county commissioner proceedings, court proceedings, real estate transfers and celebrations and special events.

Although many issues are missing, and some of the surviving newspapers are badly damaged and illegible, newspapers remain an often overlooked vital research tool for those wishing to glean either genealogical information about the early inhabitants of the county or to understand the county's early history.

List of Newspapers

Wayne County Review   August 17, 1876 -
                           August 25, 1876

Logan Valley Herald   January 4, 1884 -
                           August 8, 1884

Wayne Herald-Tribune   August 15, 1884 -
                           December 10, 1885

Wayne Herald   January 5, 1888 -
                           June 21, 1888

Wayne Journal   November 30, 1892

Wayne Republican   August 17, 1895 -
                           December 27, 1899

Wayne County Review
August 17, 1876 (Vol. 2, No. 3)

Wayne County Directory:
   Commissioners: Joseph BOEKENHAUER, Charles
       ERXLEBEN, and I.O. RICHARDSON.
   Clerk: R. B. CRAWFORD
   Treasurer: Solon BEVINS
   Sheriff: J.W. AGLER
   County Judge: E.P. THOMPSON
   Surveyor: John T. BRESSLER

History of Wayne County Neb.
BY R.B. CRAWFORD, M.D.

    Having been honored with an appointment to write the history of Wayne county, I reluctantly accept the task, believing that abler hands might have been selected to pen paint many interesting incidents connected with the early settlement of this beautiful and fertile county but asking the forbearance of Criticism by those who for the past seven years have shared the many ups and downs incident to a pioneers life in the west, I will proceed to give such facts as I may be able to gather from various sources, and which I hope may in a measure prove interesting.
    Wayne county is situated in the northeastern part of the State and is bounded on the north by Cedar and Dixon counties; on the east by Dixon county, the Winnebago and Omaha Indian Reservation; on the south by Cuming and Stanton counties; and on the west by Pierce county.
    Geographically it is in latitude forty-two degrees north, and in longitude ninety-seven degrees west, and has an area of 444 square miles.
    The county is wholly a beautiful undulting prairie, with a dark rich, alluvial soil; and not five acres of waste or poor land can be found within its borders.
    The streams are the Logan creek, Plum creek, Coon creek, with a few others of miner importance; but the principal one is the Logan; which is really a beautiful stream, rising near the southwest corner of the county it meanders along with many a crook and turn, in a northeasterly direction receiving on its way several tributaries from the west and north, and eventually leaving the county about two miles south of the northwest corner. The stream has high abrupt banks, and swift current, and supplied with an abundance of fine fish. Eventually, and probably ere long the banks of this stream will be dotted with mills and factories, for

such superior water power as the Logan presents, will not long remain without being utilized.

Game of nearly all kinds, has been, and is still very abundant, and the hunstman here find rare sport in pursuing the chase.

For a few years previous to organization the territory now comprising this county was under the jurisdiction of Dixon county for judicial purposes, but during the summer of 1870 a petition was circulated through the county, signed and presented to Hon. David BUTLER, then Governor of the State, and he in accordance with law, ordered an election which was held at the house of George SCOTT on Coon creek in the eastern part of the county, on the 5th day of September, A.D. 1870, and the following named persons elected for officers.

For County Commissioners, W.E. DURIN, M.T. SPERRY, and Isaac MINER.
County Clerk, C.E. HUNTER.
County Treasurer, B.F. WHITTEN.
Sheriff, A.D. ALLEN.
Probate Judge, A.A. FLETCHER.
County Surveyor, Wm. G. VROMAN.
Supt. Pub. Ins't, R.B. CRAWFORD
Coroner, Nathan ALLEN

Judges of Election, Geo. HUNTER and Geo. SCOTT. Nearly all who were elected qualified and entered upon the duties of their several offices, B.F. WHITTEN failing to qualify for Treasurer Geo. SCOTT was appointed to fill the vacancy.

The first action for the erection of a building in which to do county business was taken April 19th 1871, and a house 18 by 24 feet in size was soon thereafter erected near the present town site of La Porte, at a cost of about three hundred and fifty dollars.

Previous to the erection of said building the books and papers belonging to the county were kept at the residence of the different officers, and the transaction of a small amount of business often required many miles of travel.

After the building was completed, it was occupied by the Treasurer and Clerk, and the transaction of county business became more systematic and convenient. On the 24th day of February, 1874, at a special election, bonds to the amount of fifteen thousand dollars were voted for the erection of a brick Court House, 40 by 50 feet in size, and on the 16th day of May the contract for building was let to John P. WALL for $7,993 but he failing to give bonds, the contract was awarded to SAWYERS and LEACH of Covington, for $11,993, and the building was completed by them Dec. 8th 1874, and has since been occupied by the county officers and used for county general purposes. The building is located on the public square in the town of La Porte the county seat, and is one of the finest in the State.

The first town site was laid out May 22nd, 1874, by Solon BEVINS, on his land, on the north half of the northwest quarter of the northwest quarter of section 25 in township 26 north of range 4 east, and was named, and is known as La Porte.

This town, besides being the first located in the county, is the county seat, and with a beautiful, and fertile country surrounding it, and a railroad soon to pass through, it is destined to become a business town of marked importance.

The first house in the county was built by B.F. WHITTEN about the 1st of April 1869, and he has the honor of being the first white man to settle in the county.

During the month of May 1869, a small colony came from Illinois and settled in the eastern part of the county, most of whom took homesteads on Coon creek, and after building their sod "dug outs," did some breaking, and made such improvements as would best meet the exigencies of a pioneer life.

From this date the actual settlement of the county began, and of this little band, who first braved the hardships of the actual settler on the western wilds; nearly all remain; possessed of a good farm and proud title "The pioneers of Wayne county."

In the spring of 1870 a colony of Germans settled in the southwest township of the county, on Spring branch, which colony has since been steadily increasing in number and is now a thriving and prosperous settlement.

Stock of nearly all kinds have been brought in but farming has been the principal avocation of most of the settlers.

The first census was taken by Geo. HUNTER in the spring of 1870, and showed a total population of 180. The first assessment after the organization of the county was made in March 1871, and showed the valuation of personal property to be $8,640, and of real estate, $319,500, total valuation $328,140.

This assessment of 1876 shows the valuation of personal property to be $13,329.09 and of real estate $563,722.62, and of town lots $900.00; making a total of $577,951.51, and a gain of $149,811.61 since 1871. There was deducted from the above valuation $5,900 for 87 acres of trees now under a fine state of cultivation in different parts of the county, which, if added, would make our actual gain $155,911.51. The census returns of 1876 shows the natority of the present inhabitants to be as follows, viz from Germany 62, Illinois 38, Nebraska 55, England 3, Canada 10, Pennsylvania 20, Ohio 4, Indiana 7, New York 15, Maine 2, Vermont 6, Denmark 16, Michigan 7. *Continued next week.*

• • •

SOLON BEVINS
TREASURER OF WAYNE CO.
NEBRASKA,

• • •

E. P. THOMPSON
COUNTY JUDGE,
Office in the Court House, La Porte
Wayne County, Nebraska

• • •

JAMES BRITTON
Attorney at Law.
LA PORTE   NEBRASKA

• • •

R. B. CRAWFORD, M.D.
ECLECTIC PHYSICIAN,
OFFICE
At Residence, La Porte, Wayne Co, Nebraska

• • •

CENTENNIAL HOUSE
LA PORTE   NEBRASKA
J.E. HARMON, PROP.
Stages leave for all points
North, South and East.

• • •

R.B. CRAWFORD
Clerk of Courts and Recorder
La Porte   Nebraska

• • •

C.E. HUNTER
REAL ESTATE AGENT

Wayne County Review
August 25, 1876 (Vol. 2, No. 4)

History of Wayne County Neb.
BY R.B. CRAWFORD, M.D.
(continued from last week)

Iowa 9, Scotland 2, Wisconsin 31, New Jersey 5, Minnesota 2, Dist. of Columbia 1, Norway 1, Virginia 1, Ireland 1, Kentucky 1. The occupation as shown by the report is 71 farmers, 2 carpenters, 1 physician, 1 attorney, and 2 blacksmiths. The number who could neither read or write 3. The first wedding which took place in the county was M.T. SPERRY, age 25 years, and Miss Sarah EAYRS, aged 20, on May 14th, 1871, A.A. FLETCHER, Probate Judge officiating. Since then there has been eleven marriages consumated making a total of twelve.

The first child born in the county was a son to Mr. and Mrs. Charles PHILLIPS on the first day of June, 1869, near the Logan bridge in the eastern part of the county. The first death was a son of Mr. and Mrs. Wm. VROMAN, who died Aug. 6th, 1870, aged 8 months. Seventeen deaths have occured since making a total of 18 in all.

The first sermon was preached by Mrs. M.B. RICHARDSON at the residence of Alex SCOTT, the last of September, 1870.

The first law suit occured in June, 1871, before George HUNTER, J.P.

The first blacksmith shop in the county was put up in the summer of 1869 on what is now known as the old MINER place in the eastern part of the county, near Logan creek, and consisted of a sod forge, a pair of bellows, a pair of tongs, an anvil and hammer; the tools belonged to Willard GRAVES, and every man who had work to do was his own blacksmith. Since then shops have been put up in several places, but that of Wm. P. AGLER who is now doing business at La Porte, is the principal one.

The first regular practicing physician was R.B. CRAWFORD M.D. who came here the first of June, 1869 and who has been since, and is now the only practicing physician in the county.

The first serious case requiring a surgical operation occurred in February, 1873, to A.S. MINER, who had a portion of both feet amputated on account of freezing. G.W. WILKINSON M.D. from Dakota City performing the operation.

The first general celebration was held on the 4th day of July, 1871, near the present town site of La Porte, and was entered into with a spirit, and enthusiasm, which made it a day that will be remembered with pleasure as long as the memory of the earliest settlers shall last. Since that time several celebrations have been held, and the spirit of 1776 manifested in a manner to do honor to the sires who fought, and died for the freedom, which we now enjoy.

The first map of the county, showing the boundary lines, the location of streams, and the general features of the land, was drawn and furnished the county by Wm. G. VROMAN, on the 6th day of March 1871, and for which he was paid twenty dollars.

The first store was opened up in June, 1872, and kept by C.E. HUNTER and Solon BEVINS in the west end of the old county building, near the present town of La Porte.

The first school district included the whole county and was organized Feb. 11th 1871, and was known as school district No. 1. The first school meeting was held Feb. 11th 1871, at the residence of C.E. HUNTER, and the following officers elected, viz: A.A. FLETCHER moderator, A.S. MINER director, and George SCOTT treasurer; the whole number of votes present being nine. In April, 1871 the county was divided into three school districts, in May 1872 into six and again July 1st 1876 into nine. The first census returns made March 21st 1871 showed the whole number of children between the ages of five, and twenty-one years, to be fifty; twenty-seven females, and twenty-three males.

The first teacher examined was Miss Jane OLIN July 1st 1871 who was granted a third grade certificate, and taught the first school in district No. 2 during the same summer. The first school house was built in school district No. 3, in October 1871, the contractor was Solon BEVINS and the contract price was $1,400 in district orders. Since then five more good substantial school buildings have been erected, which are all used, and a credit to the county. No church has yet been built, but public worship is held in the various school houses, and at private residences.

The first Post Office was established Sept. 8th 1870 near the Logan bridge in the eastern part of the county and was called Toffe, Wm. P. AGLER was appointed Post Master and held the office until October 1871, when he moved to his farm and O.F. CRANE was appointed to fill his place; he holding the office until Jan 27th 1874, when it was discontinued.

The second P.O. was established at La Porte Feb 21st 1871 with C.E. HUNTER Post Master.

This office receives a daily mail from the north, east, south and west, and being located in the center of a large settlement is readily reached by all. A post office was established at Leslie Dec. 18th 1871, on the mail route from West Point to Ponca, in tp. 25, range 5, with Joseph BOEKENHAUER, post master who held the office until April 12th 1875 when J.W. MAHOLM was appointed to fill the vacancy caused by the resignation of Mr. BOEKENHAUER. The office and mail route was discontinued Oct. 12th 1875.

The first printing press brought in, and operated in the county, was by C.E. HUNTER Aug. 5th 1876, and he has the honor of publishing the first paper printed in the county, viz. THE WAYNE COUNTY REVIEW.

It is a weekly paper devoted to the interest of Wayne county and deserves the unanimous support of the people.

The finance of the county is in an excellent condition, warrants on all the county funds are at par and have been since the organization of the county, except for a short time during 1871.

Thus it will be seen from the few statistics given that Wayne county has made sure and positive progress. With present prospects for facilities, and the many superior inducements held out to the actual settler, this county will soon stand in the front ranks with any in the State.

None but those who have had actual experience in the western pioneer life can judge of the pains and pleasures incident to establishing a home on the verge of the borders of civilization.

The picturesque scenery which meets the gaze at almost every step fills the heart with awe, and wonder and thrills the very soul with emotions, which neither pen can paint, or words describe. Here the mind untrammeled with the din and noise of the city can roam o'er the past, and reach forward to the future, and plan for the present with all that freedom which gives pleasure and recreation to an active brain; while the vici-itude to be met with calls for an unusual amount of forethought and planning in order to meet the emergencies. Thus it is doubtful whether there is any sphere in life where a greater extreme of pleasure and vexation can be found than in that of the pioneer.

But many of the disadvantages under which we have labored for want of railroad facilities, will soon be overcome, and we are led to rejoice in the prospect of a bright and prosperous future. While Wayne county may not be able to show as rapid increase in population as some of the older counties bordering on the river, and possessed of railroad facilities, yet with nearly every acre of the black, rich, loam soil within her borders tillable, with beautiful streams of pure running water, a climate as healthy as can be found in the wide world, she is destined to become one of the most attractive, as well as the richest in the State, and while equaled by few, will be excelled by none.

Concluded

BIRTH: And now comes William of the House of HUNT and with a wink of both eyes says; "Who cares for the Grasshoppers now" It's a boy. No cards.

• • •

HUNTER & BRITTON
Dealers in General
Merchandise
La Porte   Nebraska

• • •

WILLIAM P. AGLER
BLACKSMITH
Horse shoeing done on short notice.
Terms Cash
LA PORTE   NEBRASKA

• • •

Logan Valley Herald
January 4, 1884 (no Vol. No. assigned)

County Directory.
D. W. BRITTON . . . . . Co. Treasurer . . . . .Wayne
T. J. STEELE . . . . . Co. Clerk . . . . .Wayne
E. MARTIN . . . . . Co. Judge . . . . .La Porte
A. S. MINER . . . . . Sheriff . . . . .Wayne
J. S. HAKE. . . . .Co. Sup't . . . . .Wayne
H. K. HARRIS . . . . . Co. Surveyor . . . . .Wayne
J. W. BARTLETT . . . . . Coroner . . . . .Wayne
J. J. W. FOX . . . . . Co. Com'r . . . . .Wayne
O. F. CRANE . . . . . Co. Com'r . . . . .Wakefield
A. T. CHAPIN . . . . . Co. Com'r . . . . . Wayne

Wayne county has one veteran of the Mexican war in the person of W.H. ALLEN.

George STALLCUP was severely hurt Saturday, by the breaking of a chain, while engaged in moving Sheriff MINER's house.

FINNELL & BRASSFIELD'S blacksmith shop was sold at Sheriff's sale on Wednesday. BRITTON and NORTHROP were the purchasers.

The following are the improvements for 1883 as far as THE HERALD has been able to garner them. If there are any omissions, it will be pleased to be informed of it, that they may be published next week.

Town Hall Association, Hall	$4,000
G. B. STONE, Creamery	1,500
G.B. STONE, barn, etc.	750
SLATER & CONE, coal office, etc.	1,500
W. G. VROMAN, house	500
W. G. VROMAN, house	400
Peter COYLE, house	400
Geo. BEARDSHEAR, house	600
Wm. CARNELL, house	400
D.A. VROMAN, house	750
S.B. RUSSELL, house	400
C.C. WHITING, addition to house	250
Henry REESE, house	400
N.N. VROMAN, house	250
J. BROD, restaurant	2,000
S.F. ROBINSON, harness shop	800
Frank FULLER, law office	150
C.A. MORTON, house	400
MORTON Bros. addition to barn	600
John PHILLIPS, house	800
John PHILLIPS, shop	150
L. ROOTH, house	500
J.D. SLATER, bakery, etc.	400
Henry MERRIMAN, house	500
A.G. HOWARD, house	750
Andrew WHEATON, house	500
Alex. HOLZ, brick house	600
D.R. HANCOCK, house	800
R.B. CRAWFORD, house	750
Al. MINER, house	750
J.W. CHAFFEE, house	600
Charles HUNT, house	300
E.J. PORTER, addition to house	400
J.H. JOHNSON, addition to house	300
Charles JOHNSON, barn	300
Charley COREY, house	450
T.J. STEELE, barn	400
Herald Pub. Co., add'n to office	300

H.A. MOORE, house	$1,400
H.A. MOORE, addition to store	500
LINN Bros., addition to store	400
George WHITTON, millinery store	800
Logan Valley Bank, vault	600
Paul ENGLISCH, house	1,500
Paul ENGLISCH, house	750
G.M. LODGE, add'n to house	250
I.N. FLICKINGER, store building	800
J.D. SLATER, store building	300
Henry MYERS, house	1,250
James BRITTON, house	2,500
H. VAN VELSOR, house	750
R.L. OXFORD, house	2,000
W.H. HAMILTON, house	1,250
W.R. WALLACE, house	400
J.D. SLATER, house	300
A.O. MYERS, house	1,500
I.P. MARTIN, house	400
L.C. DEARBORN, barn	300
Boyd House, addition	100
Henry LEY, improvements	250
J.F. HEILNER, improvements	50
B.F. FEATHER, improvements	100
Geo. BEARDSHEAR, ice house	200
L. GROH, improvements	100
A.B. SLATER, improvements	150
O.E. CHAFFEE, improvements	350
A.S. MINER, barn	200
S.W. SMITH, house	2,000
FINNELL & BRASSFIELD, shop	100
O. RICE, barn	250
CUTLER & SEWELL, house	500
F. WOODALL, improvements	50
J.O. MILLIGAN & Co., improvements	100
WARNER & COYLE, improvements	100
John LAWRENCE, improvements	500
Total,	$48,800

THE BAR BANQUET

As was briefly noted in our last weeks issue, the members of Wayne County Bar, gave a Banquet at The Boyd, last evening, to the outgoing and incoming officers, which was probably the toniest or most *rechere* affair of the kind ever held in Northeastern

Nebraska.

About 35 guests were invited of whom 28 put in appearance, as follows:

    James BRITTON and lady
    Judge C.E. HUNTER
    D.W. BRITTON and Miss BRITTON
    Frank FULLER and lady
    T.J. STEELE and lady
    O.F. CRANE
    J.J.W. FOX
    Enoch HUNTER and lady
    D.C. PATTERSON and Miss GAMBLE
    A.A. WELCH and the Misses DAVIES
    Ernest BEHMER
    Judge MARTIN and lady
    F.M. NORTHROP and Miss FERMAN
    A.S. MINER and lady
    A.P. CHILDS and lady
    I.N. FLICKINGER

The spread was laid in the spacious dining room of The Boyd, the tables being arranged in the form of a T. Attorney BRITTON presided; with Mr. PATTERSON at the foot, and Messrs. FULLER and NORTHROP at the end of the arms of the T. The cuisine was admirable and fully sustained the reputation of The Boyd in that respect. The following is the

MENU

which was elegantly printed on white satin:

Soups:
Vermicelli   Oyster   Maccaroni

Fish:
Columbia Salmon   Sardines
Spiced Brook Trout   Lobster
Mackerel with Tomato Sauce
Sardines with Mustard

Oysters:
Raw   Fried   Escalloped

Cold Meats:
Ham   Suckling Pig   Beef
Lamb   Heart
Tripe   Pig's Feet   Tongue

Game:
Venison   Quail   Rabbit
Prairie Chicken

Snipe   Turkey   Chicken

Relishes:
Mixed Pickles   Chow Chew   Celery
Mustard   Tomato Catsup
Worcestershire and Lestershire Sauce

Salads:
Lobster   Chicken   Salmon   Potato

Fruits:
Apples   Grapes   Oranges

Pastries:
Cream Tarts   Fruite Cake   Jelly Cake
Cranberry Tarts   Lemon Tarts
Marble Cake   Nut Cake   Orange Cake
Lemon Cake   Chocolate Cake
Cocoanut Cake   Doughnuts

Nuts   Confectionary   Raisins

Tea   Coffee   Chocolate

Wines:
Catawba   Claret   Sherry
Widow Clicquot

THE TOASTS

    The first toast of the evening. The Profession was responped to in a few happy but appropriate remarks by A. WELCH.

    Judge MARTIN responsed to the toast Our Country, in the only really impromptu speech of the evening.

    In responding to the toast of Great Extremities, D.W. BRITTON made some very happy hits at the hosts of the evening, which elicited rounds of applause.

    Enoch HUNTER responded to the toast of Wayne, the Banner County of Nebraska, in a few brief but pertinent remarks.

    Tom STEELE informed the assembly what he knew about "Running for Office" and Frank CRANE indulged in a few humorous remarks concerning The Babies.

    The editor responded to the sentiments of The Press, while J.J.W. FOX brought down the house in his response to The Bachelors, admitting that if the ladies would avail themselves of the privileges of leap year, it would not be his fault if he was a bachelor at the next Bar Banquet.

When the sentiment of The Ladies was given Frank NORTHROP as the most poetically inclined member of the profession was called upon, and did honor to himself and to the subject.

Mr. FLICKINGER described the connection of Law and Literature, and Mr. PATTERSON told us about Our Courts, illustrating his ideas with humorous stories about justices, blunders.

Judge HUNTER gave us in response to Pioneer Journalism, an interesting account of the founding of the Review.

In response to the sentiment of The Wayne County Bar - Past and Present, Mr. BRITTON delighted his hearers with anecdotes of early days in Wayne, and concluding with stating that but few counties had ever had a better official for the position than the retiring County Judge, and that on behalf of his fellow practitioners he now had the pleasure of presenting Judge HUNTER with a cane as a small testimonial of their regard, and appreciation of his merits as an official.

This presentation was an utter surprise to all present except the donors and especially to the Judge, who was visibly affected by it, and whose voice faltered considerably, as, choking down his emotion, he rose and accepted the present. The cane is a beautiful one, and on its gold head is inscribed

PRESENTED TO
JUDGE C.E. HUNTER,
BY THE
WAYNE COUNTY BAR,
JAN 3D, 1884.

The last toast of the evening, The Lawyer in Politics, was responded to in his happiest vein, by Frank FULLER, after which O.F. CRANE on behalf of the guests, returned thanks to the Bar for their generous hospitality, and at 12:30 o'clock, all retired to their homes, "too full" for further utterance, and satisfied that the first banquet of the Wayne County Bar was a grand success in every particular, and one which will long be remembered.

We might say in conclusion, that the toilets of the ladies on this occasion were superb, and that their presence added much to the enjoyability of the evening.

• • •

MARRIED: JOHNSON - NORLING - In Wayne, Neb. Dec. 31st, 1888, by Judge C. E. HUNTER, Andrew JOHNSON, jr. and Miss

Anna NORLING, both of Bega, Neb.

ANNIVERSARY: Mr. and Mrs. C.D. MARTIN will celebrate the twenty-fifth anniversary of their marriage at their residence two miles south of Wayne on Saturday Jan. 12th.

Teacher Examination

I will hold a public examination of teachers at the school house in Wayne on the third Saturday of every month, between the hours of 9 a.m. and 4 p.m. No private examination can be legally held. A fee of $1 will be required for every examination or for a certificate endorsed.

Jesse S. HAKE
Co. Sup't of Pub. Instruction

• • •

NOAH ROBITAILLE
Harness Maker
Wayne, Nebraska

• • •

BROD'S
RESTAURANT
AND
ICE CREAM PARLOR
Wayne, Neb,

• • •

JOHN LAWRENCE,
GEORGE BEARDSHEAR
Proprietor of the
WAYNE
THE MONARCH
BILLIARD HALL
And Dealer in
The Best Brand of Cigars,
Cider, Lemonade,
and
SODA POP!

WAYNE, NEB.

WAYNE DRUG STORE
DR. LOVE
Drugs   Medicines
Paints, Oils, Varnishes
And Druggist's Sundries.

• • •

W. A. LOVE, M.D.
PHYSICIAN AND SURGEON
WAYNE, NEBRASKA

• • •

Tin and Sheet Iron Ware
Barb wire, pumps, well wheels,
Buckets, lanterns,
And a full line of
Shelf and Heavy Hardware
LINN BROS.

• • •

READY MADE CLOTHING
AT COST!
At the Brick Corner Store
HENRY LEY
Wayne, Neb.

• • •

WE SELL LUMBER.
J.O. MILLIGAN & CO.

• • •

BRESSLER & PATTERSON
Real Estate Brokers.

• • •

WARNER & COYLE,
City Livery & Feed Stable

Logan Valley Herald
January 11, 1884 (Vol. IX, No. 25)

BIRTH: A boy, at Henry KELLOGG's Sunday morning.

Fashionable Wedding

Fennville, (Mich.) Dispatch.

One of the most happy events of the season took place in the spacious parlors of the bride's parents, Mr. and Mrs. Charles H. HARRISON, of New Richmond, which were pleasantly filled last Thursday evening, Dec. 20, to witness the marriage of their daughter Clara E., to Edgar M. SMITH of Wayne, Neb.

The ceremony was performed precisely at half past seven by Rev. Mr. BAXTER, of Douglas. Miss Ida HANSON and Prof. J. WARNOCK assisted as bridesmaid and groomsman. The tables were gracefully arranged, and groaned beneath the weight of good things, and were well calculated to feast both eye and body. The guests numbered over thirty and consisted of elite of Fennville, Douglas, Richmond and Holland. The bride was beautifully dressed in garnet colored satin and looked charming as usual.

The many friends of the young couple wish them long life and continued happiness, and will miss them sadly as they are to depart for their new home in Wayne, Neb. next Monday. Below we give a complete list of the presents which were numerous and costly.

An elegant family bible from the bride to her husband; gold bracelets, from Mr. SMITH to his wife; silver dinner castor, bride's father; silver butter dish, bride's mother; silver butter knife and sugar spoon, from brother Charlie; silver cake basket, Mr. and Mrs. GOODRICH of Benton Harbor; glass cake dish, Mrs. Mary D. PENDLETON, Chicago; silver butter knife, Mrs. Charles DELEVAN, Pierport; one half dozen silver teaspoons, Ida HANSON; silver cream pitcher, John LEAMON, Fennville; knit baby shoes and pair towels, Mrs. George McNUTT, Freemont Center; silver fruit dish, Mrs. Jennie DYE, Fennville; pair vases, Miss Jane WARNOCK, Douglas; towel rack and towels, Mr. and Mrs. Wilmot OWEN, Manilus; pair towels, Mr. and Mrs. E.S. APPLETON, Richmond; glass breakfast castor, Ami COATES; silver pickle castor, Carrie KINGSLEY; china fruit plates, Madge HINMAN, Fennville; silver knives and forks, Mr. and Mrs. HALL; silver napkin ring and perfume bottle, Genie HANSON; rattle box, Mr. and Mrs. J. RAYMER; two dolls and whistle, unknown friend; hand painting, Miss Emily PIERCE; Waterbury, Maine; ?, Miss Elsie COATES; photograph of homestead, bride's father; china moustache cup, Miss Linda WADE; china cup and saucer, Charlie LEAMON; one dozen napkins, Mr. and Mrs. J. INGHAM; pressed glass toilet set, Miss Linda WADE; carving knife and fork, Miss E. FRY.

The happy couple started for home on Monday (Wayne, Neb.) but will remain in Chicago several days visiting relatives and friends. They will then go to Albany, Ill, at which place, Mr. SMITH being a member of the B.L.K Club, that honorable body will give a grand banquet on Monday eve, Dec. 31, in honor of their brother's new advent in life. From there they will go to Wayne, Nebraska, Mr. SMITH's former home, where the gentleman is doing a thorough business in the mercantile trade. On their arrival there a reception will be given the happy bride and groom. Mr. SMITH and his amiable lady are both well respected in the circle in which they move, and we have no doubt but that their life will be one of pleasure and profit.

COMMISSIONER PROCEEDINGS. Wayne, Neb. Jan. 2, 1884.
    Commissioners met pursuant to adjournment.
    Present: Ernest BEHMER, J.J.W. FOX and O.F. CRANE, Commissioners, and Enoch HUNTER, clerk.
    Minutes of last meeting read and approved.
    The Treasurer reporting that he was not ready for settlement, the Board took up regular business.
    It appearing that Lots 1, 2 and 8 in block 4 in the town of Wayne, had been assessed and it appearing that at time of assessment the property belonged to the Lutheran church, and that same had been sold for taxes of 1882. On motion the clerk was directed to draw a warrant on county general fund for the sum of $4.61 in favor of the county treasurer to redeem the same.
    The following official bonds on file were approved.
    J.R. MANNING, assessor, Deer Creek precinct.
    Joseph BOEKENHAUER, assessor, Leslie precinct.
    Eugene H. EMERSON, assessor, Wayne precinct.
    L.W. ROOT, supervisor, road district No. 8.
    M.S. DAVIES, Justice of the Peace, Wayne precinct.
    Official bond of J.W. BARTLETT for coroner was on motion referred back for additional surety by reason of his sureties being on other official bonds.
    Bond of A.A. HARDY for constable was referred back for the same reason that none of the Board are acquainted with the financial standing of his sureties.
    The following bills were audited and allowed on County General Fund.
    G.M. LODGE, Co. sup't of Pub. Instruction,
        fees, claimed $51.20, allowed $49.40
    PERKINS Bros, tubs   2.00

State Journal Co., bank books	$8.60
Enoch HUNTER, fourth quarters salary and expenditures	101.40
Ernest BEHMER, comr's fees and mileage	5.30
J.J.W. FOX, comr's fees and mileage	3.50
O.F. CRANE, comr's fees and mileage	4.10

On motion of O.F. CRANE the thanks of the county officers and of the county at large were extended to Ernest BEHMER, the outgoing commissioner for his kindly, courteous and efficient manner in which he has discharged the duties of his office during the past six years, and for the watchful care he has ever had over the finances of the county. Its present standing, financially being due, in a great measure to his solicitude for the welfare of the county at large, and for which he has the thanks of his constituents and the best wishes of this Board and of all citizens will follow him in his future walks through life.

On motion adjourned to meet Jan 3, 1884.

Attest

         E. HUNTER, Clerk.

ADJOURNED SESSION. Wayne, Neb. Jan. 3, 1884.

Commissioners met pursuant to adjournment.

Present: J.J.W. FOX and O.F. CRANE, Commissioners, and Thos. J. STEELE, clerk.

Minutes of last meeting read and on motion approved.

On motion the official bond of A.A. HARDY, as constable of Wayne precinct, as amended was approved.

On motion the bond of David HERNER road supervisor of district No. 10, was approved.

In the report of the overseer of the poor, bill of F.M. SKEEN for services as overseer of the poor for $6.00 was allowed, and warrant drawn on County General Fund. All other bills in said report having been already audited, no further action was taken.

On motion of O.F. CRANE, a vote of thanks was tendered the outgoing clerk of the board, Mr. Enoch HUNTER, on behalf of ourselves, for the uniform courtesy, promptness and efficiency he has shown during his official connect with us, and as a mark of the esteem of this Board we desire to tender to Enoch HUNTER a Gold Pen and Holder as a token of respect; as the representatives of the county at large, we would tender the thanks of the county for the accuracy, economy and fidelity that has in so marked a degree characterized his official career, and has done so much toward making Wayne the Banner county of the State in the matter of records, as it is in everything else.

On motion the Board adjourned until Jan. 4th, 1884.

Attest

Thos. J. STEELE, Clerk.

ADJOURNED SESSION. Wayne, Neb. Jan. 4, 1884.
Commissioners met pursuant to adjournment.
Present: J.J.W. FOX and O.F. CRANE, Commissioners, and Thos. J. STEELE, Clerk.
Minutes of last meeting read and on motion approved.
On motion stoves were ordered procured for sheriff's and judges offices.
On motion the clerk was requested to notify Martin REDMER, road supervisor of road district No. 5 to appear Jan. 8th to settle the accounts of his disctrict.
The treasurer reporting lock on vault out of repairs. He was directed to get same repaired.
It appearing that William P. AGLER has finished moving and setting up the coat house according to contract, it was ordered that he be allowed the agreed price of $25.00 and the same be credited on his note to Wayne county.
Certified bill of Chris JENSEN, road district No. 3, in favor of Wm. P. AGLER for setting piles for $10.00 allowed and ordered credited on his note to the county.
On application of J.S. HAKE, county superintendent of public instruction for an office, he was assigned joint use of office with county judge.
On motion the clerk was requested to procure coat hooks for his office and that of the treasurer.
Sheriff was instructed to procure and put in glass in his and clerks office.
On motion adjourned until Jan. 5, 1884, at 9 o'clock A.M.
Attest

Thos. J. STEELE, Clerk.

ADJOURNED SESSION. Wayne, Neb. Jan. 5, 1884.
Commissioners met pursuant to adjournment.
Present: J.J.W. FOX and O.F. CRANE, Commissioners, and Thoa. J. STEELE, clerk.
Minutes of last meeting read and on motion approved.
On motion the official bond of Henry KELLOGG, assessor, of La Porte precinct be accepted.
The county treasurer reporting that he was ready for settlement on motion the board proceeded to settle with treasurer.
The settlement with the treasurer not being completed on motion the board adjourned until Monday, Jan. 7th, at 9 o'clock.
Attest

Thos. J. STEELE, Clerk.

ADJOURNED SESSION. Wayne, Neb. Jan. 7, 1884.
    Commissioners met pursuant to adjournment.
    Present: J.J.W. FOX and O.F. CRANE, Commissioners, and Thos. J. STEELE, Clerk.
    On motion minutes of last meeting be approved as read.
    On motion the official bond of J.W. BARTLETT, coroner, be approved as amended.
    On motion the following bill were audited and allowed on County General Fund.

CHACE, NEELY & Co., stoves and hardware	$21.52
MYERS & CHAFFEE, clerks and treasurer's desks	12.70
LINN Bros., stove and pipe in judge's office	12.55
A.S. MINER, guarding prisoner 2 days	4.00
Total	$50.77

    The settlement with the treasurer being incomplete, on motion adjourned to meet Jan. 8th, at 9 o'clock.
    Attest
                      Thos. J. STEELE, Clerk.

ADJOURNED SESSION. Wayne, Neb. Jan. 8th, 1884.
    Commissioners met pursuant to adjournment.
    Present: J.J.W. FOX and Otis F. CRANE, Commissioners, and Thos. J. STEELE, Clerk.
    Minutes of last meeting read and on motion approved.
    On motion the settlement with the several road supervisors was taken up.
    On motion the following bills were taken up and allowed to the several road supervisors and warrants drawn on the several districts named below:
    C.A. FOX, supervisor of road district No. 10, $29.93.
    F. STRATE, supervisor of road district No. 4, $4.50.
    L. ROOT, supervisor of road district No. 8, $40.28.
    George CULVER, supervisor of road district No. 9, $45.00.
    John GABLER, supervisor of road district No. 2, $26.25.
    J.H. MITCHELL, supervisor of road district No. 1, $31.36.
    Chris JENSEN, supervisor of road district No. 3, $31.70.
    James E. HARMON, supervisor of road district No. 6, $28.25.
    The report of Martin REDMER supervisor of road district No. 5 not accepted on account of its being imperfect.
    On motion the following bills were audited and allowed

and warrants ordered to be drawn on County General Fund.

    Ernest BEHMER, interpreter $3.00

    I.O. RICHARDSON, for collections   285.12

    On motion Thirty dollars be transferred from the General Road Fund to District No. 10.

    On motion the settlement with the treasurer was taken up.

    On settlement with the outgoing treasurer, there was found to be in his hands the sum of $8,600.97 which amount was produced and verified by the commissioners.

    On motion adjourned to meet Jan. 9th, 1884, at 9 o'clock.

Attest
                                          Thos. J. STEELE, Clerk

• • •

BRITTON & NORTHROP,
ATTORNEYS AT LAW
WAYNE,   NEB

• • •

FRANK FULLER,
ATTORNEY AT LAW,
WAYNE,   NEB

• • •

A. A. WELCH
Attorney at Law
Wayne,   Neb.

• • •

THE BOYD
WILKINS & FEATHER, Prep'rs.
WAYNE,   NEB

• • •

J. P. GAERTNER,
Dealer in
FURNITURE
Wayne, Nebraska

Gunsmithing!
G. W. THOMPSON

• • •

W. L. HARRIS
JEWELER

• • •

Well Digging
L. L. ALLEN

• • •

FARMS FOR SALE
LINDLY & GAMBLE,
Wayne,   Neb.

• • •

CASH PAID FOR GRAIN
J. N. LAWRENCE

• • •

SLATER & CONE
Dealers in SOFT and HARD COAL.

• • •

CLOAKS
OVERCOATS
H. A. MOORE

• • •

HENRY MERRIMAN
House Painting
Graining a Speciality

PIONEER
Milinrey and Notion House.
Mrs. M. P. AHERN
Wayne, Neb.

• • •

A Full Blood
Mammoth Jack,
now standing at the stables of
PERRY & WARNER

• • •

Logan Valley Herald
January 18, 1884 (Vol. IX, No. 26)

DIED: Henry NEIBUHR, who has resided in or near Dakota City for the past twenty years, died on Sunday, aged 74 years.

Silver Wedding Anniversary

The silver wedding of C.D. MARTIN and his estimable lady, on Saturday evening, drew together a large concourse of their friends at their residence, two miles southeast of Wayne. A bountiful super was provided, and all passed off as pleasantly and smoothly as possible. The following is a list of presents: Picture frames, Luther. SCHNUR; Glass Dish, Chas. A. MARTIN; Mantle Ornament, Sammie ALEXANDER; Individual silver set, Mr. and Mrs. H.A. MOORE; China cups, saucers and plates, Mr. and Mrs. R.J. MORGAN; Set tea spoons, Mr. and Mrs. E. MARTIN; Castor, F.O. MARTIN and Miss Annie ZIMMERMAN; Sugar Tongs, Mrs. M.J. REED; Butter Dish, Lewis MORGAN and Mr. and Mrs. W.L. HARRIS; Butter Knife, Mr. and Mrs. A.P. CHILDS; Sett Knives, Mrs. and Mrs. J.W. BARTLETT; Sett of Forks, H.E. HARRIS and Miss Susie DAVIES; Silver Dollar, Mrs. J.F. HEILNER; Lace Bed Set, Misses REED, MARTIN and RAYMOND; Painting, Mr. and Mrs. W.F. SEARS; Ladies Gold set, Mr. and Mrs. Henry LEY; Shakespeare and Burns Works, Mrs. and Mrs. M.S. DAVIES; Engraved Silver Butter Dish, Mr. and Mrs. J. DECKER and Mrs. and Mrs. W.D. FERGUSON, Clarence, Iowa; Silver Pickle Castor and Tongs, Mr. and Mrs. George McLOOD, Clarence, Iowa; elegant hand painted Picture, Miss Carrie DECKER, Clarence, Iowa; Shelf Lambrequm, Miss Lillie DECKER, Clarence, Iowa.

COMMISSIONERS PROCEEDINGS. Wayne, Neb. Jan 9, 1884.
Commissioners met pursuant to adjournment.
Present: J.J.W. FOX and O.F. CRANE, Commissioners, and Thos. J. STEELE, Clerk.
Minutes of last meeting read, and on motion approved.
On motion the county superintendent's fees shall be fixed at $3.50 per diem, for every day actually and necessarily engaged in the duties of his office for the ensuing year.
On motion the county clerk's salary be fixed at $400.00 for the ensuing year.
On motion the estimate for expenses were made for the ensuing year, and ordered spread upon the records, as follows, to wit:
Estimate for County General Fund
8 mills on the dollar, $7,677.58
Estimate for the Bridge Fund
4 mills on the dollar, $3,838.76
Estimate for General Road Fund
3 mills on the dollar, $2,879.07
The report of J.L. MERRIAM, Henry MYERS and J.S. FOX, commissioners on the vacation of certain streets and alleys, read and accepted, and the same were ordered vacated.
On motion, the title of CRAWFORD and BROWN to Block 2 of Crawford & Brown's Addition to the Town of Wayne, being perfected, we accept the donation of said block to county of Wayne, and State of Nebraska.
On motion the clerk was directed to procure one-half dozen copies of the Compiled Statutes of Nebraska, edition of 1881.
On motion adjourned to meet Feb. 1, 1884.
Attest
Thos. J. STEELE, Clerk.

At the annual meeting of the Stock holders of the Wayne Town Hall Association held on Tuesday evening the following officers were elected: R.B. CRAWFORD, President; W.O. GAMBLE, Vice President; F.M. NORTHROP, Secretary; Henry LEY, Treasurer; the President, Secretary and Treasurer constitute the executive committee. It was voted to borrow on mortgage money to complete the hall.

Northside Notes
Northside, Neb. Feb 18, '84
An accident occurred here the 9th, as Willie TROTTER and our much respected teacher, Mr. ZEIGLER were preparing for a little

hunt about the snow capped hills and broad valleys of Northside, a loaded shell was exploded in the hands of Willie TROTTER, through some defects of the gun, while attempting to place it in the breech, sending the charge of load in close proximity to his head, the powder into his face and one eye, while the bursted shell severely cut one of his hands and we are pleased in the belief that he has escaped a permanent injury.

• • •

F. M. SKEEN
Real Estate Agent
Wayne, Neb.

• • •

Logan Valley Herald
January 25, 1884 (Vol. IX, No. 27)

MARRIED: R.E. TEMPLIN, of Hoskins, is to be married to day, to a daughter of Jesse HAMILTON of Northside.

DIED: Judge E.P. THOMPSON of Decatur, a former resident and for two years judge of this county, died last week.

DIED: Phillip GREENWALD, living south of town, lost a child Monday evening. We did not learn of the disease.

DIED: BROWN. - In Wakefield, Jan. 12th Carrie, daughter of George and Emma BROWN aged 13 years, 6 months and 13 days.

To All Whom It May Concern.

Know ye that all delinquent taxes on personal property must be paid within the next thirty days, or I shall proceed to collect as the law directs.

D.W. BRITTON, Treasurer
Wayne, Neb. Jan 23d, 1884.

A divorce suit is pending between Mr. and Mrs. Clarence W. LANE in the Illinois courts. The parties were formerly residents of this county, Mr. LANE having been a compositor on the Review.

Logan Valley Herald
February 15, 1884 (Vol. IX, No. 30)

BIRTH: A.W. CHAFFEE. Boy, Friday night, Standard weight.

BIRTH: The census is increased by one at E.B. STEWART's. A boy born Wednesday morning. One day to early for a Valentine, Ed.

Almost A Fire.

On Wednesday morning when going up stairs in the WILKINS house, Mr. WILKINS discovered a fire in one of the rooms. The fire had caught in the carpet where the pipe passes through the floor, and burned a large hole through the floor, ran up the partition on the inside, necessitating the tearing down of the plaster and lath for a space about 6 feet square. A chair on which were some bed clothes also caught fire, and the five bed quilts were destroyed. By hard work, Mr. WILKINS and his son Jesse succeeded in putting out the flames, but were severely scorched themselves. The heat in the room was so intense as to break a looking glass, and the glass in the windows. As it was, it was a narrow escape from a disastrous conflagration, and gives us warning that the town should provide for water for such emergencies as this. A few wells in the most exposed portions of town, with water tanks would answer every purpose and would not require a large outlay of capital.

A slight furore occurred in town last Saturday over the arrest of Charles GOURGHAN, one of the bridge building force here with FOX & Co., by Sheriff A.S. MINER of Wayne county, on suspicion of being one of the parties to a burglary committed on the store of JOHNSON, SMITH & Son, at Wayne, some two weeks ago. The arrested party was taken to Wayne last Sunday, but was almost immediately turned loose, it being ascertained by the authorities that they had the wrong sow by the ear. Mr. G. is now back here attending to his own business like any other good citizen (Hartington Herald).

To All Whom It May Concern
Notice is hereby given that all persons are forbidden to trust my wife or any other person on my account, without my written order.
Wayne, Neb Feb. 2, 1884
John G. MESTHALER

CITY
Meat Market
Two Doors north of Chace's Store.
PETER & MENTIS, Propr's

...

M. S. DAVIES,
Book and Music Store
Wayne, Nebraska

...

Logan Valley Herald
February 22, 1884 (Vol. IX, No. 31)

LEGAL NOTICE
In the County Court of Wayne County Nebraska.
In the matter of the estate of NIELS NIELSON, Deceased.
To Sarah DAVENPORT, Niels NIELSEN, Jens V. LARSEN, Andreas RASMENSEN and DeGrosse W. BRITTON, Administrator of said Estate:
You are hereby notified that we will apply to E. MARTIN, County Judge of said county, at his office in Wayne, Nebraska, on the 7th day of April, 1884, or as soon thereafter as the application can be heard, to have the order of distribution, allowance of the account of the Administrator, and his discharge heretofore made in this matter vacated and set aside. And that affidavits will be used in the hearing of said motion.
Dated Feb. 22d, 1884
ANE MARIE SOPHIA NIELSEN,
SIDSEL NIELSEN, Insane
By NIELS JENSEN, her guardian,
ELSIE MARIE NIELSEN,
By A.A. WELCH
Their Attorney

Injunction Suit. A suit has been commenced in the county court to set aside the order of distribution in the estate of Niels NIELSEN, the Dane who committed suicide, and an injunction issued restraining the payment of the money. The suit is brought by A.A. WELCH, attorney for the deceased's sisters, who reside in Denmark.

The jury in the case of Dr. SCHUHARDT, formerly of this place, indicted for assault with intent to kill, on trial in the Cuming county district court, were unable to agree, and the prisoner was discharged.

NORTHSIDE

Northside is the name given by the railroad company to the first station west of this city. It is about 14 miles west of Wayne, and is surrounded by as good farming lands as can be found anywhere in the state. At present, no town has been laid out, but we believe it would be to the interest of the railroad company to build a good station house, and lay out a town site. The country around about is rapidly settling up, with good substantial farmers, and it must eventually become a trading point. The farmers there have organized an Immigration Association with a view to induce people to locate with them. The officers of the Association are: R.G. SINES, President; Perrin LONG, Treasurer; James A. ELLIOTT, Sec'y; Warner STARR, Ass't Secretary, any of whom will be glad to furnish further information to parties seeking homes in this county.

Logan Valley Herald
February 29, 1884 (Vol. IX, No. 32)

MARRIED: ZIEMER - ANDERSON. In Hoskins, Feb. 24th by Esq. R.G. SINES, Mr. Louis ZIEMER and Miss ANDERSON, all of this county.

DIED: LUTH - At Wakefield, Feb. 25th, of diptheria, Martha, daughter of Henry LUTH, age about 3 years.

DIED: LEEDON, in Wakefield, Neb., Feb. 25, 1884, of lung lever, Winnie Wigton, second son of B.S. and Ella M. LEEDON, age four months, and twenty six days.

> "Ere sin could blight, or sorrow fade,
> Death came with kindly care.
> The opening bud to heaven conveyed,
> and bade it blossom there."

"Baby is dead." Only three short words, yet only God, and others whose baby is dead, know the heart ache they bring. The hopes of future years wrecked like some bright ship, and suddenly gone out of sight. Yesterday here, to day gone, and with all our grief we are glad it is not for him to know life's hard realities, its bitter sorrows, its heavy burdens, nor the thorny path which human feet must tread, nor the cloud of sin which hangs overall. And as we feel the touch of angel fingers, we feel the hand of Him who "doeth all things well." "It is well with the child."

• • •

D. W. BRITTON,
AUCTIONEER,
Wayne, Neb.

• • •

Logan Valley Herald
March 7, 1884 (Vol. IX, No. 33)

BIRTH: To Mr. Theo. BENRHARDT and wife, on Feb. 25th, a girl. Mother doing well, and Theo. feeling as jolly as usual. (Hoskins)

BIRTH: Feb. 29th, 1884, to Mr. and Mrs. Henry REES, a son.

BIRTH: In Wayne, March 2d to Mr. and Mrs. W.S. BAKER, a daughter.

But Four Birthdays in 21 Years.

The young son of Henry REES, born last Friday, will, should he live to be 21 years old, see but 4 birthdays, one when 4 years old, one at 8, one at 12, and one at 20, his first birthday after 1896 occurring in 1904, 1900 not being a leap year.

Serious Accident.

This morning about 9 o'clock, a serious accident occurred to A.B. SLATER. He had just left his office to go to the depot, and while walking down the middle of the street, a runaway team came down Main street, and before he could get out of the way the horses were upon him. The tongue of the wagon, or the neck yoke, struck him in the back knocking him down, and the wagon passed over him. He was carried into the office of Mr. SKEEN where his wounds were dressed by Dr. CRAWFORD and Dr. WINSTON, of Foreston, Ill. who happened to be present. How serious the injury is, we are, as yet, unable to learn, but from surface examination the doctors report nothing dangerous. We sincerely hope this may prove true.

School Report.
Report of Wayne school for month ending Feb. 29th, 1884.
PRIMARY SCHOOL.
Anna B. DAVIES, Teacher.

No. of boys enrolled,	27
No. of girls enrolled,	26
No. of boys not absent,	7
No. of girls not absent,	4
Average daily attendance,	38.0

CHURCH SCHOOL
Susie DAVIES, Teacher.

No. of boys enrolled,	40
No. of girls enrolled,	37
No. of boys not absent,	8
No. of girls not absent,	12
Average daily attendance,	66.3

SUMMARY

Total No. enrolled,	130
Total No. not absent,	31
Average daily attendance,	105.3

A.A. WELCH, Principal

Logan Valley Herald
March 14, 1884 (Vol. IX, No. 34)

BIRTH: To Mr. and Mrs. D. REES, March 10th, a boy, 9 lbs. Mother and child doing well, and REES one of the proudest men in Wayne county. (Hoskins)

BIRTH: March 11th, to Mr. and Mrs. O.P. ANDERSON, a daughter.

Jens NELSON was made a full-fledged citizen of the United States, by the district judge yesterday.

District Court.

The term of Court held here this week drew together a large concourse of people from all parts of the county. In addition to Hon. James C. CRAWFORD, the district judge, Eugene MOORE, Stenographer, and Wilbur F. BRYANT, the district attorney, we noticed the following gentlemen from abroad in attendance: Judge BARNES and William E. GANTT, of Ponca, John D. HOWE the well known practitioner of Omaha, but better know throughout the state as one of the real personages in Father MARTIN's delightful romance, Watson PARRISH, of Oakland, H.C.

BROME, of Norfolk, N.H. BELL, of Fremont, and others with whose faces we were not familiar.

A.A. WELCH was admitted to the bar of this district court.

On call of the docket the cases names below were disposed of as follows:

DISMISSED

BRUNER, vs. NICHOLS, SHEPARD & Co.
KLOSTERMAN, vs. NAFZINGER. Costs taxed to plaintiff.

CONTINUED

HARDENBURGH & JOHNSON, et al, vs. HERNER.
LAMB, vs. F.E. & M.V.R.R. Co.; two cases.
PETERSON, vs. GOULD.
McCormick Harvesting Co., vs. AGLER, 30 days to file petition.
Deft. 30 days to answer

DEFAULTS

Case Threshing Maclime Co., vs. WHITTAKER
CHACE, NEELY & Co., vs. J.G. and D.A. MAURER. Default against last named defendant.
BLACK, vs. DUGAN. Special order for services against unknown heirs.
CLARK, vs. Michael & Mary BRASCH.

SETTLED

Hulda ODEEN, vs. Charles BINDERUP. This is the case noted some time since in THE HERALD, where the plaintiff sued under the statute for a prospective incumbrance. The parties met at the office of CRAWFORD & FLICKINGER on the first day of court, and settled their differences through the aid of Judge MARTIN, who joined them in the Holy bonds of matrimony.

Other cases were disposed of as follows:
MONROE, vs. FINLAYSON. Judgement for defendant.
CRAWFORD & FLICKINGER, vs. SLATER. Continued - Leave to answer in 30 days.
GREEN, vs. GREEN. Divorce. Dismissed.

The grand jury failed to find an indictment against Richard HAMMOND, and he was accordingly discharged. Ham. GRAYSON was indicted for burglary, plead guilty, and was senteced to 3 years in the penitentiary.

The indictments against Geo. BEARDSHEAR, William CARNELL and S.B. RUSSEL for selling liquor were quashed.

• • •

F. KELLER, M.D.
Homeopathic Physician
Wayne, Neb.

Logan Valley Herald
March 21, 1884 (Vol. IX, No. 35)

BIRTH: March 14th, at La Porte, to Mr. and Mrs. J.P. LARSEN, a boy.

HYMENEAL.
Patterson - Gamble
Who Were There - What They Wore - &c, &c.

The much talked-of and long-expected social event of the season took place at the Presbyterian church of this city on Tuesday morning, March 18th, at which time David C. PATTERSON and Miss Maude A., oldest daughter of William O. GAMBLE, were united in holy bonds of matrimony by Rev. Thomas C. HALL, of Omaha. The church, which had been beautifully decorated for the occasion, was crowded with spectators, among those present from abroad, being, Attorney General POWERS and wife, of Lincoln; Mr. DORN, of Omaha; District Judge J. C. CRAWFORD and Eugene MOORE, of West Point; District Attorney Wilbur F. BRYANT, of Aten.; John T. SPENCER and wife; Dr. George W. WILKINSON and wife; Atlee HART and wife, and Mrs. Geo. HOLMAN, of Dakota City; J.H. PATTERSON and wife, of Austin, Minn.; W.C. PATTERSON of Kansas; R.C. PATTERSON and Rudolph PATTERSON, of Omaha; Miss Belle WOODS and Miss Fannie GAMBLE, of Woodhill, Ill.; besides a large concourse of friends in Wayne.

THE BRIDE

looked charming in her exquisite bridal toilet of cream-colored satin, trimmed with Spanish guipure lace, and Lilies of the Valley; long flowing veil of Tulle caught gracefully on the right side of the coiffure; held there by natural flowers; slippers and gloves of cream-colored kid. Miss Fannie GAMBLE, the first bride's-maid was dressed in cream mull, with pink satin basque; Miss Belle WOODS, the other attendant was dressed in cream-colored mull, and cream satin basque. The brides traveling dress was a beautiful toilet of ruby velvet and satin. The toilets of the bride were designed and executed by Mrs. B.F. TALBERT, of this city.

THE RECEPTION

was held at The Boyd where for an hour, Mr. and Mrs. PATTERSON were kept busy shaking hands and receiving the congratulations of their friends after which the company were invited to partake of a bountiful breakfast, the *menu* for which was elegantly printed on white satin. The breakfast did honor to the people of The Boyd, but the time was too limited for all to get their fill, before the special train which had been ordered to bear

Mr. PATTERSON and his bride away signalled "All Aboard," and a hasty leave-taking was the order of the day. The bride and groom accompanied by a large number of their friends were soon on board, and off for Sioux City, where their friends saw them safely on board the S.C. & P. train for Council Bluffs. The happy couple will visit friends in Woodhill, Illinois, Pennsylvania, Washington and New York, and on the 10th proximo, will sail in the steamer Hammonia for Europe. They expect to spend the entire spring and summer in England, France and Italy, and will return home some time in September. The Herald wishes them *bon voyage* and a safe return.

• • •

PINE LUMBER
Building Material
REES, of Hoskins

• • •

Logan Valley Herald
March 28, 1884 (Vol. IX, No. 36)

MARRIED: HOUSER - ZIEMER - At the residence of the bride's parents in Hoskins on March 25th, Al. HOUSER and Miss Lizzie, daughter of L. ZIEMER, all of Hoskins, Esq. R.G. SINES, officiating.

MARRIED: Miss Maggie BARCKLEY, a former resident of La Porte, was married recently at her home in Elgin, to a Mr. CURTIS, of that city.

An Old Settler Gone
DEATH: Jerome AGLER, one of the old settlers of Wayne county, and father of Joseph W. and W.P. AGLER, and Mrs. C.E. HUNTER, Mrs. P. MERRIMAN, Mrs. W.H. HUNT and Mrs. Henry MERRIMAN, of this county, died at the residence of his daughter, Mrs. P. MERRIMAN in La Porte precinct on Monday evening last, in the 78th year of his age. The deceased was a native of Pennsylvania and was one of the earliest settlers of Lee county, Illinois, from which county he removed to this in 1878. He had been confined to his bed nearly all the winter, and his death was not unexpected. He leaves behind him, besides the children above mentioned three sons in Illinois. His remains were buried at his own request, in the cemetery at Wakefield.

Logan Valley Herald
April 4, 1884 (Vol. IX, No. 37)

BIRTH: In this village, March 31st, to Mr. and Mrs. O.M. ELLSWORTH, a son.

DIED: We are pained to learn that Mrs. James BUSH's father, Alex STRACHAN, died on Saturday night at Howard, Kansas. Mrs. BUSH left Tuesday morning for there; having only just returned from burying a sister in Illinois.

The following correspondence explains itself:
  To the Jennie Holman Combination:
  The undersigned citizens of Wayne respectfully request you to give us another season of one week at the Academy of Music, commencing on Monday next, and we pledge ourselves to take season tickets, and to guarantee your expenses. And we further state that we are induced to do this because of the uncalled for attack made in one of our pulpits on Sunday last.
                Very Respectfully Yours.

E.M. SMITH	W.F. SEARS
J. BROD	Henry LEY
W.J. METTLEN	Arthur ENGLISCH
J.P. GAERTNER	L.C. DEARBORN
W. CARNELL	F.A. DEARBORN
Ed. PERRY	John T. BRESSLER
John LAWRENCE	Chas. WILKINS
J.W. ROCK	A.P. CHILDS
Peter COYLE	F.L. NEELY
H. WRIGHT	A.O. HENRY
J.F. SHERBAHN	N. ROBITAILLE
T.W. MORAN	Chas. JOHNSON
S.B. RUSSELL	W.J. PERRY
F.H. WALLACE	J.W. WOODS
H. MYERS	R.J. ARMSTRONG
M.W. BENSON	George L. COOK
John PHILLIPS	Richard JOHNSON
N. LEIBFRIED	Geo. BEARDSHEAR

            Wakefield, Neb., April 2d
A.P. CHILDS, E.M. SMITH and others:
Your request lies before me, but it is impossible for us to come on account of previous engagements. With thanks for your unsolicited testimonial, I am
            Yours Respectfully, Otto H. KRAUSE, Manager.

CRAWFORD & WIGHTMAN
Physicians And Surgeons.
WAYNE, NEBRASKA

• • •

Lumber, Lath Shingles,
Sash and Door Posts, Paper.
Lime, Cement Hair &C.,
E. L. JONES.

• • •

Logan Valley Herald
April 11, 1884 (Vol. IX, No. 38)

DIED: WILBUR - At the residence of his son, R.H. WILBUR, of paralysis, on April 8th, 1884, Stephen V. WILBUR, aged 82 years and 27 days. The deceased was born at Stephentown, Renssellaer county, N.Y. He removed to Connecticut at an early age, where he was married in Litchfield county, to Polly CAMPBELL, and removed to Chemung county, where his wife died in 1859, since which time he has resided with his children the last few years of his life being spent with his oldest son, Russel, in Nebraska. He was the father of seven children, four of whom survive him. His was ever an active busy life and now at a ripe old age he has been called to meet her again whose smiles and prescence enlivened his life in her earlier years.

A Card
To the many friends who surprised us by their visit on the eve of our 16th marriage anniversary, and to all those who contributed to the pleasant occasion, who left such substantial tokens of good-will we return our heart felt thanks. The concise yet comprehensive presentation address of J.A. LINDLEY was fully appreciated. Dear friends you have added a golden link to the chain of friendship that binds us. Such generous marks of esteem and confidence cheer and strengthen us in our labors for Christ and humanity. Heaven's choicest blessing be yours and may prosperity and peace attend you everymore.
G.M. LODGE
N.S. LODGE

Logan Valley Herald
April 18, 1884 (Vol. IX, No. 39)

BIRTH: April 11th, to Mr. and Mrs. C.E. HUNT, a son.

Logan Valley Herald
April 25, 1884 (Vol. IX, No. 40)

BIRTH: Near Wayne, on Saturday, April 19th, to Mr. and Mrs. J.E. BENNETT, a son.

BIRTH: In Wayne, April 23d, to Mr. and Mrs. James BRITTON, a daughter.

MARRIED: ZOOK - WEAVER - At the residence of the bride's parents, April 13th, by Rev. J.R. GEARHARD, Wm. ZOOK and Miss Ella, daugther of Noah WEAVER, of this county.

MARRIED: ANDERSON - JOHNSON - At the parsonage in Wayne, April 24th, by Rev. G.M. LODGE, John ANDERSON and August JOHNSON, both of Wakefield.

Suicide Near Wisner

M.H. RUSSELL, a former resident of this county, but of late years a resident and for two years a commissioner of Cuming county, committed suicide by shooting himself in the head while on his way home from Wisner on Thursday last, at about 6 o'clock. For some months past, the deceased had given evidence of a failing mind, and it is highly probable that it was during a fit of temporary insanity that he committed this rash act.

Death of Dr. J.C. BROWN

The many friends who knew Dr. J.C. BROWN during his residence in this county, will regret to learn of his death at Shelby, Iowa, on Saturday, April 12th, of an overdose of hydrate of chloral. Dr. BROWN came to this county at an early day and was, for many years an associate of Dr. CRAWFORD in the practice of medicine, and from 1879 to 1881 was county surveyor. In the spring of 1873 he removed to Iowa, where he had succeeded in building up an extensive practice. He died at the supper table, almost in an instant, and was buried on the following day.

Destructive Prairie Fire.

On Wednesday afternoon, a prairie fire came in on the tenants of J. M. STRAHAN'a place on section 9, 20, 3, and despite all their efforts, burned a barn, breaker's stable, all their hay and grain, two wagons, plows, harness, etc., in fact everything that they had out there. The losers are John KEEFOOT, Henry BURNHAM, William RITCHIE, and another whose name our informant was unable to learn.

Look out for stray stock. J.E. HARMON has been appointed the pound master.

Logan Valley Herald
May 2, 1884 (Vol. IX, No. 41)

MARRIED: On April 24, 1884, at the residence of the bride's parents, by Rev. Dr. SNOWDEN, and assisted by Rev. J.L. GUARD, Rev. G.H. SCHNUR, of Wayne, Neb. to Miss Caroline DOCK, of Delphia, Ind.

New Lodge Instituted.

Wayne Lodge No. -, A.O.U.W. was instituted Monday evening with 28 charter members by D.G.M.W. FORMAN. The officers of the Lodge are A.B. SLATER, P.M.; S.W. SMITH, M.; J.H. BROWN, F.; A.P. CHILDS, O.; Frank FULLER, Recorder; Charles JOHNSON, Fin'r; F.A. DEARBORN, Receiver; J.K. RYTHER, Guide; F.L. NEELY and B.F. FEATHER, Watchmen; Drs. WIGHTMAN and LOVE are the medical examiners. T.J. STEELE, E.H. EMERSON and Henry LEY were elected trustees. The regular nights of meeting of the new lodge will be held on the first and third Fridays of each month, commencing Friday, May 16th, 1884.

Odd Fellows Lodge Instituted.

Wayne Lodge No. 118, I.O.O.F., was instituted in Masonic Hall of this City, yesterday, by Grand Master HUDSON of Columbus, with eleven charter members. The officers are as follows: Charles WILKINS, P.G.; A.A. WELCH, N.G.; John T. BRESSLER, V.G.; M.S. DAVIES, Sec'y; R.B. TAYLOR, Treas'r; E.J. NANGLE, Warden; F.M. STRICKLAND, Conductor; A.S. MINER, O.S. The regular nights of meetings are Monday.

• • •

F. E. MOSES,
COLLECTOR & CONVEYANCER,
Wayne,   Neb.

Logan Valley Herald
May 9, 1884 (Vol. IX, No. 42)

Almost a Fatal Accident.

Bertie, a young son of C.F. CARPENTER, was thrown from a pony near the residence of J.E. HARMON, on Wednesday evening last, his foot catching in the stirrup strap, in which shape he was dragged along the ground until the saddle girth broke. The pony evidently stepped on him once or twice, cutting and bruising his head severely. No bones were broken, but the left arm was dislocated at the elbow, while he was pretty badly shook up and bruised considerably about the body. Dr. CRAWFORD and WIGHTMAN were called and attended to his injuries, and the boy is getting on very nicely.

Building Notes.

M.P. AHERN is erecting a large sized addition to his house on Main street. The front room, which is now used as a business room, will hereafter be used exclusively for Mrs. AHERN's Millinery department, while the next room back will be devoted to the dress and cloack making business. Mrs. AHERN has built up and extensive business here, having been one of the pioneers of the town; and we are pleased to note that her growing business now demands more room.

Charles JOHNSON has the foundation laid, and carpenters are now at work on an addition to his house, which will greatly improve its appearance.

More residences for rent are greatly needed in town, and parties having means can make a good investment by building a few tenant houses.

Dr. CRAWFORD's new house is nearly completed.

Al. MINER's house is completed, and he has moved into the same.

James BRITTON has let the contract for a new store building 25x70 on the site now occupied by JOHNSON, SMITH & Son. The present building will be moved on to the next lot and a brick veneer, two-story building erected in its place.

L.C. DEARBORN has built an Oil room addition to his drug store during the past week.

• • •

H. G. LEISENRING, M.D.
Physician and Surgeon,
Wayne, Neb.

CHACE, NEELY & CO.
We have a full line of
SHELF & HEAVY HARDWARE,

• • •

SOENNEKEN'S New Store
Dry Goods, Groceries,
and Notions.

• • •

Logan Valley Herald
May 16, 1884 (Vol. IX, No. 43)

BIRTH: May 13th, to Mr. and Mrs. Aug. RANNOW, a son.

MARRIED: At the residence of the bride's brother, S.J. BOWERS, in Dixon county, by W.H. GIBSON, J.P., Mr. Elmer BLOODHART and Miss Carrie BOWERS.

HOSKINS

The Herald man made a trip to Hoskins on Monday evening, and is pleased to note that the town is prospering and that the country around about it is settling up rapidly, thus insuring a future for the town that will make it one of the best along the line. The old settlers of Spring Branch precinct, most of whom are frugal industrious farmers, have by that frugality and industry secured for themselves competency, and are as thriving a class of citizens as can be found in any country. The soil is excellent and the country around about the village exceedingly well-watered, while speculation has not raised the price of the land beyond the means of the average farmer. Good land, within a short distance of town, can still be bought at from $5 to $8 per acre; and that this land is productive, one only needs to look at the well-filled granaries and corn-cribs of the residents. Parties desiring to secure homes would do well to correspond with
HOWSER & ZIEMER
the energetic real estate agents at that place, whose list embraces nearly all the land in the western part of our county, and who will take pleasure in showing you about, and will sell you as low as the lowest.

David REES
is the postmaster, and does a large business in lumber, coal, and general merchandise, his store being well filled with a general

stock; and his trade large enough enable him to sell at bed-rock prices.

William LALK,

an old settler, does a large trade in shelf and heavy hardware, farm machinery, etc. Mr. LALK is at present visiting his parents in Wisconsin, and during his absence, his business is looked after by Mr. REES and his brother-in-law, Mr. WILKINSON.

L.P. RIDGE

is the Vulcan of the town, and attends to all the blacksmithing in a first class manner. Among the urgent needs of the village is

A Hotel,

a want which will probably soon be supplied, as Mr. WILKINSON is now talking of building one, to be 22x40, and two stories high. At present, travelers are entertained by

J.P. WRIGHT,

the enterprising section foreman of the Railroad, to whose hospitality The Herald man testify.

A Brick Yard,

about two miles from town is being successfully run by Frank PULS, a local adv't of which will be seen in another column.

A shoemaker would find this an excellent place to locate, and the inhabitants all inform us that a saloon would pay well.

Logan Valley Herald
May 23, 1884 (Vol. IX, No. 44)

BIRTH: May 19th, in Wayne, to Mr. and Mrs. F.M. SKEEN, a son.

Another Suicide
Gus. HAGELIN, Tired of Life,
Hangs Himself in his Stable.

On Saturday last, a little after noon, our citizens were startled by the report that Gus. HAGELIN, the village shoemaker, had hung himself in his stable, about three quarters of a mile northeast of town. A number of our citizens including a Herald representative immediately went out to the place, where we found the body lying on the manure in the stable just where it had been cut down by Anton KLEUVER. An inquest was held by Sheriff MINER, acting as Coroner, with the following gentlemen as jurors: J.A. LINDLY, E.H. EMERSON, W.O. GAMBLE, John LAWRENCE, A.P. CHILDS and Edward PERRY. From the evidence before the jury, it was found that for a week or more past, Mr. HAGELIN had not drawn a sober breath; that his nerves were all unstrung, and his actions and talk wild and meaningless; that on this morning he had evidenced a desire to be alone, sending one of the children to town, another out to herd the cattle, while the third one at home with her mother was sent to PELLEREN's. About 11 o'clock; Mrs. H. was returning when she met her youngest boy, a lad of 10 years, who said his father was hanging in the stable. She immediately returned to Mr. KLEUVER's, a near neighbor, who drove over as fast as possible, and cut the body down, but too late, as the spark of life had already fled. From the position of the body which was hanging with the knees almost touching the ground, it is evident that he had exercised great will power and deliberately choked himself to death. In the pockets of the deceased were found nothing but some snuff, a few matches, and a copy of a summons with which he had been served only the day before. The deceased when he first came to this county, was one of the most sober, industrious men we ever met, kind and loving to his children, of whom he was very proud, especially of little Jennie, the pride of his home, but the demon of drink got hold of him, and in two years all the manliness of his nature was driven out of him. His time was given to drunkeness, and from a loving kind parent, he became morose and ugly, and his children instead of running to meet him, now shunned his presence. During the week that preceeded his death, it was noticed by those with whom he came in contact that his mind appeared to be clouded, and there is no doubt now of his insanity. The verdict of the jury was that he came to his death by his own hands by strangulation, produced by hanging with a rope. He leaves a widow and five children.

Wayne Station. We are indebted to station agent MORAN for the following interesting facts concerning the business of this station:
The earnings for the month of April amounted to nearly $8,000.
During the past two weeks, thirty-four cars of cattle were received at this station; 25 being consigned to J.A. and Wm. FRAZIER, and 9 to J.M. STRAHAN.
The total number of cars of stock shipped from Wayne during the past year was 108, divided as follows:

Ran. FRAZIER	39
J.A. & W. FRAZIER	15
H.B. MILLER	7
W.H. HINES	2
Richmond & P.	2
L.K. MEAHAN	9
John GOSS	2
P.W. OMAN	2
Frank WOODALL	2

STEELE & FRAZIER	6
SHERMAN Bros.	4
A.B. SLATER	10
J.M. STRAHAN	4
G.W. WAITT	1
C.C. BROWN	<u>3</u>
Total,	108

• • •

FASHIONABLE MILLINERY WEAR
Mrs. B.F. TALBERT   **Mrs. L.A. GALLAGER**

• • •

CHAS. M. WALTERS
House, Sign, Carriage
- and -
Ornamental Painter

• • •

MERRIMAN & McMAKIN,
House, Sign and Carriage Painters,

• • •

Logan Valley Herald
June 6, 1884 (Vol. IX, No. 46)

Letter From London

The Herald has been permitted to make the following extract from a letter from Mrs. D.C. PATTERSON, giving some of her impressions concerning London and vicinity. Next week we will publish a similar extract from a Paris letter, and after that from one written from Italy, where they now are:

London, May 2, 1884

Wednesday morning we went to the Tower of London, a very ancient pile to which is attached much historical interest, once the residence of sovereigns, as well as prison and fortress; now it is a sort of an arsenal and fort. In it we saw 60,000 guns, and suits of armor from the Grecian period down to the present time. Saw also various instruments of torture, the block and axe which were used at the beheading of Lords Lovett, Killmanock and

Belineri, after the rebellion of 1745 and the executioner's mask; also the Regalia or Crown Jewels. These are kept in an immense glass case, surrounded by an iron cage, the most conspicuous of which is the "Queen's Crown" of purple velvet, enclosed in hoops of silver, and surrounded by a ball and cross, all of which are resplendent with diamonds (2,783 in number) a magnificent sapphire and a very large ruby, the whole said to be worth £111,900, or over a half a million of dollars. There is also the Prince of Wales' crown of pure gold, unadorned with jewels, St. Edward's crown of gold, diamonds, rubies, pearls and sapphires, ancient Queen's Crown, Queen's Diadem, Sceptre, rod, Coronation bracelet, spurs, annointing vessel and spoon, all used in the coronation ceremonies, baptismal font, used at the christening of the royal children, gold wine fountain, dishes, spoons and salt cellars of pure gold. We saw the places where many people who were prominent in English history were imprisoned and executed.

On Wednesday afternoon, we went to the Regent's Park and Zoological Gardens, where we enjoyed ourselves very much until evening. The Park is a very beautiful one, containing 400 acres, and the Zoological Gardens are grand. One sees birds, reptiles, fishes, mammals, etc. of every zone and every country in the world, the finest and largest collection of animals ever made. In the evening we went to hear Lawrence Barrett in Richelieu, which was good indeed.

Yesterday we visited Windsor castle, by rail, a distance of thirty miles. This, you know, is the residence of the Queen. The castle was founded by William the Conqueror as a mere fortress or hunting post. It has been added to since by his successors who made it their residence, until it is now one of the most imposing royal palaces in existence. It has been greatly enlarged and modernized since George IV. The castle is on a high eminence, overlooking the Thames for many miles; parts of twelve counties can be seen from the tower where we had a grand view of the beautiful country; could see from where we stood Eton College, the residence of William Penn, and the home of the poet Gray, who wrote his "Elegy in a Country Churchyard" at the church nearby. The state apartments were not open, St. George's chapel is the most beautiful room, and the Albert Memorial Chapel, which Victoria erected in memory of her husband is the most beautiful room I was ever in; it is impossible to describe it. We have a picture of it, together with nineteen other views of Windsor which you can see when we return. The drives, grounds, deer park, etc., around Windsor are very beautiful. We saw the Queen's carriages, horses and ponies. There are 80 or 90 horses;

and as many as thirty carriages. They are, of course, very grand and in keeping with everything else. On our return to London, we had a pleasant drive through the lovely fields. After dinner, we visited the Prince's Theatre where we saw Claudian played. It was the grandest thing I ever saw. We start Monday for Paris, and thence to Italy. Send our mail as usual.

Maude

• • •

BIRTH: On convention day, June 3d, 1884, to Mr. and Mrs. John E. HANSON, a son. Our friend HANSON ought to name his boy after the nominee of the convention.

BIRTH: John BOEKENHAUER feels proud over a new girl, born June 4th. (Leslie)

MARRIED: At the Baptist Parsonage, on Tuesday evening, June 3d, 1884, by Rev. J.F. HEILNER, John ZWALD to Matilda J. SHAW, both of Wayne, Neb.

Obituary
DIED: At her residence, about 8 miles west of Wayne, on Wednesday morning, June 4th, 1884, of consumption, Mrs. Nora, wife of Arthur T. CHAPIN, aged about 30 years.

The deceased was a daughter of Dr. P.C. COOPER, of Blair, Nebraska, and was born in Harrison county, Iowa. Her parents removed when she was but a child to the then young territory of Nebraska, where they have since resided. In 1870 she was united to Mr. CHAPIN, at that time a prominent farmer of Washington county. About the year 1877 they removed to Boston, where they resided for nearly two years, Mr. CHAPIN being engaged in the real estate business. Returning again to Nebraska, they resided in Washington county until the spring of 1881, when Mr. CHAPIN acquiring large land interests in Wayne county, removed here and opened up the ranche which bears his name. Here in the early days, when circumstances compelled them to rough it, she caught a severe cold, which steadily increased until it had developed into consumption, being the first case known to us originating in Nebraska. Fearing that she could not stand the rigorous winters we are subject to, Mr. C. took her to San Antonio, Texas, where they remained during last winter, and where they cherished the delusive hope that she might regain her health. But the dreaded monster's fangs were too firmly fastened, and it was evident to all on their return this spring that her days were but few here and it was but a question of time when the devoted wife and loving mother should be called away from her little family. Everything that could be possibly done for her comfort and to relieve her pain was done but without avail. She was sensible to the last moment, and expressed but one regret, that of leaving her husband and children. Although not a member of any church, she had that faith and resignation of a believing christian, and died in the hope of a christian resurrection. She leaves behind her to mourn her loss, a husband and three children, the oldest child is nine and the youngest 4 years old. May they turn for comfort to Him who has said "Blessed are they that do mourn for they shall be comforted."

The funeral services take place at the house Monday at 1 o'clock. Rev. G.M. LODGE officiating.

CENSUS RETURNS

The assessors having turned in their books, we make the following notes in regard to the population of the county.

SPRING BRANCH

No. of families	61
No. of Males	131
No. of Females	88
No. of Males over 20	20
No. of deaths last year	1
No. of births last year	0

HANCOCK

No. of families	27
No. of Males	69
No. of Females	64
No. of Males over 20	34
No. of deaths last year	3
No. of births last year	0

DEER CREEK

No. of families	27
No. of Males	86
No. of Females	55
No. of Males over 20	39
No. of deaths last year	0
No. of births last year	8

WAYNE

No. of Males	742
No. of Females	558
No. of Males over 20	390
No. of deaths last year	6
No. of births last year	38

LA PORTE

No. of families	82
No. of Males	257
No. of Females	197
No. of Males over 20	129
No. of deaths last year	5
No. of births last year	3

LESLIE

No. of families	82
No. of Males	361
No. of Females	270
No. of Males over 20	172
No. of deaths last year	3
No. of births last year	25

The total population of the county by precinct is as follows:

	M	F	Total
Spring Branch	131	88	219
Hancock	69	68	137
Deer Creek	86	55	141
Wayne	742	558	1,300
La Porte	257	197	454
Leslie	361	270	631
Total,			2,882

Logan Valley Herald
June 13, 1884 (Vol. IX, No. 47)

Letter From Paris

Paris, May 7th, 1884.

On Monday evening at 6 o'clock we left London for Paris; reached Dover at 9:36 p.m., lunched there and took the steamer for Calais, across the English Channel. It was a beautiful moonlight flight, and the sea was very smooth "for the Channel", but to us quite rough; but we were not troubled with *mal de mer* at all. We were a little over an hour and a half in crossing, and many were sick but happily we were not. Many dread the trip

because the channel is always so rough, that it makes them sick, but we had a delightful trip. At 11:45 we took the train for Paris, arriving at that beautiful city on Tuesday morning; and taking a cab were driven to the London and New York hotel, where I sat down to the best breakfast I ever had in my life. We joined one of Cook's parties and drove out into the country, about 14 miles, passing a very fine church [St. Augustine] through one of the loveliest of parks, Park Moncean, the magnificent Arch de Triumphe, the lakes, Grand Cascade, and race course, the last two just outside of the city; the road leading through a beautiful or par view of the citadel of Mont Valberien, the town park and ruins of an old palace of St. Cloud. These places were about 8 miles from Paris and the route was one of the loveliest I have ever seen. After these places were visited we went through another beautiful park and walked to a palace built for Mme. Maintuen, afterwards the residence of Napoleon I. It was a grand old place, containing some twenty or thirty rooms, some of them containing the original furniture used by Napoleon and Josephine. Saw the private apartments of the unfortunate Empress, and a suite of rooms fitted up for Victoria in 1856, when she was visiting France. They are fitted up in red and gold, bed and hangings of red and gold silk. We saw many other things of interest, among them the state carriages, with their trimmings of gold, and linings of silk and satin. We then walked up to the palace of Versailles, built by Louis XIV, and since converted into a picture gallery and containing the largest and finest assortment of painting and statuary in the world. Drove to Sevres to visit its porcelain manufactory, back by way of Billancourt, Fortifications of Paris, Viaduct of Anteniul, along the banks of the Seine, passing many beautiful chateaux, and arriving at our hotel at 6 in the evening. Paris is truly the Frenchman's Paradise, and I regret that our stay here is so short, as we start to morrow morning for Italy. On our return, however, we will make amends, and after a visit to Scotland will do Paris before returning in September.
                                                            Maude.

Robert FINLAYSON was arrested on a warrant issued by 'Squire DAVIES, charged with having beaten and maltreated his wife. Before the prisoner was arraigned for trial, the affair was settled by FINLAYSON promising to go away and remain until Sept. 1st.

Logan Valley Herald
June 20, 1884 (Vol. IX, No. 48)

MARRIED: At the residence of the bride's parents, in Wayne precinct, on Wednesday, June 18th, 1884; W.H. GILDERSLEEVE, and Miss Katie CUNNINGHAM. Rev. G.M. LODGE officiating. There were quite a goodly number of friends and relatives present at the wedding, who by their gifts to the newly married pair showed the high esteem in which they are held. Below we give a list of the presents together with the names of the donors: Quilt, Grandmother; Family Bible, Father; Carpet, Mother; Silver Butter Knife, Sister Lillie; Picture Frame, brother Holmes; Large Lamp, Mr. and Mrs. NANGLE; Table Cloth and Napkins, Misses REED and MARTIN; a beautiful collection of flowers, Miss RAYMOND; Set silver Tea Spoons, Mr. and Mrs. W.D. SEIBER, Syracuse, N.Y.; Set Glass Ware, Mr. and Mrs. John T. MARRIOT, Wakefield; Pickle Dish, Mrs. G.W. COOK; Glass Cake Stand, Charles RICE, Wakefield; Set Silver Knives and Forks, Mr. and Mrs. E. CUNNINGHAM, Gilman, Iowa; Silver Pickle Dish and Castor, Charles COLEBURN and sisters, Gilman, Iowa; Table Cloth and Napkins, Miss Beckie GRANGER, Patterson, Pa.; Glass cake and fruit stand and dessert dishes, Miss Celia COYLE; Glass butter dish, Mrs. RICHARDSON; $5, Mrs. E. HAINING, Middletown, Pa.; Table Cloth and $5, Mr. and Mrs. W.T. CUNNINGHAM, Patterson, Pa.; Set Glassware, sister Ellen and brother Lloyd.

A Deplorable Death: Miss Angie, a 14-year old daughter of Mr. Henry B. MILLER, of this county, died at her house 9 miles west of this city, on Monday last, of lockjaw. Just a week previous in jumping off the porch at home, she had run a rusty nail in her foot. But little attention was paid to the slight wound, which apparently was healing rapidly until Saturday when she commenced to complain of pains in her neck, which grew worse until Sunday morning, when lockjaw set it. Drs. LOVE and CRAWFORD were at once summoned, but medical skill was of no avail and after enduring the most terrible agony, death put an end to her sufferings at 9:30 o'clock on Monday morning. Her mother was absent on a visit to her old home in Emerson, Iowa, and a telegram was sent her, but she did not receive it until after her daughter's death, but arrived in time for the funeral which took place on Wednesday morning. The family have the sympathy of the community in this hour of afflication, when death has invaded their home and taken a lovely girl just budding into womanhood.

Attempted Suicide.

Garret HARMSEN, a breaker, engaged in breaking about two miles west of this city, attempted suicide yesterday by shooting himself in the head. The gun used was an ordinary shot-gun, loaded with

No. 7 shot. He had evidently placed the muzzle of the gun at the base of the forehead, the charge ranging upwards and tearing off a sliver of bone from the *os frontis*, while his face was badly powder burnt. Dr. WIGHTMAN was called, and found the man rational, and on examination, discovered that but two or three of the shot had pierced the skull. Should inflammation of the brain not set in, he may recover. The patient claims that the shooting was the result of an accident, but Mr. NORRIS, with whom he is stopping says he has threatened to suicide several times, add in confirmation of this, HARMSEN said when first discovered that he had been kicked by one of his horses.

ROLL OF HONOR

of the Wayne Public Schools for the month ending June 13th, 1884. Names of those neither tardy nor absent.

PRIMARY DEPARTMENT

Amy BEARDSHEAR
Bessie WALLACE
Ella BENNETT
Edna SEWELL
Gracie ROBINSON
Pearl SEWELL
Maud WISE
Artie QUINN
David MORTON
Frank NANGLE

Frank GAERTNER
Frank MINER
Homer SKEEN
Henry GAERTNER
Monte GAERTNER
Norton HARRIS
Roscoe BENNETT
Vernie TAYLOR
Fred BEARDSHEAR
Bertie CARPENTER

Anna B. DAVIES, Teacher

HIGHER DEPARTMENT

Lalla MAURER
Helen LODGE
Emma SLATER
Louie BENSON
Dottie BROWN
Lizzie HAYES
Bertha ARMSTRONG
Grace MAURER

Carrie WISE
Fred ARMSTRONG
Geroge NANGLE
Charlie MORTON
John WISE
Harry FISHER
*Volney PORTER
*Wesley PORTER

Pupils marked thus * entered the second week of the month. For the remaining two weeks of school, we hope to have a "Roll of Honor" twice as large as the present one. Let pupils and parents make an extra effort to prevent tardiness and absence.

Respectfully Yours,
Susie B. DAVIS, Asst' Teacher
W.J. McCOY, Principal
Wayne, Neb., June 13, 1884

JULY 4TH
CELEBRATION IN WAYNE.

The coming anniversary of American Independence will be appropriately celebrated in Wayne, under the auspices of
CASEY POST, NO. 5, G.A.R.,

The committee on arrangements have made the following selection of officers and committees:

President of the day,	Jas. BRITTON
Vice Presidents,	John T. BRESSLER
	L.C. DEARBORN
	A.T. CHAPIN
	O.F. CRANE
	R.H. WILBUR
	J.P. CULVER
	O.H. BURSON
Marshal,	D.W. BRITTON
Ass't Marshal,	Peter COYLE
Chaplain,	Rev. G.M. LODGE
Orator,	Hon. W.F. NORRIS
Reader,	Frank FULLER

COMMITTEES:

Racing and Sports - E. H. EMERSON, Henry WARNER and Ed. MORTON.

Dancing - D.W. BRITTON, A.P. CHILDS and E.H. EMERSON.

Ragamuffins - Hon. Theoprastus Nonesuch HIGGENBOTHAM.

Stands - A.O. MYERS and Jas. E. HARMON.

Dinner - J.E. HARMON, Newton KROW, and Ladies of the Post.

An old fashioned army dinner of baked beans, sowbelly, hard tack and coffee will be served at 25 cents a plate. Complete program will be announced in city papers next week, and by posters.

By order of the Post.

• • •

American House.
Wayne, Neb.
Wm. G. VROMAN, Prop.

Logan Valley Herald
June 27, 1884 (Vol. IX, No. 49)

DIED: Mrs. J.J. MOORE living about 8 miles northwest of Wayne, died Monday morning, June 23, 1884. She, with her husband and family, had removed from eastern Iowa last spring. When she was 17 years of age she joined the M.E. church and lived a devoted christian life till the time of her death. The funeral took place from her home Tuesday morning, June 24th, conducted by Rev. H.G. PITTENGER, Pastor for the M.E. church. She leaves a husband and six children to mourn her loss.

Recovering. - Garret HARMSEN, the man who endeavored to secure a passage to the other world via a shotgun last week is recovering. He was removed Wednesday to Wayne. Since his shooting scrape, he has had the misfortune to lose a horse.

Mrs. PATTERSON's Letters.
Impression of Rome.

We arrived in Rome on May 19th at 6 o'clock in the morning, stopping at the "Allemagne Hotel" after breakfast we drove to the Vatican, which is the residence of the Pope, and went through the picture galleries and halls of statuary. We next visited St. Peter's, which, as you know, is the finest church in the world, I shall not attempt the impossible feat of describing it, beyond saying that it is very grand, and we were charmed with its magnificent beauty. After luncheon we drove out to see Ancient Rome, "the Rome which sat on her seven hills, and from her throne of beauty ruled the world," visiting the Forum, Pantheon, Arch of Titus, Palace of the Caesers, old Temples, the Coliseum and other interesting scenes. The Coliseum was a grand old theatre, four or five stories high, with no roof, merely an out-door affair, in which were given gladitorial fights, bull fights, circuses and other performances. All of them were just enough "ruined" to make them interesting. We purchased views of them all. In the afternoon we drove out to the Catacombs, the burial place of ancient Rome, and the meeting place of the early Christians. We descended some very steep steps, into a labyrinth of cells, with passages leading in every direction, and tombs all about us. The passages are very numerous and circuitous, and I was frightened all the while we were down them, and only felt relieved, when we emerged from the dismal place.

I like Rome very much. There are some very handsome streets, and very many poor ones, as is the case with all Italian cities we have visited. We were shown what is said to be the table on which "the last supper" was laid, and at another the staircase from the home of Pontius Pilate, which Christ descended after the judgement. No foot is allowed to profane the staircase, every one ascending on bended knees, and repeating a prayer at every step. Also the church built on the spot where Christ met St. Peter when the latter was fleeing from Rome.

Maude.

A Card.

The undersigned take this method of returning their thanks to their friends and neighbors for the many kind offices of affection shown during our recent trial and bereavement.

Henry B. MILLER
Adaline M. MILLER
Wayne, Neb. June 24th, 1884

Logan Valley Herald
July 4, 1884 (Vol. IX, No. 50)

BIRTH: Sunday, June 29th, to Mr. and Mrs. D.W.C. HOOD, a daughter.

MARRIED: At Scribner, June 23d, Mr. William BORKENHAGEN and Miss Antoinette ENGLISCH. The bride is a sister of Paul and Arthur ENGLISCH of this city.

DIED: Garret HARMSEN, a laborer employed two miles west of Wayne, shot himself in the forehead on Thursday of last week with a gun loaded with No. 7 shot, and has since died. No cause is given for the rash act. For a dead man, HARMSEN presents the liveliest kind of an appearance. (West Point Republican)

ROLL OF HONOR
of the Wayne Public Schools, June 27th, 1884.
PRIMARY DEPARTMENT

Bessie WALLACE	David MORTON
____ WACHOB	Fred BEARDSHEAR
Carrie PHILLIPS	Frank MINER
Gracie ROBINSON	Monte GAERTNER
Ella BENNETT	Henry GAERTNER
Mabel BENSON	Morton HARRIS
____ WALTERS	Vernie TAYLOR
Artie QUINN	Anna B. DAVIES, Teacher

HIGHER DEPARTMENT

Nora CRAWFORD
Alice MINER
Lalla MAURER
Maude WALLACE
Helen LODGE
Emma SLATER
Dottie BROWN
Mable GAMBLE
Lizzie HAYES
Pauline WACHOB
May DAVIES
Gracie BEARDSHEAR
Bertha ARMSTRONG
Fred ARMSTRONG

Gracie MAURER
Robbie ARMSTRONG
Geo. MEIRMAN
_____ MORGAN
Eddie LAWRENCE
George NANGLE
George MOORE
Frank GAMBLE
Charlie MORTON
John ELLSWORTH
John WISE
Fred HAGELIN
Harry FISHER
Wesley PORTER

Susie B. DAVIES, Ass't Teacher
W.J. McCOY, Principal

• • •

N.J. JUHLIN,
BOOT AND SHOE MAKER,
Wayne, Neb.

• • •

Logan Valley Herald
July 11, 1884 (Vol. IX, No. 51)

BIRTH: July 4th, 1884, to Mr. and Mrs. A.H. ELLIS, a son. Mr. ELLIS is now the father of two boys, both of whom were born on Independence day, while his only daughter was born on election day.

DIED: July 3d, near Wayne, Danna, infant son of J.E. and E.J. GLASS, aged 14 months.

A Card.

To the neighbors and friends who so kindly lent their assistance during our recent bereavement, we tender our sincere and heartfelt thanks.

J.E. GLASS
E.J. GLASS

An Assault Case. On Thursday evening last, W.R. TOWNS, a carpenter and painter who came to this city this spring, enraged at being refused more whisky at the saloon, threw a heavy leaden knuckle at Geo. BEARDSHEAR, barely missing his head and smashing a hole in the wall. Mr. BEARDSHEAR swore out a complaint charging TOWNS with assault with intent to kill, and after a preliminary hearing, Justice MEARS held him in $500 bail to await the action of the grand jury. Unable to procure bonds the prisoner was remanded to the care of the sheriff from whom he escaped on Sunday evening, and the sheriff now offers a reward of $25 for his arrest and detention.

Logan Valley Herald
July 25, 1884 (Vol. X, No. 1)

BIRTH: July 18th, near Wayne, to Mr. and Mrs. Robert LAPSELY, a son.

BIRTH: On Saturday, July 19th, in Wayne, to Mr. and Mrs. Alex. HOLZ, a daughter.

BIRTH: July 13th, near Wayne, to Mr. and Mrs. E.J. WALTON, a daughter.

MARRIED: At the home of the bride's parents in Mongaup Valley, N.Y., John S. WHEELER of Valley county, Neb., and Miss Ida WHEELER. The groom is a brother of the editor's wife, and accompanied her on her eastern trip.

Teacher's Institute

The following are the names of those who have attended the Institute during the past two weeks.

W.J. McCOY	Charles McLEOD
W.H. KENNEDY	Grace M. MAKIN
Anna B. DAVIES	Cella R. COYLE
Ada M. RAYMOND	Anna M. CHACE
Susie DAVIES	Juetha MILLER
Susie HUNTER	Augusta FLOHR
Eldona CLARK	E.B. SHERMAN
Prof. M.S. DAVIES	Edward NIELSON
Effie WISE	Blanche WISE
Chas. E. BARBOUR	Emma BUSBEE
Edith MEARS	Mamie McGINNIS

Logan Valley Herald
August 1, 1884 (Vol. IX, No. 50)

MARRIED: In Wayne, July 26th, by Rev. G.M. LODGE, Daniel ANDREWS of Stanton county and Miss Fannie May LEWIS of Missouri Valley, Iowa.

Grand Larceny

On Thursday of last week, having considerable money (about $125) in his pocket, the weight of which was uncomfortable, John F. SHERBAHN, our brick manufacturer, laid the sack containing it in a crevice in the shanty occupied by him when burning kiln, and at dinner time forgot to take it. After dinner he went down, but the money was gone. He at once suspected A.O. HENRY and employee in the yard, and a search warrant was obtained, and Andrew's person and premises searched, but without avail. The matter was then apparently dropped, but the eye of Justice in the person of Sheriff MINER was upon HENRY and every step he made, and every cent he spent was noted, and when the sheriff discovered that on Wednesday, HENRY had had a twenty-dollar gold piece changed at Wakefield, it was determined to arrest him. The arrest was accordingly made about 8 o'clock last evening, after which another search of his house was made, resulting in the finding of $90 of the money concealed in an album. When HENRY found that the money had been recovered, he weakened and confessed, telling when he took the money and just where he concealed it.

The examination was held before Justice MEARS this morning, resulting in the prisoner's being bound over to the District court in the sum of $500. Attorneys BRITTON and FULLER appeared for the prosecution, and W.M. WRIGHT for the defense.

The prisoner is a young man, 23 or 24 years of age, is married, and has a child about a year old. Has lived in Wayne about two years, and during most of that time has worked at well-digging, or as a laborer in the brick yard.

Logan Valley Herald
August 8, 1884 (Vol. IX, No. 51)

DIED: Rev. Wm. McCANDISH, an aged Presbyterian minister well known throughout the state and who will be remembered by many Wayne people, died in Omaha, Tuesday.

Wayne Herald-Tribune
August 15, 1884 (Vol. IX, No. 52)

The annual meeting of the Greenwood Cemetery Association will be held at the Citizen's Bank, Tuesday evening, August 19th, at 8 P.M. All members are requested to be present. M.S. DAVIES, Clerk.

A Pleasant Party

Dr. and Mrs. R.B. CRAWFORD dedicated their pleasant new home to the goddess of hospitality by sending over a hundred neat cards to their married friends in Wayne announcing that they would be "At Home" Thursday evenng. The amiable goddess herself must have presided on the occasion for last evening was as pleasant as could be wished for.

The guests were greeted by the host and hostess with a hearty cordiality that put everyone in a good humor at once, and the house, the porches and the grounds were filled with a laughing, chatting crowd. Soon after the guests arrived the cornet band put in an appearance and for half an hour or more enlivened the scene with a number of their best selections. Two long tables with seats to accomodate over a hundred persons at once were placed in the grounds which were gaily lighted up by Chinese lanterns and one table was filled the second time. In addition to the usual delicacies for such occasions, the Dr. had at considerable troubled procured plums, peaches, pears and grapes from California. It was a late hour when the guests bade the Doctor and Mrs. CRAWFORD good night. The occasion will long be remembered by those present, and if the writer ever attended a more social gathering he is unable to recall it.

Wayne Herald-Tribune
August 22, 1884 (Vol. X, No. 1)

BIRTH: Monday, Aug. 18th, to John GOSS and wife, a daughter.

BIRTH: Tuesday, August 19th, to L.C. ALLEN and wife, a son.

BIRTH: Wednesday, August 20th, to Jas. BUSH and wife, a daughter.

A difficulty between O.M. ELLSWORTH, Geo. GRONER and Al. SHERBAHN in the saloon Saturday night, culminated in a row in which ELLSWORTH was badly bruised.

I hereby notify all persons not to sell intoxicating liquors of any kind to O.M. ELLSWORTH, nor give nor procure them for him. Any person doing so will be prosecuted to the full extent of the law. J.P. GAERTNER.

PROGRAMME

Of First Annual Sunday School Convention of Wayne County, to be held at the Presbyterian Church in Wayne, Aug, 29th, 30th, and 31st, 1884, commencing at 8 o'clock, P.M.

Order of Exercises

FRIDAY EVENING.

8:00. Singing and Devotional Exercises.
8:30. Address of Welcome by Rev. G.M. LODGE.
8:45. What do I expect to Learn at this Convention? Rev. G.J. TRAVIS.
9:00. Singing.
9:05. The purpose and Importance of Sunday School Conventions. Rev. H.G. PITTENGER.

SATURDAY MORNING, AUG. 30TH.

9:00. Singing and Devotional Exercises.
9:30. Election of Officers.
9:55. Singing.
10:00. Tendency of Sunday Schools to Promote Christian Union. Rev. G.M. LODGE and others.
10:40. Singing.
10:45. The Relation of the Church to the Sunday School and the Duties Growing out of that Relation. Rev. G.J. TRAVIS, C.D. MARTIN and others.
11:10. Singing.
11:15. Relation of the Pastor to the Sunday School. Rev. G.H. SCHNUR, Rev. H.G. PITTENGER, Wm. MILLER.

AFTERNOON.

1:45. Devotional Exercises.
2:00. How best to secure the attendance of Sunday School Scholars at Church, E. MARTIN, J.L. FREEMAN and others.
2:25. Singing.
2:30. How to Retain the Older Scholars in the Sunday School, J.S. LOVE.
2:55. Singing.
3:00. Teacher and his Class outside of the Sunday School. J.R. MANNING and E. MARTIN.

EVENING.

8:00. Address by Rev. G.H. SCHNUR.
8:25. Singing.

8:30. The Evil Results of Closing Sunday School during Winter. J.S. LOVE, S.S. Missionary.
SUNDAY MORNING, AUG. 31ST.
10:30. Address by Rev. J.N. HICK of Wakefield.
AFTERNOON.
2:30. Children's Meeting. Singing. Addresses by Superintendents and Workers.
EVENING.
8:00. Self Culture of Teachers, G.J. TRAVIS. Music. History of Sunday School Music, Prof. M.S. DAVIES. Music. The Sunday School and American Citizenship, Rev. G.M. LODGE. Bring your Gospel Hymns, Music conducted by Prof. DAVIES.

• • •

FREEMAN & WELCH
General Insurance Agents
Wayne, Nebraska

• • •

MORTON BROS.
Livery & Feed
Stable

• • •

Wayne Herald-Tribune
August 29, 1884 (Vol. X, No. 1)

BIRTH: To Sylvester TAYLOR and wife, Saturday, August 23d, a daughter.

DIED: The sixteen months old son of Mr. and Mrs. Warner STARR, of Northside, Aug. 27th.

A Dangerous Ride.

The following extracts from a letter by Mr. D.C. PATTERSON to his brother, we take from the Omaha Bee of July 19th, but of which we were not able to obtain a copy at the time. It relates a very thrilling experience.

Cologne, Germany,
On the Rhine, June 4th, 1884.

My Dear Brother: -
Your favor of June 6th and 10th to hand yesterday. We

are always glad to hear from home. It has now been more than six weeks since we crossed the Alps - of which we have not written a word home, as I was afraid Maud's folks would feel very uneasy about us.

The morning of June 3d found us in a *diligence* (or post wagon) attached to five strong horses on our way up the Gnudo gorge on the Italian side of the Alps. There was scarcely room enough in the bottom of this gorge for the swollen stream and the road. The rain was pouring down, and waterfalls without number were constantly in sight. Sometimes we passed under them and sometimes through them. Dreary as our way seemed it was not without the greatest interest as we wound our weary way up the mountain side. We passed from the land of rain to the heat of sun; from the land of foliage to that of snow and ice, and when we reached the summit the snow was 24 inches deep. After taking a view of all Italian creation we began our descent. The dangerous portion of the road was yet to be traversed. We had had come but one-half mile when an avalanche encountered us. We could go no farther, neither could we retrace our journey as it was impossible to turn round. We did not know what to do. We were within two feet of a perpendicular precipice several thousand feet high. In fact it makes me dizzy yet when I think of the bottomless abyss it appeared to be on the one side of us and when I think of the cold, icy, merciless avalanche, suspended thousands of feet above us, it makes me tremble with terror and fright. To now return or attempt to return was equally perilous. Our driver and conductor were in an earnest and excited conversation. The other sole passenger (an Italian) sat stupefied. If you can imagine our feelings, do so, for I can not describe them. After a short wait three connisseurs (snow shovellers) came to our rescue. They went to work, making way for us. It was three-quarters of an hour, the longest we ever lived, that we sat in breathless silence and painful suspense, watching them work and at the same time keeping watch, turn about, to see if an avalanche would start to fall five or six thousand feet above us. Just as the workmen had made the way passable another avalanche came tearing down the mountain side and filled the road before us. The result of this was three-quarters of an hour of indescribly anxious suspense. I shall never forget how bravely those men worked.* The way was again passable and the heavy coach with those stout horses moved on with the utmost difficulty. They succeeded in drawing us through. The coach swayed so much we were sure we were going over - and down too. We moved on slowly for a few rods, in fact we could not go fast as I thought they would certainly stall in the deep snow, and that down a steep grade. We had gone I should think ten rods when a third avalanche stopped us - another wait of thirty long minutes. To look down into that abyss would try the strongest of unexperienced hearts. *

The passage was again declared to be clear, and the driver of 30 year's experience mounted the box and the coach moved on. We had almost gotten through when, horror of horrors, the *diligence* upset. Knowing too well what was below and what was not below, we gave up all as lost.

*But Providence interfered in our behalf. The horses so noble and trusty, kept their ground and with the assistance of the three connisseurs, kept that heavy stage coach on the edge of that frightful and bottomless abyss, with the hind wheels dangling over. I was on the upper side and lost no time in crawling through the coach-door window, drawing Maude after me - feeling though that the coach would certainly drop every second as it was so heavy and unweildy the men and horses could no longer hold it. The poor driver lost his balance and fell about 200 feet and landed on a ledge of rock projecting out, which was covered with four or five feet of snow. How they ever got him up I don't know. This I do know, if one had to go I wish it had been the conductor instead, as I attributed the accident largely to his negligence. The Italian passenger crawled out after us, lacerating his hands and face most terribly on the glass door. Being back on our feet in that narrow pass we felt it was a "haven of rest." The *diligence* being broken, we had to wade a mile through the snow to a house of refuge, where we remained till evening, when the next *diligence* came up the mountain and was turned around and carried us down to the foot of the Alps. We spent a couple of days in the Rhine valley; from there we went to Geneva, from which place I sent a complaint to the Swiss authorities, setting forth negligence on the part of the conductor. I herewith enclose their reply. If you have not forgotten your French you will be able to read it. Suffice it to say, Mr. conductor is now engaged in other business. We spent a day at Waterloo, one at Brussels, and are now on our way to England, where we will spend the time till the 29th of July, when we sail for New York.*

Your Bro.. D.C.P.

Notice is hereby given that L.O. DEARBORN did, on the 31st day of August, 1884, file his petition in the Clerk's office of the village of Wayne, asking that a druggist's permit may be granted him for the sale of malt, spirituous and vinous liquors, for medical, mechanical and chemical purposes.

A.P. CHILDS, Village Clerk.

Baseball.

The game of base ball between the Wakefield and Wayne clubs took place Saturday afternoon and after a closely contested game, the result was announced in favor of Wakefield by a score of 12 to 11. The Wayne club were considerably dissatisfied with the score as declared, insisting that several runs they had made were not counted. An additional reason for dissatisfaction was that in the 8th inning the Wakefield club sent their strong men to bat out of their regular order, which by the rules puts the batsman out, virtually making the score 11 to 9 in favor of the Wayne club, provided 11 scores were all they were entitled to. For these reasons the Wayne boys refused to pay over the stakes which were upon the game, but they offer to play over and increase the amount of money to $100. The following is the score as announced, by runs and outs:

WAYNE

	R.	O.
LIEBFRIED, s.s.	1	2
BRYANT, rf.	1	4
DEARBORN, 1b.	1	4
MORGAN, 2b.	2	3
DEARBORN, 3b.	2	3
O'HARA, lf.	1	2
SMITH, cf.	1	4
TOLLINGER, c.	0	3
McNEAL, p.	2	2
Total	11	27

WAKEFIELD

	R.	O.
PATCH	1	3
BENU, p.	1	2
SHUMWAY, ss.	1	4
VANDERSHULE, 1b.	1	3
RHEA, 2b.	2	3
DRAKE, 3b.	2	3
HERRINGTON, cf.	1	4
HAMMON, rf.	0	3
FRINK, lf.	3	2
Total	12	27

Wayne Herald-Tribune
September 5, 1884 (Vol. X, No. 3)

DIED: Thursday, Sept. 4th, Clifford, the infant son of Mr. and Mrs. C.H. JOHNSON. The funeral occurred this morning at 10 o'clock. The parents, who have been residents of Wayne but a few days, will have the sympathy of the entire community in their bereavement.

Tom LOUND, who lives near Northside, was arrested Saturday on the charge of an attempt to commit a rape upon the person of Mrs. R.E. TEMPLIN, and was brought before Esquire MEARS for examination. He waived examination and was placed under bonds of three hundred dollars to secure his appearance at the District Court.

The following committees have been appointed to take charge of the preparations for the exhibit by Wayne County at the Sioux City District Fair: Stock, D.W. BRITTON and P.C. MAURER; Grain and Vegetables, A.B. SLATER; Fruits &c., R.B. CRAWFORD; Fancy Articles, The Herald-Tribune.

Wayne Lodge No. 120, A.F. and A.M. was constituted Saturday last by Past Grand Master HAYES, with the following officers: W.M., James BRITTON; S.W., John T. BRESSLER; J.W., A.P. CHILDS; Treas., D.C. PATTERSON; Sec'y, B.F. FEATHER; S.D., W.L. HARRIS; J.D., C.O. FISHER; Stewards, D.W. BRITTON and M.F. GIDDINGS; T., Frank FULLER.

Wayne Herald-Tribune
September 12, 1884 (Vol. X, No. 4)

BIRTH: To R.H. MORGAN and wife, Thursday, September 4th, a girl.

BIRTH: To Mr. and Mrs. E.H. EMERSON, Friday, Sept. 5th, a daughter.

MARRIED: At the residence of M.P. AHERN, in Wayne, Monday September 8th, Mr. Richard GRANFIELD and Miss Ella MALONE, Rev. Father KEARNEY, of Norfolk, officiating.

DIED: Monday September 8th, in Wayne, of consumption, Geo. R. AMENT, aged 26 years. Mr. AMENT came to Wayne a few weeks since from Yorkville, Ill., in the hope that he might be benefitted by the change, but the disease had too strong hold on him. He leaves a widow, and a child three months old, who will return to Illinois. The body was taken to Illinois for burial.

Will TOLLINGER had both hands cut very badly in a scuffle with Dell STRICKLAND the first of the week, by the latter drawing his hand in which he had an open pen-knife through Will's hand. Will gets a vacation of a couple of weeks by it and is considering whether he will get some circulars to hand out to every one asking him what's the matter with his hands.

We are informed that among those badly injured at the fall of the grand stand at the Fremont re-union last week, was Jesse HAMILTON, of Northside in this county. We have been unable to learn the extent of his injuries, beyond the fact that his name appeared in the list of seriously injured. He was brought home by the way of Norfolk.

About two weeks ago, the wife of Wm. H. HUNT, one of the old residents of La Porte, developed symptoms of insanity. She was taken to Wakefield for treatment, but has grown rapidly worse, and is now violently insane. She will probably have to be sent to the asylum at Lincoln for treatment.

Wayne Herald-Tribune
September 19, 1884 (Vol. X, No. 5)

BIRTH: To Mr. and Mrs. Henry MYERS, of this city, September 13th, a daughter.

BIRTH: Wednesday morning, September 16th, to Mr. and Mrs. C. WHITING, a daughter.

• • •

THE CHICAGO STORE,
WHITTON & WOOLSTON,
Successors to
H.A. MOORE,
General Dealers in
Dry Goods, Boots and Shoes, and
Groceries

W. H. WORDLEY
is prepared to take contracts for digging
Wells, Cellars & Cisterns
Wayne, Nebraska

• • •

NEW LUMBER YARD.
BAILEY & DYER,
Yards on Second Street, East of the Boyd.

• • •

Wayne Herald-Tribune
September 26, 1884 (Vol. X, No. 6)

MARRIED: H.P. SHUMWAY and Miss Nellie HOWARD, two of Wakefield's most worthy young people, were married on Wednesday night.

Jesse HAMILTON is improving slowly from the injuries he received at the reunion at Fremont. (Northside)

Proceedings of the District Court.
Cases coming before the Court at the present term were disposed of as follows:

E.L. MONROE vs. Robert FINLAYSON and Elizabeth FINLAYSON, dismissed.

E.L. MONROE vs. Watson PARISH and M.A. FREELAND, case transferred to the United States court.

HARDENBURG and JOHNSON vs. Benjamin HERNER, dismissed.

C.L. LAMB vs. The Fremont and Elkhorn Valley Railroad, continued.

R.B. CRAWFORD vs. Wayne county Demurer overruled and defendant allowed 30 days to answer.

J.H. JOHNSTON vs. J.O. MILLIGAN & Co., Appeal from Justice's court, Judgment reversed.

Frank FULLER, Admr. vs. Emily PRATT, et al, order granted for sale of real estate.

John LAKE vs. Wayne county, continued.

PETERSON & DAVIES vs. A. GOULD, continued for service.

J.I. CASE & Co. vs. B.C. WHITTAKER, continued.

L.C. BLACK vs. James DUGAN, et al, continued for further proof.

E.B. CLARK vs. Michael BRAASCH and Mary BRAASCH, sale of property confirmed.

McCormick Harvesting company vs. John AGLER, continued by consent.

McCormick Harvesting company vs. Annie B. BLACK and Joseph A. DUKE, continued by consent.

John T. BRESSLER vs. James McQUINN, default judgment and decree.

A.B. SLATER and C.C. MERRIAM vs. R.B. CRAWFORD and I.N. FLICKINGER, motion to make more specific, sustained and plaintiffs allowed time to amend.

H.B. BOYD vs. W.O. GAMBLE, continued.

H. LEY vs. H.B. BOYD & Co., dismissed.

School District No. 17 vs. Wayne county, continued.

L.C. CLARK vs. Jamed DUGAN, et al, default.

H.A. MOORE vs. Joseph QUINLIN, order for conveyance of real estate.

J.A. GRAY vs. AGLER & WILKINS, default and judgment.

State of Nebraska vs. A.O. HENRY, plea of guilty of grand larceny; sentence to 15 months hard labor in penitentiary.

State vs. Wm. R. TOWNS, no arrest, continued.

State vs. Thomas LOUND, continued.

Wm. M. WRIGHT vs. W.K. MOORE, dismissed.

F.M. SKEEN vs. B.S. GIBSON, judgment for deft.

P.A. ENGLISCH vs. James J. JOHNSON, dismissed.

A.O. HENRY plead guilty to the charge of grand larceny yesterday and was sentenced to fifteen months in the penitentiary by Judge CRAWFORD.

Accidental Shooting.

A.H. CROSBY of Wakefield was accidentally shot Wednesday evening, it is feared fatally. So far as we have been able to learn the accident happened as follows. He was out hunting with some friends and his gun was handed him by one of the party, when it slipped through a hole in the bottom of the buggy and the hammer striking against something the gun discharged, the entire charge entering his left breast inflicting a ghastly wound. He was at once taken to the resident of J.H. SECHLER, a physician summoned, and everything possible was done. We are informed that there is but small hope of his recovery.

The grand jury found indictments against A.O. HENRY for grand larceny, against Thomas LOUND for assault with intent to commit rape, and against W.R. TOWNS for assault with intent to commit murder.

Yet Another Suicide.
An Unfortunate Woman Hangs Herself.

Consirable excitement was caused yesterday morning by the report on the streets that Wayne had been the scene of another suicide, the victim being Mrs. Matilda ZWALD, who with her husband has been living in the shanty just east of DEARBORN's drug store. Coroner BARTLETT was notified at once and a jury was summoned and the following facts were elicited by the inquest. The deceased and ZWALD has been married about three months and their marriage life had been an almost continuous quarrel, Mrs. ZWALD being a woman with an almost ungovernable temper. She had been more than usually quarrelsome for a few days, and the evening before had driven her husband out of the house and he slept in a barn across the way. When he returned in the morning he found the door locked and cooked his breakfast in the shed, and then called to the children, who got up and opened the door. When the door was opened the body of the deceased was found hanging by a rope within a foot or two of the door, with the feet firmly planted on the floor, the rope having cut into the neck until it was out of sight. The jury after hearing the testimony of the members of the family, and of Dr. CRAWFORD, who was called as a medical expert, rendered their verdict that the deceased came to her death by her own hand while laboring under a fit of temporary insanity. She was about 40 years old and had been twice married before.

• • •

H. E. NYE
Attorney at Law
Wayne, Neb.

• • •

TAILORS
LEVIN & REINART
Have opened a Tailor Shop in Wayne with a full line of
Imported and Domestic Suitings.
First Class Cutting and Workmanship Guaranteed.

Wayne Herald-Tribune
October 3, 1884 (Vol. X, No. 7)

SOCIETIES.

I.O.O.F., Wayne Lodge, No. 118, meets Monday evening in Masonic Hall. A.A. WELCH, N.G., M.S. DAVIES, Secretary.

A.O.U.W., Wayne Lodge, No. 38, meets the first and third Friday evenings in each month. Frank FULLER, M.W.; T.J. STEELE, Recorder.

A.F. & A.M., Wayne Lodge, No. 120, meets in Masonic Hall the second and fourth Fridays in each month. James BRITTON, W.M.; B.F. FEATHER, Secretary.

G.A.R., No. 5, meets second and fourth Wednesday evenings in each month, in Masonic Hall. Chas. JOHNSON, Com.; A.P. CHILDS, Adjt.

CHURCH DIRECTORY.

Presbyterian Church. Services every Sabbath morning and evening, Sabbath school at 12 M. Prayer meeting Wednesday evening. Rev. G.M. LODGE, Pastor; J.A. LINDLEY, Supt. S.S.

Methodist-Episcopal Church. Services every Sabbath at 11:00 A.M., and 8:30 P.M. Sabbath School at 10:00 A.M. Rev. H.G. PITTINGER, Pastor; Wm. MILLER, Supt. S.S.

Evangelical Lutheran Church. Services every Sabbath mornng at 11 o'clock, Sabbath School at 10 A.M. Prayer meeting Wednesday evening. Rev. G.H. SCHNUR, Pastor.

Baptist Church. Services every alternate Sabbath at 11 A.M. and 8:45 P.M. Sabbath School at 12 M., every Sabbath. Rev. G.J. TRAVIS, Pastor.

MARRIED: On the 24th of September, 1884, in Wayne, Wayne county, Nebraska by E. MARTIN, county judge, Mr. Enos ADAMSON of Hastings, Nebraska, to Miss Nancy NEASHET, of Iowa.

MARRIED: On the 25th of September, 1884, in Wayne, Neb., by E. MARTIN, county judge, Mr. Carl THOMPSON to Miss Hannah KAY, all of Wayne county, Nebraska.

DIED: A.H. CROSBY, the man who was accidentally shot last Thursday morning died Saturday morning.

Wayne Herald-Tribune
October 17, 1884 (Vol. X, No. 9)

Wayne County

Wayne County, Nebraska is situated on the northeastern part of the State, in the second tier of counties from the Missouri River. The soil is of the greatest fertility, and no county in the state is better adapted to farming and stock-raising than Wayne. The county now has a population of between four and five thousand, principally well-to-do and intelligent farmers from Iowa, Illinois and other western states. The character of farm buildings and improvements is remarkably good for a new country, and is noticed by all strangers visiting us. The county is well supplied with schools, there being now 29 school districts. Parties seeking homes will do well to visit Wayne county and investigate the advantages it offers.

WAYNE,
the county seat of Wayne county, is a rapidly growing town of nearly 1,000 inhabitants, situated about 45 miles from Sioux City, on the C. St. P. M. & O. R'y, in the famous Logan Valley. Wayne is the market for a large scope of country, and has a large and increasing trade. Its business houses, residences and improvements testify to the push, taste and intelligence of its inhabitants. The improvements for 1884 will aggregate over $60,000, and already a large amount of building for the coming year is being planned. Persons wishing any information in regard to the best, handsomest and most promising new town in Nebraska can obtain it by addressing a letter of inquiry to the Herald-Tribune.

BIRTH: To R.C. OSBORN and wife, October 4th, a son.

BIRTH: To H.C. WRIGHT and wife, on Saturday, October 11th, a daughter.

ROLL OF HONOR
of the Wayne Public Schools for the month ending October 10:
PRIMARY DEPARTMENT
(neither tardy nor absent)

Enda SEWELL
Grace ROBINSON
Pearl SEWELL
Chettie WITTER
David MORTON

Henry GAERTNER
Monte GAERTNER
Mattie COYLE
*Geo. THOMPSON
*Louise THOMPSON

Frank GAERTNER

*Seward TRAVIS
Anna B. DAVIES, Teacher

HIGHER DEPARTMENT

Katie PORTER
Grace MAURER
Mary NUSBAUM
Lizzie HAYES
Bertha ARMSTRONG
Dottie BROWN
Cora SIMMONS
Lalla MAURER
Mabel GAMBLE
Daisy WITTER

Helen LODGE
Eva BEEBE
Clint SLATER
Geo. COYLE
Rollin OXFORD
Charlie MORTON
Frank GAMBLE
Richard COYLE
Robbie ARMSTRONG
*Lee TRAVIS

* Did not enter at the beginning of the month, but have not been absent or tardy since entering.

Susie B. DAVIES, Ass't Teacher

Next Monday, we hope to begin school in the new building and in our new quarters will be glad to receive calls from any of the patrons. We take this opportunity of extending an invitation to call.

Yours Respectfully,
W.J. McCOY, Principal

Wayne Herald-Tribune
October 24, 1884 (Vol. X, No. 10)

MARRIED: At the residence of the bride's parents in Sioux City, on Sunday, October 9th, Mr. N. ROBITAILLE of Wayne, and Miss Augustine REDOUTY, of Sioux City. Their many friends will join in wishing them a long and happy married life.

Wayne Herald-Tribune
October 31, 1884 (Vol. X, No. 11)

John CUMMINS, the baggageman on Conductor INGRAHAM's train, while endeavoring to climb on a moving car at Hoskins Monday night, fell from the car and the wheel passed over his leg crushing it so badly that it was necessary to amputate it above the knee. The unfortunate man has been generally regarded as one of the best men on the Nebraska division, and was a universal favorite among the railroad boys.

Wayne Herald-Tribune
November 7, 1884 (Vol. X, No. 12)

Notice of Application for the Appointment of an Administrator of the Estate of Jane ZWALD, Deceased.

Application having been made this 27th day of October 1884, for the appointment of Frank FULLER as administrator of the estate of Jane ZWALD, deceased.

Notice is hereby given that the said application will be heard at my office in Wayne, Wayne county, Nebraska, on the 17th day of November, 1884, at one o'clock P.M., and it is hereby ordered that the foregoing notice be published for three successive weeks in the Herald-Tribune.

E. MARTIN
County Judge.

Wayne Herald-Tribune
November 20, 1884 (Vol. X, No. 14)

Precinct Officials.

The following persons have received certificates of election from the county clerk:

GARFIELD

Assessor, F.A. BERRY; Justice, M.J. ROOT; Constable, James HARMON.

DEER CREEK

Assessor, J.R. MANNING; Overseers of Highways, Dist. 24, J.A. BROWN; Dist. 27, I.D. HICKERT.

WAYNE

Assessor, H.C. WRIGHT; Overseers of Highways, Dist. 23, John PERRY; Dist. 20, Wm. RICHIE; Dist. 3, W.P. AGLER; Dist. 17, Geo. STERRETT; Dist. 7, D.W.C. HOOD; Dist. 22, J.D. ADAMS; Dist. 11, Chas. FIGGINS; Dist. 12, O.P. ANDERSON.

LOGAN

Assessor, Ira B. WILSON; Overseers of Highways, Dist 1., Geo MITCHELL; Dist. 16, John T. METTLEN.

LESLIE

Assessor, C.A. FOX; Overseers of Highways, Dist 10, L. WARNOCK; Dist. 15, L. KELLER; Dist. 14, J.W. WHITE.

PLUM CREEK

Assessor, Charles ERXLEBEN; Overseers of Highways, Dist. 18, W.H. GILDERSLEEVE; Dist. 2, Wm. BIERMAN.

BRENNA

Assessor, James KELLEY; Overseers of Highways, Dist. 9, James BAIRD; Dist 19, J.A. GRAY; Justices, Fletcher PRICE and Wm. BENSCHOFF; Constables, Edward ADAMSON and C. FRINK.

HANCOCK

Assessor, Warner STARR; Overseer of Highway, Dist. 5, Perrin LONG.

SPRING BRANCH

Assessor, Wm. BERNHARDT; Overseer of Highways, Dist 4, J. WEATHERHOLT; Justices, A.L. HOWSER and J.W. POWELL; Constables, Wm. WINTER and Wm. LALK.

Wayne Herald-Tribune
December 4, 1884 (Vol. X, No. 16)

MARRIED: At the residence of Rev. G.M. LODGE in Wayne, Thursday Nov. 27th 1884, Louis E. HUNTER and Miss Susan KNAGGS, both of Wakefield, Rev. G.M. LODGE officiating. Both bride and groom are well known here, and their many friends will unite with us in wishing them a happy and prosperous married life. Mr. HUNTER was formerly one of the proprietors of this paper, but he has abandoned the joys and sorrows of country journalism for the more certain and satisfying rewards of a mercantile life.

Wayne Herald-Tribune
December 11, 1884 (Vol. X, No. 17)

MARRIED: At the residence of the bride's parents at Mt. Sterling, Ills., Saturday, November 29th, J.S. HAKE of Wayne, and Mrs. Lucy ALLEN, of Mt. Sterling.

Mr. and Mrs. HAKE returned to Wayne last Friday evening and the Professor has been since receiving the congratulations of his friends, which includes about all the people of the county. To Mrs. HAKE the people of Wayne and vicinity will extend the heartiest greeting, with the hope that she may ever find the new scenes and the new associations pleasant. Mrs. HAKE is an accomplished musician and a cultured lady, and will be a welcome acquisition to the musical and social circles of Wayne.

We take from the Mt. Sterling Democrat the following

account of the wedding and the very complimentary notice regarding Mrs. HAKE.

"On last Saturday evening, at the palatial residence of Dr. J.B. GLASS, his charming and accomplished daughter, Mrs. Lucy ALLEN, was united in marriage with J.S. HAKE, Esq., of Wayne, Neb., Rev. S.M. MORTON of Jacksonville, officiating, Rev. Mr. LOWRIE, pastor of the Presbyterian church of this city, of which Mrs. ALLEN is an earnest and consistent member, being absent from the city. No cards were issued and only a few intimate friends were present. After the ceremony an elegant collation was spread of which those present partook and which was greatly enjoyed. The happy couple left on the evening train for Jacksonville, Mr. HAKE's old home, where they remained only long enough to receive the hurried but most hearty congratulations of hosts of friends, the bride having graduated at one of the universities in that city, where she was beloved by all who knew her. They proceeded the same night to Chicago, where they remained a few days and from there to their home in Nebraska.

Of the bride it is unnecessary to speak. She was raised in our city, everybody knew her, and to know her was to love and respect her. She was one of our most accomplished young ladies, the finest musician, perhaps in the city and for years presided at the organ of the Presbyterian church.

A wedding was never consummated under more favorable auspices, "two hearts that beat as one," were never joined whose lines promise to fall in pleasanter places. The Democrat, one and all extend their congratulations."

Wayne Herald-Tribune
December 18, 1884 (Vol. X, No. 18)

ROLL OF HONOR

of Wayne public schools for the month ending December 3, 1884.
PRIMARY DEPARTMENT
(neither tardy nor absent)

Daisy OXFORD	David MORTON
Ella BENNETT	Frank NANGLE
Grace ROBINSON	Frank GAERTNER
Lena ZWALD	Henry GAERTNER
Maud WISE	Mont GAERTNER
____ WALTERS	Harry BEEBE
Pearl SEWALL	Homer SKEEN
Jessie WACHOB	Lloyd SMITH
Lois CHILDS	Mattie COYLE
Osie TAYLOR	Roscoe BENNETT

Della COOK
Maud BRITTON
Alice FORDYCE
August SALTZWEDEL
Berti WALLACE
Chettie WITTER

Bertie CARPENTER
*Robert HEFTI
*Rudolph HEFTI
*Annie HEFTI
*Johnnie ZWALD
*Jamie AHERN

Anna B. DAVIES, Teacher

INTERMEDIATE DEPARTMENT

Kate PORTER
Daisy WITTER
Lizzie HAYES
Bertha ARMSTRONG
Dotta BROWN

Harry FISHER
Charlie MORTON
Richard COYLE
Robert FORDYCE
*Wesley PORTER

Susie DAVIES, Teacher

HIGHER DEPARTMENT

Ivan MAURER
Ed. LODGE
Samuel ALEXANDER
*Charlie BEEBE
*Willie BEEBE
*Raymond TRACY
*Gus TRACY

*Bert PORTER
*Frank TRACY
Mabel GAMBLE
Laura MINER
Eva BEEBE
May CHACE

* Did not enter at the beginning of the month.

The scarlet fever has affected the length of the "Roll of Honor" to some extent.

W.J. McCOY, Prin.

Wayne Herald-Tribune
December 25, 1884 (Vol. X, No. 19)

Cotton Wedding

A houseful of guests joined with Mr. and Mrs. E.M. SMITH last Saturday evening in the celebration of the first year of their married life. The chilly blasts that made being out doors unpleasant, only made the scene within more attractive, while every guest received a hearty welcome that made all feel at home. The evening passed pleasantly and rapidly until the clock told the hour of twelve, and the guests bade host and hostess a reluctant good night. Mrs. SMITH received a large number of presents, useful, ornamental and suggestive, to assist her in recalling the pleasant occasion.

Wayne Herald-Tribune
January 1, 1885 (Vol. X, No. 20)

BIRTH: To Wm. MOREY and wife, a splendid Christmas present in the shape of a bouncing boy.

BIRTH: To S.R. GIBSON and wife, Friday Dec. 26, a son.

BIRTH: To F.M. GRIFFITHS and wife, Wednesday Dec. 31st, a son.

MARRIED: At the residence of H.E. MYERS, Wayne, Wednesday, Dec. 24th, 1884, Mr. Axel KOEFOED and Miss Christina JENSEN, Rev. G.J. TRAVIS officiating.

MARRIED: Wm. ALBEE, of Wayne county, and Miss Gertie JENKINS, daughter of W. JENKINS, of Logan Grove, were married at the residence of the bride's parents on Thursday, Dec. 11th. Miss JENKINS is the most popular young lady in the neighborhood in which she lives, and from a personal acquaintance with Mr. ALBEE for over two years, we know he is worthy of the bride he has won. (Ponca Advocate)

ROLL OF HONOR
of Wayne Public Schools (neither tardy nor absent)
PRIMARY DEPARTMENT

Anna BEARDSHEAR
Bessie WALLACE
Edna SEWELL
Ellen BENNETT
Jessie WACHOB
Bertie WALLACE
Chettie WITTER
Dave MORTON
Frank GAERTNER
Freddie BEARDSHEAR

Harvey BEEBE
Henry GAERTNER
Harry GAMBLE
Homer SKEEN
Mattie COYLE
Roscoe BENNETT
Tommy COOK
Vernie TAYLOR
Seward TRAVIS
Plummer HUFF

Anna B. DAVIES, Teacher
INTERMEDIATE DEPARTMENT

George COYLE
Rollin OXFORD
Harry FISHER
John ELLSWORTH
Charlie MORTON
Frank GAMBLE
John WISE

Robbie ARMSTRONG
Lee TRAVIS
Martin TOLANDER
Robert FORDYCE
Lemmie MEARS
Daisy WITTER
Pauline WACHOB

Geo. MOORE
Cora SIMMONS
James COYLE
James WACHOB
Clint SLATER
John COYLE
Ed LODGE
Mark MILLER
Charlie BEEBE
William BEEBE

Bertha ARMSTRONG
Susie DAVIES, Teacher
HIGHER DEPARTMENT
Gus TRACY
Frank TRACY
John REES
Carrie WISE
Mabel GAMBLE
Helen LODGE
Nora CRAWFORD
Nelie AMENT
W.J. McCOY, Principal
Wayne, Neb., Dec. 19, 1884

Wayne Herald-Tribune
January 8, 1885 (Vol. X, No. 21)

Wayne County Finances
A List of the Tax Payers who have
Contributed Fifty Dollars or More
to the County Fund.

The following list, taken from the county treasurer's cash book, gives the names of persons paying taxes in Wayne county to the amount of fifty dollars or more. The amounts are given in even dollars, odd cents being disregarded.

J.A. BENT	$138
Thos. HUGHES	61
O.S. WHITHAM	80
C.A. BUCKS	58
J. BROD	63
R.H. GODDARD	52
E.A. GAMMEL	448
C. St. P.M. & O R'y	4602
R.M. WALLACE	51
John LAKE	72
J.C. HAVEMEYER	204
Jerusha MILLS	51
Geo. Warren SMITH	150
H.B. SCOTT	51
A.J. PRESTON	62
R.J. TIRRILL	60
Jno. WEIR	69
H.R. WOODALL	103
J.T. BRESSLER	90
I.N. FLICKINGER	107

L.V. Land Co.	$111
J. DAVENPORT	515
W.M. BENNETT	64
G. WEATHERHOLT	81
Fred SCHRODER	73
N. ORCUTT	84
STARR & Co.	73
P.A. ENGLISCH	352
O.H. CONE	79
T.J. STEELE	69
A.W. CROSS	73
O.D. BROWN	105
W. STOWE	82
D.L. STRICKLAND	99
LINN Bros.	91
O.D. REINKING	51
R. ARMSTRONG	54
E.B. KING	223
S.W. SMITH	96
F. THOMPSON	68
L. NEWTON	111
B. KELLEY	64
JOHNSON, SMITH & Son	66
M. HETTINGER	88
J. BOEKENHAUER	67
Thos. PAUL	74
Jas. MACK	67
H.A. MOORE	85
S.W. RAWSON	56
J.W. JONES	91
J.C. BROWN	168
C.R. GODDARD	499
J.P. GAERNTER	60
D.W. COMSTOCK	61
Seth RICHARDS	169
R.B. TAYLOR	577
E.B. BILLS	99
A.E. PLATNER	63
A.T. CHAPIN	157
J.M. STRAHAN	297
G.M. LODGE	70
D.W. and L.J. BRITTON	87
DUFF Bros.	57
BRESSLER & PATTERSON	553
C.E. GILL	237

Jno. ZWALD	$65
G.H. SCHNUR	52
E. SEWELL	58
J.H. PINGERY	113
E.L. JONES	120
J.M. PULLEN	55
W.H. SHEPHERD	51
SLATER & MERRIAM	725
H. LEY	108
W.E. CARLIN	129
E.J. NANGLE	54
Geo. WHITTON	64
A. WHITE	83
Wm. HOUSE	99
D. LATHAM	58
E.K. SMITH	142
CHACE & NEELY	78
F.M. NORTHROP	73
C. JOHNSON	68
E.A. HOWARD	57
L.C. DEARBORN	65
C. MOORE	148
CARTWRIGHT & Co.	77
F.E. MOSES	99

The list gives only the names where taxes have been paid. Quite a number of additional names would appear if all taxes had been paid.

Report

Of school in District No. 14, for the month ending December 26, 1884:

No. of pupils enrolled	20
Average attendance	15.6

Names of pupils not absent during the month: Jacob MILLER, Edward MILLER, Guy EMERSON, Nettie KLUEVER.

Those whose deportment was 97 or better in a scale of 100: Fred MILLER, 100; Harvey SPHAR, 100; Sarah CAVANAUGH, 100; Mont. SPHAR, 99; Dillie FLOHR, 99; Flora FLOHR, 99; Jacob MILLER, 98; Fred HAGELEN, 97.5; Nettie KLUEVER, 97.

Hoskins Items.

I will give you a list and cost of the improvements made in 1884 in our town and surrounding neighborhoods:

TOWN IMPROVEMENTS.

J.L. CLINE, house	$300

R. WILKINS, house	$250
W.E. GLEASON, house and stables	600
C.W. WOOLEY, house and stables	700
J.P. WRIGHT, stable	100
Carl DANIELS, house and stable	300
A.L. HOWSER, house and stable	800
	$3,050

COUNTY IMPROVEMENTS.

John BERNHARDT, stable	$200
F. SHRADER, granary	200
School house dist.	800
Mr. JOHNSON, imp. house, stable	700
Mr. CHAPMAN, imp. house, stable	250
Mr. ANDERSON, imp. house, stable	200
John ELLIOTT, house and stable	800
Chas. MASS, house and stable	500
Chas. WENDT, granary	200
Aug. HOHNEKE, house	300
Jas. ELLIOTT, imp. house, stable	150
L. ZEIMER, Jr., imp. house, stable	150
Mr. ECHARDT, house	350

The improvements have been light and with small amounts, owing to close times for money this year. Reporter.

Wayne Herald-Tribune
January 15, 1885 (Vol. X, No. 22)

Pasadena, Cal., Jan. 1, '85

Ed., Herald-Tribune:

I wish all my Logan Valley friends a happy new year. With me it is the happiest New Year I ever saw. The theremometer stands at 65 degrees above zero this morning, though it has been down to 40. The hardest wind that I have seen here was just hard enough to turn a wind mill fast enough to pump, have been waiting for winter to come, but it don't come. I have come to the conclusion that this is the place God has prepared for man, and his situation will depend on his money, and instead of crossing the River Jordan to reach this evergreen shore you will have to cross one thousand miles of a terrible desert.

I can remember one year ago today my brother and I were snowed in for three days at Mr. CHAONS'. We managed to send to Wayne and get a keg of beer, and had what they call a good time. I don't know what a man in this country would call it. I know that you have a good country there for a poor man to get a start and can stand the cold winters I think I have had my share and I don't wish for any more of it.

If a man has anything in this country he has to work for it as well as anywhere. California is about a hundred and fifteen years old, and yet is new country. It has improved more in the last two years than in all the rest of the time. In twenty years southern California will be all in town lots from one to twenty acres each and valued at from $500 to $1500 per acre.

Oranges are ripe now. Come and get some.

I have my grain all sowed and now I am getting out grapevines and trees. I shall take the boat for San Luis Obespo on business to morrow and have no more time to write.

Yours Truly, J.T. BUTLER

Wayne Herald-Tribune
January 22, 1885 (Vol. X, No. 23)

MARRIED: JONES - ENGLISCH. Married at the residence of the bride's parents near Scribner, Nebraska, Thursday Jan. 15th, 1885, E.L. JONES of Wayne, and Agnes ENGLISCH, Rev. M.B. HARRISON officiating. The wedding was a very quiet one only the family and a few intimate friends being present.

The above announcement tell of the union for life of two of Wayne's most estimable young people. Mr. JONES is the resident member of the lumber firm of E.L. JONES & Co., and is widely known and respected throughout the county. Miss ENGLISCH was one of the most popular of our young ladies, and among her friends were numbered all who knew her. To Mr. and Mrs. JONES the Herald-Tribune extends its heartiest congratulations, with the hope that the new life thus happily begun may be an unclouded one of peace and prosperity. They returned to Wayne Friday having driven across the country from Wisner, accompanied by F.A. DEARBORN and Miss Nettie MASON, who went over to attend the wedding.

The following is a list of the presents to the bride: China Tea Set, Miss Nettis MASON and Frank A. DEARBORN; Silver Castor, Miss Lizzie SMITH; Silver Butter Dish, Knife and Table-Spoons and Mantel Clock, Mrs. ENGLISCH and Mrs. BORGENHAGEN, mother and sister of bride; Silver Cake Basket, brother Arthur ENGLISCH; Camp Rocker, Mr. and Mrs. P.A. ENGLISCH; Solid Silver Teaspoons, Father JONES; Carving Set and Napkins, Mr. and Mrs. H.C. WRIGHT; Handsome Tidy, Miss Emma BONNAWITZ, Milwaukee, Wisconsin; Silver Knives, Forks, Tea and Tablespoons, Groom.

Below we give a list of the officers of the Philomathean society, the literary organization of the higher department of the Wayne schools:

James COYLE, President; Bert PORTER, Vice President; Minnie GAMBLE, Secretary; Clint SLATER, Editor; Ida SLATER, Assistant Editor; James WACHOB, Prosecuting Att'ry; Stewart JOHNSON, Serg't-at-Arms; Eva MYERS, Critic; Minnie SMITH, Treasurer.

The following officers of Wayne Lodge No. 118, I.O.O.F. were installed Monday night by E.E. PARKER, of Covington, special D.D.G.M.: Jno. T. BRESSLER, N.G.; M.S. DAVIES, V.G.; R.J. MORGAN, Sec.; J.J.W. FOX, Treas.; E.J. NANGLE, War.; Chas. JOHNSON, Cond.; A.S. MINER, O.G.; I.O. RICHARDSON, I.G.; James BRITTON, R.S.N.G.; B. CUNNINGHAM, L.S.N.G.; R.H. SKILES, R.L.V.G.; R.B. TAYLOR, R.S.S.; Jas. A. ELLIOTT, L.S.S.

Wayne Herald-Tribune
January 29, 1885 (Vol. X, No. 24)

Report

Of school in district No. 14, for the month ending Jan. 23, 1885:

No. enrolled   21
Average attendance   16.8

Names of those not absent - Geo. KLUEVER, Guy EMERSON, Sarah CAVANAUGH.

Names of those having a deportment of 97 or better in a scale of 100: Mont SPHAR, 100; Harvey SPHAR, 100; Dillie FLOHR, 100; Flora FLOHR, 100; Emma KLUEVER, 100; Sarah CAVANAUGH, 99; Nettie KLUEVER, 99.7; Jabob MILLER, 99.4; Amanda FLOHR, 99.4; Fred MILLER, 99; Fred HAGELIN, 97.4.

Wayne Herald-Tribune
February 5, 1885 (Vol. X, No. 25)

BIRTH: To J.S. LEWIS and wife, Tuesday, January 3d, a son.

BIRTH: To August DANBURG and wife, Sat. Jan 31, twin boys.

DIED: Mrs. W.M. WITTER received sad news by telegram Monday, of the death of her grandmother, Mrs. CONET, of Monroe, Wisconsin, who died at an early hour that morning after a protracted illness of several days. Our sympathy is with the bereaved.

Wayne Herald-Tribune
February 12, 1885 (Vol. X, No. 26)

Last Sunday the following persons united with the Presbyterian Church: Mr. and Mrs. J.S. HAKE; Mr. and Mrs. G. COOK; Mr. and Mrs. BRYANT; Mr. and Mrs. C.O. JOHNSON; Mr. and Mrs. C.H. JOHNSON; Mr. and Mrs. F.A. PHILLEO; Mrs. E.M. SMITH; Mrs. G.E. LINN; Mrs. PORTER; Mrs. Margaret FORDYCE; Misses Anna DAVIES, Irene BOYER, Maud WACHOB, Katie PORTER, Lallah MAURER, Mable GAMBLE, Helen LODGE and Mertie FORD; H.A. MOORE; Wm. WOODS; Ed. LODGE.

Wayne Herald-Tribune
February 19, 1885 (Vol. X, No. 27)

BIRTH: To Mr. and Mrs. Lewis MAUK, six miles northeast of Wayne, Friday, February 13th, a son.

Service by Publication.

In the District court of Wayne County, Nebraska.

To Jane WHITE, Mary F. HOLLINGSWORTH, Henry HOLLINGSWORTH, John WHITE, Mary F. WHITE, Lelila J. WOOD, James A. WHITE, Elzena WHITE, A.E. WHITE, Dillie D. WHITE, Leonard W. WHITE, Hannah J. WHITE, Sarah E. BURTON, A.M. BURTON, and A.H. STUCKEY, heirs of John WHITE, deceased:

Defendants:

You and each of you will hereby take notice that on the 18th day of February 1885, the plaintiff, George T. HANLY, filed his petition in the District Court of Wayne County, Nebraska, against you as defendants, the object and prayer of which are to remove a cloud upon plaintiff's title to the following described real estate to-wit:

The southwest quarter of Section number Twenty-seven, the northeast quarter of Section number Thirty-three and the northwest quarter of section number Thirty-four, all in Township number Twenty-six, North, Range number Three, East of the sixth principal meridian, caused by failure to record a certain lost deed conveying said real estate from one John WHITE and wife to one Isaac A. HAVILAND. That defendants be decreed to execute a quit claim deed conveying said land to plaintiff, and that a master commissioner be appointed to execute such deed in case said defendants neglect or refuse so to do. You are required to answer said petition on or before the 30th day of March 1885.

Dated Feb. 18th 1885.

George T. HANLY
By A.A. WELCH, His Attorney

Wayne Herald-Tribune
February 26, 1885 (Vol. X, No. 28)

The Busy Bee is the name of the literary society of the Intermediate department of the schools. Its officers are: Rolla OXFORD, President; Irene BOYER, Vice Pres.; George COYLE, Secretary; Daisy WITTER, Critic; Mary NUSBAUM, Editor; Dottie BROWN, Treasurer.

Wayne Herald-Tribune
March 5, 1885 (Vol. X, No. 29)

MARRIED: John E. BENNETT and Miss Helen PORTER were married last Sunday evening, and took the Monday morning's train for Wayne, where they will make their home. The best wishes of the Herald go with them, may they live long and prosper. Both Mr. BENNETT and wife were residents of Hartington. We are sorry to lose them and hope they will soon make up their minds to return and live among us again. (Hartington Herald)

Rabies.

Monday afternoon a dog belonging to J.D. SLATER was observed to act strangely and though usually very quiet and inoffensive, became ill-natured and uneasy. He was continually snapping and fighting with other dogs, a number of which he is said to have bitten, and he finally bit Mr. SLATER's little boy on the hand and in the leg. From the dog's actions it was feared he had gone mad, and parties hunted him with guns with the intention of killing him. He was finally secured and fastened in a shed, where he has since been kept with a view of ascertaining whether he has rabies or not. The matter naturally excited a great deal of interest and considerable alarm which will not be allayed until the nature of his disorder is determined. There is much anxiety felt over the possibly horrible fate of the boy who was bitten.

As a measure of precaution the board of health instructed the marshal to require all owners of dogs to keep them securely chained and none will be permitted to run at large at present.

Wayne Herald-Tribune
March 12, 1885 (Vol. X, No. 30)

BIRTH: To M.N. CONOVER and wife, Sunday March 8th, a son.

BIRTH: To Eugene GIDDINGS and wife, Tuesday, March 10th, a daughter.

SLATER's dog, of which mention was made last week, has since died. It is still a question whether or not he was mad, but the general belief among those best able to judge is that he was. Sunday a dog belonging to Jno. ZWALD became quite sick, and as he was one of the dogs supposed to have been bitten he was killed the following morning.

Wayne County

The attention of all persons seeking homes is respectfully called to the advantages offered by Wayne county. The purpose of this notice is to set forth as clearly as possible those advantages, without any misrepresentations or high coloring.

LOCATION AND CLIMATE.

Wayne county is situated in northeastern Nebraska, in the second tier of counties from the Missouri River on the east and north. It is in about the same latitude as Marshalltown and Cedar Rapids, in Iowa, Chicago, Illinois, and Toledo, Ohio. The climate is nearly the same as that of central Iowa, and Illinois; but owing to the greater elevation the atmosphere is drier, there are more bright days, and the air is more invigorating. It is a peculiarly healthy climate, especially for persons troubled with weak lungs. There is less snow in winter, and the thermometer during all the past winter has registered from six to ten degrees higher than in corresponding latitudes in Iowa and Illinois.

CHARACTER OF THE SOIL.

There is no timber in the county, the entire surface being an undulating prairie. The soil is a deep, rich, dark loam, underlaid with a light porous subsoil of great depth, that on exposure to the air and light becomes as dark and productive as the surface soil. The soil is of almost exactly the same quality as the best of the "Missouri Slope" in Iowa.

The surface of the county in the eastern part is chiefly, composed of long sweeping undulations with no lands so flat that they have not good drainage. In the western part the land is more rolling, but in very few places is it so broken as to interfere with cultivation. In answer to many inquries as to whether there is any sand hills in the county it needs only be stated that sand for building purpose in Wayne, the county seat, is brought from the Missouri River, fifty miles away. *There is not a quarter section of land in the county that will not make a good farm.* There is absolutely no waste land.

STREAMS.

The county is well watered by the different branches of the Logan and their tributaries, streams that never dry up, and in which the amount of water varies but little throughout the year.

PRODUCTIONS.

The productions of the county are those usually raised in the same latitude. All the cereals are produced in great abundance and of the best quality. Fruit growing is yet in its infancy, though there are a number of bearing orchards in the county that are producing apples equal to the best. Small fruits of all kinds thrive and produce largely.

RAIL ROAD FACILITIES.

The C. St. P.M. & O. Railway runs diagonally through the county from northeast to southwest, and south along the east line giving connections with Sioux City and Omaha. The Sioux City & Pacific runs through the counties south a few miles from the Wayne county line.

VACANT LANDS.

A large part of the county is yet unbroken, but is nearly all in the market at prices from $5 to $20 per acre, according to the quality and nearness to the railroads. Thousands of acres of as good land as can be found in northern Nebraska can yet be obtained, that are suitable for farming and stock raising. More definite information regarding prices and lands can be obtained of any of the real estate dealers in Wayne, who will take pleasure in answering any questions. The best method however is to make a personal visit and inspect the lands.

STOCK RAISING.

Stock raising has already become a leading industry and is being engaged in more largely every year. It is destined to be the great industry of the county, the soil being especially adapted to the culture of corn and growing the tame grasses on which it depends. As yet there are thousands of acres of wild land for grazing though that can be expected to be available but for a few years.

SCHOOLS.

The county now has thirty-five school districts and more are being formed as they are needed. No part of the county is without school facilities.

INHABITANTS.

The county now has a population of about four thousand people, composed almost entirely of well-to-do people from Iowa, Illinois, Wisconsin and other western states. No county in the state is being settled with a better class of people, as a view of the farm building and improvements will convince anyone. The county has much more than the usual number of energetic public spirited men of large means, who are able and willing to assist in the development of the county. The person who is seeking a home in the West, where he will have the advantages of a healthy climate, and excellent soil, of schools and churches and agreeable neighbors can find it in Wayne county, which he is most cordially invited to visit.

WAYNE.

Wayne, the county seat of Wayne county, is a handsome, growing village of a thousand inhabitants, situated on a south and east slope in the Logan Valley. Its people are enterprising and public spirited, and ready to lend a helping hand to anything that will be of benefit to the town. No other town of the same size in Nebraska has as many good residences, as many sidewalks and other public improvements. It has four churches, Methodist, Lutheran, Baptist and Presbyterian, all with comfortable and commodious buildings. A public school building was erected in 1884, at a cost of $6,000 and the schools are in excellent condition. The improvements last year amount to $61,000, and an equal or greater amount will be expended in 1885.

• • •

Farmer's Hotel,
Wayne, Nebraska
ALEX SCOTT   Proprietor.

• • •

Wayne Herald-Tribune
March 19, 1885 (Vol. X, No. 31)

Monday morning George PETERS started to Dixon county with a load of lumber. A falling board frightened his mules and they started to run, throwing him against the wagon. His head struck the frozen ground and he received an ugly but not dangerous wound, from which the blood poured profusely. He managed to overtake the mules and stop them, and then was assisted into Dr. LOVE's drugstore where the doctor dressed his wounds.

A German boy named Karl SCHNEIDER who has been working for W.J. WHITE on the STAMBAUGH ranch in Brenna precinct was kicked by a horse Sunday and his face terribly cut up. His nose was broken, the frontalbone fractured, one eyelid torn off, and a quantity of hardened earth driven into the flesh and eye. Dr. WIGHTMAN was summoned and dressed the wounds but his recovery is doubtful, as it is thought the brain was injured.

• • •

F. HINRICHS
Blacksmith Shop

• • •

**Wayne Herald-Tribune
April 2, 1885 (Vol. X, No. 33)**

MARRIED: At the residence of his honor, Judge MARTIN, Wednesday Apr. 1st, Edwin HESTEN and Miss Mary NEEL, both of Holt county.

The following officers have been elected by the M.E. Sabbath school for the ensuing year. Supt., Wm. MILLER; Asst. Supt., Dallas BRIGGS; Sec., Ida SLATER; Treasurer, W.M. LINN; Librarian, F.P. TAYLOR.

• • •

LEWIS BERRY
PAINTER.
Wayne, Neb.

• • •

T. H. WALLACE
House Moving & Raising
Wayne, Neb.

• • •

J. A. WILCUT,
Dealer in Fruits & Confectionery,
Cigars, Tobacco & Candies,
Vegetables, Oysters and Ice Cream

Wayne Herald-Tribune
April 9, 1885 (Vol. X, No. 34)

MARRIED: At Wayne, Neb, Apr. 6th, by county judge MARTIN, Alexander WALKER of Gibbon, Neb. to Miss Neoma BENN of Wakefield, Neb.

City Election.

The city election passed off very quietly, not enough interest being manifested to draw out even a fair numerical vote. Two tickets were in the field, one containing the names of the old council - A.B. SLATER, E.R. CHACE, Chas. JOHNSON, L.C. DEARBORN and F.M. NORTHROP. The other contained the names of Chas. JOHNSON, E.R. CHACE, A.H. ELLIS, R.B. TAYLOR and A. WHEATON. Both tickets were recognized as being composed of excellent men, and so no especial effort was made to bring out votes. The count resulted as follows, the total votes numbering 112. CHACE 112, JOHNSON 100, TAYLOR 71, ELLIS 62, WHEATON 73, SLATER 50, DEARBORN 48, NORTHROP 36. There is no especial significance in the result, and no change in the policy of the city government is anticipated.

• • •

JOHN PHILLIPS
Is Prepared to Polish and Grind
Plows and all Farm Machinery.

• • •

R. H. ROBINSON
Will do all Wagon Making
and Repairing in the best manner.

• • •

DEARBORN'S
Pharmacy
Wayne, Nebraska

• • •

TOLLINGER BROS.
Contractors & Builders
Wayne, Neb.

W. O. GAMBLE,
Real Estate Agent
Wayne, Nebraska

• • •

NYE & HATCH,
Attorneys at Law,
Wayne,   Neb.

• • •

Wayne Herald-Tribune
April 16, 1885 (Vol. X, No. 35)

MARRIED: Saturday, April 11th, at Hoskins, Mr. Christoph PEIPER and Miss Mina ALBERT, Rev. Otto KUHN officiating.

MARRIED: At Hoskins, Mr. Gottlieb KLAWAN and Miss Louis WITT, A.L. HOUSER, J.P., officiating. This wedding is an interesting one from the fact that the bride is of but twenty summers, but the groom of sixty-two winters.

MARRIED: At the residence of the bride's mother, in Hartington on Saturday April 11th, H.E. HARRIS of Wakefield and Miss Susie DAVIES, of Wayne, Reb. G.J. TRAVIS officiating. The above announces the marriage of two estimable young people, well known and universally esteemed in Wayne. Their friends, who number every one in Wayne, will unite in wishing them a long life of wedded bliss.

MARRIED: John BRITTON and Miss Ada RAYMOND, two of Wayne county's best young people, were married in Sioux City last week and are receiving the congratulations of their many friends. We were not able to get the particulars.

• • •

WALTERS BROS.
House, Sign, Carriage
- and -
Ornament'l Painter

RICKABAUGH & LARISON
Barbers
Shaving, Hair Cutting & Shampooning

• • •

Logan Valley Drug Store,
ADAMS & DUTCHER

• • •

Wayne Herald-Tribune
April 23, 1885 (Vol. X, No. 36)

MARRIED: At the residence of the brides' parents in Wayne, Saturday April 18th, T.H. WALLACE and Miss Effa WISE, and W.H. McNEAL and Miss Blanche WISE, Rev. G.M. LODGE officiating. Two of Wayne's most estimable young ladies and two of her best young men have thus united their fortunes' "for better of worse," they start on their married life with the universal good will and congratulations of their friends and acquaintances. The affair was a quiet one only the intimate friends of the family being present.

• • •

G. G. SEBALD
City Barber,
Shaving, Hair-Cutting & Shampooning

• • •

Wayne Herald-Tribune
April 30, 1885 (Vol. X, No. 37)

MARRIED: OLESON - PETERSON. At the residence of N.L. JUHLIN in Wayne, Monday, April 27th, Magnus OLESON and Miss Bertha PETERSON, both of Dixon county, Rev. G.J. TRAVIS officiating.

MARRIED: EMERY - SCOTT. At the residence of the bride's parents in Wayne, Sunday, April 26th, Ward EMERY and Miss Emiline SCOTT, Rev. G.M. LODGE officiating.

MARRIED: SOENNEKEN - LUTZ. At St. Paul's church in Norfolk, Monday April 27th, 1885, Mr. Wm. SOENNEKEN of Wayne and Miss Minnie LUTZ of Norfolk, Rev. M.H. PANKOW officiating.

MARRIED: RENNICK - PRESCOTT. Thursday eve, April 16, 1885, at the residence of the bride's parents, Mr. and Mrs. J.H. PINGREY, by Rev. E.L. BRIGGS, Mr. E.T. RENNICK, of Wayne, Neb., and Mrs. R. O. PRESCOTT of this town. The groom was formerly a resident of this vicinity, but is now a prosperous farmer of Neb. The bride has long been known and highly respected by all our people and it will be regretted by many that she is to permanently leave our midst. They leave for their home in Wayne, Wayne Co., Neb., the last of this week. (Wilton, Iowa Review)

• • •

PEAVEY & CO'S
Elevator.
J.C. SUING, Agent.

• • •

Wayne Herald-Tribune
May 7, 1885 (Vol. X, No. 38)

BIRTH: To W.M. JAMES and wife, April 30, a daughter.

BIRTH: To August SAMUELSON and wife, May 3d, a boy.

BIRTH: To J.C. CRIST and wife, April 30th, a boy.

• • •

ALEX HOLZ.
Contractor and Builder,
Brick Layer and Plasterer,
Wayne, Neb.

• • •

Wayne Herald-Tribune
May 14, 1885 (Vol. X, No. 39)

BIRTH: To J.H. BROWN and wife May 13th, a girl.

MARRIED: WHEATON - STANLEY. Saturday, May 9th, by County Judge MARTIN, Mr. Homer WHEATON and Miss Lizzie STANLEY, both of Wayne.

• • •

New Harness Shop,
Wayne, Nebraska
JOHN S. LEWIS, JR.

• • •

Wayne Herald-Tribune
May 28, 1885 (Vol. X, No. 41)

BIRTH: To John ANDERSON and wife, Sunday, May 24th, a son.

MARRIED: PHIEL - HANKE. Carl PHIEL and Miss Caroline HANKE, both of Wayne, at the County Judge's office May 22nd.

MARRIED: BECKENHAUER - HELVA. Monday, May 25th, Jos. BECKENHAUER and Mrs. Margaret HELVA, Judge MARTIN officiating.

MARRIED: John W. POPE, of Columbus, Neb. and Miss Fannie SHORT of Brenna Precinct will be married at the residence of Robert PERRIN this evening, Reb. G.M. LODGE officiating.

The Turf.

Last Saturday an exciting horse race occured at the race course between horses owned by Henry WARNER and a stranger passing through. The latter winning - Purse $20 - Distance 300 yards.

The foot race at the race course Monday between Dan BLUE of Wayne and the foot runner of Pender resulted in the victory for the former; Distance 75 yds, purse $10.

The trotting race between T.J. STEELE's and Luther DEARBORN's trotting horses yesterday resulted in a victory for the former; time 3:45, best two out of three. Mile heat, purse $20. A large crowd gathered at the race course to witness the race.

PHOTOGRAPHS
GEO. W. KORTRIGHT,
Wayne Studio, Wayne, Nebraska

• • •

Wayne Herald-Tribune
June 4, 1885 (Vol. X, No. 42)

BIRTH: To Chas. COREY and wife May 28th, a boy.

MARRIED: June 3d, by Rev. G.M. LODGE, Mr. W.H. SMITH and Miss Emma BUSBY, both of Wayne county. The bride and groom are two of the very best of Wayne county's young people, and they will begin their married life with the universal good wishes of their many friends. They will live on Mr. S.W. SMITH's farm in Logan precinct.

Charlie WALTERS stepped on a needle while in his bare feet about two weeks ago and it broke off inside about three quarters of an inch from the surface. It passed through a tendon and resisted all attempts to get it out for more than a week when Charlie set to work to dig for it and get it. It proved to be an inch and a half long.

Coon Creek Items.
BIRTH: It is a little late to mention it, but Nels NELSON and wife have a bouncing boy at their house, about three weeks old.

The officers of School District No. 8 are Fred THOMPSON, Director; Geo. SCOTT, Moderator; P.P. NELSON, Treasurer.

Wayne Herald-Tribune
June 11, 1885 (Vol. X, No. 43)

BIRTH: To Mr. and Mrs. James CONNOR, June 7th, a daughter.

BIRTH: To Mr. and Mrs. Howard ROBINSON, June 9th, a daughter.

MARRIED: TAYLOR - REED. At the Methodist church, Wednesday evening, June 10th, Frank P. TAYLOR and Miss Jennie E. REED, both of Wayne, Rev. J.W. LEWIS of Emerson, Iowa, officiating.

Wayne Herald-Tribune
June 18, 1885 (Vol. X, No. 44)

MARRIED: MONSON - OBERY. In Wayne June 11th, 1885, by E. MARTIN, Co. Judge, Mr. John S. MONSON of Wayne Co. to Miss Ellen OBERY of Wakefield.

Drowned in the Logan.

A sad case of drowning took place last Sunday afternoon a short distance from town in the North Logan at a point where the Hartington branch crosses the creek. Jonas RYTHER, Miner ACTON and J. STONER went to that point to take a swim. It seems that ACTON and STONER went into the water first and upon coming out and resting on the bank RYTHER went in the creek for the first time. At the beginning he did not go into deep water, but after a while ventured to deeper places, endeavoring to swim to the railroad bridge near by. He could not swim and went tunder, the boys on the bank having not the remotest idea that he was drowning as he gave no signs or utterance of distress. They watched him going some distance down the stream and when under water thought he was intentionally diving. It did not take long before suspicion as well as fear was aroused by the boys when RYTHER failed to come to the surface after the usual time. They soon became conscious of the sad fact that their comrade had drowned. Some search was made by them but without effect, and they came to town and told the cheerless story of RYTHER's fate. The news was at once sent to Wayne, and about twenty of the boys came down the same evening on two hand cars; with the intention to assist in the search. Little could be done that evening in view of the approaching storm. The next day the search for the body was continued by Wayne and Wakefield people, but without the desired result. On Tuesday a cannon was brought from Norfolk in the hope to raise the body by means of its effects, but this, too, failed to bring him to the surface. On Wednesday, the third day, the water raised the body and he was found one and a half miles below the bridge, floating along. He was a member of the Masonic fraternity, and both lodges made noble efforts to find him. In the afternoon he was taken to Wayne for burial. He came toWayne about two years ago from Cattaraugus county, N.Y., to his uncle, John LAWRENCE. A portion of the time he worked for his uncle, ran a dray line at Hartington three months, and has during the past year been employed by F.H. PEAVEY & Co., a portion of the time at Wayne and during the past four or five months at Wakefield. He was about 23 years of age, unmarried, received an academic education in the Alfred Seminary, N.Y. His parents are both living. He was a young man of more than average general intelligence, was liked by all who knew him, and his untimely end in the very acme of health and strength is deeply deplored by all.

The parties who were here from Wayne assisting in the search were:

Lon ELLIS, W.H. McNEAL, F.A. DEARBORN, Will METTLEN, C. CHACE, H.E. NYE, J.W. ROCK, R.W. WILKINS, I.P. MARTIN, Del. STRICKLAND, E.T. JOHNSON, J.M. CHERRY, S.B. RUSSEL, A.P. CHILDS, T.H. WALLACE, Geo. SMITH, Bert PORTER, Grant MEARS, E.D. SUSSENHAM, Chas. BRYANT, Ed. PERRY, Jas. BRITTON, J.T. BRESSLER, SIMMONS, AHERN, A.S. MINER, John LAWRENCE, C.W. WATTERS, J.W. ROCK and W.S. SHERBIN. (Wakefield Republican)

Wayne Lodge A.F. & A.M. and a large crowd of friends of deceased were at the train last evening to receive the body which was accompanied by Wakefield lodge A.F. & A.M. At the toll of the bells the large procession headed by mourners and Wayne and Wakefield lodges procceded to the cemetery where the funeral services took place under the rules of the masonic fraternity. A beautiful wreath of flowers made by a number of young ladies was placed upon the caskets, and the body laid to its last resting place. The relatives of deceased have the sympathy of the entire community.

Dr. FOGG, W.P. AGLER, Moses HERNER, Jos. BECKENHAUER, Martin ANDERSON, T.H. GUERNSEY, S.F. NELSON, C. E. WAKEFIELD, Rev. HICKS and others of Wakefield whose names we did not learn were in Wayne last evening attending the funeral services.

Wayne Herald-Tribune
June 25, 1885 (Vol. X, No. 45)

JULY 4TH
CELEBRATION IN WAYNE.

The coming anniversary of American Independence will be appropriately celebrated in Wayne, under the auspices of
WAYNE CORNET BAND,

The committee on arrangements have made the following selection of officers and committees:

President of the day, Jas. BRITTON
Vice Presidents, L.C. DEARBORN
T.J. STEELE
R.B. CRAWFORD
A.P. CHILDS

Marshal,	R.M. GOSHORN
	A.T. CHAPIN
	Frank CRANE
	E.H. EMERSON
	Chas. H. JOHNSON
Ass't Marshal,	John PERRY
Chaplain,	Rev. G.J. TRAVIS
Orator,	Frank FULLER
Reader,	A.A. WELCH

COMMITTEES:

Racing and Sports - D.W. BRITTON, Ed. PERRY, R.B. CRAWFORD, Will FRAZIER and T.J. STEELE.
Dancing - W.H. McNEAL.
Ragamuffins - Hon. Comeandfetchit.
Stands - J.E. BENNETT and W.H. McNEAL.
Fun - B.F. FEATHER, E.M. SMITH and Ed. L. HATCH.
Dinner - Members of band.

PROGRAMME.

Salute at day break.

At 9:30 A.M. a procession will be formed headed by the Wayne Cornet Band, and march to the ground where the following exercises will take place.

1. Music by band.
2. Prayer by Rev. G.M. LODGE.
3. National air by Glee Club.
4. Reading of the Declaration of Independence by A.A. WELCH.
5. Music by the band.
6. Oration by Frank FULLER.
7. Song by the Glee Club.
8. Benediction by Rev. G.M. LODGE.
9. Dinner at Town Hall.

AFTERNOON SPORTS.

Trotting race - $100 purse - Blood Blood.

1. Horse race, free for all, quarter mile dash, best two in three, $10 to 1st, $5 to 2d, five to enter and three to start, entrance fee $1.00.

Pony race to ponies that have never run for money - half mile heats best two in three, $10 to 1st and $5 to 2d, entrance fee $1.00.

Pony race, half mile heats, best 2 in 3, $10 to 1st and $5 to 2d, entrance fee $1.00.

Slow mule race, prize $5, entrance fee 50cts.
Races to be called at 2 P.M. and run alternately.
Entries for horse races can be made with Ed. PERRY at Wayne and will positively close on July 4th at 12 M.
2. Foot races $5.00.
3. Sack race $3.00.
4. Bicycle race $5.00.
5. Greased pig race $2.00.
6. Potato race $3.00.
7. Roller Skating at the rink from 1 to 6 o'clock. Prizes given at 5 o'clock.
8. Grand ball in the evening.
9. The committee will pay a prize of $5 to the best dressed rafamuffin.
10 per cent of each purse will be charged for entrance fee.
Let every body attend.
By order of WAYNE BAND.

Wayne Herald-Tribune
July 2, 1885 (Vol. X, No. 46)

MARRIED: At the residence of the bride's parents, Wednesday evening, July 1st, John DERICK and Miss Rebecca TRIPP, both of Wayne, Rev. J.W. LEWIS, of Emerson, Ia. officiating. The Herald-Tribune shies the customary old shoe after the bride and groom, wishing them long life and prosperity.

Wayne Herald-Tribune
July 9, 1885 (Vol. X, No. 47)

BIRTH: To Mr. and Mrs. Jno. F. FISHER of Wayne Precinct, July 7th, a son.

MARRIED: WARREN - ROBB. At Wayne, July 4th, by E. MARTIN, County Judge, Mr. Chas. H. WARREN of Dakota county and Miss Etta M. ROBB, of Wayne county.

Teacher's Institute

The following is a list of the teachers attending the Wayne county Teachers Institute, commencing July 6, 1885:

J.S. HAKE	W.J. McCOY
W.E. HOWARD	L.F. PANABAKER
Eva TAYLOR	Cella COYLE
Anna M. CHACE	August FLOHR
M.S. DAVIES	J.J. GILDERSLEEVE

Rosa M. BEACH
J.S. HALL
F.A. BERRY
Lutie BROWN
Carrie WISE
Edith MEARS
Sadie HUNTER
Judson GARWOOD
Minnie JOHNSTON

Grace McMAKIN
Mrs. Sallie McFEE
Cora BROWN
Sadie M. AITKEN
Susie HUNTER
J.E. HUNTER
Edward NEILAN
Maria S. SPEER

Supt HAKE informs us that the attendance is 25 per cent greater than last year. Nearly all the teachers of the county are present. Twenty-seven visitors attended since the Institute began.

How The Fourth Was Celebrated in Wayne.

A more auspicious morning than that with which we were favored last Saturday could not be desired. The rain of the evening before had settled the dust and given everything a bright appearance. Early in the day wagon loads of people came pouring in from all directions, until the universal wonder was where so many people came from. Nearly every business house and many residences were decorated with the national colors, and Main street presented a gay appearance. By ten o'clock it had become almost oppressively warm and the lemonade and ice cream stands were doing a rushing business. At half past ten the procession formed with the band and proceeded to the court house where the morning exercises were to take place. Prayer was offered by Rev. G.J. TRAVIS, and the Declaration of Independence was well read by A.A. WELCH. Frank FULLER, the orator of the day, delivered a most excellent and appropriate address, which was attentively listened to by the audience. The band and glee club furnished some good music during the exercises.

After dinner the crowd assembled at the grounds that had been prepared for the races on the banks of the Logan.

The first race called was the one between Dr. CRAWFORD and L.C. DEARBORN's horses for a purse of $100. There was considerable interest in this race as it had been postponed a number of times before and has been talked of considerably about town. The Doctor's horse captured the purse.

There were four entries for the next trot, purse $65; $50 to first, $15 to second; best three in two. The first place taken by Jim Fisk, belonging to BROWN of Pierce; second by Old Tom, belonging to HALE of Battle Creek.

In the running race BROWN's mare took first and ROWE's second, Purse $50; $35 to first and $15 to second.

In the foot race J.F. COLEMAN came in ahead, FRINK second.

The game of ball between the Pierce and Wakefield clubs attracted a large crowd, but did not prove as interesting as had been expected, as the Pierce club was badly over matched and it was evident from the first that they had not the slightest chance to win the game. Seven innings were played, the game resulting 22 to 0 in favor of Wakefield.

The sports of the day closed with a very successful hop at the rink.

Taken all through the celebration was the most successful that has been held in Wayne, and the band boys can congratulate themselves on the result.

NOTES.

It was the biggest crowd that has ever gathered in Wayne.

Not a drunken man was to be seen on the streets, and no arrests were made. A fact that the village and county may well feel proud of.

No town in the country could show a better looking or better acting crowd of people than were in Wayne that day.

Among the many decorated buildings WITTER & Co.'s bore away the first prize.

The calaboose didn't get dedicated as was expected.

• • •

New Jewelry Store,
A. W. TAYLOR

• • •

Wayne Herald-Tribune
July 16, 1885 (Vol. X, No. 48)

Card of Thanks.

Lyndon, N.Y. June 29th, 1885.
Eds. Herald-Tribune.
Wayne, Neb.

Dear sirs: The Family of which Jonas K. RYTHER was a member wish to express through the columns of your paper their sincere and heartfelt thanks to the people of Wayne, Wakefield and vicinity for the assistance so freely and promptly rendered by them in the search for the missing body of their son and brother Jonas K. RYTHER. We would also thank the Wayne Lodge 120 A.F. and A.M. for the good work performed by them of burying the body decently and we also appreciate the sympathy extended by them to us. We also extend our thanks to the ladies that in token of their esteem for him while living prepared the floral wreath to decorate his casket.

Other papers will please copy, especially the Wakefield Republican.

Yours &c
Nelson RYTHER.

Wayne Herald-Tribune
August 6, 1885 (Vol. X, No. 51)

DIED: A little daughter of A.L. DAVIS and wife, aged 20 months, died Sunday evening of cholera infantum.

Sheriff Sale.

Notice is hereby given that by virtue of three executions to me directed; one in favor of Alonzo W. STRAW, Winslow W. THAYER, William H. ELLSWORTH and William C. MIDDLETON against Cyrus E. HUNTER, Louise K. HUNTER, and Joseph E. HUNTER, one in favor of Horace PITKINS and Augustus THOMAS against C.E. HUNTER and Joseph E. HUNTER, issued out of the District Court of Wayne county Nebraska.

I will, at 3 o'clock P.M. on the 9th day of September, 1885, at the door of the court house in said county, offer for sale at public auction, the following real estate to wit: The interest of Cyrus E. HUNTER in the North East Quarter of Section Twenty Six (26), Township Twenty Six (26), Range Four (4), Wayne county Nebraska, taken as property of Cyrus E. HUNTER on said executions.

A.S. MINER, Sheriff:
Wayne Co., Neb.

Dated this 6th day of August, 1885.

• • •

Dry Goods and Groceries,
Boots and Shoes, Hats and Caps,
Clothing and Gents' Furnishing Goods,
Trunks and Valises,
OXFORD & STRICKLAND

The Herald-Tribune
Published Every Thursday At
Wayne, Nebraska.
GOSHORN & McNEAL
Editors and Proprietors.

• • •

Wayne Herald-Tribune
August 13, 1885 (Vol. X, No. 52)

BIRTH: To N.I. JUHLIN and wife, Monday August 10th, a son.

MARRIED: Wednesday, Aug 5th, by Rev. G.J. TRAVIS at his residence, George W. JONES and Miss Anna DE LONG, both of Burnett. The happy couple slipped quietly up here thinking to take in the good people of their neighborhood and keep the marriage a secret, but with malice aforethought the editor spoiled the programme by sending a telegram to the editor of the Burnett Blade, who gave the whole thing away.

DIED: Francis, infant child of M. CARROLL, Wednesday morning, of cholera infantum.

Baseball.

A large crowd from Wayne went to Wakefield Friday afternoon to witness the game of ball between the Wayne and Wakefield nines. The match had been a common topic of conversation here for some time as the Wakefield club had easily beaten every club they had met during the season, and had had a great deal of practice, while the Wayne club had been organized but a short time and had not played a single game. Under the circumstances it was generally believed that our boys would be beaten, and in all probability badly beaten. The result of the game shows that they are able to cope with the Wakefielders and we expect to see them come out victorious in the next contest. In making the game a tie they certainly did well, and but for the unfortunate accident that happened to Frank DEARBORN, who had his hand so badly hurt while running between bases that he had to play the last two innings with but one hand to use, the victory would almost certainly have been with Wayne. The score at the close of the ninth inning stood 9 to 9 and the game was declared a draw. The following is the score.

WAYNE

	R.	O.
MORAN, 2d b.	3	2
TOLLINGER, s.s.	1	4
DEARBORN, 3d b.	1	3
McNEAL, p.	1	0
HOLTZ, c.	1	2
McLEOD, lf.	0	4
HATCH, cf.	0	5
BRYAN, rf.	0	4
DEARBORN, 1st b. & p.	<u>2</u>	<u>3</u>
Total	9	27

WAKEFIELD

	R.	O.
DRAKE, 3d b.	1	4
BENN, cf.	0	5
CONRAD, lf.	1	3
HAMMOND, 2d b.	0	4
ACTON, 1st b.	2	1
COOK, s.s.	1	3
SHUMWAY, rf.	0	4
PATCH, c.	2	2
CONRAD, p.	<u>2</u>	<u>1</u>
Total	9	27

A Bit of Local History.

In view of the fact that such a howl has been raised about the existence of a ring in Wayne county, and the attempt being made to injure the present county clerk by using the cry of "clique," "ring" and such like phrases, a few words on the subject may enlighten some of the newer residents of the county who are not posted on its past politics. To one who knows the history of the past few years in the county the repeated howl that "The ring must go," coming from the source it does is as ridiculous a piece of nonsense as could well be imagined, and there is no danger of its imposing on the older residents, but lest some might be led estray by it it may be well to consider what there is in it.

Several years ago, while the population of the county was still very small and the votes very few, the number who could receive any offices included nearly all the voters in the county. They naturally formed a "ring" for mutual protection and as newcomers came into the county those who showed any disposition to give the "ring" trouble were gently taken into it, and it soon had so firm a grip on the political affairs of the county that no one could hope to get any recognition politically except by their consent. The affairs of the county were not mismanaged in their hands however, and no pretence was made that the ring was any particular injury to the county. Of this ring James BRITTON, who was then as he probably is now the shrewdest politician and best political organizer in the county was the recognized head and the organization was generally known as the "Britton Ring." He was seconded by such men as John BRESSLER, Charles JOHNSON, DeGrasse BRITTON, Frank CRANE, Cy HUNTER, A.P. CHILDS and a number of others whom it is not necessary now to name, thought the duties of some of these were confined to executing the plans of their superiors who were too shrewd to show their own hands.

When the county seat was moved to Wayne and the population of the county began rapidly to increase the membership of the ring was considerably enlarged and it began to carry on things with a high hand. The domineering way in which it began to assert its power created a good deal of opposition. To this feeling the defeat of James BRITTON for District Attorney a year ago was largely due. His reduced vote in this county was not due to the fact that he was not considered competent to fill the position, but that he was generally regarded as the chief of the ring and therefore objectionable. Two years ago the ring was supposed to include beside those mentioned above, and quite a number of others, all the county officials with the exception of County Superintendent HAKE, who had been elected in spite of the most determined efforts to defeat him.

X

Continued Next Week.

• • •

Pioneer Grocery
WITTER & CO.

• • •

Wayne Herald-Tribune
August 20, 1885 (Vol. XI, No. 1)

BIRTH: W.L. DUTCHER and wife are rejoicing over the arrival of their first born, a daughter, who put in her appearance in this vale of tears Monday.

DIED: The infant daughter of Dr. and Mrs. W.A. LOVE died

Tuesday evening and was buried yesterday afternoon. The funeral services were largely attended.

A window in BRITTON & NORTHROP's office fell on Maud BRITTON's hand Saturday bruising and smashing her hand very badly. The window was a heavy one and the force with which it fell may be imagined from the fact that the impression of Maud's hand was plainly left in the sash where it struck it.

Wayne Herald-Tribune
August 27, 1885 (Vol. XI, No. 2)

RING.
(Continued From Aug. 13)

In the last two years a change has come over the "ring." Its members do not regard each other with that warm and enthusiastic affection so beautiful to see in this sinful world. How the unfriendly feeling originated is a matter of some uncertainty to the writer, but it is certain that the ring, as formerly constituted is not taking any special part in politics this year. One faction however, composed of the men who were most thoroughly identified with the most objectionable features of the ring, is doing everything in its power to defeat the re-nomination of the present county clerk by means of all kinds of abuse and misrepresentation. They have the assurances to pretend that they are doing it only for the public good. Heaven save the mark! It looks to a disinterested observer as though there was some other reason for their frantic efforts, and as though there was more than a mere personal ill will back of it all. They represent that all the present county officials but one is actively opposed to Mr. STEELE. This I happen to know is not true, but it is on a par with many of their other misrepresentations. They have started out with claiming everything and profess the greatest confidence that they will have things all their own way. It is a game of bluff to deceive those who do not see through their plan of making the public believe STEELE is beaten in advance.

They say they have Wayne precinct two to one. I don't know much about the feeling in the rest of the precinct, but in this part of it STEELE will get five sixths of the vote. Don't forget it. The editor of the Gazette is the special spokesman for the disgruntled fraction of the ring. A beautiful specimen he is to howl about a ring! He, who ever since he has been in the county has been the most abject tool and puppet of the ring, and has always danced when his superiors pulled the string. His explanation of his grounds for personally opposing Mr. STEELE is the silliest thing he has yet attempted. He poses before the people of Wayne county as a martyr, when it is well known that whatever business troubles he had he brought them by his own conduct, and Mr. STEELE had no more to do with them than the Emporer of China.

We do not believe that the people of Wayne county will permit themselves to be deceived by such a mass of bosh. They certainly will have enough judgement to decide whether they wish Mr. STEELE to fill the office of clerk for a second term without the interference or dictation of a set of men who are working for their own advancement only.

X

T.B. DEMAREE, of Louisville, Ky., employed by the state temperance society, delivered a temperance lecture in the Methodist church Sunday afternoon and at the close of the lecture a Good Templars Lodge was organized.

The following are the officers appointed:

R.B. CRAWFORD, W.C.T.	Mrs. N.E. MILLER, W.V.T.
Jno. E. BENNETT, W.S.	A.P. CHILDS, W.F.S.
W.E. HOWARD, W.M.	Mrs. N.S. LODGE, W.T.
Miss Stella WOODROW, W.D.M.	Miss Juetta MILLER, N.I.G.
G.L. COOK, W.O.G.	A.O. MYERS, P.W.C.T.
Mrs. J.E. BENNETT, W.A.S.	Mrs. Chas. JOHNSON, R.H.S.
Mrs. Chas. WALTERS, L.H.S.	A.P. CHILDS, L.D.G.W.C.T.

Wayne Herald-Tribune
September 3, 1885 (Vol. XI, No. 3)

MARRIED: WARNER - SCOTT. At the residence of the bride's parents in Wayne, Thursday, Aug. 27th, Henry WARNER and Miss Rebecca SCOOT, Rev. J.R. GEARHART, officiating. The happy couple will please accept the sincere wish of the Herald-Tribune for their happiness and prosperity.

MARRIED: TOLLINGER - OXFORD. At the residence of the bride's parents in Wayne, Monday, Aug., 31st, H.M. TOLLINGER and Miss Delia OXFORD, Eld. C.H. LOTSPIECH, of Wakefield, officiating. The many friends of the bride groom join us in extending their heartiest congratulations.

Wayne Herald-Tribune
September 10, 1885 (Vol. XI, No. 4)

BIRTH: To J.R. WASHBURN and wife, Thursday, Sept. 3rd, a daughter.

BIRTH: To Chas. DAHLBERE and wife, Friday, Sept. 4th, a son.

BIRTH: To A.H. MILLER and wife, Friday, Sept. 4th 1885, a son.

BIRTH: To A.L. DAVIS and wife, Monday, Sept. 7th, 1885, a son.

BIRTH: To J.E. HANSON and wife, Tuesday, Sept. 8th, a son.

BIRTH: To Henry WITTLER and wife, Tuesday, Sept., 8th, a son.

BIRTH: To W.M. BENNETT and wife, Wednesday, Sept. 9th, a daughter.

The above is a pretty good showing even for this productive country, and the Herald-Tribune extends its heartiest congratulations to the parents one and all. We hope that the example may prove contagious and that many others will go and do likewise. This country must be settled up and a native population to the "manor born" is to be most desired. Keep it up.

MARRIED: LUTT - PETERSON. In Wayne Sept. 5th, 1885, by E. MARTIN, county judge, Mr. John LUTT to Miss Hannah PETERSON, all of Wayne county.

MARRIED: ROCK - SLATER. At the residence of the bride's parents in Wayne, Saturday, September 5th, James W. ROCK and Miss Ida SLATER, Rev. G.W. LODGE, officiating.

MARRIED: MORAN - COYLE. At the residence of the bride's parents in Wayne, Tuesday, Sept. 8th, Thomas W. MORAN and Miss Cella COYLE, Rev. Father MORIARITY of Lyons, officiating.

The young people whose marriages are announced above are among the best and most popular in Wayne, and begin their married life with the best wishes of their many friends.

• • •

W. A. IVORY,
Dentist
Wayne, Neb.

Wayne Herald-Tribune
September 17, 1885 (Vol. XI, No. 5)

MARRIED: RICHEY - ROEBER. Thursday, Sept. 10th, Oscar A. RICHEY and Miss ROEBER, Rev. G.H. SCHNUR officiating. The Herald-Tribune extends congratulations.

MARRIED: HARTPENCE - MARTIN. At the residence of W.F. SEARS, Sept. 16, 1885, J.W. HARTPENCE, of Hartington, and Miss Almena MARTIN, of Wayne, E. MARTIN, County Judge, father of the bride, officiating. Mr. HARTPENCE takes one of Wayne county's best young ladies with him to Hartington, and has our congratulations.

DIED: BRESSLER. On Sunday, Sept. 13th, 1885, of cholera infamtum, George, son of John T. and Julia BRESSLER, aged two years and seven months. The funeral took place from the Presbyterian church Tuesday at 10 o'clock and was very largely attended. The bereaved parents have the sympathy of the entire community in their afflication.

Card of Thanks.
Wayne, Neb. Sept. 16, '85

We return our heartfelt thanks to the friends who gave us their sympathy and aided us in ministering to the wants of our child during his last illness.

John T. BRESSLER, Julia BRESSLER

The following is a list of petit jurors drawn for the ensuing term of court. No grand jurors were summoned.

Robert CARR, T.T. CLARK, F.L. NEELY, Jno. BENNING, Christian JENSEN, C.A. GROTHE, James RENNICK, Wm. EMERICK, John O'HARA, R.J. ARMSTRONG, S.M. CUTLER, H.D. OSBORN, John ELLIOTT, D. BRIGGS, S. TAYLOR, S.W. SMITH, M.P. NELSON, Herman RIDDLER, M.O. HINMAN, W.S. SHERBAHN, Jacob WEATHERHOLT, Geo. HORNBY, Homer J. SHIELDS, L.E. SHERMAN.

ANNOUNCEMENTS.

I hereby announce myself as a candidate for County Clerk, subject to the decision of the Republican County Convention.

Thos. J. STEELE.

I hereby announce myself as a candidate for the office of Register of Deeds, subject to the decision of the Republican county convention.

B.F. FEATHER.

Wayne Herald-Tribune
September 24, 1885 (Vol. XI, No. 6)

BIRTH: To J.A. WILCUT and wife, Saturday, Sept. 19th, a daughter.

MARRIED: BRYANT - SHUFELT. At the Boyd, Thursday, Sept. 17, Henry G. BRYANT of Jackson County, Iowa, and Eva F. SHUFELT, of Wayne county. E. MARTIN, County Judge, officiating.

MARRIED: NEWMAN - NEWMAN. At Wayne Sept. 21st 1885, by E. MARTIN, county judge, John NEWMAN, of Page county, Iowa, and Emily NEWMAN, of Lucas county, Iowa.

DIED: COOK. In Wayne, Sept. 21st 1885, Daniel COOK, aged 87 years. The deceased was the father of Mrs. A.S. MINER, with whom he had been making his home. The funeral services took place at the Methodist church Tuesday and were largely attended.

ANNOUNCEMENTS.

I am a candidate for the office of Register of Deeds, subject to the action of the Republican County Convention.

W.K. HOWARD.

At the request of many friends I am a candidate for County Treasurer, subject to the decision of the Republican County Convention.

Enoch HUNTER.

I hereby announce myself a candidate for the office of County Superintendent of Wayne county, subject to the decision of the Republican county convention.

J.S. HAKE.

Upon request of numerous friends, I hereby announce myself as candidate for County Treasurer, subject to the decision of the Republican County Convention.

J.L. MERRIAM.

Wayne Herald-Tribune
October 1, 1885 (Vol. XI, No. 7)

BIRTH: To H.M. SEWELL and wife, Thursday, Sept. 24th, a girl.

MARRIED: At Wayne Sept. 24th by E. MARTIN, county Judge, J.H. KELLER and Miss Maryetta PECK, both of Wakefield.

MARRIED: TOLLINGER - OXFORD. At the residence of the bride's brother-in-law, R.L. OXFORD, in Wayne, Monday evening, Sept. 28th, W.F. TOLLINGER and Miss Emma May OXFORD. Elder E.B. LOTSPIECH of Wakefield, officiating.

Martha, daughter of A.N. CHILDS, ran a nail into her cheek one day this week, tearing it so badly that it was necessary to sew it up.

ANNOUNCEMENTS.

I hereby announce myself as a candidate for Register of Deeds, subject to the will of the voters of Wayne county in the Republican County Convention.

F.M. SKEEN.

• • •

Citizens Bank
Wayne, Neb.
R. B. TAYLOR

• • •

First National
Bank,
Wayne, Nebraska

Officers and Directors:
JOHN T. BRESSLER, President
D. C. PATTERSON, Cashier
E. L. JONES, Ass't Cashier.
HENRY LEY,   J. W. JONES

Wayne Herald-Tribune
October 8, 1885 (Vol. XI, No. 8)

MARRIED: LARSON - MORGANSON. Oct. 2d 1885 at Wayne, Neb., by E. MARTIN, county Judge, James P. LARSON and Miss Anna MORGANSON, both of Cedar county.

Wayne Herald-Tribune
October 22, 1885 (Vol. XI, No. 10)

MARRIED: PERRY - GILCHREST. At the residence of W.J. PERRY, on Thursday evening, Oct. 15th, Rev. G.H. SCHNUR officiating, Edward PERRY and Miss Nellie GILCHREST. The Herald-Tribune extends its heartiest wish for the future happiness and prosperity of the happy couple.

MARRIED: CROSS - MEARS. At the residence of the bride's parents in Wayne, Wednesday evening, Oct. 21st, Louis CROSS and Miss Mary MEARS, Rev. G.J. TRAVIS officiating. The happy couple left this morning for a short visit to Lyons.

Wayne County Fair.

List of premiums awarded continued from last week [missing issue]:
FARM PRODUCTS.
Spring wheat 1/2 bu or more, H.B. MILLER.
  Second J. FISHER.
Oats 1/2 bu or more, Jas. CONNOR. Second H.B. MILLER.
Rye 1/2 bu or more, H.B. MILLER.
Barley 1/2 bu or more, Jno. KOEFORD.
Yellow dent corn in ear, H.B. MILLER. Second R. SNEATH.
White corn, T.H. MITCHELL. Second J. FISHER.
Elint corn, L. NEWTON.
Sweet corn in ear, M.F. GIDDINGS. Second J.D. SLATER.
Buckwheat, M.F. GIDDINGS. Second R. LAPSLEY.
Table potatoes, Art CHAPIN, J.E. SPAHR.
  Second J.W. BARTLETT, J.D. SLATER.
Sweet potatoes, J.W. BARTLETT. Second J.D. SLATER.
White turnips, A.F. CHAON. Second J. BARTLETT.
Beets, A. MILLER. Second A. KLEVER.
Carrots, Hud FEATHER.
Pie Melon, J.D. SLATER.
Six heads of cabbage, A.F. CHAON. Second H.B. MILLER.
Onions, E. CHENAUR. Second J. CONNOR.
Tomatoes, J.D. SLATER. Second G. STERRETT.

Display of pumpkins, A. KLEVER.
Display of squashes, H.E. KETCHUM.
Variety of farm products, H.B. MILLER.
Variety of potatoes, Geo. STERRETT.
Dried sweet corn, J.D. SLATER.

BUTTER AND CHEESE.
Best tub of butter, Mrs. C.D. MARTIN.
Best package of roll butter, Mrs. H. SHIELDS, Mrs. E.J. NANGLE, Mrs. J.J. TRACY, Mrs. L. NURNBURGER, NEWTON Bros.

FRUITS AND WINES.
Variety of apples, R.B. CRAWFORD.
Collection of fall apples, R.B. CRAWFORD.
Collection of winter apples, R.B. CRAWFORD.

PRESERVED FRUITS, ETC.
Three Cans Blackberries, Mrs. A.B. SLATER.
Three Cans Raspberries, Mrs. E. CHAFFEE.
Three Cans Strawberries, Mrs. A.B. SLATER.
Three Cans Crab apples, Hannah BAYES.
Three Cans Peaches, Mrs. A.B. SLATER.
Three Cans Plums, Mrs. John FISHER.
Three Cans Cherries, Mrs. A.B. SLATER.
Three Cans Grapes, Mrs. F.L. NEELY.
Three Grape Jellies, Mrs. James BRITTON,
    Second Mrs. J.T. BRESSLER.
Three Crab apple Jellies, Mrs. James BRITTON,
    Second Mrs. Chas. JOHNSON.
Three Strawberry Jellies, Mrs. A.B. SLATER.
Three Apple Jellies, Mrs. Wm. MILLER,
    Second Mrs. Ida ROCK.
Glass Can Cucumber Pickles, Hannah BAYES,
    Second Mrs. A.W. TAYLOR.
Glass Can Sweet Pickles, Mrs Ida ROCK.
Glass Can Tomato Catsup, Mrs. Ida ROCK.
Collection Dried Fruits, Mrs. A.B. SLATER.
Crab Apple Marmalade, Mrs. A.B. SLATER.
Plum Marmalade, Mrs. A.B. SLATER.
Crab Apple Pickles, Mrs. A.B. SLATER.
Lemon Jelly, Hannah BAYES.
Muskmelon Butter, Emma CHAFFEE
Collection Pickles, Mrs. M.F. SHAW
Melon Preserves, Mrs. Ida ROCK.

Ground Cherry Jelly, Mrs. F. NUSBAUM

PORTRAITS.
Display from 1 Gallery, G.W. KORTRIGHT.
Crayon portrait, Mrs. E.M. SMITH.

FLOWERS.
Floral design, Mrs. M. HARTPENCE.
Collect'n cut flowers, Mrs. M.E. BENTLEY,
    Second Mrs. F.L. NEELY.
Everlasting flowers, Mrs. L. NURENBERGER,
    Second Mrs. C.D. MARTIN.
Foliage Plants, Mrs. A.O. MYERS.
    Second Mrs. D.W. BRITTON.
Green house plants, Mrs. D.W. BRITTON.
Relics, Mrs. George SHAW.
Mineral fancy work, Mrs. F. MITCHELL
Crystal Boquet, Mrs. Wm. FRAZIER.

FINE ARTS, PAINTINGS, ETC.
Flowers in oil, Ida FORD.
Oil painting, Mrs. O.H. CONE. Second Effie WALLACE.
Animal picture, Mrs. E.E. EVANS. Second Ida FORD.
Marine view, Ida FORD. Second Mrs. E.M. SMITH.
Winter scene in oil, Ida FORD.
Fruit piece, Ida FORD.
Oil paint'g on plaque, Mrs. O.H. CONE.
    Second Ida FORD.
Fancy piece in oil, Mrs. O.H. CONE.
    Second Ida FORD.
Oil pt'g on porcelain, Ida FORD.
Flowers in water colors, Mrs. E.M. SMITH.
Pen drawing, S.B. RUSSEL

VEHICLES, HARNESS, ETC.
Two horse carriage, J.O. MILLIGAN & Co.
Top Buggy, J.O. MILLIGAN & Co.
Farm wagon, J.O. MILLIGAN & Co.
Display of carriages, J.O. MILLIGAN & Co.
Open Buggy, John BEIRMAN.

• • •

S. V. JOHNSON
Carriage Painter

AUGUST STONE
Merchant - Tailor,
Wayne, Nebraska.

• • •

Wayne Herald-Tribune
October 29, 1885 (Vol. XI, No. 11)

BIRTH: To Fred RABER and wife, Saturday, Oct. 24th, a son.

MARRIED: At the residence of J.A. WILCUT, Sunday evening, Oct. 25th, 1885, H.E. NYE of Wayne, and Miss Cora E. GILES, of Sioux City, Rev. H.G. PITTENGER officiating. Mr. NYE is one of the most energetic of our young professional men and during his residence of a year in Wayne has made many friends in the town and county and the firm of NYE & HATCH of which he is a member, have built up an excellent and increasing business. Mrs. NYE is comparatively a stranger to Wayne, but will be heartily welcomed to the social circles of the village. The Herald-Tribune extends its heartiest congratulations.

DIED: HAKE. Mrs. HAKE, wife of Prof. J.S. HAKE, died last evening in childbirth. The above is a peculiarly sad death, and will bring sorrow to many a heart outside of the family. Mrs. HAKE lived at Wayne only since the time of her marriage, less than a year ago, but had made many warm friends here who extend to Mr. HAKE their heartfelt sympathy in his bereavement. The funeral will occur from the residence Saturday forenoon at 10:30.

M. E. Conference.

The first district conference of the M.E. church for the Norfolk district met in Wayne Tuesday and closes its sessions today. The following ministers and others are in attendance: Rev's. Dr. MAXFIELD of Omaha, W.G. OLINGER of Central City, W.A. DAVIES of Homer, J.R. GEARHART of Humphrey, Jno CREWS of Leigh, J.B. PRIEST of Norfolk, S.L. PARKER of St. James, S.W. MARTIN of Wakefield, C.S. MOORE of Stanton, D. MARQUETTE of Omaha, O.H. LAKE of Homer, W.J. BEELS of Norfolk, and H.G. PITTINGER of Wayne; Prof. E.B. ALLEN of Wakefield, and G.A. CULVER of Wayne. Quite a number of ministers who were expected were kept away by the rain.

Tuesday evening an interesting sermon was preached by Rev. J.W. MARTIN.

On Wednesday morning after the opening exercises and the transaction of some business the time was devoted to a discussion of the "The Church," with especial reference to her mission, conditions of success, elements of power and means of grace and how to make them effective. In the afternoon an educational address was delivered by Rev. W.G. OLINGER; followed by a general discussion of the subject, "Church Officers; Their duties and qualifications."

In the evening a very interesting temperance meeting was held and addressed by Rev.'s Dr. MAXFIELD, W.G. OLINGER and J.W. MARTIN. A fair audience was present, but it would have been much larger if the meeting had been more generally announced.

The principal subject discussed this morning was "Revivals." The afternoon is devotedly principally to the transaction of business and the conference will close this evening with a sermon to which all are invited.

Wayne Herald-Tribune
November 5, 1885 (Vol. XI, No. 12)

MARRIED: GIDDINGS - DUMM. At Sioux City, Iowa, Thursday, October 29th, M.F. GIDDINGS of Wayne and Mrs. Emma DUMM of Ligonier, Indiana. Our friend GIDDINGS has done a sensible thing in thus completing his home and that it may be a happy and prosperous one for many years is the wish ot the Herald-Tribune.

Card of Thanks.
Wayne, Neb. Nov 2nd, 1885.

We desire to tender our sincere acknowledgements to the many friends for their kind aid and sympathy, and to the church for its consolation at this time of our severe affliction.

J.S. HAKE,
Mrs. Dr. GLASS.

Advertised Letters.

List of letters remaining uncalled for in the Wayne Post office Oct. 31, 1885.

Gentlemens List.

A.G. ARNOLD	W.M. ANDERSON
Andrew BENTH	G. BASTIAN
Rob't CHAPIN	Willie B. CUTTER
John B. CURTIS	Alexander CATTNACH
Edward J. DAVIS	Chas. DECKER

DAVIDSON Bros.
Frank GAERTNER
E. Herman KRUEGLER
C.G. LEDER
James MURRY
Eaber MARSH
James McCOLLOUGH
Carter OLSON
D.A. SHARP
W. TOLANDER
J.W. TAYLOR
William WJEESE
A. WOODWARD
M.L. WHITNEY

M.A. DICKSON
I.R. JOHNSON
H.H. LARSON
Oscar MILLER
Chas McKAY
R.B. MARTIN
P.N. NELSON
O. RICE
M.G. STEECE
W.O. TAMBEAGE
R.L. WARNOCK
N.O. WRIGHT
M.F. WISE

Ladies List.

Mrs. Lewis ANDERSON
Mrs. Mary COLLINS
Mrs. Lodisa HINDS
Mrs. Sophia LARSON
Miss Ada TAYLOR
Miss H. WILKINSON

Miss Cally CRISSWELL
Mrs. Chas. H. GROESBECK
Miss Lizzie HINES
Mrs. Anna RICHMOND
Mrs. Wm. WALLACE

Persons calling for the above letters will please say "advertised". M. DEARBORN, P.M.

Election Results.

The following was the vote in the different precincts on the state ticket last year. It will be convenient for comparison with this year's vote.

STATE.

	Rep.	Dem.
Wayne	240	93
Logan	36	19
Deer Creek	19	5
Garfield	5	3
Leslie	39	35
Plum Creek	21	16
Brenna	21	13
Hancock	14	8
Spring Branch	19	31

Results in Wayne County.

STATE TICKET.

	Rep.	Dem.
Wayne	324	114
Spring Branch	26	31

Logan	31	25
Plum Creek	36	36
Leslie	65	43
Brenna	27	31
Deer Creek	38	6
Hancock	21	10
Garfield	10	13
Total	578	309

Wayne Precinct.

Rep.		Dem.	
Chas. JOHNSON	232	F.A. DEARBORN	125
D.W. BRITTON	255	Wm. MILLER	186
E. MARTIN	324		
A.A. WELCH	311	James A. ELLIOTT	118
A.S. MINER	333	M.D. WEBER	107
A.L. HOWSER	275	F.E. MOSES	158
O.F. CRANE	195	J.T. METTLEN	240
J.W. BARTLETT	318	L. NURNBURGER	115
J.J.W. FOX	262	C.O. JOHNSON	131
F.H. ROBINSON	263	A.A. HARDY	95
Henry G. WRIGHT	270	S.R. RUSSEL	136
M.S. DAVIES	270	D. WISE	93
J.E. RENNETT	260		

Logan Precinct.

Rep.		Dem.	
Chas. JOHNSON	29	F.A. DEARBORN	27
D.W. BRITTON	32	Wm. MILLER	24
E. MARTIN	30		
A.A. WELCH	31	James A. ELLIOTT	25
A.S. MINER	23	M.D. WEBER	23
A.L. HOWSER	27	F.E. MOSES	24
O.F. CRANE	19	J.T. METTLEN	32
J.W. BARTLETT	34	L. NURNBURGER	20

Deer Creek Precinct.

Rep.		Dem.	
Chas. JOHNSON	19	F.A. DEARBORN	20
D.W. BRITTON	14	Wm. MILLER	25
E. MARTIN	34		
A.A. WELCH	30	James A. ELLIOTT	8
A.S. MINER	32	M.D. WEBER	7
A.L. HOWSER	7	F.E. MOSES	32
O.F. CRANE	18	J.T. METTLEN	21

| J.W. BARTLETT | 34 | L. NURNBURGER | 6 |

Garfield Precinct.

Rep.		Dem.	
Chas. JOHNSON	11	F.A. DEARBORN	11
D.W. BRITTON	9	Wm. MILLER	14
E. MARTIN	20		
A.A. WELCH	6	James A. ELLIOTT	17
A.S. MINER	13	M.D. WEBER	10
A.L. HOWSER	13	F.E. MOSES	10
O.F. CRANE	6	J.T. METTLEN	17
J.W. BARTLETT	10	L. NURNBERGER	13

Leslie Precinct.

Rep.		Dem.	
Chas. JOHNSON	56	F.A. DEARBORN	49
D.W. BRITTON	63	Wm. MILLER	45
E. MARTIN	64		
A.A. WELCH	66	James A. ELLIOTT	42
A.S. MINER	61	M.D. WEBER	40
A.L. HOWSER	66	F.E. MOSES	40
O.F. CRANE	49	J.T. METTLEN	56
J.W. BARTLETT	61	L. NURNBURGER	44

Plum Creek.

Rep.		Dem.	
Chas. JOHNSON	17	F.A. DEARBORN	54
D.W. BRITTON	23	Wm. MILLER	46
E. MARTIN	36		
A.A. WELCH	36	James A. ELLIOTT	36
A.S. MINER	28	M.D. WEBER	44
A.L. HOWSER	38	F.E. MOSES	32
O.F. CRANE	15	J.T. METTLEN	57
J.W. BARTLETT	36	L. NURNBURGER	36

Brenna.

Rep.		Dem.	
Chas. JOHNSON	27	F.A. DEARBORN	21
D.W. BRITTON	22	Wm. MILLER	26
E. MARTIN	28		
A.A. WELCH	30	James A. ELLIOTT	18
A.S. MINER	27	M.D. WEBER	21
A.L. HOWSER	5	F.E. MOSES	43
O.F. CRANE	24	J.T. METTLEN	23
J.W. BARTLETT	27	L. NURNBURGER	21

Spring Branch.

Rep.		Dem.	
Chas. JOHNSON	32	F.A. DEARBORN	24
D.W. BRITTON	26	Wm. MILLER	30
E. MARTIN	32		
A.A. WELCH	25	James A. ELLIOTT	31
A.S. MINER	34	M.D. WEBER	23
A.L. HOWSER	41	F.E. MOSES	16
O.F. CRANE	16	J.T. METTLEN	39
J.W. BARTLETT	30	L. NURNBURGER	27

Total Votes and majorities:

CLERK.
Chas. JOHNSON, Rep.	463
F.A. DEARBORN, Dem.	402
Majority	61

TREASURER.
D.W. BRITTON, Rep.	463
Wm. MILLER, Dem.	408
Majority	55

JUDGE.
E. MARTIN, Rep.	596

CORONER.
J.W. BARTLETT, Rep.	565
L. NURNBERGER, Dem.	297
Majority	268

COMMISSIONER.
J.T. METTLEN, Dem.	516
O.F. CRANE, Rep.	347
Majority	169

SHERIFF.
A.S. MINER, Rep.	586
M.D. WEBER, Dem.	287
Majority	299

SUPERINTENDENT.
A.A. WELCH, Rep.	544
J.A. ELLIOTT, Dem.	316
Majority	228

SURVEYOR.

A.L. HOWSER, Rep.	495
F.E. MOSES, Dem.	363
Majority	132

Wayne Herald-Tribune
November 12, 1885 (Vol. XI, No. 13)

BIRTH: To G.D. ROE and wife, Thursday November 5th, a boy.

BIRTH: To Wm. KETTLER and wife, Tuesday Nov. 10th, a girl.

Wayne Herald-Tribune
November 19, 1885 (Vol. XI, No. 14)

MARRIED: HUGHES - RICHMOND. Nov. 18th 1885, at the residence of J.S. RICKABAUGH, Mr. Thomas B. HUGHES of Wayne to Miss Retta RICHMOND of Malvern, Iowa, Rev. H.G. PITTENGER officiating. Mr. HUGHES is one of the solid farmers of Brenna precinct, and we supposed from all appearances that he was proof against Cupid's wiles. The Herald-Tribune extends its congratulations.

MARRIED: WELCH - DAVIES. At the residence of the bride's mother at Sioux City, Iowa Tuesday, Nov. 17th 1885, Anson A. WELCH and Anna B. DAVIES.

MARRIED: NORTHROP - FORD. At the residence of the bride's parents, near Earlham, Iowa, Monday Nov. 6th 1885, Frank M. NORTHROP and Ida M. FORD.

The above announcements tell of suits prosecuted by two of Wayne's attorneys in another court than that of the dry and musty law. The gentlemen are among the foremost members of the Wayne bar, and have been deservedly popular and successful in their business. We heartily congratulate them on their enlistment into the ranks of the benedicts.

Mrs. WELCH was for two years a teacher in the public schools of Wayne, and was one of the most popular of teachers, and an active member of the church and social circles of the village.

From a long acquaintance with Mrs. NORTHROP we know her to be possessed in a rare degree of the social and domestic graces and accomplishments that are the ornament of true womanhood. The ladies will be welcome additions to the social life of the village.

Mr. and Mrs. WELCH have rooms in the residence of J.A. LINDLEY, Mr. and Mrs. NORTHROP are "at home" in Mr. DEARBORN's residence north of the Methodist church.

DIED: WALTERS. In Colton, Thursday Oct. 22nd, J.E. WALTERS, a native of Ohio, aged 56 years. The deceased was born in Tuscarora county, Ohio, Oct. 27, 1839. He united with the church and was converted when 14 years of age, and when 8 years old was much impressed by hearing a sermon on the text John 14-2, which impression never left him, and since that time lived in anticipation of entering his mansion when called hence. By request the same text of Scripture was used as his funeral text by Rev. I.G. SIGLER. At the time of his death he was a member of the M.E. church and the I.O.G.T. (Colton, Cal., Semi-Tropic). The deceased was the father of Chas. and Geo. WALTERS of this place.

Advertised Letters.

List of letters remaining uncalled for in the Wayne Post office Oct. 31, 1885.

Gentlemens List.

A.G. ARNOLD	W.M. ANDERSON
Andrew BENTH	G. BASTIAN
Willie B. CUTTER	John B. CURTIS
Alexander CATTNACH	Edward J. DAVIS
Chas. DECKER	DAVIDSON Bros.
M.A. DICKSON	I.R. JOHNSON
E. Herman KRUEGLER	H.H. LARSON
C.G. LEDER	Chas. McKAY
Eaber MARSH	R.B. MARTIN
James McCOLLOUGH	P.N. NELSON
Carter OLSON	O. RICE
D.A. SHARP	M.G. STEECE
W.M. TOLANDER	W.O. TAMBEAGE
J.W. TAYLOR	R.L. WARNOCK
William WJEESE	A. WOODWARD
M.L. WHITNEY	

Ladies List.

Mrs. Lewis ANDERSON	Miss Cally CRISSWELL
Mrs. Mary COLLINS	Mrs. Chas. H. GROESBECK
Mrs. Lodisa HINDS	Miss Lizzie HINES
Mrs. Anna RICHMOND	Miss Ada TAYLOR
Mrs. Wm. WALLACE	

Persons calling for the above letters will please say "advertised". M. DEARBORN, P.M.

Wayne Herald-Tribune
December 3, 1885 (Vol. XI, No. 16)

A.N. CHILDS has been sick for several days this week and is not yet so far recovered as to be able to be out.

Advertised Letters.

List of letters remaining uncalled for in the Wayne Post office Nov 30, 1885.

Gentlemens List.

J.F. ANDVENS	George O. ANDERSON
F.W. BAWDEN	Joseph BRIDAL
Wm. BRANMER	Alex CATTNACH
Floyd CUNNINGHAM	A.A. CRAMER
John COABOSE	James FLETCHER
Flinny FORD	F.L. FRINK
H. FREWIER	C.P. JOHNSON
Jeppa JEPPSON	Louis KERCHEUR
C.W. LANSON	J.B. McDONALD
Harry LUS	F. MILLER
McHENEKY & GEISE	Willhelm MERCER
Lot MORRIS	Louis NURENBERGER
R.E. RICHMOND	M.T. ROBINSON
Jas SALTER	J.W. SAUNDERS
N.D. SHOENHOLZ	TRYON & WRIGHT
Christ UTRECHT	Chas. WELDON
Wenzel WAGNER	Chas. WITMAN

Ladies List.

Miss Anna BOOK	Mrs. H.K. JONES
Mrs. E. JOHNSTON	Mrs. Ed LORD
Mrs. Francis MITCHELL	Miss Bertha POLLEY
Mrs. Emma REALE	

Persons calling for the above letters will please say "advertised." M. DEARBORN, P.M.

Wayne Herald-Tribune
December 10, 1885 (Vol. XI, No. 17)

BIRTH: To T.H. WALLACE and wife, Wednesday, Dec. 9th, a son.

BIRTH: To A.W. CHAFEE and wife Thursday, Dec. 3rd, a boy.

Wm. LALK, Wm. WINTER, Wm. PHEIL, Herman WILKINS and John WENDT all went to Wayne Saturday, but only the latter in company with Sheriff MINER. Mr. WENDT had been guilty of assaulting his neighbor Conrad WILLS and was called to appear in Wayne for doing so. (Hoskins)

Tuesday morning while engaged in shelling corn for Dan KOENTY, S.W. GAYLORD in some way got his right hand in the power sheller and had his hand so badly injured as to lose his fingers and perhaps his whole hand. Lewis ZIEMER drove over to Norfolk with him, at present writing we have not heard how he fared in the hands of the surgeons. (Hoskins)

• • •

JOHN D. KING
Attorney at Law,
Wayne, Nebraska.

• • •

The Wayne Herald
January 5, 1888 (Vol. XII, No. 52)

Brenna Precinct.

Jan. 1, 1888.
 Editors Herald: - This being the first of the new year, I have resolved (if agreeable to you) to note some of the events that may occur in Brenna Precinct the present year, and as this first day of 1888 has furnished nothing of importance, so far as I know, I will devote this letter to some of the more important events of 1887.
 So, to begin, I will say, good bye to dear old 1887. Thy memory is fraught with much to cheer; and but little to sadden the heart of our people. The only deaths were those of the infant children of Messrs. BROWN and HUGHES; very little sickness; three weddings; 9 or 10 births. A number of new settlers have come among us and are proving themselves worthy neighbors. A good many substantial improvements have been added to the farms and homes of our people, among which I might mention the fine new residence of D.B. TOLLMAN, in north Brenna. Our soil has proven itself worthy of the hand of toil by producing the finest crops I have ever seen grown, thereby more firmly attaching our people to their homes, dispelling discontent, and creating new life and energy among us. Brenna people are becoming somewhat noted for their sociability, getting together publicly and privately as often as possible, thereby getting intimately acquainted with each other.
 Well, lest I should get this letter too long I will note a few of

the present happenings in our midst.

Brenna lyceum is running this winter at the Gray school house, time of meeting every Friday evening. The question for next meeting: - Shall "Brenna" build a hall or a church?

Jolly little Jimmy RENNICK feels as big as any man since he became "papa" to a nice little girl.

Mr. and Mrs. Thomas HUGHES are spending their holidays in southwestern Iowa.

Johnny CREAMER returned Wednesday from a vist to Malvern, Iowa, where he says corn is selling at from 45 to 50 cents.

Josiah BLACK's little baby boy is very sick. (We have learned that the child has since died. Ed.)

Miss Minnie SWEET, sister-in-law of Dock TOLLMAN, has been very sick for some time. Her father arrived from Davenport, Iowa, last week.

Well, I presume this letter is too already.

B.

• • •

VAN CAMP & PERRINE,
Dealers in
Drugs and Druggists Sundries,
Patent Medicines,
Stationery, Perfumery,
Cigars - and - Tobaccos.
Perscriptions a Speciality.
Wayne, Nebraska

• • •

CROCKERY!
P. L. MILLER'S.
Elegant Hanging Lamps, Mustache cups,
Castors, Decorated setts.

• • •

The Peoples Store
CORBIT & LINDLY, Proprietors.
Dry Goods, Boots and Shoes,
Hats, Caps, Gloves and Mittens.
Wayne, Nebraska

Moline Wagons, Deer Plows, Columbus Buggies.
On hand and for Sale by
SLATER & FISHER

• • •

J. E. McFARLAND,
Druggist,
Wayne, Nebraska.

• • •

GEO. W. RILEY
Att'y at Law
Wayne, Neb.

• • •

JOHN KLEVER,
Carpenter, Contractor, and Builder.
Wayne, Nebraska.

• • •

Wayne Meat Market
ROE BROTHERS

• • •

H. A. WHITAKER,
Wagon & Carriage Maker
Wayne, Nebraska

• • •

J. H. BUCHANAN,
Piano Tuner and Organ Repairer.
MABEL BUCHANAN,
Music Teacher
Wayne, Nebraska.

L. F. RAYBURN.
Blacksmith,
Wayne, Nebraska

. . .

The Wayne Herald
January 12, 1888 (Vol. XIII, No. 1)

COMMISSIONER PROCEEDINGS. Wayne, Neb. Jan. 5, 1888.
Commissioners met pursuant to adjournment.
Present: J.T. METTLEN, chairman, and A.T. CHAPIN and Wm. FRAZIER, commissioners, and Wm. MILLER, clerk.
On motion the official bonds of Wm. MILLER, county clerk, John CONNOR, treasurer, W.E. HOWARD, county supt., and George CHILDS, justice of the peace, were approved.
On motion the following bills were allowed and warrants ordered drawn on the county general fund to pay the same.

D.W. BRITTON, fees	$333.25
Chas. JOHNSON, salary, etc.	104.60

On motion it was ordered that the county clerk pay the city marshal of Wayne $8.00 per month for watching county buildings, and charge same to county.
On motion board proceeded to settle with the county treasurer, which occupied all the time of the 5th and 6th, and up to the 7th day of January, 1888.
On motion the completion of the settlement with the treasurer was postponed until such time as treasurer shall produce proper vouchers for moneys paid to state.
On motion the following bonds were approved:
County Judge - E. MARTIN.
Sheriff - A.S. MINER.
Coroner - George SHAW.
County Surveyor - C.D. MARTIN.
R.C. OSBORN, assessor, Strahan prec't.
Jas. KELLY, assessor, Brenna precinct.
A.O. MYERS, assessor, Wayne precinct.
J.J.W. FOX, assessor, Hunter prec't.
S.A. DUGAN, assessor, Spring Branch.
J.A. GRAY, supervisor, Road Dist. 19.
E.J. NANGLE, supervisor, Road Dist. 8.
R. BENSER, supervisor, Road Dist. 4.
W. DELAHOYDE, supervisor, Road Dist. 18.
John OLSON, supervisor, Road Dist. 11.
E. BEHMER, supervisor, Road Dist. 34.

O. McANNICK, supervisor, Road Dist. 38.
David SHAW, supervisor, Road Dist. 5.
L.W. ROOT, supervisor, Road Dist. 37.
R.Q. WARNOCK, constable, Wayne.
J.C. BONAWITZ, constable, Plum Creek.
R.E. TEMPLIN, constable, Spring Branch.
David SHAW, constable, Hancock.
J.E. CREAMER, constable, Brenna.
A.B. CLARK, justice peace, Hancock.
W.H. ROOT, justice peace, Deer Creek.
W. DELAHOYDE, justice peace, Plum Creek.
Jno. E. BENNETT, justice peace, Brenna.
J.M. HUGLIN, justice peace, Spring Branch.

On motion the county clerk was directed to draw warrants on county general fund for the following commissioner's services:

J.T. METTLEN,	$18.60
A.T. CHAPIN,	15.20
Wm. FRAZIER,	18.00

On motion adjourned to regular meeting Jan. 10th, 1888.
Attest:
Wm. MILLER, County Clerk.

Advertised Letters.

List of letters remaining uncalled for in the Wayne post office for the week ending Jan. 4.

Lewis JONES, Andrew SPANNAN, Henrich WRIGHT, James E. MOORE, W.F. LEWIS, John HASSIN, John HOLTGRENEVE, F.C. MULM.

Fannie FENTON, 2, Miss Belle JONES, 3, Charlotte HOLMES, Mrs. Lesior HILGIT.

Parties calling for the above will say "Advertised" and give date.
M. DEARBORN, P.M.

• • •

WM. PIEPENSTOCK,
Harness Maker
and Upholsterer.

• • •

HARRY WORKMAN'S
Barber Shop

A. E. VAN CAMP, M.D.
Physician & Surgeon,
Wayne, Nebraska.

• • •

J. H. SPEARS
Veterinary Surgeon,
Wayne, Nebraska.

• • •

FRED LILLJEBERG,
The only Exclusive Boot & Shoe Store
in the County.

• • •

The Wayne Herald
January 26, 1888 (Vol. XIII, No. 3)

Advertised Letters.

List of letters remaining uncalled for in the Wayne post office for the week ending Jan. 21.

J.B. CUMMINGS, Wm. CASS, James KELLER, Ira LIEBERSTEIN, Mrs. Alice I. GOFMAN, Mrs. Freddie McBURNEY, Mrs. Elizabeth WERNICK

Parties calling for the above will say "Advertised" and give date.

M. DEARBORN, P.M.

• • •

The Citizens Bank
A. L. TUCKER, President
D. C. MAIN, Cashier
BENJ. LEMOBARD, Jr. Vice Pres't
C. B. FRENCH, Jr. Ass't. Cash
C. B. FRENCH, Jr. Ass't Cash.

Directors,
BENJ. LOMBARD, Jr. • **A. A. WELCH**
JAMES PAUL • **D. C. MAIN**
NELSON GRIMSLEY • **A. L. TUCKER**
C. B. FRENCH, Jr.

HAYES & KING
Jewelers,
Wayne, Nebraska

• • •

PHILLEO & SON,
Successors to Philleo & Son and J.O. Milligan & Co.,
Dealers in all Kinds of
Lumber, Lime, Coal

• • •

P. A. ENGLISH
Dealer in
Grain, Lumber, Lime and Farm Machinery
Winside, Neb.,
J. M. CHERRY, Agent.

• • •

CITY MEAT MARKET
J. H. GOLL, Prop'r.

• • •

HINRICHS & SHIRTS,
Blacksmiths.
Wayne, Nebraska

• • •

A. J. FERGUSON,
Pension, Bounty and Claim Solicitor.
Wayne, Nebraska

• • •

West Side Creamery and Feed Mill,
NEWTON & CO., Pr's.

• • •

West Side Pharmacy!
B. J. KASS, Prop.

The Wayne Herald
February 9, 1888 (Vol. XIII, No. 5)

County Directory.

John CONNOR . . . . . County Treasurer . . . . .Wayne
Wm. MILLER . . . . . County Clerk . . . . .Wayne
E. MARTIN . . . . . County Judge . . . . .Wayne
A. S. MINER . . . . . Sheriff . . . . .Wayne
W. E. HOWARD. . . . .County Sup't . . . . .Wayne
J. D. KING. . . . .County Attorney. . . . .Wayne
Geo. SHAW. . . . .Coroner. . . . .Wayne
Wm. FRAZIER. . . . .County Com'r. . . . .Wayne
A.T. CHAPIN. . . . .County Com'r. . . . .Wayne
J.T. METTLEN. . . . .County Com'r. . . . .Wakefield

Fourth monthly report of school district No. 30 for the month ending January 20th, 1888.
No. pupils enrolled, 10
Average attendance, 7
No. days taught, 20
Sallie McFEE, Teacher.

Advertised Letters.

List of letters remaining uncalled for in the Wayne post office for the week ending Feb. 4.

F.M. EDWARDS, Charlie STILES, Tilten WEBER, A.C. NEWMAN, C.A. ANDERSEN, C.E. ANDERSEN, Jesse HAMILTON, Miss May HARRINGTON, Mrs. Jane ALDEN.

Parties calling for the above will say "Advertised" and give date. M. DEARBORN, P.M.

The Wayne Herald
February 16, 1888 (Vol. XIII, No. 6)

MARRIED: John W. BROWN and Miss Minnie ELLISON were married at the Caroll parsonage Sunday, Feb. 5th.

MARRIED: At the home of the bride Wayne, Neb., on February 14th, 1888, John BAYES and Miss Eva B. MYERS, Rev. F.P. BAKER officiating.

DIED: The eight year old daughter of Jno. FOLEY died on Sunday night from the effects of lung fever. The burial took place at Wayne on Wednesday. (Wakefield Republican)

Obituary.

TOLLMAN. Darius TOLLMAN was born in Duchess county, N.Y., June 18th, 1800, and died at the home of his son, D.B. TOLLMAN, in Wayne county, Neb, Feb. 9th, 1888. In early life he was married and soon moved to Saratoga county, N.Y., where he was converted at the age of 32 years and joined the M.E. church. He at once became a true representative of his ancestors, in that he was an earnest laborer in the Lord's vineyard, a liberal contributor of his means to the support of the gospel and the various benevolent enterprises of the church, and home at once became a home and place of rest and refreshment for any and all preachers of the gospel, and this class of persons in large numbers were continually his guests for nearly sixty years, the whole time during which he and the wife of his youth walked hand in hand over life's toilsome journey. In 1856 he left New York and settled in Scott county, Iowa, where he lived until April 17th, 1886, when he came to Nebraska to reside with his son. About eight years ago his life companion stepped down in to the cold river and passed over in great triumphs of faith. Since then he has been waiting and watching for the close, the meanwhile doing what he could in the Lord's vineyard, which at times seemed to be but little, since he suffered so greatly from a cancer on his hand, which finally ended his career on earth. Though a great sufferer for several years he was always cheerful, expressing the most boundless confidence in his future prospects, and when the end finally came he met it with great fortitude and that conquering faith which is the "substance of things hoped for, the evidence of things not seen."

The funeral services were conducted by Rev. Wm. GORST in the Gray school house at 12 M. last Sunday where a large congregation had gathered in expression of their esteem of the deceased and the family. The remains will be sent to Poughkeepsie, N.Y., for interment.

• • •

A meeting of the stockholders of the Wayne County Agricultural Society was held at the town hall yesterday afternoon. As the attendance was small the only business transacted was the election of officers for the ensuing year. The officers elected are as follows:

President, A.T. CHAPIN.
Vice President, John CONNOR.
Secretary, L.C. DEARBORN.
Treasurer, A.L. TUCKER.

Directors: J.R. MANNING, Wm. FRAZIER, D.W. BRITTON, Ran. FRAZIER, A.B. SLATER, T.J. STEELE, E.J. NANGLE, R.H. GIBSON, W.S. ANDERSON, H.H. MOSES.

A meeting will be held at the town hall next Monday afternoon at 2 o'clock, and it is urgently requested that every stockholder, and especially every officer shall be present.

Advertised Letters.

List of letters remaining uncalled for in the Wayne post office for the week ending Feb. 11.

Peter BACKER, Chas. BALLARD, E.W. COOPER, Fleming CUNNINGHAM, Robert DEVINE, Wm. HEFT, C. JENTON, J.A. JOHNSON, Gust JOHNSON, R. JOHNSON, Fred KEPE, W. KUGLER, Henry LEHMAN, John A.D. PORTER, O. PETERSON, Anson RICKARDSON, H.D. ROGERS, Willhelm VOSK, V.A. YOUTZ, Jane ALDEN, Lyda GALLAGHER, Mrs. S.J. JOHNSON, Mrs. Mattie KENYON, Miss E.D. WISE.

Parties calling for the above will say "Advertised" and give date.

M. DEARBORN, P.M.

• • •

First National Bank
Wayne, Nebraska,

Officers and Directors:
JOHN T. BRESSLER, President
HENRY LEY, Vice Pres.
F.A. DEARBORN, Cashier
W.S. GILLETTE, Ass't Cash'er

Directors.
JOHN T. BRESSLER
D.C. PATTERSON,
F.A. DEARBORN
HENRY LEY
J.W. JONES,
F.M. NORTHROP
FRANK FULLER

• • •

P. W. OMAN,
Auctioneer!

The Wayne Herald
February 23, 1888 (Vol. XIII, No. 7)

BIRTH: Mr. and Mrs. Wm. WEBER are rejoicing over the advent of a fine son and heir, born on Tuesday of this week.

BIRTH: Mr. and Mrs. MOCK are the happy parents of a bouncing boy. (Deer Creek)

MARRIED: At the residence of the bride's parents, Wednesday, February 22nd, W.A. IVORY and Miss Nellie B. FRENCH, Rev. F.P. BAKER officiating. This event, which has been expected for some time, unites two most worthy young people for life. Both bride and groom are well-known and very popular in the community, and their many friends will unite in congratulating them, and wishing them all the favors of fortune for their future.

Obituary.

DEARBORN - Elizabeth A. OWENS was born at Cincinnati, Ohio, June 22nd, 1820, and died at Wayne, Nebraska, February 18th, 1888, of dilation of the heart She was married to Marcelius DEARBORN at Havana, Illinois, September 12th, 1850. Mr. and Mrs. DEARBORN lived at Havana until 1864, when they moved to Minnesota, where they remained for eight years, returning to Havana in 1872, and made their home there until their removal to Wayne in 1881.

They had three children, Charles E., who died in infancy, Luther C., who has lived in Wayne since the town was founded, and Eugene C., who lives at Jacksonville, Florida.

The funeral services were conducted at the residence Monday afternoon by Rev. F.B. BAKER, according to the ceremony of the Episcopal church, of which Mrs. DEARBORN had been a member since 1866. Only the intimate friends of the famly were present.

Her body ws taken to Havana, Illinois, Tuesday, for interment and was accompanied by her husband, her son, and F.A. DEARBORN.

Mrs. DEARBORN had been an invalid for a number of years, and her life in Wayne was a very quite one, but she enjoyed the respect and esteem of all who knew her, and her more intimate friends loved her for her uncomplaining christian life and conduct, and her true womanhood. The afflicted family has the heartfelt sympathy of the entire community.

Obituary.

NEWTON - Anna M., wife of I.L. NEWTON, Monday, February 20th, 1888, aged 26 years, of _____ of the heart, after an illness of but two days.

It was but a short time ago that we chronicled the marriage of Miss Anna M. SPAHR to O.L. NEWTON on Thanksgiving day, and now the sad news of her death follows close after, ending the hope of a long and happy life. The funeral service was conducted at the Methodist church Tuesday afternoon by Rev. Wm. GORST, and was attended by a large number of the friends of the deceased and the family.

SOCIETIES.

I.O.O.F., Wayne Lodge, No. 118, meets Monday evening in Masonic Hall. Jno. T. BRESSLER, N.G., R.J. MORGAN, Secretary.

A.F. & A.M., Wayne Lodge, No. 120, meets in Masonic Hall the second and fourth Fridays in each month. J.T. BRESSLER, M.W., B.F. FEATHER, Secretary.

K. of P., Lotus Lodge, No. 65, meets the 1st and 3rd Mondays of each month in the Masonic Hall. Jas. BRITTON, C.C., D.L. STRICKLAND, K. of R. and S.

A.O.U.W., Wayne Lodge, No. 103, meets 1st and 3rd Fridays of each month in Masonic Hall. Geo. W. KORTRIGHT, M.W., G.W. RILEY, Rec.

W.C.T.U. meets the 1st and 3rd Thursdays in each month. Mrs. J.D. KING, Pres., Mrs. N.F. BENNETT, Sec'y.

G.A.R., No. -, meets the First and Third Mondays of each month. B. CUNNINGHAM, Com.

• • •

S. D. RELYEA,
Contractor & Builder
Wayne, Nebraska

• • •

The Wayne Herald
March 1, 1888 (Vol. XIII, No. 8)

BIRTH: To R.M. FARR and wife Feb. 20th, 1888, a daughter.

BIRTH: To J.H. GOLL and wife, Feb. 21st, a son.

BIRTH: To C.C. BOSTEDER and wife, Feb. 22nd, a son.

BIRTH: To G.W. KORTRIGHT and wife, Tuesday, February 28th, a daughter.

BIRTH: M.S. ENGLERT is the happiest man on Coon Creek. They have a 15 lb. boy.

Court Proceedings.

The following is the dispostion of the cases before the district court so far as any action has been taken.

McCormick Harvesting Machine Co. vs. ALGER, continued.
McCormick Harvesting Machine Co. vs. DURKE, continued.
MILLIGAN & Co. vs. CHAFFEE, contd.
Catherine LEJEUNE et al vs. HARMAN, continued.
TAYLOR vs. GAMBLE & PATTERSON, cont.
SAUNDERS vs. McCANDLISS, continued.
TOLLES vs. STEELE, continued.
HORNICK vs. LAUMAN, continued.
METCALF vs. NOBLE, improperly on the docket.
GODDARD vs. GODDARD, report of referees confirmed.
ROOT vs. PATRICK, continued.
FREELAND vs. MOORE, continued.
Nolin, Blinkeron & Co. vs. BROWN, judgment for plaintiff, $524.34.
BROWN, RECEIVER vs. SECHLER, improperly on docket.
GARRETTSON vs. BENNETT, improperly on docket.
McNISH vs. LONG, continued.
YALE vs. NELSON, sale confirmed.
TAYLOR vs. KREBS, improperly on docket.
TAYLOR vs. Julia A. KREBS, improperly on docket.
HIND vs. HIND, decree for divorce granted.
In the matter of the estate of Norman B. HARVEY, sale confirmed.
Norris, Alister & Co. vs. CASE, continued.
Giles Bros & Co. vs. CASE, continued.
NEIGENFIND vs. Wayne county, settled.
Paul A. ENGLISH vs. John O. MILLIGAN et al, demurrer sustained as to Kate A. MILLIGAN, overruled as to defendant GARDNER.
HOGUEWOOD vs. MINER, continued.
Stark & Co. vs. JORDAN, judgment for plaintiff and attached property ordered sold.
BENNETT vs. COOKSIE, default.
SHAW vs. SHAW, continued.
HIGMAN vs. ZIEMER, motion to dissolve attachment overruled.

FELDENHEIMER vs. ZIEMER, motion to dissolve attachments overruled.
Same order in other ZIEMER cases.
MARQUARDT vs. CASE, judgment for plff., and property ordered sold.
HERRICK vs. TOWL, judgment for plaintiff and mortgaged property ordered sold.
BROWN vs. FLEMING, default.
MILLIGAN vs. SCOTT, improperly on docket.
CHACE vs. CHAFFEE, imporperly on the docket.
BRITTON vs. DAVIS, special appearance overruled and case continued.
Giles Bros & Co. vs. TAYLOR, default.
SLATER vs. SHIRTS, default.
SUNDALL vs. BARNES, continued.

The following are the newly elected officers of the Tyro debating society on Coon Creek: Pres., Will SEARS; V. Pres., Canvas MILLER; Sec., Will DELAHOYDE; Treas., Ben KITE. The question for debate to night is: Resolved - That a man has more love for money than for women.

The ladies of the Monday Club give a "Musical" at the residence of A.L. TUCKER this evening, for the benefit of the library. The following is the program:

Overture	Mr. BUCHANAN
Instrumental	Miss TRAIN
Quartette	Misses SPRAGUE and WRIGHT
	Messrs McCOY and HOWARD
Instrumental	Miss BRAMHALL
Vocal Solo	Mrs. WELCH
Instrumental	Mrs. PHILLEO
Vocal Solo	Mrs. McFARLAND
Instrumental	Mrs. PERRINE
Talk on Music	Mr. BAKER
Violin Solo	Mr. BUCHANAN
Instrumental	Miss WRIGHT
Duet	Miss SPRAGUE and Mr. HOWARD
Instrumental	Miss WITTER
Vocal Solo	Nettie CHILDS
Instrumental	Miss TRAIN
Bass Solo	Mr. McCOY
Instrumental	Miss MILLER
Chorus	

COMMISSIONER PROCEEDINGS. Wayne, Neb. Feb. 21st, 1888.
Commissioners met pursuant to adjournment.
Present: J.T. METTLEN, chairman, and Wm. FRAZIER and J.R. MANNING, commissioners, and Wm. MILLER, clerk.
Minutes of last meeting read and approved.

Board then examined the accounts of the following road overseers, and certificates ordered drawn on the different road districts to pay the amounts due.

District No. 26,	$8.76
District No. 30,	27.10
District No. 32,	22.95
District No. 24,	17.17
District No. 23,	22.91
District No. 25,	15.88

remaining in the hands of old supervisors.

A false tax appearing against D.A. PITTENGER it was ordered stricken from the list.

It appearing on the tax list of 1887 that certain personal property had never been entered on said list the Board instructed the clerk to correct the same.

On motion of Wm. FRAZIER, the clerk was instructed to call a special election for Wayne Precinct for the election of two Justices of the Peace, said election to be held on the 13th day of March, 1888.

G.W. WALTERS was appointed constable for Wayne precinct and W.M. JAMES was appointed assessor for Sherman precinct.

The following official bonds were then approved for overseers of highways:
> District No. 22, J.L. ADAMS,
> District No. 3, Jacob LONGNECKER,
> District No. 25, J.R. MORRIS,
> District No. 15, August JOUST,
> District No. 16, Levi DILTS,
> District No. 1, Claus JOHNSON,
> District No. 30, P. COLEMAN,
> District No. 24, J.A. BROWN,
> District No. 26, J.W. JAMES,
> District No. 14, J.W. MAHOLM,

Assessors bonds approved:
> Hancock precinct, John ELLIOTT,
> Logan precinct, James BUSH,
> Leslie precinct, J.W. MAHOLM

G.W. WALTERS, constable for Wayne precinct.

The commissioners then took action in the case of the

inquisition of O.D. SAWYER, and the claims examined and allowed.

On motion the clerk was ordered to draw a warrant on the county general fund for $30.00 in favor of M.S. DAVIES to pay transportation of paupers from Wayne to Burlington, Iowa.

On motion the clerk was instructed to draw a warrant on road fund for $6.00 to pay Frank FULLER, administrator of Nelson Bros. deceased, a poll tax which he had paid under protest.

The following claims were audited and allowed:

J.H. BUCHANAN, Lettering office doors,	$1.25
H.G. LEISENRING, salary as county physician,	50.00
LINN Bros, hardware,	2.95
M.S. DAVIES, supplies for pauper,	74.11
F.M. NORTHROP, rent for county offices,	112.50
E. MARTIN, services in ZIEMER case,	6.10
John CONNOR, supplies,	13.62
J.P. GAERTNER, window shades,	1.00
GIBSON, MILLER & RICHARDSON, supplies,	7.10
State Journal Co., supplies,	24.70
Omaha Republican Co., tax receipts,	15.00
A.P. CHILDS, printing and stationery,	26.68
GOSHORN & McNEAL, printing and stationery,	62.77
J.L. CLINE, work on bridge,	3.00
Frank FULLER, poll tax Nelson Bros.	6.00
Geo. SHAW, expenses of inquest,	41.25
W.E. HOWARD, county sup't,	71.70
A.S. MINER, services and fees as jailor,	38.00
A.S. MINER, money paid for pauper,	4.00

On motion adjourned to appraise land.

Feb. 22, 1888.

Board met, same present as yesterday, and on motion the consent road was vacated along railroad right of way through sections 14 and 23, township 25, 2.

At the request of the clerk the board rescinded its action in regard to deputy hire.

Following bills were allowed:

J.T. METTLEN, commissioner,	$7.80
Wm. FRAZIER, commissioner,	7.20
J.R. MANNING, commissioner,	8.40

On motion the Board adjourned to meet March 20th, 1888.

Attest: Wm. MILLER, Co. Clerk.

The Wayne Herald
March 8, 1888 (Vol. XIII, No. 8)

MARRIED: FOSTER - SINES. At the residence of the bride's parents, on February 28th, 1888, Mr. John G. FOSTER, and Miss Anna, youngest daughter of R.G. SINES, M.H. DODGE, J.P., officiating. (Hoskins)

Advertised Letters.

List of letters remaining uncalled for in the Wayne post office for the week ending Feb. 11.

Joel BOLIN, Geo. A. BENNET, R.W. COOK, John DEAN, Anderson FAVAR, Rev. Ellis M. JONES, M. JOHNSON, Matt KOMMER, E.W. POTE, J. PRICE, A.J. RAND, Andrew SPARMAN, 5, Malachy SHEHAN, Charles THOMPSON, Eli THOMPSON, Chas. WARNER, Amanda RIDWELL, Miss Laura WIDLEY.

Parties calling for the above will say "Advertised" and give date.

M. DEARBORN, P.M.

The Wayne Herald
March 15, 1888 (Vol. XIII, No. 9)

Advertised Letters.

List of letters remaining uncalled for in the Wayne post office for the week ending March 10.

Henry ULRICH, Sylvanus TAYLOR, Adam LILLEY, Milo LACROIX, C. Add. ANDERSON, Mrs. Belle COOK, Mrs. C.H. LEWIS.

Parties calling for the above will say "Advertised" and give date.

M. DEARBORN, P.M.

The Wayne Herald
March 22, 1888 (Vol. XIII, No. 10)

MARRIED: Mr. James REED and Miss Nettie TALLMAN were married at Stanton on the 15th inst. Thus two of our young people have joined hands, hearts and fortunes to journey together, through sunshine and blizzards, until the matrimonial ship shall land them safely upon the evergreen shore, and so may it be. (Brenna Precinct)

Election Notice.

Notice is hereby given that on the 3rd day of April, 1888, from nine o'clock A.M. until seven o'clock P.M., at the office of R.B.

CRAWFORD, in the village of Wayne, an election will be held for the purpose of electing five members of the board of trustees for said village of Wayne.

Dated Wayne, March 3rd, 1888.
Henry LEY
F.A. DEARBORN
W.H. LINN
W.A. LOVE
W.J. PERRY
Board of Trustees of said Village of Wayne.
Attest, F.L. NEELY, Clerk.

Advertised Letters.

List of letters remaining uncalled for in the Wayne post office for the week ending March 17th.

Mr. Bill SKEENS, Frank MANGAN, Mrs. Hans SVAGERSON, Mrs. Lucy MILLER, Mrs. Callie MILLER, Mrs. Annie ANDERSON, Mrs. ___ter ____troufrect, Miss Anne PIOFESEL.

Parties calling for the above will say "Advertised" and give date.

M. DEARBORN, P.M.

COMMISSIONER PROCEEDINGS. Wayne, Neb. March 20, 1888.

Commissioners met pursuant to adjournment.

Present: J.T. METTLEN, J.R. MANNING and Wm. FRAZIER, commissioners, and Wm. MILLER, county clerk.

The following official bonds were approved:
A.P. CHILDS, Justice of the Peace, Wayne Precinct.
Henry JOYNER, Assessor, Chapin Prect.
C.A. GROTHE, Assessor, Garfield Prect.
I.W. STEELE, Assessor, Deer Creek Prect.
Edwin ADAMSON, road overseer, Dist. 9.
Archie LINDSAY, road overseer, Dist. 31.
Andrew SHINN, road overseer, Dist. 21.
James BAIRD, road overseer, Dist. 32.
S. TIMMONS, road overseer, Dist. 36.

The board then appointed road overseers for the following districts:
No. 2, C.C. BASTIAN.
No. 7, D.W.C. HOOD.
No. 12, Jas. BARBOUR.
No. 27, A.T. CHAPIN.
No. 33, Perrin LONG.
No. 35, G.W. SAUNDERS.

On motion the board settled with Elias LONG, road

overseer of district number 35, and instructed the clerk to issue certificate on road district fund to pay the balance due him: $4.44.

On motion the clerk was instructed to confer with the lumber dealers at the different railroad stations in the county, and also with the dealers at Pender, Randolph and Wakefield, Nebraska, asking them to furnish sealed bids for bridge lumber, of the following dimensions, to the board at their meeting on the 1st day of May, 1888.

3 x 12, 12 to 20 feet; 2 x 12, 12 to 20 feet.

The clerk was instructed to advertise the vacation of road No. 3 across sec. 33, 25, 1.

On motion the clerk was authorized to purchase one half dozen automatic ink stands for county, and pay $4.50 for the same.

At this time, C.D. MARTIN tendered his resignation as county surveyor, and on motion of J.R. MANNING, F.E. MOSES was appointed to fill the vacancy.

On motion of Wm. FRAZIER the clerk was instructed to notify the Wayne Cornet Band that they have failed to comply with their written contract entered into with the county commissioners and that unless they pay their rent immediately and also bill of A.S. MINER for cleaning room, their contract will be cancelled by said board of commissioners.

The following bills were audited and allowed, and warrants ordered drawn on the county general fund to pay the same.

Wm. MILLER, Jury fees,	$157.30
M.S. DAVIES, Supplies for pauper,	27.15
A.P. CHILDS, printing &c.,	8.84
CHACE & NEELY, Hardware,	14.30
J.D. KING, road damages paid to H. NEIGENFIND,	56.25
S.T. SIMMONS, services,	8.50
A.P. CHILDS, clerk of election,	2.00
GOSHORN & McNEAL, printing,	4.34
HARRINGTON Bros., Matting,	16.80
Wm. MILLER, cash advanced,	11.75
A.S. MINER, sheriff's fees,	33.50
J.E. BENNETT, supplies for pauper,	10.70
W.E. HOWARD, official services,	51.85
J.W. POWELL, lumber,	9.00
J.T. METTLEN, commissioner,	3.90
J.R. MANNING, commissioner,	8.70
Wm. FRAZIER, commissioner,	7.80

On motion adjourned to May 1st.

Attest: Wm. MILLER, County Clerk.

The Wayne Herald
March 29, 1888 (Vol. XIII, No. 11)

DIED: A.N. CHILDS, who was for some time a resident of Wayne, and associated in the publication of the Gazette, died at Norfolk Monday, of comsumption. Mr. CHILDS came here from New York about three years ago, hoping to benefit his health. He went to Norfolk from here and resumed the practice of his profession of law. Last fall he went to California, thinking the climate there might restore him to health. He grew steadily weaker however, and returned to Norfolk about two weeks ago. His body was taken to New York for burial, and was accompanied by his brother, A.P. CHILDS, of this place.

An Unfortunate Affair.

A party of young men and boys of Brenna precinct went to the house of Frank PERRIN, who was recently married, last night to shivaree him and his bride. PERRIN had evidently suspected that this attention wo'd be paid to him and prepared for it by loading a shot gun with salt. He fired this into the crowd, almost the entire charge taking effect in the face of Hi OMAN, son of P.W. OMAN, a young man about twenty years old. As it was evident that OMAN had been seriously hurt this ended the shivaree. Young OMAN was taken home and Dr. WIGHTMAN was summoned to attend to his injuries. His face is badly scarred and it is almost certain that he will lose both his eyes. PERRIN was arrested late in the night, brought to town and lodged in jail. It is a lamentable affair all around and the foolish sport on one side and the unnecessary anger on the other will be a sad lesson to all concerned as long as they live.

The Wayne Herald
April 5, 1888 (Vol. XIII, No. 12)

MARRIED: On Wednesday April 4th, 1888, by Rev. WM. GORST at Wayne, Nebraska, Mr. William DAVIES, son of Thomas DAVIES, Panderry Farm, Wydrim, Carmarthenshire, S.W. England, to Miss Poebe RICHARDS, Llanbordy, Carmarthenshire, S.W. England. Wish you prosperity, W.D. Home papers please copy.

                        Yours Respectfully,
                        Lewis JONES
                        Pilger, Stanton Co., Neb.

DIED: B. CULVER, March 31st, 1888, aged 67 years, 3 months. The subject of this sketch was born December 29th, 1822, in Cayuga county, New York, and at an early age removed with his parents to Athens county, Ohio, where, on February 20th 1845 he was married to Miss N.A. SPRING. In 1865 he removed with his family to Mills county, Iowa, where he remained until 1882, when he removed to Nebraska and settled in Wayne county, where death closed a most worthy and profitable life. For a number of years he had a strong desire to return to his childhood's home, and in January, 1886, in company with Mrs. CULVER he made an extensive visit to New York, Ohio and Iowa, returning after an absence of six months with the conviction that the disease that had afflicted him for fifteen years would soon terminate his life. In early life he was converted and for 43 years was a faithful and consistent member of the M.E. church, and of him it can truly be said that he thoroughly vindicated the Pauline theory of a christian life. With a deep sense of the value of the present, and a firm conviction that to do the highest possibly good to his fellow man, was the most sacred obligation of life, he laid hold of the forces of nature and made them subservient to this end. Added to a heart naturally sympathetic and generous were the qualities of mind only obtained by a deep religious experience. He was always ready to help the unfortunate and cheer the discouraged. He leaves his family the heritage of a spotless name and character. With a life of trust and faith in Him who said, "I am the resurrection and the life" he went down to the grave with the full assurance that He who conquered death would also give him the victory, and the last intelligible words of peace and joy, and the voice that had so often sang His praise and witnessed to his power to save, became silent in death with His holy name on his lips.

Rest on, dear Father, until that final day when the grave shall yield its treasures at the mandate of the Prince of Live and your family will all join you in the everlasting song, "Unto Him who loved us, and washed us from our sins in His own blood, and hath made us kings and priests unto God and His Father, to Him be glory and dominion for ever and ever." Geo. A. CULVER.

The SHERMAN Tin Wedding. On Tuesday, April 3rd, occurred the 10th or tin wedding anniversary of Mr. and Mrs. E.J. SHERMAN, and if the day is to be an omen of their future life it will be beautiful and serene indeed for it would seem that nature had caught the spirit of the occasion and kindly assisted in making this one of the happiest and most joyful of all our social gatherings. Notwithstanding the invitations were "no presents" a few of the guests took the liberty of making a few presents, in the shape of mementoes or keepsakes. Just prior to refreshments Mr.

and Mrs. SHERMAN were placed in the midst of their friends when J.E. BENNETT, Esq., after a few remarks upon the subject of matrimony, asked the bride and groom if under the circumstances they were still willing to continue in the relationship assumed ten years ago, and by an affirmative answer, he, by virtue of his office, pronounced them husband and wife. Then came refreshments or the wedding dinner, in which the bride displayed her skill in the culinary art, and her desire to sumptuously entertaining her friends.

After the repast the guests engaged in short speeches, declamations, resitations, and singing. Not an illtimed word or look occured to mar the happiness of the occasion, and from the number present, and the demonstrations of the guests, it is evident that Mr. and Mrs. SHERMAN have the respect and confidence of all.

The following guests were present: H.B. MILLER and wife, D. SHAW and wife, Chas. MILLER and wife, E.T. RENNICK and wife, J. RENNICK and wife, J. BAIRD and wife, W. BAIRD and wife, F.E. MOSES and wife, Mrs. H.H. MOSES, E. ADAMSON and wife, T.B. HUGHES and wife, J.E. BENNETT and wife, R. PERRIN and wife, J.A. GRAY and wife, Miss Emma GRAY, F. and D. PITTENGER, Miss Mate PITTENGER, Miss Julia ROOT and Herbert SHERMAN.

Quite Wet. The hot contest that marked the village election last year made both the high license and the no license advocates expect an equally doubtful one this year, but the decided stand taken by the majority of the business men of this town for high license, evidently had more effect than had been looked for, and the high license ticket was easily elected by an average majority of fifty in a total vote of 228. The ubiquitious jake brown again attributed to the defeat of the side he championed by standing at the polls all day and challenging voters whose right to vote was in question.

The following is the vote.

CITIZENS TICKET.

W.J. PERRY,	138
Henry LEY,	136
D. HARRINGTON,	139
J.S. LEWIS,	135
S.B. RUSSELL,	138

NO LICENSE TICKET.

Jas. CONNOR,	94

W.H. LINN,	88
F.J. BENNETT,	95
L. NEWTON,	84
August STONE,	84

Advertised Letters.

List of letters remaining uncalled for in the Wayne post office for the week ending March 17th.

J.S. CRAWFORD, J.H. CRAWFORD, Mr. Lewis JONES, Mr. Chas. JOHNSON, Mrs. Mary COOK.

Parties calling for the above will say "Advertised" and give date.

M. DEARBORN, P.M.

Sheriff's Sale.

By virtue of an order of sale issued by the clerk of the district court of Wayne county, Nebraska, upon a judgement of foreclosure and sale rendered in said court, in favor of Eugene K. HERRICK, and against Erwin B. TOWL and Sarah C. TOWL, and to me directed, I will on the 9th day of May, 1888, at the front door of the building used as a court house of said county at Wayne (the same being the building in which the last term of the district court of said county was held) sell

The North West Quarter of Section Twenty-one, in Township Twenty-five north, of Range One east, in Wayne county, Nebraska.

Taken as the property of the said Erwin B. TOWL and Sarah C. TOWL, at public auction to the highest bidder for cash, to satisfy said order of sale, in the aggregate amounting to $661.85 and $4.78 costs, accruing costs and interest.

Dated this 2nd day of April, 1888.

A.S. MINER,
Sheriff of Wayne county, Nebraska.

• • •

OLMSTEAD & BRANT
Moving and Raising of Buildings
Wayne, Nebraska

• • •

The Wayne Herald
April 12, 1888 (Vol. XIII, No. 13)

MARRIED: VAHLKAMP - MORNE. At the Presbyterian church, Wayne, on April 4th, by Rev. J.F. MUELLER, German Lutheran pastor, Henry VAHLKAMP and Miss Mina MORNE.

MARRIED: VOSTEEN - BOKELOH. At the Lutheran church, Wayne, on April 6th, by Rev. J.F. MUELLER, John VOSTEEN and Beta BOKELOH.

MARRIED: George WEATHERHOLDT and Miss Nettie HUGLIN were married at the residence of the bride's father last Thursday. Quite a number of young people were present to witness the ceremony. The happy couple will begin housekeeping immediately.

Advertised Letters.

List of letters remaining uncalled for in the Wayne post office for the week ending April 4th.

Ed. ANDERSON, 2, A.L. CLARK, 2, J.P. CURRAN, John H. COOK, Wm. DAVIES, Davis DAVIES, Frank EVERT, Wm. J. EDWARDS, A.A. JANSAN, Frank LOVELACE, Henry LAGE, Andrew LAKE, F. McUMBER, D. MARQUETTE, A.C. NEWMAN, Evert ROBERTS, M.B. PASSON, Georg Adam RELG, Y.A. SHARP, Caroline KRISTENSEN, Mrs. Fannie FENTON, Miss Hester WRIGHT.

Parties calling for the above will say "Advertised" and give date.

M. DEARBORN, P.M.

Programme for the entertainment given by the Ladies' Aid Society at the Presbyterian church this evening.

1.	Song	Messrs McCOY & HOWARD, Miss SPRAGUE & Mrs. McFARLAND
2.	Address	Prof. McCOY
3.	Music	Orchestra
4.	Reading	Mrs. GOSHORN
5.	Solo	Miss SPRAGUE
6.	Declamation	Frankie NANGLE
7.	Reading	Miss GOLDIE
8.	Duett	Mr. BENNETT & Mrs. BRITTON
9.	Recitation	Bertha ARMSTRONG
10.	Reading	Mrs. PHILLEO
11.	Song	Male Quartette
12.	Recitation	Jas. WACHOB

13.	Solo	Mrs. NORRIS
14.	Recitation	Mr. HOWARD
15.	Music	Orchestra
16.	Declamation	Kate PORTER
17.	Duett	Frank NANGLE and Frank GAMBLE
18.	Remarks	Rev. BAKER
19.	Song	Quartette

The Wayne Herald
April 19, 1888 (Vol. XIII, No. 14)

BIRTH: To John MARKLEY and wife, of Carroll, Wednesday, April 18th, a daughter.

BIRTH: To C.W. WALTERS and wife Friday, April 13th, a son.

MARRIED: JOHNSON - PRESCOTT. At the residence of the bride's mother, Mrs. E.T. RENNICK, in Brenna precinct, on Sunday April 14th 1888, Erick T. JOHNSON and Miss Effie PRESCOTT, Rev. Wm. GORST officiating.

MARRIED: MIDTGAADT - JASPERSON. At Wayne, April 14th 1888 by E. MARTIN, County Judge, Martin MIDTGAADT and Miss Magdalena JASPERSON, all of Wayne county.

Advertised Letters.
List of letters remaining uncalled for in the Wayne post office for the week ending April 14th.
Paul G. HAMLIN, T.M. TAYLOR, Henry ULRICH, T.E. MOTTER & Co., John WAGNER.
Parties calling for the above will say "Advertised" and give date.
M. DEARBORN, P.M.

• • •

L. S. WINSOR'S
Blacksmith Shop

• • •

The Wayne Herald
April 26, 1888 (Vol. XIII, No. 15)

DIED: McCOOL. Emily Ruth, infant daughter of Prof. and Mrs.

W.C. McCOOL, Tuesday, April 24th, of pneumonia, aged 11 months. The stricken parents have the sympathy of the entire community in their sad affliction. The funeral services were conducted at the Lutheran church at 10 o'clock this morning.

DIED: GILLETTE. At Glen Ellen, Io., Friday evening, April 20, at 6 o'clock, William Stewart GILLETTE, aged 23 years.
Will GILLETTE, the eldest child of Austin S. and Evelina R. GILLETTE, was born in Mercer, PA., where his grandfather, Hon. William STEWART, had lived for many years. His parents removed to Sioux City in 1869, when he was quite young, and he has here grown up to manhood. He was educated in Washington, Pa., and after leaving college was taken by Mr. John T. BRESSLER into the First National Bank of Wayne, Neb., where he has made so many friends that he was recently promoted to be assistant cashier of the bank. (Sioux City Journal)
The above announcement is one that caused the deepest sorrow to many a heart in Wayne. During his residence here his pleasant, affable manner made every one he met his friend. Those who knew him best held him in the tenderest regard, and were most deeply shocked by his untimely death. To the officers of the bank especially the sad event brought the most poignant sorrow. With the young people of Wayne he was a universal favorite, and his death came to them as would that of a dearly loved brother. Of sterling integrity, excellent business qualifications, and brilliant prospects, a career that promised more than usual success was cut short by death. It will be long before he will be forgotten by his former associates, or the memory of the sad ending of a bright young life will not be remembered with regret. His remains were taken to the old home of his parents in Pennsylvania, for interment.

Advertised Letters.

List of letters remaining uncalled for in the Wayne post office for the week ending April 14th.
Lewis BON, A.A. JANSEN, Em. MICHELS, N.J. MILLER, H.E. WALKINS, Miss L. ARCHER, Miss Hattie D. BUSH, Miss Hattie LEWIS, Kristen MADSEN, Mrs. John PHILLIPS, Miss Florence SHOWGO.
Parties calling for the above will say "Advertised" and give date.

M. DEARBORN, P.M.

The Wayne Herald
May 3, 1888 (Vol. XIII, No. 16)

BIRTH: April 26th, to Mr. and Mrs. O.B. KORTRIGHT, a daughter.

BIRTH: April 27th, to Mr. and Mrs. Wm. SOENNEKEN, a daughter.

MARRIED: SAID - HARRISON. At Wayne April 30th 1888, by E. MARTIN, Co. Judge, J.S. SAID and Martha Ann HARRISON, all of Wayne Co.

MARRIED: Horace GREGORY, of Wayne, and Miss Alice STONE, of New York, were united in the bonds of matrimony at Anita, Ia., last Thursday. They arrived at Wayne this morning.

MARRIED: HINDES - LIKES. On the 29th day of April at 12:30 P.M. in the M.E. church at Wayne, by Rev. Wm. GORST, Mr. H.L. HINDES from near Concord, Dixon county of this state to Miss Rose LIKES of the same vicinity.

Here is a sample of what will be done in the way of converting wild land into fertile farms in Wayne county this year. In one locality near Winside W.M. WRIGHT will break out 450 acres, E.R. CHACE 150 acres, a Mr. HAAS 200 acres, and J.T. BRESSLER 100 acres.

The Wayne Herald
May 10, 1888 (Vol. XIII, No. 17)

BIRTH: To Judson GARWOOD and wife, Wednesday, May 9th, a boy.

BIRTH: To Mr. and Mrs. H.E. HARRIS, of Pavilion, Illinois, formerly of Wayne, May 2nd, a son.

MARRIED: At Wayne, May 8th, 1888, by E. MARTIN, County Judge, August J. ZIEMER and Maud J. WOOLEY, all of Wayne county, Neb.

MARRIED: At the residence of the bride's parents in Plum Creek precinct, Chris. JENSTENSON and Miss Ricka NELSON, Justice DELAHOYDE, officiating.

Advertised Letters.

List of letters remaining uncalled for in the Wayne post office for the week ending May 5th.

Ed. ANDERSON, Y. Emil CARLSON, O.M. DARNER, Peter Henrih HANSON, W. Reed HEFMER, Ed. KELLEY, Milow LeCROIX, V. MUELLER, W.B. ROE, F. SANDERS, W.W. TAYLOR, W.B. WETHERBY, Emile BROWN, Lottie M. GILBERT, Sophia JOHNSON.

Parties calling for the above will say "Advertised" and give date.

M. DEARBORN, P.M.

The Wayne Herald
May 17, 1888 (Vol. XIII, No. 18)

DIED: A telegram was received from Eric T. JOHNSON yesterday afternoon stating that his wife had died at Chicago very suddenly, and the remains would be taken to Durant, Iowa, for interment. No particulars were received. Only a month ago Eric and his bride left Wayne on their wedding tour, their hearts full of the hope of long and happy lives, little thinking that their dreams of happiness would be so soon dispelled. The sympathy of the entire community will go out to the afflicted young husband and the bereaved family.

Advertised Letters.

List of letters remaining uncalled for in the Wayne post office for the week ending May 14th.

Geo. L. AMADON, Mac. SOHNSON, Charlie WYDAHL, A. THOMPSON, D.E. A. METON & Co., Maggie McFARLAND.

Parties calling for the above will say "Advertised" and give date.

M. DEARBORN, P.M.

The Wayne Herald
May 25, 1888 (Vol. XIII, No. 19)

BIRTH: To J.A. GREEN and wife, Tuesday, May 8th, a daughter.

A Card of Thanks.

To the friends who extended us their kindest offices in the last sad rites over the remains of wife and daughter, we return our sincerest thanks.

E.T. JOHNSON.
Mr. and Mrs. E.T. RENNICK.

Programme
Sunday, May 27th

Memorial services at the Lutheran church by Rev. M.L. MELICK. Committee on music, A.J. FERGUSON.

1. Opening services at Masonic Hall 12:30 P.M.
2. Procession formed, G.A.R., school children and other bodies to march to Presbyterian church.
3. Oration by Rev. F.P. BAKER.
4. Services by G.A.R.
5. March to Grave.
6. Memorial services at grave.

The following committees have been appointed:

Music: J.D. KING.

Decorations: The ladies of the town.

Flowers: George SHAW, assisted by Mrs. A.O. MYERS, Mrs. A.J. FERGUSON, Mrs. J.D. KING, Mrs. J.A. LINDLY, Mrs. M.S. DAVIES, Miss BUCHANAN, Miss KLEVER, Miss SHAW, and Miss PHILLEO.

Gun Squad: J.B. STALLSMITH.

All the people in town are not only cordially invited, but requested to take part in the exercises.

A.P. CHILDS, P.C.

The Wayne Herald
May 31, 1888 (Vol. XIII, No. 20)

MARRIED: At Wayne May 27th by E. MARTIN, Co. Judge, Mr. J.H. WEAVER and Miss Sarah NEFF, all of Wayne Co. Neb.

Advertised Letters.

List of letters remaining uncalled for in the Wayne post office for the week ending May 14th.

F.J. DEVLIN, A.W. BUCKER, Frank LOVELACE, Wm. W. WORTHING, Harriet BALDWIN, Isabel BENNETT.

Parties calling for the above will say "Advertised" and give date.

M. DEARBORN, P.M.

• • •

DAISY
The Home made Cigar manufactured at
Wayne, Nebraska,
by **JOHN MATSON**.

The Quiet Saloon
F. NUSBAUM, Prop.
Dealer in
Fine Wines, Ale, and Beer.
Wayne, Nebraska.

• • •

H. GREGORY'S
Blacksmith & Wagon Shop

• • •

EDWARDS & McCULLOCH
Lumber Company
W. H. BRADFORD, Agent
Wayne, Neb.

• • •

LUND & ANTHONY,
Successors to
CONNOR & HUGHES,
Dealers in
Farm Machinery, Wagons, Carriages,
Threshers and Binders.

• • •

The Wayne Herald
June 7, 1888 (Vol. XIII, No. 21)

BIRTH: To O.W. MILLIGAN and wife, May 30th, a boy.

BIRTH: To Geo. HURD and wife, May 31st, a girl.

BIRTH: To E. BOCKEMULE and wife, June 1st, a girl.

MARRIED: At the residence of Frank PERRIN, May 29th, Harry WORKMAN and Miss Jennie BAYES, Rev. GROST, officiating. The happy couple have the hearty congratulations of the Herald.

MARRIED: At Waterloo, Iowa, May 23rd, 1888, D.C. MAIN, of Wayne, Nebraska, and Miss Winnifred McELROY, of Waterloo.
Mr. MAIN is well known to our people as the popular and

efficient cashier of the Citizens Bank, and is in every way worthy of one of the best prizes in the matrimonial lottery. The people of Wayne will extend him their heartiest congratulations and the merriest wishes for his happiness. Mrs. MAIN is as yet a stranger to Wayne, but is said to be a lady of culture and refinement, and will make a welcome addition to the social circles of Wayne. The happy couple are expected home this evening and will occupy their residence in the northern part of town.

Obituary.
Mrs. Effie PRESCOTT JOHNSON
(From the Wilton (Iowa) Review, May 24.)

But a few weeks ago the Review chronicled the happy marriage of Miss Effie PRESCOTT, formerly of this place, to Mr. JOHNSON, at Wayne, Neb. which place had been her home during the past two years. Picture if you can the surprise and pain which was occasioned by the sudden announcement of this young lady's death occuring in Chicago, while on her bridal tour, on May 16th, just one month after marriage! Pen cannot describe the feelings of the husband and friends thus bereft of their loved one.

The couple were returning home from an extended eastern tour by way of Chicago and intending to spend a few days there calling with friends, when Mrs. JOHNSON was suddenly taken ill with inflammation of the bowels. Her illness was not considered serious until about the fifth day after taking sick, when her case took a sudden change for the worse and with scarcely any warning she passed away before the eyes of the heartbroken and loving husband of one month. The remains were brought to Wilton Friday evening, and were conveyed to the home of Mr. and Mrs. PINGREY, her grandparents. The funeral services were held in the Presbyterian church of this place on Sunday afternoon, the sermon being preached by Rev. E.L. BRIGGS. The edifice was crowded with sorrowing friends and former acquaintances of the deceased, and scarcely a dry eye could be found during the solemn services. Rev. BRIGGS' discourse was one of comfort to the bereaved husband, mother and friends, dwelling on the beauties of the land to which she had passed, and exhorting all to be prepared to meet her when the final summons came.

Effie PRESCOTT was born in Durant about 20 years ago, moved when a child to Avoca with her parents, where she lived for a number of years, she then came to Wilton and resided up to two years ago with her grandparents. She was loved by all who knew her - always cheerful and making those associated with her as cheerful as herself. She was a student of both our public school and academy, and no pupil was more loved by classmates than

Effie. That a life so full of promise should be called to an end at this early stage is heart-rending, but He who wills all things for good, knows what is best for His children.

The remains were taken to Wayne, Neb., on Monday morning, for interment.

Advertised Letters.

List of letters remaining uncalled for in the Wayne post office for the week ending June 4th.

Jesse HAMILTON, Billie SKEEN, H. LOWENBERG, Susie BEAM, Mrs. Bella COOK, Janey DILLARD, Sarah HART.

Parties calling for the above will say "Advertised" and give date.

M. DEARBORN, P.M.

The Wayne Herald
June 14, 1888 (Vol. XIII, No. 22)

BIRTH: To E. HUNTER and wife, Wednesday, June 13th, a son.

The following officers for the ensuing year have been elected by Wayne Lodge No. 120 A.F. & A.M.:

A.P. CHILDS, W.M.; F.A. DEARBORN, S.W.; J.H. ROMAN, J.W.; J.S. LEWIS, Treas.; B.F. FEATHER, Sec.

The Wayne Herald
June 21, 1888 (Vol. XIII, No. 23)

BIRTH: To Henry JOYNER and wife, of Chapin precinct, Monday June 18th, a daughter.

DIED: At his residence two miles north of Wayne, on Tuesday, June 19th, 1888, Adam Henry MILLER, Sr., aged 75 years. Mr. MILLER was born in Hanover, Germany, in 1813 and came to America in 1845 living in Indiana two years, and in Nebraska fourteen years. He was married for more than fifty years, and his wife survives him. He had ten children; seven daughters and three sons. Of these, six, one son and five daughters are living. He had twenty-six grandchildren living at the time of his death. The funeral will take place from the Lutheran church this afternoon.

Advertised Letters.

List of letters remaining uncalled for in the Wayne post office for the week ending June 18th.

J.B. KEYS, James O'NEAL, Wm. TAYLOR, H.H. WOLF,

Anna DAMME.
Parties calling for the above will say "Advertised" and give date.

M. DEARBORN, P.M.

• • •

AUG. PIEPENSTOCK,
City Bakery and Grocery.

The Wayne Journal
November 30, 1892 (Vol. 2, No. 27)

COMMISSIONERS PROCEEDINGS.
Commissioners met pursuant to adjournment. Present Henry WITTLER, chairman, C.D. MARTIN and P.W. OMAN and S.B. RUSSELL, clerk. The following proceedings were had and entered of record, to wit:

On the 8th day of August 1892, J.R. MANNING and others filed a petition in the county clerk's office asking that a public road be established as follows: Commencing at the southeast corner of the town of Carroll, thence south to the half section line intersecting section 34 and 35 thence East on said section line to section 36 all in Town. 27, range 2E. A special commissioner having been appointed and reported in favor of said road and the same having been advertised for damages, six parties have filed claims for damages, appraisers appointed to appraise said damage having filed their report, parties interested were notified to appear and show cause why said road should be established, and to prove claim for damages. Now on this 10th day of November 1892 upon hearing said petition the said road was established and the following claims for damages were allowed:

J. BAILEY,	$35.00
T.M. HURLBERT,	18.00
J.A. BROWN,	70.00
Wm. BOVEE,	35.00
C.H. WOLF,	53.00
T.J. HOWORTH,	35.00

The following bills were allowed:

Wm. ZUTZ, election expenses claimed, $20 allowed,	5.00
B. CUNNINGHAM, grading,	3.00
HUGHES & LOCKE, goods for pauper,	8.63
J.R. MANNING, election expenses,	2.00
Fred VOLPP, goods for pauper,	4.40

Herman MOHKE, repairing grader, $5.65
W.S. GOLDIE, printing, 12.00
W.P. AGLER, repairing bridges, 99.00
R.J. ARMSTRONG, coal, 65.40
Board adjourned until December 24, 1892.
S.B. RUSSELL, Clerk.

• • •

First National Bank
Officers and Directors:
J.M. STRAHN, *President*
GEO. BOGART, *Vice President*
H.F. WILSON, *Cashier*
Directors:
**J.M. STRAHN • FRANK E. STRAHN
GEO. BOGART • J.W. JONES
F.M. NORTHROP • FRANK FULLER
H.F. WILSON**

• • •

**The Wayne Republican
August 17, 1895 (Vol. 2, No. 26)**

MARRIED: KRUGER - UTECHT. On August 18, Judge MARTIN pronounced the magic words that united in marriage Albert KRUGER of California and Paulina UTECHT of this county.

DIED: Mr. and Mrs. Frank STEWART mourn the death of their little girl aged five months who died last Thursday and was interred in the Carroll cemetery Friday afternoon. They have the sympathy of all in their great loss.

Real Estate Transfers.
W.J. PERRY to Harry JOHNSON, et al.,
    part nw 1/4 sw 1/4, 18-26-4 $1.00
PERRY Bros. & Co. to Henry JOHNSON, et al.,
    part sw 1/4, 18-26-4 1.00
U.S. to Martin REDMER, patent (tree claim),
    w 1/2 ne 1/4 and e 1/2 nw 1/4, 28-25-2
Elizabeth JONES to Robert H. JONES,
    w 1/2 ne and e 1/2 nw 1/4, 2-26-1 2,400.00

W.E. GLEASON and W.J. WEATHERHOLDT to Jas. E. NELSON, ne 1/4, 19-25-1	$3,200.00
Martin REDMER to Alf. WOODWARD, e 1/2 nw 1/4 and w 1/2 ne 1/4, 28-25-1, blk. 4 Winside	5,000.00
Wm. HUNT to Alf. WOODWARD, nw 1/4, 17-26-2	3,200.00
St. Mary's Catholic church to Richard SCANNELL, lots 7, 8 and 9, blk. 10 n Ad. to Wayne	1.00
S.R. WARNOCK to J.H. MERRILL (Contract), lot 9, blk. 27, Wayne	744.00
Sheriff to Adelbert FRENCH, se 1/4, 11-27-1	3,053.50
C.B. TOMLINSON to Wm. F. SCHRIEBER, ne 1/4 and ne 1/4 of se 1/4, 11-25-1	3,800.00
C.B.&Q.R.R. Co. to E.W. MULLER, ne 1/4, 35-25-2	1,200.00

Advertised Letters.

The following is a list of letters, etc., remaining in the post office at Wayne, Nebraska, for the week ending Aug 13, 1895:

BISHOP, Mrs. May
CRANE, Nina
DOVEE, F.J.
DOFFINY, James
ENDERS, Miss Ethel
EVANS, Mrs. R.J.
GARDILE, A.H.
HARVEY, W.B.
KAMPE, Miss Anna
McBRIDE, A.F.
PAYNE, Byron L. (2)
ULRICH, Henry
VENNERBERY, Hilma
WILLIAMS, Stella

Parties calling for the above please give date when advertised.

A.P. CHILDS, P.M.

• • •

Central Meat Market
FRED VOLPP, Prop.

• • •

The Wayne Republican
August 24, 1895 (Vol. 2, No. 27)

BIRTH: At Perris, California, Aug. 23, to Mr. and Mrs. W.L. SEDGEWICK, a boy.

MARRIED: Jesse T. BURCH, aged 29, a native of South Carolina and Mary Belle SHAW, aged 21, a native of Iowa, both residents of Los Angeles. (Los Angeles (Cal.) Times)

The marriage of the above couple occurred in Los Angeles on July 26. Many of our citizens will quickly recognize in the bride the youngest daughter of George SHAW of this place. The bride was until three years ago a resident of our city and the best wishes of a large circle of friends will be extended to the newly wedded pair.

The Winside Tribune says there are three candidates for commissioner in the third district, M.S. MOATS, of Sherman, Geo. HARRIGFELDT, of Hoskins, and James BAKER, of Deer Creek, every one of them good men and the district can make no mistake in electing any of them. It also says Ed. CULLEN of Winside can have the democratic nomination if he wants it.

• • •

EDWARDS & BRADFORD
Lumber Company
Successors to **EDWARDS & McCULLOCH** Lumber Co.

• • •

STONE & FRIDOLPH
Merchant Tailors
Wayne, Neb.

• • •

The Wayne Republican
August 31, 1895 (Vol. 2, No. 28)

BIRTH: To Mr. and Mrs. L.F. HOLTZ on Monday, Aug. 26, a boy.

Pounded His Wife.

Albert FEUCHS living east of the city seems to think that it is his duty to administer corporal punishment upon any and all members of his family whenever they don't dance obedience to his orders. One day during the latter part of last week his wife, who, at present, is in a rather delicate condition, didn't exactly suit his lordship so he went at her with his fists and was pummeling her most unmercifully when a couple of neighbors passing heard her cries of agony and went in and caused the brute to detist. He had pounded her about the face and head unmercifully and when upbraided for it by a neighbor said it was not the first time and that he had to whip her to make a good woman of her. It may be that such is the idea of fellows of his stripe as to what is right and what is wrong, but a good dose of law administered properly would teach him that such is not the way people of this day and land, and they do not believe that any man has a right to strike a woman. None but the brute of the lowest type would be guilty of a deed of this kind and especially under the circumstances.

Real Estate Transfers.

I.J. COONS to H.G. LEISENRING, lots 7, 8 and 9, blk. 2, north ad. to Wayne	$2,750.00
Frank KRUGER to Rose KRUGER, lots 7, 8 and 9, blk. 7, B.&P.'s ad to Winside	2,500.00
John D. KNEEDLER to Frank BROWER, lot 1, blk. 4, Winside	150.00
Josephene W. TAYLOR to Homer J. GRAVES, n 1/2 nw, 5-25-4 and other lands	6,800.00
Mary E. TEMPLIN to Josephine W. TAYLOR, lot 9, blk. 6, east ad. to Wayne	600.00
McCLUSKY & NEEDHAM to Jas. HAMILTON, lot 5, blk. 6, east ad. to Wayne	98.00
BRESSLER & DEARBOW to J.A. BENEDICT, lot 2, blk. 7 and s 1/2 lot 2, blk. 8, B&B's ad. to Wayne	600.00

• • •

JAS. DOBBINS
Buggies and Wagons
Wayne, Neb.

• • •

Empire Clothing & Shoe House
T. COLLINSON

• • •

The Wayne Republican
September 7, 1895 (Vol. 2, No. 29)

MARRIED: Henry SMITH and Miss RANTENBURG were married at the German church on Sunday. (Hoskins)

MARRIED: WIGHT - WILKERSON. At high noon on Wednesday, August 28, at the Methodist church in Mt. Ayr, Iowa, Rev. Edward Van Dyke WIGHT and Kate Olive WILKERSON were joined in wedlock. It is scarcely necessary for us to undertake to say anthing regarding the contracting parties, because the groom is well known to a great portion of our readers as they very able young minister of the Presbyterian church at this place. He is held in the very highest regard by all without regard to church and of his bride we cannot speak from the standpoint of acquaintanceship but believe that she is a fit helpmeet for the able young pastor. That she will meet with a cordial reception by our people there is no doubt and while the lot of Mr. and Mrs. WIGHT shall be cast among us or wherever else it may be we feel that we but voice the sentiment of the entire community when we say that it is our hope that their lines be always pleasantly cast and that their ship may have a peaceful, happy voyage.

The first literary of the year will be given by the Philomathean Society next Friday evening, September 6th. The following program has been arranged:

Inaugural Address	W.O. SAND
Music	
Oration	Elmer LUNDBERG
Review of the Philomathean Literary Society	Henrietta SCHLOTFELDT
Recitation	Miss Grace NEIHART
Essay	Bert BROWN
Oration	George WILBUR
It	Bennie SKILES
Prophesy	Miss Jennie METTLEN
Music	

Everybody is cordially invited to attend the literary.

• • •

LESLIE BAKER
Has just opened a new
Barber Shop
at Hoskins

• • •

W.M. SHARP
Contractor and Builder.

The Wayne Republican
September 14, 1895 (Vol. 2, No. 30)

BIRTH: Joe WILLIAMS is all covered with smiles because of the arrival of a new boy at his house last Thursday of the usual weight. All lovers of the weed are smoking at Joe's expense. (Carroll)

MARRIED: Frank METTLEN and Emily BERGUSON were married at the home of the bride's mother at Lynn Grove, Illinois, on Sept. 12.

DIED: Mrs. Paul NINDEL died at Wakefield on Sept. 9.

The Wayne County Fair.

The Exhibits are Spendid and a Credit to the Grand County. Especially is this so in Grains, Fruits, Vegetables & the Fine Arts. The first or "entranse day" the 11th, was an extremely hot one and the circus kept away hundreds from the grounds, but as it was the entries came in fully as rapidly as anticipated and of a character that was surprising to even the management. Grains, vegetables and fruits came by the wagon load until exhibition space was almost at a premium before nightfall, the secretary was unable to receive the entries as fast as offered, while the immense tent that was put up to be used as an art hall was filled with beautiful paintings, crayons and unexcelled work with the needle. It is an utter impossibility to go into detail in telling of what is on exhibition and we shall only attempt to summarize.

Horses and Colts

are being shown by Jacob BRUGER, Wm. BRUNE, Sam BARNES, J.H. ATKINS, F.H. CAMPBELL, D.L. STRICKLAND, Wm. PRINCE, George PALMER, Jame McINTOSH, E.B. GIRTON, George ROE, F.M. NORTHROP, John GUSTAFSON, Ran FRAZIER, W.D. HAMMOND, Minnie DANBERG, R.H. GIBSON, N. GRIMSLEY, S.P. MILES, F.M. GRIFFITH, H.J. GRAVES, James GRIER, T.E. HILL, H.E. FOOTE, H. KLOPPING, Wm. KOCH, J.A. WASHBURN, Fred NEIMAN, Geo. PALMER, Geo. ROE.

The Art Hall

Here is where the lover of the beautiful delights to dwell and drink in the beauties of the pencil and brush, behold the handiwork of the needle. Too much praise cannot be bestowed upon the different exhibits in the mammoth tent and if you do not take it in you are missing a rare treat indeed. Space will not permit us to go into any details even as to what the different exhibitors have here for your entertainment, we can only give the names of those who have entries and say to you "see for yourself" if you would be convinced that in all that pertains to the beautiful our county is well to the front. The exhibitors so far as we can learn are Meddames WHITE, LEY, BRENNER, FRAZIER, ROE, FORTNER, PETERSON, PHILLEO, ANDRESS, SMITH of Winside, FISHER, ASH, BRESSLER, CULLER, SULLIVAN, SOULES, CROSSLAND, GOODYEAR, HAMMOND, WINTERBURN, the Misses Nora HILL, Mary and Reba NANGLE, Lena HITCHCOCK, Lulu COOK, Maud TUCKER; the Mesdames James BARBOUR, Susie BRENNER, J.M. CHERRY, T. DUERIG, L. COCHRAN, F.W. BURDICK and Lulu NEIHART; A.F. BRENNER, Will Weber, H. GRIGGS; Dr. HECKERT: special plate work, Wm. SONNEKEN, N. GUSTAFSON. Mary and James AHERN, Luther MASON, Mesdames Wm. MILLER, C.D. MARTIN, H.E. CORBIT, H.M. DAMME, J.J. DILTZ, Jas. ELLIOT, G. HARRISON, HENCH, A.M. JACOBS, S. JONES, P.H. KOHL, Frank KRUGER, LAUGHLIN, H.W. LESSMAN, E.P. OLMSTEAD, TOWER, WILBUR and SWAN. Misses Lena LERNER, Annie LUND, JACOBSEN, Coar KIEFER, C.M. CRAVEN, Bert COOK, J.J.W. FOX, In this same bulding is the girls department and here is displayed some very fine work, among the exhibitors were Pearl MILLER, Libbie ELLIS, Ruby and Josie FRAZIER, Blanch HOSTETTER, Emma LARIMER, Reba NANGLE and Clara PHILLEO.

Products of the Fields, Orchards, Vineyards and Gardens.
Under this head comes one of the greatest displays ever put on exhibition in the state. Everything imaginable is here and cannot be surpassed in excellence. The grains of the field, the vegetables of the truck patch, the grand sugar beets, the garden's rich yield, fruits of all kinds, green, canned, dried of every kind and description are here in abundance entirely unlooked for even by the most enthusiastic of our people. If in giving the list of exhibitors in this line we should omit any one we trust you will pardon the oversight as it is almost an impossibility to get everyone. The list as we have it is Ed SANDAHL, James ELLIOT, W.A. HUNTER, Wm. BENSHOOF, J.W. MAHOLM, A.F. CHOAN, J.W. CAMPBELL, C.S. ASH, F.M. GRIFFITH, James BARBOUR, Al MINER, Mrs. Ran FRAZIER, Maud BENSHOOF, Jacob BRUGER, Pat COLEMAN, W.J. WHITE, Robt. SNEATH, M.K. RICKABAUGH, L. ROE, F. SORENBERGER, W.H. SWARTZ, Mrs. Geo. H. PORTER, Mrs. R. PHILLEO, A.J. PETERSON, A. CHRISTIANSON, H.M. DAMME, August HANSON, C.E. HEIKES, Adam GRIER, Mrs. T.S. GOSS, Mrs. Geo. COOK, J.W. MAHOLM, Mrs. D.S. McVICKERS, Josie FRAZIER, Mrs. GILDERSLEEVE, W.H. GILDERSLEEVE, Mrs. GOODYEAR, Tom HILL, Louie LARSON, H.W. LESSMAN, H. LAYMAN, M.C. LOWER, G.B. NETTLETON, Mrs. W.A.K. NEELY, Mrs. PERDUE, J.L. SOULES, W.F. SEARS, Mrs. TUCKER. We

have grouped under this head all exhibits that were in class L, N, O and R, thus taking in all the cereals, grains, grasses, vegetables, fruits in all forms, and in fact everything that was in the Floral Hall. The display is a grand one and it is a source of regret to us that we cannot go into detail in telling what each exhibitor had there and it certainly ought to forever silence the croaker as to the possibilities of our county.

Poultry.

Here is every variety of the feathered fowl from the saucy little bantam to the great awkward Shanghai, in chickens, with a liberal sprinkling of turkeys, ducks and geese. The birds are not only of the kinds that are beautiful to behold but are well chosen for their qualities of usefulness. The exhibitors are H. GREGORY, Will WEBER, C.E. MARTIN, I.W. ALTER, Ralph SULLIVAN, Fred WADSWORTH, Clarence COCHRAN, Arthur BECKENHAUER, Mrs. Ran FRAZIER, Bert COOK, Alfred FURCHNER, Charley and Ray REYNOLDS, Henry GAERTNER, E.P. OLMSTEAD, E.B. GIRTON, R.H. GIBSON, Clark CAMPBELL, George H. PORTER, Mary E., John and L. PAULSKI. This exhibit is a grand one and ought to be seen by every lover of useful fowls.

Girls' Department.

This of course if a part of the exhibition at the art hall but we desire to call your attention to the elegant display and trust if you have not given it a careful inspection you will do so and see that the hands as well as minds are being taught to be useful. The exhibitors here are Lizzie and Ella WILLIAMS, Bessie WINTERBURN, Winnie ROMAN, Ruby, Josie and Willie FRAZIER, Eva and Blanch HITCHCOCK, Lulu COOK.

The School Department.

Here is an exhibit in the art hall that deserves special notice of all those interested in the work of our schools. The entries were made by George GELDER, H. BUSH, Caroline BOCK, Anna BARRET, Edith and Myrtle MOSES, Sadie MICK, Mabie MARTIN, Luella MICK, Luella MUNDHENKE, Earl GIBSON, Mamie PERFECT, Clara SAHO, Charley and Clyde WINTERBURN, Fred, Rose, Pearl and Henry WOLF, district No. 72 and No. 29.

Cattle.

The entries here were few, but they were good ones and it is a matter of surprise that so few compete for prizes where a county is so filled with grand herds. The exhibitors were R.H. GIBSON, F.M. NORTHROP, Franz MOSES, A.H. MILLER, A.F. CHOAN.

Hogs.

The prevalence of cholera in this section came pretty nearly knocking this part of the exposition entirely out, most of the raisers being afraid to bring their stock for fear of contracting the disease; however the animals on exhibition are good ones. The exhibitors are F.M. NORTHROP, W.H. GILDERSLEEVE, H. KLOPPING and Geo. PORTER.

Twenty-one bold bad Masons went down to our neighboring city of Winside on Friday night and assisted in organizing a new Lodge at that place and were very nicely entertained by the brethren while there. The officers of the new lodge are A.A. WELCH, W.M.; A.B. CHERRY, S.W.; I.O. WOOLSTON, J.W.; W.H. McCLUSKY, secretary; A.T. CHAPIN, treasurer; Frank BENSER, S.D.; A.H. CARTER, J.D.; John CASSEL, Tyler.

• • •

SULLIVAN BROTHERS
Fresh Fruits and Vegetables

• • •

A.F. COLLINS
Contractor and Builder

• • •

W.D. HAMMOND
Veterinary Surgeon

• • •

The Wayne Republican
September 21, 1895 (Vol. 2, No. 31)

BIRTH: Ed. ZELKIE and wife are rejoicing over the arrival of a daughter Sept. 16.

BIRTH: Mr. and Mrs. VAASE have a new boy baby. (Hoskins)

BIRTH: Mr. and Mrs. MORT are the proud parents of a little girl who came to gladden their home on the 13th.

BIRTH: Mr. and Mrs. Chas. SULLEN are rejoicing over the arrival of a baby boy who came on the 12th.

MARRIED: WELBAUM - CLARK. At the office of Judge MARTIN, on Sept. 18, F.I. WELBAUM and Mary I. CLARK.

MARRIED: SMITH - KLOPTON. On Sept. 16, at office of Judge MARTIN, F.A. SMITH to Josie KLOPTON.

MARRIED: OLIVER - MUSTIFER. On Sept. 16, Judge MARTIN officiating, C.E. OLIVER and Alice MUSTIFER.

MARRIED: PRESCOTT - TIDRICK. At the home of Mr. and Mrs. A. TIDRICK on Wednesday afternoon at 4 o'clock their daughter Edith was joined in wedlock to True PRESCOTT, Rev. W.W. THEOBALD officiating. It is hardly necessary to say anything in regard to the newly wedded pair, so well and favorably are they known. The groom is one of the best known men of Brenna precinct, while the bride has heretofore been one of Wayne county's most prominent teachers. They start in life with the fairest of skies over them, and none will have any other wish that that the sun may always shine brightly for them. On Thursday morning they took their departure for Missouri, where they will visit for a fortnight or more.

DIED: STEVENS. On Sept. 18, the eighteen months old boy of Geo. and Etta STEVENS, of cholera infantum.

Maimed for Life.

On Friday afternoon September 18, a terrible accident happened to Wm. McCLOUD while threshing at Charley MILLERs' north of the city a few miles. He is part owner of one of the new automatic feeding and stacking threshers and while in the performance of his duties in connection with the machine had his left arm cut or torn off near the elbow and was otherwise severely injured. It appears that something had gone wrong with the belt that drives the self feeder and that Mr. McCLOUD had taken it off and was fixing it at the machine while it was in motion and one of the other belts caught it and quick as a flash he was jerked around the shaft several times until the hand was torn off and thrown several feet distant and he mangled and bleeding hurled in a different direction. Besides losing the arm the gentleman received some terrible bruises on other parts of his body from which he is suffering intensely. Drs. WIGHTMAN and LEISENRING dressed his injuries and did all in the power of surgical skill to make him as comfortable as possible and at this time he is reported as doing as well as can be expected.

Thos. COLBERT and W.C. TALBOTT, living in the neighborhood of Winside, got into a dispute on Monday. Words led to blows, blows to COLBERT skipping out and being taken in by Deputy

GILDERSLEEVE in the vicinity of Pilger, a hearing before Judge MARTIN, a fine of $10 and costs, an over-night in jail and payments of costs and fine and a departure for home a poorer but wiser man.

Advertised Letters.

The following is a list of letters, etc., remaining in the post office at Wayne, Nebraska, for the week ending Sept. 17, 1895:

Ed ANDERSON, J.S. EGELER, Herman FREESE, J.H. FERGUSON, F.A. FARIS, S.L. GULDBERG, John GUNSOLLY, Frank HUFFER, J.F. JUDKINS, Miss Allie ROE, L.F. SA___ANSON, Wm. TOWNSEND.

Parties calling for the above please give date when advertised.

A.P. CHILDS, P.M.

• • •

M. STRINGER
Blacksmith

• • •

H. GREGORY
Wagon Maker

• • •

GUY WILBER
Attorney at Law
Wayne, Neb.

• • •

The Wayne Republican
September 28, 1895 (Vol. 2, No. 32)

BIRTH: Ira TAYLOR and wife are the proud parents of a pair of twin girls, born one day last week. (Carroll)

MARRIED: Arlone BRADFORD neice of W.H. BRADFORD of this place was married at Sioux City on the 25th to D.N. KINKAID. Many of our readers are quite well acquainted with the bride and will wish her and husband a happy voyage.

MARRIED: At the parsonage of Sept. 23, Rev. H.E. MILLARD officiating, Ira WILHELM and Nellie MANNING, both of Wakefield.

DIED: SPAHR. On Tuesday, Sept 23, the spirit of the infant daughter of Mr. and Mrs. Wilbur SPAHR passed into the hand of Him who hast said "suffer little children to come unto me and forbid them not, for such is the kingdom of heaven."

Delegates to County Convention.

The following is a list of delegates chosen at the republican caucuses on the 25th to meet in convention at the court house on the 28th:

Brenna - Ed. RENICK, A. LINDSAY, C.J. LUND.

Hoskins - John DONNER, W.C. PARSONS, E. BEHMER, John SHANNON, J.G. FOSTER.

Hunter - J.J.W. FOX, Mark JEFFREY, W. RICE, D. CUNNINGHAM.

Deer Creek - W.A. LOVE, R.D. MERRILL, L.R. THORPE, James BAKER.

Chapin - W.C. LOWRY, Geo. LEWIS.

Plum Creek - Wm. POWELL, S.K. WEST, Aug. SAMUELSON, C.E. GILDERSLEEVE.

Strahn - Frank SPAHR, Geo. PORTER, C.C. BROWN, J.B. STALSMITH.

Winside - Frank TRACY, F. PETERS.

Sherman - R. WADSWORTH, Evan JENKINS, O.W. JONES.

Leslie - C. WORTH, H. SLAUGHTER.

Wilbur - A.M. JACOBS, H. HANSEN, C. SHEULTHEIS, S. FRIDOLPH.

Wayne - 1st ward, C.A. CHACE, G.A. BENSON, S.H. McMACKEN, C.B. OWEN. 2nd ward, I.W. ALTER, W.H. BRADFORD, Chas. BEEBE, W.D. HAMMOND, A.G. HOWARD. 3rd ward, N. GRIMSLEY, E.D. MITCHELL, J.G. MINES, F.M. NORTHROP, Jas. BARBOUR.

Garfield - Wesley STEELE, A.A. BELL, E.C. BROOKS.

Hancock - H. WITTLER, Perrin LONG.

Logan - Eph. ANDERSON, Eli McCONOUGHY, Nels UTTER.

Real Estate Transfers.

Fred KAY to Theodore LORGE,	
nw 1/4 ne 1/4 and ne 1/4 nw 1/4, 25-26-4	$2,800.00
August WEDNT to Jas. BAKER,	
lot 1, blk. 1, Carroll	300.00
Randolph Real Estate & Inv. Co., to E.F. WALDEN,	
ne 1/4, 3-26-2	4,000.00

F.A. DEARBORN to Geo. W. TROTTER,	
lot 5, blk. 4, Wayne	$1,500.00
G.A. BURGERSON to Nels J. BJORKLAND,	
w 1/2 nw 1/4, 186-26-5	2,280.00
A.C. CROCKETT to D.S. McVICKER,	
w 1/2 lots 1, 2 and 3, blk. 15, Wayne	700.00
Wm. GREEK to Citizens Bank,	
lots 14 and 15, blk. 4, n. ad to Wayne	1,636.00
James HAMILTON to Ella K. MORRISON,	
lot 5, blk. 6, Northside	425.00
Margaret and Jesse HAMILTON to Jesse HAMILTON,	
lot 5, blk. 6, Northside	400.00
John BRUGGEMAN to Claus REESE,	
sw 1/4, 28-26-2	3,600.00
G.F. SEBALD to Otili SEBALD,	
lot 5, blk. 20, and lot 6, blk. 9, Wayne, and part nw 1/4, 13-26-3	1.00
E. CHICHESTER to Geo. E. ROE,	
ne 1/4, 2-26-3	4,200.00
C. ROSLMAN to W.C. WIGHTMAN,	
ne 23-26-2	4,000.00

Advertised Letters.

The following is a list of letters, etc., remaining in the post office at Wayne, Nebraska, for the week ending Sept. 24, 1895:

Heinrich BEHRNIDE, F.M. DOUGLASS, John DORNICE, Henry KAISER, J.W. LASE, John LEVERINGHOUSE, E.C. ROSE, E.A. WARD.

Parties calling for the above please give date when advertised.

A.P. CHILDS, P.M.

ANNOUNCEMENTS.

We are authorized to announce E. HUNTER as a candidate for county judge subject to the action of the Republican convention.

Please announce me as a candidate for clerk of the District Court, subject to the action of the republican county convention.

John H. ROMAN.

Please announce me as a candidate for clerk of the District Court subject to the action of the republican county convention.
O.L. TAYLOR.

Please announce my name as a candidate for the office of county judge, subject to the action of the Republican County Convention.
Peter MEARS.

Please announce me as a candidate for the nomination of county judge subject to the action of the republican county convention.
Sam DAVIES.

• • •

C.M. CRAVEN,
Photographer
Wayne, Nebraska.

• • •

MRS. ROBERT UTTER
Piano or Organ Instruction

• • •

BARTLETT & HIESTER
Furniture

• • •

The Wayne Republican
October 5, 1895 (Vol. 2, No. 33)

BIRTH: On Sept. 20, to Mr. and Mrs. PETERS southwest of the city, a boy.

BIRTH: A new boy has come to make a permanent stay at the home of Hans HANSEN, the arrival was on the 2nd.

DIED: HOGUEWOOD. On Friday, September 27, the spirit of the eight months old daughter of Mr. and Mrs. Newt HOGUEWOOD winged its way to the great Beyond. The funeral services were held at the M.E. church on Sunday and the remains of the little one laid to rest in the cemetery.

At the caucus held in Carroll Sept. 25 the following officers was placed in nomination for Deer Creek precinct: Assessor, Leander SIMMERMAN; justices, Jas. BAKER, Geo. YARYAN; constables, Geo BELFORD, Fred WILCOX; judges of election, J.A. BROWN, Geo. YARYAN, J.R. MANNING; clerks of election, Geo. A. BAILEY, Geo. C. MERRILL. M.S. MERRILL was elected precinct committeman.

Republican Convention.
Not an Absent Delegate, But the Entire
Fifty-nine Present and Voting.
A Good Ticket Was Named.

The Most Enthusiastic Convention in the County's History. Saturday, Sept 28 saw one of the best attended and most enthusiastic conventions ever held in our city assembled at the court house. It was one of complete harmony from the calling to order and reading of the call by Chairman FULLER of the county central committee to the final adjournment. That "scrap" that some of our friends of an opposite political faith so often predicted and so earnestly hoped for, failed to materialize. The utmost good feeling prevailed and the ticket will get an enthusiastic support from every delegate present, and they will serve to spread the contagion of republicanism to every part of the county. As a matter of course there must be disappointments in every convention; every one cannot possibly realize their desires and when the will of the majority is expressed by a free ballot then it is certainly the duty as we feel certain it is the intention of everyone to give their best efforts to the success of the entire ticket at the polls in November. With an exceptionally good ticket the party can elect each one of its nominees to the places for which they are named. The ticket is headed by I.O. WOOLSTON, treasurer; M.O. CUNNINGHAM, county clerk; E. CUNNINGHAM, sheriff; Mrs. Myra FLETCHER, superintendent; E. MARTIN, county judge; Bert BROWN, clerk of the district court; L. ZEIMER, surveyor; John P. GAERTNER, coroner. The convention passed a resolution requesting Anson A. WELCH to name the men he desired for delegates to the judicial convention, in accordance with that resolution he named the following who were approved: R. WADSWORTH, N. GRIMSLEY, J.R. MANNING, M. JEFFREY, E. CUNNINGHAM, F. FULLER, D.H. CARROLL, W.H. McNEAL, C.A. CHACE, M.S. DAVIES.

The following were chosen as delegates to the state convention: John T. BRESSLER, F. FULLER, A.T. CHAPIN, G.

HARRIGFELDT, N. GRIMSLEY, Jay WILSON, J.W. FOX, F.M. NORTHROP, E.D. MITCHELL.

Nelson GRIMSLEY was elected chairman and Dorr CARROLL secretary of the county central committee for the ensuing year.

• • •

R.W. WILKINS & CO.'S
Soda Fountain

• • •

EDWARD S. BLAIR, A.M., M.D.
Professor of Hygiene, Sioux City College
Office over Sedgewick Drug Store
Wayne, Nebraska.

• • •

The Wayne Republican
October 12, 1895 (Vol. 2, No. 34)

BIRTH: On Oct. 5 to Mr. and Mrs. Dan. WOOLEY, a girl.

The following are the republican precinct committeemen elected at the different caucuses:
    Leslie - Geo. BUSKIRK.
    Chapin - Albert SALTERS.
    Hunter - Mark JEFFREY.
    Strahn - B. CUNNINGHAM.
    Deer Creek - M.S. MERRILL.
    Winside - A.H. CARTER.
    Wilbur - A.B. JEFFREY.
    Hoskins - Geo. HARRIGFELDT.
    Sherman - Evan JENKINS.
    Garfield - Wesley STEELE.
    Wayne - 1st ward, J.P. GAERTNER; 2nd ward - Chas. BEEBE; 3rd ward - Frank FULLER.

Next week court will be in session with Judge ROBINSON on the bench and the following named Wayne county gentlemen will act as arbiters between their fellow men and receive the plaudits and curses of the litigants, they are jurors: O.P. ANDERSON, E. BEHNER, A.F. BRENNER, Geo. BEALE, J.V. FRANCIS, Wm.

FRAZIER, J.J.W. FOX, John GREENWOALD, H. HUTCHNSON, Eli JONES, Perrin LONG, M.S. MERRILL, C.B. OWENS, P.W. OMAN, F. PETERS, C. RITCHEY, E.T. RENICK, D.W. SHAW, H. SHIELDS, A.T. WADDEL, R. WADSWORTH, J.E. WILSON, C.H WOLF, Geo. WEATHERHOLT.

• • •

Law Office of
A.B. CHARDE

• • •

Depot Restaurant
J.R. HOOVER, Prop.

• • •

**The Wayne Republican
October 19, 1895 (Vol. 2, No. 35)**

MARRIED: At Hoskins on Oct. 15, Robert RANTENBURG and Martha ROGGOW.

MARRIED: PITTENGER - REICHERT. At the home of the bride's parents near Winside on the 16th ist., Rev. LEHRER officiating, FRANK PITTENGER of Albion, Boone county and Tillie REICHERT. The groom will be remembered by our readers as one of the PITTENGER Bros. formerly well known residents of this county, but now residing in Boone county. The bride is the daughter of Jacob REICHERT a well known farmer of the western part of the county. May long life, prosperity and happiness be the lot of the newly wedded pair.

MARRIED: At the residence of the bride's parents, Mr. and Mrs. T. COLLINSON, in this city, Wednesday, October 9th, 1895, at 11 o'clock a.m., Mr. S.H. ALEXANDER of Wayne, Nebraska, and Miss Edith L. COLLINSON. The ceremony which united the two lives for better or for worse was very beautifully performed by Rev. L. SESSUP, pastor of the Presbyterian church and was witnessed by only a few invited guests. After the ceremony congratulations were offered and the company invited to partake of an elegant dinner. Mr. and Mrs. ALEXANDER will visit a few days here and with friends in Iowa and then proceed to housekeeping in their own home in Wayne which the groom has already nicely furnished. The Record acknowledges the receipt of a plate of the wedding cake and extends to the newly wedded couple its sincerest congratulations. (Jefferson County (Neb.) Record)

Court Proceedings.

Court convened on Monday afternoon and at once began to grind out the usual gist of joy and grief.

WIGHTMAN vs. LAUMAN, continued.

SLOAN & JOHNSON vs. RUNDELL, Plaintiff to file brief in ten days.

Nebraska Loan and Trust Co. vs. CUNNINGHAM, A.A. WELCH appointed guardian ad litem of minor Bertie CUNNINGHAM.

WATTS vs. GANTT, sale confirmed. GANTT excepts and given forty days to settle bill of exceptions.

John T. BRESSLER, et al. vs. PRINCE, et al., sale confirmed and deed ordered.

C.St.P.M. & O.R.R. vs. county of Wayne. Motion in equity, motion overruled, deft. RICHARDSON excepts.

GUY vs. SHULTHEIS, motion for new trial overruled, Defendant excepts, judgment on verdict and forty days given to settle bill of exception.

LEISENRING vs. RILEY, Judgment for Defendant.

JONES vs. KELLEY, continued.

STEPHENS vs. KAUFFMAN, continued.

Citizens Nat'l Bank of Norfolk vs. BARNES and TYLER, confirmed. Deed ordered.

MAIN & FRENCH vs. WOOD, confirmed, deed ordered.

BRESSLER vs. PORTER, default.

C. ASMUS, guardian vs. Frank HEWINS, et al. Actions dismissed by plaintiff each party to pay their own costs.

STONE vs. BOSTROM, continued.

Carroll State Bank vs. KEMP and BURKS, stricken from docket.

Ellanor MORRILL vs. BLENKIRON default, Decree ordered as prayed.

WARDDRIP vs. WARDDRIP, decree of divorce ordered, plaintiff to pay costs.

First National Bank of Ft. Scott, Kan. vs. H.M. HENRY et al. Default against defendants. Judgment for plaintiff $3187 and interest at 8 per cent.

EDWARDS & BRADFORD Lumber Co. vs. H.M. HENRY et al. Judgment for plaintiff $549 and foreclosure ordered.

Carroll State Bank vs. KLAPMEIR. Settled and dismissed.

BAYES vs. Wayne National Bank. Leave granted sheriff to file amended return. Defendants to in reply thirty days and plaintiff to answer in thirty days thereafter.

HURLBURT vs. SUNDALL, dismissed on payment of costs by plaintiff.

MONROE vs. MONROE, divorce granted, plaintiff to pay costs.

BURR vs. MODING, et al. Default against MODING and Frank KRUGER for $721. Foreclosure is prayed.

BLAKE vs. BLAKE, decree of divorce granted. Plaintiff to pay costs.

A.L. TUCKER vs. PERRY, at al., default against Matilda MYERS and Union Stockyard National Bank, Judgment $1110 and interest at 10 per cent. Judgment for M. MYERS $131. Judgment for Stock Yards National.

Mary TILLSON vs. WOHLER, defendant to answer in 30 days, plaintiff to reply in twenty days thereafter.

BRYANT vs. BRYANT, decree of divorce granted plaintiff.

State of Nebraska vs. BRUECKNER, costs paid and defendant discharged.

BURR vs. BEALE. Default against all defendants except J.T. BRESSLER, judgment for cross petitioner BRESSLER for $171. Action dismissed by plaintiff.

City of Wayne vs. J. SINGER, et al., default against defendants.

HENRY vs. GIBSON, plaintiff 30 days to file petition. Defendant 20 days to answer.

Nebraska Loan & Trust Co. vs. CUNNINGHAM, et al. Judgment for plaintiff, foreclosure ordered.

OLMSTED vs. Wayne Agricultural Society. Judgement for defendant.

HAMILTON BROWN Shoe Co. vs. SINGER & Co. Judgment for plaintiff.

Coats Thread Co. vs. SINGER & Co. Judgment for plaintiff.

PETTYS vs. PETTYS. divorce granted.

GUY vs. LEWIS, dismissed.

GODRICH vs. RUDAT, et al., settled.

FRENCH vs. MILLER, dismissed.

BROWN vs. WROBEL, et al., foreclosure ordered.

Talcott & Co. vs. HONEY, continued.

HILDER vs. HILDER, continued.

Tollerton & Stetson Co. vs. WOLF, et al., judgment for plaintiff $1760.

Kilpatrick Koch Co. vs WOLF, et al., dismissed.

SNYDER vs. VAN CAMP, et al., foreclosure ordered.
McCONNELL vs. LEWIS, judgment against defendant for $155. Allowance made defendant for damaged leather.
WATKINS vs. WATKINS, divorce granted.
FRENCH vs. GAINES, judgment for plaintiff $1799.

Real Estate Transfers.

Christian RASHMAN to W.C. WIGHTMAN, ne 1/4, 23-26-2	$4,000.00
Dettef KAY to H.F. MOUK, e 1/4, 31-26-5	5,600.00
Logan Valley Land Co. to Wm. F. LALK, Lots 11 and 12, blk. 7, Hoskins	45.00
J.R. MORRIS to T.J. THOMAS, n 1/2 ne 1/4 and ne 1/4 se 1/4, 26-27-1	3,000.00
H.F. MOUK to Louise MOUK, n 1/2 ne 1/4, 31-26-5	5,600.00
W.R. MICK to C.A. GROTHE, se 1/4, 30-27-8	4,800.00
J.T. BRESSLER to McCLUSKEY and NEEDHAM, lots 3 and 3 blks. 14 and lots 2, 3, 4, 5, and 6, blk. 15, Winside	200.00
Joseph CARROLL to Rachael A. CARROLL, nw 1/4, 20-25-1	2,000.00
Cornelius HARRINGTON to Geo. WATTS and J.H SMITH, lots 1, 2 and 3, blk. 6, Lakes ad to Wayne	3,000.00
Alpheus WELLS to John FREITLE and C.A. CHACE, lot 4 and n 1/2 lot 5, blk. 26, Wayne	1,000.00

• • •

A. SCHWAERZEL
Wayne Shoe Shop

• • •

E. CUNNINGHAM
Auctioneer

• • •

ROE & FORTNER
Second Street Meat Market
Wayne, Nebraska

The Wayne Republican
October 26, 1895 (Vol. 2, No. 36)

BIRTH: To Mr. and Mrs. Dan BYRD, a fine girl.

BIRTH: To Mr. and Mrs. TUHN a fine girl.

Real Estate Transfers.

O.D. BROWN to F.M. SKEEN, lot 6, blk. 12 n ad, Wayne	$150.00
Ed. REYNOLDS, sheriff to Andrew LINN, W 75 a of se 1/4, 4-21-5	3,200.00
E.W. BROWN to David HERNER, s 1/2 ne 1/4, 19-25-5	1,365.00
E.W. BROWN to H. FISHER, n 1/2 ne 1/4, 19-25-5	1,843.00
E.W. BROWN to Mrs. Wm. KORTH, nw 1/4, 19-25-5	2,720.00
Neb. Normal College to N. GRIMSLEY, lots 19, 20 and 21, blk. 20, College Hill	105.00
N. GRIMSLEY to G.W. RILEY, lots 19, 20 and 21, blk. 20, College Hill	1.00
G.W. RILEY to J.M. PILE, lots 19, 20 and 21, blk. 20, College Hill	1.00
Ed. REYNOLDS, sheriff, to Adolph KEEFER, s 50 ft, lot 27, T&W ad, Wayne	185.00
Siefried ANDERSON to A.L. TUCKER, se 1/4, 14-27-2	3,200.00

Garfield precinct is alive to her best interests this year and will be found in line when it comes election time this year. The rally at the Maze school house out there on Saturday night was well attended. Before the addresses were delivered a caucus was held and the following put in nomination for the precinct offices: Assessor, J.V. FRANCIS; Judges of election, W.I. STEELE, F.C. SCHROEDER and J.V. FRANCIS; Clerks of election, F.E. FRANCIS, A.A. BELL; Road supervisors, district 28, John KNOUSE; 49, F.C. SCHROEDER; 36, Mell GROAT; 26, Jos. BORDERS. The speakers of the evening were A.A. WELCH of Wayne and Dorr CARROLL of Winside. They gave the audience good straight republican talk and the marked attention shown by those in attendance clearly indicated that the opposition can hope for but little in that precinct this year. There are some pretty enthusiastic republicans in Garfield that age going to do the party lots of good and make the other fellows wonder what hit them.

District Court.

Court adjourned Friday afternoon. Only a few cases were disposed of other than mentioned in last week's Herald.

OLMSTEAD vs. Wayne Agricultural Society, verdict for defendant.

MULKEY, et al. vs. Wm. BRUNE, judgment for defendant.

C.St.P.M. & O.R.R. Co., vs. The County of Wayne, default against HUNTER.

ELDRED vs. DODGE, sale confirmed.

Coats Thread Co. vs. SINGER, judgment for plaintiff.

FRENCH vs. Chas. MILLER, dismissed.

First National Bank vs. BROWN, et al., judgment for plaintiff.

Almeda BROWN vs. Chas. WROBEL, sale confirmed, deed ordered.

Allen MAHER vs. WROBEL, confirmed, deed ordered.

Tollerton & Stetson Co. vs. WOLF, et al., judgment for plaintiff, $1,700.14.

S.R.&I.C. McCONNELL vs. John LEWIS, verdict for plaintiff.

Alice PETTYS vs. Merritt PETTYS, judgment for plaintiff.

WATKINS vs. WATKINS, divorce granted.

EDWARDS & BRADFORD Lumber Co. vs. S.S. STARKS, judgment for plaintiff.

Almeda BROWN vs. Ole HOGAN, judgment for plaintiff.

• • •

The Turf Exchange
WORKING & KRUGER, Proprietors
Pure Wines & Liquors

• • •

L.S. WINSOR
Practical Horseshoer

• • •

The German Store
FURCHNER, DUERIG & CO.

• • •

The Wayne Republican
November 2, 1895 (Vol. 2, No. 37)

MARRIED: SMITH - RICHARDSON. At the M.E. parsonage by the Rev. MILLARD, Tuesday evening, Oct. 29, Sophia SMITH to Fred RICHARSON. The young people have our best wishes.

MARRIED: At the court house by Judge MARTIN, Chas. HULT, and Christine BROLINE, both of Wausa, Nebraska.

MARRIED: On Thursday evening, Oct. 24th at the home of Mr. Will ROOT, Mrs. Alice PETTY and Mr. GUDGLE.

MARRIED: The following clipping from the Woodhull (Ill.) Dispatch gives an account of the wedding of Miss Nonnie GAMBLE to Mr. WOODS of that place; and will be of interest to everyone in Wayne, as the young lady in question was beloved by all who knew her, and her many friends have the deepest interest in her future.

The residence of Mr. and Mrs. S.A. GAMBLE on South Division street was the scene of a happy home wedding on Tuesday evening, at which time Nonnie D., second daughter of Mr. and Mrs. GAMBLE, was united in marriage to Mr. John Lyle WOODS. At 6:30 the well known strains of Mendelssohn's wedding march, played by Master Sammie GAMBLE, brother of the bride, announced the coming of the bridal party, which consisted of Mr. Forest T. PRITCHARD and Miss Myrtle GAMBLE, first groomsman and bridesmaid; Mr. Fred GAMBLE, brother of the bride, and Miss Nellie GRIFFITH, second groomsman and bridesmaid, followed by Mr. WOODS and Miss GAMBLE, who stood beneath an arch of autumn leaves, while the Rev. Grant STROHN repeated the sweetly solemn words which bound together the lives of two more young people who thus publicly promised "to walk the long path together until death do us part."

The bride wore a silk gown with a girdle of pearls, and carried blush roses. After congratulations a bountiful supper was served. The guests numbered fifty, all, with a few exceptions, relatives of the bride and groom.

The presents, which were displayed in an upper room, were numerous and handsome, testifying not only to the regard of the guests but also to the appreciation by the church people of the bride's services as a "sweet singer in Israel."

Mr. and Mrs. WOODS left for St. Louis at 8:30, carrying with them the loving thoughts and kind wishes of many friends whose hearts re-echoed the pastor's benediction, "The Lord bless thee and help thee, the Lord make his face to shine upon thee, and be gracious unto thee; the Lord lift up his countenance upon the and give thee peace."

DIED: Mrs. GUTKNECHT, wife of the German pastor, 9 miles north of town, last Saturday from puerperel convulstions, aged 33 years. She was a model wife and mother, worshiped by her family and esteemed by all who knew her. She leaves a family of six children, the youngest three years old. The services were held in the German church Tuesday morning and conducted by Rev. HANSEN of Martinsburg, assisted by Rev. HILBREDS of Laurel.

The election this year will be held in the Wineland building, and the board consists of the following persons: Judges, J.R. MANNING, James BAKER and M.S. MERRILL. Clerks, Geo. BAILEY and Carleton HURLBURT.

Advertised Letters.

The following is a list of letters, etc., remaining in the post office at Wayne, Nebraska, for the week ending Oct. 29, 1895:

Wm. BLAGG (2), B.H. CARVER, G.G. DEPLER, Miss Maggie E. DAVIES, O. GARRISON, Biet HENSON, R.L. LIVINGSTON, E.N. NELSON, Lonies ROHDE, L.M. SMITH, Charlie SHAFEE.

Parties calling for the above please give date when advertised.

A.P. CHILDS, P.M.

The Wayne Republican
November 9, 1895 (Vol. 2, No. 38)

BIRTH: On Oct. 29, to Mr. and Mrs. J.E. WILSON, of Leslie, a fine girl.

BIRTH: Mr. and Mrs. Jas. MULVANEY rejoice over the arrival of a nice boy at their residence on November 3.

MARRIED: The pleasant home of Mr. and Mrs. McCLURE near Silver City, Iowa, was the scene of a happy home wedding on Wednesday, October 30 at 12 o'clock, noon, at which time Mina, daughter of Mr. and Mrs. McCLURE was united in marriage to William JACKSON of Wayne county, Nebraska. After congratulations a grand dinner was served. The presents were many and handsome and after wishing the young people a safe journey the many friends of the bride and groom departed for their homes.

The following is the precinct officers elected for Deer Creek: For assessor, Leander SIMMERMAN; for justice of the peace, James BAKER, George YARYAN; for constable, George BELFORD, Fred WILCOX; for judges of election, J.A. BROWN, J.R. MANNING, George YARYAN; for clerks of election, George A. BAILEY, George C. MERRILL; for road overseer, dist. no 24, C.A. McVAY, dist no. 42, L. SIMMERMAN.

The Wayne Republican
November 16, 1895 (Vol. 2, No. 39)

County Directory.

L.F. RAYBURN ..... County Treasurer ..... Wayne
S.B. RUSSELL ..... County Clerk ..... Wayne
E. MARTIN ..... County Judge ..... Wayne
Ed. REYNOLDS ..... Sheriff ..... Wayne
Charlott M. WHITE ..... County Sup't ..... Wayne
A.A. WELCH ..... County Attorney ..... Wayne
J.P. GARTNER ..... Coroner ..... Wayne
Ludwig ZIEMER ..... County Surveyor ..... Wayne
Mark JEFFREY ..... County Com'r ..... Wayne
A.M. JACOBS ..... County Com'r ..... Wayne
A.H. CARTER ..... County Com'r ..... Winside

Words, Blows and Arrest.

Tom McCAFFREY living down in the southwest part of Brenna got on his fighting clothes on Friday last and went into the cornfield of his neighbor, Mike EICHE and began a quarrel with him and after a few words lit into the latter, knocked him down and severely pummeled his face, bruising and scratching him up badly. On Saturday the sheriff interviewed the beligerent Tom and brought him to town where he answered to Judge MARTIN's court to the charge of assault and battery. He plead guilty to the accusation and was assessed $5 and costs the total amounting to something over $16.

Advertised Letters.

The following is a list of letters, etc., remaining in the post office at Wayne, Nebraska, for the week ending Nov. 12, 1895:

Louis ANDERSON, Oran ANDREWS, John COTTRELL, Louis S. CLARK, H.J. MEAN, Rev. A. MARTIN, Fred MACKEN (2), J.P. RAWLINGS, C.W. KNAPP.

Parties calling for the above please give date when advertised. A.P. CHILDS, P.M.

Real Estate Transfers.

Oran D. BROWN to F.M. SKEEN, lot 8, blk. 12, n. add. to Wayne	$150.00
A.S. MINER to Frank A. DEARBORN, w 20 ft. of lot 3, T&W's add. to Wayne	150.00
Ed. REYNOLDS to Ellen MAHER, 1 acre in nw 1/4 sw 1/4, 18-25-4	488.00
F.L. WELSCHLAGER to Caroline WELSCHLAGER, nw 1/4, 10-25-2	1.00
Nels SWANSON to Louis S. JOHNSON, n 1/4 ne 1/4, 8-26-4	2,800.00
John DONNER to Albertine MAAS, lots 13, 14 and 15, blk. 4, Hoskins	450.00
E. CULLEN to Lucius WELLS, sw 1/4, 33-26-1	4,080.00
North Neb. Land & Imp. Co. to J.A. BERRY, lot 14, blk. 8, Carroll	85.00
Julius WANTOCH to Fred MULLER, w 1/2 nw 1/4, 34-25-2	2,400.00
J.T. BRESSLER to Sol SLAUGHTER, nw 1/4, 21-25-5	5,000.00
Sol SLAUGHTER to J.T. BRESSLER, se 1/4, 21-26-4	5,000.00
First Nat'l Bank to Louis S. JOHNSON, s 1/4 ne 1/4, 3-26-4	2,400.00
F. ULRICK to Anna ULRICK, sw 1/4, 17-27-3	4,000.00

Sarah A. WRIGHT to Wm. H. WEBER,
    lots 7, 8 and 9 and e 1/2 lot 3,
    also part of e 1/2 s 1/2 lot 2,
    all in blk. 10, Wayne
	6,000.00

Wm. H. WEBER to Sarah A. WRIGHT, e 1/2 lots 4, 5 and 6, blk. 6, n. add. to Wayne	---

The Wayne Republican
November 23, 1895 (Vol. 2, No. 40)

MARRIED: PHILLIPS - THOMPSON. At office of county judge on Wednesday afternoon, November 20, Charley PHILLIPS and Mary A. THOMPSON, both of Wayne county, Judge MARTIN officiating.

MARRIED: GUDGEL - GATES. At the M.E. parsonage, Rev. MILLARD officiating, on Saturday, November 16, M.N. GUDGEL and May GATES.

MARRIED: ZEIMER - KRUGER. At the office of county Judge on November 21, Ludwig ZEIMER of Hoskins and Mrs. Henrietta KRUGER of the same place were joined in wedlock by Judge MARTIN.

DIED: At her home northwest of Carroll, Sunday, November 17, Mrs. CLINGMAN wife of William CLINGMAN. The remains were interred in the Carroll cemetery Monday afternoon. The deceased was a daughter of Jacob MORT and leaves a husband and one child a few days old. Her bereaved husband and family have the sympathy of all in this, their great loss.

COMMISSIONER PROCEEDINGS. Wayne, Neb. Nov. 15, 1895.
Commissioners met pursuant to adjournment. Present, A.B. CARTER and A.M. JACOBS.
The following bills were examined and allowed:

F.H. ROMJINE, road work	$25.00
J. SIMMERMAN, road work	5.00
Ed PRINCE, road work	2.50
Char. SCHROER, road work	2.00
Foed KOEBKE, road work	25.00
Adam GREAR, road work	52.50
A.H. CARTER, Waddell, road work	36.00
O.C. LEWIS, road work	78.00
Mrs. E. HUNT, road work	5.00
Wm. HILL, road work	6.25
M. CASE, road work	60.00
H.W. BRUGGERMON, road work	2.50
N.B. CULLEN, road work	6.25
R.H. SKILES, road work	5.00
Robt. H. JONES, road work	18.50
Claus OTTE, road work	27.50
F.A. RUSSELL, road work	22.50
Joseph BROWN, road work	3.75
L.R. JOHNSON, road work	2.50
John HARDER, road work	15.00
Fred SCHRODER, road work	12.50
C.D. SIEFKEN, road work	3.75
P.M. PETERSON, road work	5.62
Wm. HARRISON, road work	2.50
S. SLAUGHTER, road work	6.25
Aug. LOHBERG, road work	48.25
L. SIMERMAN, road work	40.00
C.A. McVAY, road work	113.50
Wm. VINCENT, road work	30.00

C.D. JONES, road work	$10.00
D. SHEA, road work	7.50
Aug. WITTLER, road work	6.25
P.L. MILLER, goods for needy	6.75
Dan ROUSE, boarding pauper	15.00
R.J. ARMSTRONG, coal for pauper	8.15
Benser & Son, goods for pauper	17.95
John HARRINGTON, goods for pauper	10.83
Fred VOLPP, goods for pauper	2.40
Fanny LOUND, rent for pauper	5.35
Zenan & Heffner, goods for pauper	6.80
L.C. MITTLESTADT & Co., goods for pauper	3.75
Jacob REICHERT, goods for pauper	5.00
Ed's & B Lumber Co., lumber	70.57
SMITH & ELLIS Co., lumber	212.80
L.C. MITTLESTADT & Co., lumber	20.88
L.F. RAYBURN, supplies	9.50
C.A. BAGGERT, janitor, court work	6.75
McNEAL & BEEBE, printing	10.75, 9.50
State Journal Co., poll books	24.50
E. MARTIN, office expenses	3.71
Hugh HALL, ditching	102.50, 97.50
Carl F. LONG, repairs	4.25
Ed. REYNOLDS, court, jailor fees	95.95
S.B. RUSSELL, election expenses	167.10
W.M. GUE, overseer poor	8.00
A.M. JACOBS, com. fees	3.70
A.H. CARTER, com. fees	29.00

Report of S.B. SCACE, overseer dist. No. 13 approved.

On motion the clerk was ordered to advertise for the leasing of a building for a poor house and superintending the same for the paupers of Wayne county, Nebr., said bids to be filed with the county clerk on or before noon of the 29th day of Nov., 1895.

Attest: S.B. RUSSELL, County Clerk.

The Wayne Republican
November 30, 1895 (Vol. 2, No. 41)

BIRTH: George KINGSTON and wife are rejoicing over the birth of a son which arrived a few days ago. (Carroll)

DIED: Mr. and Mrs. Carter COX mourn the loss of their youngest boy, Roy, aged about eight years, who died November 21 of typhoid fever. The funeral was conducted by Rev. BERKLEY at the Baptist church on Friday afternoon. The bereaved parents and family have the sympathy of all in their sorrow. (Carroll)

The Wayne Republican
December 7, 1895 (Vol. 2, No. 42)

BIRTH: Aug. PIEPENSTOCK and wife rejoice over the arrival of a girl baby at their home.

MARRIED: On November 30, C.J. CAGLY and Nora FREBERG, judge MARTIN officiating.

MARRIED: On December 3, Albert ANDERSON and Louisa NELSON, judge MARTIN officiating.

Real Estate Transfers.

Randall FRAZIER to Anna McLAUGHLIN, n 1/2 nw 1/4, 24-27-2	$2,700.00
Edw. SUHR to Alex SUHR und 1/4 n 1/2 nw, 18-25-3	---
Wm. FRAZIER to L.S. WINSOR, lot 11, Skeen's ad., Wayne	13,000.00
J.A. and Wm. FRAZIER to S.O. Nat'l Bank, Sec 18-26-3, except e 1/2 se 1/4	17,300.00
J.A. and Wm. FRAZIER to J.V. HINCHMAN, sw 1/4, 17-26-3	5,110.00
O.C. HOLTZ to Alex HOLTZ, lots 7, 8, 9, 10, 11 and 12, blk. 1, College Hill	1.00
K. LEARNER to Jas. SNEATH, lot 4, blk. 20, Wayne	2,000.00
Jas. SNEATH to R.P. WILLIAMS, lot 4, blk. 20, Wayne	3,000.00
G.W. SERANTON to FURCHNER D & Co., lots 6, 7 and 8, blk. 4, e ad. Wayne	1,000.00

Lodge No. 118, I.O.O.F. held their annual election of officers on Saturday evening and elected M.O. CUNNINGHAM, N.G.; James PORTERFIELD, V.G.; Otis STRINGER, secretary; Henry LEY, Permanent secretary and treasurer; A.A. WELCH, George GELDER and J.J. FOX, trustees.

Casey Post G.A.R. held their regular annual election of officers on Monday evening and elected Mark STRINGER, commander; A.W. TAYLOR, S.V.A.; A.J. HYATT, J.V.; J.W. BARTLETT, Quartermaster; B.F. FEATHER, surgeon; G.W. CULLER, chaplain,

Ed REYNOLDS, Officer of Day; Jim PRESTON, Officer of Guard. On January 7 they will hold their installation of new officers, have a grand camp fire and supper to which old soldiers are cordially invited.

・・・

Harness Shop
A.W. TAYLOR & SON

・・・

City Livery Barn
S.H. RICHARDS, Proprietor

・・・

The Wayne Republican
December 14, 1895 (Vol. 2, No. 43)

DIED: The 6-months-old child of Mr. and Mrs. Ben ELLIOTT died during the night of the 11th. The cause of death is unknown as the child appeared to be in good health on retiring in the evening and when the father went to take the child up in the morning found the spirit had taken its flight.

DIED: The infant daughter of Mr. and Mrs. Jas. STEPHENS died on Saturday night and was buried in the Carroll cemetery on Sunday afternoon. The parents have the sympathy of the entire community.

        He has called for many a love one,
        We have seen them leave our side.
        With our Saviour we shall meet them,
        When we too have crossed the tide.

Real Estate Transfers.

J.T. BRESSLER to McCLUSKY & NEEDHAM,	
Lot 3, blk. 12, Winside	$60.00
J.S. FRENCH to Chas. NENNSON,	
se, nw, ne 1/4, 9-26-4	3,500.00
A.E. CHAMBERS to FURCHNER D & Co.,	
d 1/2 sw 1/4, 9-27-3	1,600.00
J. SHELLINGTON to H.B. HARRISON,	
s 1/2, ne 1/4, 33-26-5	2,800.00

Thos. WESTON to A.W. CHAPIN,	
w 1/2, 19-26-5	$2,800.00
T.K. THOMPSON to E.W. LUTZ,	
ne 1/2, 23-25-1	1,600.00
J. DIMMEL to J.H. SHERE,	
lots 10, 11, blk. 1, Winside	500.00
N.N. MOORE to J.H. SHERE,	
lot 12, blk1, Winside	90.00
E.J. NANGLE to F. WEBER,	
n 1/2 ne 1/4	
E.J. NANGLE to W. BAUMGARDNER,	
s 1/2 ne 1/4, 24-23-2	3,464.00
24-26-8	3,764.00
M.D. TYLER to F. SHROEDER,	
sw 1/4 and se 1/4 of nw 1/4 and	
nw 1/4 se 1/4, 18-25-1	3,400.00
Winside Mill Co. to H.H. SHERE,	
lot 19, blk. 5 and blk. 1 B&P ad, Winside	160.00
F. STEWART to P.F. PETERSON,	
s 1/2 sw 1/4, 8-27-1	1,900.00

The Wayne Republican
December 21, 1895 (Vol. 2, No. 44)

BIRTH: On Tuesday Dec. 17 to Dr. and Mrs. BLAIR, a boy.

Card of Thanks.

To the many friends who so kindly assisted us in the burial of our little Hilda, we wish to extend our sincere thanks. May God bless you and be your Comforter in such sorrows.

Mr. and Mrs. B.E. ELLIOTT

Logan Valley Camp M.W.A. held their annual election of officers on Tuesday evening and elected W.H. HOGUEWOOD, V.C.; T.W. MORAN, W.A.; Met GOODYEAR, Banker; P.H. KOHL, Clerk; John COYLE, escort; J.J. WILLIAMS and E.S. BLAIR, physicians; A. JETT and M.P. AHERN, Managers; M.P. SAVIDGE, inside sentry; Henry MERRIMAN, outside sentry. Two new members were initiated into the mysteries of the craft. The camp now has over 100 members in this place and is constantly adding new members to its list.

Poultry Show.

The Northeast Nebraska Poultry association have been holding their show at this point this week and have had quite a successful exposition. Several coops of birds were exhibited by parties from abroad and when it comes to a "chicken show" Wayne easily takes the cake in that line. She has more "chicken men" to the acre than any other place far or near and is today looked upon as one of the leading points in the west for that purpose. Below we give a list of the entries. Let us say that while many people look upon poultry breeding as a small business, that instead of its being such that it stands well up in the lists as a leader.

There were about 250 birds on exhibition by 30 different exhibitors. The following is a complete list.

Golden Wyandottes - H. GREGORY, O.H. MISKIMMENS, L. HOLTZ, Frank OSBORN, R.E.Q. MELLOR.

Buff Cochins - H. GREGORY, Thomas HUGHES, L. ROOT, Randolph.

Barred Plymouth Rocks - C.D. MARTIN, H. GAERTNER, Bert COOK, L. HOLTZ, Mrs. R. FRAZIER, J.C. FORBES, Frank OSBORN, M. GOODYEAR, B.S. DART, Hartington, L.A. BOWDEN, Beemer.

Light Brahmas - C.D. MARTIN, John JUHLIN, L.A. BOWDEN, Beemer.

S.C. White Leghorns - Will WEBER, W.H. BRADFORD, J.H. RIGGS, Randolph, L.A. BOWDEN, Beemer, H. GAERTNER.

R.C.B. Leghorns - Will WEBER, H. SHERBAHN, J.S. LEWIS, Thos. HUGHES.

Silver Wyandottes - Ralph SULLIVAN, J.H. RIGGS, Randolph.

White Wyandottes - W.H. BRADFORD, M. GOODYEAR.

White Brahmas - I.W. ALTER.

B.B. Red Game Bantams - O.H. MISKIMMENS, Frank HOOD.

S.S. HAMBURGS - Bert COOK.

R.C.W. Leghorns - Albert FURCHNER, M. GOODYEAR.

White Bantams - Robt. OSBORN.

S.D.W.G. Bantams - Robt. OSBORN, Art BECKENHAUER.

S.C.B. Leghorns - J.S. LEWIS, L. A. BOWDEN.

Black Langshans - E.P. OLMSTED, B.L. DART, Hartington.

Golden Polish - Charley REYNOLDS.

Partridge Cochin - L.P. ROOT, Randolph.

Houdans - R.G. COFFIN, Randolph.

Black Leghorns - L.A. BOWDEN, Beemer.

• • •

Dry Goods, Groceries
L.J. HANSEN

The Wayne Republican
January 1, 1896 (Vol. 2, No. 46)

MARRIED: New Year's Day at John HAMER's place in this precinct, Harry HUGHES and Miss Annie HAMER, both residents of Wayne county. (Garfield)

COMMISSIONER PROCEEDINGS. Wayne, Neb. Dec. 27, 1895.

Commissioners met pursuant to adjournment. Members all present. The following official bonds were examined and approved:

Mrs. Myra FLETCHER, Co. Supt; E. MARTIN, Co. Judge; Ed. REYNOLDS, Sheriff; W.M. GUE, Justice of the Peace; Walter GOELDER, Justice of the Peace; G.W. YARYAN, Justice of the Peace; James BAKER, Justice of the Peace; B.F. FEATHER, Justice of the Peace; D.J. CAVANAUGH, Constable; Richard KARO, Constable; J.J.W. FOX, Assessor Hunter Precinct; G.A. LEWIS, Assessor Chapin Precinct; P.C. COLEMAN, Assessor Plum Creek Precinct; John O. DOBBIN, Assessor Garfield Precinct; John HARDER, Overseer Dist. No. 7; P.M. PETERSON, Overseer, Dist. No. 11; J.A. BARBOUR, Overseer Dist No. 12; Henry BRUSE, Overseer Dist No. 49; Ed. MILLER, Overseer Dist No. 50; Michael EICH, Overseer Dist No. 32; Clause OTTE, Overseer Dist No. 41; Patrick COLEMAN, Overseer Dist. No. 30.

The following claims were examined and allowed:

ROE & FORTNER, goods to needy, before Dec 5, 1895	$1.55
John HARRINGTON, goods for poor house	8.50
J.H. GOLL, goods for needy, before Dec 5, 1895	2.45
H.E. CORBIT	8.95
L.E. HUNTER, Overseer Poor	8.00
HARRINGTON & ROBBINS, goods for needy, before Dec 5, 1895	4.65
J.W. INGALLS, goods for needy, before Dec 5, 1895	4.15
P.L. MILLER, goods for needy, before Dec 5, 1895	6.35
J.P. GAERTNER, goods for Poor House	9.30
PHILLEO & Son, coal for jail	52.10
D.L. HAINES, cleaning court house	4.00
E. HUNTER, witness fees for county	6.00
SHUMWAY & EVERET, claim of $16.24 allowed at	14.61
Sam HUNT, road work	37.50
Aug. PEIPENSTOCK, goods for needy, before Dec 5, 1895	2.00
SMITH & ELLIS Co., lumber	178.65
D.T. ROUSH	13.88

R.J. ARMSTRONG, coal for needy, before Dec 5, 1895	$8.55
EDWARDS & BRADFORD Lbr. Co.	38.90
PERKINS Bros. Co.	51.70
Carl F. LENZ, repairs on grader	2.80
Ed. REYNOLDS, jailor's fees	45.75
Western Wheel Scraper Co., grader	210.00
CHACE & NEELY, hardware	92.65
Hugh HOUSE, road work	2.50
A.G. JOSLYN, road work	1.75
McNEAL & BEEBE, printing	19.50
Charles KNAPP, road work	2.50
A. ANDERSON, road work	6.25
R. WADSWORTH, road work	7.50
Geo. BERRIS, road work	2.50
F.M. JAMES, road work	8.10
W.P. AGLER, road work	29.28
Thos. JAMES, road work	1.50
Camp POWELL, road work	5.00
H. BEUTHEIN, road work	3.00
H.M. DAMME, road work	3.00
S.K. WEST, road work	18.00
Richard RITZE, road work	2.00
Christ SYDOW, road work	3.75
L. NURENBERGER, road work	10.00
H. PFLUGER, road work	5.00
C.E. BENSHOOF, road work	5.00
FURCHNER DUERIG & Co., goods for needy, before Dec 5, 1895	7.55
John GILFERT, road work	1.88
M.P. SAVIDGE, repair on grader	1.45
Carl C. THOMPSON, road work	2.50
Fred MULLER, road work	2.50
P.M. PETERSON, road work	5.62
EDWARDS & BRADFORD Lbr. Co.	20.67
J.T. ARMSTRONG, account BOWMAN	46.17
E. MARTIN, costs	22.90

Bond of Adam GRIER for road Dist. No. 40, approved.

Bond of J.E. WILSON road Dist. No. 15, approved.

On motion the county treasurer is ordered to deduct from warrant of Hugh HALL the amount due for his personal tax.

W.C. PARSON, hardware	$2.00
Chas. ERXLEBEN, road work	10.00

Resignation of Carl C. THOMPSON overseer of Dist. No. 3, accepted.

On motion the county clerk is directed to notify the publishers of all newspapers published in the county that bids will be received to Jan'y 8th, 1896 at 12 o'clock M., for all printing required to be published at the expense of the county for the coming year, the county reserving the right to reject any or all bids.

On motion county clerk is directed to prepare estimates of books, blanks and stationery required for the use of the county officers for the coming year and send same to PERKINS Bros., Co., of Sioux City, Ia., State Journal Co., Lincoln, Neb., Omaha Mercury & Omaha Printing Co., of Omaha, together with notice that bids for furnishing the same will be received to Jan'y 8th, 1896, at 12 M. Said bids to specify the prices per item for each kind at which the same will be furnished as needed or ordered by the county. Articles in the clerk's estimate not needed shall not be furnished nor paid for by the county. Commissioners reserving the right to reject any and all bids.

The petition of James FRY, et al. asking for the establishing of a public road between sections 4 and 5, tp 26, r 3, e, and it appearing from the claims on file that damages are claimed, the clerk is instructed to appoint appraisers to appraise the damages by reason of the location of said road.

Mark JEFFREY, commissioner's fees	$10.00
A.H. CARTER, commissioner's fees	12.60
A.M. JACOBS, commissioner's fees	11.80

On motion board adjourned until Jan. 8th, 1896.
Attest: S.B. RUSSELL, Clerk.

Real Estate Transfers.

Richard SCANNELL to M.T. HEALEY, lots 1 and 2, blk. 4, Lake's Ad to Wayne	$200.00
Evald KOEFOED to Sophius THOMPSON, quit claim deed to se 1/4, 12-26-2	1.00
Logan Valley Land Co. to School Dist. 9, lots 4, 5 and 6, blk. 14, Hoskins	62.70
D. LONGNECKER to D.M. KITE, ne 1/4, 32-26-5	6,000.08

The Wayne Republican
January 8, 1896 (Vol. 2, No. 47)

MARRIED: GRIFFITH - VINCENT. At the Baptist church in this city at 12 o'clock high noon on Tuesday, January 7, 1896, occurred the marriage of Miss Estella VINCENT of this city to J.A. GRIFFITH of Seward, Nebraska. Rev. W.W. THEOBALD pronounced the magic words that made the parties husband and wife. The bride is one of the best known young ladies of this vicinity, is highly respected and accomplished. Of the groom we cannot speak from a personal knowledge but he is highly spoken of by those acquainted with him. The best wishes our our readers will go with the newly married couple wherever their lot may be cast and the Republican joins a host of friends of the bride in extending congratulations.

DIED: At his farm in Sherman precinct on Tuesday morning, January 7, 1896, Richard WADSWORTH passed from this life to the great unknown.

It don't seem possible that "Uncle Dick," as we all have been accustomed to call Mr. WADSWORTH, is dead, but it is so. Only a few days ago he was on our streets greeting friends with a hearty shake of the hand, a kind word for everyone. Apoplexy was the immediate cause of his death and he had only been confined to his room for a few days more than a week. None were better or more favorably known than was the deceased and in his death the community has lost a good man and the state a valuable citizen. His remains will be taken to Dixon, Illinois, at which place the funeral will occur.

Advertised Letters.

The following is a list of letters, etc., remaining in the post office at Wayne, Nebraska, for the week ending Dec. 28, 1895:

Mr. Henry ALBERS, Mr. W.F. AUSENHEIMER, Mr. O.L. ANDERSON, Chas. ACKLEY, Mr. Chas. ACKLIN, Julius GOLDSTIEN, William MAY, Mr. John O'BRIEN.

Parties calling for the above please give date when advertised.

A.P. CHILDS, P.M.

The Wayne Republican
January 15, 1896 (Vol. 2, No. 48)

BIRTH: On Sunday evening to Mr. and Mrs. Will WEBER, a boy.

MARRIED: RUSSELL - SHAWGO. At the M.E. parsonage, Thursday evening January 9, Rev. MILLARD said the words that made Frank A. RUSSELL and Florence SHAWGO man and wife.

MARRIED: HICKS - BRECKENRIDGE. At the Catholic church, Rev. Father McGRATH on Monday tied in the bonds of matrimony, J.F. HICKS and Ollie BRECKENRIDGE.

MARRIED: FINN - McALEN. On Monday forenoon, January 13 at the Catholic church, Rev. McGRATH officiating, John FINN and Mary McALEN were joined in the bonds of matrimony.

DIED: R. WADSWORTH died Jan. 7th at 8:55 a.m. of paralysis. He was taken ill Dec. 24th about 9 o'clock p.m. soon after he had retired. Mr. WADSWORTH had not been feeling well for some time, but kept at his business (i.e.) bought 30,000 to 40,000 bushels of corn which he weighed, gave tickets and checks for all of it. He had got through buying corn only a few days previous to the date that he was taken ill. He was one of the first settlers in the western part of Wayne county; he owned 1,760 acres of land here which he divided into several farms and made good improvements on all of them. Wayne county lost one of its best citizens in him. He had built up this part of Wayne county; he generally bought all the grain in the neighborhood and paid the highest prices for it; whatever he promised to do he would always do it. The remains were taken to Dixon, Ill., for interment, accompanied by Morris WADSWORTH, his nephew also a partner of R. WADSWORTH in business. The neighborhood sympathize with M. WADSWORTH and all the family in their bereavement. We have lost a friend and neighbor from among us that we will wish back for all time to come. The deceased was 67 years of age.

Attempted Hanging.

Eugene MUELLER the German that languishes in the county bastile because of the elegant job of thrashing done sometime ago by him on the frame of Constable Tom BELL, attempted to climb the golden stairs by the rope route on Monday. When incarcerated he had a short rope around his waist in order to hold his pants in place, this he used as the means to cross the river Styx, and would have succeeded but for accident. He had taken the rope made a noose in one end, took a chair and fastened the other end over a bar on top of his cage, slipped his head into the noose and was just going to jump into eternity when a couple of his old neighbors who had come to visit him put in an appearance at one of the windows of the jail, discovered what he was about to do, gave the alarm and prevented his carrying out his design.

The public installation of new officers of I.O.O.F. 118 and banquet at this place on Saturday evening was all that the most ardent could desire. An excellent program of music by the male quartet and the orchestra, address of welcome by Rev. KUNKELMAN preceded the installation of the officers. The installation was by David EWING of Hartington, District deputy Grand Master of

Nebraska; the ceremonies were fitting and well conducted. The new officers are: M.O. CUNNINGHAM, N.G.; James PORTERFIELD, V.G.; Otis STRINGER, Secretary; Henry LEY, Permanent Secretary and Treasurer; G.A. BENSON, Warden; Mark JEFFREY, R.S.N.G.; A.A. WELCH, L.S.N.G.; J.J. WILLIAMS, Conductor; C. WARNER, Inside guardian; J.J.W. FOX, Outside guardian; Wm. VINCENT, R.S.S.; N.I. JUHLIN, L.S.S.; R.C. OSBORN, R.S.V.G.; Geo. FOX, L.S.V.G. After the completion of the installation ceremonies a very neat and appropriate address was delivered by the District Deputy Grand Master, then came more music. This was followed by an invitation to all in attendance to repair to HOOVER's restaurant there to partake of a banquet fit for the gods. The evening was one that will long be remembered by the guests and will leave a warm place in the hearts of all for Wayne Odd Fellows.

COMMISSIONER PROCEEDINGS. Wayne, Neb. January 8, 1896.
Commissioners met pursuant to adjournment. Members all present. Minutes of last meeting read and approved.
The following claims were examined and allowed:

E.S. BLAIR, county physician, salary	$50.00
C.M. WHITE, county superintendent, salary and expenses	187.95
A.A. WELCH, county attorney, salary	162.50
Town Hall Association, rent	112.50
Henry KREBBS, repair on grader	2.25
F.C. SCHROEDER, blacksmithing	1.25
R.D. MERRILL, hardware	5.00
R.D. MERRILL, hardware	2.02
R.J. ARMSTRONG, coal	8.40
G.E. WILLIAMS, road work	1.25
E.J. DAVIS, road work	2.50
John BANISTER, road work	4.70
George GREEN, road work	5.00
Earnest BEHMER, road work	6.25
S.B. PERFECT, road work	2.50
J. GARWOOD, road work	2.50
S.F. NELSON, road work	.62
P.N. NELSON, road work	1.25
H.J. NURENBERGER, road work	10.00
W.F. BANISTER, road work	1.25

The following official bonds were examined and approved:
A.T. WITTER, justice of the peace, Wayne precinct.
I.H. WEAVER, justice of the peace, Logan precinct.

W.J. WEATHERHOLT, justice of the peace, Hoskins precinct.
J.L. CLINE, justice of the peace, Hoskins precinct.
J.H. PORTER, justice of the peace, Sherman precinct.
S.H. McMAKIN, constable, Wayne precinct.
Frank HOOD, constable, Wayne precinct.
A.T. WADDELL, constable, Hoskins precinct.
George BELFORD, constable, Deer Creek precinct.
Fred WILCOX, constable, Deer Creek precinct.
R.C. OSBORN, assessor, Wayne precinct.
O.W. JONES, assessor, Sherman precinct.
C.C. BROWN, assessor, Strahan precinct.
N.H. NYE, assessor, Leslie precinct.
J.L. CLINE, assessor, Hoskins precinct.
Levi DILTZ, assessor, Logan precinct.
N.B. CULLEN, overseer dist. No. 6.
Levi DILTZ, overseer dist. No. 16.
I.O. RICHARDSON, overseer dist. No. 17.
A.B. JEFFREY, overseer dist. No. 23.
J.R. MORNS, overseer dist. No. 44.
Hayden HUTCHINSON, overseer dist. No. 48.
A.T. WADDELL, overseer dist. No. 52.
Fred KRAUSE, overseer dist. No. 53.
L.C. GILDERSLEEVE, deputy sheriff.
S.B. RUSSELL, county clerk.
J.M. CHEERY, deputy county clerk.
Bert BROWN, clerk of district court.
Bonds of the First National Bank, State Bank, Citizens Bank, Wayne National Bank for depositories of county funds for year 1896 approved.
T.E. BURCHART, road work $5.00
Alf JONES, road work 2.50
Report of C.M. WHITE, county superintendent, showing balance in institute fund $28.35.
On motion all bids for county printing are hereby rejected.
The following official bonds are hereby approved:
Jenkins DAVIS, overseer dist. No. 25.
T.E. EVANS, constable, Sherman precinct.
A.H. CARTER, commissioners fees $4.00
On motion A.H. CARTER was tendered a vote of thanks by the officers of Wayne county for his conscientious and efficient services as county commissioner, after which board adjourned until January 9, 1896.
Attest: S.B. RUSSELL, Clerk.

COMMISSIONER PROCEEDINGS. Wayne, Neb. January 9, 1896.
Commissioners met pursuant to adjournment; board organized with Mark JEFFREY as chairman and George HARRIGFELDT entered upon his duties as county commissioner with ease and dignity.

Bond of Phil KOHL, treasurer, approved.

On motion the county attorney was asked to furnish an opinion as to the existence of the office of the clerk of the district court of this county, and therefore the same was prepared, filed and presented to the board, in words and figures as follows, to wit:

IN THE MATTER OF THE OFFICE OF THE CLERK OF THE DISTRICT COURT OF WAYNE COUNTY, NEB.

To the Hon. Board of County Commissioners of said county.

GENTLEMEN:

The sole question to be determined in this matter is, whether Wayne county at the time of the general election in 1895, had a population of 8,000 inhabitants.

If it had such population or more there is such office of clerk of the district court for Wayne county, and the person elected thereto at the general election in 1895 is entitled to such office. Neither the calling of [illegible] to the number of votes in a county is evidence tending to prove the number of inhabitants.

In case the court held that a county which in 1883, contained less than 8,000 inhabitants at the time the census was taken in that year but more than that number 30 days before the general election was authorized to elect a clerk of the district court. I would advise that the person claiming the office be requested to produce his proof before the board that the county contained a population of 8,000 inhabitants or more at the time of the general election in 1895. And if you find that the county did contain such population at that time, that you provide a place for him to perform the duties of his office.

Your action in this matter would in no manner stop or prevent any other person from questioning his right to hold the office.

Very Respectfully, A.A. WELCH, County Attorney.

The following official bonds were examined and approved:

Ludwig ZEIMER, county surveyor. J.P. GAERTNER, coroner. D. SHAY, assessor, Deer Creek precinct.

Now comes the county treasurer and makes settlement with the county commissioners showing amount of money collected and disbursed since July 1, 1895.

(See Statement.)

The following claims were examined and allowed:

Mrs. SEBALD, rent needy before Dec 5, 1895	$5.00
John OTT, rent needy before Dec 5, 1895	12.00
Thomas PRINCE, road work	7.50
N.B. CULLEN, bridge work	10.00
McNEAL & BEEBE, printing	5.00
R.C. OSBORN, oil	4.20

The following settlements were made with road overseers:

Eli McCONOUGHEY, district No. 1, showing balance due him	$26.14
S.K. WEST, district No. 2, showing balance due him	30.00
C.C. BOSTEDER, district No. 3, showing balance due him	43.24
C. SCHROEDER, district No. 4, showing balance due him	48.26
N.B. CULLEN, district No. 6, showing balance due him	34.50
John HARDER, district No. 7, showing balance due him	44.50
Sam HODSON, district No. 8, showing balance due him	- - -
G.H. CULLER, district No. 9, showing balance due him	34.50
L. NUREMBERGER, district No. 10, showing balance due him	26.00
P.M. PETERSON, district No. 11, showing balance due him	8.36
J.A. BARBOUR, district No. 12, showing balance due him	27.58
J.E. WILSON, district No. 13, showing balance due him	18.08
Wm. VINCENT, district No. 15, showing balance due him	30.00
W.M. HILL, district No. 18, showing balance due him	31.00
S.A. BRUNER, district No. 20, showing balance due him	3.10
A.B. JEFFREY, district No. 23, showing balance due him	35.50
C.A. McVAY, district No. 24, showing balance due him	39.00
S. HUNT, district No. 25, showing balance due him	42.47

Robt. H. JONES, district No. 26, showing balance due him	$27.00
C.D. JONES, district No. 27, showing balance due him	24.50
August SAMULESON, district No. 29, showing balance due him	31.50
P. COLEMAN, district No. 30, showing balance due him	30.00
J.M. CASSELL, district No. 32, showing balance due him	29.46
Cal RITCHIE, district No. 31, showing balance due him	42.00
B.P. PETERSON, district No. 35, showing balance due him	51.20
W.B. GROAT, district No. 36, showing balance due him	60.00
James MULVANEY, district No. 38, showing balance due him	53.80
O.P. ANDERSON, district No. 39, showing balance due him	49.62
Adam GRIER, district No. 40, showing balance due him	28.50
Clause OTTE, district No. 41, showing balance due him	36.00
Aug. LOBERY, district No. 43, showing balance due him	34.50
J.R. MORRIS, district No. 44, showing balance due him	41.00
L. SIMMERMAN, district No. 42, showing balance due him	30.00
W.A. PICKARD, district No. 46, showing balance due him	36.50
Thos. PRINCE, district No. 47, showing balance due him	30.0
F.C. SCHROEDER, district No. 49, showing balance due him	52.50
Herman DECK, district No. 51, showing balance due him	47.25
F. SCHROEDER, district No. 52, showing balance due him	67.25

On motion that the county printing be let to the Wayne Republican and the Winside Tribune. Each to receive one-fourth legal rates, except the publication of the delinquent tax list, for which they are each to be paid one-half legal rates. Ayes and nayes being called showing the result, JACOBS and

HARRIGFELDT aye and JEFFREY naye.

On motion that the clerk of the district court be allowed to office with the county clerk, ayes and nayes being called, resulting HARRIGFELDT and JACOBS aye and JEFFREY naye.

The matter of blanks, books, etc., was deferred until next meeting.

On motion board adjourned until January 14, 1896.

Attest: S.B. RUSSELL, Clerk.

COMMISSIONER PROCEEDINGS. Wayne, Neb. January 14, 1896.

Commissioners met pursuant to adjournment. Members all present. The following official bonds were examined and approved.

James MULVANEY, overseer Dist. No. 38.
H.W. BURNHAM, overseer Dist. No. 45.
W.B. GROAT, overseer Dist. No. 36.
W.B. EASTBURN, overseer Dist. No. 26.
W.H. PECKARD, overseer Dist. No. 25.
Perrin LONG, assessor, Hancock precinct.

The following settlements were made with road overseers:

John KNOUSE, district No. 48, showing balance due him	$30.25
Jacob MORT, district No. 48, showing balance due him	29.43
Oscar CASE, district No. 34, showing balance due him	22.09
H.H. CHILDS, district No. 16, showing balance due him	2.74

The following claims were examined and approved:

H.H. CHILDS, road work	$13.25
Jacob MOST, bridge work	4.00
L.E. HUNTER, printing	8.25
Oscar CASE, road work	10.00
John NELSON, road work	.62
W.M. GUE, justice blanks	5.90

Bonds of Leander SIMMERMAN, assessor Deer Creek precinct and overseer Dist. No. 42, approved.

The following estimates were made for the year 1896:

County General Fund	$30,000.00
County Bridge Fund	9,000.00
County Insane Fund	800.00
County Bond Fund	6,500.00

On motion J.R. SHAWGO was appointed road overseer of Dist. No. 2. Bond of J.R. SHAWGO's Dist. No. 2 approved.

Bond of C.A. KILLION, overseer Dist. No. 10, approved.

Claim of L.F. RAYBURN collecting taxes, $245.88.

A contract was entered into by and between W.P. AGLER and the county of Wayne for the leasing of the old court house on the public square in the old town of La Porte in Wayne county, Neb., the same to be used for a county poor house for the sum of one hundred and twenty-five dollars ($125.00) from January 14th, 1896 to January 14th, 1897, he to superintend the same and care for all inmates, furnish all fuel, lights and board for the same at $2.50 per week for each inmate thereof, unless in case of any inmate being sick and required extra nurse, then such expense should be paid by the county, said AGLER to receive $125.00 in advance by his giving bond the same to be approved by the county commissioners.

On motion the salary of the county superintendent was fixed at $700.00 for the ensuing year.

On motion the county attorney's salary is fixed at $650.00 for the ensuing year.

On motion S.B. RUSSELL is allowed a salary of $400.00 for the ensuring year, as clerk of county commissioners.

On motion S.B. RUSSELL is allowed the sum of $700.00 for deputy for the ensuing year.

On motion E.S. BLAIR is appointed county physician for the ensuing year at a salary of $200.00, payable quarterly, he to enter into a contract and furnish all medicines at his own expense.

On motion J.W. AGLER was appointed road overseer of Dist. No. 3.

On motion that the matter of the county printing be reconsidered, ayes and nays being called, resulting JACOBS and HARRIGFELDT nay; JEFFREY aye.

On motion the matter of stationery and supplies be deferred until next meeting with privilege for bidders to file bids until that time to wit, February 1, 1896.

Bond of Perry BENSHOOF, assessor Brena precinct, approved.

On motion Perry BENSHOOF was appointed assessor for Brenna precinct.

W.P. AGLER, lease court house	$125.00
Mark JEFFREY, commissioner fees	9.90
A.M. JONES, commissioner fees	11.10
Geo. HARRIGFELDT, commissioner fees	10.00

On motion board adjourned until February 1, 1896.

Attest: S.B. RUSSELL, Clerk.

The Wayne Republican
January 22, 1896 (Vol. 2, No. 49)

LICENSED TO WED: Aug. J. SCHEEL and Olive JOHNSON.

MARRIED: BURNHAM - SCOTT. At the M.E. parsonage at Carroll on January 22, H.W. BURNHAM and Mamie SCOTT were united in marriage, Rev. BERKLEY officiating.

DEATH: On last Friday the dread messenger, Death, entered the NELSON family of our village and took from it the ninteen-year-old son, Nels; the cause of death being lung fever. The bereaved family have the sympathy of the entire community. (Hoskins)

He Had an Ax.

A family quarrel at the home of John GREENWALD south of the city on Monday resulted in the arrest of John GREENWALD, jr., charged with a felonious assault upon his father. The complaint alleges that the son did assault and menace the father in a threatening manner. The story is that for several years the father and son have not dwelt together in the sweetest of harmony and on the day above named a quarrel between them resulted in the son getting hold of an ax and making the father seek refuge in the house. Then followed the warrant, arrest and confinement in jail of the son.

Advertised Letter List.

The following is a list of letters, etc., remaining in the Post office at Wayne, Nebraska, for the week ending Jan. 21, 1896.

Joe MARTIN; Mr. Louig VAN NOONAN (2); Otto WAECHTER.

Parties calling for the above please give date when advertised.

A.P. CHILDS, P.M.

The Wayne Republican
January 29, 1896 (Vol. 2, No. 50)

BIRTH: A son was born unto Leslie BAKER and wife on the 22nd.

MARRIED: TOFT - JENSEN. At the office of the county Judge on January 29, Hans TOFT and Sophia JENSEN.

MARRIED: RITCHEY - MOSSMAN. At the home of the bride's parents today, Wednesday January 29 at 11:30 a.m. Rev. H.H.

MILLARD pronounced the words that bind for life in marriage James RITCHEY and Louie MOSSMAN. the groom is one of our well known and respected young men and the bride is the daughter of Mr. and Mrs. Byron MOSSMAN of Deer Creek precinct and has for some time been one of Wayne county's successful teachers. Mr. RITCHEY and his bride will have the very best wishes of a large circle of friends and acquaintances go with them as they start upon life's sea of matrimony.

MARRIED: Wednesday evening, Jan. 22, 1896 at 8 o'clock at the bride's home, Mr. S.M. CLAYBAUGH and Miss Clara E. MELTON were joined in marriage, Rev. A.B. BUCKNER officiating.
    The guests were a select crowd of young people, those from a distance being Miss May CLAYBAUGH of Wayne, Neb., and Robt. CLAYBAUGH of Greenfield, Iowa, and Miss Hattie DYER from Villisca, Iowa. At the appointed hour a wedding march was played, and keeping step with the music the bride and groom marched into the parlor which was beautifully decorated. After the ceremony all expressed good wishes for the young couple, after which the guests partook of an elegant and bountiful wedding supper, which was enjoyed by all. After an evening of conversation and music the guests retired to their homes, feeling delighted with the occasion, and leaving behind them a number of useful and beautiful presents.
    Mr. CLAYBAUGH was formerly a resident of Montgomery county, but for the last three years has made his home at Wayne, Nebraska. Miss MELTON's home has always been in Montgomery county where she is well known by many young people, who will miss her very much. They will soon depart for their future home at Wayne, Nebraska. (Red Oak Express)

DIED: At her home near Laurel on Monday January 27th, Emma BECKMAN aged about 16 years. Inflammation of the bowels was the immediate cause of death. The funeral took place from her home on Tuesday the 28th. The bereaved parents, brothers and sisters have the sympathy of the entire comunity in this hour of overwhelming sadness.

BURIAL: The remains of Welbert LaCROIX, whose parents reside west of the city, were brought to this place from Iowa on Thursday for interment. The young man died of pneumonia.

The Masquerade.

    The lovers of the light fantastic had an evening of rare enjoyment at the opera house on last Thursday evening. The managers of the ball are certainly to be congratulated on the excellent entertainment furnished their patrons. The costumes were not only elegant, but in many cases were quite fantastic and were varied enough to suit the most exacting. Below we shall attempt to give at least a partial list of the characters represented: Mesdames A.H. ELLIS, E.P. ELLIS, Frank FULLER, Topsys; Mrs. NEELY, carnation; Mrs. WEBER, queen of clubs; Mesdames C.E. COLE and R.E.K. MELLOR, flower girls; Mrs. INGALLS, good luck; Mrs. BRENNER, bat; Mrs. HARRISON, butter cup; Mrs. WHITE, babe; Gertie WEBER, huntress; Lulu THOMPSON, Theo. SCACE and Pearl REYNOLDS, tambourine girls; Bertha ARMSTRONG, babe; Lois CHILDS, Marguerite; Miss VOSE and Mary HENRY, flower girls; Leta CORBIT, gypsy; Maud BRITTON, poppy; Minnie SMITH, black diamond; Mrs. FLETCHER, Troubadour; Susie EDWARDS, school girl; Ed SULLIVAN and George NANGLE, English gentlemen; R.J. ARMSTRONG, Mr. ZEINER, W.L. SEDGWICK, Harry JONES and Emil WEBER, monks; Dr. HECKERT, Mr. DITTLE and Rollie LEY, bicyclists; E.P. ELLIS, knight; Gus TRACY, devil; Mr. EVANS, Sailor; A.F. BRENNER, German; W.H. McNEAL, Irishman; Clarence CORBIT and James MILLER, dudes.

Advertised Letter List.

The following is a list of letters, etc., remaining in the Post Office at Wayne, Nebraska, for the week ending Jan. 28, 1896.

Adolph BRUGGERMAN, Louis BRUGGERMAN, Chan. BROWN; A. CROFFER, P. FRAYER, Arthur B. SMITH, Rod BENUTH, Eathel WILLIAMS, Francis FILKNER.

Parties calling for the above please give date when advertised.

A.P. CHILDS, P.M.

Public Sales.
E. CUNNINGHAM, Auctioneer.

On Saturday, February 1, at 2 o'clock at feed yards in Wayne, Chas. McCONNELL will sell horses, wagons and harness.

S.M. CLARK 6 miles south and 2 miles west of Wayne, 7 1/2 south and 1 1/2 miles east of Laurel, at 10 o'clock a.m., Thursday Feby. 6, 22 head of horses and colts, 8 head of cattle and all kinds of farming implements and household furniture. Free lunch at noon.

On Tuesday, February 11, at 12 o'clock noon, 10 miles east of Wayne, 3 miles south and 2 miles east of Wakefield, H.E. MONICLE will sell all his horses, hogs, implements and household furniture.

On Wednesday, Feby. 12 at 12 o'clock noon 3 miles east of Wayne, Mark JEFFREY will sell horses, hogs and implements.

W.S. COOK will sell at the stock yards in Wakefield on Saturday, Feb. 15 at at 1 p.m. 40 head of brood sows, 40 stock hogs, 10 cows, 10 yearlings and calves, wagons and other implements.

Otto FREDERICKSON, three miles south of Wakefield on Friday, Feb. 7 at 12 o'clock. Horses, cattle, hogs and implements.

Dedlauf KAY, at 12 o'clock, Tuesday, February 18, 5 miles east and 3 south of Wayne, 5 miles south and 1 1/2 west of Wakefield. All his horses, cattle, hogs and farming implements. Terms easy. Come everybody.

Wm. FRAZIER 6 miles west of Wayne at 10 o'clock a.m., Wednesday and Thursday, February 19 and 20, 70 head of horses of all kinds, several head of cattle and all kinds of implements and household furniture. Free lunch both days.

The Wayne Republican
February 5, 1896 (Vol. 2, No. 51)

LICENSED TO WED: Jay LEATHERBY and Ollie M. DARNELL.

MARRIED: KING - McGRAIL. At the office of the county Judge January 29, W.R. KING and Anna McGRAIL.

DIED: LILLARD. At Appleton, Mo., on Sunday, January 26, Mrs. Mary LILLARD, aged 56 years. The deceased was the mother of our fellow worker, W.H. McNEAL of the Herald and today we extend to him a sympathy that is born of experience. The loss is irreparable, none can ever take the place of the dear departed one and we believe that ours is but an expression of the sympathy of the entire community as our brother is thus so deeply afflicated. The news of the mother's serious illness came to the son too late to reach her bedside before the spirit had passed away, as he did not receive the telegram until the day she died. He at once left for her home and telegraphed from Omaha that he was on his way but through some error the telegram was not delivered and when he arrived, he found that the funeral had taken place just a few hours previous.

DIED: THOMPSON. At her home near Concord on Monday, February 3, Mrs. Ida THOMPSON, aged 24 years. The deceased was well known to many of our readers as the daughter of James ALEXANDER. She was a graduate of our high school and a lady beloved by all of her acquaintances. The Republican offers its condolence to the husband, parents, brothers and sisters.

Real Estate Transfers.

B.F. SWAN to August DANBURG, nw 1/4, 21-27-3	$1.00
Dora and John HOLST, to N.H. MEIRE, se, 22,26-1	3,680.00
Hugh N. CUNNINGHAM to Hannah C. CUNNINGHAM, lot 12, blk. 24, Wayne	40.00
E.D. VANPELT to John STROMBERG, lts. 7 and 8, blk. 28, Wayne	200.00
Marcellos DEARBORN to Wm. MOYER, lts. 27 and 28, blk. 22, College Hill	90.00
D.J. RAWHOUSER to Pat MINIHAN, w 1/4 se 1/4 and 3 60 a of sw 1/4, 31-26-4	2,000.00
H.W. EATON to Margret BUSH, lts. 19 and 20, blk. 15, College Hill	125.00
Anna B. JEFFERSON to Carrie POND, w 1/2, lts. 8, 9 and 10, blk. 1, e ad to Wayne	900.00
Carrie POND to Anna B. JEFFERSON, s 1/2 se 1/4, 35-27-3	3,125.00
J.B. CARNS to Henry OTTO, sw 1/4, 20-27-3	2,600.00
C.F. MIDDLETON to J.S. FRENCH, ne 1/4, 8-27-3	3,200.00
L.R. THORP to Anna ASHLEY, ne 1/2 nw 1/4, 43-27-2	2,000.00
E.J. VAUGHN to Mary E., se 1/4, 10-26-3	4,800.00

Following is the names of the scholars who have neither been absent nor tardy during the two months ending Jan. 30: First month, Pearl BLACK, Jessie BLACK, Della BLACK, Lillie HAINES, Mary HAINES, Mattine HAINES, Clara HAINES, Francis SCHUTT, Edgar STEPHENS, Oscar STEPHENS, Archie STEPHENS. Second month, Della BLACK, Jessie BLACK, Mary HAINES, Lillie HAINES, Edgar STEPHENS.

COMMISSIONER PROCEEDINGS. Wayne, Neb. February 1, 1896.
 Commissioners met pursuant to adjournment. Members all present.
 The following appointments were made:
 J.H. WEATHERHOLT, overseer District No. 4 and bond approved.
 O.C. LEWIS, overseer District No. 19 and bond approved.

A.G. METTLEN, overseer District No. 20 and bond approved.
C.A. McVAY, overseer District No. 24 and bond approved.
Alfred JONES, overseer District No. 29 and bond approved.
C.D. JONES, overseer District No. 27 and bond approved.
Jacob RIECHART, overseer District No. 33 and bond approved.
O.P. ANDERSON, overseer district No. 39 and bond approved.
Wilhelm SCHULZ, appointed road overseer District No. 51 and bond approved.
J.P. MARVIN, appointed assessor of Winside precinct and bond approved.
The following settlements were made with road overseers:
O.C. LEWIS, District No. 19, showing balance due him, $29.50.
Andrew HARPER, District No. 45, showing balance due him, $48.00

The following claims were examined and allowed:

Henry ALTERS, road work	$3.50
James BAIRD, road work	1.25
Andrew HARPER, road work	5.00
Fred JENSEN, road work	2.50
Aug. KRAUSE, road work	5.00
E. LONGNECKER, road work	2.50
D.W. SHAW, road work	2.50
Christ SYDOW, road work	2.50
Wm. WINTER, road work	5.00
S.B. RUSSELL, 4th quarter salary, tax list and office expenses	667.00
E. MARTIN, costs, State vs. LINCH	2.20
E. MARTIN, office expenses	4.71
S.B. RUSSELL, appraisers road damages	15.00
PERKINS Bros. Co.	19.50
Wm. HART, repairs on grader	6.50
C.A. BAGGERT	1.25
EDWARDS & BRADFORD Lumber Co.	9.79
R.J. ARMSTRONG	10.00
Ed REYNOLDS, jailers fees, etc.	39.55
McNEAL & BEEBE, printing	13.50
Dorr H. CARROLL	9.60
EDWARDS & BRADFORD Lumber Co.	19.22
Fred PFLUGER, road work	3.75
E. CUNNINGHAM, printing	15.60
A.M. JACOBS, commissioner fees	3.70

Mark JEFFREY, commissioners fees $3.70
Geo. HARRIGFELDT, commissioners fees   5.00
Claim of Mrs. SEBALD for rent, rejected.

Jas. STEPHENS was appointed road overseer District No. 27 and bond approved.

On motion the matter of the appointment of the County Physician was reconsidered and W.C. WIGHTMAN was appointed for the ensuing year at a salary of $300.00 payable quarterly; he to enter into a contract with the County for the faithful performance of his duties.

Now at this time the bids for printing stationery and blanks for county were opened and examined, and it appearing that the Wayne Democrat was the lowest bid, the contract was awarded to it for the ensuing year.

On motion the bid of PERKINS Bros. Co. for furnishing books and supplies was accepted.

On motion J.L. CLINE was appointed Soldier's Relief Commissioner for a term of three years.

On motion J.W. BARTLETT was appointed Soldier's Relief Commissioner for a term of one year.

On motion the Board decided to engage an expert for the purpose of examining the records of the County Judge, County Clerk and Sheriff.

Bond of L.E. HUNTER for printing approved.

Bond of PERKINS Bros. Co. for furnishing books and supplies approved.

On motion John KOEFOED was appointed road overseer District No. 22 and bond approved.

Report of Soldier's Relief Commission, approved.

Settlement was made with the following road overseers:

Ed MULLER, District No. 50,
    showing balance due him $27.27
John KOEFOED, District No. 22,
    showing balance due him   .65

On the first day of January comes the C.St.P.M. & O.R.R. Co., by J.B. BARNES, its attorney and presents its application for an order to the county Treasurer, to refund the following taxes for the year 1895, paid this day under protest for the reason that said amounts are levied on property not subject to city and village taxes, to wit:

City of Wayne, water bond tax $94.35
City of Wayne, city tax   140.00
Village of Winside   82.80
Village of Carroll   32.40

The Board thereupon proceeded to hear evidence as to the

amount of property of said Railroad company subject to taxation in said villages and city, on consideration whereof the Board finds that in apportioning the mileage of said Railway Company in the city of Wayne, the Clerk entered the same on the tax list as 4.84 miles assessed at $24,000.00 and extended its tax with accordance therewith. The Board also finds that the actual mileage of said Railway Company in the city of Wayne is 2.63 miles and its true assessment for taxation in the city of Wayne is $10,150.00, whereof the taxes in said city as entered by the county clerk were as follows, to wit:

 Water Bond $169.40
 City Tax   242.00

The Board further finds that the taxes of said city of Wayne on the true mileage of said Railway Company are:

 Water Bond $71.05
 City Tax   101.50

and that the following sums have been entered on the tax list of 1895, on property not subject to taxation in the city of Wayne:

 Water Bond $98.35
 City Tax   140.50

The Board also finds that in apportioning said mileage in the village of Carroll, the Clerk entered on the tax list for said year 2.18 miles assessed at $10,900.00 and entered taxes in accordance therewith, that its true mileage in said village of Carroll is 1.1 miles and true assessment is $3,500.00; that the village of Carroll tax as entered on the tax list is the sum $65.40, that the tax in said village of Carroll is on property not subject to taxation thereof.

The Board also finds that in apportioning said mileage in the village of Winside, the Clerk entered on the tax list for said year 3.18 miles assessed at $15,900.00 and entered village tax in accordance therewith; that the true mileage in said village of Winside is 1.11 miles and true assessment $3,550.00; that the village of Winside tax as entered on the tax list is the sum of $127.20; that the said village tax on the true mileage and assessment thereon is the sum of $44.40 and that $82.80 of the village tax of Winside entered on said tax list is on property not subject to taxation thereon.

The Board further finds that said Railway Company have paid the full amounts of said city and village taxes paying the sums herein before set forth, is on property not subject to said taxes under protest. It is therefore ordered that the County Treasurer refund the said Railway Company the following from the sums as entered on tax list from:

City of Wayne, Water Bond	$98.35
City of Wayne, City Tax	140.00
Village of Winside	82.80
Village of Carroll	32.40

Board adjourned until March 14th, 1896.
Attest: S.B. RUSSELL, Clerk.

The Wayne Republican
February 12, 1896 (Vol. 2, No. 52)

BIRTH: A new boy has taken up his abode in the home of George CULLEN.

BIRTH: Born, Friday, Feb. 7, to Mr. and Mrs. Warren BISHOP, a daughter.

BIRTH: Prof. CONN and wife are the proud parents of a baby girl that arrived on Friday.

BIRTH: The home of Mr. and Mrs. John SHERBAHN was made glad on Sunday by the advent of a nice baby girl.

BIRTH: Mr. and Mrs. Mike MOORE are the proud parents of a baby girl.

MARRIED: CLARK - JONES. On Feb. 6 1896 at the Baptist church at this place, Rev. THEOBALD united in marriage Emmet CLARK and Leta JONES. The groom is a son of S.M. CLARK one of the best and most respected farmers of the county. The bride is a young lady well known to many of our people and highly respected by all. The young couple start out in life with the best wishes of a large circle of friends and acquaintances accompanying them. They will make their home on the farm of the father of the groom in the north part of the county. The Republican family desire to return thanks for their kindly rememberance in the shape of a bountiful supply of wedding cake.

MARRIED: OLIVER - SMITH. At the Baptist church Wayne on Wednesday, Feby 12, Rev. THEOBALD officiating, Wilham C. OLIVER and Susan SMITH.

DIED: At his home near St. Peter, Dixon county, Nebraska, on Monday Feb. 10, Dennis O'FLAHERTY. The deceased is the father of Mrs. Dennis SULLIVAN of this city and was one of Dixon county's oldest and best known settlers.

Advertised Letter List.

The following is a list of letters, etc., remaining in the Post office at Wayne, Nebraska, for the week ending Feb. 11, 1896.

Dan BURK, Mary E. HANARTH, Mrs. Mary KEGIR.

Parties calling for the above please give date when advertised.

A.P. CHILDS, P.M.

Public Sales.
E. CUNNINGHAM, Auctioneer.

W.S. COOK will sell at the stock yards in Wakefield on Saturday, Feb. 15 at 1 p.m., 40 head of brood sows, 40 stock hogs, 10 cows, 10 yearlings and calves, wagons and other implements.

Dedlauf KAY, at 12 o'clock, Tuesday, February 18, 5 miles east and 3 south of Wayne, 5 miles south and 1 1/2 west of Wakefield. All his horses, cattle, hogs and farming implements. Terms easy. Come everybody.

Wm. FRAZIER 6 miles west of Wayne at 10 o'clock a.m., Wednesday and Thursday, February 19 and 20, 70 head of horses of all kinds, several head of cattle and all kinds of implements and household furniture. Free lunch both days.

Geo. ROHWER, 2 miles north and 1 mile west of Wayne at 10 o'clock a.m., Thursday, Feb. 13. will sell all his horses, cows, implements and househould furniture. He is going to Montana.

On Friday, Feb. 14th Frank LEMMON 2 miles west of Winside, will sell horses, cows, hogs, and implements. Sale to commence at noon.

On Tuesday, Feb. 25th, Victor SANDAHL, 4 miles east and one-half mile south of Wayne will sell horses, cattle, hogs, and implements.

On Thursday, Feb. 27th, Geo. BUSH, northwest of Wayne, will sell his entire stock of horses, cattle, hogs and implements.

On Friday, Feb. 21, at 1 o'clock p.m., W.R. MICK will sell at his farm 9 miles northwest of Wayne all his personal property.

The Wayne Republican
February 19, 1896 (Vol. 3, No. 1)

BIRTH: To Mr. and Mrs. Wendell BAKER on last Friday, a girl.

BIRTH: Mr. and Mrs. SPENCER are the proud parents of a baby girl.

BIRTH: Born to F.M. WOODS and wife Monday, February 17, a daughter of the standard weight.

DIED: A fatal case of trichinosis occurred in the family of Charley THOMPSON, who lives six miles south of La Porte. About six weeks ago Mr. THOMPSON butchered, and the members of the family ate some of the meat without cooking. The family were all taken with what they supposed was rheumatism. Before the true character of the disease was known it had progressed so far that it resulted in the death of Clara PATES, a sister of Mrs. THOMPSON, 16 years old, who was staying with the family, who died on Tuesday last. The rest of the family are recovering. (Wakefield Journal)

Those interested in the creamery held a meeting at the rooms of the First National on Monday and proceeded to put the project on a firm footing by the election of officers. They are F.M. NORTHROP, president; W.O. GAMBLE, secretary; H.W. LESSMAN, Henry MYERS, S.G. GRIMSLEY, W.O. GAMBLE, A.B. CLARKE, L.O. RICHARDSON, H.J. GRAVES, H.M. EVANS, directors. It is to be co-operative and the stock dividend into 150 shares of $20 each, to be paid in monthly payments of $5 each until paid.

State of Nebraska, Wayne county, ss. Before me, A.T. WITTER, a justice of the peace in and for said county, personally came Anson A. WELCH, county attorney within and for said county, who being duly sworn according to law, deposeth and saith, that on or about the 12th day of February, 1896, at the county of Wayne in the state of Nebraska, Ed REYNOLDS and Liffie C. GILDERSLEEVE did then come there, willfully disturb, molest and interrupt a certain public school duly organized under the laws of the state of Nebraska to wit: the school taught by W.W. BONER, Willis E. HOWARD, and E.C. PARK in the school district of Wayne in the county of Wayne in the state of Nebraska then and there being, by entering the building wherein said school is kept and talking in a loud and indecent manner therein, and by assaulting and striking the said E.C. PARK all while pupils of said school were engaged in the proper exercises thereof, the said school being organized under the laws of the state of Nebraska for the intellectual improvement of its members, and this deponent says that said Ed REYNOLDS and Liffie C. GILDERSLEEVE are guilty of the facts charged; and further this deponent saith not.

Anson A. WELCH.

Subscribed and sworn to before me this 14th day of February, 1896. A.T. WITTER, Justice of the Peace.

The above named parties waived arrest and appeared in court, plead guilty as charged and Ed REYNOLDS was fined $15 and costs and Liffie C. GILDERSLEEVE $10 and costs.

The Wayne Republican
February 26, 1896 (Vol. 3, No. 2)

Wayne had quite a sensational case in Jusitce WITTER's court last week. It seems that one of the teachers in the city schools had thrashed one of the county sheriff's ill-behaved boys, and said sheriff becoming enraged proceeded to the school house and pummeled Mr. Teacher to his satisfaction, taking along his deputy "to see fair play." The principal was fined $15 and costs and his deputy $10 and costs, and the whole county is humiliated over the affair. (Laurel Advocate)

The Wayne Republican on Wednesday contains the information that the high sheriff of Wayne county, Ed REYNOLDS, went on a recent date to the public school and various other persons proceeded to administer a pounding to a teacher in the public school, because said teacher had punished the said sheriff's boy. The deputy sheriff, L.C. GILDERSLEEVE accompanies his chief to prevent interference from others present, but the combatants were separated before any one was seriously hurt. It seems that this affair occured a week ago Wednesday afternoon and there was no mention of it in either the Wayne Herald or Democrat of last week, both published after the disgraceful affair occurred. The Republican being issued on Wednesday, was unable to mention it last week but this week gives a full account of the affair and demands the impeachment of the sheriff and his deputy. After the attack, the two beligerants appeared before a justice of the peace and pleaded guilty to practically what we have published above and paid costs amounting to $15 and costs for the sheriff and $10 and costs for the deputy. An attack of the kind described by the Republican would be bad enough for a common everyday citizen, but for peace officers whose sworn duty it is to uphold the peace and dignity of the state, it is an outrage that should not be condoned and deserves the severest condemnation. (Randolph Times)

Advertised Letters.

The following is a list of letters, etc., remaining in the Post office at Wayne, Nebraska, for the week ending Feb. 25, 1896.

Veuzeng KRUITGER.

Parties calling for the above, please give date when advertised.

A.P. CHILDS, P.M.

Public Sales.
E. CUNNINGHAM, Auctioneer.
    On Thursday, Feb. 27th, Geo. BUSH, northwest of Wayne, will sell his entire stock of horses, cattle, hogs and implements.
    On Monday, March 2, 9 miles north of Wayne, H.A. LOWER will sell cattle, hogs and implements.
    On Tuesday, March 3, 5 1/2 miles north of Wayne, A. WATSON will sell all his horses, cattle, hogs, implements, etc.
    On Wednesday, March 11, W.J. WHITE southwest of Wayne will sell cattle, hogs, horses and implements.
    On Thursday, March 12, at his home one mile west of Wayne, Ran FRAZIER will sell horses, cattle, hogs and implements. This will be a big sale.

The Wayne Republican
March 4, 1896 (Vol. 3, No. 3)

BIRTH: A nice girl baby has taken up her abode with Mr. and Mrs. BRAASCH. (Hoskins)

BIRTH: Johnnie PETERS and wife are the proud parents of a bouncing baby boy.

MARRIED: Saturday, February 29, Mr. Frank HOLMES of this precinct and Miss Huldah CARLSON of Wakefield. (Hunter precinct)

MARRIED: CUNNINGHAM - RITCHEY. At the home of the bride's mother in the city of Wayne on Thursday, Feb. 27, Rev. MILLARD united in marriage Howard F. CUNNINGHAM and Etta L. RITCHEY. Only the relatives and immediate friends of the contracting parties were present at the ceremony. Both bride and groom are well known to the people of this section and are highly respected. The Republican along with the numerous friends desires to extend congratulations and bid them God speed on life's journey.

MARRIED: NELSON - ANDERSON. At the M.E. parsonage on Friday evening, Feb. 28, Rev. MILLARD officiating, Andrew NELSON and Tena ANDERSON were united in wedlock.

MARRIED: At the elegant home of Peter N. NELSON in Hunter precinct on Feb. 27th Rev. SWANSON of Wakefield in the presence of about 80 guests pronounced the words that united in marriage Charles JOHNSON and Anna CARLSON. After the ceremony and the extension of congratulations to the happy couple all present sat down to the wedding feast where the table groaned under its load of good things of this world. The young couple start in life with the best wishes of a large circle of friends and acquaintances to go with them.

DIED: At the home of her parents, Mr. and Mrs. James SPENCE near Laurel, Neb., on Saturday, Feb. 29, 1896, Edna SPENCE aged seventeen years, the immediate cause of death being pneumonia. The funeral occured at Laurel on Tuesday and was largely attended. The Republican joins the many friends of the bereaved family in extending to them sympathy in this dark hour.

DIED: Mr. CLINGMAN's baby died last Saturday and was buried in the Carroll cemetery on Monday.

Real Estate Transfers.

H.B. BOYD to R.E.K. MELLOR,	
Und. 1/2 of lot 12, blk. 21, Wayne	$500.00
Elizabeth WERNICK to Alvin M. NICHOLS,	
3 1/2 ne 1/4 16 and w 1/2 nw 1/4, 15-25-5	6,500.00
A.L. DAVIS to D.J. CAVENAUGH,	
lot 5, blk. 4, Winside	2,000.00
D.J. CAVENOUGH to A.L. DAVIS,	
lot 9, blk. 5, Winside	700.00
Joseph FREED to Stephen C. DURHAM,	
lots 17, 17 and 18, blk. 14, College Hill	70.00
Thomas C. MORRIS to Daniel ISAAC,	
nw 1/4, 34-27-1	4,000.00
R.E.K. MELLOR to J.T. BRESSLER,	
Und. 1/2 of lot 17, blk. 12 and all of lot 12, blk. 21, Wayne	2,500.00
Catherine C. FOSTER to Robt. and O.T. RUBECK,	
ne 1/4, 13-26-4	1,700.00
Robt. and O.T. RUBECK to David LONGE,	
e 1/2 ne 1/4, 13-26-4	2,400.00
Neb. Normal College to S.M. CLARK,	
lots 4, 5 and 6, blk. 22, College Hill	- - -
Helen M. HENRY to F. FULLER,	
quit claim ne 1/2 and part nw 1/4, 17-26-4	6,000.00
G.L. LARSON to C.W. WORTH,	
ne 1/4, 29-25-4	4,480.00
Alvin M. NICHOLS to John McGUIRE,	
w 1/2 nw 1/4, 15-25-5	2,400.00

Randall FRAZIER to Joseph MILLARD, trustee, 1,427 acres in Wayne county	$59,245.00
Nancy A. CULVER to A.W. and E.E. CULVER, ne 1/4, 1-25-5	6,000.00
Geo. MORRISON to H.E. PETERSON, se 1/4 and e 1/4 of ne 1/4, 20-26-5	8,000.00
Guy R. WILBUR to Lucy L. MILLER, w 1/2 lots 1, 2 and 3, blk. 7, Wayne	1.00
Emma L. VAN CAMP to Lucy L. MILLER, w 1/2 lot 4, blk 11, C&B's ad to Wayne	- - -

The Wayne Republican
March 11, 1896 (Vol. 3, No. 4)

BIRTH: Mr. and Mrs. MIESKY are the parents of a baby girl. (Hoskins)

MARRIED: David THOMAS and Ida EDWARDS both of this place were united in matrimony March 4. Rev. HUGHES performed the matrimonial services, then the bridal party drove to the home of the bride where a number of guests were invited to partake of a grand supper. We wish the young couple much success. They will move into their new home three miles west of Carroll, probably in a few days.

MARRIED: LUTH - LESSMAN. At the home of the bride's parents, Mr. and Mrs. H.W. LESSMAN, in Logan precinct, on Feb. 27th, occurred the marriage of Fred LUTH and Annie LESSMAN. Over 200 guests were present and the new couple start life with the best wishes of all accompanying them.

MARRIED: COPPLE - WILCOX. By Judge MARTIN on Feb. 26th, Elmer COPPLE and Sophronia WILCOX.

MARRIED: HENSCHKE - FOUSS. Feb. 27th, Ernest HENSCHKE and Rosa FOUSS.

MARRIED: LAASE - KAUFLE. March 2, Amos LAASE and Mary KAUFLE.

MARRIED: HUNT - WEBER. Feb. 26th, Harry HUNT and Annie E. WEBER, Rev. J.M. BOTHWELL officiating.

MARRIED: FISHER - HERRON. At the office of County Judge MARTIN on March 5, H.P. FISHER and Florence E. HERRON.

MARRIED: Emil ANDERSON of this county and Helen ANDERSON of Oakland were married at the home of the bride on Wednesday, March 4.

Public Sales.
E. CUNNINGHAM, Auctioneer.

On Wednesday, March 11, W.J. WHITE southwest of Wayne will sell cattle, hogs, horses and implements.

On Thursday, March 12, at his home one mile west of Wayne, Ran FRAZIER will sell horses, cattle, hogs and implements. This will be a big sale.

Sophus THOMPSON 6 miles west of the city at 12 o'clock on the 13th of March. Horses, cattle, hogs and implements.

Chas. NYDAHL 3 1/2 miles south of Wayne on Monday, March 16. Horses, hogs and implements.

Paul HEYER 2 miles northeast of Winside on Thursday, March 19 at 12 o'clock. Horses, cattle, hogs and implements.

• • •

I.W. ALTER
Bonded Abstractor, Writes Insurance
and makes Collections.
Wayne, Nebraska

• • •

The Wayne Republican
March 18, 1896 (Vol. 3, No. 5)

BIRTH: Griffie GARWOOD and wife are rejoicing over the arrival of a boy at their home March 12. (Carroll)

BIRTH: The home of F.M. NORTHROP was made glad this morning by the birth of a fine boy.

LICENSED TO WED: A license to wed was issued by Judge MARTIN on the 14th to Harry G. OGDEN and Reba BROWN.

MARRIED: HUTCHINS - SNELL. At the home of the bride on March 10, William HUTCHINS and Viola SNELL were united in marriage by Rev. F.M. CLARK.

MARRIED: RETHWISCH - STOLTENBERG. At the office of the county judge today, March 18, Adolph RETHWISCH and Annie

STOLTENBERG both of this county.

MARRIED: March 11 Everett ROBERTS and Kate HUNT were married at the bride's home, the young couple have the good wishes of their numerous friends.

DIED: March 13 at 8 o'clock p.m., Byron HOLMES a son of Hans HOLMES of Sherman precinct, 11 years old. He was taken ill about 10 days previous to his death with lagrippe which terminated in brain fever, which ended his time here on earth.

DIED: The infant child of Dr. and Mrs. CHERRY of Winside died at their home on yesterday and will be buried today. The sympathy of friends will be extended to them in the loss of the dear one.

Real Estate Transfers.

Fred SHELLENBERG to August SHELLENBERG, w 1/2 nw 1/4, 22-23-1	$1,600.00
Wm. FAIRBAIN to Wm. McMILLAN, n 1/2 ne 1/4, 4-25-3	3,400.00
Carl THOMPSON to Louis MUELLER, e 1/2 nw 1/4, 29-25-4	2,640.00
R.J. and J.J. TRACY to BUOL & BUOL, se 1/4 sw 1/4 and n 1/2 of se 1/4, 14-26-3	2,500.00
J.E. HAYES to E.W. CULLEN, lots 24, 25 and 26, blk. 4, Winside	600.00
A.B. CHARDE to B.W. ASHLEY, lots 10, 11 and 12, blk. 26, College Hill	75.00
Neb. Normal College to J.L. WINGERT, lot 10, blk. 1, College Hill	35.00
C.E. PERKINS to Erick STAMM, sw 1/2, 4-25-1	1,500.00
Ed REYNOLDS (sheriff) to S. HARDENBAUGH, s 1/2 lot 1, blk. 9, B&B ad to Wayne	675.00
Margaret AVERILL to John C. BENDER, lot 13, blk. 2, Winside	800.00
A.M. NICHOLS to First National Bank, e 1/2 ne 1/4, 16-25-5	2,400.00

Jurors for the April 1896 Term.

W.P. AGLER, W.S. BROWN, James BUSH, John DONNER, Christ ECKMAN, A.C. GOLTZ, W.E. GLEASON, Charles JONES, Evan JENKINS, W.C. LOWRY, Joe A. LOVE, J.R. MANNING, J.R. MORRIS, J.P. MARVIN, S.H. McMAKIN, Dan McMANIGAL, W.H.

ROOT, S.D. RELYEA, I.W. STEEL, Fred SCHROEDER, Jr., Frank STEWART, John SHANNON, C.W. WORTH.

**The Wayne Republican
March 25, 1896 (Vol. 3, No. 6)**

MARRIED: MONTGOMERY - DAMME. At the M.E. parsonage March 25, Rev. MILLARD officiating, Geo. MONTGOMERY, of Coon Rapids, Iowa, and Anna DAMME, of this county.

DIED: A small child of H.H. JONES living 7 miles southwest of Carroll died on the 20th and was buried in the Welch cemetery.

Billy Was Loose.
Last evening was one long to be remembered by Logan Valley Camp of Modern Wodsmen. For some time the members of the Camp and the Royal Neighbors, the Ladies' Auxiliary had been looking forward with considerable anticipation to this date. The neighboring Camps of Pilger, Laurel, Dixon, Carroll, Hoskins, Winside and Wakefield had been extended invitations to be present and participate in the work and be entertained by the home Camp and Royal Neighbors. How well they responded to the invitation is best told by a list of those present from abroad. Winside headed the list with 22 members and several of them brought their wives, they were: M.H. DODGE, Dorr CARROLL, H. WOODWARD, F. BROWER, Paul HEYER and wife, John MORIN, John JASZKOYIACK, Anton JENSEN, Peter SWENSON, Chris HANSEN, Frank METTLEN, H.P. PETERSON, F. PERRIN and wife, Andrew HUPP, Geo. WRIGHT, Wm. GUE, Geo. WESTROPE and wife, W.I. LOWRY, D.J. CANANAUGH, Henry PACKRANDT, John BILLMAN, Herman PIEPGRASS, D.W. SHAW. Next in point of numbers come Wakefield with an even 20 and some of their wives, here they are: C.W. LONG, Wm. WHEELER, C.L. HERRINGTON and wife, J.M. JOHNSON and wife, J.A. BLOTCKY, R. WALDEN, J.C. CRAMER, J.B. CARY, J.E. HEYL, Thos. RAWLINGS, W.S. EBERSOLE, Newell SIMPSON, Geo. BANNON, L. LeMAY, J.L. ROWSE and wife, Frank JOHNSON, Detlef KAY, Eph. ANDERSON, C.FOLTZ, E. WICKE. Pilger sent 9, they were: J. DOTY, F. SIMONS, W. LAYTON, Ed. ABBOTT, H. ELLIS, D. GANDY, H. VAIL, F. LOWDER, Theo. OLK, D.R. ROUSS. Carroll responded with R.D. MERRILL, B.W. WINELAND, Geo BELFORD, M.S. LINN, J.B. TAYLOR, J.H. BEACH and J.H. BUTLER. Dixon sent John OTT, John ROBINSON and Joshua ROBINSON, AW. ROUSS and two others whose names we failed to get. Laurel had present Will SERBER, Alex and Roy JEFFREY. Hoskins received an invitation

but for some reason or other was unable to send any delegation except Commissioner HARRIGFELDT who was in the city and present. First thing on the program was the adoption ceremony of several new members by the camp and about the time the ceremonies were concluded sweet strains of music were wafted to the ears of the assembled neighbors as the Wayne Band came marching toward the camp, quickly the doors were opened and in came the ladies who informed the weary waiting workers that a banquet was in waiting. To the banquet hall the assemblage wended its way and what a layout. The Royal Neighbors proved conclusively that they were of blood royal as entertainers for mortal men never sat down to a board more heavily laden with the fruits of a land filled with plenty. The quartette of WOODMEN, HOLTZ, GOODYEAR, McINTOSH and WINTERBURN and the band discoursed vocal and instrumental music while all partook of the abundant and excellent solids and dainties provided by the ladies. About 250 persons were present and enjoyed the evening after the banquet in music by the trio, COOK, HAYS and TITSWORTH, and the quartette and in listening to remarks by the neighbors from visiting camps and some of the boys of the home camp. It was a red letter day for the camp of this city and the boys all feel that too much cannot be said in praise of the ladies of the Royal Neighbors who made the occasion one of the happiest and most successful events in the history of all the city's social entertainments. The camp feels itself under lasting obligations to the visiting neighbors for the manner in which they turned out and helped to make the event so grand a success, and to the Wayne Band for the excellent music that added so greatly to the happiness of the occasion.

Real Estate Transfers.

Wm. BENSHOOF to C.A. GROTHE, part ne 1/4 se 1/4, 13-26-3	$480.00
BENSHOOF & GROTHE to BENSHOOF & TOWER, lot 6, & n 15 ft lot 15, blk. 28, Wayne	1,055.00
C.B. FRENCH jr., to J.C. BENDER, lot 28, blk. 2, Winside	500.00
J.M. SHERO to A. GOLTZ, lot 19, blk. 5, B&P's ad to Wayne	40.00
J.W. TILLSON to John BENDER, lot 14, blk. 2, Winside	450.00
Carl DANIELS to Aug SCHUMACHER, lots 1, 2, 3 and 5, blk. 5 in Hoskins, also 13 acres adjoining Hoskins on east	- - -
Douglas GAADY to F.A. DEARBORN, part ne 1/2 nw 1/4, 18-26-4	1,000.00

G.G. WESTROPE to J.C. BENDER,
　　75 ft lot 22, blk. 4, Winside　　　　　　　　$250.00
A.J. HONEY to H. HONEY,
　　n 1/2 nw, 20-27-2　　　　　　　　　　　　2,000.00

The Wayne Republican
April 1, 1896 (Vol. 3, No. 7)

BIRTH: It is a great big fine boy that came to take up his abode at the home of John KOEFOED on last Friday.

LICENSED TO WED: Louis TRAVER and Mary J. STONE.

DIED: PERFECT. At her residence northwest of this city Saturday, March 28, Mrs. S.B. PERFECT. The remains were taken to Harlan, Ia., for interment on Monday.

DIED: On Friday evening March 27, 1896, the spirit of Dedrich LESSMAN took its departure from this earth and its cares and sorrows. The deceased was just 70 years of age, the day of his death being the anniversary of his birth. For several years he has lived in what is known as the German settlement northeast of the city and has been one of the most respected members. He leaves behind a wife, several sons and daughters, besides a host of friends to mourn his departure.

The Wayne Republican
April 8, 1896 (Vol. 3, No. 8)

BIRTH: John STEPHENS is the happiest man in this county. Why? Because a bouncing big boy came to make his home with him last Sunday night.

MARRIED: SCHULZ - LENSER. On April 2 at the office of Judge MARTIN, Wm. SCHULZ and Emma LENSER were united in marriage.

The city election on Monday resulted in the election of Mark STRINGER, mayor; Charles BEEBE, clerk; L. ROE, treasurer; S.H. RICHARDS, councilman 1st ward; E.P. OLMSTED, 2nd ward; C.O. FISHER, 3rd ward. E.D. MITCHEll and A.F. BRENNER for full term board of education and J. TOWER fo till vacancy. A light vote was polled and but little interest manifested.

To the memory of little Johnnie, son of Mr. and Mrs. Henry JONES, who died at their home southwest of Carroll, March 20th, 1896:

  Cease your weeping, loving parents,
  For your Jonnie, bright and fair,
  He has left this world of sorrow,
  He has climbed the golden stair.

  You will miss your little Johnnie,
  You will miss him everywhere,
  At the hearth and 'round the table,
  There will be one vacant chair.

  He is with the happy angels,
  And no sorrow will he know,
  He is singing loud the praises,
  To the God that loved him so.

  May we all be ever ready,
  When the chilling summons come,
  So that we may meet our darlings,
  In that bright and heavenly home.

    Mrs. Evan JENKINS, Carroll, Neb.

Real Estate Transfers.

G.S. SHOEMAKER to D.J. RAWHOUSER,	
sw 1/4 & w 1/2 of w 1/2 se 1/4, 31-26-4	$1.00
Gus ECKMAN to Magnus ECKMAN,	
n 1/2 sw 1/4, 34-26-1	1,600.00
D.C. PATTERSON undivided 1/2 int. in Lots in	
sections 2, 11, 14, 23 and 35 in 26-5	750.00
R.L. OXFORD to Bloomfield State Bank,	
s 1/2 nw 1/4, 11-27-2	1,600.00

Court Proceedings.

 WIGHTMAN vs. LAUMAN, continued.
 STEVENS vs. KAUFMAN, dismissed at plaintiff's cost.
 TACKERBERRY vs. C.S. INGLES, sale confirmed; deed ordered.
 NORTHROP vs. BARRETT, sale confirmed, deed ordered, judgment against A. HEILSEN in favor of D. OLESON for $713.17.
 GOSHORN vs. NELSON, sale confirmed, deed ordered.
 STONE vs. BOSTROM, continued by agreement.

GOODRICH vs. RUDAT, et al., sale confirmed, deed ordered, motion to retax costs sustained.

FRENCH vs. John DELFS, deed ordered.

HARDENBURG vs. J.J. GILDERSLEEVE, judgment for plaintiff, $463.30.

SNYDER vs. VAN CAMP, on motion sustained and charge for printing reduced to $13.

State vs. SNEATH, dismissed on payment of costs.

SCHNIEDER vs. SORENBERGER, funds ordered paid to intervenor, plaintiff excepts, 40 days to prepare bill or exceptions, motion for new trial overruled.

MILLER vs. WORKINGS, settled and dismissed.

BRESSLER vs. VAUGHN, foreclosure as prayed.

WRIGHT vs. HANSEN, judgment for plaintiff, $756.90.

Wayne Co. Bank vs. WOOD, et al., default against August and Ursala LOHBERG, Gustave and Augusta WENT, Decree ordered.

EVERETT & WAIT vs. BOUCHER, finding for plaintiff, $161.38, decree as prayed.

Decrees of foreclosure in the following cases:

BRESSLER vs. KING; BURR vs. HAM; same vs. BRYANT; BURR vs. R.J. TRACY; same vs. WILBUR; same vs. BEALS; same vs. J.J. TRACY.

Rialto, et al., vs. SEIFKEN; MEYER vs. HUTH; Citizens Bank vs. WOLF; TUCKER vs. STEWART; MELLOR vs. VAUGHN; Merchants State Bank vs. Winside Roller Mill Co.; GOLTZ vs. MAHIKE; HAM vs. JAMES; PINGREY vs. BEALE; HARRINGTON & ROBBINS vs. WELBAUM.

BRADY vs. MAHER, judgment for plaintiff, attached property ordered sold.

SHUMWAY & EVERETT vs. LONGNECKER, judgment for plaintiff, attached property ordered sold.

State vs. WEICH, not guilty, defendant discharged.

NEFF vs. C.St.P.M. & O. Ry Co., continued.

MILLER vs. KARO, appeal dismissed, costs taxed to KARO.

BARTELS vs. BARTELS, decree of divorce granted.

MIDDLESTADT & Co. vs. VANSHUER, continued by consent.

MERRIMAN vs. STUBBS, F.M. NORTHROP appointed guardian ad litem of minor defendants.

TALBOTT vs. JAMES, A.A. WELCH appointed guardian ad litem of minor defendants.

Wayne National Bank vs. SMITH, continued by agreement.

SMITH & ELLIS Co. vs. FRAZIER, leave given sheriffs of Wayne and Douglas counties to amend returns.

FURCHNER, DUERIG & Co. vs. Home Fire Ins. Co., settled and dismissed; same vs. Home Ins. Co. of N.Y.; same vs. above; same vs. Phila. Underwriters; same as above.
    WELCH vs. BEALE, continued.
    WATTS vs. GANDT, judgment for plaintiff.
    MULLER vs. WESSELSCHMIDT, confirmed, deed ordered.
    MIDDLESTADT vs. BENTHIAN, decree for plaintiff.
    SEVERNS vs. SEVERNS, default against defendant.
    SHUEL vs. HUNT, decree for plaintiff.
    Decrees entered for plaintiffs, as follows:
    MIDDLESTADT vs. ECKMAN.
    WALDREF vs. CAHOON.
    McBRIDE vs. BUCHOLTZ.
    DODGE vs. KRUGER.
    Citizen's Bank vs. DOBBIN.
    TALBOT vs. JAMES.
    BOGART vs. TALLMAN.

The Wayne Republican
April 15, 1896 (Vol. 3, No. 9)

BIRTH: To Carter COX and wife Friday April 10 a girl of the regulation size and weight. (Carroll)

BIRTH: To Joe BELDON and wife a boy on Sunday April 12. (Carroll)

DIED: Mrs. Martha E. PERFECT was born in Kentucky the 26th day of April, 1844, and died at her home near Wayne Thursday March 26th 1896, making her 51 years and 11 months. Her maiden name was HARLAN. At the age of 17 she moved with her uncle's family to Greencastle, Ind., where she was united in marriage to Oliver T. GREEN. Unto them was born six children, two of those children died in infancy and preceded her to that better world, while four remain with us, two sons and two daughters. In her 33rd year she was united in marriage to Mr. S.B. PERFECT; unto them has been born one child, a daughter. Our sister leaves a husband, three daughters, two sons, a step son and a large number of other relatives and friends to mourn her departure.

    Our beloved sister gave her heart to Jesus at the early age of 14, and thus became identified with the church of Christ, of which she was a faithful member until her death. She was a true wife and model mother. Through all of her trials in life and in the trying hours of her sickness she put her trust in God and her Lord

Jesus Christ. Her life was exemplary both in the church and at home. Her loved ones can truly call her "blessed," and thank God for such a mother. Her friends who loved her because they knew her will ever feel that the world is better because she has lived in it. Her influence will rest over all as a sweet benediction. She has gone to her reward and her works do follow her.

Court Proceedings.
(Continued from last week)

C.B. FRENCH vs. ROHLFS, confirmed, deed ordered.

BAYES vs. Wayne National Bank, jury failed to agree, discharged and cause continued.

TILLSON vs. WALLOR, plaintiff to file brief.

BRESSLER vs. HURLBURT, continued.

HURLBURT vs. SUNDALL, continued by consent.

BOYD vs. MELLOR, demurrer overruled, defendant to plead in 20 days.

State of Nebraska ex rel. Bert BROWN vs. S.B. RUSSELL, evidence submitted, given time to file brief.

HURLBURT vs. SUNDALL, motion to disolve, attachment denied.

Citizens Bank vs. GLEASON, et al., plaintiff: 1st lien; EDWARDS & BRADFORD Lbr. Co.: 2nd lien; Aultman Taylor Machine Co.: 3rd lien.

SAWYER vs. OXFORD, default against all defendants except John MARUE.

OLMSTED & Co. vs. MIDDLETON, judgment lower court affirmed.

H.P. SHUMWAY trustee vs. CRANE, finding for defendants.

Republican Convention.
Ex-Senator BRESSLER gets the Delegation
to Norfolk by a vote of 29 1/2 to 20 1/2.

The convention was called to order by Nelson GRIMSLEY, chairman of county central committee. Frank FULLER was elected termporary chairman and George HARRIGFELDT, Secretary. A committee of five consisting of John SHANNON, R. PHILLEO, Chas. BEEBE, E. HUNTER and W.F. SEARS were appointed on credentials and reported credentials for delegates from every precinct in the county being a total of 53 delegates, but when it came to voting it was found that although credentials were in the hands of the convention for three delegates from Garfield there was none of them present to cast the vote. The report of the committee on credentials was accepted and a motion prevailed to make temporary organization permanent. A motion then prevailed to proceed by vote of precinct to designate choice of convention for district delegate and that the one receiving highest number of votes be permitted to name his delegates. Roll of precincts called and BRESSLER received 29 1/2 votes and GRIMSLEY 20 1/2. BRESSLER then named the following as delegates to Norfolk for April 22. Frank FULLER, Robt. UTTER, W.H. HOGUEWOOD, A.W. TAYLOR, W.H. McNEAL, A.T. CHAPIN, Perrin LONG, F.M. NORTHROP, E.D. MITCHELL, George HARRIGFELDT. On motion a committee of five was appointed to select delegates to state convention and W.H. McNEAL, J.J. WILLIAMS, R. RUSSEL, John DONNER and A. GOULD were appointed such committee and they named the following delegates: J.T. BRESSLER, E. HUNTER, F.M. SKEEN, M.S. MERRILL, W.F. SEARS, Lert HOILE, Mark JEFFREY, Eli McCONOUGHY and R. PHILLEO. The following was then passed with a whoop:

RESOLVED: That we fully recognize the importance at this time of the success of the principles established and maintained by the Republican party. Believing that the welfare of the people can be best promoted by the election of a Republican president at the coming election.

We believe that it is the sentiment of the people of this country that the political theories of the present administration are producing serious business distrubances and have worked great injury to the materal welfare of our people, and we, the republicans of Wayne county, reaffirm our belief in the principles of protection and reciprocity as advocated by the republican party since it came into control of national affairs.

Believing, therefore, in these principles, we affirm that in our judgment there is no man more fully represents the great mass of republicans, no man who can be better intrusted with the final decision of all questions effecting the welfare of the people, no man who can better command the support of Republicans than that brave soldier, distinguished citizen, and eminent statesman, William McKINLEY, Jr., of Ohio.

We therefore ask our representatives in the state and district convention to use their influence to the end that the delegates from Nebraska to St. Louis shall be unanimously in favor of this great Republican leader.

The Wayne Republican
April 22, 1896 (Vol. 3, No. 10)

BIRTH: To Melvin CASE and wife, April 18, a daughter.

MARRIED: WHIPPERMAN - BECKENHAUER. On April 15, in the city of Wayne, George WHIPPERMAN and Louise BECKENHAUER.

MARRIED: At Wayne on April 21, Arthur ZEIGLER and Emma ZEIMER, both of Hoskins. The entire community heartily extends congratulations to the newly wedded pair and bid them God speed on life's voyage.

DIED: A little child of Wm. SCHREIBER living at Apex, died on Saturday.

Sixteen to One.
That's What the Democratic Convention of Saturday Was.
The Administration Fellows Refuse to
Participate in Its Deliberations.

The democratic convention as called by the central committee of the party in the county met at the court house on Saturday afternoon April 18 and was called to order by the chairman of the central committee, J.W. ZEIGLER. On the roll of precincts being called it was shown that Chapin, Brenna, Deer Creek, Garfield, Hunter, Leslie, Logan, Sherman, Second and Third Wards of the city of Wayne had no accredited delegates. The delegates present proceeded by motion to fill delegations from these precincts by electing any democrat present as delegate to represent their precincts. Temporary organization was effected by electing Andy SHINN chairman and Walter GAEBLER Secretary. A committee on resolutions was then appointed by the chair consisting of J.W. ZEIGLER, D.B. TALLMAN and E.R. LUNDBURG. Then by motion the temporary organization was made permanent.

On motion Fred VOLPP, Ed. CULLEN and R. FENSKE were appointed a committee to select delegates to the convention to be held at Lincoln today. The following were named as the delegates: R. FENSKE, D.B. TALLMAN, D.A. JONES, Wm. WOLVERTON, C.A. BERRY, E.R. LUNDBURG and Andy SHINN. The committee on resolutions reported resolutions endorsing the platform as enunciated by the convention held at Omaha, August 22, 1895. ZEIGLER made a motion that was adopted expressing the sentiment of the convention as being in favor of W.J. BRYAN as their favorite for president, and convention adjourned after instructing the chairman of the county central committee to call the next convention for the nomination of county officers and selecting delegates to the different conventions of the party.

The Wayne Republican
April 29, 1896 (Vol. 3, No. 11)

BIRTH: Tuesday, April 28, at the home of P.H. KOHL, a girl.

MARRIED: RUNYON - GILSON. On Saturday, April 25, John T. RUNYON and Cora M. GILSON were united in marriage by Rev. MILLARD at the parlors of the Boyd.

James PORTERFIELD, J.R. HOOVER, Wm. VINCENT, J.J.W. FOX, M.O. CUNNINGHAM, Chas. HOLTGREEN, M.I. JUHLIN, H. LEY, A.A. WELCH, I.W. ALTER and Charley WARNER were Wayne Odd Fellows in attendance at the big celebration in Sioux City on Tuesday.

Real Estate Transfers.

J.W. ZEIGLER to Enno HEREN, w 1/2 sw 1/4 & sw 1/4 nw 1/4, 6-26-3	$3,050.00
Logan Valley Land Co. to M.S. DAVIES, lot 4, blk. 5 n ad Wayne	100.00
F. KRUGER to John ZWIGHT, se 1/4	4,000.00
Sheriff to H. BUCHOLZ, nw 1/4, 19-25-1	1,604.56
Sheriff to W. WORTHING, nw 1/4, 15-26-2	1,100.00

Someone on Friday morning undertook to bring to an end the earthly career of a canine by the gun route, and evidently was a very poor marksman in so far as hitting dogs was concerned, but came very nearly enacting a tragedy. The bullet in its course passed through a window in the residence of Geo. GELDER, passed over a couch where the children were sleeping and struck the hard coal burner where it was picked up by a member of the family. It would be well for dog exterminators to exercise greater care, as there are hardly enough dogs on earth to pay for injuring one human being.

The Pie Biters Meet.
Thirteen by Actual Count Come Together
and Declare That They are not Dead.
No Resolutions, No Nothing, Only to do
the Will of To Be, The Dispenser.

The post office pie-biter rustled around on Monday afternoon and got together, so he says, thirteen, a very unfortunate number, democrats who believe in GROVER and held a county convention of about ten minutes duration. Guy R. WILBUR was elected chairman and A.P. CHILDS secretary. The following were named as delegates to the pie biters' convention to be held at Lincoln today. A.B. CHARD, A.P. CHLDS, Guy R. WILBUR, J.T. METTLEN, H.F. WILSON, J.H. MITCHELL, J. REICHERT and Al HOUSER. Convention then adjourned.

The Wayne Republican
May 6, 1896 (Vol. 3, No. 12)

BIRTH: To Henry KREBS and wife Monday, May 4, a boy of regulation weight and size.

MARRIED: At the residence of the bride's mother in Carroll, Wednesday, May 6, 1896, Mr. Hugh HOUSE to Miss Mae McVAY, Rev. HATHERALL officiating. The bride is well known here, having lived in Carroll for several years. The groom is one of Wayne county's prosperous farmers. The happy couple start out in life with them the best wishes of their many friends.

MARRIED: HOLTZ - McCRARY. At the home of June CONGER on Tuesday evening, May 5, Alex HOLTZ and Miss Maggie McCRARY were united in marriage. The ceremony was performed by Rev. THEOBALD. The newly married couple will carry with them in their new relations the best wishes of a host of friends who will join the Republican in extending to them congratulations.

DIED: WATSON. At his home 5 1/2 miles north of the city of Wayne on Tuesday morning, May 5, Andrew WATSON aged 70 years. The deceased was quite well and very favorably known and while his death was not wholly unexpected yet it gave to his neighbors quite a shock. He had been ailing for quite a length of time but was not confined to his room until last Thursday. The immediate cause of death was heart disease. The funeral services will be held at his late home at two o'clock today and the interment will be at the Wayne cemetery.

The old council wound up its affairs on Monday evening and adjourned sine die. Mayor STRINGER promptly called the new council to order and proceeded at once to business. The following committees were appointed: Streets and Alleys, OLMSTED FISHER and VOLPP; Finance, MAIN, RICHARDS and PIEPENSTOCK; Water, PIEPENSTOCK, VOLPP and MAIN. Geo L. MINER was appointed city marshal and Peter COYLE water commissioner. The bonds of clerk and treasurer accepted. Applications of D.T. WORKINGS, KRUGER & MILLNER, and O.A. BURSON for license to sell liquors and remonstrance against issuing of same read and Tuesday evening appointed for a hearing on same. Committees were appointed to inquire into the responsibility of parties signing bonds for applicants for saloon license and also to see that each applicant had the requisite number of resident freeholders attached thereto. Council will meet again tonight for the purpose of action on granting or refusing license to saloons.

Real Estate Transfers.

F. HOOD to John KRETTLE, lots 11 and 12, blk. 17, College Hill ad	$750.00
Sheriff to F.G. HAAS, ne 1/4, 33-26-3	450.00
W.E. GLEASON to Ernest BEHMER, lots 13, 14, 15, 16, 17, and 18, blk. 11, Hoskins	1,200.00
Ran FRAZIER to T.J. STEELE & Co., part sw 18-26-4, 1 1/2 acres	500.00
Ran FRAZIER to Anna McLAUGHLIN, lot 23, T&W's ad Wayne	400.00
John C. HAVERMEYER to Jas. MULVANEY, se 1/4, 9-27-1	2,000.00
L.F. HOLTZ to J.V. HEWER, lots 1, 2 and 3, Skeen's ad. to Wayne	500.00
Ed REYNOLDS to Peter N. NELSON, sheriff's deed, nw 13-26-4	3,450.00
Ed REYNOLDS to Daniel OLSEN, sheriff's deed, ne 26-27-2	160.00
Aug. SCHUMACHER to Martha E. LUTZ, lots 1, 2, 3, 4, and 5, blk. 5, Hoskins and 13 acres in ne 1/4, 27-25-1	800.00
Walter S. TAYLOR to James BARBOUR, lots 4, 5 and 6, blk. 4, College Hill ad to Wayne	100.00

The Wayne Republican
May 13, 1896 (Vol. 3, No. 13)

MARRIED: TRACY - BROWN. At Hartington on Tuesday, May 5, 1896, R.J. TRACY and Miss Ollie BROWN were united in marriage. The groom is a well known young man of our city. The bride is highly spoken of but to most of us is a stranger.

DIED: At her home in Sherman precinct, on Thursday, May 7th, Mrs. Vaughn DAVIS. The bereaved husband and family have the sympathy of many friends in the great loss occasioned by the death of wife and mother.

Obituary.

Mr. Andrew WATSON was born in Paisley, Scotland in October, 1826. A portion of his boyhood days was spent in Ireland. In the year 1884 he came to America bringing with him a paper signed by the Presbyterian minister at Letterkenny, Ireland. This minister (Andrew SPRAT) has known him from infancy and speaks of his integrity and Christian character in the highest degree. He resided in New York for a few years, then moved to Galena, Ill., where he remained until the year 1849 when he went to California. In 1857 he returned to Galena, Ill. In 1858 he was married to Miss Sarah HOPE. Five children were born to them, two sons and three daughters. Two of the daughters died in infancy. Mr. WATSON and family spent a part of their lives in Virginia and Wisconsin before moving to Nebraska. They lived near Scribner, Neb., from 1885 to 1890. The remainder of his life has been spent with his family on his farm six miles north of Wayne, where he passed peacefully away May 5th, 1896. He has always been a devoted member of the Presbyterian church until he came to Nebraska, never uniting with the church in this state, but always remaining firm in his belief. All who knew him honored him for his integrity and honesty. His loss is deeply felt by his friends and neighbors.

Real Estate Transfers.

McCLUSKY & NEEDHAM to Margaret C. AVERHILL,
    lot 28, blk. 4, Winside $225.00
Geo SMITH to Adolph KEIPER,
    s 1/2 se 1/4   1,200.00
O.O. WHITED to M.S. MERRILL,
    lots 1, 2, 3, 4, 5, and 6, blk. 6 1st ad to Carroll   - - -
F.M. SKEEN to J.T. BRESSLER,
    lot 8, blk. 12, n ad Wayne   75.00

The Wayne Republican
May 20, 1896 (Vol. 3, No. 14)

MARRIED: WATSON - SHINKLE. At the home of John LARISON in this city on Tuesday evening May 12, W.H. WATSON and Lucy SHINKLE, Rev. THEOBALD officiating. The contracting parties are well known young people of this county. They have gone to housekeeping on the farm of Mr. WATSON, northwest of the city and have the best wishes of their friends in their new relationship.

Sheriff's Sales.

The southeast quarter of southeast quarter of section 28 and north half of northwest quarter and southeast quarter of northwest quarter of section 33, township 25, range 2, sold as property of August and Herman HUTH on Monday June 8 at 10 o'clock.

On Monday June 15, at 10 o'clock: Lots 1 and 2, blk. 12, College Hill addition to Wayne, sold as property of Grant BOUCHER.

On Monday June 8 at 10 o'clock: Out lot 2 in C & B's addition to Wayne and part of out lot 1 in C & B's addition to Wayne, sold as property of Chas. DOBBIN, et al.

On Monday June 8 at 10 o'clock: the northeast quarter of 34, and southeast quarter of northwest quarter of 84-27-2, sold as property of C.H. WOLF, et al.

On June 15 at 10 o'clock, property of John and Ellen MAHER.

The graduating exercises of the high school will be held at the opera house Friday evening, May 29th. The following is the program.

Invocation	Rev. E. Van Dyke WIGHT
Music	Pupils of Intermediate Department
Necessity of Universal Education - Salutatory	Walden E. TUCKER
Does It Pay?	Pearl E. SEWELL
Unamerican Americana	Elsie M. MERRIMAN
Music	High School Chorus
Need of Strict Immigration Laws	Thos. COOK
The Old Woman	Mae L. CUNNINGHAM
Unwritten Biographies	Theo. E. SCACE
Music	Pupils of Grammar Department
Value of Competition	Chas. W. REYNOLDS
Class Poem	Pearl E. REYNOLDS
Stepping Stones to Higher Things - Class Will	Luke G. THOMPSON
Vocal Solo	Mae L. CUNNINGHAM
Value of Self Education - Valedictory	Edward B. PHILLEO
Presentation of Diplomas	A.A. WELCH
Music	High School Chorus
Benediction	Rev. H.H. MILLARD

The Wayne Republican
May 27, 1896 (Vol. 3, No. 15)

BIRTH: It's a great big girl and Carl and Mrs. FURCHNER are the proud parents.

MARRIED: At the residence of the bride's parents, Mr. and Mrs. ROBINSON northeast of Carroll, on Tuesday at 10:30, Mr. Louis LEWIS of Shubert, Neb., and Miss Della ROBINSON of Carroll, Neb., Rev. W.J. HATHERALL officiating. The friends of Mr. and Mrs. LEWIS will wish them much success in life. They took the afternoon train for their future home at Shubert, Neb.

DIED: JONES. At his home in Sherman precinct on Sunday afternoon, May 24th, the spirit of Owen W. JONES winged its way from earth to that other and better world on high. The deceased was 34 years of age and had been a resident of our county but four years, coming here from Montgomery county, Iowa, but in those four years had become quite well known throughout the county and was held in respect by all. In his death the community loses one of its best citizens and his neighbors a friend true at all times and under all circumstances. The immediate cause of his death was appendicitis for which an operation was performed on last Friday evening but it was too late and within 48 hours the lamp of life ceased to burn. He leaves to mourn his untimely going a loving wife, mother, brothers, sisters and friends by the score who feel that there is by his death a vacancy caused that cannot easily be filled. On Monday morning the remains were followed to Carroll by a large concourse of friends and neighbors and from thence shipped to Wales, Iowa, where the funeral occurred on Tuesday, May 26. It seems impossible that he is dead. Only a few days ago he was among us apparently in the full vigor of life, with grand prospects of usefulness, but the fell destroyer has come and taken him away. His remains were accompanied to his old home in Iowa by his wife, the companion of his joys and sorrows, and his aged mother and brother D. W., who arrived only a few hours prior to his death, and by his sisters, Mrs. J.A. JONES and Mrs. Howell REESE and the parents of his wife and J.A. JONES, Rev. and Mrs. Samuel JONES.

Wayne Lodge No. 120 A.F. & A.M., held its annual election of officers on Friday evening resulting as follows: E. CUNNINGHAM, M.W.; J. TOWER, S.W.; J.M. CHERRY, J.W.; Henry LEY, Treasurer and E. HUNTER, Secretary.

The Wayne Republican
June 3, 1896 (Vol. 3, No. 16)

MARRIED: BONER - BECKENHAUER. This morning June 3, at the home of the bride's parents in this city in the presence of a few of the chosen friends of the high contracting parties, Rev. E. Van Dyke WIGHT pronounced the magic words that bind for life William W. BONER and Lily May BECKENHAUER.

The groom is the present very efficient principal of the schools of the city, a position he has filled acceptably for the past two years. During his stay in our midst he has made a host of friends by this gentlemanly manners and straightforward course as a citizen and teacher.

The bride is the daughter of Mr. and Mrs. Henry BECKENHAUER and has made the city her home since early childhood. She has a host of friends who have always respected and admired her and who will today join in wishing the newly married pair a happy and successful voyage in life. Mr. and Mrs. BONER left on this morning's west bound train for Lincoln where they expect to remain for a few weeks and then go to Missouri, returning to Wayne and being at home to their friends after August 17th.

MARRIED: CONKLIN - McGUIRE. At Pleasant Valley M.E. church in Leslie precinct on May 26, Rev. D.W. McGREGOR united in marriage Charles L. CONKLIN and Anna M. McGUIRE. The groom is a resident of Red Oak, Iowa, and is highly spoken of by those acquainted with him. The bride is the daughter of John McGUIRE of Leslie, one of its oldest settlers. She numbers her friends by the hundred and many were the valuable and useful presents she and her husband received on the wedding day. We had intended to give a list of the presents but find it impossible on account of our limited space this week. Soon after the ceremony the couple left on a bridal trip to Denver and other western points after which they will return to Red Oak to make their future home. The Republican desires to join their host of friends in bidding them God speed on life's journey.

MARRIED: CARLSON - CARLSON. At the office of Judge MARTIN on May 26, John A. CARLSON and Anna M. CARLSON, both of Randolph, were joined in matrimony.

MARRIED: SPAHR - BRUNER. On Tuesday June 2, at the M.E. parsonage, Rev. MILLARD officiating, J.H. SPAHR and Maude

BRUNER. Mr. SPAHR and his bride are quite well known in this vicinity and are highly respected by all who have the privilege of their acquaintance. The Republican wishes to join in congratulations.

DIED: SPAHR. On May 7th at his home in Lamberton, O., Rev. Gideon SPAHR. Deceased was born in Virginia, Feb. 16, 1813, and was the eldest of twelve children. Four brothers survive him, Matthias, of Red Key, Ind.; James E., of this county; David and Thomas of Green county, Ohio. The funeral services were held in the M.E. church at Lamberton, on May 9th. The sympathy of our community will be with his brother James E. who is one of our best and most respected citizens.

Court.

Bert BROWN wins his suit as clerk of district court.

The railroad company was beaten in its claim for overpayment of taxes.

J.H. WILSON, the wheat thief, plead guilty to burglary and was sentenced to two years in the penitentiary.

The Wayne Republican
June 10, 1896 (Vol. 3, No. 17)

The Loyal Legion effected an organization on Friday evening and elected A.P. CHILDS, W.C.; Mrs. NEIMAN, W.V.C.; P.M. CORBIT, Prophet; F.W. BURDICK, Sec'y and M. STRINGER, Treas.

Real Estate Transfers.

D.T. HALLETT to Marion HALLETT, e 1/2, 8-25-5	$8,000.00
James BARBOUR to Andrew HUFF, lots 10, blk. 8, B&P ad to Wayne	80.00
F.M. NORTHROP to L. PRESTON, lots 8 and 0, blk. 15, Wayne	150.00
Calantha AMENT to Nellie AMENT, lots 7, blk. 23, Wayne	1.00
L. NURENBERGER to H.J. NUERENBERGER, se 1/4, 25-5	1.00
J.T. METTLEN, south 100 ft lot 19, blk. 3, Winside	27.00
H.J. NUERENBERGER to Adam NURENBERGER, s 1/2 of sw 1/4, 27-26-5	1.00

J.J. HAYES to Fred KOHL,
  lots 11 and 12, blk. 2, and lot 1, blk. 3,
  B&P ad to Winside $558.00

The Wayne Republican
June 17, 1896 (Vol. 3, No. 18)

MARRIED: FREY - GILFERT. At Judge MARTIN's office, he presiding on June 16, Thomas FREY and Lydia GILFERT were married.

COMMISSIONER PROCEEDINGS, Wayne, Neb., June 15, 1896.
  Board met in regular session. All members present. The following proceedings were had and done, to wit:
  Settlement was made with C.A. McVEY road overseer Dist No. 24, amount found due him $1.96 and warrant ordered drawn on general fund for same.
  The following claims were examined and allowed and warrants ordered drawn on county general fund for same:

Perry BENSHOOF, assessing Brenna	$63.00
C.C. BROWN, assessing Strahn, claimed $81.00, allowed	79.40
J.L. CLINE, assessing Hoskins, claimed $64.00, allowed	62.00
P. COLEMAN, assessing Plum Creek	72.00
Jno. O. DOBBIN, assessing Garfield	78.00
Levi DILTS, assessing Logan	41.90
J.J.W. FOX, assessing Hunter	70.00
J.A. JONES, assessing Sherman	75.00
L. SIMMERMAN, assessing Deer Creek	93.00
Perrin LONG, assessing Hancock	75.00
G.A. LEWIS, assessing Chapin	42.00
J.P. MARVIN, assessing Winside	40.50
N.H. NYE, assessing Leslie	47.00
R.C. OSBORN, assessing Wayne	130.00
D. SHAY, assessing Wilbur	75.00
St. L. Ref. & W.C. Co., car piling	165.18
Harry BENSER, unloading piling	2.50
SMITH & ELLIS Co., lumber	71.50
SMITH & ELLIS Co., lumber	284.35
Gus WENDT, unloading tile	2.00
W.C. PARSONS, hardware	3.50
E. & B. Lbr. Co., Hoskins, lumber	40.37
E. & B. Lbr. Co., Hoskins, lumber	67.39

W.M. GUE, viewing road and dray	$3.50
A. HUPP, viewing road and dray	3.00
J.R. MORRIS, viewing road and dray	4.60
John AGLER, road work	6.25
Ray AGLER, road work	8.90
W.P. AGLER, road work	8.90
J.A. BARBOUR, road work	5.00
N.B. CULLEN road work	2.50
B.F. EASTBURN, road work	22.50
Adam GRIER, road work	7.50
Bell GROAT, road work	12.50
Fred KAY, road work	2.50
Jacob REICHERT, road work, claimed $9.00, allowed	7.50
Jno. REINHART, road work	1.25
I.O. RICHARDSON, road work, claimed $15.00, allowed	12.50
Fred TRUEDLER, road work	1.25
E.K. WILLIAMS, road work, claimed $35.35, allowed	34.95
A.T. WADDELL, road work	27.50
A.T. WADDELL, road work	13.75
John ZEIMER, road work	40.62
PERKINS Bros. Co., supplies	32.15
PERKINS Bros. Co., supplies	4.25
PERKINS Bros. Co., supplies	52.00
E. CUNNINGHAM, printing and circulars	13.25
Dorr H. CARROLL, printing	12.25
L.E. HUNTER, stationery	11.40
Otto VOGET, repairs at jail	6.25
P. COYLE, water at jail	10.00
R.W. WILKINS & Co., paper for jail	20.50
W.C. BONHAM, papering jail	18.00
Howard COEN, moving pauper	2.00
R.P. WILLIAMS, boarding pauper	1.50
A. PIEPENSTOCK, provisions for tramps	.75
R.J. ARMSTRONG, coal for court house	5.45
E.S. BLAIR balance salary as county physician (Jan.)	16.50
G.A. BENSON, grader repairs	3.25
Carl F. LENZ, grader repairs	4.90
Albert JOHNSON, refund tax	1.13
Carl F. LENZ, blacksmithing	4.90
L.A. MARVIN, cutting weeds	.50

T.J. WELTY, expert work	$36.00
T.J. WELTY, expert work	36.00
T.J. WELTY, expert work	36.00
P.H. KOHL, refund taxes	6.00
Geo. HARRIGFELDT, transportation of pauper	3.00
Geo. HARRIGFELDT, commissioner fees	61.60
Mark JEFFREY, commissioner fees	50.70
A.M. JACOBS, commissioner fees	52.80

This being the day set for the letting of contracts for furnishing the county lumber for the ensuing year, and the board having carefully examined the bids filed, the contracts were let as follows:

Wakefield - Geo. CHILDS; Wayne - SMITH & ELLIS Co.; Winside - L.C. MITTELSTADT & Co.; Hoskins, Carroll and Randolph - EDWARDS & BRADFORD Lumber Co.

Each of said contractors to sign contract and furnish a bond in the sum of $500 with approved sureties.

The following appropriations were made to the several road districts of the county, hereby authorizing the overseers to hire work done on the road in an amount not to exceed the amount set aside hereby for their district, they to issue receipts therefor, which receipts shall be attached to the claim of the person performing said labor as a voucher:

No. 1.	60.00	Eli McCONOUGHEY.
No. 2.	55.00	J.R. SHAWGO.
No. 3.	50.00	J.W. AGLER.
No. 4.	100.00	John WEATHERHOLT.
No. 5.	40.00	Herman ROHMUS.
No. 6.	40.00	N.B. CULLEN.
No. 7.	50.00	John HARDER.
No. 8.	40.00	F.O. MARTIN.
No. 9.	65.00	- - -
No. 10.	60.00	C.A. KILLIAN.
No. 11.	40.00	P.M. PETERSON.
No. 12.	30.00	J.A. BARBOUR.
No. 13.	- - -	Wayne.
No. 14.	- - -	Winside.
No. 15.	60.00	Jay E. WILSON.
No. 16.	65.00	Levi DILTS.
No. 17.	30.00	I.O. RICHARDSON.
No. 18.	55.00	E.B. CHICHESTER.
No. 19.	70.00	O.C. LEWIS.
No. 20.	40.00	A.G. METTLEN.
No. 21.	40.00	O.W. MILLIKEN.

No. 22.	40.00	John KOEFOED.
No. 23.	50.00	A.B. JEFFREY.
No. 24.	45.00	John I. STEWART.
No. 25.	40.00	Jenkin DAVIS.
No. 26.	40.00	W.H. EASTBURN.
No. 27.	40.00	C.D. JONES.
No. 28.	- - -	Carroll.
No. 29.	50.00	Alf JONES.
No. 30.	45.00	Pat COLEMAN.
No. 31.	50.00	- - -
No. 32.	50.00	Michael EICH.
No. 33.	40.00	Jacob REICHERT.
No. 34.	50.00	Peter LIEF.
No. 35.	40.00	- - -
No. 36.	45.00	W.B. GROAT.
No. 37.	45.00	James STEPHENS.
No. 38.	40.00	James MULVANEY.
No. 39.	40.00	O.P. ANDERSON.
No. 40.	40.00	Adam GRIER.
No. 41.	40.00	Clause OTTE.
No. 42.	45.00	Leander SIMMERMAN.
No. 43.	40.00	August LOHBERG.
No. 44.	45.00	J.R. MORRIS.
No. 45.	40.00	H.W. BURNHAM.
No. 46.	40.00	W.H. PICKARD.
No. 47.	40.00	John BOOCKE.
No. 48.	45.00	Hayden HUTCHINSON.
No. 49.	45.00	Henry BRUSE.
No. 50.	40.00	Ed MILLER.
No. 51.	45.00	Wm. SCHULZ.
No. 52.	55.00	A.T. WADDELL.
No. 53.	55.00	Fred KRUSE.

No further business appearing the Board adjourned until June 23rd, 1896.

Attest: S.B. RUSSELL, Clerk.

In the First ward in the city 48 votes were cast at the primary on Friday evening. W.H. McNEAL and E. HUNTER received 9 votes each; W.H. HOGUEWOOD 8; their opponents, O.A. CHACE received 34; J.H. GOLL 33; and R.C. OSBORN 35. In the Third ward the tickets ran as follows: GRIMSLEY 37; SHERBAHN 37; CRAVEN 36; WADSWORTH 35; PHILLEO 36; FULLER 36; WILLIAMS 38; DAVIES 37, electing GRIMSLEY, SHERBAHN, WILLIAMS and DAVIES. In the Second: NEELY 30;

BUSH 29; McVICKERS 29; HOLTZ 29; BEEBE 20; GILDERSLEEVE 20; COOK 19; TOWER 20, electing the four first named. In Hunter, Plum Creek, Brenna, Hoskins, Chapin and some other precincts were all one sided and all had large attendances. Garfield held its caucus on Monday evening, but up to going to press we have been unable to learn the result, while Logan, Deer Creek, Sherman and Wilbur have not held theirs yet, but will undoubtedly elect delegates.

The republican caucuses in Wayne on last Friday evening resulted in the election of the following delegates to county convention: C.A. CHACE, R.C. OSBORN, J.H. GOLL, F.L. NEELY, James BUSH, Alex HOLTZ, D.S. McVICKERS, J.J. WILLIAMS, M.S. DAVIES, Nelson GRIMSLEY and John SHERBAHN. In Hunter precinct the delegates are J.J.W. FOX, O.P. ANDERSON, O.S. GAMBLE, H. CLAYBAUGH. In Plum Creek, Dan McMANIGAL, W.H. GILDERSLEEVE, S.K. WEST. Winside, A.H. CARTER, I.O. WOOLSTON. Brenna, James BAIRD, C. BENSHOOF, O.C. LEWIS. Chapin, Albert SALTER, W.C. LOWRY. Hancock, Perrin LONG, George HORNBY. Hoskins, Geo. HARRIGFELDT, John SHANNON, C. LENZ, W.C. PARSONS, John DONNER. Garfield held the caucus on Monday evening but the names of delegates chosen we have not learned. Sherman, Deer Creek, Strahn, Wilbur, Logan and Leslie are yet to be held.

The Wayne Republican
June 24, 1896 (Vol. 3, No. 19)

MARRIED: SAMSON - HAYE. At Fremont, Neb., on June 18, Rev. BUSS officiating, Roy SAMSON of Marion, Ia., and Grace HAYE were joined in wedlock. The bride will be recognized as a teacher in our primary department of schools a few years ago. She made many warm friends during her stay among us and they all join in extending congratulations.

DIED: On Thursday afternoon a 2-year-old child of Fred EICHOFF living about 11 miles southeast of the city fell into a tub of hot water and was so badly scalded about the head and upper part of the body as to cause its death the day following. It seems the mother was washing and had filled the tub with hot water and while her attention was called elsewhere the little one in playing about ran against the tub and fell in head first with the result indicated.

DIED: The 14-year-old son of John ROSEKA who lives on James BUSH's farm northwest of the city was overcome by the extreme heat of last Thursday forenoon and made his way to the barn of his employer, Mr. STONKE, where he lay down and was found shortly afterwards in a very precarious condition. Dr. WIGHTMAN was at once summoned but found the boy beyond human aid when he reached his bedside and in a little while the lad breathed his last.

The Wayne Republican
July 1, 1896 (Vol. 3, No. 20)

MARRIED: CHACE - WACHOB. At the home of the bride in Allegheny City, PA., on June 30, Nathan CHACE and Maude WACHOB. The groom is the well known assistant cashier of the First National Bank and is one of Wayne's best young men. The bride is a former resident of this place and numbers her friends here by the extent of her acquaintance. It goes without saying that the young couple will have the best wishes of their many friends and the Republican joins in extending its congratulations.

The Wayne Republican
July 8, 1896 (Vol. 3, No. 21)

BIRTH: On July 4th a new boy took up his residence at the home of O.H. MISKIMMONS.

DIED: PHILPOT. On July 2, Frank PHILPOT, aged 44 years. The cause of Mr. PHILPOT's death was diabetes from which he had been a sufferer for a considerable time. His mother, Mrs. WHIPPLE of Faulkton, S.D., and sister, Mrs. PETERSON, of Alta, Iowa, were with him at the time of death.

COMMISSIONERS PROCEEDINGS, Wayne, Neb., July 6, 1896.
    Commissioners met pursuant to adjournment. Members all present. The following proceedings were had and done, to wit:
    Comes now Myra D. FLETCHER and gives her report of the Institute Fund for the quarter ending June 30th, 1896, as follows, which report was approved:

On hand April 17, 1896	$145.65
Received from examinations	10.00
Total	$155.65
Paid to CUNNINGHAM for printing Institute announcements	$17.50

Amount on hand $138.15

Report of B.F. FEATHER showing no fines received by him and belong to the county to June 14th, 1896, approved.

The following claims were audited and allowed and warrants ordered drawn on the county general fund for same:

T.J. WELTY, examining records	$90.00
S.B. RUSSELL, salary and expenses	151.14
S.B. RUSSELL, freight car piling	93.33
Dorr H. CARROLL, printing	10.45
Dorr H. CARROLL, checking up car lumber	1.00
E. CUNNINGHAM, printing	17.90
A.A. WELCH, salary	162.50
Myra D. FLETCHER, salary and expense, claim $212.42, allowed	187.42
Henry LEY, rent court house	112.50
Ludwig ZEIMER, surveying road Dist. No. 38	22.20
E. MARTIN, costs State vs. WILSON	5.80
J.P. GAERTNER, coffin etc., PHILPOT	28.50
Ira RICHARDS, care PHILPOT	74.48
C.A. BAGGERT, cleaning	3.00
W.P. AGLER, bridge work	255.26
Harry BENSER, unloading lumber	3.00
Perry BENSHOOF, hauling lumber	5.00
Fred VOLPP, meat for tramps	.50
Carl F. LENZ, repairs grader	11.60
Perry BENSHOOF, road work	8.75
Fred J. BRUSE, road work	17.50
John BRUSE, road work	22.50
N.B. CULLEN, road work	7.50
Morse EVERINGHAM, road work	2.50
W.H. EASTBURN, road work	16.25
W.B. GROAT, road work	30.00
John KOEFOED, road work	7.50
J.L. HUNTER, road work	2.65
Mark JEFFREY (assignee) r'd wr'k	1.25
Peter LIEF, road work	35.00
Cal RITCHEY, road work	5.00
Cal RITCHEY, road work	15.00
I.W. STEELE, road work	2.50
Alex SCOTT, road work	2.50
A.T. WADDELL, road work	17.50
A.T. WADDELL, road work	12.50
Fred WEBBER, road work	3.35
Geo. WEATHERHOLT, road work	28.12

John WEATHERHOLT, road work	$28.38
John ZEIMER, road work	21.25
John ZEIMER, road work	16.25
SMITH & ELLIS Co., lumber	121.55
SMITH & ELLIS Co., lumber	197.95
Ed REYNOLDS, fees, State vs. BRADY	78.85
Ed REYNOLDS, fees, T.J. BRADY insane	10.05
Bert BROWN, fees, T.J. BRADY insane	11.25
E. MARTIN, witness, T.J. BRADY insane	2.00
L.C. GILDERSLEEVE, witness, T.J. BRADY insane	2.00
A.M. JACOBS, witness, T.J. BRADY insane	2.00

Contracts were made with the following parties for lumber for the following year: Geo. CHILDS, Wakefield; SMITH & ELLIS Co., Wayne; I.C. MITTELSTADT & Co., Winside.

On motion the county clerk is ordered to procure and keep as required by law, a register of instruments filed in his office, beginning with the first day of October, 1896.

On motion the county clerk is ordered to procure and keep a book in which he shall keep an account with each road district, showing the amount of money used in each, commencing with January 1st, 1896.

On motion board adjourned until tomorrow morning (July 7th) at 9 o'clock.

Attest: S.B. RUSSELL, Clerk.

The Wayne Republican
July 15, 1896 (Vol. 3, No. 22)

BIRTH: The home of Rev. WIGHT was made happy on Monday by the advent of their first born and it is a boy.

MARRIED: WOLVERTON - PALMER. At Judge MARTIN's office July 15, Samuel S. WOLVERTON and Ada PALMER.

Real Estate Transfers.

Aug. HUTH to Lena KIPKE, outlots 2, B&P ad to Winside	$2,400.00
Ira DAVENPORT to Mary E. REED, ne 1/4, 27-26-2	70.00
Tom LONND to Aug. DECK, lot 1 of outlot 2, B&P's 1st ad to Winside	3,000.00
Alvia LONGNECKER to C.C. MERRIMAN, nw 27-26-4	80.00

Logan Valley Land Co. to Ludwig ZEIMER,	
lots 1, 2, 3, 4, 5 and 6, blk. 12, Hoskins	$80.00
Ludwig ZEIMER to John SHANNON,	
lots 1, 2, 3, 4, 5 and 6, blk. 12, Hoskins	80.00
COONS MT and IJ to RICHARDS Bros.,	
part e 1/3 se 12-26-3 (Oliver property)	800.00
Chas. MAST to Minnie WILL,	
lot 12, blk. 8, Carroll	1,200.00
Logan Valley Land Co. to W.H. BUCHOLZ,	
lots 1, 2, and 3, blk. 14, Hoskins	78.00
Carl KIPKE to Aug. NEHRING,	
n 1/2 se 28 and e 1/2 ne, 34-25-2	1,000.00
Aug. NEHRING to Lena KIPKE,	
n 1/2 se 28 and e 1/2 34-25-2	1,000.00
L.W. POUTY to H.B. BOYD,	
n 100 ft lot 27, T&W's ad to Wayne	1,600.00
A.T. CHAPIN to HARDING Creamery,	
lot 14, blk. 6, B&P's ad to Winside	40.00
Elizabeth WERNICK to HOHNQUIST Grain & Lumber Co.,	
se 1/4, 18-27-1	3,250.00
E.B. MASON to Henry C. MOWRY,	
e 1/2, 29-27-1	1.00
E.B. CHICHESTER to C.C. MERRIMAN,	
n 1/2, 16-25-4	1,836.00
N.A. RAINBOLT to Wm. F. LALK,	
lot 5, blk. 3, Hoskins	400.00
H.B. BOYD to F.A. DEARBORN,	
lot 3, blk. 20, Wayne	5,000.00
W.A. IVORY to W.H. BILLITER,	
s 1/2 nw 1/2, 10-27-2	1,320.00
John ZWIGHT to Henry C. MATRAN,	
se 1/4, 19-25-2	4,000.00
F.M. SKEEN to Dan ROUSH,	
lots 7, 8 and 9, blk. 9, College Hill	130.00
James BRITTON to Henry LEY,	
the e 70 ft of lot 18, blk. 21, Wayne	7,000.00
Martin REDMER to Albert REDMER,	
se 1/2 29 and se 1/4 sw 1/4 28-25	6,000.00
John T. BRESSLER to James EVANS,	
lot 5, blk. 1, Winside	80.00
John T. BRESSLER and W.S. GOLDIE to Elizabeth A. FOLCK,	
lots 4, 5 and 6, blk. 6, east ad to Wayne	- - -
Elizabeth JONES to Thos. H. JONES,	
se 2-26-1	3,500.00

Robert H. JONES to Elizabeth JONES, w 1/2 ne 2-26-1	$2,400.00
G.W. TROTTER to Alf WOODWARD, lot 5, blk. 4, Wayne	1,500.00
Alf WOODWARD to G.W. TROTTER, nw 1/4, 17-26-2	4,000.00

The Wayne Republican
July 22, 1896 (Vol. 3, No. 23)

BURIAL: The infant child of Mr. and Mrs. Chas. KNAPP was buried in the Carroll cemetery Friday.

Advertised Letter List.

The following is a list of letters, etc., remaining in the Post office at Wayne Nebraska, for the week ending July 21, 1896.

W.A. COTTERELL, Mrs. Ella JONES, Wayne Clothing Co.

Parties calling for the above please give date when advertised.

A.P. CHILDS, P.M.

The Wayne Republican
July 29, 1896 (Vol. 3, No. 24)

BIRTH: A brand new baby girl took up her abode at the home of Geo. ROBERTS on yesterday.

BIRTH: A great big 10 pound boy came to gladden the home of Dan ROUSH on Saturday.

BIRTH: Mr. Gus WENT and wife are rejoicing over the arrival of a little girl a few days ago.

DIED: At his home in Henry, Illinois on July 14, 1896, Robert CLARK aged 72 years, 5 months, 26 days. The deceased was the father of our citizen, A.B. CLARK. He was one of the most high respected citizens of his community, and held many important offices and places of trust during his life. He was always a consistent christian whose hand was over extended in aid of the needy.

The Sixth Annual Sunday School Convention
Saturday Afternoon Session.
The convention was called to order by Pres. H.E. MASON.

It had been thought best that the evening division be also rendered in the afternoon.

Despite the small attendance on Saturday a great deal of interest and spirit was shown throughout the meeting. The convention was opened by a devotional meeting conducted by Chas. HOSTETTER, led in prayer by Rev. ECKHART. A short talk on "Why We Organize Sunday Schools," was given by Lloyd CUNNINGHAM. The subject was discussed by a number. An able address was given by Rev. W.D. REAUGH upon the subject, "How to Make County Organizations More Efficient." He emphasized the thought of unity and oneness in Christ. He showed the importance of selecting the best man for the head of the organization. He spoke of the importance of educating men and women, especially along the lines of Sunday school work.

H.J. THEOBALD being absent, his subject was not taken up. "Child Conversion, Its Importance and Our Duty," was the subject of Mrs. NEIHART's excellent paper. She laid emphasis upon the thought of surrounding the little ones with such influences so that they would not need conversion. This subject was discussed with considerable interest.

Prof. U.S. CONN was not present to give his paper.

The convention met in the opera house on Sunday morning with a full attendance. A spirited "Promise Meeting," conducted by H.E. MASON, after which a "Chalk Talk," by W.E. HOWARD, which was made very interesting and instructive, especially adapted to the little ones.

T.L. MATTHEWS of Fremont, chairman of the board, gave the principal address of the day. His subject was, "The School and the Book," an address which no one could well afford to miss. He said, "the future success of the church depends upon the success of the Sunday school."

The afternoon meeting was in charge of the Y.M.C.A., led by Dr. W.A. IVORY, who wondered what the world looked like to God after sin entered it.

"Why do the Boys From 16 to 18 Leave the Sunday School," brought out much discussion. It was, however, well stated that many boys who do leave the schools are brought into the Y.M.C.A.

President MASON announced that 12 schools in the county had made written reports. Personal reports by delegates from Winside, Carroll, La Porte, Pleasant Valley, Welch, Grace church and the Wayne schools were made together, with "What I Like and What I Don't Like About Our Sunday Schools."

The nominating committee reported the following names:

President, W.E. HOWARD; vice president, W.A. IVORY; secretary, W.W. THEOBALD; treas., Mrs. WALKER. Dr. IVORY declined to serve and the name of G.W. CROSSLAND was substituted and the report adopted. On account of the storm no evening session was held.

The Wayne Republican
August 5, 1896 (Vol. 3, No. 25)

BIRTH: Born on Thursday July 30, a girl to Mr. and Mrs. Herman HONEY.

BIRTH: A girl baby came to take up her permanent abode with Mr. and Mrs. L.C. TITSWORTH on Sunday.

Real Estate Transfers.
L.R. THORPE to Catherine CHAFFIE,
    lots 4, 5 and 6, blk. 10, College Hill $100.00
Ole HOGAN to Wm. WOEHLER,
    ne 35-25-3   4,160.00
S.W. BLACKWELL to John REINHART,
    w 1/2 w 1/2 30-25-4   4,100.00
W.H. BUCHOLZ to Nettie E. WEATHERHOLT,
    lots 1, 2 and 3, Hoskins   1.00

Dance, Beer and a Knife.
On Sunday at Germania Beer Hall Northwest of Winside.
Results in a Free-for-All Fight in
Which John SPRINGER Uses a Knife.

A few miles northwest of Winside is located what is known as Germania Hall, a place used for dancing purposes by an element of the people residing in that part of the county. Beer is always kept there in abundance and is dealt out in unlimited quantities to the thirsty without regard to age, sex or condition. The day usually selected for the greatest jamborees is Sunday, when at times the attendance will run well into the hundreds. On last Sunday one of the regular roundups was being held when for some cause or other the fellows that had an extra jag aboard got on their fighting clothes and from fists it went to knives when one Henry SPRINGER got in his work in terrible shape of some of his fellowmen. It was a genuine case of blood-letting and some of the women present were literally covered with the blood of the victims of his murderous knife. It has been very difficult to get at the exact facts in the case as those present seem to be desirous of hushing the matter up entirely and try to make it appear that it didn't amount to much and even the fellow that dished out the beer and at whose home it is said one of the victims of the murderous knife is stopping, pretends he don't know the name of the injured man.

It appears as nearly as we can be learned that SPRINGER went out to the beer hall with the avowed intention of doing harm of the parties there and he armed himself with a butcher knife. Chris ROTEMAN was the most severely cut, mainly about the chest and shoulders; several other were cut more or less severely. It would seem as if the condemnation of such places and actions cannot be too severe.

The Wayne Republican
August 12, 1896 (Vol. 3, No. 26)

DIED: FISHER. On Saturday afternoon Aug. 8, of heart failure, Mary, wife of Charles FISHER, aged 59 years. Deceased had been ailing for some time but at noon on Saturday felt improved and greatly encouraged but in less than two hours afterwards she was dead. She was born in Ohio and has been a resident of this state for about twenty years and leaves to mourn her decease a husband and eight children besides a host of friends. The funeral was held Monday the services being conducted by Rev. WIGHT.

DIED: ALGER. At her home one mile south of this city on Monday August 10, Mrs. Susan, wife of Pierson ALGER, passed from this to the great beyond leaving to mourn her departure an aged husband and several children. The funeral services were held at the M.E. church this morning and the interment of all that was mortal was made at Greenwood Cemetery immediately after.

John COYLE, S.B. RUSSELL, F. VOLPP, A.P. CHILDS, J.M. CHERRY, E.R. PANKRAUTZ, A.H. ELLIS, P.H. KOHL, L.E. HUNTER and Guy R. WILBUR are the delegates from the city to the democratic convention to be held on Saturday next.

The Wayne Republican
August 19, 1896 (Vol. 3, No. 27)

LICENSED TO WED: Jacob PAULSEN to Dorothy JAEGER.

Real Estate Transfers.

John T. BRESSLER to Ida FORD NORTHROP, outlot 1, B&B's ad to Wayne	$750.00
Sydney O. REESE to Security State Bank, sw 1/4, 17-27-1	320.00
Joseph A. BENT to Lars LARSEN, ne 1/2 n 1/4, 19-27-2	1,200.00
LILLEJEBERG, Mary and Fred to Robert UTTER, e 1/2 lots 1, 2 and 3, Blk. -, Wayne	1,000.00

The Wayne Republican
August 26, 1896 (Vol. 3, No. 28)

MARRIED: KORTH - FREY. At the home of the groom's mother on Friday Aug. 21. Rev. WIGHT joined in the marriage William KORTH and Mabel FREY, two of Leslie's most respected young people.

Obituary.

ALGER - Susan DeMASSE was born Nov. 24th, 1814, in Butler county, Ohio, and died at her home one mile north of Wayne, Neb., Aug. 10th, 1896. She married Pierson ALGER Sept. 28th, 1836. They spent the early part of their married life in Ohio. They removed to Iowa in the year of 1840 and settled near West Liberty, Muscatine county, where they remained until the spring of 1885 when they removed to Wayne, Wayne county, Neb. Mrs. ALGER was a woman of extraordinary character and was loved best by those who knew her best. She was reared by christian parents, her grandfather having left France for America in the time of oppression that he might enjoy his religion. And she gave her heart to God in her early childhood, and after a busy, well spent life she passed to her reward. She was a woman that could enjoy prosperity or could bear adversity or whatever might fall to her lot, and was never heard to complain. In an early day in Iowa she did much to the support of the church, always ready to entertain its ministers and laymen. She was sick for over one year, and for the last three weeks of her life was a great sufferer. She was ready and willing to go to that glorious home where so many loved ones were awaiting her coming. And while the dear, tender mother is missed so greatly in the home, 'tis sweet to know that she is in that blissful rest, where, as she was heard to murmur near the last, "where moth and rust doth not corrupt." She leaves an aged husband, seven sons and daughters, and three brothers to mourn her loss. These are Joseph M. ALGER, St. Louis, Mo, John D. and

James I. ALGER, of Wayne, Mrs. C.O. FISHER, of Wayne, Mrs. W.C. HUDSON of West Liberty, Iowa, Ola G. ALGER of Wayne, and Mrs. W.D. DICKERSON of Rising City, Neb. The brothers are Peter DeMASSE of Muscatine, Iowa, Dr. Morton DeMASSE of Nedosha, Kansas, and James DeMASSE of Oklahoma. The funeral took place on the 12th at the M.E. church. The sermon was preached from the 21 v of the 1st chap. Phillippians by the pastor, H.H. MILLARD. The floral tributes from friends were many and beautiful.

The Wayne Republican
September 2, 1896 (Vol. 3, No. 29)

MARRIED: GRIFFITH - JOHNSON. At the M.E. parsonage Sept. 2, by Rev. MILLARD, R.H. GRIFFITH of Bloomfield and Irilla JOHNSON of Winside.

DIED: On Saturday Aug. 29 after nearly eight years of suffering from cancer in the face, Roy GRAY, grandson of Jacob WEATHERHOLT.

COMMISSIONER PROCEEDINGS, Wayne, Neb., Sept. 1, 1896.
Commissioners met pursuant to adjournment. All members present.
The proceedings were had and done, to wit:
The following list of names of the persons selected from which to draw a jury for the October, 1896, term of the District Court was furnished the Clerk of said Court:
Hunter - Henry KELLOGG, John SNODDY, O.S. GAMBLE, P.N. NELSON, Grant MEARS.
Leslie - Frank BRESSLER, C.A. KILLIAN.
Logan - J.H. MITCHELL, Nelson UTTER.
Plum Creek - Henry HANSEN, Phillip GREENWALD, Chas. PFELL, Wm. DAMME.
Wayne - 1st ward, W.B. LARRISON, Dennis NEWTON, Enoch HUNTER; 2nd ward, Henry MERRIMAN, Chas. S. BEEBE, Henry LAYMAN, D.H. SULLIVAN, O.B. KORTRIGHT; 3rd ward, E.D. MITCHELL, R.M. FARR, Eli JONES, Mark STRINGER.
Strahan - J.D. ALGER, J.W. ZIEGLER, Oscar MILLIKEN, Chas. SPAHR.
Brenna - A.E. GILDERSLEEVE, James BAIRD, G.H. CULLER, T.B. HUGHES.
Hoskins - Mell CASE, Simon STRATE, H.W. MANK, Fred WICHMAN, Wm. WINTER.

Sherman - J.A. JONES, Jas. MULVANEY, M.S. MOATS.
Hancock - John KAUFL, Henry ULRICH, Chas. LONG.
Deer Creek - Rodney MANNING, John HAINES, Geo. A. BAILEY, H.C. PAULSON.
Chapin - Geo. LEWIS, Tom PRINCE, Andrew GOULD.
Winside - D.H. CARROLL, A.H. CARTER, A.L. WOODWARD.
Wilbur - T.S. GOSS, Sam BARNES, Adam GRIER.

It appearing that local freight from Wayne to Winside and Hoskins on two cars of piling had been charged to S.P. MacCONNNELL and deducted from his bill allowed Aug. 6th on motion his additional claim for $32.42 is allowed to correct error and warrant ordered drawn to pay same.

The County Treasurer is instructed to transfer $2000.00 from county bridge fund to county General fund.

On motion Board adjourned sine die.

Attest: S.B. RUSSELL, Clerk.

The Wayne Republican
September 9, 1896 (Vol. 3, No. 30)

BIRTH: There is a new boy at the home of Mr. and Mrs. Frank SPAHR.

BIRTH: Abner ROBINSON and wife are rejoicing over the birth of a boy at their home a few days ago. (Carroll)

The Wayne Republican
September 16, 1896 (Vol. 3, No. 31)

The Old Soldiers' Picnic.

The morning of Sept. 15 dawned with the sky overcast with heavy clouds and a slight mist falling. The appearances were that the day would be anything but a pleasant one for the pleasure planned, but about 10 o'clock the clouds began to break away and in a little while the sun came forth, the old veterans and friends who had made preparations for the day were quickly on the move and in a little while were on their way to STALSMITH's grove.

When the beautiful grove was reached the Wayne Corn Palace Band, one of the best musical organizations in the state, made the hills and valleys ring with their excellent music. Then came the welcome by President METTLEN and an address by J.D. KING, followed by H.B. BOYD, these were interspersed with songs by the Glee club. The time for dinner having arrived a foraging party was selected and from the amount of the good things of earth that burdened the tables it was very evident that their duty was well done. Dinner over the afternoon was passed with music, song and short addresses by Comrade FERGUSON, followed by the pioneer, Mrs. RICHARDSON, and after her came CHILDS, KING, WRIGHT, MORRISON and others.

The election of officers for the ensuing year resulted as follows: J.D. KING president; Fred WEBER vice-president; J.P. MATTHEWS secretary; A.W. TAYLOR quartermaster; Geo. L. COOK quartermaster sergeant; B. CUNNINGHAM paymaster. Executive committee A.P. CHILDS, B.F. FEATHER, S.H. McMAKIN. The picnic was a success in every particular, but did you ever know the old soldiers to take hold of anything they didn't make a success of, and this was no exception to the rule. The attendance was very good and everybody seemed to be enjoying themselves hugely and will look forward to next year's reunion and picnic in anticipation of another glorious time. J.B. STALSMITH went to considerable trouble in the preparation of the grounds, but seemed to be more than repaid when he saw how the comrades and friends enjoyed their surroundings. The picnic was all right.

The Wayne Republican
September 23, 1896 (Vol. 3, No. 32)

MARRIED: KEMP - SANDERS. At Keokuk, Iowa, on September 16, Rev. George H. KEMP and Rose SANDERS were joined in matrimony. In the bride our readers will recognize one of the teachers in our schools last year and the congratulations of a host of friends will be extended to the newly wedded pair.

DIED: At his home 5 miles west of Hoskins Sept. 19th, Charles WOOLEY. The deceased was an old soldier, a true friend and kind neighbor. In his family he was a loving husband and father.

The Wayne Republican
September 30, 1896 (Vol. 3, No. 33)

BIRTH: Sunday a brand new girl arrived at the home of D.S. McVICKERS.

Program of Wayne section of Teacher's Reading Circle October 3, at 10 o'clock:
    Music - Direction of W.E. HOWARD.
    Patriotism in the Schools: -
        a Should it be encouraged? Rena RITCHEY.
        b How Stimulated? Anna HANSEN.
        c Its Value. Gertie CULLER.
    Recitation - Maude BRITTON.
    North American Indians - Mrs. FLETCHER.
    Discovery of American by the Norsemen - Hilma PETERSON.
    Recitation - In American History - Conducted by E.C. PARK.
    Child Study - Finishing Chap. I of Tracy - Mabel PRESTON.
    Value of This Work at Outlined for the Year - Marie BROWN.
    Discussion - Earl GIBSON.
    Current Events - Everybody.
                          E.C. PARKS, Local Manager.

The Wayne Republican
October 7, 1896 (Vol. 3, No. 34)

MARRIED: PLIMPTON - BARTLETT. In Omaha on Wednesday, Oct. 1, 1896, Dr. W.W. PLIMPTON of Glenwood, Iowa, and Laura BARTLETT of this place, were married. The bride is the daughter of Mr. and Mrs. J.W. BARTLETT, one of the best known and most highly respected of our young ladies. A graduate of our high school, also a graduate of the Des Moines, Iowa, Baptist College, and for several years one of the leading teachers of this county, quite prominent in church work and one of whom all have always thought and spoken well. The newly married couple will make their home at Glenwood, where the husband is a successful practitioner of medicine. The best wishes of this entire community will follow them to their home.

MARRIED: TOWER - RIED. At the home of the bride in Chicago on Sept. 30th, Rev. A.M. WHITE officiating. Rev. Fred TOWER and Mabel S. RIED were joined in marriage. Mr. and Mrs. TOWER arrived in this place on Friday afternoon and are visiting at the home of the groom's parents and receiving the congratulations of the many friends in and about the city.

Roll of honor of the Third and Fifth grades in the Ward Building during the month ending Oct. 3, the following pupils have not been absent or tardy and have not whispered. They have also had thoroughly prepared lessons: Third grade pupils - Nellie DEARBORN, Jennie OLMSTED, Linn WELKER, Baker ECKHART, Myrtle FARR. Fifth grade - Helen PILE, Lelia OLMSTED, Birdie CROSS and Mamie BLANCHARD. Mrs. COON.

The republicans of Hunter on Monday evening nominated the following officers: Assessor, J.J.W. FOX; judges of election, O.S. GAMBLE, Mark JEFFREY, C.H. CLAYBAUGH; clerks, J.J.W. FOX, Grant MEARS; road overseer Dist. No. 3, J. LONGNECKER; 17, I.O. RICHARDSON; 11, P.M. PETERSON; 8, Henry STUMP; 39, O.P. ANDERSON; 12, J.A. BARBOUR; justice of the peace, D. CUNNINGHAM; constable, Grant MEARS.

COMMISSIONER PROCEEDINGS, October 6th, 1896.
 Board met in regular session. All members present.
 The following bills were audited and allowed and warrants ordered drawn on county general fund to pay same.

Jas. MULVANEY, road work	$40.00
W.H. BURNHAM, road work	47.50
James STEPHENS, road work	45.00
P.L. MILLER, road work	20.40
Carter COX, road work	7.50
Andrew SPIKE, road work	20.75
Henry GARMEN, road work	2.50
Herman FISHER, road work	5.00
Olaf YUNGDAHL, road work	32.50
Alfred HAGELAND, road work	3.50
Mark JEFFREY, road work	0.62
W.A. JONES, road work	7.50
Ray GLEASON, road work	8.00
John LARISON, road work	7.50
Herman KRUEGER, road work	5.00
H.H. KREBBE, road work	2.50
R.B. LEONARD, road work	6.00
John L. STEWART, road work	42.50
F.S. BENSER, road work	27.50
G.W. CULLER, road work	27.50
H.F. WILSON, road work	17.50
John ZIEMER, road work	91.25
A.T. WADDELL, road work	27.50
J.R. SHAWGO, road work	37.50
Adam GRIER, road work	7.50

W.T. SCHULZ, road work	$5.00
Sophus THOMPSON, road work	17.50
Wm. THOMPSON, road work	0.75
W. ELLIOTT, road work	18.75
Luther J. MASON, road work	1.10
Chas. SODERBERG, road work	1.25
Erick STAMM, road work	2.50
R.M. GALBRAITH, road work	20.00
Cal RITCHEY, road work	21.25
Claus KAY, road work	5.00
N.B. CULLEN, road work	1.25
Ed WILLIAMS, road work	28.20
J.H. MITCHELL, road work	8.40
C.D. JONES, road work	55.00
R.M. GALBRAITH, road work	28.75
A.T. WADDELL, road work	22.30
R.M. GALBRAITH, road work	13.75
Jay E. WILSON, road work	60.00
J.S. WELLBAUM, road work	30.00
A.T. WADDELL, road work	7.50
J.P. LARSEN, road work	2.50
F.O. MARTIN, road work	2.50
Eli McCONAGHEY, road work	7.50
F.O. MARTIN, road work	12.50
A.G. METTLEN, road work	12.50
J.T. PERDUE, road work	5.00
J.A. BARBOUR, road work	2.50
R.J. ARMSTRONG, coal for jail	12.25
Ludwig ZIEMER, surveying	6.00
Ludwig ZIEMER, surveying	8.20
Western W&S Co., grader repairs	16.00
W.P. AGLER, boarding paupers	21.25
Tim COLLINS, land for road	40.00
S. NELSON, blacksmith	8.25
P.H. KOHL, postage	8.00
D.C. AARON, pens	4.50
BUOL Bros., hardware	4.75
Dorr H. CARROLL, printing	12.86
Carl F. LENZ, blacksmithing	10.20
Bert BROWN, postage	1.50
G.L. MINER, watchman	2.00
Dorr H. CARROLL, printing	3.35
S.B. SHORT, dray pauper	1.50
G.L. MINER, watchman Sept.	2.00

A.T. WITTER, fees State vs. REAL	$75.00
A.T. WITTER, fees State vs. STRANE	25.85
Met GOODYEAR, oil	2.00
E. MARTIN, costs	3.05
State Journal Co., supplies	11.00
PERKINS Bros. Co.	91.10
W.S. GOLDIE, stationery	32.00
B.P. SORRENSON, repairing grader	2.15
Hugh HALL, work for county	30.00
E. CUNNINGHAM, printing	13.80
Geo. CHILDS, material (lumber)	15.57
KIESAU & BRAASCH, material (nails)	1.83
Wm. P. AGLER & Son, building bridges	287.11
Wm. P. AGLER & Son, bridge work	165.35
Wm. P. AGLER & Son, bridge work	350.55
E & B Lbr. Co., Randolph, lumber	89.30
E & B Lbr. Co., Carroll, lumber	68.69
E & B Lbr. Co., Hoskins, lumber	55.13
SMITH & ELLIS Co., lumber	158.75
CHACE & NEELY Co., hardware	73.82
R.D. MERRILL, hardware	9.61
Walter GAEBLER, hardware	18.92
Geo CHILDS, lumber	182.78
L.O. MITTLESTADT & Co.	99.30
A.A. WELCH, County atty's sal 3d qr	162.50
J.D. KING, insane com. fees	6.00
D. MARTIN, witness fees	2.00
Bert BROWN, insane com	11.25
A.M. JACOBS, commissioner	10.00
Mark JEFFREY, commissioner	16.60
Geo. HARRIGFELD, commissioner	15.40
S.B. RUSSELL, tax list, salary and expns	584.53
Town Hall Ass'n, rent 3d qr	112.50
Myra D. FLETCHER, sal 3d qr	188.75

The following claims for High school tuition fees were audited and warrants ordered drawn on county school fund to pay same.

School dist. 45, Cedar county	$35.50
School dist. 39, Wayne county	18.00
School dist. of Wayne	13.50

The following claims for damages by reason of the location of a public road between the Sec. 34, 35, 4 E. and 26, 25, 4 E were rejected:

Maria JONES - $75.00; George I. JONES - $75.00.

Upon the presenting of the petition of John HARDER et al for the changing of the voting place in Wilbur precinct from the Mason School house to the Wilbur school house and upon motion in that behalf made such change is hereby ordered.

On motion Board adjourned until Wednesday morning, Oct. 7th at 9 o'clock.

The Wayne Republican
October 14, 1896 (Vol. 3, No. 35)

MARRIED: At the home of the bride's parents Sunday, Oct. 11, Rev. St. CLAIR officiating. Isaac CARR and Loretta TEMPLIN.

The Wayne Republican
October 21, 1896 (Vol. 3, No. 36)

DIED: At his home in Hoskins on Oct. 17, Charles MAAS, aged 72 years. The funeral was from the M.E. church on Tuesday afternoon.

The republicans of Sherman precinct held a caucus on Oct. 14 and nominated the following candidates for precinct officers: Assessor, James MULVANEY; judges of election, D.M. DAVIES, M.S. MOATS, James HANCOCK; clerks of election, Daniel ISAACS, J.L. DAVIS; justices of the peace, Howard PORTER, Joel HANCOCK; constables, T.E. EVANS, Jarvis CONN; road overseers, No. 25, Jenkin DAVIS; No. 30, Howard PORTER; No. 28, James MULVANEY; No. 44, Joel HANCOCK.

Court Proceedings.

Court convened Monday afternoon, Judge ROBINSON on the bench. The following cases have been disposed of and findings as follows:

WIGHTMAN vs LAUMAN, continued.
State vs BOSTROM, continued.
HILDER vs HILDER, continued.
SAUNDERS vs SAUNDERS, continued.
HENRY vs GIBSON, continued.
LEWIS vs TALLMAN, continued.
FLYNN vs McGRATH, continued.
WRIGHT vs CARROLL, continued.
State vs ZEILKE, stricken from docket.
RALPH vs WILSON, dismissed.
JONES vs. KELLY, dismissed.

JONES vs Wayne Co., dismissed
Same vs same, dismissed
SHELDON vs BARGHOLZ, et al., dismissed
Madison Bldg. Ass'n vs HART, et al., foreclosure ordered.
Same vs McGILL, et al., foreclosure ordered.
Same vs. MEARS, et al., foreclosure ordered.
First National Bank vs WALDEN, et al., foreclosure ordered.
BRESSLER vs NYGREN, et al., foreclosure ordered.
BEARDSLEY vs WILBUR, et al., foreclosure ordered.
Same vs TRACY, et al., foreclosure ordered.
BURR vs KLAWOON, et al., foreclosure ordered.
HARRISON vs McCORKENDALE, et al., foreclosure ordered.
GOSHORN vs COONS, et al., foreclosure ordered.
WAFFLE vs KOEFOED, et al., foreclosure ordered.
BRESSLER vs LOUND, et al., foreclosure ordered.
FRIENDS Bros vs Wayne Clothing Co., property ordered sold.
BRADY vs EVERETT, sale confirmed, deed ordered.
SHUMWAY & EVERETT, sale confirmed, deed ordered.
SPENCER, HARDENBAUGH vs DOBBIN, sale confirmed, deed ordered.
MEYER vs HEATH, sale confirmed, deed ordered.
Citizens Bank vs WOLF, sale confirmed, deed ordered.
Same vs DOBBIN, sale confirmed, deed ordered.
FELKER vs HAYES, et al., judgment for plaintiff.
E.T. & Co. vs HONEY, judgment for plaintiff.
State Bank of Crawford vs TILLSON, judgment for plaintiff.
Madison Co. B&L Ass'n vs IRELAND, judgment for plaintiff.
GARMAN vs HORN, judgment for plaintiff.
VAIL vs CAHOON, judgment for plaintiff.
McCLUSKY vs WEATHERHOLT, judgment for plaintiff.
TILLSON vs WOELLER, judgment for defendant.
WILHELM vs W. U. Tel. Co., execution issued to carry out judgment.
BRESSLER vs HURLBERT, continued.
M & NEEDHAM vs HURLBERT, continued.
McCormick H Co. vs ALSTADT, continued.
JOHNSON vs Village of Winside, decree for plaintiff.
MIDDLESTADT vs VANSHUR, foreclosure ordered.
WELCH vs BEALE, foreclosure ordered.
N.E. Trust Co. vs HENRY, foreclosure ordered.
1st Nat'l Bank vs ZEIMER, foreclosure ordered.
BURR vs KEATING, foreclosure ordered.
STRAHN vs OMAN, foreclosure ordered.

McCLUSKY vs WEATHERHOLT, foreclosure ordered.
M Co. B & L Ass. vs HEYER, dismissed.
FOGG vs TONLINSON, leave given, EOUGHN to intervene.
MYERS vs LEY, motion overruled, defendant 30 days to answer.

List of judges and clerks of election for the year 1896:
WAYNE - 1ST WARD.
JUDGES - George GELDER, W.B. LARRISON, E. HUNTER.
CLERKS - Henry GAERTNER, Will RICKABAUGH.
WAYNE - 2ND WARD.
JUDGES - N.G. BENTLY, O.J. BUFFINGTON, Chas. MARTIN.
CLERKS - Chas. BEEBE, E.R. LUNDBERG.
WAYNE - 3RD WARD.
JUDGES - C.O. FISHER, S. DAVIES, W.O. GAMBLE.
CLERKS - B.F. FEATHER, George WILCOX.
WINSIDE PRECINCT.
JUDGES - John ELLIOTT, R.R. SMITH, Andrew HUPP.
CLERKS - D.H. CARROLL, John W. ZEMAN.
HOSKINS PRECINCT.
JUDGES - Ernest BEHMER, Ludwig ZEIMER, F.O. JOHNSON.
CLERKS - J.G. FOSTER, John SHANNON.
STRAHN PRECINCT.
JUDGES - Joel ATKINS, N.B. CULLEN, Ran. FRAZIER.
CLERKS - June CONGER, Charles SPAHR.
WILBUR PRECINCT.
JUDGES - Adam GRIER, Chas. SCHROEDER, A.B. JEFFREY.
CLERKS - Edward SCHULTHIES, Hans HANSEN.
PLUM CREEK.
JUDGES - Charles ERXLEBEN, Peter MERTEN, Dan McMANIGAL.
CLERKS - C.C. BASTIAN, M.S. ENGLERT.
HUNTER PRECINCT.
JUDGES - Henry KELLOGG, J.W. ALGER, E.B. GIRTON.
CLERKS - Geo. NANGLE, Arthur MILLER.
LESLIE PRECINCT.
JUDGES - C.A. KILLIAN, D.L. CHAMBERS, F.P. BRESSLER.
CLERKS - Jay E. WILSON, James MACK.
LOGAN PRECINCT.
JUDGES - Levi DILTS, A. ANDERSON, C.L. BARD.
CLERKS - Eli McCONOUGHEY, Leslie WEAVER.
SHERMAN PRECINCT.
JUDGES - Jenkin DAVIES, L. HUNT, J.R. MORRIS.
CLERKS - Daniel DAVIES, J.A. JONES.

GARFIELD PRECINCT.
JUDGES - John R. HAMER, Peter JENSEN, John LUMSDEN.
CLERKS - Wm. M JAMES, Everett ROBERTS.

HANCOCK PRECINCT.
JUDGES - Fred KRAUSE, Fred MILLER, Albert REDMER.
CLERKS - Jacob REICHERT, Samuel REICHERT.

CHAPIN PRECINCT.
JUDGES - Geo BARNES, Paul HEYER, C.W. REED.
CLERKS - J.R. WASHBURN, J.E. JAMES.

DEER CREEK PRECINCT.
JUDGES - J.R. MANNING, J.A. BROWN, Geo. YARYAN.
CLERKS - Geo A. BAILEY, Geo. C. MERRILL.

BRENNA PRECINCT.
JUDGES - Wm. BAIRD, O.C. LEWIS, E.T. RENNICK.
CLERKS - O.H. BERKHEIMER, James BAIRD.

The Wayne Republican
October 28, 1896 (Vol. 3, No. 37)

BIRTH: To A.G. METTLEN and wife, Oct. 21, a ten pound girl.

BIRTH: Frank FRANCIS and wife of Garfield are the proud parents of a boy baby born on last Friday.

BIRTH: Wm. KLAPMEIR and wife are rejoicing over the birth of a son a few days ago.

MARRIED: McMANIGAL - KNUTSON. At M.E. parsonage on October 28, Rev. MILLARD officiating, E.G. McMANIGAL and Lottie KNUTSON. Our readers will recognize in the groom one of Plum Creek's well known young farmers and the Republican wishes with the other friends of the contracting parties to extend congratulations.

Court Proceedings.

HURLBERT vs SUNDALL, judgment for plaintiff in sum of $41.53.

Wayne National Bank vs SMITH, submitted to court by stipulations.

State of Neb vs A. REAL, McPHERSON and Grant STRAINE, defendants plead guilty and sentenced to one year in the penitentiary.

TILLSON vs WOELER, judgment for plaintiff.

VAIL vs CAHOON, continued.

BRADY vs MAHER, sale confirmed.
McCLUSKY vs KRUEGER, foreclosure ordered.
CROSS vs BENTHIER, decree for plaintiff sum of $2705.77.
SHUMWAY & EVERETT vs LONGNECKER, sale confirmed.
STONE vs BOSTROM, continued.

The Wayne Republican
November 4, 1896 (Vol. 3, No. 38)

BIRTH: D.C. MAIN and wife are very happy over the arrival of a fine boy baby at their home on Thursday evening.

Roll of honor for Third and Fifth grades in the Ward building for the month ending Oct. 30. The following pupils have not whispered, been tardy, and have had the best prepared lessons: Fifth grade - Helen PILE, Lelia OLMSTED, Opal OLMSTED, Frank CHAFFEE, Mamie BLANCHARD, Birdie CROSS and Ethel BROWN. Third grade - Nellie DEARBORN, Baker ECKHART, Myrtle STUBBS, Myrtle FARR, Jimmey PILE, Guy CHANCE, Hazel MILLARD, Jennie OLMSTED, Flora CROSS and Effie NORTON.

COMMISSIONER PROCEEDINGS, Wayne, Neb., Oct. 31st, 1896.
Board met in regular session. Present, Mark JEFFREY, A.M. JACOBS, Geo HARRIGFELD and S.B. RUSSELL, clerk.
On motion the following claims were audited and allowed, and warrants ordered drawn on County General fund to pay same:

Chas. S. BEEBE, juror fees	$4.00
Sam BARNES, juror fees	4.60
Wm. DAMME, juror fees	2.50
R.M. FARR, juror fees	2.00
P. GREENWALD, juror fees	3.20
T.S. GOSS, juror fees	4.50
T.B. HUGHES, juror fees	4.40
Enoch HUNTER, juror fees	4.00
J.A. JONES, juror fees	6.00
John KAUFL, juror fees	5.50
Henry KELLOGG, juror fees	4.40
O.B. KORTRIGHT, juror fees	4.00
Chas. LONG, juror fees	5.50
M.S. MOATS, juror fees	6.30
J.H. MITCHELL, juror fees	5.00
Rodney MANNING, juror fees	3.30
P.N. NELSON, juror fees	4.60

H.C. PAULSON, juror fees	$3.20
Henry ULRICH, juror fees	5.30
Fred WISHMAN, juror fees	4.50
Wm. WINTER, juror fees	4.50
A.L. WOODWARD, juror fees	5.20
C.D. MARTIN, juror fees	2.00
James BARBOUR, juror fees	2.00
C.E. BROKS, road work	2.50
Isaac CARR, road work	20.00
D. CUNNINGHAM, road work	5.75
G.W. CULLER, road work	7.50
Levi DILTZ, road work	39.50
Jenkin DAVIS, road work	45.00
W.H. EASTBURN, road work	5.00
M.S. ENGLERT, road work	20.00
Michael EICH, road work	25.00
Michael EICH, road work	15.00
R.M. GALBRAITH, road work	50.00
J.C. HANSEN, road work	11.00
Chas. HERZBERG, road work	7.50
John HARDER, road work	35.00
W.A. HUNTER, road work	2.65
A.W. JEFFREY, road work	35.00
J.L. HUNTER, claimed $3.54, allowed	2.39
C.A. KILLIAN, assignee	9.00
C.A. KILLIAN, assignee	11.50
John KOEFOED, assignee	13.50
C.W. LARSEN, assignee	8.75
John LEE, assignee	1.25
F.O. MARTIN, assignee	3.75
W.A.K. NEELY, assignee	2.50
Claus OTTE, assignee	15.00
B.P. PETERSON, assignee	20.00
L. PETERSON, assignee	2.50
Jacob REICHERT, assignee	22.50
I.O. RICHARDSON, assignee	5.00
A.A. SMITH, assignee	10.00
S. SLAUGHTER, assignee	10.25
Fred C. STONE, assignee	37.50
Aug. SAMUELSON, assignee	2.50
L.E. SWANSON, assignee	6.25
G.W. TROTTER, assignee	5.00
Karl THOMSEN, assignee	2.50
T.J. THOMAS, assignee	40.00

Fred VAHLKAMP, assignee	$8.75
Ed. K. WILLIAMS, assigned	52.25
George WERT, assigned	6.25
John E. AGLER, boarding pauper	20.00
John E. AGLER, bridge work	23.00
TOWER & BENSHOOF, tile	187.00
Ed. & Br'd Lbr. Co., Hoskins, lumber	46.14
Ed. & Br'd Lbr. Co., Randolph, lumber	11.36
Robert UTTER, paper	3.75
Robert UTTER, supplies	3.70
PERINS Bros., supplies	37.10
Dorr H. CARROLL, printing	146.05
E. CUNNINGHAM, printing	148.03
L.E. HUNTER, printing supplies	42.00
L.E. HUNTER, printing tickets	34.00
L.E. HUNTER, printing bar dockets	14.25
L.E. HUNTER, printing supplies	3.00
N.P. NYBERG, hardware	1.00
S.M. SLOAN, draying	.75
D. BRYANT, repairs	3.00
C.A. BAGGERT, work	3.25
P.H. KOHL, postage	3.50
KORTRIGHT & NEWTON, repairs & booths	12.56
E.P. OLMSTED & Co., ballot boxes	19.85
Wm. HART, repairs	11.15
L.F. RAYBURN, repairs	2.00
W.M. GUE, land for road	12.00
L. ZIEMER, surveying	9.75
L. ZIEMER, surveying	10.50
T.J. WELTY, witness, claim $17.00, alw'd	12.00
A.T. WITTER, costs vs STRAIN	11.75
Ed. REYNOLDS, jailors fees, etc.	91.20
Ed. REYNOLDS, costs vs SEBALD	63.70
Bert BROWN, court costs	19.25
Guy R. WILBUR, defending prisoners	45.00
Mark JEFFREY, com'r fees	9.80
A.M. JACOBS, com'r fees	16.40
Geo. HARRIGFELD, com'r fees	30.80

Comes now B.F. FEATHER and makes report of fines showing total receipts to be $1.00, which said report is approved.

On motion the County Clerk is instructed to notify coal dealers that sealed bids will be received for Hard and Soft coal to be delivered as wanted, said bids to be filed with the County Clerk on or before noon, November 14, 1896.

On motion E.B. CHICHESTER, road overseer of Road District No. 18, is ordered to open section line road, No. 99, between sections 31, 32, 33, 34, 35, 36, Twp. 26-4, E. and sections 1, 2, 3, 4, 5, 6, Twp. 25-4, E.

It appearing that it is impracticable for a railroad crossing where public road on west line of section 7, township 25, range 2, crosses the right of way of the Chicago, St. Paul, Minneapolis and Omaha Railway, on motion it is ordered that said road be changed and a consent road 2 rods wide be located and ordered opened as follows:

Commencing where the said right of way crosses said road, running thence 2 rods wide east along the south side of said right of way 18 rods, thence north 4 rods wide across said right of way, thence west along the north side of said right of way 2 rods wide to said section line, all owners of land taken therefor having conveyed the same to the County.

Also the crossing where the public road on the west line of section 12-25-1 crosses the said right of way, on motion it is ordered that said road be changed and a consent road 2 rods wide be located and ordered opened as follows:

Commencing where the said right of way crosses said road, running thence 2 rods wide east along the south side of said right of way 8 rods, thence north 4 rods wide across said right of way, thence west along the north side of said right of way 2 rods wide to said section line, all owners of land taken therefor having conveyed the same to the County.

Settlement was made with the following road overseers and warrants ordered to pay same:

C.A. KILLIAN, Dist. No. 10, amt. due him	$30.00
Jno. KOEFOED, Dist. No. 22, amt. due him	28.00
John BOOCK, Dist. No. 47, amt. due him	34.50

On motion the Board adjourned until November 14, 1896.
Attest: S.B. RUSSELL, Clerk.

The Wayne Republican
November 11, 1896 (Vol. 3, No. 39)

BIRTH: R.C. OSBORN and wife are the parents of a new boy at their home.

BIRTH: J.R. HOOVER and wife are rejoicing over the arrival of a fine boy baby at their home on last Saturday morning.

MARRIED: HICKS - ROBERTS. On Nov. 4, at Paw Paw, Ill., George H. HICKS and Della L. ROBERTS. The bride is a sister of George L. ROBERTS, Mrs. James BRITTON, Mrs. W.M. GOODYEAR, Mrs. J.W. AGLER of this county and Mrs. R.J. MORGAN of Jerico, Mo., and is well known in the city.

Minutes of Teachers' Meeting Held Nov. 1, 1896.

Meeting was called to order at 10:30 a.m., Miss WEAVER acting as president. After announcing the subject of the County Schools was taken up and discussed by Mrs. FLETCHER, Mrs. CONN, E.C. PARK, Miss WEAVER, Mr. BONER, Mr. CUNNINGHAM and Mr. WOLF. On the next topic, Language and Grammar, papers were read (a) Ends to be Attained, E.B. PHILLEO, (b) Methods, Mrs. CONN, (c) In the City and Country, Miss DORMAN. Discussion by Mrs. WOLF, Miss Dottie BROWN, Mrs. FLETCHER, Mr. PARK. Adjourned until 1:30 p.m.

In the afternoon reading circle work came first. The preparations of notes and outlines was taken up and discussed by Mr. BONER. Narratives on the early history of Virginia were read by Mr. BONER and Miss Anna HANSEN. Remarks on the preparation of next month's work, E.C. PARK. Discussions also by Mrs. WOLF, Mrs. FLETCHER and Miss BRITTON. Work of Child Study was led by Mr. BONER in the absence of Miss THOMPSON. The discussion on this subject was quite general. Current events by everybody.

Moved and carried that our next meeting be called at 1 o'clock p.m. Dec. 5, and that we have but a single session. The following program was then announced for the next meeting:

1. What should pattrons reasonably expect from teachers, Miss WARNOCK.
2. Reading - End to be Attained, Miss WEAVER.
3. Use of Supplementary Reading, Miss Anna HANSEN, Miss DICKEY, Mr. HOWARD.
4. Preparation of Work . . . Miss Mary SCACE.
5. Book Review, Miss Preston.
6. Reading Circle Work - History - North American Indians, Mrs. FLETCHER, Mrs. WOLF.
7. History of Massachusetts Through Colonial Period, Miss Marie BROWN, E.C. PARK.
8. The French in the Mississippi Valley, Misses CULLER, METTLEN and SEWELL.
9. Cause of French and Indian War, Mr. SURBER, Miss DORMAN, Mrs. CONN.
10. French and Indian War in the West, Mr. NANGLE,

Miss Dottie BROWN, Mr. WOOLSTON.
11.   French and Indian War in the East, Miss BURSON, Mr. CUNNINGHAM, Mr. PHILLEO.
12.   Life on the New Frontier, Mr. BLAKESLEY, Miss SMITH, Miss RICHEY.
13.   The Colonial Chatters, Misses BRITTON, THOMPSON, and Lizzie BROWN.
President for meeting.
E.B. PHILLEO.
Adjourned.   E.C. PARK, Sec'y.

The vote cast in Wayne county was 2,185, which indicates a population of nearly 11,000 in the county. The following is the vote by precincts.

Winside 89; Hoskins 153; Logan 93; Leslie 87; Plum Creek 142; Strahan 158; Deer Creek 169; Hancock 125; Garfield 100; Wayne 1st ward 104; Wayne 2nd ward 133; Wayne 3rd ward 144; Hunter 185; Wilbur 112; Brenna 156; Chapin 125; Sherman 120.

The following are the assessors elected in the different precincts:

Hoskins - J.L. CLINE; Garfield - W.M. JAMES; Sherman - Vaughn DAVIS; Hancock - Perrin LONG; Chapin - J.R. WASHBURN; Deer Creek - L. SIMMERMAN; Brenna - Perry BENSHOOF; Strahan - N.B. CULLEN; Wilbur - David SHAY; Plum Creek - Pat COLEMAN; Hunter - J.J.W. FOX; Leslie - Neal NYE; Logan - J.H. WEAVER; Wayne - A.T. WITTER; Winside - G.F. WRIGHT.

The following road overseers were elected:

Dist.	Name	Dist.	Name
4	Chas. NEISS	34	Wm. PFIEL
52	A.T. WADDELL	53	Henry GREEN
26	W. EASTBURN	36	Robt. FRANCIS
48	H. HUTCHISON	44	C. ECKMANN
25	Jenkin DAVIS	49	J.J. CARROLL
45	H. BURNHAM	5	H. PRESCOTT
33	Jacob REICHERT	50	Ed. MILLER
51	Aug. DECK	46	W. PICKARD
35	C.M. SUNDAHL	27	Jacob BRUGER
47	John BOOCK	29	E.J. DAVIS
37	Jacob MORT	42	W. GARWOOD
43	O. ANDERSON	19	F. BENSHOOF
32	Anton JENSON	9	Geo. CULLER
31	Cal RITCHIE	6	Chas. SPAHR

Dist.	Name	Dist.	Name
20	Gus METTLEN	21	O. MILLIKEN
22	Jno. KOEFOED	7	John HARDER
23	W.R. MICK	40	G. KRUGER
41	Claus OTTE	2	J.R. SHAWGO
18	Jas. FINN	29	Alf JONES
30	Pat COLEMAN	3	J.W. AGLER
8	H. STUMPF	12	J.A. BARBOUR
17	Martin MUTH	39	Ottis STRINGER
10	C.A. KILLIAN	15	Aug JOOST
16	Levi DILTZ	1	J. MITCHELL

Advertised Letter List.

The following is a list of letters, etc., remaining in the Post office at Wayne Nebraska, for the week ending Nov. 10, 1896.

George JORGENSEN, A.C. JOSLYN, Jess HANSON, Nellie E. McCLINTOC.

Parties calling for the above please give date when advertised.

A.P. CHILDS, P.M.

**The Wayne Republican
November 18, 1896 (Vol. 3, No. 40)**

BIRTH: O. ANDREWS and wife are the proud parents of a fine girl baby. (Carroll)

MARRIED: OTTE - PAULSEN. On Nov. 6, Rev. GRABER officiating, Claus OTTE and Christine PAULSEN.

MARRIED: SHELLENBERG - BINGER. At the county judge's office on Nov. 11, C.F. SHELLENBERG and Minnie A. BINGER.

COMMISSIONER PROCEEDINGS, Wayne, Neb., Nov. 14, 1896.

Board met pursuant to adjournment. Present: Mark JEFFREY, A.M. JACOBS and G. HARRIGFELDT, commissioners, and S.B. RUSSELL, clerk.

The following claims were examined and allowed and warrants ordered drawn on the county general fund to pay same:

A.F. JONSEN, election expenses	$4.00
William BEEMER, election expenses	4.00
Herman ZIEMER, election expenses	4.00
J.G. FOSTER, election expenses	6.20
John SHANNON, election expenses	6.20

John R. HAMER, election expenses	$4.00
J.D. LUNDSEN, election expenses	4.00
Peter JENSEN, election expenses	7.40
W.M. JAMES, election expenses	4.00
Everett ROBERTS, election expenses	4.00
J.H. PORTER, election expenses	4.00
J.A. JONES, election expenses	8.00
Jenkin DAVIS, election expenses	4.00
S. HUNT, election expenses	4.00
David DAVIS, election expenses	4.00
Wm. BRUCKNER, election expenses	4.00
E.A. REDMER, election expenses	4.00
Fred MILLER, election expenses	4.00
Samuel REICHERT, election expenses	4.00
Jacob REICHERT, election expenses	7.80
C.W. REED, election expenses	4.00
Paul HEYER, election expenses	4.00
George BARNES, election expenses	4.00
David E. JAMES, election expenses	4.00
J.R. WASHBURN, election expenses	6.00
C.L. BAIRD, election expenses	4.90
Levi DILTZ, election expenses	.90
Almond ANDERSON, election expenses	4.00
M. KROGER, election expenses	4.00
Eli McCONOUGHEY, election expenses	4.00
Leslie WEAVER, election expenses	4.00
Geo. C. GILDER, election expenses	4.00
R.P. WILLIAMS, election expenses	4.00
E. HUNTER, election expenses	4.00
J.H. GAERTNER, election expenses	4.00
Will RICKABAUGH, election expenses	4.00
J.W. BARTLETT, election expenses	4.00
C.A. MARTIN, election expenses	4.00
Chas. S. BEEBE, election expenses	4.00
N.G. BENTLY, election expenses	4.00
Elmer LUNDBERG, election expenses	4.00
C.O. FISHER, election expenses	4.00
B.F. FEATHER, election expenses	4.00
F.A. DEARBORN, election expenses	4.00
W.O. GAMBLE, election expenses	4.00
Samuel DAVIES, election expenses	4.00
W.M. GUE, election expenses	4.00
Walter GAEBLER, election expenses	4.00
John ELLIOTT, election expenses	6.40

R.R. SMITH, election expenses	$4.00
A. HUPP, election expenses	4.00
C.C. BASTIAN, Treas. Dist. No. 34, rent	4.00
B.W. WINELAND, rent	2.00
H. WORKMAN, rent	2.00
A.W. TAYLOR, rent	2.00
Joe LOVE, rent	2.00
C.O. FISHER, canvassing returns	4.00
F.L. NEELY, canvassing returns	4.00
J.R. MANNING, board of election	6.40
F.A. BERRY, board of election	4.00
G.W. YARYAN, board of election	4.00
Thomas BELL, board of election	4.00
Geo. A. BAILEY, board of election	4.00
E.T. RENNICK, board of election	4.00
Wm. BAIRD, board of election	6.20
O.C. LEWIS, board of election	4.00
James BAIRD, board of election	4.00
O.H. BIRKHEIMER, board of election	4.00
June CONGER, board of election	4.00
C.E. SPAHR, board of election	4.00
J.I. ALGER, board of election	4.60
Henry KLOPPING, board of election	4.00
J.H. ATKINS, board of election	4.00
E.A. SCHULTHEIS, board of election	4.00
H.E. HANSON, board of election	4.00
Chas. SCHROEDER, board of election	4.00
A.B. JEFFREY, board of election	4.00
Adam GRIER, board of election	5.00
C.C. BASTIAN, board of election	6.00
Pat COLEMAN, board of election	4.00
Chas. ERXLEBEN, board of election	4.00
Peter MERTEN, board of election	4.00
Daniel McMANIGAL, board of election	4.00
Henry KELLOGG, board of election	5.20
J.W. AGLER, board of election	4.00
E.B. GIRTEN, board of election	4.00
Wm. MILLER, board of election	4.00
Geo. E. NANGLE, board of election	4.00
C.A. KILLIAN, board of election	6.80
D.L. CHAMBERS, board of election	4.00
F.P. BRESSLER, board of election	4.00
Jay E. WILSON, board of election	4.00
James MACK, board of election	4.00

J.T. BRESSLER, rent	$3.00
P.H. KOHL, ink	3.99
J.R. MORRIS, trip for booth	2.00
KORTRIGHT & NEWTON	20.63
PERKINS Bros. Co., poll books, etc., claimed $12.50, allowed	11.75
PERKINS Bros. Co., supplies, claimed $28.50, allowed	22.10
PERKINS Bros. Co., blanks for Supt., $18.00, rejected	
P.H. KOHL, postage	3.00
E & B Lbr. Co., coal	10.00
Hugh HALL, hauling tile	10.00
G.L. MINER, night watch	2.00
W.C. WIGHTMAN, 3rd quarterly salary	50.00
E & B Lbr. Co., Randolph	.84
E. MARTIN, postage and express	2.35
PHILLEO & Son, coal	20.38
R.J. ARMSTRONG, coal	8.50
Ed REYNOLDS, boarding prisoners	8.20
S.B. SHORT, draying	.75
H.G. LEISENRING, Com'r of Insane	11.00
C. SCHROEDER, land for road	6.00
Elizabeth SINES, land for road	6.60
Dorr H. CARROLL, special Com'r and expenses	6.00
E. CUNNINGHAM, printing and supplies	18.35
A.T. WADDELL, road work	15.00
O.C. LEWIS, road work	52.00
F.M. HOSTETTER, road work	2.50
A.T. WADDELL, road work	50.00
Eli McCONOUGHEY, road work	13.35
John ZEIMER, road work	56.25
Adulf LARSEN, road work	5.30
Harry PRESCOTT, road work	5.00
L. NUERNBERGER, road work	5.00
Herman REHMUS, road work	35.00
C.M. SUNDALL, road work	2.50
A.B. JEFFREY, road work	10.00
Lee FITZSIMMONS, road work	5.00
Ed K. WILLIAMS, road work	11.10
Jenkin DAVIS, road work	4.50
Adam GRIER, road work	21.25
W.A. JONES, road work	24.00
Aug. HANSEN, road work	2.50

Peter LIEF, road work	$22.50
H. MILLNER, road work	35.00
Andrew STANN, road work	7.50
B.P. PETERSON, road work	2.50
Chas. ERXLEBEN, road work	6.00
N.B. CULLEN, road work	10.00
J.W. BARTLETT, soldiers' relief	100.00
Geo. HARRIGFELDT, Com'r fees	11.00
A.M. JACOBS, Com'r fees	8.20
Mark JEFFREY, Com'r fees	9.20

Settlement was made with the following road overseers, and warrants ordered drawn on county general fund to pay balances:

Herman REHMUS, Dist. No. 5, due him	$30.00
N.B. CULLEN, Dist. No. 6, due him	30.00
Jenkin DAVIS, Dist. No. 25, due him	30.00
Jacob REICHERT, Dist. No. 33, due him	31.00
Peter LIEF, Dist. No. 34, due him	32.45
C.P. ANDERSON, Dist No. 39, due him	24.50

On motion the county clerk was instructed to notify County Superintendent Myra D. FLETCHER not to have any printing done at the expense of the county, except such supplies pertaining to the superintendent's office as are mentioned in the printing contract entered into with L.E. HUNTER.

This being the day set for letting the contract for coal for the county use for the ensuing year, and sealed bids being filed by PHILLEO & Son, SMITH & ELLIS Co., PEAVEY & Co., and the EDWARDS & BRADFORD Lbr. Co., the bids were opened and examined by the board.

On motion the contract was awarded to the EDWARDS & BRADFORD Lbr. Co., they to sign contract and furnish said coal at the several coal bins when ordered, at the following prices:

Hard coal $9.50, Hocking Valley Lump coal $6.50, Rock Springs nut coal $6.00, said contract to be for one year from this date.

On motion the county attorney is instructed to take the mandamus case of the State of Nebraska ex rel the County of Wayne vs. Stephen B. RUSSELL to the Supreme Court for review of the decision of the Disrict Court therein.

On motion board adjourned to December 12, 1896.

Attest: S.B. RUSSELL, Clerk.

The Wayne Republican
November 25, 1896 (Vol. 3, No. 41)

BIRTH: To Chas. STEVENS and wife, Saturday, Nov. 21, a boy of the standard weight.

MARRIED: Mort McMANIGAL and Miss LEUCKE are to be married this evening.

DIED: The infant child of F.E. FRANCIS, of Garfield precinct, died on last Tuesday, and was buried in the Welsh cemetery.

DIED: McDONNELL. In Wayne on Sunday morning Nov. 21, Thomas McDONNELL, aged 42 years. The deceased was taken sick on Wednesday with inflamation of the bowels which caused his death. His remains were shipped to LaSeur, Minnesota, on Sunday afternoon accompanied by his sister. His wife and five children had gone to the latter place some months since on account of Mrs. McDONNELL's health and were there at the time of his death.

The Wayne Republican
December 2, 1896 (Vol. 3, No. 42)

MARRIED: PUTZIER - McGILL. At the office of Judge MARTIN, Nov. 30, Charles E. PUTZIER and Harriet McGILL.

The Wayne Republican
December 9, 1896 (Vol. 3, No. 43)

MARRIED: NINDELL - KLOTH. On Dec. 2, at the residence of Justice WITTER in Wayne, Paul NINDELL and Dora KLOTH, of Wakefield.

MARRIED: NELSON - JORGENSEN. At the office of Judge MARTIN, Dec. 4, James NELSON and Hannah JORGENSEN.

DIED: At her residence in Wilbur precinct on Tuesday December 8, Mrs. R.H. WILBUR, aged 66 years. The deceased was among the earliest settlers of the county and leaves to mourn her demise several sons, daughters and a host of friends. The funeral services will be held at the Presbyterian church in this city tomorrow (Thursday) afternoon at 2 p.m.

Report of Teachers' Meeting.

Meeting called to order at 1:15 p.m., by W.E. HOWARD. After reading of minutes of the last meeting the following subjects were taken up:

Paper - "What should patrons reasonably expect from teachers," Mrs. WARNOCK.

Reading - "End to be attained," discussed by teachers.

Supplementary Reading - Miss HANSEN, Miss DICKEY, Mr. HOWARD; discussed by Mrs. FLETCHER, Miss Marie BROWN, Miss METTLEN, Miss WEAVER, Miss SHULZ, Mr. NANGLE, Mr. BONER, Mr. PARK, Miss STRINGER, Mr. SURBER.

Book Review - "Old Curiosity Shop," Miss PRESTON.

In the Reading Circle work papers were read on North American Indians by Mrs. FLETCHER. Early History of Massachusetts, Mr. PARK. The French in the Mississippi Valley, Miss METTLEN. Causes of the French and Indian War, Mr. SURBER and Miss DORMAN. The French and Indian War in the West, Mr. NANGLE, Miss Dottie BROWN, Mr. WOOLSTON. The French and Indian War in the East, Mr. CUNNINGHAM, Mr. PHILLEO. Life on the New Frontier, Mr. BLAKESLEY.

Discussion, Messrs. CULLEN, NANGLE, HOWARD, BONER, PARK, SURBER, WOOLSTON.

The Colonial Characters, Miss BRITTON, Miss Lizzie BROWN.

Owing to the absence of Miss SIMONTON the Child Study work was not taken up. Miss STRINGER reviewed the November Journal for good things in History, and Mr. BONER in Child Study.

Current events by everybody.

Announcements for next meeting: Advantages vs. Disadvantages of Rural Schools - Advantages, Misses PETERSON and MATTHEWS. Disadvantages, Lulu THOMPSON, E.B. PHILLEO.

Number work and Arithmetic: (a) In first and second years, Misses CULLEN, SCACE, SHULZ. (b) Mental Arithmetic, Misses STRINGER, Marie BROWN. (c) Sticking to the Text, Miss SIMONSON, Frank NANGLE.

Reading Circle work. (a) How I am using the History of what I think of the Source Study Method, Mr. CULLEN, Mr. WOOLSTON, Misses SEWELL, BRITTON, HANSEN, PRESTON, WEAVER, Lizzie BROWN. (b) General Lesson, Group IV to page 177. (c) Practical Value of the Work in Child Study, Misses METTLEN. (d) Chapter Three in Tracy, first half led by Mrs. WOLF.

Current Events.

President for next meeting, Miss DORMAN.
On motion it was decided to hold next meeting second Saturday in January.
E.C. PARK, Secretary; W.E. HOWARD, President.

The following is the program for the High School entertainment to be given at the Presbyterian church on Friday evening of this week:

Address	President
Song	Quartette
Oration	Arthur L. TUCKER
Recitation	Louie A. SULLIVAN
Oration	John L. JUHLIN
Solo	E. Grace LUDEKE
Recitation	Carrie V. KORTRIGHT
Recitation	E. Maude BENSHOOF
Original Poem	E. Grace LUDEKE
Class Analysis	Frank W. HITCHCOCK
Oration	Byron J. HOILE
Pantomine	- - -
Song	Quartette

Wayne, Neb., Dec. 7, 1896.
Casey Post No. 5 Department of Nebraska met in regular session, and under the order of new business was the election of officers for the ensuing year, as follows: Post Commander, John T. METTLEN; Senior Vice-Commander, G.W. CULLER; Junior Vice-Commander, A. ANSON; Quartermaster, J.W. BARTLETT; Surgeon, B.F. FEATHER; Chaplain, Mark STRINGER; Officer of Day, T.J. MURRILL; Officer of Guard, K.S. BARGER; Sentinel, A.P. CHILDS; Delegate to Department Encampment, A.W. TAYLOR; Alternate, Jno. P. MATTHEWS.

Jno. P. MATTHEWS.

**The Wayne Republican
December 16, 1896 (Vol. 3, No. 44)**

BIRTH: A bright baby girl came on Monday morning to brighten the home of Magnus WESTLUND and wife.

LICENSED TO WED: Licensed to wed on Dec. 15, Bert BROWN and Clara KNEBLE.

The Y.M.C.A. elected on last Sunday the following officers for the ensuing year: President, S.R. THEOBALD; Vice President, H.L. KIMBALL; Treasurer, Ralph GRIER; Secretary, Everett LAUGHLIN; Corresponding Secretary, D.C. MAIN; Devotional Committee, S.R. THEOBALD, A.L. TUCKER, Dr. IVORY, S.H. ALEXANDER, Geo. BLAKESLEY, Frank NANGLE, W.H. HOGUEWOOD, G.W. CROSSLAND, A. McINTOSH; Business Committee, Dan HARRINGTON, G.E. FRENCH, E.S. BLAIR, F.L. NEELY, Geo. COOK; Chorister, Frank GAMBLE; Organist, Homer SKEEN; Ushers, Walden TUCKER and Frank HITCHCOCK.

There will be a meeting of the above officers and committees at the office of BRESSLER & DEARBORN, Friday evening, Dec. 18 at 7:15 to talk over the future work of the association. This is an important meeting.

The Wayne Republican
December 23, 1896 (Vol. 3, No. 45)

BIRTH: A bright baby girl baby arrived at the home of Mr. and Mrs. BIGLER on Friday.

BIRTH: Born, at the home of Herman DECK a boy on the 7th inst.

BIRTH: To Mr. and Mrs. LINN on Friday, a girl.

MARRIED: MASON - PAUL. At the residence of the bride's sister, Mrs. McLAUGHLIN, 211 Main street, Sioux City, at 12 o'clock noon today, Wednesday, Dec. 23, Harvey E. MASON and Agnes PAUL were united in marriage. Harvey MASON, the groom, is one of the best known and highly respected young men of our county who ranks quite high in educational circles of the state and is at present the principal of the Oakdale schools. His bride is quite well known to many in the county, being for some time a student at the College here. Her acquaintances all esteem her very highly and the very best wishes of all will be with the newly wedded pair in which the Republican heartily joins.

MARRIED: While we were at press last week our young and efficient clerk of the district court, Bert BROWN, and Clara F. KNEBLE were united in marriage at the bride's home southwest of Winside. They have the very best wishes of all their friends who are limited only by the circle of their acquaintance as they start on their journey.

MARRIED: At 12 o'clock noon today the marriage bells rang out their glad notes at the home of H.F. CUNNINGHAM and wife south of the city while Rev. MILLARD spoke the magic words that bind for life Charles JEFFREY and Rena B. RITCHEY as man and wife. The newly married couple are among the best known young people who will have the best wishes of all as they launch their boat on life's sea where it is hoped no storms will ever be encountered, but only peace, prosperity and happiness be theirs.

The Knights of Pythias elected the following officers last night: Nathan CHACE, Chancelor; Aug. PIEPENSTOCK, V.C.; Dr. HECKERT, Prelate; W.H. McNEAL, M.W.; W.K. HIESTER, K.R.S.; H.D. BLANCHARD, M.F.; Sam DAVIES, M.E.; R.J. ARMSTRONG, M.A.

The following were elected officers last night of the Camp M.W.A.: V.C., Frank FULLER; Adviser, D.C. McVICKER; Banker, E.P. OLMSTED; Clerk, E. HUNTER; Escort, A. JETT; I.W., M.P. SAVIDGE; O.W., J.C. LUDEKE; Manager, M.P. AHERN; Delegate State Convention, W.A. HOGUEWOOD.

The Wayne Republican
December 30, 1896 (Vol. 3, No. 46)

BIRTH: W.B. GAMBLE and wife are the parents of a fine boy baby born about a week ago.

MARRIED: BENNER - STONE. At the home of the bride on Christmas day Rev. H.H. MILLARD joined in matrimony John F. BENNER and Bessie U. STONE. The newly married pair have the best wishes of a host of friends.

MARRIED: NEFF - SWANSON. On Dec. 25, Rev. SHAFER officiating, Geo. H. NEFF and Armadale SWANSON.

MARRIED: SPIKE - MATTSON. On Dec. 26, Judge MARTIN officiating, Andrew SPIKE and Anna MATTSON.

MARRIED: ANDERSON - ERICKSON. On Dec. 28, at office of county Judge, John ANDERSON and Christine ERICKSON.

MARRIED: STONE - HEFTI. On Dec. 29, at the Lutheran parsonage Rev. ECKHART joined in matrimony Fred STONE and Emma HEFTI.

DIED: The father of L.S. NEEDHAM of Winside died at Sioux City on Thursday, Dec. 24 from the effects of poison administered by his own hand.

DIED: Neil CUNNINGHAM aged about 64 years died at La Porte on the 24th, and was buried at this place on Christmas day.

DIED: Frederick LENZ, aged 68 years, died at the home of his son Carl on the 24th. (Hoskins)

The Wayne Republican
January 6, 1897 (Vol. 3, No. 47)

MARRIED: George SKIFF was married at St. Paul one day last week. We did not learn the ladies name but we all extend congratulations. (Hoskins)

DIED: GOLL. On Saturday, January 2, of membranous croup, John, the 3-year-old son of Mr. and Mrs. J.H. GOLL. the summons came very unexpectedly as but a few hours intervened between the attack and death. The funeral of the little one occurred on Tuesday. The stricken family have the sympathy of the entire community in their time of affliction.

The Wayne Republican
January 13, 1897 (Vol. 3, No. 48)

BIRTH: A girl baby was born to Ed MOORE and wife on Tuesday. (Carroll)

MARRIED: TIDRICK - PRESTON. At the home of the bride's parents in Brenna, at high noon on Wednesday, January 6th, Rev. HODGETTS, of Norfolk, united in marriage Harry TIDRICK and Mae PRESTON, in the presence of from forty to fifty invited guests. The high contracting parties are well known young people and need no words of introduction or commendation from us. Their friends are almost numberless each one of whom will bid them God speed on the voyage of life and with them will always be their best wishes. The presents received were many and valuable showing the esteem in which the young couple are held.

DIED: Mrs. L. FOWLER west of town died a few days ago of pneumonia. (Carroll)

Roll of honor of the Third and Fifth grades in the Ward building for the month ending Dec. 22, 1896: Fifth Grade - George WINGERT, Birdie CROSS, Mamie BLANCHARD, Opal OLMSTED, Ethel BROWN, Helen PILE, Edward STUBBS, John AHERN, Frank WINGERT, Frank CHAFFEE, Lela OLMSTED, Hattie WEBER. Third Grade - Flora CROSS, Nellie DEARBORN, Linn WELKER, Myrtle STUBBS, Myrtle FARR, Jennie OLMSTED, Guy CHANCE, Vernie TAYLOR, Eddie MERRILL, Effie NORTON, Roscoe LEAGON, John WINGERT, Hazel MILLARD, Jimmie PILE and Baker ECHART.

A lodge of the Sons of Herman was instituted at this place on the evening of the 6th, with the following officers: Fred VOLPP, president; H.J. LUDERS, vice president; Otto VOGET, secretary; H. MILDNER, treasurer; E.R. PANKRATZ, F.; Geo HOFELDT, I.W.; F. STAHN, O.W.; A. BIGLER, ex-Pres.

Real Estate Transfers.
M.L. GOREHAM to Anton JORGENSEN,
    nw 1/4, 11-26-2 $4,800.00
O.B. KORTRIGHT to S.R. WARNOCK,
    w 1/2 of lots 7, 8 and 9, blk. 11,
    n ad to Wayne   1,500.00
Carrie and Wm. POND to OLMSTED & MELLOR,
    w 1/2 of lots 8, 9 and 10, blk. 1,
    e ad to Wayne   567.00

COMMISSIONER PROCEEDINGS, Wayne, Neb., Jan. 11, 1897.
    Board met pursuant to adjournment. All members present.
        On motion the following appointments were made:
        Gustave KRUSE, Road overseer Dist. No. 40.
        O. ANDREWS, Road overseer Dist.No. 42.
        Perry BENSHOOF, Assessor Brenna.
        On motion the following official Bonds were approved:
        J.R. SHAWGO, Road overseer Dist. No. 2.
        J.W. AGLER, Road overseer Dist. No. 3.
        John H. WEATHERHOLD, Road overseer Dist. No. 4.
        John HARDER, Road overseer Dist. No. 7.
        C.A. KILLIAN, Road overseer Dist. No. 10.
        P.M. PETERSON, Road overseer Dist. No. 11.
        J.A. BARBOUR, Road overseer Dist. No. 12.
        August JOOST, Road overseer Dist. No. 15.
        Levi DILTZ, Road overseer Dist. No. 16.

Martin MUTH, Road overseer Dist. No. 17.
Fred BENSHOOF, Road overseer Dist. No. 19.
Gus METTLEN, Road overseer Dist. No. 20.
Jenkin DAVIS, Road overseer Dist. No. 25.
W.A. EASTBURN, Road overseer Dist. No. 26.
W.A. JONES, Road overseer Dist. No. 29.
Patrick COLEMAN, Road overseer Dist. No. 30.
Wm. PFEIL, Road overseer Dist. No. 34.
F.E. FRANCIS, Road overseer Dist. No. 36.
Otis STRINGER, Road overseer Dist. No. 39.
Gustave KRUSE, Road overseer Dist. No. 40.
O. ANDREWS, Road overseer Dist. No. 42.
Perry BENSHOOF, Assessor Brenna.

On motion a resolution was adopted in the following, to wit: It is hereby ordered that the county treasurer for the six months ending Dec. 31, 1896, present statement of the county's finances in form substantially the same as sample furnished him by this board and that the same from be adhered to in the future.

Comes now P.H. KOHL County Treasurer and files amended report as requested. No further business having been completed, board adjourned to Jan. 12, 1897, at 8 o'clock a.m.

Attest: S.B. RUSSELL, Clerk.

The Wayne Republican
January 20, 1897 (Vol. 3, No. 49)

BIRTH: A nice girl baby was born to Lewis STYRES and wife on Monday. (Carroll)

DIED: CAMPBELL. On Tuesday evening, January 19, T. Milton CAMPBELL aged 25 years. The deceased was the second son of J.W. CAMPBELL residing about 4 miles northeast of the city. His death was caused by lung troubles. He was an exemplary young man and one that patiently bore his sufferings. The parents, brothers and sisters will sadly miss him in the family circle and can only be comforted in their great bereavement by Him who doeth all things well. The sympathy of the entire community will go out to the afflicted ones. The funeral will be held tomorrow (Thursday) afternoon at 1 o'clock.

The Wayne Republican
January 27, 1897 (Vol. 3, No. 50)

BIRTH: To Fred SCHROEDER and wife a 10 pound boy. (Carroll)

BIRTH: A new boy arrived at the home of Marshal MINER on last Saturday.

MARRIED: SUHR - PAULSON. At the office of Judge MARTIN January 20, 1897, George W. SUHR and Anna PAULSON were united in marriage.

DIED: In Wayne on January 20, Emily Mabel GRACE, aged 22 years, 3 months, 26 days. The funeral occurred from the family home in the city on the 21st.

DIED: KREITLE. On Saturday, January 23, the infant daughter of Mr. and Mrs. John KREITLE. The little life had scarcely begun on earth until the summons of the reaper came and the little one was called unto Him who hath said "suffer little children to come unto me, and forbid them not, for of such is the kingdom of heaven." To Him who doeth all things well can the bereaved parents alone look for comfort. The funeral was held on the 25th and all that was mortal of the dear babe laid to rest in the silent city.

District Deputy Grand Master B.A. JONES, of Belden, installed the following officers of Wayne Lodge, No. 118, I.O.O.F. on Monday evening. G.C. GELDER, N.G.; Geo. FOX, U.G.; Chas. H. WARNER, Sec.; Henry LEY, Treas.; J.R. HOOVER, R.S.N.G.; Ira RICHARDS, L.S.N.G.; R.T. CARPENTER, W.; A.A. WELCH, C.; Fred VOLPP, R.S.V.G.; Andrew NELSON, L.S.V.G.; Chas. HOLTGREEN, L.S.S.; Mark STRINGER, L.G.; Jas. PORTERFIELD, S.P.G.

The Workmen of our city held their installation ceremonies on Thursday evening having present with them their wives and ladies of the Degree of Honor. The new officers are: L.C. GILDERSLEEVE, P.M.; H.E. GRIGGS, M.W.; Fred VOLPP, F.; Geo. C. GELDER, O.; T.W. MORAN, Receiver; I.W. ALTER, Recorder; E. HUNTER, Financier; W.H. HOGUEWOOD, Guide; R.Q. WARNOCH, I.W.; Axel KOEFOED, O.W. Following the installation an elegant banquet was spread and good cheer reigned supreme for a time around the banquet board.

Real Estate Transfers.

James KEATING to Chas. McKENZIE,
    nw 1/4, 35-27-2 $5,000.00

Harry MATRAN to Harry THOMPSON, se 1/4, 19-25-2	$4,000.00
Chas. McKENZIE to C.L. PROUTY, nw 1/4 35-27-2	4,000.00
F. and S. VRENDENBERG to E.D. MITCHELL and D.C. MAIN, sw 1/4, 32-26-2	3,800.00
John C. HAVEMEYER to Mel BENEDICT, w 1/2 sw 1/4, 5-25-1	1,000.00
R.R. JAMES to Elias HAIN, lot 4, blk. 22, Wayne	350.00
Ernest BEHMER to Peter BRUMMELS, se 1/4 of sw 1/4, 33-25-1	1,000.00
J.W. MAHOLM to Henry LAYMAN, ne 1/4 of ne 1/4, 19-26-4	1,500.00
A.J. PRESTON to E.W. ZUTZ, w 1/2 of se 1/4 and e 1/2 of sw 1/4, 4-24-1	2,400.00
J.W. MASON to C.M. YOCUM, Und 1/2 of section 6-27-3	4,857.00

The Wayne Republican
February 3, 1897 (Vol. 3, No. 51)

MARRIED: KARNES - BATTAM. At the office of Judge MARTIN on Feb. 2, H.B. KARNES of Dixon County and Julia BATTAM of Saunders County.

MARRIED: HEFTI - BENNING. On Tuesday January 26, Rev. ECKHARDT united in married Fred HEFTI and Bertha BENNING. The groom is one our industrious substantial young farmers and the bride is a daughter of John BENNING residing northwest of the city a few miles. The Republican but voices the sentiment of the entire community in extending to the newly married pair its best wishes for their future.

DIED: NELSON. On Wednesday, January 27, Mrs. P.N. NELSON, aged 32 years, 3 months, 29 days. On Sunday, January 31, the infant child of not quite a week followed its mother to that other better land. Mrs. NELSON leaves to mourn her demise a husband, four children, quite a number of relatives and a host of friends who will sadly miss her. On Thursday she was laid to rest in the silent city. The sympathies of all will be with the bereaved ones in their days of darkness.

DIED: STINER. On Sunday, January 31, John STINER, aged

about 60 years. The deceased has been ailing for some time and on the date named breathed his last at the home of his brother, J.L., east of the city. The funeral occurred on Monday.

An Awful Tragedy.
An Inhuman Husband and Father Brutally Murders His Wife and Three Children.
THE MURDERERS STORY.
The Wife Pleads for the Lives of Herself and Children, but Finds no Mercy at his Hands.

Wayne county on last Wednesday night had one of the most inhuman crimes committed within her confines that is recorded in the west. C.K. RASH, a farmer living ten miles southwest returned from a revival meeting at Grace M.E. Church where he secured a soapstone used for warming the feet and with it pounded the life out of his wife and three children consisting of a bright boy of 10 years, a fair haired girl of 8 and a boy baby not quite two years old. At present it is impossible to give the motive that prompted the inhuman act and the most charitable view is that he who so heartlessly took the lives of his wife and innocent babies is that he was deranged and knew not what he was doing. The awful act became known when one of the neighbors whom RASH had promised to help in corn shelling went to his abode to see why he didn't come. The neighbor opened the door of the house and there found the fiend in the midst of his victims without apparent concern as to his surroundings. The community was at once aroused and in a short time dozens had gathered on the premises and one of their number was at once dispatched to this city after the sheriff and coroner, while the rest stood guard to see that the guilty one should not escape. The coroner quickly summoned a jury and in company with the sheriff at once proceeded to the scene of the crime. When the officers entered the house they found RASH there entirely unconcerned and on the floor lay his wife with her head beaten to a jelly and within three feet of her lay the eldest boy cold in death and on the bed the two younger children. The stone with which the deed was committed had been broken into several pieces and with one of these he had crushed the heads and faces of the victims in a terrible manner. On RASH's face were some scratches showing that the wife and mother had evidently defended to the last the lives of herself and babes. The murderer was at once secured and ironed and after the surroundings were carefully noted by the coroner and jury they adjourned to meet in the court house on Friday. The sheriff brought RASH to the city and lodged him in jail. The murderer refuses to talk or give any intimation as to the reason for his awful act and steadfastly rejected both food and water until Sunday when he drank some water but up to Monday had not touched a mouthful of anything to eat. The coroner's jury convened on Friday afternoon and the testimony of the witnesses called at that time failed to show any cause for the deed until his brother, Charles RASH, was put on the witness stand when he testifed that their father had several years ago became mentally deranged and took his own life by hanging and that an older brother had gone insane and died in an asylum at Fulton, Mo. The inquest was adjourned until Tuesday of this week for the purpose of getting the testimony of additional witnesses. After the sheriff and coroner had left the abode of death, kind hearted neighbors took charge of the remains of the victims and prepared them for their last resting place. On Saturday occurred the funeral, the services being held in the M.E. church of this city and it was one of the sights that will never be forgotten by those who saw the coffin containing all that was mortal of the wife and mother carried out of the church followed by the other three coffins having within them the bodies of the three little children. They were all laid away in the same grave there to await the great final.

    On Monday afternoon the sheriff with a physician forced liquid food into the stomach of the prisoner which seemed to arouse a further desire for it and several times during the night he called for and ate what was given him and has since seemed to relish food as well as anyone. On Monday night or Tuesday morning the murderer confessed all to the sheriff who as a matter of course cannot divulge what he is in possession of until the proper time and place and pending that time it will be best for all concerned that cool counsel prevails. Since Monday afternoon visitors cannot gain admittance to the jail except by express permission of the sheriff and in this he is certainly doing the right thing.

    On Tuesday afternoon the inquest was continued and several additional witnesses examined, among the number being Mrs. BONAWITZ, to whom Mrs. RASH had communicated some family history that Mrs. B. thought might have caused trouble between husband and wife. She also testified that on Tuesday prior to the murder RASH had insisted on the oldest boy and girl going to school and the mother believed it too cold and told the children to go to the BONAWITZ' and stay there until time to come home, and to tell Mrs. B. to come over to Mrs. RASH's as she wanted to see her. The lady complied with the request and found

RASH and his wife at home and during his absence from the house while she was there Mrs. R. imparted to her the history referred to, but Mrs. B. didn't go into details as to what it was that Mrs. R. related, except that she thought that the brother residing near Laurel ought to be sent for to see if he could not do somethng with C.K. Mrs. B. made known to her husband and several others who were shelling corn at their place the desires of Mrs. RASH and after talking it over the neighbors didn't seem to think it necessary to send for the brother. In all the testimony before the coroner's jury there didn't anything appear as to the conduct of RASH prior to the time of committing the murder indicating insanity, and none of the witnesses, all of whom were neighbors, had observed anything to lead them to believe that he was deranged. The soapstone with which he committed the deed was presented before the jury and identified by the minister who had been conducting the meetings at Grace church as the one that RASH had taken from that place on the night when the deed was committed. After the testimony was all in it took but a very few minutes for the jury to decide on their verdict and it is as follows:

STATE OF NEBRASKA }
 } ss.
Wayne County }

At an inquisition holden at the residence of C.K. RASH and at Wayne, each is said Wayne county, on Jan. 28 and 29, 1897, and Feb. 2, 1897, before me, J.P. GAERTNER, coroner of said county, upon the body of said Julia RASH lying dead, by the jurors upon their oath do say that the said Julia RASH came to her death on or about the 27th day of January, 1897, from the effect of being struck and beat on and about the head of her the said Julia RASH with a certain stone in the hands of one Clarence K. RASH, and the said jurors upon their oath do say that the said blows were inflicted by the said Clarence K. RASH intentionally and feloniously.

P.M. CORBIT,
F.E. GAMBLE,
Ira. G. RICHARDS,
M.S. STRINGER,
E. HUNTER,
C.A. CHACE,

Attest: J.P. GAERNTER, Coroner.

The verdict was the same in regard to death of the children as the above. After the inquest was concluded some parties visited RASH in the jail and to them he gave his version of the murder. He says that God commissioned him to kill his family, and that he went home from the church entered the home and told his wife he was going to slay her and the children. She tried to persuade him from his course and begged for their lives to which he turned a deaf ear and struck her on the head with the stone and broke it in several places but did not knock her down. They got into a scuffle for the pieces, she endeavoring to get the instrument of death away from him, but he got possession of one of the larger pieces and with it struck her again and again until she was dead. The oldest boy was in bed and called, "Papa, papa don't," and then started to get out of bed, but he paid no attention to his cries, and after he had disposed of the wife and mother he found it awful hard to kill the children, but felt he was commanded to destroy them, and with the same stone struck and killed the oldest boy and then dragged him out to where he was found beside the mother. The little girl had waked up and while he was murdering the others and to her he next turned and crushed her head with the stone and following that he took the life of the babe. RASH further told the parties referred to that he never loved his wife and children as he ought and he manifests no apparent remorse for the awful crime he has committed.

John BRANDT the man brought back last week from Iowa charged with rape on the person of Sophie SCHROEDER was arraigned before Judge MARTIN and bound over to court in the sum of $500 which he could not furnish and now languishes in jail awaiting the action of the District Court in April.

The RASH murder seems to be the all-absorbing topic anywhere and everywhere in this section since the occurrence. All kinds of stories are afloat in regard to the matter, and opinion is pretty evenly divided as to the sanity or insanity of the murderer. The reports that have gone out as to threats of lynching are certainly without any foundation. Wayne county people will not take the law into their own hands even though the crime may be without a parallel. The courts will be left to do their work without hindrance and we feel certain that exact justice will be meted out to the perpetrator of the terrible crime.

The Wayne Republican
February 10, 1897 (Vol. 3, No. 52)

DIED: J.H. GOLL received a telegram from his brother John who was formerly a resident of this place and now lives at Streetor, Ill., that his son, Adam, a lad of 11 years had broken through the ice at that place and was drowned on the 2nd of February.

DIED: SAVIDGE. On Saturday afternoon, the 8 months old girl baby of Mr. and Mrs. M.P. SAVIDGE was called unto the Father of all. The funeral was held on Sunday afternoon.

DIED: NELSON. On the evening of February 9, Peter N. NELSON aged 37 years, 9 months. The deceased was a native of Sweden and came to this country about 22 years ago settling first in Know County, Illinois. He came to Wayne county, Nebraska, 13 years ago and has been during those years one of her very best citizens, a man that by his industry and thrift has been very successful in life. He leaves three orphan children, the oldest eight years and the youngest two years, the wife and mother passed away but two weeks ago. It seems as though the hand of affliction has been laid upon this family very heavily for within the space of two short weeks three of its members have been called to the great Unknown. To the bereaved ones, brothers, sisters and orphans will the sympathies of the entire community go out.

There was quite a tremor of excitement in the city on Saturday night and Sunday. For several days prior men were to be seen in groups talking in rather strong language and threats of summary dealings with RASH, the murderer were frequently indulged in until Saturday afternoon the sheriff seemed to partake of the spirit of nervousness prevailing and at once proceeded to prepare to thwart any attempt to remove the prisoner from the jail. Extra help was deputized and ugly looking guns carried to the county bastile with the evident expectation of trouble. As soon as darkness covered the land on Saturday evening men came from different directions and gathered at the saloons and from there wandered away singly, in pairs and otherwise to what seemed to be a desire on the part of some of the assemblage to make short work of the prisoner in the jail, while others seemed only to have come for the purpose of being onlookers. No one cared to lead in the fight that all believed would follow the making of an attempt to secure the man they wanted and finally all wandered away as they had come. It seems that while this was happening south of the track that another lot of men had congregated in the neighborhood of the court house, but their numbers were too limited as they believed to accomplish what they desired and it is said that at one time an emmissary was sent to the other rendezvous to size up the crowd there, but his report was not of a very encouraging nature so they, like the others, folded their tents and silently stole away. Whether there was serious danger of an attack on the jail or not for the purpose of getting possession of RASH we are unable to say, but one thing we are sure, it created considerable sleeplessness on the part of the sheriff and created within his breast a burning desire to get his man away from this community and on Monday morning early he put him in a carriage and drove to Wakefield and there took the train for Lincoln where RASH now is in the penitentiary for safe keeping until the time of his trial in April.

Real Estate Transfers.

John T. BRESSLER to A.C. GOLTZ, lot 8, blk. 1, Winside	$20.00
Albert SALTER to PEAVEY Elevator Co., Lot 8, blk. 4, B&P's ad to Winside	25.00
Ed STEPHENS to J.H. PINGREY, lot 30, blk. 5, P&B's ad to Winside	30.00
Wm. T. AVERILL to PEAVEY Elevator Co., lot 10, blk. 4, B&P's ad to Winside	15.00
J.T. BRESSLER to A.C. GOLTZ, lot 9, blk. 1, Winside	20.00
John GLANDT to John RAHDER, n 1/2 nw 1/4, 29-26-2	1,800.00
Bert BROWN has purchased the J.J. GILDERSLEEVE residence on N. Pearl street through I.W. ALTER, agent, consideration	1,100.00

The Wayne Republican
February 17, 1897 (Vol. 4, No. 1)

DIED: JUHLIN. On Monday, February 15, Mrs. Bengta JUHLIN, aged 73 years, 7 months, 27 days. The deceased was the mother of N.I. JUHLIN of this place and Mrs. P.N. NELSON, deceased. She was a native of Sweden and came to this country about ten years ago. The funeral was from the Lutheran church of this city on yesterday.

There seems to be no doubt as to the death of Peter N. NELSON which occurred about a week ago being caused by the drinking of about a pint of alcohol that had been used for the purpose of bathing him during his sickness. Those who knew him best do not believe that he was in a condition at the time to realize what he was doing, but think that his mind had become deranged as he had been delirious at different times during his sickness, and that his taking it was because of being in that condition at the time. It is certainly a very sad case and deprives three little children of the protecting care of their father when so sadly needed.

The Wayne Republican
February 24, 1897 (Vol. 4, No. 2)

BIRTH: On Friday, February 19, to Mr. and Mrs. Mark JEFFREY, a daughter.

DIED: H.R. NEFF, of Logan precinct, aged about 85 years, died on the 17th, and his remains were sent to Illinois on the 18th for interment.

Public Sale.

The undersigned, administrator of the estate of Peter N. NELSON, will sell at the late residence of deceased, 5 1/2 miles east of Wayne at 10 o'clock a.m. sharp on Thursday, March 4th, 1897.

Thirteen head of work horses, from 3 to 7 years old. Seventy-five head of cattle: 63 steers, coming 2 years old; 7 yearling steers and heifers; 3 good milch cows; 1 fat cow; 1 black yearling Polled Bull. 97 head of hogs, 60 of these are Poland China brood sows, all safe in pig; 3 thoroughbred boars; balance stock hogs. About 200 chickens and turkeys. Farm Implements: Harness, saddles, fly-nets, plows, cultivators, 2 planters, 2 seeders, 1 disc, drags, mower, 2 binders, hay stacker, and sweep, hay rake, 4 wagons, hay rack, bob-sleds, spring wagon, about 100 tons of hay, 4 bushels of timothy seed, a lot of lumber. Household furniture: Sewing maching, bed room sets, beds, matresses, chairs, tables, cooking and heating stoves, carpets, canned fruit, and other articles too numerous tomention. Terms of sale: On cattle six months' time, on everything else ten months' time on all sums over $10, purchaser giving approved not bearing 10 per cent interest. Sums of $10 and under, cash; 2 per cent discount for cash on cattle, all other articles 5 per cent on time sums.

Free lunch at noon.

E. CUNNINGHAM, Auctioneer   C.J. LUND, Administrator.

Real Estate Transfers.

F.A. BERRY to Citizens Bank,
    lots 9 & 10, blk. 4 & lot 14, blk. 8, Carroll $800.00

J. Christ SORENSON to Jens,	
n 1/2 ne 1/4, 11-26-2	$2,000.00
H.B. BOYD to S.R. THEOBALD,	
lot 4, blk. 11, Wayne	1,450.00
T.S. MATTHEWS to Mary BARBOUR,	
lts. 16 & 17, blk. 10, College Hill	400.00
Winside Mill Co. to W.T. AVERILL,	
lot 10, blk. 4, B&P ad Winside	80.00
Warren B. GOREHAM to P.P. GOREHAM,	
nw 1/4, 22-25-5	4,800.00
Wm. PRINCE to PEAVEY Elevator Co.,	
lot 22, blk. 4, B&P ad to Winside	20.00
Henry TREVERT to Herman TREVERT,	
e 1/4 se 1/4, 7-25-4	2,800.00
HARDENBERGH, S. to Clara F. BROWN,	
s 100 ft lot 1, blk. 7 B&P ad Wayne	1,000.09
W.H. McCLUSKY to Pv Elevator Co.,	
lot 2, blk. 4 B&P ad to Winside	25.00
R.J. TRACY to Anna E. KOHL,	
s 1/2 ne 14-26-3	3,000.00
J.S. FRENCH to J.O. BARRON,	
n 1/2 sw 1/4 11-26-3	1,400.00
H.B. MILLER to Pv Elevator Co.,	
lot 9, blk. 4, B&P 1st ad Winside	25.00
C.W. SIMON to E.M. LAUGHLIN,	
n 50 lt 1, blk. 9, B&P ad Wayne	600.00
Peter OMAN to Wm. MELLOR,	
s 1/2 9-25-3	7,000.00
Edward ADAMSON to John RITCHEY,	
n 1/2 se 1/4 23-25-3	2,200.00
Carroll State Bank to T.I. SHAFER,	
lots 8 & 9, blk. 9, Carroll	600.00
J. SHANNON to G.J. KAUTZ,	
lot 8, blk. 3, Hoskins	50.00
F.G. PHILLEO to W.R. GRACE,	
lots 7, 8 and 9, blk. 18, College Hill	530.00
Geo. W. BRIGGS to O.L. BRIGGS,	
n 1/2, 22-26-1	7,000.00

The Wayne Republican
March 3, 1897 (Vol. 4, No. 3)

BIRTH: Hugh HOUSE and wife are rejoicing over the arrival of a fine girl at their home.

BIRTH: Some few weeks ago in our budget from here we said a girl baby had been born to Mr. and Mrs. C.E. JAMES and by some hocus pocus or other when the paper came here it read C.E. JONES instead of JAMES, and as JONES is a confirmed old bachelor it naturally complicated matters considerable.

MARRIED: ROLAND - HOUSE. By Rev. W.W. THEOBALD, Harry U. ROLAND and Miss J. HOUSE. They live 12 miles west.

MARRIED: At high noon today the wedding bells will peal forth their glad notes in the town of Carroll, where at the hour named Miss Abbie M. MERRILL of Carroll and George R. DUNLAP of Vermillion, S.D. will be joined in wedlock. Of the groom we know only as others tell us, but he is spoken of very highly, while of the bride her friends who are numbered only by the circle of her acquaintance, cannot speak too many words of praise. The young couple start out under very favorable circumstances and it is the hope of all that theirs may be a journey of pleasure. After March 10 Mr. and Mrs. DUNLAP will be at home to their friends at Vermillion, S.D.

The Wayne county devil who pounded his wife and little children to death with a stone, is now safe in Lincoln. He was taken to protect him from mob violence, but we are of the opinion that a people who would allow him to live at all after the murder, is too cowardly to touch him. A mad dog would be safe in Wayne county and would receive much sympathy on account of a loss of reason. (Dixon Tribune)

There is no cowardice in being law abiding citizens and Wayne county people are not going to lose any sleep over the opinions of anyone who would wish to see them commit an act of lawlessness in order to gratify a brutal desire for revenge. The courts will do their work.

Real Estate Transfers.

Alice M. DODGE to Pv Elevator Co., lot 3, blk. 4, B&P ad Winside	$25.00
C.B. FRENCH to Pv Elevator Co., lot 1, blk. 4, B&P ad Winside	25.00
Peter DALL to S.O. HOGUE, se 1/4, 18-26-2	264.00
Fred RANTONBERG to Robt. RANTONBERG, n 1/2 nw 1/4 28-26-1	2,600.00

Winside Mill Co. to Ludwig REHMUS,
lot 5, blk. 6, B&P's ad to Winside $80.00

The following is the list of jurors drawn on February 24, 1897, for the April term of court. They are to appear April 20, 1897:

John BOOK, George BUSH, Charles BAGGART, David CUNNINGHAM, Dorr H. CARROLL, Thomas E. EVANS, Charles ERXLEBEN, Adam GRIER, J.H. GOLL, H.L. KIMBALL, Archie LINDSAY, J.P. LARSEN, Eli McCONOUGHY, Thos. MULVANEY, F.E. MOSES, Ed OWENS, Thomas PRINCE, C.A. SLAUGHTER, Frank SINES, Wm. SHULTZ, Charles SHELLENBERG, Henry WITLER, H.C. WRIGHT, O.C. LEWIS.

The Wayne Republican
March 10, 1897 (Vol. 4, No. 4)

The Wayne cooperative creamery held its regular annual meeting on last Friday and elected the following officers for the ensuing year. President, Homer GRAVES; Secy., Chris WISCHOFF, Directors, Homer GRAVES, H.E. EVANS, B.W. LESSMAN, Henry MEYER, A.B. CLARK. Last years business was very satisfactory and the company are in better shape than ever to take care of the business and if you will bring in your milk they will accord you fair treatment and prompt settlement each month.

The work of the Nebraska Children's Home Finder Society is a work that should commend itself to every person in Wayne. Many of our people heard either Mr. or Mrs. MARKLEY, who recently spoke from the various pulpits relative to this organization. For some time Wayne has been represented in this work, not alone by contributions, but homes for three children have been found and one has been sent from here to a home in another part of the state. The local board has recently been reorganized by appointing from the names of those who contribute, representatives of the various churches as follows: Baptist - J.W. BARTLETT, president; Methodist - Mrs. MYERS, W.A. IVORY, Mr. J.D. KING; Lutheran - B.F. FEATHER, Miss STAMBAUGH; Episcopal - A.P. CHILDS, Mrs. BRENNER, vice president; German Lutheran - J.H. GOLL, Mrs. Wm. PIEPENSTOCK. Presbyterian - W.E. HOWARD, secretary and treasurer, Mrs. ANDRESS. All who have recently subscribed to the cause are requested to hand the amount to the treasurer who will receipt for it, or to a member of the board from your church, who will receive a receipt from the treasurer for the amount. Anyone knowing of destitute children or of a good home that would receive a child, are requested to communicate with the officers or members. Children will be placed only in homes where they will receive the same training and care that an own child would receive.

A union literary and musical entertainment was held at the Congregational church Monday afternoon and evening, March 1st. The entertainment consisted of declamations and songs, also a chance was given parties to compete on different things, such as writing, papers on different subjects, competition for children reciting psalms, also in writing and singing. Evan D. JONES captured first prize on paper No. 1 Thos. D. JONES on paper No. 2. Paper No. 3 was for ladies only, Miss Mary ISAACS took first prize on this one. Next competition was in writing, these were divided into two classes. First for children under 15 years of age. Lizzie JENKINS took first prize in this class. Second class was under 20 years; Luther EVANS captured this prize. Next was competition in speaking. Class 1st, under 15 years of age; Robert JONES first in the class. No. 2, under 20 years. Bonner MORRIS was the lucky man here. Next came the singing; only one double quartette was ready to sing, so there was no competition in the class. Next was a tenor solo, contestants were, Thos. D. JONES and Lot MORRIS, prize divided. Next was solo and chorus for ladies; only one in this class, Mrs. Thos. E. EVANS. Next came solo singing for children under 15 years of age. Eddie EVANS first prize. Next came singing at first sight by note in the "So, Fa" system, in the first class under 15 years of age Eddie EVANS first prize. Class No. 2, under 20 years, Lot MORRIS came out victorious. W.J. JAMES was judicator in all the singing contest. A very interesting five minute discussion was had to try to determine which was the most influential the pulpit or the printing press, the discussion was decided in favor of the pulpit. Miss HITCHCOCK of Wayne was present and favored us with a selection of instrumental music which was appreciated very much. Mr. JAMES of Carroll sang to solos very acceptably. Let us hope that we may have more entertainments of this nature in the future as they are both instructive and interesting, and much good may be derived from them.

Real Estate Transfers.

Carl BRONSYNSKI to Herman BENTHEIRE,
    se 1/4 ne 1/4 and n 1/2 nw 1/4 and se 1/4 nw 1/4
    all in 33-25-2 $3,200.00

Herman BENTHEIRE to Marie BRONSYNSKI, Same land as above	$3,200.00
Ed REYNOLDS (sheriff) to Citizens' Bank, ne 19-25-1	500.00
Ed REYNOLDS (sheriff) to Wm. HARRISON, nw 1/4, 5-26-5	1,900.00
Peter LIEF to Andrew LIEF, ne 1/4 and e 85 acres of se 1/4, 4-25-1	6,125.00
Aury M. MYERS to Wm. M. WRIGHT, lot 3, blk. 9, C&B ad Wayne	1,500.00
Ed REYNOLDS (sheriff) to Wm. MELLOR, se 1/4, 10-26-3	3,600.00
Ed REYNOLDS (sheriff) to Citizens' Bank, sw 1/4, 24-26-3	1,400.00
Ed REYNOLDS (sheriff) to A.L. TUCKER, s 1/2 sw 7-27-2	1,200.00
Sarah A. WRIGHT to Kate A. MYERS, e 1/2 lot 4, 5 & 6, blk. 6	- - -
Wm. MILLER to Edwin SOWERS, e 1/4 nw 1/4 and n 1/2 sw 1/4, 19-26-4	5,600.00
Geo C. GELDER to Kate E. GELDER, w 1/2 lots 1, 2 & 3, blk. 26, Wayne	660.00

The Wayne Republican
March 17, 1897 (Vol. 4, No. 5)

MARRIED: GEMMELL - SHARP. At the home of the bride's parents, Rev. THEOBALD officiating, Robert GEMMELL and Miss Ellen SHARP. Both of the young people are Christian workers and have their church home with the Baptists. They begin their housekeeping in their new home, seven miles west of Wayne, the latter part of this week.

MARRIED: PARK - BLAKE. On Malrch 10 at the office of County Judge MARTIN, Ralph PARK and Etta A. BLAKE.

MARRIED: RUFF - CUNNINGHAM. On March 16, Rev. MILLARD officiating, Xavier J. RUFF and Mrs. Gora CUNNINGHAM, at the home of the bride's father, W.S. BROWN south of the city.

DIED: FISHER. On Tuesday March 16, the 8-months-old daughter of William FISHER, living southwest of the city. The funeral will be held from the M.E. church at this place at 11 a.m. tomorrow (Thursday).

Advertised Letter List.

The following is a list of letters, etc., remaining at the Post office at Wayne Nebraska, for the week ending March 16, 1897.

Webeck ATLES; H.M. BISSELL, Chas. DAHLBERG, Lizzie KLEINE.

Parties calling for the above please give date when advertised.

A.P. CHILDS, P.M.

The Wayne Republican
March 31, 1897 (Vol. 4, No. 7)

BIRTH: George THEIS and wife rejoice over the birth of a son on the 28th.

BIRTH: On March 25 a baby girl came to cheer and bless the home of Fred VAHLKAMP.

BIRTH: Mac CLAYBAUGH and wife are the proud parents of a beautiful girl baby.

LICENSED TO WED: Herman BENTHIER and Emma EHLUS.

MARRIED: At the office of Judge MARTIN on March 25, Albert HAMLOTH and Lena ROHDE.

DIED: The 10-months-old child of D. BATEMAN living seven miles southwest of the city died on Monday and was laid to away to rest on Tuesday.

The following is the village ticket of Carroll to be voted for at the election next Tuesday, five of whom are to be elected trustees: Republicans - J. BAKER, H. BASSFORD, F.M. HURLBURT, Gus WILL, C.H. WOLF. By petition - J. BELDEN, George BELFORD, A.J. SWARTZ.

Eight little Misses following in the steps of their mammas have organized a club that meets each Saturday afternoon for the purpose of self improvement. The name of the club is "The Juvenile History Club" and its membership is composed of Helen and Winifred NORTHROP, Florence WELCH, Ruth and Kate BRESSLER, Lela and Jessie TUCKER and Nellie DEARBORN. This is certainly commendable on the part of the members of the club and we trust they may succeed beyond their fondest expectations.

Real Estate Transfers.

W.M. WRIGHT to Chas. PFEIL,	
s 1/2 sw 1/4 34-26-4	$1,800.00
Lulu L. FOOTE to Chas. ROLAND,	
sw 1/4, 30-26-3	5,000.00
Geo W. JONES to Lucy WATSON,	
n 1/2 ne 1/4 15-27-3	2,000.00
Nelson UTTER to F.M. NORTHROP,	
nw 1/4, 30-26-5	4,800.00
Alex HOLTZ to Mary D. CHANCE,	
lots 15, 16, 17, 18, 19 & 20, blk. 22,	
College Hill ad to Wayne	210.00
J.T. BRESSLER to C.F. BOMERMASTER,	
sw 1/4, 10-25-1	2,500.00
Winside Roller Mill to G. REHMUS,	
lot 2 sub Div. outlot 1 B&P 1st ad to Winside	80.00
O. OAK to M. KRUGER,	
sw 1/4, 13-26-4	5,200.00
H. KRUGER to F. KRUGER,	
all lands and lots of	
Aug. KRUGER, deceased	10,000.00
Aug. BUSS to H. BUSS,	
se 1/4, 35-25-1	3,200.00
C.W. MILLER to Margareta BRUGGERMAN,	
s 1/2 nw 1/4, 8-27-3	1,840.00
Winside Roller Mill to Wm. HOFFMAN,	
lot 3, blk. 3, B&P's 2nd ad to Winside	80.00
R.E.K. MELLOR to L. NURENBERGER,	
ne 1/4, 10-25-5	4,000.00

The Wayne Republican
April 7, 1897 (Vol. 4, No. 8)

DIED: CLARK. On Saturday, April 3, the 10-weeks-old boy baby of Mr. and Mrs. Emmett CLARK living northwest of the city passed to the great beyond.

DIED: WALLACE. In the city of Wayne on Friday morning April 2, Ruby WALLACE aged 22 years. The deceased was a daughter of Mr. and Mrs. WALLACE, living southwest of the city two miles, and was a young lady highly respected by her entire circle of acquaintances and friends. The funeral was held from the home of H.C. WRIGHT in this city on Sunday where the young lady was stopping at the time of her death. The parents, brothers and sisters of the departed have with them the sympathy of our entire community.

The RASH murder case is set for trial at the April term of court, but it is not very likely that it will be tried. RASH has employed no attorney and when court convenes and he is brought in for trial in all probability the court will have to appoint an attorney to defend and he in turn will ask for time to prepare his case so that in all probability the case will go over to the November term and then a change of venue will carry it still further into the future while the county will foot the bills.

The election on Tuesday resulted in electing Henry LEY mayor over Mark STRINGER by a majority of 5, and Everett LAUGHLIN clerk over Will RICKABAUGH by three votes. Lambert ROE was elected for treasurer and A.T. WITTER Police judge. The councilmen elected are 1st ward J.H. GOLL, 2nd ward Ran FRAZIER, 3rd ward D.C. MAIN. The school board members are: for three years' term, C.O. FISHER and J.J. WILLIAMS; Two years' term to fill vacancy, A.F. BRENNER and J.P. GAERTNER; one year's term to fill vacancy, W.H. BRADFORD.

Wayne, Neb., April 6, 1897.
Executive committee appointed by Commander METTLEN of CaseyPost No. 5, at their regular meeting April 5, met in J.D. KING's office to organize and transact such business proper to observe Memorial day. J.D. KING, elected chairman, Jno. P. MATTHEWS was appointed secretary. Committee on Speaker, A.P. CHILDS, J.T. METTLEN; Finance Committee, F.L. NEELY, A.J. FERGUSON, Dan HERRINGTON, Mark STRINGER; Decoration Committee, J.W. BARTLETT, A.W. TAYLOR, Chas. BAGGART, Mr. and Mrs. FERGUSON, Miss Mary METTLEN, Miss C. STRINGER, Mrs. L.E.A. SMITH, Mrs. BRENNER, Mrs. F.L. NEELY; Music, George L. COOK, J.D. KING, Rev. THEOBALD; Commander METTLEN takes charge of procession; B. CUNNINGHAM takes charge of Firing Squad; John STALLSMITH, charge of Colors; Commander METTLEN and Jno. P. MATTHEWS, committee on invitations which will include all ex-soldiers in this and adjoining counties, also all church organizations, civic societies, college and schools with their professors and teachers. Committee adjourned to meet Monday evening, April 19, at 7:30 at J.D. KING's office.

Jno. P. MATTHEWS, Secy.

The Wayne Republican
April 14, 1897 (Vol. 4, No. 9)

BIRTH: To Mr. and Mrs. Walter HURLBERT on Monday a fine girl. (Carroll)

MARRIED: LUNDINS - PEARSON. At the office of County Judge MARTIN on April 9, F.A. LUNDINS and Anna PEARSON.

MARRIED: WITSAMUN - WEAVER. At the M.E. parsonage on Tuesday April 13, Rev. MILLARD officiating, H.U. WITSAMUN and Alice WEAVER, both of Wayne county.

DIED: THOMPSON. On Saturday death entered the home of Mr. and Mrs. Fred THOMPSON and claimed as his own their daughter Eriea, aged 20 years. The immediate cause of death was measles and in the passing of this young lady a family circle is broken. Now sorrow reigns where a few short days ago all was joy. The funeral was held from the Baptist church in this city on Monday, Rev. THEOBALD conducting the services. The sympathies of a vast circle of friends will be extended to the bereaved parents, brothers and sisters in their time of great bereavement, yet we are assured there is but one that can give a consolation that is lasting.

At the recent village election H.C. WOLF, Gus WILL, H. BASSFORD, Joe BELDEN and James BAKER were elected on the town board.

On last Friday Sheriff REYNOLDS brought C.K. RASH, the murderer, from the penitentiary at Lincoln to this place for trial at court next week. It didn't require any extra precaution to keep the citizens of Wayne from resorting to lynch law while the fiend was being taken from the depot to the county bastile, where he is safely ensconsed and apparently free from any danger of mob violence.

The Wayne Republican
April 21, 1897 (Vol. 4, No. 10)

LICENSED TO WED: On Monday Judge MARTIN issued a marriage license to H.C. HECKT and Mabel PHILLIPS, both of Hoskins.

MARRIED: CARROLL - HEFNER. In the city of Wayne at the home of the groom's grandparents, Mr. and Mrs. A.G. HOWARD on Monday evening, April 19, Rev. THEOBALD pronounced the words that bind for life in the holy bonds of wedlock, Dorr H. CARROLL and Gertrude HEFNER. In the groom our readers will readily recognize the young man who for the past three years has guided the destinies of the Winside Tribune. He is a young man of whom our people are justly proud. The bride is a former Winside lady of whom all speak in the highest terms as being a lady of rare accomplishments and one fitting to be a helpmeet to her excellent husband. For this young couple only the best wishes of all will prevail and that theirs may be a happy journey through life is the desire of everyone. Dorr and bride accept congratulations.

MARRIED: JASTRAM - SMITH. At the home of the bride's parents at Homer, Nebraska on Monday, April 19, Rev. H.J. HAPEMAN officiating, W.C. JASTRAM and Mary J. SMITH. The groom is one of the best known young men of our city and one who numbers his friends by the hundreds. The bride is not an entire stranger to our people, having been a student at the College during the years of '92 and '93. She has been a teacher for some time in the schools of Dakota county and is very highly spoken of by all her acquaintances. To "Will" as we are all accustomed to calling him and to his bride the Republican on behalf of itself and readers desires to extend its heartiest congratulations.

Death of Maude BUSKIRK.

Miss Maude BUSKIRK, the oldest daughter of Mr. and Mrs. George BUSKIRK, living north of town in Wayne county, died last Wednesday afternoon of congestion of the lungs, following an attack of measles. Miss BUSKIRK was one of the successful teachers of Wayne county and a young lady who was highly esteemed by all who knew her. Her death brings a double load of afflication to the mother who was absent from home, having been called to Wisconsin last week to attend the funeral of her father. She was unable to reach home until last evening after the funeral which made the circumstances peculiarly sad for her.

The funeral took place yesterday from the Congregational church, Rev. J.W. WHITE conducting the services, after which a large concourse of friends attended the burial of the remains in the family plat in the Wisner cemetery. The Chronicle voices the feelings of the entire community when it expresses heartfelt sympathy with the members of the sorrowing family in their deep bereavement. (The Wisner Chronicle)

The Presbyterian congregation held their annual business meeting on Monday evening and elected as elders D. CUNNINGHAM and John T. METTLEN; trustees Dan HARRINGTON, J.G. MINES, John T. BRESSLER, W.A.K. NEELY and E.D. MITCHELL; morning chorister, Mrs. UTTER; evening, Maude BRITTON; ushers, Walden TUCKER, Ted PHILLEO, George WILBUR and Tom HOLTZ; Sunday school superintendent, W.E. HOWARD; assistant, Frank NANGLE; council Boys' Brigade, E.D. MITCHELL, F.G. PHILLEO and E. CUNNINGHAM.

On Sunday monring last Sheriff REYNOLDS and Deputy GILDERSLEEVE brought RASH the murderer and two other prisoners confined in the jail down through the streets of our city to one of the barber shops to be shaved. They brought them down on foot without so much as a handcuff on RASH and at a time when as many or more persons were on the streets as at any time during the day, it being just about the time that the train was due from the east at 9:30. No demonstration was made by any one or any talk of doing violence to the wretch in any manner whatever, and yet we candidly believe that there was just as much real danger of mob violence then as at any time since the commission of the crime that has but few paralels in the history of fiendish brutality. Wayne county people are law abiding citizens and believe in the law dealing with all that commit offenses no matter how grave that offense may be, and should the trial of RASH be had in our county the offender will receive exact justice at the hands of a jury composed of our citizens.

Court Proceedings.

Court convened on Monday afternoon and at once began to grind and up to noon of today the following cases have been disposed of:

DECREES OF FORECLOSURE GRANTED.

Monticello State Bank vs HANSEN; Maria D. MITCHELL vs KELLY; ELTING vs W.A. LOVE; ERKSHIRE vs E. HUNTER; BURR vs F.P. WILBUR; M. Louise MITCHELL vs GLASER; C.A. CHACE vs HEYER; McCLUSKY & NEEDHAM vs HURLBURT; First National Bank, Wyoming, Ia., vs ASH; HENRIQUE vs GAEBLER, Admr.; J.D. KING vs BRUECHNER.

DODGE vs KRUGER.
Mary MITCHELL vs JOHNSON.
McCLUSKY & NEEDHAM vs HURLBURT.
BURR vs VENNERBURG.
SPENCER HARDENBERG vs LILLIGEBERT.

BARGHOLZ vs KAUFL.
CONTINUED.
WIGHTMAN vs LAUMAN.
STONE vs BOSTROM.
HILDER vs HILDER.
MIDDLESTADT vs KRUGER.
MIDDLESTADT vs BENTHEIR.
MIDDLESTADT vs ECKMAN.
MIDDLESTADT vs VANSHUR.
County of Wayne vs S.B. RUSSELL.
DISMISSED.
McCormick Harvesting Co. vs ALSTADT.
MIDDLESTADT vs BAKER, at plaintiff's cost.
Benton County Bank vs TRACEY.
WHITTON vs LEWIS.
SAUNDERS vs SAUNDERS.
BRESSLER vs WINTER.
BURR vs R.J. TRACEY.
SAWYER vs OXFORD.
HORNICK, HESS & MOORE vs KASS.
DEFAULTS AGAINST DEFENDANTS.
MIDDLESTADT vs. BOOCK.
ECKROTH & CARLSON vs SLAUGHTER.
FURCHNER, DUERIG & Co. vs REIBOLD.
SALES CONFIRMED.
WRIGHT vs HANSEN.
C.H. BURR vs J.J. TRACY.
BOGART vs TALLMAN.

In state vs John BRANDT the charge was statutory rape; the defendant entered a plea of "Guilty" and was sentenced to three years in the penitentiary at hard labor.

Stave vs C.K. RASH, defendant entered plea of "Guilty" but claims not with malice. The case will be the last one of the jury trials and will probably begin tomorrow or Friday.

Frank KRUGER vs Wayne National Bank was the first case submitted to a jury and resulted in a verdict for the plaintiff.

BREWER vs BREWER, decree of divorce granted to plaintiff.

The case of State vs Eugene MUELLER is being tried today. MUELLER is charged with shooting at John KNOUSE with intent to kill.

The Wayne Republican
April 28, 1897 (Vol. 4, No. 11)

The Democrat of last week charges that the commissioners have run bills for the keeping of the poor for the months of January, February and March, 1897, of $683.44, including commissioners charges for attending to the same. We have looked the matter up carefully and find the amount to be about $642.34 in which we include $10.90 for charges of commissioners and we append a statement as to what these expenses were incurred for in order to show the exact conditions as nearly as possible:

W.P. AGLER, board of H.N. CUNNINGHAM, Dec. '96	$5.00
W.P. AGLER, rent poor house Jan. 1, '97 to Jan. 1, '98	125.00
J.P. GAERTNER, coffin and funeral expenses of H.N. CUNNINGHAM on Dec. 25, '96	36.00
Home of Feeble Minded, bills of 1896	21.15
W.P. AGLER, care of H.N. CUNNINGHAM, 1896	12.50
EDWARDS & BRADFORD Lbr. Co., coal for paupers	19.50
H.G. LEISENRING, county physician, 1st qtr.	50.00
John ZEIMER, care of poor	5.00
J.P. GAERTNER, coffin for Mrs. BOCKEMUEHL and KLANAN	44.00
Aug. DECK, shroud	.95
A.B. CHERRY, physician for Mrs. BOCKEMUEHL	14.00
Mrs. STRICKLAND, groceries and care for Mrs. BOCKEMUEHL and children	56.15
A.H. CARTER, supplies	13.00
Miss McCAULEY, dress for Mrs. BOCKEMUEHL	5.00
D.J. CAVANAUGH, funeral for Mrs. BOCKEMUEHL	7.00
Bert BROWER, expenses Mrs. BOCKEMUEHL	6.00
W.R. OLMSTED, expenses Mrs. BOCKEMUEHL	6.00
Mrs. G.B. CARTER, expenses Mrs. BOCKEMUEHL	28.00
EDWARDS & BRADFORD Lbr. Co., coal	14.95
P.L. MILLER, supplies	4.95
W.C. PARSONS, suplies	24.29
John ZEIMER, care of poor	2.50
J.P. GAERTNER, four coffins and funeral expenses, burial of the murdered family of RASH	125.00
EDWARDS & BRADFORD Lbr. Co., coal	6.50
A.M. JACOBS, care of poor	3.00
Geo. HARRIGFELD, care of poor	7.90
TOTAL	$642.34

If the reader will observe, of this amount $17.50 paid to AGLER and $36.00 to GAERTNER for H.N. CUNNINGHAM, belongs to 1896, also the charge of Home of Febble Minded of $21.15.

Now by looking up the records for 1895, the year before the present system went into vogue, we find the total poor bills for that year were $2,369.93, and of this amount $186.50 was paid to justices of the peace for acting as overseers and of this amount one justice was paid $112. The amount paid out for the support of the poor and for justices to act as overseers for the months of January, February and March of the year 1895 was $1,202.36, and of this the justices got $107.50, and one of them had as his share of this $62. Let us look a little further into the charges for the three months of 1897 alluded to. There is a charge of $125 for rent of poor house for the entire year, while only $37.50 is properly chargeable to the three months named. Then again there comes in the funeral expenses attendant upon the RASH murder of $125 and also two others of $44 for coffins, and in the same months of 1895 there were no such expenses. However, comment is unnecessary as the facts set forth will show the intent of the Democrat to mislead in the article referred to, and of its desire to try to throw the board of commissioners into disrepute in order that a member may be elected in the Second district this fall that will be ready to return to the old methods that put taxpayers completely at the mercy of a lot of fellows whose aim in life is and has been to loot the treasury at every turn.

Hoskins Public School.

Number of days all pupils attended, 3,160 days.
Number of visits of County Superintendent, 3.
Number of visits of Directors, 3.
Number of actual days taught, 140 days.

Pupils who were never tardy: Harry and Vernie ZEIMER, Ethel WEATHERHOLT.

Miss Pearl GREEN drew the prize for attending 133 of 140 school days this year.

Visitors of this term are as follows: Mrs. J.R. HOYLE; M.E. ZUTZ; Mabel PHILLIPS; Agnes PAUL; M.D. FLETCHER, three times; W.J. WEATHERHOLT, three times; J.W. WINTER; C.H. CLINE; Mrs. PARSON, three times; Thos. WEISEMANN; A. STORTZ, three times; Geo. LICHTY, three times; Rev. E. LOHAER, two times; Geo. HARRIGFELD, two times; Jennie WADDELL and Miss LEE.

Court Proceedings.
(Continued from last week.)

HENRY vs GIBSON, dismissed without prejudice at plaintiff's cost.

EVERETT & WAITE, confirmed, deed ordered.
GOLTZ vs MAHLKE, confirmed, deed ordered.
BOGART vs TALLMAN, confirmed, deed ordered.
McCLUSKY & NEEDHAM vs WEATHERHOLT, confirmed, deed ordered.
N.E.L.&T. Co. vs HENRY, foreclosure as prayed.
VAIL vs CAHOON, foreclosure as prayed.
BRESSLER vs ADAMS, foreclosure as prayed.
HOWE vs MILLER, foreclosure as prayed.
TALBOT vs CARSTENS, foreclosure as prayed.
E. & B. L. Co. vs BRADY, foreclosure as prayed.
University VT. vs SMITH, foreclosure as prayed.
MELLOR vs CADWELL, foreclosure as prayed.
STRAHN vs NIEMAN, foreclosure as prayed.
BOYD vs MELLOR, judgment for defendant.
BRESSLER vs WINTER, dismissed at plaintiff's cost.
HARDENBERG vs DOBBIN, judgment for plaintiff.
Citizen's Bank vs GLEASON, judgment for plaintiff.
LOVE vs LUNDBERG, judgment for plaintiff.
MEYERS vs LEY, judgment for plaintiff.
Wayne County vs RUSSELL, continued.
HANSEN vs HOUSE, continued.
FRUECHTE vs MONK & WALTER, judgment for plaintiff.

JONES vs Wayne County, plaintiff given 30 days to file petition, defendant 30 days thereafter to answer.

BARTLETT vs HEISTER, judgment for plaintiff.
HALBERT vs BRITTON, settled, dismissed at plaintiff's cost.
SCHMILL vs ERICKSON, continued.
GIBSON vs CHENAUER, leave to file petition.
GIBSON vs NORTHROP, same as above.
BREWER vs BREWER, divorce granted Elsie BREWER.
GERARD vs LEWIS, continued.
REYNOLDS vs Wayne County, dismissed at plaintiff's cost.
HANSEN vs HANSEN, new trial granted.

REYNOLDS vs Wayne County, judgment for plaintiff for $48.20, defendant given 40 days to file bill of exceptions.

FRENCH vs MILLER, demurrer of defendant sustained, plaintiff given 60 days to file amended petition.

State vs MUELLER, defendant found guilty and sentenced to 18 months in penitentiary at hard labor.

FEATHER vs Wayne County. This is the case in which plaintiff as a taxpayer appealed from bills of A.M. JACOBS for $3.00 and Geo HARRIGFELD for $7.90 for acting as overseers of the poor. Court sustains appellant, but in giving decision admitted the justice of the bill, but finds no law allowing same.

Real Estate Transfers.

G.W. TROTTER to Perrin LONG,	
lots 1, 2, 3, 4, 5 & 6, blk. 10, Winside	$1,300.00
J.O. MILLIGAN to Lewis M. WATSON,	
lot 18, F&W ad to Wayne	600.00
Wm. GODDARD, et al., to Moses B. I. GODDARD,	
nw 1/2, 3-27-1	1.00
Wm. GODDARD, et al., to Wm. GODDARD,	
se 1/4, 30-27-1	1.00
Wm. GODDARD, et al., to Elizabeth SHEPHARD,	
se 1/4, 1-27-1	1.00
Chas. M. KNAPP to J.S. FRENCH,	
s 1/2 sw 1/4 3 and n 1/2 nw 1/4, 10-27-2	2,000.00
J.S. FRENCH to Henry SCHLUNS,	
s 1/4 sw 1/4 3 and n 1/2 nw 1/4, 10-27-2	- - -

The Wayne Republican
May 5, 1897 (Vol. 4, No. 12)

DIED: McMANIGAL. On Friday, April 30, E.G. McMANIGAL, aged 25 years and one month died at the home of his father, Dan McMANIGAL, 11 miles southeast of this city. The deceased had been ill for about two weeks of lung fever or pneumonia, was apparently improving when with scarcely any warning the dreaded messenger entered the home and called him away. He leaves to mourn his seemingly untimely going a wife, father, mother, one sister and three brothers whose hearts are bleeding today as never before and who have the sympathies of the entire community in their great affliction. The great procession of neighbors and friends that followed all that was mortal of this young man to their last resting place on Sunday plainly indicated the high estimation in which he was held by those who knew him best. The funeral services were held in the M.E. church in this city and were conducted by Rev. MILLARD after which the remains were conveyed to our silent city there to rest from life's cares and pains.

On Monday evening the old city council met and transacted the business before it adjourned sine die. Mayor LEY then called the new council together after the qualification of the members elect and proceeded to the organization of that body. The following committees were appointed: Finance, D.C. MAIN, E.P. OLMSTED, J.H. GOLL; Streets and Alleys, C.O. FISHER, S.H. RICHARDS, Ran FRAZIER; Water, OLMSTED, FISHER, RICHARDS; Marshal, Geo. L. MINER; Water Commissioner, Peter COVIE; City Attorney, Frank FULLER. On the matter of application of Frank and Otto KRUGER for license to sell liquors it was voted to grant same at $120.

One day last week Frank HITCHCOCK, a member of the High School graduating class got into a dispute with the assistant principal, Mr. HOWARD and used language that showed him to be a hoodlum and then followed it up by striking the teacher. At the time Principal BONER was out of the city and HITCHCOCK was suspended until BONER's return. On Monday evening the matter was brought before the school board and they decided to let the young man return to school again if he would make an apology to the school and Mr. HOWARD which he did on yesterday. It may be that the board did what was best in the premises, but public opinion is not very unanimously with them in the action taken.

The Wayne Republican
May 12, 1897 (Vol. 4, No. 13)

BIRTH: Dr. LEISENRING informs us that Gotleib HALLER and wife are the proud parents of a fine boy born Saturday.

LICENSE TO WED: On Monday afternoon Judge MARTIN issued a license to marry to Peter ULRICH, jr., and Lena MAAS.

MARRIED: NEITZKE - PODDOLL. On Sunday, May 9 at High noon in the German Lutheran church at Winside, Rev. Alfred KRAUS joined in matrimony H. NEITZKE and Gertie PODDOLL.

Sheriff REYNOLDS conveyed C.K. RASH to Pierce on Monday afternoon there to remain until a jury of his fellowmen shall determine the punishment that shall be his for the murder of his wife and children.

An Open Letter.
TO THE EDITOR OF REPUBLICAN:

Yes sir, I did apologize to Mr. HOWARD, the school board and the school, and I am not ashamed of it either. I was largely in the wrong, and Mr. HOWARD more than acted the man in helping me out of the difficulty, and I can assure you we shall be the best of friends in the future.

As to the hoodlum part - Men were conveniently born with two eyes, two ears and one tongue, that they may hear both sides of anythng, see it from more than one standpoint and then speak of it once for each time he hears and sees it twice. But it seems that the honorable Editor of the Republican is blind in one eye, deaf in one ear and has more than one tongue, or else the one he has is his chief weapon which is hung on a pivot and cracks at both ends. A loquacious mouth is like a badly managed bank. It makes large issues on no solid capital. The calibre of a man's brain is inversly proportional to the calibre of his mouth. If the calibre of his mouth is large the calibre of his brain is small. Any writer who uses weak arguments and strong epithets makes quite as great a mistake as the landlady who furnishes her customers with weak tea and strong butter. I think also that the school board can manage the affairs of the district without the counsel or dictation of the wise editor.

Frank W. HITCHCOCK
- In Democrat

The Wayne Republican
May 19, 1897 (Vol. 4, No. 14)

BIRTH: Another fine daughter is making her home with Mr. and Mrs. J.G. FOSTER. (Hoskins)

Real Estate Transfers.

Geo. BOGART to Wm. MELLOR, w 1/2 nw 1/4 9-25-3	$1,550.00
Jas. SHORTEN, et al., to Jas. H. & W.T. SHORTEN, ne 1/4, 14-25-3	5,600.00
I. IVANSON to Laurel State Bank, lot 12, T&W ad to Wayne	300.00
Wm. HOUSE to N.A. RAINBOLT, s 1/2 and nw 1/4, all 13, ne 1/4 24 all in twp 26-1; ne 1/4 7, w 1/2 of 18, all in 56-2	44,000.00

E. BRAASCH to Ellen SHANNON,
    lots 10, 11 & 12, blk. 11, Hoskins $50.00
W. COLLARD to R.E. PATE,
    nw 1/4, 32-25-3   3,200.00

The Wayne Republican
May 26, 1897 (Vol. 4, No. 15)

DIED: J.H. CUNNINGHAM, very suddenly of conjestion of the lungs, aged 72 years. Deceased was the father of E. CUNNINGHAM, editor of this paper, and brother David CUNNINGHAM of this place. He was a resident of Patterson, Pa., where he has lived all his life. He leaves one daughter and two sons to mourn his demise.

The class of '98 gave a very pleasant entertainment at the Presbyterian church on Tuesday evening. It consists of seven girls and two boys: Misses Rena OLMSTED, Reba NANGLE, Alice RUNDELL, Ethel TUCKER, Julia ANDREAS, Mary PAWLSKI, Laura HOLTZ, Messrs. Jim WRIGHT and Lester SURBER. Space will not permit a definite account as we would like, but we will say that one and all acqitted themselves admirably. They were assisted in their music by Miss Anna GAMBLE who sang a very pleasing solo, and Misses BECKENHAUER, Grace COOK and Lulu COOK who rendered a beautiful quartette, Miss Reba NANGLE whistling an obligato like a bird.

The Wayne Republican
June 2, 1897 (Vol. 4, No. 16)

MARRIED: Chas. WATSON, our popular furniture man was married on Wednesday to a Miss RILEY of Pierce. Mr. WATSON has lived in Wayne and vicinity for some time and has made many friends who rejoice to see him lay aside single blessedness and trot in dual harness the rest of his natural life.

Chris NELSON was locked in the calaboose on Saturday charged with being drunk and disorderly. During the night he tired of his quarters and decided to go home which he did by prying off the bars.

At a meeting of the school board Tuesday night the following teachers were retained: Miss SHULTZ, Miss BROWN, Miss DICKEY, Mrs. CONN, Mr. HOWARD. The new teachers elected are

Miss BYRNE and Miss FRASER.

The Wayne Republican
June 9, 1897 (Vol. 4, No. 17)

MARRIED: Henry FREVORT and Martha BEHMER were married at the home of the bride a few days ago. Congratulations are extended. (Hoskins)

MARRIED: WATSON - RILEY. At the home of the bride's mother, south of town, on Wednesday, June 2, Mr. C.A. WATSON, of Wayne, and Miss Emma RILEY, of Pierce, Rev. G.M. COUFFER officiating. The ceremony was performed in the parlors of the residence, the couple taking their vows underneath a beautiful arch of green. After this the guests to the number of seventy-five, were invited to a feast that was elaborate and sumptous. Mr. and Mrs. WATSON left the same afternoon for their future home in Wayne. The bride was the recipient of many useful and costly presents, tokens of the love and esteem in which she is universally held by her friends in Pierce and elsewhere. The Call extends congratulations and wishes them all the joys and comforts this life can afford. (Pierce Call)

DIED: The people of this place were shocked to learn on Saturday morning that Mrs. JOHANSEN, wife of drayman JOHANSEN, had taken a large dose of paris green with the determination of ending her life. For some time past her health had been failing and those who knew her best noticed that her mind often wavered. About 8:30 p.m. Mr. JOHANSEN who was out in the yard heard the children crying and going to the house found what his wife had done. He immediately summoned Dr. NEIMAN who worked with her all night and left her at 4 o'clock a.m. resting quite easy, but later in the day she grew rapidly worse, and suffered until noon on Sunday when she passed away. Mrs. JOHANSEN was born in Denmark and was 26 years old at the time of her sad death. She leaves three little children, the oldest being ____ years old. The funeral took place Monday afternoon.

Chris NELSON was arraigned before Justice WITTER on Friday, on the charge of being drunk and disorderly. He plead guilty and was given $5 and costs or 15 days in jail. He took the latter.

On Monday afternoon the attorneys and witnesses in the RASH murder case left for Pierce. The prosecution took to that place about twenty-five or thirty witnesses and the defense seven or eight. Several other parties from the city and county are also in attendance at court to watch the proceedings.

The school board met on Monday evening and completed the election of their corps of teachers for the ensuing year and they are as follows: W.E. HOWARD, ass't principal; Mrs. CONN, grammar; Miss BYRNE, intermediate; Miss MORROW, intermediate; Miss SHULZ, 1st primary; Miss BROWN, 2nd primary; and the Misses FRAZIER and DICKEY in the ward building. We believe the corps of teachers just chosen will prove to be one of the best ever in charge of our schools and that those who fought so hard to prevent the reelection of several members of the present school board will ere many months have reason to believe that the members in question were ever ready to do all in their power for the advancement of our schools. The position of a member of a school board is not one to be particularly desired at any time and when members are found that have the stamina to stand up for what they believe to be the interests of the district they should receive proper credit.

Cour Proceedings.

KRUGER vs Wayne National Bank, motion for new trial taken under advisement.

MELLOR vs CADWELL, et al., judgment for cross petitioner, B.F. SWAN for $136 and interest at 10 per cent. Foreclosure ordered.

State of Nebraska vs Frank MYERS, plead guilty and sentenced to three years in the penitentiary. This is the case where defendant robbed the store of Bruce ROOSA a few weeks ago.

MELLOR vs VAUGHN, et al., motion of plaintiff to retax costs overruled, plaintiff excepts and given 40 days to file bill of exception.

First National Bank vs BROWN, et al., sheriff ordered to make deed.

RASH Murder Trial.

On yesterday the trial of C.K. RASH for the murder of his wife and three children was commenced at Pierce.

It will probably be well to give here a short history of the case in order that the testimony and findings of the jury will be better understood. For a few years prior to January 27, 1897, C.K. RASH and his wife and children lived on a farm two miles west and about eight miles south of the city of Wayne. On the evening of the date above given RASH attended a protracted meeting being held at Grace M.E. church located a few miles north of where he resided and while there got possession of a soapstone belonging to Rev. WRIGHT and used as a footwarmer while driving. After services were concluding at the church RASH got into his wagon and started for home singing and shouting along the way in a manner that attracted the attention of neighbors whose homes he passed. Arriving at home, he left his team standing and taking the stone mentioned, entered the house and found his wife awaiting his return and the three children in bed asleep. He told his wife that God had commanded him to destroy her and the children consisting of a boy of 10 summers, a little girl of 8 and a baby boy not quite two years of age. The wife and mother plead for the lives of herself and babes but it was all of no avail and the fiend dealt her a blow on the head with the stone smashing it into pieces but failed to knock her down. She then fought for her life, but he secured one of the larger pieces of the stone and with it pounded her head to jelly. The oldest boy awakened by the noise rose and begged his father to spare his mother's life but the appeals of the child like those of the mother were unheeded and when he had killed the mother he turned upon the innocent lad and took his life with the same stone and then with it killed the little girl and babe as they lay in bed. After completing his awful work he went out, unhitched and put his horses in the barn while the blood of those he should have protected to the last was warm upon his hands, leaving the bloody imprints of his hands upon horses and harnesses. He then returned to the home he had so ruthlessly destroyed and without any fire sat all the cold winter night alone with the dead until neighbors during the following day discovered his horrible deed, reported to the officers, and he was arrested, brought to the city and locked up. His case was called at the April term of court in this county when an application was made for a change of venue which was granted and trial fixed for June 8 at Pierce.

RASH is about 5 feet 10 inches tall, weighs about 160 or 170 pounds is of light complexion, with a dull blue eye and a shock head of brown hair and wears a stubby reddish mustache. He has gained in flesh since his incarceration and although a plea of insanity will be entered by his attorney, Frank FULLER, yet he seems perfectly rational on all subjects and talks calmly of the awful deed, giving as his only excuse that God commanded him to do it.

The Wayne Republican
June 16, 1897 (Vol. 4, No. 18)

RASH NOT GUILTY.
So Says the Pierce County Jury - -
The Evidence in the Case.

The attorneys appearing were M.H. LEAMY, County Attorney of Pierce County, and A.A. WELCH, County Attorney of Wayne County, for the State, and Frank FULLER of Wayne, and Douglas CONES and H.F. BARNHARDT for defendant.

Five brothers of the defendant were at the trial, two from near Wayne, one from Fremont, and two from Missouri; also one sister from Missouri.

Court convened at 9:30 June 8, 1897, at the court house. Selection of the jury commenced at 11 o'clock and with an adjournment of one and one-half hours lasted until 3:50 p.m. Thirty-six jurors in all were examined before twelve were selected. The jurymen as selected are as follows: C.W. SCOTT, Henry KUHL, Heimer RHODES, Samuel FITCH, Robert SCHOENFELDT, H.L. LUECK, Wm. WALKER, Julius KUHL, C.S. MARTIN, Geo FRIEDRICH, Horace WOODWORTH, and Charles ULRICH.

The attorneys then opened the case by making a statement to the jury of what they proposed to prove. The statement on behalf of the State made by Mr. WELCH consisted principally in what our readers already know from report of coroner's inquest.

Mr. FULLER on behalf of the defense stated that they were not here to deny that an awful crime had been committed, we are not here to say that it was not one of the worst crimes ever committed in this part of the state, but we are here to show that before you can convict a man of the charge of murder there are certain ingredients must enter into that charge. The story of this man's life is very brief. He was raised on a farm, always lived upon a farm; come to the state of Nebraska about eight to ten years ago with wife and two children, resided in Wayne county for last three or four years. Is a man of peculiar disposition, of peculiar acting temperament; some time before the offense was committed had been attending meetings; had been attending these revivals for something like a week. Took his wife and children; was along in the month of January, very cold severe weather. Did not take his family all the time, weather got so cold concluded to leave his family at home and he attended church alone. Prior to this time had been a member or made application for membership in the Methodist church, but he had (what is called in common parlance) back-slidden, as he had failed to live up to some of the doctorines of the church. The idea again seized him that he would become a church man and change his mode of living, so when these revivals began he commenced to attend. He became very earnest and very devoted, reading his Bible, had it with him constantly. Three or four evenings before the terrible calamity took place he was on his way to church and he thought he heard a command. In obedience to the command he went to a straw stack near by, unhitched his horses, and got down and prayed. Looking up he saw three bright lights, like moons, coming directly towards his home. He asked the Lord what that meant and the Lord said it was enemies come to destroy himself, his family and his property. He immediately hitched up and drove as fast as he could to his home. He went to the house and looked in and saw no one there. He then went in, and he and his wife talked on religious subject and finally retired. On blowing out the light he thought he heard some one knock at the door. Asked his wife who that was that knocked. She said she heard no one. He said for them to come in. He said the Lord come in and up to the side of the bed, saw Him distinctly and conversed with Him, told Him he was going to follow in His foot steps. The Lord told him to keep right on as he was and it would be all right. The Lord then turned and went out. He then began to sing religious songs and to pray, and asked his wife to sing and pray and they both sang religious songs and sang themselves to sleep.

The night of the crime went to church, was not many there, the minister asked him to pray; went to the altar and kneeled down and prayed, and when he got up thought he saw a bright star coming towards him. It hit him in the forehead and blinded him. When services were over he started to go out and took a stone laying on the stove. Drove home very fast and sang and exorted all the way home. When he got home went to the barn, threw the lines over his horses' backs and went to the door and knocked; his wife came to the door and let him in. He thought he heard a command to sacrifice his wife and children to the Lord; that he then with the soap stone killed his wife and children, and remained in the house all night reading his bible.

WITNESSES CALLED AND SWORN AT 4:40:

P.M. CORBIT, testified in substance as follows: Was acquainted with Julia RASH (wife of C.K. RASH.) Saw her body last on the 28th day of January, 1897, at her residence on farm 10 miles south of Wayne. Body was lying on the floor in terrible mutilated condition her head being mashed out of all resemblance to life, no eyes or nose being distinguishable; wore an ordinary wrapper as would wear around the house. (While witness was describing condition of Julia RASH's body the defendant RASH became very much affected, sobbing out aloud, and the Sheriff had to request him to keep still) Witness testified he had known the defendant some six years.

Henry GAERTNER, testifed that he was called to prepare the body of Julia RASH for burial about three days after the crime. Testimony in regard to condition of body about same as CORBIT.

W.S. GUTHRIDGE said he was acquainted with defendant and wife Julia RASH. Lived about 3/4 of a mile from them, his being about the nearest house to theirs on the south. Assisted in preparing body of Julia RASH for burial.

Charles MAXWELL, lived 2 3/4 miles from defendant RASH; was not much acquainted with him. Saw the body of Julia RASH on the evening of the 28th day of January, 1897, at house where defendant and wife resided. Testimony in regard to condition of body same as foregoing witnesses.

Gus ANDERSON, resided January 27th, 1897, about 3/4 of mile from RASH, south east; was acquainted with defendant and knew his wife Julia RASH, when he saw her; had known RASH four years; helped lay out bodies of RASH's family on the evening of January 28. Testimony in regard to the condition of bodies same as foregoing witnesses. Had conversation with defendant in October. Witness asked to repeat conversation; object to by defendant and objection over-ruled, followed by other objections and rulings, until witness hardly knew what he was testifying to. The substance of the testimony was that he (RASH) had had some trouble with Nels ANDERSON whom he had given a thrashing, and Nels had said that if he did not come over and settle before the next Monday he would sue him. RASH had said to Gus ANDERSON that he would follow the thing up if he was sued if it cost him a divorce from his wife. Witness saw buggy next morning after the crime, looked as if had been upset, the tongue being broken. Witness before Mr. ANDERSON were not cross-examined; a cup was here introduced with blood marks on it, and on cross examination witness said that when found it looked as if someone had drank blood out of it, as there marks on it indicating fingermarks, and also marks which looked as if it had been touched by some person's lips.

Joe BONAWITZ, was acquainted with defendant and wife, Julia RASH, had known them three years, lived within half mile of them, was at their place January 28th, 1897, at 8 o'clock; was at house of RASH Tuesday before crime, talked with him and his wife. Defendant passed by my house singing the night of the crime. On cross-examination did not know what he was singing.

They had three children. Saw nothing peculiar in conversation of RASH on Tuesday, talked about the weather, price of corn, etc. Saw defendant at coroner's inquest, had known him about three years, neighbored with him.

Ben RHEMUS, acquainted with C.K. RASH and wife Julia RASH. Lived one mile southwest from defendant; was in his house night before crime, asked RASH if he would come next day and help shell corn, RASH finally said he would. Did not show up next morning, went over, looked in door, saw RASH, saw body lying on the floor, says Ugh! and run away, scared. No cross-examination.

Ray McNIGHT, lived in Stanton Co., near RASH. Saw him next day after crime in the house, about 10 o'clock. Was in the kitchen when I first saw him, did not say anything to him.

Stephen RASH, testified he lived in Stanton Co., was a brother of the defendant; was at defendant's place about two months before crime; talked about various subjects, did not have any conversation about trouble between defendant and his wife.

Ed RENNICK, testified was acquainted with RASH; lived about four miles from him, saw him at Grace church on the night of January 27, 1897. After singing RASH led in prayer, had heard him pray before, did not remember anything unusual in his prayer. After dismissal he shook hands with witness and Mr. GILDERSLEEVE and went down towards the stove, heard Mr. WRIGHT speak something to him about himself and wife uniting with the church, did not hear defendant answer, defendant then went out. Saw him at church before that; do not remember of hearing him say anything before, did not notice him take any part.

Mrs. BONAWITZ, am wife of Joe BONAWITZ, acquainted with defendant and his wife, known them about two years, lived about half mile from them. Saw defendant on the 27th day of January, 1897, at home in the house; talked with him and wife about the weather, corn, and that was about all the conversation we had while he was there. Had some conversation with Mrs. RASH (Witness not allowed to state any conversation with Mrs. R. while Mr. R. was not present.) Defendant sat by the stove whittling, was not there all the time I was there; was there about two hours; Mrs. RASH did not seem cheerful as sometimes. RASH always seemd to treat his wife all right so far as witness knew.

Enoch HUNTER, acquainted with defendant, never met wife. Testimony in regard to bodies about the same as has been given. No new evidence.

Nels ANDERSON, lived near RASH, defendant drove by his house on the night of January 27, 1897. No new evidence.

Charles GILDERSLEEVE, acquainted with defendant, saw him on the 27th of January, at Grace church; defendant led in prayer, thought it a little peculiar, did not think he prayed as he used to, had heard him pray before, about a year before. Most of testimony in regard to defendant's actions at church same as Mr. RENNICK's. On cross-examination thought his actions were peculiar and that he looked peculiar out of his eyes.

Rev. WRIGHT testifed in part as follows: Lived in Winside, conducted services at Grace church during part of January, 1897, including the 27th. His testimony in regard to actions of defendant at church on the night of the 27th same as former witnesses. The balance of his testimony consisted of a re-statement of a conversation he had had with RASH at the jail after the crime, brought out by questions on the part of WRIGHT, being a statement of the circumstances of the crime with which our readers are familiar. He also stated that defendant had told him when asked why he had killed his wife that he did it because she was an adulteress and was not worthy to live, he did not love her, and she had no right to live, did not love the children because they were her children and he could not love them. He also testifed in regard to some slight quarrels defendant had had with his wife, some of them so remote that Judge would not admit them as evidence, some being as long as eight years before they were married.

Adjourned at 10 o'clock until 9 Wednesday morning.

WEDNESDAY MORNING.

Ed REYNOLDS testified he had been acquainted with RASH 6 or 7 years; knew his wife when he saw her; saw RASH at his home southwest of Wayne at the time he was arrested, on the 28th of January; saw four bodies lying in the house; supposed they were the bodies or RASH's familiy; found several pieces of soap stone there at that time, supposed they were the insruments used by RASH to commit the deed; on the way to Wayne defendant complained of being cold; wanted witness to get to Wayne as soon as possible, as he was afraid when his neighbors got into the house and saw the bodies they would want to hang him; requested witness half a dozen times to hurry up and get to Wayne; witness talked with him that night in jail about the crime, and he seemed to feel bad over it; the next morning defendant was morose and sullen and would not talk, would not eat, and did not eat or drink for three days; on the third day witness told him if he did not eat he would make him do so; RASH said he would like to see him, said he guessed a man did not have to eat unless he wanted to; witness went down and got Dr. LEISENRING and they fed him, forcing it down his throat through a rubber tube; from that time on he was the same as any other man, had good appetite and would eat more than he dared give him; during his fasting RASH had tried to make an assault on witness, and also wanted to fight his brother when he went in to see him; RASH told the witness that he had not intended to kill the children, but thought he was commanded by some higher power to kill the woman; when the boy came to the rescue he hit him with the stone, and then thought he might as well kill the rest of them and have done with it; never heard the defendant say anything in regard to his wife's character.

L.C. GILDERSLEEVE had known defendant 5 or 6 years, saw him on the night of his arrest, sat in the front seat of the carriage coming from RASH's place to town, while RASH and the sheriff sat in the rear seat; defendant objected to going a certain road, because he said it led back to the crowd, saying to witness, "now you have always been my friend, you would not allow a mob to take me, would you?" witness said he would not and that there was not one in the crowd that would; RASH requested the witness to take the lines from the driver and drive to Wayne as fast as he could; RASH did not talk much the first night in jail; said he had killed his family and that the Lord had directed him to; would commence to say something and then hesitate and say "I guess I won't say it, don't know that I have any friends, but don't know that I can trust you;" commenced the same way the second night; witness told him he did not care whether he talked to him or not; defendant said he had got to talk to some one, and it seemed as though he was directed to talk to him; inquired about his family and wanted to know if Charles GILDERSLEEVE and Rev. WRIGHT had been witnesses; when asked why he thought they would be witnesses he said, "they saw me at the church the night I committed the crime and saw how I acted;" defendant said he was jealous of his wife, was jealous of two persons in the neighborhood, and that he had found out that they had put up a job on him, that one of them would go to town with him and get him drunk and the other would go up to his house and stay with his wife; said the Lord had directed him to kill them; that he warned his wife repeatedly to stop it, but that she did not heed his warning, and that the Lord had commanded him to kill her; also told witness about seeing the stars; witness did not know if RASH had told him when he first determined to kill his wife, but that he had intended to kill her for some time, and made up his mind to kill her some time before that, but his courage failed; had made up his mind when he left church that night to go home and kill her, and drove very fast all the way home to keep up his courage; when he got home left the horses stand for fear if he waited to unhitch he would not kill her; he seemed anxious to talk at night but would not talk in the day time; went up one day to get him to sign a waiver of advertising in chattel mortgage sale, and he was standing in the corner; spoke to him several times, but he paid no attention, finally told him there was nobody there but me, that I wanted to see him on business; he then came up to the bars but refused to sign the waiver, said he was afraid it would go against him; in the evening of the same day, about 10 o'clock, he approached the subject again and asked what I thought about it, that it was simply to save cost, and he then said to make out waiver and he would sign it, which he did; talked with him every night a great deal, but do not remember all he said; on cross examination witness said defendant spent most of his time standing in the corner in day time, when not lying down on cot; sometimes read to witness from bible at night; read 2nd chapter of Revelation, where it refers to the white stone; said he saw stars on the night before the crime, told his wife he was going to church and started in that direction, saw the stars and went to the straw stack, found a good place for his team where someone had hauled out a few loads of straw, unhitched his horses and tied them to the buggy, knelt down and prayed and then got up and followed the star which led him to his house; said he went to the house and looked in at the window; said something about a battle he said was going on, looked in at the window and saw his wife, that he watched the premises; said he told his wife when he started that he was going to church, but that he did not intend to go, went to the straw stack for the purpose of leaving his team and going back to watch the house for those fellows he had told me about; said he watched the premises until about the time for church to be out; and then went back and got his team; told his wife what he had seen; after retiring said he heard a rap at the door and said, "Come in, Lord," and the Lord opened the door and came in; there was a bright light in the room, asked his wife if she could see it, and she said she could not; think he said there was a noise something like a cannon going off at the time he was saved in the night; did not say anything about being afraid he would be poisoned when he refused to eat, said he would eat when he got ready. On re-direct examination witness said defendant had told him that he went out to the straw stack for the purpose of waiting for two men he supposed would be at the house that night; that he told his wife he was going to church, but did not intent to go; said he followed the star back to the house.

Mr. REYNOLDS recalled, testified that he had asked defendant what his object was not to eat or talk to him when first put in jail, and that he said he did not care to say anything, that if he talked there was a good many people in, and he might say something that would hurt him; witness asked him if he intended to make people believe he was insane, and he said no, he did not want to talk for fear he would say something that he hadn't ought to say.

The State here rested its case.

Geo. WEATHERALL testified, had been acquainted with the defendant and his wife for 5 or 6 years; was at their home Tuesday proceeding the crime; was there about two hours, talked about religion, argued on religion; defendant got his bible and wanted to prove his side, got up in front of witness with his knees against witness' knees and got hold of his hand and read out of the bible to him; witness would say I must go, and RASH would say I just want to read you one more verse now; told witness about seeing the stars in heaven, felt a great pain in his breast one night, and than a great crash, and says to his woman did you hear that Julia, what was that, and she said it was the dog coughing under the house, and then he says the pain left him and he felt as humble as a little child, and said that was when he went into heaven; did not think much about his actions, just supposed he had got religion and was excited over it; never talked with him on religion before; never saw him ill-treat his wife.

James T. RASH testified, am the brother of defendant, resident of Putnam county, Missouri, lived there 41 years; father dead, died about 11 or 12 years ago, by suicide. On cross examination testified, father was 65 years old when he died; was in fair health; do not know that he ever had any domestic troubles, was in poor financial condition; owned 80 acres of land and little personal property; land was not incumbered.

Mrs. HICKMAN, resident of Missouri, sister of defendant; had a brother named Joseph H. RASH, who is dead, was confined in the asylum in Missouri for over a year, finally died in the asylum; before going to asylum he was insane for about two years, kept him at home, had to watch him all the time, and sometimes had to tie him, as he was vicious; he claimed to be Christ the living God, and thought everybody had to come to him to be saved; had been attending religious revivals for five weeks previous to becoming insane; he was a cripple, kind of club foot, but done as much work as anyone.

Charles H. RASH, lives near Laurel, brother of defendant;

had a brother named Joseph H. RASH, is now dead, was about 30 years old when he died, died at Fulton, Missouri, in the insane asylum; I was at home while we kept him before sending him to the asylum; watched him most of the time; he would imagine he was commanding a great army, and would ask me if I did not hear the great noise and see that smoke of battle; when he had these spells we would humor him, for if crossed he would resent it and get angry.

James RASH recalled, stated that his father had committed suicide by hanging himself with a rope.

Clarence K. RASH, defendant, testified as follows: Am 33 years old; am a farmer, was born in Missouri, lived there until was near 22 years old; went from there to Platte county, Nebraska, lived there two years, then went to Colorado, lived there 2 or 3 years, went from there back to Platte county and in the fall up to Wayne, about 8 years ago; was married at 21, in Iowa, went from there home, to Missouri, and then up into Nebraska; had three children last winter, boy 9, girl 7 and baby about 2 years old; have been farming for myself for last 3 or 4 years; my wife was 28 years old; when I was a boy went to Sunday school until I was 21, lived at home until 21, but went to Mills county, Iowa, one summer; joined church sometime during December, 1895; parents were members of Christian church; attended meetings last winter, they commenced about two weeks prior to the 27th of January; think I attended about five times; meetings were conducted by Rev. WRIGHT, same denomination I had formerly belonged to, the Methodist; Tuesday night I shook hands with the minister and told him I had been gloriously saved Saturday night, and asked him to come down; on Tuesday evening started for church, and went out to the straw stack on the leased land of Mr. WOEHLER, about 1/4 of a mile from where I lived, stopped there and prayed awhile and then went to another one; seemed as though there was something leading me, something told me to go, did not hear any sound or anything of that kind, but seemed like I was led out there; asked Him to guide me and lead me in everything, asked God, was praying to God, went to second straw stack, seemed like better place for team, just seemed like something just appeared like something was leading me, didn't hear no word, but just seemed to come to me, in thinking you know. Q. What made you go back home, why didn't you go on to church instead of stopping there? A. Why, heard a great noise like lots of chariots running, seemed like they were coming in from every direction, seemed like chariots running around Ringling's show; I had been there, then heard a great noise in the east, took it for a lot of angels coming to battle, then saw a couple of stars coming across the sky, one coming from the northeast and one from the north, that was time for me to start for battle, thought that was the signal for me to start to battle, I went down to the corner of my place, and I stayed down there quite a while, then I started back, and it seemed like I was commander of a big army, don't know what made me do it, but seemed like something told me I had to be careful and had to watch; I crawled from the barn to the house, and don't remember whether I went to the door or not, anyhow I went to the window, don't know what led me to do it, did not see anyone but my family, and it just come to me like I was doubting her, you know, or something of that kind, and it made me feel so bad; instead of going back and not letting her know anything about it I went in and told her what I had done, and what I had seen, told her about slipping up from the barn to the house, I said that is for something, showing me what he will do, slip up on me like a thief in the night, if I don't do right; that's in the bible, you know; I took it that way; told my wife where I had left the team, and she says didn't you go to church? then I went up and got the team and put them up; on Wednesday evening, the 27th, made arrangements to go to church; while doing chores I noticed myself staggering, and didn't know what it meant, know it was not drunkness, for I had not drank any whiskey for two weeks; went to church, only a few there, 6 or 8; minister called on me to pray, afterwards I went up to the altar, and when I got up to come back seemed to me I saw a bright star, and fire come in my eyes, I felt kind of faint; after the services were out I got up and went down to the stove and saw this stone lying there, and seemed like something told me to take it, and I just reached down and took it up; Mr. WRIGHT said something, and seems to me I said I have need of it; I went out and there was a light streak in the west across the sky, from one foot to 16 inches long and from 4 to 6 inches across, right across this star; it seemed to get me all unstrung and nervous seeing this, and I remember I hurried up and unhitched my team and got into the buggy, and run the team all the way home, hollering "Glory be to God in the highest, my only Redeemer still liveth, and he always was and always will be;" when I show up the star would commence to fall; when I got home I just threw the lines in the buggy and jumped out and got this stone and went to the house (witness here got off on how he had read the bible on the Tuesday afternoon before the crime to his wife, from the 20th to the 25th verses of the 2nd chapter of Revelations, and had asked her what she had to say to that, she had said he had no right to judge her, etc.) (Coming back to the

27th) After going in the house I says Julia, you must die; she said oh don't, or something like that; I am not ready to die (Witness here began to weep, which continued for some time), resuming: well, I struck her then, I struck her one lick right on the temple, on the left or the right temple, I think it was temple; when I struck her she said, "now Doc I just allowed you'd do that;" well, I struck her, and it looked so bad I almost thought better of it, and it seemed like something just said it had to be the whole family, and I tell you I got through with it as quick as possible, and that is the reason I mutilated them as I did, to get them out of their misery. (Witness was again overcome with emotion); after that I put my team up and read some; I did not unharness the team, for something seemed to tell me they would be used before long; did not know what they would be used for, as I did not think of using them; went into the house and kept up the fire until morning.

Witness here related how he went out during the night and saw a bright crown in the sky, and falling stars like hail; how he had blowed fire out of his mouth, and kept blowing at the screen door, blowing it open all night, and a lot of stuff along the same line, and said when his neighbors came over in the morning he did not want to blow this fire on them. Witness here looked around and said: "If you people are all right, I am all wrong." On cross examination witness stated that he had no intention of killing his wife until he got in the house the night of the crime. When asked why he did not blow fire on the sheriff when he come, he said: "I had lost this here fire business."

Dr. WIGHTMAN, of Wayne; Dr. GREEN, of Lincoln; Dr. MACKAY, of Norfolk; Dr. WILLIAMS and LEISENRING of Wayne all gave expert testimony, all tending to show that the defendant was insane at the time he committed the act. The State then recalled a number of its witnesses who lived in the neighborhood where the crime was committed, in order to get their testimony in regard to RASH's actions during the two or three years immediately before the crime. The pleas were made on the afternoon of Thursday, June 10th, and the case went to the jury at 6 o'clock that evening, and at 7:30 on Saturday morning they returned a verdict of "not guilty." The verdict is far from satisfactory to the majority of Wayne county people who have felt all along that the fiend would at least receive a sentence of imprisonment for life. There are yet three other cases pending against RASH for the murder of his three children, the case just disposed of being the charge of murdering his wife. In face of the verdict of the jury in the case just ended it would seem to be almost a criminal waste of time and public money to prosecute the other cases. RASH will now be sent to the insane hospital for a time and then pronounced cured and turned loose to again wreak his insane fury on some other innocent persons and then claim God commanded him to do so. It will, in all probability, be well for him to hear now a command from above to steer clear of Wayne county because today we believe an outraged community is liable to make short work of him if he puts himself where they can get hold of him.

• • •

Celebration Committees.

The Band has selected the following committees for the celebration:

Marshals of the Day: Ed REYNOLDS and Ran FRAZIER.

Parade Arrangements: Captain J. P. MATTHEWS, assisted by Marshals.

Decorations: S.R. THEOBALD.

Morning Salutes: R. GALBRAITH.

Bicycle Races: E.P. OLMSTED and S.H. ALEXANDER.

Pony Races, Foot Races and other Amusements: Frank STRAHAN, A.J. TRACY, Peter COYLE, Robert ARMSTRONG, Jim PORTERFIELD.

Balloon: R.W. WILKINS.

Collector and Treasurer: Charles CRAVEN.

Fire Works: S.B. RUSSELL, Dick GALBRAITH and Walt COOK.

At the regular communication of Wayne Lodge No. 120 A.F. & A.M., on last Friday evening, A.A. WELCH was elected M.W.; J.M. CHERRY, S.W.; F.L. NEELY, J.W.; A.T. WITTER, Sec., and C.O. FISHER, Treas. The new officers will be installed on Thursday evening June 24.

The Wayne Republican
June 23, 1897 (Vol. 4, No. 19)

BIRTH: On Sunday a son was born to Mr. and Mrs. Frank GRIFFITH.

BIRTH: G.P. ARTLEY and wife are the parents of a fine girl baby.

LICENSED TO WED: Henry POCKRANDT and Mary REDMER.

MARRIED: PEARSON - PEARSON. On June 10, Justice FEATHER officiating, Oscar PEARSON and Emily PEARSON.

MARRIED: KLUG - KLAWAN. At Hoskins June 20, Rev. DAWIDAT officiating, Leopald KLUG and Mrs. Louise KLAWAN.

DIED: JEFFREY. On June 21 at her home southwest of Wayne, Hattie, wife of Alex JEFFREY, passed from life to the great beyond. The deceased was 21 years of age and died of dropsy from which she had been a sufferer for a long time. The funeral will be held from the M.E. church this afternoon. An affectionate husband and large circle of friends will mourn the seemingly untimely going of the loved one and to them the sympathies of our community will go out.

The Wayne Republican
June 30, 1897 (Vol. 4, No. 20)

BIRTH: A girl baby was born to Mr. and Mrs. DEARBORN yesterday.

Celebration Day Program.

The following is the program of exercises and amusements for the Fourth of July celebration in Wayne on Monday July 5th.

MORNING AND FORENOON.

Salute of 20 guns at sun rise.

Decoration of business houses.

10:00 - Boys Brigade Drill.

10:30 - Parade - Marshals, Ed. REYNOLDS and Ran FRAZIER - Band, Young Ladies representing States, Orator of Day and Mayor in carriage, Boys Brigade, under Captain MATTHEWS, Sons of Herman, Woodmen, Workmen, Firemen, Displays and Citizens in Carriages and Bicyclists.

11:00 - Music be Glee Club, directed by Prof. KELLER.

Oration by Hon. T.L. MATTHEWS of Fremont.

AFTERNOON SPORTS.

At the Fair Grounds. Everything free.

Bicycle Races - 1/2 mile boys' race; 1st prize, Cyclometer, 2nd Sweater.

1/2 mile Club race - Prize, Medal.

1 mile race - 1st, Kodak; 2nd, Sweater.

2 mile handicap - 1st, Kodak; 2nd, Bicycle Shoes; 3rd, Bicycle Pants.

Pony Race - 1/4 mile Wayne county; $5 to 1st; $3 to 2nd.

Pony Race - 1/2 mile free for all; $6.50 to 1st; $3 to 2nd.

Base Ball Game - Wayne vs Laurel, for championship of Northeast Nebraska.

AFTERNOON SPORTS, in the City.
On Pearl Street.

4:00 - Foot Race, free for all - $3.50 to 1st; $1.50 to 2nd.

Boys' race - $1.00 to 1st; 50c to 2nd.

Fats Men's race - $2.00 and $1.00.

Sack race - $1.50 and $1.00.

5:30 - Balloon Ascension by Prof. B.J. DEARING of Sioux City, who will be accompanied by a lady if the weather is favorable.

EVENING SPORTS.

8:00 - Illuminated parade in which everybody is invited to take part.

This parade will be in command of Marshals REYNOLDS and FRAZIER. After this a large display of fire works will be witnessed on the court house square.

There will be dancing during the afternoon and evening for those who enjoy it.

The Wayne Republican
July 7, 1897 (Vol. 4, No. 21)

BIRTH: Mr. and Mrs. SELLON are the proud parents of a baby boy which was born on Wednesday.

BIRTH: On July 5th a son was born to Mr. and Mrs. Isaac CARR. (Hoskins)

DIED: LEMHKUHL. On July 2, at her home southeast of the city of Wayne Mrs. George LEMHKUHL, aged 41 years. The deceased was a native of Germany and was a woman much beloved and respected by friends and neighbors. She was the mother of twelve children ten of whom survive her, the youngest being but a few hours old at the time of the mother's demise. The funeral was held at Wisner on Sunday the 4th and was largely attended. To the bereaved husband and children and aged father and mother the sympathy of all will go out in this their day of sadness.

DIED: ALGER. On Sunday morning July 4th Pierson ALGER breathed his last at the ripe age of 87 years, 3 months and 5 days. Mr. ALGER was born at Oxford, Butler county, Ohio, March 28th, 1810, and was married to Susan DeMOSS Sept. 28, 1836. For almost sixty years they traveled life's journey together, she passing away less than a year ago. In the spring of 1840 they moved from Ohio to West Liberty, Iowa, and resided there until 1885, when they came to Wayne county, Nebraska, settling north of the city of Wayne about a mile. Nine children were born unto them, five being now alive, two sons and three daughters. The funeral took place from the M.E. church on Tuesday forenoon and all that was mortal of our aged citizen was laid to rest in our silent city by loving hands.

The Wayne Republican
July 14, 1897 (Vol. 4, No. 22)

President FULLER has filled the vacancies of the Fair directory and the board is now F.M. NORTHROP, D. CUNNINGHAM, I.O. RICHARDSON, John LARISON, James BARBER, T.S. GOSS, F.M. GRIFFITH, D.L. STRICKLAND, Chas. NEISS, and C.J. LUND. A meeting of the directors is called to meet at STRAHN, GRIMSLEY & Co.'s office on Saturday afternoon at 3 o'clock to fix date and complete all arrangements for the Fair.

If it is true as reported that RASH is now declared sane by the Norfolk hospital authorities it would seem as though his acquittal for the brutal muder of his wife last January was a travesty on justice and a disgrace to our boasted advancement in knowledge. If the devil is sane now we are led to believe that he never was anything else and that the Pierce county jury very seriously erred when it acquitted him. We'll bet if he is turned loose that he'll have sense enough to steer clear of Wayne county and if he don't the probabilities are very strong that court expenses on him in the future will be very light.

List of old soldiers in Wayne county as returned by the assessors for the year 1897:

NAMES:	P.O.
AGLER, J.W.	Wayne
ANSON, A.	Wayne
BENNER, P.	Wayne
BARTLETT, J.W.	Wayne
BURSON, O.H.	Wayne
BAGGERT, C.A.	Wayne
BOSTETTER, C.C.	Wayne
BARRETT, J.M.	Wayne
CUNNINGHAM, B.	Wayne
CHILDS, A.P.	Wayne

NAMES:	P.O.
CULLER, G.W.	Wayne
COOK. G.L.	Wayne
COYLE, P.	Wayne
CUNNINGHAM, D.	Wayne
DOUGLASS, F.	Wayne
FERGUSON, A.J.	Wayne
FEATHER, B.F.	Wayne
FISHER, C.	Wayne
FARRAND, T.H.	Wayne
GAMBLE, W.O.	Wayne
GRIMSLEY, J.G.	Wayne
GRAVES, H.J.	Wayne
GOSS, T.S.	Wayne
HUNTER, E.	Wayne
HAYES, Jas.	Wayne
HODSON, H.	Wayne
HILL, Wm.	Wayne
KING, J.D.	Wayne
LINDSAY, A.	Wayne
LUNDBERG, P.	Wayne
METTLEN, J.T.	Wayne
MURRILL, T.J.	Wayne
MATTHEWS, J.P.	Wayne
McMAKIN, S.H.	Wayne
McMANIGAL, D.	Wayne
NANGLE, E.J.	Wayne
OSBORN, J.H.	Wayne
OBST, F.	Wayne
OTT, J.W.	Wayne
PERRIN, R.	Wayne
PRESTON, L.	Wayne
ROBBINS, L.	Wayne
RUNDELL, C.J.	Wayne
REYNOLDS, Ed	Wayne
RAMSEY, W.F.	Wayne
STALLSMITH, J.B.	Wayne
STRINGER, M.	Wayne
SKILES, R.H.	Wayne
TAYLOR, A.W.	Wayne
THORPE, L.R.	Wayne
TAYLOR, S.	Wayne
WRIGHT, W.M.	Wayne
WILKINSON, G.W.	Wayne

NAMES:	P.O.
ANDERSON, W.C.	Winside
BENSER, R.Z.	Winside
CARTER, A.H.	Winside
CHAPIN, A.T.	Winside
HAYES, C.G.	Winside
HYATT, A.J.	Winside
JOHNSON, T.E.	Winside
JONES, W.E.	Winside
LOWRY, W.C.	Winside
MUNDY, John	Winside
ROUSH, R.J.	Winside
TILLSON, J.W.	Winside
ULRICH, Peter	Winside
BRASCH, M.	Hoskins
CLINE, J.L.	Hoskins
CASE, H.	Hoskins
GLEASON, W.E.	Hoskins
HOWSER, A.J.	Hoskins
JONES, J.M.	Hoskins
TEMPLIN, C.	Hoskins
VINCENT, J.P.	Hoskins
BAKER, J.	Carroll
BELL, T.	Carroll
DeLONG, T.E.	Carroll
HANCOCK, Joel	Carroll
HONEY, A.J.	Carroll
HOWARTH, T.J.	Carroll
MOORE, J.J.	Carroll
MERRILL, M.S.	Carroll
ROBINSON, L.F.	Carroll
WILLIAMSON, S.W.	Carroll
WHITE, J.P.	Carroll
DILTZ, Levi	Wakefield
DRISKELL, E.E.	Wakefield
OLIVER, C.	Wakefield
SWANSON, A.	Wakefield
POWELL, Gideon	Wisner
SNEATH, R.	Pender

**The Wayne Republican
July 21, 1897 (Vol. 4, No. 23)**

BIRTH: Dr. LEISENRING reports a fine girl baby at the home of

Andrew JENSEN southeast of the city.

BIRTH: Dr. NIEMAN informs us that W.D. WELKER and wife had a fine girl baby born to them on Monday.

BIRTH: An eleven pound postmaster was born to Mr. and Mrs. Frank L. METTLEN last evening, and as a consequence Frank is doing a rushing business in the cigar line. Congratulations. (Winside Tribune)

BIRTH: The home of Met GOODYEAR was brightened on Sunday by the birth of a daughter.

BIRTH: On Saturday Carl LENZ and wife became the parents of a fine boy.

The Wayne Republican
July 28, 1897 (Vol. 4, No. 24)

MARRIED: HUNGERFORD - MOORE. On July 21, at the office of county judge Edwin HUNGERFORD and May MOORE, both of Carroll.

Wayne County Crops.

A Republican representative interviewed farmers from different parts of the county Saturday afternoon as to crop conditions, yield per acre, etc., and herewith we publish replies as received:

Henry HANSEN of Plum Creek, "wheat 10 to 12 bushels per acre, oats 40, corn good but about a week to 10 days late, early potatoes small yield, late ones look well."

Adam GRIER of Wilbur, "wheat 10 to 12, oats 50, corn 25 bushels to the acre, quality of wheat and oats good."

James BARBOUR, Wayne, "wheat 12 to 14, oats 40, corn 30 bushels per acre."

A. ANSON, Wilbur, "wheat 10 to 12, oats 35, corn 25 bushels per acre."

R. LAUMAN, Hunter, "wheat 12 to 14, oats 40, corn 25 to 30 bushels."

W.G. ARCHER, Garfield, "wheat 12 to 14, oats 35, corn 25, quality of wheat and oats excellent, late potatoes look all right."

C.W. WHITE, Wilbur, "wheat 12, oats 40, corn 25."

J.R. MORRIS, Sherman, "wheat 10 to 12, oats 30, corn 25, rye good, quality of wheat the very best."

D.H. SURBER, Brenna, "wheat 12, oats 40, corn 25."
James SHORTEN, Brenna, "wheat 10, oats 40, corn 25."
J.E. SPAHR, Strahn, "wheat 10 to 12, oats 35, corn 25 to 30."
W.H. RUSH, Chapin, "wheat 12 to 14, oats 30, corn 25 to 30."
Jacob BRUGER, Chapin, "wheat 12, oats 30, corn too early to tell much about yield."
B. CUNNINGHAM, Strahn, "wheat 8 to 10, oats 25 to 30, corn 30."
E. CHENAUR, "wheat 8 to 10, oats 20 to 25, corn can't tell anything about it."
Wm. HOUSE, Garfield, "wheat 12, oats 30 to 35, corn 25 to 30."
John BAKER, Plum Creek, "wheat 12 to 13, oats 35, corn 35 to 40."
Geo. HARRIGFELDT, Hoskins, "wheat 12, oats 40, corn 30."
John SIMONTON, Brenna, "wheat 10 to 12, oats 25, corn too early to make figures on."
J.W. CAMPBELL, Logan, Dixon county, "wheat 12, oats 25, corn good, but too early to estimate."
H. CLAYBAUGH, Hunter, "wheat 10 to 12, oats 30, corn very spotted and some of it too late to amount to anything."
These opinions are given by practical farmers, with years of experience in the business and ought to be pretty nearly correct.

The Wayne Republican
August 3, 1897 (Vol. 4, No. 25)

BIRTH: To Mr. and Mrs. CLAYTON on Thursday, July 29, a daughter. (Hoskins)

The Wayne Republican
August 11, 1897 (Vol. 4, No. 26)

BIRTH: Mr. and Mrs. SHAFER are the parents of a fine boy baby. (Carroll)

BIRTH: Gus WILL is stepping pretty high owing to his being the father of a pair of twins, a boy and girl. (Carroll)

DIED: The infant child of Charles STEVENS died of cholera infantum on last Wednesday. The bereaved parents have the sympathy of the community and their many friends in their deep sorrow. (Carroll)

DIED: August MILLER living two miles from town lost a daughter two years old on last Saturday. (Hoskins)

Real Estate Transfers.

Phoebe P. HUGHES to John CONNOR,	
1/2 interest in lot 12, blk. 13, Wayne	$164.00
Phoebe P. HUGHES to Mary J. EVANS,	
lot 1 & n 1/2 lot 2, blk. 7 C&B ad Wayne	700.00
State of Nebraska to Samuel REICHERT,	
nw 1/4, 16-25-2	1,120.00
Anton JORGENSEN to M.L. GOREHAM,	
n 1/2 sw 1/4 28-26-4	3,000.00
M.L. GOREHAM to C.H. LUND,	
n 1/2 sw 1/4 28-26-4	2,500.00
Wakefield State Bank to Adam L. NUERNBERGER,	
ne 1/4 of ne 1/4 & ne 1/2 of	
se 1/4 of ne 1/4 29-26-5	1,500.00

The Wayne Republican
August 18, 1897 (Vol. 4, No. 27)

DIED: METTLEN. At his residence in Wayne, Nebraska, on Monday evening, August 16, John T. METTLEN, death caused by cancer of right kidney. Deceased was born in Milford township, Juniata county, Pennsylvania, September 6, 1831. On November 28, 1861, he was united in marriage with Salina GUSS and unto them four sons, William J., Frank L., Abraham G., and James H., two daughters, Mary A. and Jennie E., were born and until the taking away of the husband and father, death has never crossed the threshold of the family. In early life he became a professor of religion and through all the intervening years he has been a steadfast and consistent christian and for a number of years has been an elder of the Presbyterian church at this place. In March, 1865, he enlisted as a private in Company A., ____ Pa. Vol's and was soon promoted to the second lieutenantcy of the company and served as such until mustered out when the war was ended. At his old home in his native state he was elected and served a term as Register and Recorder. In the spring of 1877 he moved to Nebraska, settling first in Dakota county, remaining there two years, and then came with this family to Wayne county, settling on his farm south of Wakefield where they lived until about five years ago when he moved into the city of Wayne where he was one highly respected and beloved a very wide circle of acquaintances. He was twice elected as a member of the board of county commissioners of our county and served on that board from January, 1886 to January 1892. He was a member and at the time of his death commander of Casey Post, G.A.R., and also a member of the Masonic and Oddfellows societies. In his death his family has lost a husband and father whose council was always wise and whose love was enduring, at church his kindly face will be missed. When the veterans meet they will realize that another has answered the last call, while his brotherly handshake will never again be felt yet each of us know that while he has gone out from our midst there is a certainty of meeting in a better hereafter if we will but follow in the footsteps of this man whom years of close acquaintance leads us to believe was one that was just and upright before God and man. The funeral will be held from the Presbyterian church at 2 p.m. this afternoon and will be in charge of the Wakefield Masonic Lodge of which he is a member. Rev. WRIGHT will preach the sermon.

• • •

The Corner Restaurant
Meals Served at all Hours.
Nice Lunch on Short Notice.
MRS. POTTER, Proprietor.

• • •

The Wayne Republican
August 25, 1897 (Vol. 4, No. 28)

DIED: The 2-years-old son of Grant YOUNG died at the family home west of the city on Wednesday and was buried at Wayne on Thursday.

DIED: The twin babies of J.E. HANSEN died on Sunday at the home of his brother, H.E.

DIED: A 2-years-old daughter of Thomas FITZSIMMONS living south of Wakefield died on Monday and is to be buried at the latter place today.

Real Estate Transfers.

Wm. BINNY to Jens P. CLAUSEN, n 1/2 se 1/4 27-25-5	$1,027.00
C.O. FISHER to J.S. FRENCH, und 1/2 w 1/2 nw 1/4 26-27-3	1,000.00
O.H. BURSON to Minnie M. BURSON, lots 35, 36 & 37, blk. 23, College Hill	105.00
O.H. BURSON to Clara H. BURSON, Lots 7 & 8, blk. 27, Wayne, also that tract lying between said lot 7 & R.R.	955.00

The Wayne Republican
September 1, 1897 (Vol. 4, No. 29)

DIED: A son of George THEIS living southeast of the city died on Monday.

DIED: A child a few weeks old of John DANN living near Winside, died on Saturday.

DIED: On last Thursday Mr. and Mrs. Charles LENN lost their 1-year-old son from inflammation of the spinal column. (Hoskins)

DIED: On the same day as the LENN death, a 2-year-old child of Rudolph ROACKER died of cholera infantum. (Hoskins)

DIED: Gust WILL and family mourn the loss of one of their twin babies which had died Saturday morning. It was buried at West Point on Monday.

DIED: Chas. JONES and family, former residents of this place but now of Dickens, Clay county, Ia., are visiting at the home of Mrs. JONES' father, Jacob WEATHERHOLT, and on Sunday morning their 11-months-old child took sick with heart trouble and was dead in an hour. On Monday the stricken parents took their dead baby and left for Iowa to bury it, followed by the sympathies of the entire community. Sherman WEATHERHOLT accompanied them to their home. (Hoskins)

DIED: SHORTEN. At his recent home southwest of Wayne of Brights disease on August 26, James SHORTEN, aged 29 years. The death of Mr. SHORTEN removes from the community one of our best young farmers and one in whom all had confidence, and who was well thought of by his neighbors and the sympathy of all will be extended to his bereaved family.

The Wayne Republican
September 8, 1897 (Vol. 4, No. 30)

BIRTH: To Peter BROMMELL and wife a fine boy.

CHRISTENING: Rev. Father FITZGERALD, of Wayne, performed the ceremony of christening the little baby girl of Mr. and Mrs. Jerry HAYES on Friday. The baptismal name given the little one was Mary Adella. Father FITZGERALD was entertained at the home of John MORIN, where early mass was held on Friday morning before his return to Wayne. (Winside Tribune)

MARRIED: Miss Minnie NEELY, sister of W.A.K. NEELY, a young lady who has many friends hereabouts is to be married at her home in Juniata county, Pennsylvania, to Lisha A. BOWER, tomorrow, September 30.

DIED: Sept. 5th, 1897, Thos. W. THEOBALD, of paralysis of the brain. Aged 64 years.
        Man cannot say - Tomorrow I will live -
        Nothing in life more certain his than death.
    Again Nature and Nature's God has ordered in the immortal existence of one of His beloved children, that great change - from time on earth to eternity in heaven. How fitting that this noble man who passed so peacefully and painlessly from earth should, with the quiet Sabbath, end his day.
    At 30 minutes past 10 o'clock on Sabbath evening, Sept. 5th, passed from earth, our brother and fellow-citizen, Thos. W. THEOBALD.
    Thos. W. THEOBALD was born at Norwich, England, in the year 1833. He came to America in 1856. The following year, April 25th, at Belvidere, Illinois, he was married to Mary WIFFEN. The devoted wife and mother, whom we all so well know, preceeded him in death 3 years ago on Oct. 24th, 1894.
    After remaining in this country a short time, Mr. THEOBALD returned in 1859 to his native country. In 1874 he came again to America, and 3 years later, in 1877, moved to Nebraska where he has since continued to make his home. He was baptized into the Baptist church by his son, the Rev. W.W. THEOBALD in Wayne, Neb., on July 27, 1893. In the fall of the following year he was called upon to mourn the death of her whose companionship and sympathy had cheered his life for so

many years and whose loss had brought that deep grief which no doubt had hastened the approach of his own demise. On Sept. 5th, 1897, he departed this life surrounded by his five surviving sons, all of whom are living among us as valued and respected citizens of our community. He leaves besides these, two daughters-in-law, Mrs. S. and Mrs. W.W. THEOBALD and four grand-children.

Of this, our departed friend, it may be truly said: "The world is better for his having lived." None who knew him failed to recognize in him that nobleness of character, that upright integrity, that gentle and unselfish spirit which marks the genuine Christian and the true gentleman. His was a mind bright, intelligent and refined. A lover of music and the possessor of a voice that often, in the years preceeding his illness, charmed the delighted ears of his hearers.

Above all gentleness and purity of this good man was observed by those who best knew him and nothing could be more touching than the sweet companionship and loving devotion that so mutually existed between himself and each member of his household who so tenderly and patiently smoothed his pathway during the recent years of his illness down to the close of life.

The history of his declining health dates from the fall of 1894 when shortly after the death of his companion, he received a stroke of paralysis, from the effects of which he never fully recovered.

Three weeks ago he was compelled to take his bed from an attack of dysentery from which he was recovering, when on Wednesday last, symptoms of a second paralytic stroke which the anxious family and his attending physician feared might come, brought on the fatal stupor from which he never aroused. Death to him was painless and peaceful and came only as the "liberator of him whom freedom could not release, the physician of him of whom medicine could not cure and the comforter of him whom time could not console."

A valued citizen, a kind and gentle father, above all, a good man, earth bids farewell. God and angels greet him in a better land.

School board met on Monday evening and appointed F.L. NEELY to fill vacancy caused by removal of W.H. BRADFORD from the city. All pupils in the 4th grade and below residing east of Main Street and also all north of Sixth Street will hereafter attend the ward school. Hiram GRIGGS was elected janitor. The following bills were allowed:

R.W. WILKINS, paper	$30.00
H. GRIGGS, janitor	37.50
S.H. McMAKIN, papering	26.50
A.A. CHANCE, plastering	2.05
G.W. RILEY, cyclone ins.	40.00

COMMISSIONER PROCEEDINGS, Wayne, Neb., Sept. 4, 1897.

Board met pursuant to adjournment, all members present.

The following claims were examined and on motion allowed and warrants ordered drawn for the same.

Pierce county, costs RASH insane	$47.55
J.E. AGLER, bridge	71.00
John BOOKE, road work	26.00
R.M. FARR, jail repairs	5.36
J.H. PRESCOTT, road work	21.50
J.A. BARBOUR, road work	5.00
Fred JENSEN, bridge work	1.50
J.E. AGLER, bridges	209.60
EDWARDS & B. Lbr. Co., lumber	81.88
A.T. WADDELL, road work	12.50
Robt. UTTER, supplies (Supt)	5.25
E.P. OLMSTEAD & Co., hardware	6.05
HOGUE & PAYNE, draying	1.25
Myra D. FLETCHER, postage, etc.	11.10
Myra D. FLETCHER, furniture	5.00
C.A. BAGGERT, labor	1.00
Wm. HEYER, iron for bridges	14.40
John ZIEMER, road work	13.75
Will COLLINS, road work	2.50
B.P. PETERSON, road work	2.50
J.J.W. FOX, road work	2.50
John ZIEMER, road work	15.00
J.B. SEARIGHT, road work	2.50
Henry HODSON, road work	3.75
A. JOOST, road work	18.75
Geo. WEATHERHOLT, road work	31.50
John GLASENAP, road work	15.00
H.W. BURNHAM, road work	40.00
SMITH & ELLIS Co., lumber	154.20
L. ZIEMER, surveying	6.50
Gustave WENDT, land for road	70.00
Ed REYNOLDS, jailer fees	39.30
Anton WEIGLE, boarding pauper	24.00
A.M. JACOBS, com. fees	21.70

Geo. HARRIGFELDT, com. fees $20.00
R. RUSSELL, com. fees 22.75
On motion all that portion of the road on the south side of sec. 5-26-3, which is west of the R.R., was vacated. The board having purchased a strip of land 2 rods wide of Gustave WENTT along the north side of the R.R. for road.
Adjourned to October 2, 1897.

S.B. RUSSELL, Clerk.

• • •

Spectacles, Eye Glasses,
Colored Glasses and Goggles.
J.F. INGALLS, Jeweler.

• • •

The Wayne Republican
September 15, 1897 (Vol. 4, No. 31)

BIRTH: To Mr. and Mrs. J. MOIR of this city Thursday, Sept. 2, twins, a fine boy and girl, all doing well. (Wakefield Republican)

MARRIED: On Thursday forenoon, Rev. MILLARD at the M.E. parsonage joined in matrimony, Charle CLINE and Ella LEE, both of Hoskins. The happy couple have the congratulations of friends in which the Republican heartily joins.

MARRIED: ROYER - SIMONTON. At the home of the bride's parents, Mr. and Mrs. J.L. SIMONTON on Tuesday, September 14, their daughter Anna B. was united in marriage with Geo. D. ROYER of Gove City, Kansas. Of the groom we know nothing personally, but he is reputed to be a worthy young man in every respect. The bride is one of Wayne county's best young ladies and for some time has been a very successful teacher in the schools of the county and we know that we voice the sentiment to her and husband the congratulations of all. The newly married couple expect to make their home at Gove City, Kansas, after October 1.

MARRIED: Mr. Chas. HAASE and Miss Frida STEFFEN were married by the German minister at Wayne on Thursday afternoon, and the same evening the groom gave a big supper and dance at the German hall, south of Laurel. About forty couples were present, and all say that they were highly repaid for going out on a bad night. The rain kept them at the hall until morning. The bride and groom are two of the most highly respected young persons of the community, and the guests showed their appreciation of their friendship by contributing liberally for presents. May the path of the worthy couple be strewn with very few briars. (Laurel Advocate)

DIED: On Wednesday night the spirit of the 4-months-old child of Frank OBST winged its way to the Father who gave it. The funeral occurred on Thursday.

Premiums Awarded.
Wayne County Agricultural Society,
Sept. 8, 9 and 10, 1897.
HORSES - CLASS A

Stallions 4 yrs or over, D.L. STRICKLAND 1st, $8.

Mare or horse 4 or over, F.M. GRIFFITH 1st, $5; G. BEALE 2nd, $2.50.

Mare or horse 3 and under, S.B. SCACE 1st, $4; N. NELSON 2nd, $2.

Span draft horses or mares to wagon, J. ATKINS 1st, $5; W. GRAVES 2nd, $2.50.

Spring colt, G. BEALE 1st, $3.

Spring filley, E. LONGNECKER 1st, $3; F. GRIFFITH 2nd, $2.

Carriage team, D.L. STRICKLAND 1st, $5.

Single carriage horse or mare, R. FRAZIER 1st, $4; J. HODSON 2nd, $2.

Saddle horse or mare, D.L. STRICKLAND 1st, $4; Jas. BARBOUR 2nd, $2.

CATTLE - CLASS B
Cow 3 or over, G. BEALE 1st, $5.00.

Cow 2 or over, C.S. ASH 1st, $4.00.

SWINE - CLASS C
Boar 1 or over, M. MUTH 1st, $3.00.

Boar 1 or over, G. PORTER, 2nd $2.00.

Breeding sows 1 or over, E. LONGNECKER 1st, $3; E. LONGNECKER 2nd, $2.

Sow over 6 month and under 1 y'r, 1st Geo. PORTER, $2.

Boar pig over 4 mo and under 1 y'r, 1st M. MUTH, $2; 2nd M. MUTH, $1.

POULTRY - CLASS D
Bantams w game, W. MILLER 1st, $1.00.

Bantams B B R, G. PALMER 1st, $1.00

Bantams B B R, C. MARTIN 2nd, $.50.
Bantams S D W, C. WADSWORTH 1st, $1.00.
Bantams S D W, G. PALMER 2nd, $.50.
Langshans, E.P. OLMSTED 1st, $1.00.
Langshans, E.P. OLMSTED 2nd, $.50.
B. Cochins, S.M. PIEPENSTOCK 1st, $1.00.
B. Cochins, S.M. PIEPENSTOCK 2nd, $.50.
Leghorn R C, W. MILLER 1st, $1.00.
Leghorn W, T. BERRY 1st, $1.00.
Leghorn W, T. BERRY 2nd, $.50.
Leghorn B, A. BECKENHAUR 1st, $1.00.
Wyandottes, G.H. GREGORY 1st, $1.00.
Wyandottes silver, Mrs. G. CROSSLAND 1st, $1.00.
Plymouth Rocks, H. GREGORY 1st, $1.00.
Plymouth Rocks, H. GREGORY 2nd, $.50.
Ducks, C.S. ASH 1st, $1.00.
Guinea fowls, Geo. PALMER 1st, $1.00.
Show f'th'd stock, H. GREGORY 1st, $2.00.
Show f'th'd stock, W.A. NEELY 2nd, $1.00.
Geese, C. CAMPBELL 1st, $1.00.
Geese, C.S. ASH 2nd, $.50.
Bantams G'ld'n, S.H. GREGORY 1st, $1.00.
Bantams G'ld'n, S.H. GREGORY 2nd, $.50.
Minorcas, H. GRIGGS 1st, $1.00.
Hares and rabbits, H. GREGORY 1st, $.50.
Hares and rabbits, G. TERWILLIGER 2nd, $.25.

MANUFACTURER - CLASS G

Washing M'c'ne, L.J. HANSEN, Diploma.
Diply W'd m'ls t'ks, D.E. NEWTON, Diploma.
D'p'y S'w'g M'c'ne, J.R. HOOVER, Diploma.
D'p'y M'sc'l Instruments, R. UTTER, Diploma.
Steam Cooker, E.E. BIBLER, Diploma.

FLOWER - CLASS H

V'rty of Phlox, Mrs. C.C. BROWN, $.50
V'rty of Astors, Mrs. F. PHILLEO 1st, $.50.
V'rty of Astors, Mrs. C.C. BROWN 2nd, $.25.
V'rty of Begonias, Mrs. R. FRAZIER, $.50.
V'rty of Xenias, C.S. ASH, $.50.
V'rty of Daisies, Mrs. R. PHILLEO, $.50.
Dec'r'tive plant, Mrs. C.C. BROWN 1st, $.50.
Dec'r'tive plant, Mrs. C.C. BROWN 2nd, $.25.
C'lct'n of plants, Mrs. H. WHEATON, $.50.

LADIES WORK - CLASS J

Knit Lu'n crt'ns, Mrs. R. DURRIN 2nd, $.25.

Woolen st'k'gs, Mrs. PANKRATZ 1st, $.50.
Woolen st'k'gs, Mrs. J.P. MATHEWS 2nd, $.25.
Woolen mittens, Mrs. G. PORTER, $.50.
Wollen rug, Mrs. J.P. MATTHEWS, $.50.
Silk purse, Mrs. R. DURRIN, $.50.

LOT 2

Infants socks, Mrs. F. PHILLEO, $.50.
Cotton tidy, Mrs. G. PORTER 2nd, $.25.
Table mat, Mrs. F. PHILLEO, $.50.
Toilet mat, Mrs. F. PHILLEO 1st, $.50.
Toilet mat, Miss NANGLE 2nd, $.25.
Lace 1 yard, Mrs. S. FOLTZ 1st, $.50.
Lace 1 yard, Anna VENNERBEY 2nd, $.25.
Woolen skirt, Mrs. F. NORTHROP 1st, $.50.
Woolen skirt, Mrs. R. DURRIN 2nd, $.25.
Afghan, Mrs. PANKRATZ, $.50.
Woolen lace 1 yard, Mrs. G. PORTER, $.25.
Table cover, Mrs. PANKRATZ, $.25.

LOT 3

Handmade skirt, Mrs. F. PHILLEO, $.50.
Handmade fancy apron, Mrs. R. DURRIN, $.25.
Handmade dress, Mrs. S. FOLTZ, $.25.
Hem stitching, Mrs. F. PHILLEO 1st, $.50.
Hem stitching, Bessie WINTERBURN 2nd, $.25.

LOT 4 - DRAWN WORK

Centre piece, Mrs. Dr HAMMOND, $.25.
Sideboard Scarf, Mrs. B.F. SWAN 1st, $.50.
Sideboard Scarf, Mrs. Dr HAMMOND, $.25.
Sham, Mrs. F. NORTHROP, $.25.
Apron, Mrs. F. PHILLEO, $.50.
H'ndkrch'f, Mrs. BRENNER, $.50.
H'ndkrch'f, Bessie WINTERBURN, $.25.
Honiton Ice cntre pce, Mrs. B. SWAN, $.50.

LOT 7 - ROMAN EMBROIDERY.

Center piece, Mrs. J.W. JONES, $.50.
Doilies, Mrs. J.W. JONES, $.50.
Doilies, Mrs. SIGWORTH, $.25.

LOT 8

Shams, Mrs. PANKRATZ 2nd, $.25.
Fancy tidy, Mrs. SWAN 1st, $.50.
Pin cushion, Mrs. SIGWORTH 1st, $.50
Foot rest, Mrs. SIGWORTH 1st, $.50.
Doilies, Mrs. HAMMOND 2nd, $.25.
Infants Emb dress Mrs. S. FOLTZ 1st, $.50.

LOT 9 - LACE WORK
Battenburg sofa pillow cover, Mrs. J.W. JONES 1st,$.50.
Battenburg center piece, Mrs. J.W. JONES 1st, 50c.
Battenburg center piece, Mrs. SWAN 2nd, 25c.
Battenburg doilies, Mrs. F. PHILLEO 2nd, 25 cents.

LOT 10 - EMB. ON COTTON OR LINEN
Lunch cloth, Mrs. SWAN 1st, $.50.
Tray cloth, Mrs. P.L. MILLER 2nd, $.25.
Center piece, Mrs. P.L. MILLER 1st, $.50
Center piece, Libby ELLIS 2nd, $.25.
Doilies, Mrs. P.L. MILLER 2nd, $.25.
Set tumbler doilies, Mrs. BRENNER, $.50.

CLASS K
Hearth rug, Mrs. NORTHROP 1st, $.50.
Ptchwrk cot'n quilt, L. BRUGGER 1st, $.50.
Ptchwrk cot'n quilt, Mrs. ASH 2nd, $.25.
Ptchwrk worsted quilt, Mrs. McMAKIN 1st, $.50.
Ptchwrk worsted quilt, Mrs. PHILLEO 2nd, $.25.
Wool crazy quilt, Mrs. CROSSLAND 1st, $.50.
Wool crazy quilt, Mrs. DAVIES 2nd, $.25.
Fancy crazy quilt, Mrs. CROSSLAND 1st, $.50.
Fancy rug, Mrs. McMAKIN 1st, $.50.
Fancy rug, Mrs. C.S. ASH 2nd, $.25.
Fancy pillow case, Mrs. SIGWORTH 1st, $.50.
Fancy pillow case, Mrs. SIGWORTH 2nd, $.25.

LOT 11 - OLD LADIES' DEPT.
Worsted quilt, Mrs. DAVIES 1st, $.50.
Bed spread knit, Mrs. BRENNER 1st, $.50.
Specimen drawn work, Mrs. P.L. MILLER 1st, 50 cents.
Outline Embdy, Mrs. BRENNER 1st, $.50.
Outline Embdy, Mrs. BRENNER 2nd, $.25.

LOT 12
Patchwork quilt, Effie BRUGGER, $.50.
Patchwork quilt, Helen NORTHROP, $.25.
Crocheted lace, Libbie ELLIS, $.50.
Crocheted lace, Libbie ELLIS, $.25.
Dressed doll, Helen NORTHROP, $.50.

LOT 13
Specimen hair work, Mr.s G. PORTER, $.50.
Ice boat, R.C. OSBORN, $.50.

FARM PRODUCTS - CLASS L
Spring wheat, G. BEALE, $1.00.
Spring wheat, E. LONGNECKER, $.50.
Rye same as spring wheat.

Barley, C.S. ASH, $1.00
Corn yellow dent same $1.00
Corn yellow dent, Nels JOHNSON, $.50.
Corn white, A.T. ROBERTSON, $1.00.
Corn white, C.D. MARTIN, $.50.
Corn sweet, Jas. BARBOUR, $1.00.
Timothy seed, C.S. ASH, $1.00.
Table potatoes, E. LONGNECKER, $1.00
Table potatoes, H. HODSON, $.50.
Table beets, Jas. BARBOUR, $.50.
Cabbage, Chas. MARTIN, $.50.
Onions, C.S. ASH, $.50.
Tomatoes, J. WINTERBURN, $.50.
Tomatoes, Chas. MARTIN, $.25.
Bush Beans, C.S. ASH, $.50.
Display of Pumpkins, C. CAMPBELL, $.25.
Sugar Beets, H.E. HANSEN, $2.00.
Sugar Beets, G. GELDER, $1.00.
Water melons, R. PERRIN, $.50.
Oats black, C.G. NURENBERGER, $1.00.
Oats black, Jas. GRIER, $.50.
Oats white, C.S. ASH, $1.00.
Millet seed, same, $.50.
Flax, same, $.50.
Radishes, D. RUSSELL, 50c, Jno. GRIER .25
Dspy grains, gr'ses, J.W. BARTLETT, $1.00.

PANTRY SUPPLIES - CLASS M
Rolls, C.S. ASH, $.50.
Yeast bread, Mrs. H. WHEATON, $.50.
Display of Jelly, Helen NORTHROP, $.50.
Ginger bread, same, $.50.

LOT 1 - PICKLES, ETC.
Best Pickles, Mrs. G. PORTER, $.20.
Tomato catsup, same, $.20.
Bean pickles, Mrs. G. CROSSLAND, $.20.
Mellon pickles, Mrs. G. RILEY, $.20.
Mellon pickles, Mrs. G. PORTER, $.10.
Tomato pickles, same, $.20.
Spiced Apples, Mrs. G. RILEY, $.20.
Chow chow, Mrs. G. PORTER, $.20.

LOT 2 - BUTTERS
Plum butter, Mrs. G. PORTER, $.20
Plum butter, Mrs. G. CROSSLAND, $.10.

LOT 3 - JELLIES
Apple jelly, Mrs. G. PORTER, $.20.
Crab jelly, Mrs. SIGWORTH, $.20.
Crab jelly, Mrs. G. BEALE, $.10.
Grape jelly, Mrs. G. PORTER, $.20.
Grape jelly, Mrs. G. CROSSLAND, $.10.
Cherry jelly, same 1st and 2nd
Blackberry jelly, Mrs. G. CROSSLAND, $.20.
Gooseberry jelly, same, $.20.
Currant jelly, Mrs. G. RILEY, $.20.
Plum jelly, Mrs. G. CROSSLAND, $.20.
Plum jelly, Mrs. G. RILEY, $.10.
Rhubarb jelly, Mrs. G. CROSSLAND, $.20.

LOT 4 - PRESERVED FRUIT
Strawberry, Mrs. G. PORTER, $.20.
Plum, same, $.20.
Tomato, same, $.20.
Tomato, Mrs. E. LONGNECKER, $.10.
Currant, same, $.20.
Gooseberry, Mrs. G. CROSSLAND, $.20.
Gooseberry, Mrs. C.S. ASH, $.10.
Peach, 1st and 2nd same.
Raspberry, Mrs. C.S. ASH, $.20.
Cherry, Mrs. G. PORTER, $.20.
Cherry, Mrs. G. CROSSLAND, $.10.
Blackberry, Tillie BRUGGER, $.20.
Blackberry, Mrs. G. PORTER, $.10.
Pear, Mrs. C.S. ASH, $.20.
Pear, Mrs. G. CROSSLAND, $.10.

FRUIT - CLASS O
Variety of Apples, C.S. ASH, $1.00.
Collection of plums, F. WROBEL, $1.00.
Collection of plums, C. MARTIN, $.50.
Grapes, H. HODSON, $1.00.

ART - CLASS P - LOT 7
Mrs. L.E.A. SMITH took the premiums of 50 cents each for the following: Ice cream set, salad set and vase.

Also diplomas for fruit painting, raised paste work, rose painting, 12 pieces by one person, single plate, cup and saucer and flower painting.

MISCELLANEOUS - LOT 1
Marble clock, F.J. LEWIS, $.50.
Zephyr flwr wk, Mrs. A. SCHWEARZEL, $.50.

OIL PAINTINGS - LOT 2

Mrs. L.E.A. SMITH took the premiums of 50 cents each for landscape, panel and marine painting.

WATER COLORS - LOT 3

Landscape, Mrs. L.E.A. SMITH, $.50.
Landscape, Mrs. SIGWORTH, $.25.
Painting on satin, Mrs. R. PHILLEO, $.50.

PASTELS - LOT 8

Mrs. BRENNER took premiums of fifty cents each for fruit piece and animal.

The Wayne Republican
September 22, 1897 (Vol. 4, No. 32)

MARRIED: Today Evertee LAUGHLIN and Miss Jessie WILLIAMS are to be united in marriage at the home of the bride in Freeport, Ill. The groom is our well known city clerk and one of our best young men. The bride is a sister of Mrs. Dr. BLAIR and during her visits to the home of the latter in the city she has made a host of friends who will be glad to welcome her to our midst as Mrs. Everett LAUGHLIN.

DIED: The following is taken from the Danville, Ia., News and relates to the father of our townsman, I.W. ALTER:

Jacob ALTER was born in Washington county, Pa., March 1, 1817. He was married to Miss Jane S. KNOX, Feb. 7, 1833. Unto this union were born seven children two of whom died while quite young. They came to Des Moines county, Iowa, in 1847, settling upon the place upon which he died. His wife died February 18, 1855, and on April 3, 1856, he was married to Mrs. Elizabeth DELAPLAIN. Unto this union were born 4 children, one of which passed to the other shore.

He was converted and joined the Baptist church in September, 1847, and six years later was chosen church clerk, a position which he filled acceptably for just forty years. He also served the church as trustee for many years. His life has been one of activity and usefullness. He was an indulgent father, a devoted husband and an honored and respected citizen. He died September 8, 1897, leaving to mourn his loss a wife, eight children, besides grandchildren and hosts of friends.

The funeral services were conducted by Rev. COONEY, assisted by Rev's SHATTO and GAINES. Services were held in the Congregational church, after which the remains were laid to rest in the cemetery back of the church.

The Democrats of this city held their caucuses on Tuesday evening and the delegation as chosen from the city are a deep cherry color. They are the following gentlemen: 1st ward, Will RICKABAUGH, J.H. MERRILL, Mell NORTON; 2nd, A.H. ELLIS, J.M. PILE, W. BENSHOOF; 3rd, C.O. FISHER, Guy WILBUR, C.A. BERRY. The expectations seems to be among those well posted that Jack CHERRY will prove a winner on Saturday at the convention and secure the nomination for sheriff. It is pretty hard for an outsider to get over the court house gangs barbed wire fence and if one succeeds in breaking in they are quick to repair the fence as they realize it is much easier to bring one to time than it would be to get in several at once and try to bring them to time. Jack is slated and the other fellows will find themselves out in the cold until the boss chooses to take them in.

The Wayne Republican
September 29, 1897 (Vol. 4, No. 33)

LICENSED TO WED: Adolph HILLE and Bertha WELLSCHLAGER.

LICENSED TO WED: John HARGENS and Theresa DRIER.

MARRIED: Tomorrow afternoon at 3 p.m. Rev. SCHULZ will unite in marriage at the bride's home near La Porte, Fred UTECHT and Emma UTECHT.

MARRIED: HORNBY - WAKEFIELD. At the M.E. parsonage by Rev. MILLARD on September 23, W.B HORNBY and Lina M. WAKEFIELD.

MARRIED: MOSSMAN - HONEY. At Carroll, September 24, Justice BAKER officiating, Seth MOSSMAN and Ella L. HONEY.

The Wayne Republican
October 13, 1897 (Vol. 4, No. 35)

Real Estate Transfers.
For the week ending Sept. 27, reported by I.W. ALTER, Bonded Abstracter, Wayne, Nebraska.

Ed REYNOLDS, sheriff, to C.B. FRENCH, jr.,
    se 1/4, 14-25-2 $1,040.00
Albert SHARP to Henry BOCK,
    e 1/2 of e 1/2 of nw 1/4, 5-27-2   850.00

Winside Mill Co. to HORNBY & Sons,
    lot 8, blk. 2, lot 14, blk. 5 in B&P's
    2nd add to Winside, also lot 9, blk. 3
    in 1st add to Winside — $240.00
Geo. REIBOLD to Henry DAUM,
    se 1/4, 33-25-4 — 4,480.00
A.F. WHITNEY to C.F. WHITNEY,
    lots 15-16, blk. 11, College Hill — 100.00
W.J. WEATHERHOLT to Earnest BEHMER,
    lots 7, 8, 9, 10, 11 & 12, blk. 8, Hoskins — 300.00
Michael KELLY to E.D. MITCHELL,
    w 1/2, 20-25-3 — 5,447.00
D.F. HALLETT to W.C. WIGHTMAN,
    qt claim w 1/2, 23-26-2 — 1.00
L.M. MATSEN to W.M. WRIGHT,
    lot 18, T&W's add to Wayne — 600.00
Elias HAINES to Geo. C. MERRILL,
    lot 5, blk. 22, Wayne — 350.00
Joachin KOEHLER to Wilhelm PFIEL, jr.,
    lots 1 and 2 and nw 1/4 18-25-1 — 700.00
A.L. TUCKER to W.H. BOLING,
    se 4-27-3 — 4,000.00

The Wayne Republican
October 20, 1897 (Vol. 4, No. 36)

DIED: The 2-months-old child of A. KIEPER died on the 13th and was buried next day.

DIED: John KOHLER living four miles west of here died on Sunday of cancer from which he had been a terrible sufferer for several months. (Hoskins)

COMMISSIONER PROCEEDINGS, Wayne, Neb., Oct. 6, 1897.
    Board met pursuant to adjournment; all members present.
    The following list of names was selected from which to draw jurors for the November term of the District Court:
    Chapin - G. LEWIS, Geo. ROE, J.W. OVERMAN.
    Hancock - A.W. DORAW, Ed JONES, C. ULRICH.
    Leslie - C.A. KILLION, Geo. BUSKIRK.
    Hunter - J.G. GRIMSLEY, Chris THOMPSON, Homer GRAVES, W.A. HUNTER, Wm. VINCENT.
    Plum Creek - S.F. McMANIGAL, Peter MERTON, John LIVERINGHOUSE, J.R. SHAWGO.

Logan - R.B. LEONARD, J.W. SHIPPEY, Al DRISCOLL.
Hoskins - Wm. LALK, C.F. LENZ, E.O. BEHMER, M. CASE.
Sherman - James MULVANEY, J.E. HANCOCK, T.C. MORRIS.
Garfield - Peter ULRICH, jr., John KNOUSE, Henry BAUSE.
Deer Creek - R.D. MERRILL, C.J. N AIRN, W.W. GARWOOD, A.J. SWARTZ.
Winside - A.H. CARTER, Frank BENSER.
Brenna - Everett LINDSAY, E.T. RENNICK, Fred BENSHOOF, Jas. BAIRD, M. EICH.
Strahan - C.C. BROWN, Ed OWEN, B. CUNNINGHAM, Gus WENDT, J.B. STALLSMITH.
Wayne, 1st Ward - Wm. SOENNEKEN, Nels ORCUTT, E.R. CHACE.
Wayne, 2nd Ward - W.S. GOLDIE, I.W. ALTER, Chas. ROBBINS, R.J. ARMSTRONG.
Wayne, 3rd Ward - E. CUNNINGHAM, P.L. MILLER, J.H. PINGREY, G.W. FORTNER.
Wilbur - H.E. HANSON, Adam GRIER, A.B. CLARK.
Thereupon the Board adjourned to Friday, October 8 at 9 o'clock a.m.
Attest.   S.B. RUSSELL, Clerk.

The Wayne Republican
October 27, 1897 (Vol. 4, No. 37)

BIRTH: To Mr. and Mrs. Fred STONE, Thursday Oct. 21st, a daughter.

Real Estate Transfers.

For the week ending October 19, 1897, reported by I.W. ALTER, Bonded Abstracter, Wayne, Nebraska.

Wm. HARRISON to Malcolm McCORKINDALE, QC nw 1/4, 5-26-5	$2,000.00
Malcolm McCORKINDALE to John A. ERICKSON, QC nw 1/4, 5-26-5	54.00
D.F. HALLETT to D. MILLER, ne 1/4, 1-26-1	1,800.00
Charlotte E. GOSTICK to F.W. UTECHT, e 1/2 nw 1/4 19-26-5	2,320.00
J.C. HAVEMEYER to F.A. DEARBORN, nw 9-27-1	2,000.00
G.H. CADWELL to Wm. MELLOR, ne 32-27-3	4,000.00

J.E. HILDRETH & D.C. WOOD to Arthur G. HILDRETH,
    QC lot 10, blk. 8, Winside $1.00
Arthur G. HILDRETH to Grace CAVENAUGH,
    lot 10, blk. 8, Winside   1,000.00

The Wayne Republican
November 3, 1897 (Vol. 4, No. 38)

BIRTH: Born to Frank THIELMAN and wife, Nov. 2, a daughter. Wir gratuliren.

BIRTH: A twelve-pound boy was born to Charley MILLER and wife, of Wilbur, on Sunday last.

MARRIED: George KAUTZ and Miss HANKINS were married on Sunday last at the home of the bride's parents in Hancock precinct, four miles west of Hoskins.

Advertised List.

Of letters, etc., remaining at the post office, Wayne, Nebraska, for the week ending November 2, 1897:
    Miss Lucy BOOTH, Chas. CARPENTER, Chris DAESS, S.A. DUNCAN, W.M. MAUDE, Bert NEFF, Willie ROBSIN, Robt. SHIPPY, A.C. WILLIAMS.
    Parties calling for the above please give date when advertised.   W.H. McNEAL, P.M.

Didn't Believe It.
But Now Know Just How it was Done.
The Other Fellows had too Many Votes &
got our Scalps and Money, too.
HUNTER, ZIEMER and GAERTNER.
Are the only Republicans Elected,
and for these let us give Thanks.
Hoskins, as Usual, the Banner Republican Precinct of the County, but what's the matter with Wayne?
The Vote Not Heavy!
And the Republicans as Usual, are the Ones to Stay at Home.

ESTIMATED MAJORITIES.

Phil H. KOHL, Treasurer	216
John R. COYLE, Clerk	104
J.M. CHERRY, Sheriff	161
F. HUNTER, Judge	56

C.M. WHITE, Superintendent	55
Jacob ZIEGLER, Com'r 2d Dist.	93

Our poultry is not of the crowing variety this year and for that reason we don't propose to trot them out and have the other fellows pull out their last tail feather. The result is a surprise to the republicans as they had good reason to believe that they would elect at least a majority of the candidates on their ticket, and it is very evident that they are not good at guessing on election results. While beaten we are not discouraged, but will go after them again, and yet it is just as well to confess that constant knocking down is a little monotonous. The officers elected are all good fellows and will make efficient officials.

The following is almost a complete return of the county by precincts.

BRENNA

MANNING	23
KOHL	102 - 79
NEELY	36
COYLE	93 - 59
FRAZIER	32
CHERRY	98 - 66
HUNTER	26
TOWER	94 - 68
HOWARD	26
WHITE	102 - 76
GOSS	29
ZIEGLER	98 - 69

DEER CREEK

MANNING	88 - 36
KOHL	52
NEELY	87 - 22
COYLE	55
FRAZIER	84 - 17
CHERRY	64
HUNTER	78 - 22
TOWER	56
MARTIN	5
HOWARD	81 - 22
WHITE	59

CHAPIN

MANNING	29
KOHL	65 - 36
NEELY	32

COYLE		62 - 30
FRAZIER		22
CHERRY		67 - 45
HUNTER		31
TOWER		62 - 31
HOWARD		29
WHITE		63 - 36
	GARFIELD	
MANNING		39
KOHL		43 - 4
NEELY		42 - 2
COYLE		49
FRAZIER		41
CHERRY		41
	HUNTER	
MANNING		59
KOHL		92 - 33
NEELY		72
COYLE		78 - 6
FRAZIER		65
CHERRY		81 - 16
HUNTER		83 - 24
TOWER		61
HOWARD		71
WHITE		77 - 5
	HANCOCK	
MANNING		26
KOHL		72 - 46
NEELY		31
COYLE		68 - 37
FRAZIER		24
CHERRY		75 - 51
HUNTER		28
TOWER		61 - 33
HOWARD		36
WHITE		60 - 24
	HOSKINS	
MANNING		85 - 39
KOHL		46
NEELY		88 - 44
COYLE		44
FRAZIER		93 - 54
CHERRY		39
HUNTER		88 - 46

TOWER		42
HOWARD		84 - 39
WHITE		45
	LOGAN	
MANNING		23
KOHL		42 - 19
NEELY		26
COYLE		39 - 13
FRAZIER		26
CHERRY		38 - 12
HUNTER		26
TOWER		34 - 8
HOWARD		23
WHITE		42 - 19
	LESLIE	
MANNING		13
KOHL		45 - 32
NEELY		15
COYLE		44 - 29
FRAZIER		12
CHERRY		45 - 32
HUNTER		13
TOWER		43 - 30
HOWARD		16
WHITE		41 - 25
	PLUM CREEK	
MANNING		46
KOHL		74 - 28
NEELY		59
COYLE		62 - 5
FRAZIER		58
CHERRY		63 - 5
HUNTER		78 - 38
TOWER		40
HOWARD		68 - 13
WHITE		54
	STRAHAN	
MANNING		26
KOHL		72 - 46
NEELY		31
COYLE		68 - 37
FRAZIER		24
CHERRY		75 - 41
HUNTER		28

TOWER				61 - 33
HOWARD				36
WHITE				60 - 24
GOSS				35
ZIEGLER				101 - 66
	WILBUR			
MANNING				47
KOHL				57 - 10
NEELY				56 - 9
COYLE				47
FRAZIER				50
CHERRY				54 - 4
HUNTER				56 - 17
TOWER				39
HOWARD				52
WHITE				52
GOSS				58 - 14
ZIEGLER				44
	WINSIDE			
MANNING				26
KOHL				55 - 29
NEELY				28
COYLE				54 - 26
FRAZIER				27
CHERRY				54 - 27
HUNTER				27
TOWER				51 - 24
HOWARD				38
WHITE				42 - 4
	WAYNE			
	1	2	3	TOT.
MANNING	48	55	79	182
KOHL	71	69	71	211 - 29
NEELY	52	71	92	216 - 36
COYLE	69	53	57	179
FRAZIER	66	63	87	216 - 36
CHERRY	53	63	61	179
HUNTER	77	65	91	233 - 126
TOWER	30	34	43	107
HOWARD	64	72	94	230 - 98
WHITE	57	52	53	162
GOSS	64		89	153 - 40
ZEIGLER	56		57	113

No report from Sherman but the following majorities: Treasurer tie; NEELY 14; FRAZIER 8; HUNTER 9; HOWARD 7.

It is impossible at this writing to get complete returns on surveyor and coroner, but from all indications ZIEMER and GAERTNER are elected by about 30 to 25 each.

• • •

Merchant Tailor
L.O. MEHUS
Wayne, Neb.

• • •

The Wayne Republican
November 10, 1897 (Vol. 4, No. 39)

DIED: On last Saturday evening the wife of James BAILEY, of Carroll, was burned to death by getting her clothes saturated with kerosene, and then taking fire. The funeral occurred on Monday afternoon, and was largely attended by friends who sincerely sympathized with the sorrowing husband and children in their sad bereavement.

DIED: BAILEY. Orlinda CARVER was born at Geneva, Ill., July 6, 1845 and at the time of death was 52 years, 3 months and 28 days of age. She was united in marriage to the surviving husband in April 1866. Four children, all boys, have come to bless this union and are all living. Early in their married life they removed from Grant county, Wis., to northern Iowa, removing from there to Atlantic in the spring of 1883. In March, 1890 they removed to Carroll where they have since resided. The deceased united with the M.E. church in 1885 and has always been an active worker in the church and Sunday school as long as health permitted. A husband, four sons, five brothers, two sisters, mother and father live to mourn her loss.

The Wayne Republican
November 17, 1897 (Vol. 4, No. 40)

DIED: The eight-months-old child of William SHAWGO died in Plum Creek precinct on Thursday and was buried on Friday.

DIED: Mr. and Mrs. John STEPHENS mourn the loss of

their infant son who died on Friday of last week.

Court Proceedings.
WIGHTMAN vs LAUMAN, continued.
HILDER vs HILDER, continued.
HURLBURT vs SUNDAHL, continued.
FETKER vs HAYES, conf'mation set aside.
State vs SNEATH, dismissed.
TUCKER vs STEWART, dismissed.
JONES vs Wayne County, dismissed, pl'tf costs.
GIBSON vs CHENAUER, dismissed.
HUNTER vs GOLDIE, dismissed.
State vs LEATHERBY, dismissed.
BRESSLER vs MUELLER, dismissed.
State Bank of Crawford vs J.M. BEALE, et al., sale confirmed, deed ordered.
BEARDSLEY vs TRACY, sale confirmed, deed ordered.
GOSHORN vs COONS, sale confirmed, deed ordered.
BRESSLER vs ADAMS, sale confirmed, deed ordered.
BENTON B'k vs KING, foreclosure ordered.
BEARDSLEY vs TROTTER, foreclosure ordered.
FRENCH vs BROWER, foreclosure ordered.
State ex rel County of Wayne vs S.B. RUSSELL, Mandamus granted, clerk ordered to enter fees on fee book.
KRUGER vs Wayne National Bank, motion for new trial overruled. Judgment for plaintiff $686.30. Defendant given 30 days to settle bill of exceptions.
FRENCH vs MILLER, defendant to file answer in 20 days.
LAMBERT vs LONGNECKER, objections to jurisdiction overruled.
TOLERTON & STETSON vs HUGHES, judgment for plaintiff $611.06.
BARRETT vs BARRETT, decree granted, plaintiff given custody of children.
State vs Frank WITTIE and Walter SHERBAHN, charged with assault and battery on one GATES with intent rob. WITTIE sentenced to 2 years in penitentiary, SHERBAHN to 30 days in jail.
GIBSON vs NORTHROP, judgment for $3 for plff.
Champion Horse Co. vs BLAIR, verdict for deft.

Real Estate Transfers.
For the 4 weeks ending Nov. 15, 1897, reported by I.W. ALTER, Bonded Abstractor, Wayne, Nebraska.

PERKINS, C.E. to John SAHS,
  nw 1/4, 21-27-3 — $2,000.00
John JENKINS to J.S. FRENCH,
  nw 1/4, 14-27-2 — 2,500.00
H.J. WILSON to Mary E. PERRIN,
  lots 11 & 19, blk. 19, CH add to Wayne — .60
R.B. CRAWFORD to E.D. MITCHELL,
  s 1/2 of nw 1/4 12-26-2 — 2,000.00
Robert TAYLOR, et al., to E.C. RENNICK,
  n 1/2 nw 1/4 15-35-3 — 1,800.00
Robert TAYLOR, et al., to J.H. PINGREY,
  se 1/4, 26-26-2 — 2,400.00
Elizabeth A. SHEPARD to Edgar A. WADE,
  s 1/2 ne 1/4 17-25-5 — 2,000.00
Elizabeth A. SHEPARD to Lutheran Ch.,
  5a in ne cor 7-25-5 — 100.00
Z. BOUGHN to M.N. WINEBRENNER & J.W. HOLTZ,
  ne 4-27-1 — 4,000.00
S.A. GIBSON to HASKELL & MATHEWSON,
  se 3-25-5 — 5,348.00
J.A. LINDLEY to Ludwig BONER,
  s 1/2 nw 1/4 31-27-1 — 1,200.00
O.O. WHITED to John R. WHITE,
  blk. 4 & w 1/2 blk. 5, 1st ad to Carroll — 1.00

The Wayne Republican
November 24, 1897 (Vol. 4, No. 41)

MARRIED: SHARP - CUNNINGHAM. Today at 12 o'clock noon at the home of Mr. and Mrs. B. CUNNINGHAM, their daughter, Lois S., will be married to E. Clay SHARP. Only a few of the closest friends of the families will be present at the ceremony, but we are sure that the good wishes of a large circle of friends will be most heartily extended for their future happiness. Of the groom we can only speak from hearsay and from this we learn that he is an excellent young man and one that bears a good reputation. The bride and her family are among the best known in the county and are held in the very highest esteem by all. To the newly married couple, the Republican wishes to extend its congratulations and bid them God-speed and a happy voyage.

The CHERRY Divorce Case.

The attention of the court was occupied a portion of Monday afternoon and the entire evening with the CHERRY divorce case from our neighboring town of Winside. The court room was well filled with an audience composed of all ages of persons, there for the purpose of gratifying their curiosity as it was expected that some of the testimony would be very sensational and afford a ground work for the gossips to base a racy story on. The case was one wherein Dr. A.B. CHERRY asked to be divorced from his wife Estella, charging her with habitual drunkenness. This was resisted on the part of the wife and a general denial of plaintiff's allegations set up. Witness after witness was called by the complainant, and each of them testified to the truthfulness of the charge and even went so far as to specify dates, and some of them testifed to helping dispose of the fiery fluid in the company of Mrs. CHERRY and her mother, Mrs. MUNDY. While the evidence was pretty tough on the females as to their drink habits it didn't reflect any great amount of credit on some of the young men that gave the testimony, neither did it tend to show that the liquor laws of the state are very rigidly enforced as several lads who had testified that they had procured the stuff as far back as three or four years ago, in giving their ages to the reporter only claimed to be 21 years old now. An attempt was made to show that the doctor was responsible for the drink habit of his wife, and that he furnished her liquor prior to their marriage and at various times since. It was also claimed that he was an habitual user of liquor and while under the influence of the fiery fluid was very abusive of his wife. It was just a little bit difficult to understand how this proved that the wife was not guilty of the charge made, but it did tend to show that there was considerable rottenness on both sides. It seemed from the testimony that most of the drinking was done in company with the mother of Mrs. C., and at her home which one after another of the boys and young men testified was the rendezvous. The doctor was pretty fully examined as to his financial standing, evidently for the purpose of fixing the alimony in the case.

DIED: Died on Saturday last a three-year-old son of Mr. and Mrs. MARTEN who live four miles south of here. The funeral services were held at the German M.E. church on Sunday. (Hoksins)

DIED: Died Nov. 23 at her home near Hoskins, Mrs. Frederick SHROEDER____. She was on of the first settlers in this part of Wayne county. She leaves a large circle of friends to mourn her loss.

From a sketch of the "Senatorial Campaign of 1870, by Stephen TRIPP," in the West Point Republican, we make the following extract concerning

PIONEER DAYS IN WAYNE COUNTY.

The lengthening shadows of a crisp November afternoon brought me to the Norfolk and Dakota City crossing of the Logan, which was a short distance below where the town of Wakefield now stands. The ride from W.C. ORR's homestead, in what is now Grant township, a distance of some 15 miles, was a lonesome one. If I remember correctly the only houses in sight of the furrow were those of Mose HERNER, M.T. SPERRY, a Mr. VOORMAN, and those of two or three families by the name of ALLEN. Those of the last named I have been informed since, were near a part of the first county seat of Wayne county. In 1870 there were two families living at the Logan crossing on the east side of the creek which was spanned by a low bridge which was about half way from the water at its usual stage to the top of the bank and was reached by an excavated roadway. The occupant of one of the houses was a Mr. AGLER from Lee county, Ills., who kept the post office, the name of which I have forgotten. I have also forgotten the name of the other family which was also from Lee county. Nestled cosily under the bluffs on the west side of the creek, and some little distance below the crossing, was the residence of Capt. WHITTON, a gallant son of Mars, from the state of Maine, who tried to make it seem homelike by naming the post office at the crossing Sagadahoc after his native county, but his Illinois neighbors objected so strongly to such an outlandish name that the captain failed in his attempt and thereafter he refused to have any intercourse with his Illinois neighbors.

In 1860 Wayne county consisted principally of a broad expense of rolling and very fertile prairies. It was said by the early settlers that they did not find a tree of any kind growing within the limits of the county and all of their wood and fuel had to be hauled from the Missouri river in Dakota county, a distance of twenty-five miles or more, or from the Elkhorn in Cuming and Stanton counties, which was nearer, but as a rule had to be paid for, while that on the Missouri could be had on the sand bar for the cutting and hauling, hence was most resorted to.

The early settlers suffered great hardships from the scarcity of fuel. If I remember correctly a number of them were caught in a blizzard in the early seventies while on their way to or from the timber and some of them perished from the cold and that women and children perished at home for want of fuel. In 1870 there were only 80 odd homesteads located within the limits of Wayne county. Nearly all the rest of the land was owned by non-resident speculators, the principal one of whom was a Mr. GRAVES (generally known as old man GRAVES), of Mendota, Ill. Mr. GRAVES was a native of Vermont and emigrated to Illinois some time in the forties, bringing a considerable sum of money with him which he invested in government land which he sold at a big advance during and just after the war. This money was reinvested in government lands in Cuming, Stanton and Wayne counties; the greater portion of it being located in the last-named county. In order to make his land valuable Mr. GRAVES assisted a number of families in Lee and LaSalle counties, Ill., to emigrate to Wayne county, where they availed themselves of the benefit of the homestead law and acquired a quarter section of land. Mr. GRAVES' last investment had been made too late in life to be of any benefit to him, in fact it was a source of trouble, for after the county was organized the settlers voted bonds for a courthouse, schoolhouses and bridges. The contracts for the building of these they let to themselves at good prices and the non-residents had to foot the bills. As late as 1874 or '75 one non-resident owner of Wayne county land offered to sell 1,600 acres for $2,006, just what he had paid for it and he had paid four or five years' taxes on it. In 1870 Mr. GRAVES offered a large amount of land for the endowment of a college. I never knew the exact amount, some accounts said 10 sections, 3, and other 10,000 acres. The former is the most probable, but the conditions were such that the people were unable at that time to avail themselves of the offer. The locality receiving the benefits of the offer was required to build suitable buildings and maintain the school until land could be sold for $25 per acre; it could be rented however until that time and the proceeds go towards maintaining the school.

Court Proceedings.
(Continued from last week.)
MITTLESTADT vs VANSHUR, sale confirmed, deed ordered.
Cit Bank vs BEALE, deed ordered.
BURR vs KLAWOON, sale confirmed, deed ordered.
BURR vs KEATING, sale confirmed, deed ordered.
Estate of August KRUGER, sale of admr deed, confirmed and he ordered to execute.
CROSBY vs John DEDLA, foreclosure as prayed.
HOUSER vs HOUSE. This was a case wherein pltff claimed a commission for a sale of deft's farm which was never completed because as pltff claimed deft refused to sign agreement when presented, deft claimed the contract of sale was different from

instructions to plt'ff as his agent and after evidence of pltff was all in a motion was made by deft's counsel to dismiss case which was sustained by the court and jury ordered to find verdict for defendant.

Maria JONES vs Wayne county, dismissed at plffs costs, pltff excepts.

Champion Horse Co. vs BLAIR, verdict for deft.

GIBSON vs VOLPP, dismissed at pltff's cost.

REECE vs JAMES, continued.

1st National Bank vs HUGHES, default against all pltffs except John CONNORS $325 finding in favor of cross petitioner CONNOR $197 and given first lien judgment for pltff $2,322.50 and allowed second lien.

MITTLESTADT & Co. vs Anna KAUFL, foreclosure as prayed.

State vs Edward PERRY, deft to pay cost and is discharged, bondsmen released.

Wayne county vs S.B. RUSSELL, cont'd.
Wayne county vs S.B. RUSSELL, cont'd.
Wayne county vs S.B. RUSSELL, cont'd.

BARGHOLZ vs BARGHOLZ, divorce granted and husband given custody of child Frederick; wife allowed alimony as agreed by parties, custody of child Ella given to wife; husband to pay costs.

MITTELSTADT vs KAUFL, foreclosure ord'd.

GAEBLER vs LOUND, et al., foreclosure ord'd.

Same vs GEHRKE, et al., foreclosure ord'd.

HANSEN vs HANSEN, was a case wherein the plaintiff J.E. HANSEN sought to evict his brother from a farm northwest of the city. The jury found for defendant, Hans E. HANSEN.

The Wayne Republican
December 1, 1897 (Vol. 4, No. 42)

BIRTH: Mr. and Mrs. John HODSON are the proud parents of a bouncing boy. (Hunter)

MARRIED: FITZSIMMONS - OLIVER. On Nov. 17, Lee FITZSIMMONS and Lillian OLIVER were united in marriage by Rev. W.W. THEOBALD.

DIED: John GREENWALD, a young man 25 years of age was found dead in bed on Thursday morning. When he retired on Wednesday evening he was apparently in as good health as usual. Heart disease is given as the cause of death.

The Wayne Republican
December 8, 1897 (Vol. 4, No. 43)

BIRTH: A daughter arrived at the home of J.A. LOVE on Sunday.

The G.A.R. Post of this place held its annual election of officers at its hall on Saturday and elected A.W. TAYLOR Commander, W.R. RAMSEY Sr. and J.B. STALLSMITH Jr. vice commanders, Mark STRINGER Quartermaster, J.W. BARTLETT Officer of the Day, B.F. FEATHER Adjutant, J.D. KING Chaplain and K. BARGER Officer of Guard.

Real Estate Transfers.

For the three weeks ending Dec. 6, 1897, reported by I.W. ALTER, Bonded Abstracter, Wayne, Neb:

John T. BRESSLER to John SHERBAHN, n 1/2 lot 2, blk. 8, B&B ad Wayne	$150.00
A.L. TUCKER to J.S. FRENCH, se 14-27-2	4,000.00
Peter SWENSON to Lorenz PRESTON, lots 8, 9, 10, 11 & 12, blk. 5, College Hill, Wayne	210.00
Archie McINTOSH to Fannie McINTOSH, n 1/2 lot 1, blk. 7, C&B ad to Wayne	1.00
A.C. GOLTZ to Alice G. BAYES, lot 4, blk. 1, Winside	600.00
Mary BENSER to Gust A. BLEICH, lot 11, blk. 7, B&P ad Winside	40.00
C.B. FRENCH jr to Gust A. BLEICH, lot 10, blk. 7, B&P ad Winside	100.00
John L. NELSON to Matti C. NELSON, lot 14, blk. 1, Winside	1.00
Geo. WEATHERILL to Wm. WOEHLER, nw 36-25-3	5,000.00
Ed REYNOLDS to Chas. H. BURR, nw 4-26-3	3,517.00
Same to same, sw of n 35-25-2	400.00
Same to same, sw of nw, 2-25-2	400.00
Same to A.A. WELCH, w 3 w 1/2 26-26-3	1,850.00
J.T. BRESSLER to Mattie C. NELSON, lot 13, blk. 1, Winside	75.00

W. GAEBLER, adm'r to John BENDER,
   lot 26 & lots 1, 2, 5, blk. 1, B&P ad;
   also lot 7, blk. 3 & lot 5, outlot 2,
   1st ad to Winside $656.00
Same to I.O. BROWN,
   lot 25, blk. 3, Winside   800.00
J.S. FRENCH to Damiel MARTIN,
   se 4-27-2   3,200.00
Chas. KNAPP to J.S. FRENCH,
   se 4-27-2   2,000.00

The Wayne Republican
December 15, 1897 (Vol. 4, No. 44)

MARRIED: MINER - PARK. On Tuesday Dec. 14, by Rev. BITHEL, Benjamin E. MINER and Jane E. PARK. The groom claims to be the first white child born in Wayne county and at present is a resident of Dixon county.

The Wayne Republican
December 22, 1897 (Vol. 4, No. 45)

A Few Facts!
In Regard to the Early Settlement of Wayne County.
"The Queen of the Logan Valley!"
Her Development and Present Proud Position Among the Counties of the State!
Something About Her Homes and People, Her Schools, Churches and Societies!
The Ideal Land of the Agriculturist, Stock Breeder and Feeder!
Something of Interest for All!

Wayne County was first settled by a few families, mostly from Illinois, in the year 1869, who located in the eastern part of the county, followed a year later, by a few families of German Americans who settled in the neighborhood of the present town of Hoskins; but long prior to that time it had been visited by Eastern land speculators, who saw that is possessed unrivalled advantages as an agricultural county, and who entered for speculative purpose thousands of acres of government land so that when the first settlers came there was but little "homestead" land remaining in the county, probably not to exceed 25 sections in all. The remainder of the land was held by speculators, the B. & M. R. R. Co., which had been allowed to enter a vast tract of land here, while the state had selected several thousand acres as agricultural college lands. These facts tended to retard immigration, so that in 1870 when the county was organized, there were probably not to exceed 23 families in the county, and from that time until the building of the C. St. P. M. & O. Railway in 1880 and 1881, its growth was very slow indeed, there being but about 140 voters in 1879, while the population by the government census in 1880, was but 817, and a large number of these were graders, and others here for temporary purposes. But with the advent of the iron horse, all this changed. From Iowa and Illinois the settlers began to pour into the county almost like a stream, and purchase farms and ranches, with the result that land which had formerly gone begging at from 90 cents to $3.50 rose rapidly in value until within less than two years the same "dirt" was selling at from ten to twenty dollars per acre. These new comers were for the most part fairly well-to-do farmers, who built for themselves large and

SUBSTANTIAL FARM HOUSES,

with the result that today Wayne county possesses the finest and largest farm residences, as well as commodius barns and other outbuildings, of any county in the state.

The soil of Wayne county is peculiarly adapted to the raising of all the cereals grown in the temperate zone, including wheat, rye, oats, barley, corn, etc., but its staple production has been corn. Its native grasses furnishes abundant hay and pasturage, but tame grasses do well here, especially alfalfa. By reason of this, and the numerous small streams by which the county is abundantly watered, Wayne county has become one of the greatest, even if not the leading, stock-growing and feeding county of the state. Indeed, it was computed by representatives of the South Omaha Stock Exchange this fall, that Wayne county stood third among the counties of the state in the number of cattle held by its citizens, and both of the counties which lead it are what is known as range counties, and either of them has ten times the area of ours. A reference to the tables of shipments of stock in and out of the county during the current year, found elsewhere in this article, will show conclusively that Wayne is the

LEADING STOCK COUNTY

of this section of the state. A thing not to be forgotten in this connection is that nearly all of the corn grown in the county finds a ready market with the feeders, and nearly always at better prices than the current market rates. Another important item worthy to be remembered by eastern homseekers, is the fact that

WAYNE IS IN THE RAIN BELT,

and that never since the grasshopper times has there been a total failure of crops in this county. When corn failed here in 1894, as it did elsewhere in the state, we had a good yield of small grain, and fully a fourth crop of corn; and during the year the people of this county contributed 6 carloads of grain and provisions to the people of the burned-out counties of the state. It was not the drought so much that injured the corn as the hot dry winds which blew steadily from the south for three days, when the fields of maize were in blossom, blasting the pollen on the tassels, so that it did not fertilize the silk. The fact is that Wayne county is practically "drought-proof," as has been demonstrated during the nearly 30 years that have elapsed since the first furrow was turned, exposing the rich dark loam to the mellowing influences of God's clear sunlight.

The average rainfall for the county as shown by statistics is from 25 to 27 inches, which is amply sufficient for all purposes.

Experience has shown during the past four or five years that this is also a great

SUGAR BEET GROWING COUNTY,

the average yield being in the neighborhood of 15 tons to the acre, yielding from 12 to 16 per cent of sugar, with a coefficient purity of 80 to 85 per cent, and which is surpassed nowhere on unfertilized lands.

We have not the complete data for 1897, but quote from a pamphlet issued by the Wayne County Commerical Club, which shows that in 1895 the productions of Wayne Co. were as follows:

Corn	100,000 acres.
Wheat	60,000 acres.
Oats	18,000 acres.
Sugar beets	500 acres.
Rye, millet, flax, etc.	20,000 acres.
Hay and pasture	30,000 acres.

The value of these crops is fully $2,000,000, and to this must be added the value of the live stock, butter and other produce, amounting to not less than $1,000,000 more making a grand total of $3,000,000.

GRAIN.

By referring to the assessors reports for the year 1897, we find that there were 44,175 acres sown to wheat, 18,765 to oats and 83,223 acres planted to corn. The yield this year per acre is not nearly so great as the year of 1896, which was a phenomenal one, the corn crop being fully 5,000,000 bushels. It is safe however to put the yield of wheat per acre for the county 10 bushels to the acre yielding about 500,000 bushels that has up to this date sold at prices ranging from 65 to 80 cents per bushel, but the greater portion has sold at about 70 cents, thus making the value of the wheat crop of the county about $350,000. The 18,765 acres of oats yielded at least 30 bushels to the acre or a total of 656,775 bushels that has sold at prices ranging from 12 to 15 cents per bushel or an average of 13 1/2 cents per bushel making the total value of the crop in round numbers about $90,000. The corn crop is now practically all gathered and the yield is fully 30 bushels to the acre or a total of 2,500,000 which is today worth 15 cents per bushel or a total value of $375,000 making a grand total for these three cereals for the year 1897 of $815,000. These figures are very conservative and will be found on investigation by anyone to be under rather than over the actual value of the crops. The potato crop of the county is one of considerable value this year but it is one of the things that is very difficult to arrive at anything like definite figures.

LIVE STOCK.

This is today the greatest industry of the county in which hundreds of thousands of capital is invested and for several years past it has been a source of considerable profit to those engaged in it. We are located where the most nutritious grasses in the world are grown, and where corn and oats in abundance is always assured and at figures that do not make it hazardous to consume. The great ranges and breeding grounds of the west are in so close proximity as to be always available for the necessary supply of "stockers." When the assessors made their reports last April they found almost 20,000 head of cattle in the county. The climate here is probably the best adapted for feeding of any to be found in the whole country and stock always does well. Careful inquiry warrants us in asserting that today there are easily 10,000 more head in the county than returned by the assessors and that 10,000 to 12,000 of these are in the feed yards being made ready for the markets of the world. The remainder are young stock and cows. We are not prepared to make an estimate of the number of hogs in the county, but do know that during the past year almost or quite 20,000 have been shipped to market from the county. Hog cholera at times has been quite severe, but nothing to be compared to what it has been in many other sections of the country and indeed has never been severe enough here to have much effect on the profitableness of the business. There was a time when horse breeding was engaged in quite extensively but of late years has been sadly neglected because of the extremely low prices prevalent, and of the much surer and larger profits to be derived from hogs and cattle. There are very few sheep raised in the county and there never has been sufficient interest manifested in the business to form any basis for judgment as to its profitableness or otherwise.

THE POPULATION

of the county, now estimated at 10,000, is composed of native born Americans, and naturalized citizens of German, Swedish, Danish, Norwegian, Canadian, Irish, Scotch-Irish and Welch birth; and constitute a God-fearing, industrious and frugal people. There is not a solitary "heathen Chinee," nor a negro in the entire county.

There are 3,326 children of school age in the county, and 76 school houses. To supply the needs of these there are 100 licensed teachers in the county. The average school year throughout the county is eight months, though in Wayne and several other districts the school year lasts for nine months. The average rate of wages of teachers is about $32 per month. School houses built in 1897, 2, total value of school property $53,955, total wages paid teachers for the year $22,132.35, total enrollment 2,282, average daily attendance 1,454, total days taught by all teachers 12,974.

THE COUNTY OFFICERS FOR THE
COMING YEAR

are as follows:

County Treasurer - Phil H. KOHL.
County Clerk - John R. COYLE.
Clerk of the Courts - Bert BROWN.
Sheriff - J.M. CHERRY.
County Judge - Enoch HUNTER.
County Attorney - A.A. WELCH.
County Superintendent - Miss C.M. WHITE.
County Surveyor - A.L. HOUSER.
Coroner - John P. GAERTNER.
County Commissioners - George HARRIGFELD, Richard RUSSELL and Jacob W. ZIEGLER.

Wayne county's credit is A1. Its bonded indebtedness is small, and it has no flowing debt. Its warrants are always paid in cash upon presentation and have never been below par. It is the best county in the state for people who want pleasant homes, where the religious, social and educational privileges are unexcelled, where land is still cheap and opportunities are still numerous to better one's condition. Many fine farms and some vacant lands are in the market at from fifteen to thirty-five dollars per acre, and hundreds of opportunities exist for the safe, profitable and permanent investment of money, and where good citizenship is the highest passport to favor.

The City of Wayne founded in June, 1881, now has a population of about 2,300. It is situated on a plateau and low hillsides, and is one of the most substantially built young cities in the state, showing that its people came here to build and found HOMES, and not merely temporary abiding places. The citizenship is composed of wide-awake, hustling, representative people, largely of American birth, who take pride in their town, and are not afraid to stand up for, and to talk about it, at all times and under all circumstances. To aid them in this always laudable work they are ably assisted (although at times we are doubtful whether their work is half appreciated) by three as good country newspapers as can be found in any city of its size in this or any other state of the union. These are

THE WAYNE REPUBLICAN

published by E. CUNNINGHAM, republican in politics, and straight republican at that; the Wayne Herald, published by McNEAL & BEEBE, also republican in politics; and the Semi-Weekly Democrat, published by W.S. GOLDIE, and whose politics never belie its name. What little news escapes the vigilant eyes of the reporters of these three papers isn't worth mentioning.

RELIGIOUS AND FRATERNAL.

The city contains several church organizations as follows:
Presbyterian, Rev. MONTGOMERY.
Methodist, Rev. BITHELL.
Catholic, Rev. FITZGERALD.
German Lutheran, Rev. GRABER.
English Lutheran,
Baptist and Episcopal.

The first six of these have church buildings of their own, but at the present time the pulpits of the last three are vacant. Of a semi-religious nature there is the Y.M.C.A. and the W.C.T.U. Both of these organizations have a large membership and both, we believe, wield a powerful influence for good in the community. The former holds meetings every Sunday in its own hall, and which are usually well attended.

Wayne is peculiarly rich in the number and character of her fraternal and benevolent organizations. The oldest of these is Casey Post, No. 5, G.A.R., which was organized at La Porte in February, 1881, and is now in a pretty healthy condition, with a good membership and interesting meetings. This is the only G.A.R. Post in the county, although the 90 odd old soldiers are further organized into the Wayne County Veteran Association, which holds annual reunions in August. The next in point of age is Wayne lodge, No. 120, A.F. & A.M., organized in 1882, and which is in a flourishing condition. The only other Masonic organization in the county is at Winside, which was chartered last June. There are also lodges of Odd Fellows, A.O.U.W., Knights of Pythias, Modern Woodmen of America, Sons of Herman, Royal Highlanders, Loyal Mystic Legion, a company of the Uniform Rank, K.P., and Ladies Auxilliaries to the A.O.U.W., and M.W.A., in the Degree of Honor and the Royal Neighbors.

Winside also has a flourishing camp of Modern Woodmen and a lodge of Sons of Herman; Carroll a camp of Woodmen and a lodge of Workmen; while Hoskins has but one organization, a camp of Modern Workmen.

THE CITY OFFICERS

for the current year are as follows:
Mayor - Henry LEY.
Clerk - Everett LAUGHLIN.
Police Judge - A.T. WITTER.
Treasurer - Lambert ROE.
Marshal - George L. MINER.
Sup't Water Works - Peter COYLE.
Councilmen - J.H. GOLL, S.H. RICHARDSON, Ran FRAZIER, E.P. OLMSTED, D.C. MAIN, C.O. FISHER.

PUBLIC SCHOOLS.

Wayne has two good public school buildings, with a fine corps of teachers. The buildings are located on very sightly eminences, are large and commodious, and are, at present, able to accomodate all the pupils of the district. The schools are under the management of a Board of Education, of which A.F. BRENNER is president, and Dr. J.J. WILLIAMS, secretary. The Superintendent is U.S. CONN.

WATER WORKS.

The city possesses as fine a system of water works as can be found any where, with a capacity for more than double our present needs. The water is pumped from wells south of the railroad track to a stand pipe on one of the highest points in the city, and the pressure is great enough to furnish ample protection against fire. The entire system costs somewhere in the neighborhood of $25,000, and are owned by the city. We have also, a splendid

FIRE DEPARTMENT,

well equipped with two hose carts and a hook and ladder wagon. The offices of the department are: Nelson GRIMSLEY, president; Albert BERRY, secretary and Lambert ROE, chief. R.C. OSBORN is foreman and John O'HARA assistant of the Hose Company. Geo. C. GELDER is foreman and Will RICKABAUGH assistant of Hook and Ladder Company.

THE BUSINESS OF THE CITY

is transacted by 4 grain elevators, 3 lumber and coal yards, 1 exclusive coal dealer, 1 flour and feed mill, 4 general stores, 3 dry goods stores, 7 groceries, 1 shoe store, 3 jewelers, 3 meat markets, 1 clothing and carpet store, 1 book store, 2 bakeries, 2 saloons, 3 printing offices, 1 cigar manufacturer, 2 harness makers, 2 milliners, 3 shoemakers, 2 drug stores, 5 physicians, 2 furniture dealers and undertakers, 4 banks, 7 attorneys, 2 hardware dealers, 3 implement houses, 2 livery barns, 1 feed yard, 2 firms of stock dealers, 4 barber shops, 5 blacksmith shops, 3 wagon shops, 2 laundries, 2 plumbers, 1 tobacco store, 1 news dealer, 3 hotels, 2 restaurants, 2 merchant tailors, 8 real estate and insurance agents, 15 or 20 carpenters, 3 delivery wagons and 5 dray lines, 4 plasterers, 2 brick masons, 2 dentists and 1 vetrinarian.

Undoubtedly no institution in Wayne has a warmer spot in the affections of the people of both city and county than

THE NEBRASKA NORMAL COLLEGE,

which is a child of their own creation, for they had long felt the need of a higher educational institution, until in 1891, a plan was conceived and adopted through which their wants were supplied and the College became a living reality. The presidency of the embryo institution was tendered to

PROF. JAMES M. PILE, A.M.,

then of Fremont, where he was known as one of the leading instructors of the state. Mr. PILE accepted the offer, and the first term was held in the High School building in the summer of 1891, and afterwards in a vacant store building, until the following year when the handsome college building whose picture adorns our first page, was completed. From a small and humble beginning it has steadily grown until it is now the recognized leading educational institution of North Nebraska. Nor is its clientage confined to this portion of the state, but it has enrolled pupils from nearly every county in Nebraska, from South Dakota, Wyoming, Iowa, Minnesota and other states, and even from far-off Texas. For those who follow the profession of teaching, it has been of almost inestimable value, and there is scarcely a school in this section of the state but that numbers among its teachers graduates or students of the Nebraska Normal College. Indeed, the highest passport to the favor of school boards in the employment of teachers is the possession of a diploma from the Wayne College. As a business venture for Wayne it has been an unqualified success in the added revenue given our business men. To the revenues of the Post office alone it added at least $400 a year, and that is constantly increasing.

During the past year, President PILE has been compelled to refuse pupils for want of accommodation, and so a new dormitory 30x80 feet and 3 stories high, is in course of construction, and will be completed next month. This will give ample accommodations for 100 more students, besides creating additional class rooms by the transfer from the College building to the dormitory of the dining rooms and kitchen.

The College has five terms of 10 weeks each, but classes are so arranged that students may enter at any time. The faculty of the College is as follows:

J.M. PILE, President - Grammar and Mathematics.
Ella J. PILE - Common Branches.
O.W. CANN - Sciences, Elocution.
Emma KLINTWORT - Latin, German.
O.L. COMPTON - Comm'l Branches.
Nellie W. STEWART - Music.
Lillie M. HEALD - Shorthand.
Fred M. PILE - Librarian.

THE WAYNE BRICK YARDS

are among the most important industries of Wayne. These were started by the present proprietor, John F. SHERBAHN, in 1882, and at first only hand labor was employed, but as the town grew, and the demand increased new machinery was introduced, until now he has a well equipped steam plant, costing in the neighborhood of $15,000, and with a capacity of 30,000 bricks daily. He employs during the season a force of 14 men, whose daily wages average from $1.50 to $2.50 per day. He not only furnishes to the people of this city and county but supplies all of the towns on the Bloomfield branch, and in addition ships bricks to Laurel, Concord, Coleridge and other towns and during the present season has shipped 54,000 to go into the new wing of the Norfolk Hospital for the Insane.

THE WAYNE ROLLER MILLS

is another one of the large institutions of our city. They were erected during the summer of 1885, by WEBER Bros., who came here from Tekamah. The mills are run by steam power, and had at first a capacity of 50 barrels a day, but during the past year they have expended about $1,500 in improvements, bringing the daily capacity up to 65 barrels. The product of the mills is unexcelled in quality, and not only has a ready sale at home, but is also largely used in the adjoining towns and counties.

THE WAYNE CO-OPERATIVE CREAMERY

is the name of another manufacturing institution which is doing much for the farmers residing in the vicinity of this city, by whom it is controlled and managed. It is operated by steam, and manufactures an excellent quality of butter, as is shown by the fact that no butter commands a higher price in the markets in Chicago, New York or Boston than that made right here in our little city. The officers of the company are A.B. CLARK, president, and Chris. WISCHOFF, secretary and manager.

WAYNE'S NEEDS.

Among the most pressing of Wayne's needs is that of an electric light system and we believe that this need will soon be realized, for the mayor and city council have prepared plans for a system and are negotiating with the eastern firms with a view to the putting in of a plant by the city, or failing in that, by private parties, so that in the course of two or three months we probably will have the entire city lighted by electricity.

We need a sugar beet manufactory of sufficient capacity to work up all the beets that can be grown in this vicinity.

We need more energetic, hustling citizens who will devote their energies to the upbuilding of the Gem City of the Logan Valley.

We need a more united effort on the part of all, that together with a strong pull, we can bring desirable things our way whenever the opportunity presents itself to secure something for the benefit of our young city. The newspapers will do their part, no matter how much they apparently quarrel over trivial matters, it remains with the people of Wayne themselves to get together, and in less than five years more we shall have doubled in population and wealth. And so let it be.

WOMEN'S CLUBS.

As is well known Wayne is far ahead of most towns of her size in the state in the number of Women's Clubs. They are all literary in character. The oldest of these is the

ACME.

This club was organized in February, 1885. It began with eight charter members. Quite a number of these are still members of the club. Mrs. O.H. CONE was its first president. Its numbers are limited to twenty. The present officers are: Mrs. J.G. MINES, president; and Mrs. Hamer WILSON, secretary. Two months later the

MONDAY

Club was organized with eight charter members, Mrs. GOSHORN being the first president. During the thirteen years this club has been established it has furnished Wayne with its only circulating library. Its present officers are: Mrs. F. NORTHROP, president and Mrs. E. CUNNINGHAM, secretary. The

BACHELOR GIRLS

was next organized in October, 1896. It consists of young ladies. Its officers are: Miss Nettie CRAVEN, president and Miss Lucie BUFFINGTON, secretary.

MINERVA.

On October 19, 1896, a number of ladies not belonging to other clubs decided upon another and at once proceeded to organize one. They christened the new club Minerva. Its membership is limited to 20 members. Its present officers are Mrs. Cora BEEBE, president; Mrs. Sarah KING, vice president; Mrs. Sarah ANDRESS, secretary and Mrs. Mary FISHER, treasurer. Last and youngest, but by no means least comes the

U. D. CLUB,

Utilla Dulci, the useful with the pleasant. This, the youngest of our clubs, consists of young matrons and at present has six members. Mrs. Chas. ROBBINS, Mrs. Roland JAMES, Mrs. Nathan CHACE, Mrs. Sam ALEXANDER, Mrs. L. HOLTZ and Mrs. Willis HOWARD. Its officers are: Mrs. Nathan CHACE, president; Mrs. Willis HOWARD, vice president and Mrs. Sam ALEXANDER, secretary and treasurer.

MEN'S CLUBS.

There are two mens clubs in the city that hold regular meetings for the entertainment of the members.

* * *

Nearly every church in the city as well as those in the country have wide-awake and interesting Sunday schools which are largely attended. There are also several Sunday schools held at school houses in the country. The German Lutheran of this city also has a day school as well.

There is a Chatauqua circle in the city with a good membership of interested students.

TELEPHONE EXCHANGE.

The Iowa and Nebraska Telephone Company has put into the city one of the most complete exchanges found anywhere. Its system is one that is an ornament as well as a blessing to the city and its people. It is less than two months since the company began the erection of its lines for the exchange, and today there are over 50 phones in use, and the company has orders for many more. The same company has its lines extending to all of the leading towns of Northeast Nebraska and into Northern Iowa, Southern Minnesota and South Dakota, so that we are now able to do business with or talk to our friends whenever inclination or necessity demands.

The Wayne Republican
December 29, 1897 (Vol. 4, No. 46)

LICENSED TO WED: James H. EMCH and Della COOK.

LICENSED TO WED: James C. HANSEN and Mae BONAWITZ.

MARRIED: At the home of the bride's parents four miles east of Hoskins on December 26, 1897, Mr. Ferdinand EISENHEUER of Columbus, Neb., to Miss Emma JONES of Hoskins, Justice J.L. CLINE officiating.

MARRIED: On December 25, Justice FEATHER officiating, Chas. VAUGHN and Daisy LONGNECKER.

MARRIED: On Saturday December 25th, just as the clock was striking twelve the marriage of Mr. Ned LLOYD and Miss Gertrude CULLER took place at the home of Mr. George CULLER, Rev. Thomas BITHELL officiating. A large number of guests assembled to see the happy couple start upon the matrimonial sea and to wish them all the happiness possible. The presents were numerous and costly. After the ceremony was performred the guests sat down to tables beautifully decorated and heavily laden with the best the land could produce and to which justice was done. Their many friends wish them peace, happiness and prosperity. That he who has so far kept and preserved them may continue to do so.

COMMISSIONER PROCEEDINGS, Wayne, Neb., Dec. 27, '97.
    Board met pursuant to adjournment, all members present, minutes of last and all preceding meetings were read and on motion approved.
    On motion the county treasurer was instructed to transfer $895 from the county road fund to county general fund.
    On motion the following claims were examined, allowed and warrants ordered drawn on county general fund for same.

T.J. WELTY, attending court	$24.00
R.J. ARMSTRONG, juror	12.10
E. CUNNINGHAM, juror	12.10
E.R. CHACE, juror	14.60
B. CUNNINGHAM, juror	14.10

A.B. CLARK, juror	$8.40
Geo. W. FORTNER, juror	12.10
M. EICH, juror	18.40
J.G. GRIMSLEY, juror	15.00
W.A. HUNTER, juror	13.20
L.E. HUNTER, juror	2.00
J.E. HANCOCK, juror	19.20
Ed JONES, juror	18.80
C.F. LENZ, juror	20.00
Everett LINDSAY, juror	16.00
John LIVERINGHOUSE, juror	18.60
George LEWIS, juror	18.20
Wm. LALK, juror	16.00
S.T. McMIVAGAL, juror	14.80
P.L. MILLER, juror	12.10
James MULNANY, juror	20.60
Geo. ROE, juror	14.00
A.J. SWARTZ, juror	16.00
Peter ULRICH, Jr., juror	19.20
Gus WENDT, juror	17.20
J. JENNINGS, juror	2.00
Don WIER, juror	2.00
J.F. RAMSEY, juror	6.00
W.P. AGLER, boarding paupers	25.50
M.S. EMGLERT, road work	24.76
F.W. VAFFKAMP, road work	6.50
J.J. CARRO, road work	10.00
J.A. LOVE, boarding paupers	6.75
Paul GREENWOOD, road work	1.00
Ed K. WILLIAMS, road work	2.50
Fred KAY, road work	2.50
Martin HOLTZ, road work	7.50
Joe SLAUGHTER, road work	5.00
John T. BRESSLER, rent	15.00
G.L. MINER, Watchman	2.00
A. JETT, labor	4.00
Cal RITCHEY, road work	13.75
H.H. CHILDS, road work	2.50
W. PFIEL, road work	22.75
W.C. PARSONS, hardware	6.35
Geo. WEATHERHOLT, road work	44.30
John LEUCK, road work	2.50
Chas. GREEN, road work	7.75
F.A. BERRY, rent election	2.00

C.M. SUNDAHL, road work	$6.25
Wm. HEYER, blacksmithing	4.20
Ed REYNOLDS, boarding prisoners	88.95
A.M. JACOBS, Com. services	14.10
Geo. HARRIGELD, Com. services	22.00
R. RUSSELL, Com. services	17.60

On motion the following official bonds were examined and approved and filed for record:
J.M. CHERRY, Sheriff.
C.M. WHITE, Superintendent.
N.B. CULLEN, Assessor, Strahn precinct.
Levi DILTZ, Assessor, Logan precinct.
A.L. WADDELL, Constable, Hoskins.
Frank BROWER, Constable, Winside.
S.H. McMAKIN, Constable, Wayne.
S.C. BRESSLER, Road overseer, District 10.
T.E. HILL, Road overseer, District 12.
Jacob REICHERT, Road overseer, District 33.
Adjourned to Dec. 28, 1897.

S.B. RUSSELL, Clerk.

The Wayne Republican
January 5, 1898 (Vol. 4, No. 47)

MARRIED: Tomorrow the wedding bells will ring in our city at the home of Mrs. J.H. BROWN who will at that time be married to M.S. MERRILL the well known Carroll banker. The couple expect after March 1st to make their home in Vermillion, S.D., where Mr. M. is largely interested.

MARRIED: On Wednesday evening at the home of Mr. and Mrs. LAKE, 343 East Fourth South Street, took place the wedding of Miss Minnie SPRAGUE to Dr. W.C. WIGHTMAN, a prominent physician of Wayne, Neb. Dr. PADEN of the First Presbyterian church officiated. Miss SPRAGUE has been connected with the public schools of this city for several years past, and now that she has resigned her position, the Oquirrh school loses one of its excellent and charming teachers. While her many friends will regret their loss, their good wishes will follow her to her new home in Wayne, for which place the happy couple departed last evening. (Salt Lake (Utah) Tribune, December 31.)

DIED: The infant child of Thos. EVANS west of Carroll died on last Friday and was buried on Saturday in the Welsh cemetery.

DIED: JENNINGS. On December 28, of consumption, James JENNINGS, aged 25 years. The funeral was held at this place on the 31.

Sales.

W.W. HARDY will sell at his residence southwest of Wayne, on Monday, January 17th, 1898, commencing at 12 o'clock sharp, his horses, cattle, hogs, farming implements and household goods. Free lunch at 11:30 a.m.

Public Sales.
E. CUNNINGHAM, Auctioneer.

On Thursday January 6th, 1898. Andrew GOULD will sell horses, cows, hogs and farming implements at his home one half mile east of Winside. Sale commences at 12 o'clock noon.

Tuesday January 11th, 1898. Peter HORST living 11 miles southeast of Wayne, in Plum Creek precinct, will sell horses, cows, hogs, farming implements and all his household goods commencing at 12 o'clock.

The Wayne Republican
January 12, 1898 (Vol. 4, No. 48)

DIED: Mrs. WALKER, at the residence of her daughter Mrs. WESTROPE, on last Monday. Deceased was 68 years of age and was sick only a short time. The remains were shipped to Wisconsin for interment.

Obituary.

Mary Elizabeth COOK was born May 18, 1818, and passed into eternal sleep on January 4, 1898, at the home of her daughter, Mrs. HAINES. She was united in marriage with J.W. McPHERRON in 1841 and eight children blessed their union, six of whom with her sorrowing husband survive her. On December 6th, 1891, Mr. and Mrs. McPHERRON celebrated their golden wedding at the home of their daughter Mrs. BLACK. Deceased became a member of the Presbyterian church at the age of fifteen and has since been a faithful member. She was ever a kind and faithful wife, a fond and loving mother and a trusted friend to all who knew her. During her recent illness she has suffered patiently, knowing all that loving hands could do was being done for her. Impressive funeral services were conducted by Rev. MILLARD of Randolph at the M.E. church in Carroll on Wednesday; his text was: "Blessed are the dead that die in the Lord; they rest from their labors and their works do follow them." A host of sorrowing relatives and friends followed the remains to their last resting place in the Carroll cemetery.

    A precious one from us is gone,
      A voice we loved is stilled,
    A place is vacant in our home
      Which never can be filled.
    God in his wisdom has recalled
      The boon his love has given,
    And though the body slumbers here
      The soul is safe in heaven.

Wanted to Die.

 The Sunday daily papers of Lincoln and Omaha brought a piece of rather startling news to Wayne people. The Omaha Correspondent of the Lincoln State Journal gives it as follows: "T.E. HILL, a stock man from Wayne, Neb. who came to Omaha Thursday with a carload of cattle and sold them at South Omaha, made a persistent attempt last night and this morning to end his checkered career by the gas jet route. He was out last night with a companion named J.W. HAINES, of Carroll, Neb., and together they secured a room at the Arcade hotel about 1 o'clock this morning. After they had retired HILL got up and left his partner, taking possession of a room just across the hall. A porter passing through the hall at 4 a.m. was attracted to the room by the smell of gas, and going in he found HILL lying on the bed partially dressed and almost unconscious, the gas being turned on to its full capacity. After arousing him and raising the window to allow the gas to escape HILL was left in the room and at 6 o'clock a bell boy was again attracted to the room and again found the window closed and the gas turned on. Strange to relate, after the attendants had again raised the window and cleansed the room and had restored HILL to his normal condition of drunkenness, they again left him alone, and at 8 o'clock another bell boy was attracted to the room by the smell of gas. This time the window was again closed, and HILL was so far gone that it took several hours to resuscitate him. Immediately upon regaining consciousness he accused a police officer present of having picked his pockets. He had but 60 cents left of the proceeds of his car load of stock, unless he has placed some of it somewhere for safe keeping and forgotten it.

 The World-Herald states it in this manner:

 "J.W. HAINES of Carroll, Ia., and T.E. HILL of Wayne, Neb., are stockmen, who stopped at the Arcade hotel Friday night and drifted in at a late hour together. HILL went to his own room after a long converse with HAINES, blew out the gas and retired. He was found yesterday by a bell boy, the city physician was called, and HILL will recover and not do so again.

HILL said that he was not a drinking man, but indulged Friday night, and it so affected his head that it was not till he had been rescued from the gas blowing experiments the second time that he was able to stir about and leave the hotel. To no one about the hotel did HILL at any time intimate that he desire to commit suicide."

The above accounts are untrue in one respect at least and that is as to Mr. HILL shipping cattle and selling them and then losing the money. We understand that he did not shop any cattle and had at the time of going to Omaha but very little money on his person and we are inclined to the belief that the turning on the gas was purely accidental and was not with any intent to end his life as there seems to be no reason for any such rash step on his part. He is one of our well to do farmers and his pecuniary condition is not such as would be apt to cause him to do any thing of the kind.

The Wayne Republican
January 19, 1898 (Vol. 4, No. 49)

MARRIED: THOMPSON - BOUCK. In the city of Wayne on January 12, County Judge HUNTER officiating, Louis J. THOMPSON and Mary E. BOUCK, both of Dixon County.

Soldier Dinner.

The committee appointed by Casey Post, No. 5, G.A.R. Dept. of Neb., met at the office of A.J. FERGUSON and formulated the following program to take place on January 27, 1898 at 1 p.m., at the Y.M.C.A. hall at Wayne:

Dinner, 1:30 p.m.
Song.
Speech   Judge NORRIS
Song.
Short addresses   Wayne Clergyman.
Short talks by Com. A.W. TAYLOR, D. CUNNINGHAM, Geo. L. COOK. W.F. RAMSEY and others.
Song, America.

Committee on reception, Commander A.W. TAYLOR; committee on table arrangements and coffee, George SHAW, chairman, John OTT, George COOK, J.W. BARTLETT, and

Mesdames FEATHER, RAMSEY, BLAKESLEY and TAYLOR; committee on music, A.J. FERGUSON, J.D. KING.
W.F. RAMSEY, chairman.
Mark STRINGER.
A.J. FERGUSON.

Real Estate Transfers.

For the two weeks ending January 10 1897, reported by I.W. ALTER, bonded abstracter, Wayne, Neb:

John J. HAYES to J.R. MUNDY, lot 28, blk. 3, Winside	$2,752.00
August LARSON to Tillie OLSON, sw 1/4 ne 1/4 10-26-5	1,000.00
Nebraska Normal College to J.M. PILE, lots 1, 2 & 3, blk. 1, also lots 15, 16 & 17, blk. 2, all in Coll. Hill ad Wayne	- - -
W.C. PARSONS to Anna JOHNSON, lot 18, blk. 7, Hoskins	125.00
Samuel SUNDAHL to Amanda SUNDAHL, quit claim sw 1/4, 14-26-4	1.00
McCLUSKY & NEEDHAM to Rosa KRUGER, e 25 ft. lot 2, blk. 7, Winside	750.00

**The Wayne Republican
January 26, 1898 (Vol. 4, No. 50)**

DIED: The community was terribly shocked on Saturday morning by the intelligence that Mrs. W.S. BROWN residing four miles south of the city was found dead in bed on that morning. It seems the lady retired on the previous evening in her usual health and during the night nothing happened to awaken the family and when they went to arouse her in the morning it was found that her spirit had taken its flight. Indications all point to heart disease as being the cause of the sudden summons and in their greatest bereavement the family will have the sympathy of the entire community.

FUNERAL: On Monday forenoon occurred the funeral of the late Mrs. W.S. BROWN. The services were held in the M.E. church, the sermon being delivered by Rev. MILLARD, after which the remains were laid away to rest in our silent city.

The Wayne Republican
February 2, 1898 (Vol. 4, No. 51)

BIRTH: Mr. and Mrs. Frank NORTHROP are rejoicing over the arrival of a fine boy born Tuesday, January 24.

BIRTH: On last Friday morning a 10 pound girl took up its residence at Mr. and Mrs. A.L. HOUSER of this burg, mother and baby are doing well. (Hoskins)

BIRTH: On Sunday, January 23, a baby boy came to gladden the home of Mr. and Mrs. Wm. JACKSON.

LICENSED TO WED: Mr. George LEASE of Cuming Co. and Miss Adolphine BONESTEDT of Wayne Co.

LICENSED TO WED: January 29, Herman BUSS and Lizzie MUHLER, both of Wayne county.

DIED: The infant daughter of J.V. FRANCIS and wife died last Wednesday and was buried Thursday in the Welsh cemetery. (Welsh neighborhood)

The Wayne Republican
February 9, 1898 (Vol. 4, No. 52)

MARRIED: ROBINSON - STAARM. At the M.E. parsonage on Saturday February 5th, Rev. BITHEL joined in the holy bonds of matrimony, Ben. ROBINSON and Helen STAARM, both of Carroll. The newly married couple are among the well known young people of Carroll and it is safe to say they will receive the best wishes of the community in which the Republican desires to join.

Public Sales.

On Wednesday Feb. 16th commencing at 12 o'clock C.J. LUND will sell at public sale on his farm 5 1/2 miles south of Wayne, six work horses, 4 milch cows and 4 calves, 35 Poland and China sows, 65 shoats and all his farm implements.

On Thursday Feb. 24, at 10 o'clock J.BAILEY will sell at public sale on his farm one mile southeast of Carroll, 12 head of horses, 7 cows, 40 brood sows, 50 stock hogs, a lot of chickens and all his farm and household implements.

F.O. NELSON, west of Wakefield about two miles will sell his stock and implements on Feb. 15, beginning at 12 o'clock.

C.G. RUBECK will sell on his farm east of Wayne on Feb. 10, 5 head of work horses, 5 head of cows and calves, a number of brood sows and shotes and all his farm implements. Sale commences at 12 o'clock.

The Wayne Republican
February 16, 1898 (Vol. 5, No. 1)

LICENSED TO WED: John W. JENNINGS and Miss Gennettie SOUDERS both of Wayne county.

MARRIED: ELLIS - NETTLETON. On Wednesday Feb. 9th, W.G. ELLIS and Jennie NETTLETON. Judge HUNTER officiating.

MARRIED: HALL - CASEY. In the city of Wayne on Monday, February 14, Rev. Father FITZGERALD officiating, William HALL and Mary E. CASEY.

MARRIED: JENNINGS - SOUDERS. At the home of W.L. FISHER on Monday evening February 14, Rev. LEMON of the Baptist church of this city pronounced the words that joined for life the fortunes of J.W. JENNINGS and Gennette SOUDERS. The newly married couple start on life's journey with the best wishes of a large circle of friends in which the Republican desires to be included.

MARRIED: On Wednesday Feb. 9th at the home of the bride's parents two miles northeast of Hoskins, Herman RUSS and Lizzie MILLER, Rev. DOVEDAT officiating.

DIED: A 10-year-old daughter of Mr. and Mrs. WOLFSHIGHER who live four miles east of this place, died of diptheria on the 15th. (Hoskins)

DIED: The child of Mr. and Mrs. Fred STRATES, Jr., died on Feb. 14th of diphtheria. They reside three miles east of town. Hoskins should be quarentined against all children living in that vicinity. (Hoskins)

DIED: CLAYBAUGH. On Sunday February 13, the spirit of Grace, the seven year old daughter of Mr. and Mrs. H. CLAYBAUGH took its flight to the realms of the great unknown. Another family is berift of the charming face of a dear one and earthly things cannot fill the void, but there is a source from which consolation can be derived, a fountain that can heal every wound and though we of earth grieve with and offer our sympathies yet it is to that other friend all must turn for comfort. The cause of death was brain fever from which the little one had been a sufferer for several weeks. All that was mortal of the dear one was laid away by loving hands in our cemetery yesterday.

The Wayne Republican
February 23, 1898 (Vol. 5, No. 2)

LICENSED TO WED: Henry MAMMEN and Vena RESACKER.

LICENSED TO WED: John FOLCK and Lizzie MAMMEN.

LICENSED TO WED: Fred KRIE and Anna SOLEMELL.

LICENSED TO WED: February 19, Henry MOELLER and Lizzie DREW, both of Wayne county.

MARRIED: HULT - LARSON. At the office of the county judge on February 18, Swan P. HULT and Annie LARSON, both of Wausa.

MARRIED: JOHNSON - STONE. On Saturday, February 19, County Judge HUNTER spoke the magic words that bind the lives of Gust. A. JOHNSON of Cedar County and Mrs. Clara STONE in holy wedlock until death doth them part.

MARRIED: HANSEN - JANS. At the home of the bride's parents on Tuesday, February 22, Nick HANSEN and Mary JANS were united in marriage. The newly married couple start in life under very favorable auspices and the wish of their friends is that their journey may be a pleasant one and that success will crown their life's work.

MARRIED: Tomorrow at high noon at Omaha, occurs the marriage of Fred C. STOCKWELL and Mary E. BROWN. In the groom will be recognized by many of our readers the efficient foreman of the Republican, a young man of good standing in our community and one whom we are safe in saying possesses the confidence of all his friends and acquaintances. The bride is the daughter of John BROWN the present sheriff of Cedar county and is well known in our city having made her home here for several months a few years ago and is a young lady of estimable qualities. The newly married couple will make their home in our city and will meet a kindly reception at the hands of her people. While it is a little early yet the Republican desires to extend congratulations in advance, for don't you know we don't have weddings in the family every week.

The Wayne Republican
March 2, 1898 (Vol. 5, No. 3)

BIRTH: To L. LANGENBURG and wife on last Thursday twins. Who says that we have not got prosperity?

A Sad Accident.

A sad accident occurred at this place on Sunday afternoon, one boy lost his life and another may lose his reason. Harry RANSDALL and Hugo KRUGER started duck hunting, when about one half mile northwest of town young RANSDALL's gun was accidently discharged the entire load lodging in the upper part of young KRUGER's right thigh. Dr. SAUTTER of Norfolk was summoned and with the assistance of Dr. LEE of this place dressed the wound. On Monday he was moved to the hospital at Norfolk where other physicians were called in consultation and it was decided that amputation was necessary to prevent mortification, the limb was amputated at the hip joint and the patient died on Tuesday morning. The remains will be brought to Hoskins for interment. There is a deep feeling of sadness and sympathy in this community for the bereaved family and also for the young man who had the misfortune to be connected in the sad affair. The age of the boy that lost his life is thirteen and RANSDALL is twenty. (Hoskins)

Public Sales.

Tomorrow, Thursday, March 3, Patrick CLARK living 4 miles south of Wakefield will sell at auction his live stock and farming implements.

On Tuesday, March 15, beginning at 10 o'clock a.m. sharp, Frank KAUFLE will sell at his residence 3 1/2 miles south of Winside, horses, 10 first-class milch cows and 1 thoroughbred Jersey bull coming two years old and 3 yearling heifers, 80 head of hogs, 15 of which are brood sows safe in pig and 65 shoats. Also harness, wagons, plows, drags and 35 tons of good millet.

Live Stock at Auction.

On Tuesday, March 8, beginning at 1 o'clock, POFF Bros. residing 2 miles north of Wakefield will sell at public sale 20 excellent milch cows, 8 of which are now fresh and the balance will be very soon. Also 50 hogs, 25 of these being brood sows and the balance barrows. The cow stock is all high grade and the hogs Poland Chinas as well bred as anybody's.

The Wayne Republican
March 9, 1898 (Vol. 5, No. 4)

BIRTH: Fred HEFTI and wife are the proud parents of a fine baby.

BIRTH: A pretty girl baby came to brighten the home of Mr. and Mrs. D.L. STRICKLAND on Saturday.

LICENSED TO WED: Gustav BOETEL and Margretha ASMUS.

DIED: HANSEN. On Friday morning March 4, at the home of H.E. HANSEN and wife north of our city, was visited by the dark messenger and their seventeen year old daughter Vera HANSEN was called to that other land. Vera HANSEN was born May 3, 1880 and died March 4, 1898, making the span of her life 17 years 10 months and 1 day. The cause of death was consumption. The deceased was a bright young lady and one that numbered her friends by the circle of her acquaintance and in their hearts sadness will abide because of the departure of the loved one. The parents and family are sadly stricken by the death of the loved daughter and sister and feel most keenly the sorrow that is upon them. Human sympathy will not restore the loved one, but it goes out in a great abundance from the hearts of all acquaintances to the sorely bereaved at this time. The funeral services were held in the Presbyterian church at three o'clock Saturday afternoon, Rev. MONTGOMERY conducting the same.

DIED: STAMBAUGH. On Tuesday morning March 8, 1898, Mrs. W.B. STAMBAUGH, aged 64 years, passed from life's busy cares to the great beyond. Another home is stricken, another family mourns the loss of a loving wife and mother whose place can never be filled. The funeral will take place from the Lutheran church of this city tomorrow (Thursday) at eleven o'clock a.m. The services will be conducted by Rev. W.C. McCOOL of West Point.

Public Sales.

Having rented my farm I will sell at my home 7 miles south and 4 miles east of Wayne, 10 miles north and 1 mile west of Wisner, at 12 o'clock Wednesday March 16, 1898, 12 head of

horses, ranging in age from 2 to 11 years, all good horses. 1 span of mules weighing 2,400 pounds, 1 span of mules coming 3 years old. 10 head of milch cows coming fresh soon, 25 sows and shoats, 11 of which are brood sows safe in pig, 1 binder, 3 lumber wagons, 3 walking cultivators, 1 tricycle 14 inch gang plow used only one season, 1 Flying Dutchman 16 inch riding plow, Lister, Deere planter and check rower and other articles too numerous to mention. Terms - $10 and under cash. Sums over $10 ten months time on approved note at 10 per cent interest.
                                                    Daniel McMANIGAL.

The Wayne Republican
March 16, 1898 (Vol. 5, No. 5)

BIRTH: Frank STRAHAN and wife are the parents of a fine boy born Saturday morning.

DIED: Mr. and Mrs. WOLFSLAGER lost another child on Friday morning last, the funeral occurred on Sunday the services being conducted by the Rev. DEVIDAT of the Lutheran church. (Hoskins)

DIED: HEALEY. On Saturday, March 12, the spirit of Margaret HEALEY took its flight from its earthly tenement and returned to the God who gave it. Mrs. HEALEY was at the time of death about 84 years of age and for the past year has been confined to her room with dropsy which finally caused her death at the home of her son, M.T. HEALEY, in our city. Funeral services were conducted by Rev. Father FITZGERALD at St. Mary's Catholic church on Monday morning after which the remains were followed by a large concourse of friends to their last resting place at Wisner, Neb. The sons and daughters have the sympathy of friends in their great grief over the loss of a kind and loving mother.

DIED: RENNICK. At the home of her son James in Stanton county on Monday, March 14, Mrs. Isabel RENNICK passed from earthly cares to the great beyond. At the time of her death she was 75 years of age and has been in feeble health for some time. She leaves to mourn her death three sons and a daughter, and a host of friends. The children of the deceased who survive her are Wm. PATTERSON of Stanton county and Mrs. DOLAN of Iowa, children of her first husband, and James and Edward RENNICK. The funeral services were held in the M.E. church of this city and were conducted by Rev. WRIGHT of Winside.

Real Estate Transfers.

Real estate transfers for the week ending March 7, 1898, reported by I. ALTER, bonded abstractor, Wayne, Nebraska.

Frank DEARBORN to Henry GEISS, s 120 acres of sw 1/4, 6-26-4	$3,700.00
J.W. SCOFIELD to Frank A. DEARBORN, s 120 acres of sw 1/4, 3-26-4	2,800.00
R. BENSER to Chas. MILLER, lots 7 and 8, blk. 4, B&P's 2nd ad to Winside	- - -
D. McINTYRE to F. DINKLANG, se 1/4, 34-25-4	5,000.00
C.H. LUND to E. CUNNINGHAM, n 1/2 of sw 1/4, 18-26-4	2,000.00
Citizens Bank to R & F G PHILLEO, sw 1/2 of 24-26-3	4,800.00
A.W. CHAFFEE to Robert MICK, lots 1 and 2, blk. 5, Lakes add to Wayne	1,200.00
Soren JENSEN to Geo. MATSEN, lot 14, blk. 4, Winside	220.00
D.B. MILLER to Thomas HAMER, ne 1/4, 1-26-1	2,880.00
Floyd PETERS to Mary NEEDHAM, lot 5, blk. 3, Winside	750.00
J.W. SHELLINGTON to J.G. FUOSS, se 1/4 of the sw 1/4 and s 1/2 of the ne 1/4, of the sw 1/4, 33-26-5	1,920.00
J.W. SHELLINGTON to D.H. LANG, n 1/2 of ne 1/4 of sw 1/4 and w 1/2 of sw 1/4, 33-26-3	2,395.00
W.O. GOOLD to Jacob FUOSS, ne 1/4, 16-25-5	5,600.00

The Wayne Republican
March 23, 1898 (Vol. 5, No. 6)

BIRTH: To Fred ZIEMER and wife on March 15th, a boy of standard weight. (Hoskins)

BIRTH: Henry NURNBERGER and wife of Leslie are rejoicing over the arrival of a beautiful baby at their home Saturday.

MARRIED: J.W. WILLIAMS and Emma BOSTROM both of Wayne were married by Judge HUNTER at his home on last Wednesday evening.

DIED: The two weeks old child of M.L. WHITNEY south of the city died on last Thursday and was buried in Wayne on Friday.

DIED: Chris KRUGER died at his home one mile south of Winside Tuesday March 15 of heart trouble and was buried Thursday in the Winside cemetery.

DIED: On the evening of the 18th, little Eleanor, daughter of Wm. and Mrs. CLAYTON aged two years, two months and eleven days. The funeral services were on the 20th conducted by the Rev. Edward CASE of Hoskins. (Hoskins)

DIED: On March 18th, 1898, Maude, the little daughter of Mr. and Mrs. Jacob MORT of this place, at their home. She was born in September, 1896. The funeral was held from the house on Sunday and the remains were laid to rest in the Carroll cemetery. The stricken family have the sympathy of all in their deep bereavement.

The Sons of Herman elected the following officers last Wednesday evening: Pres., H.J. LUDERS; Vice Pres., J.H. GOLL; Sec., Aug PIEPENSTOCK; Treas., Wm. PIEPENSTOCK; trustee, Carl TOMPSON; Ex Physician, Dr. NEIMAN; Delegate to Grand Lodge, Fred VOLPP, Aug. PIEPENSTOCK.

The citizens' caucus Saturday evening met as per call and was called to order by W.M. WRIGHT. H. FISHER was chosen as secretary. On motion Henry LEY was nominated by acclimation for mayor, Will RICKABAUGH for clerk, F.L. NEELY and E. HUNTER for members of the school board and J. TOWER for police Judge. Sim RICHARDS received the nomination in the first, Frank STRAHAN in the second and C.O. FISHER in the third ward.

COMMISSIONER PROCEEDINGS, Wayne, Neb., March 15.
Board met pursuant to call. All members present.
Upon motion it was resolved that County Treasurer P.H. KOHL be allowed the excess fees of his office up to the amount of $700 for assistance.
The following is the list of names selected from which to draw jurors for the April, 1898, term of district court.
Hoskins Precinct - E.A. BEHMER, M. CASE, Jas. SHANNON, Wm. ZUTZ.
Garfield Precinct - John KOUNSE, Henry BRUSE, Hayden HUTCHINSON.

Sherman Precinct - T.C. MORRIS, Joel HANCOCK, W.H. BONHAM.

Hancock Precinct - A.W. DORAN, Carl ULRICH, Robt. FEUSKE.

Chapin Precinct - John PRINCE, Paul HEYER, Wm. WORTHNG.

Deer Creek Precinct - R.S. MERRILL, C.J. NAIRN, W.W. GARWOOD, Guy MANNING.

Winside Precinct - A.H. CARTER, Wm. HART, Frank BENSER.

Plum Creek Precinct - John COLEMAN, Frank HOOPER, J.R. SHAWGO, Charley WORTH.

Leslie Precinct - Sam. GIBSON, Geo. WHIPPERMAN.

Logan Precinct - Levi DILTZ, Al DRISCOLL.

Hunter Precinct - W.A.K. NEELY, Oliver GRAVES, O.P. ANDERSON, Jas AGLER, Jerome HUNTER.

Strahan Precinct - F.M. HOSTETTER, W.E. WALLACE, Aug. WITTLER, L.D. DYSART, Frank BAKER.

Brenna Precinct - Anton JENSON, D.H. SURBER, Highman OMAN, William BAIRD.

Wilbur Precinct - E.A. SURBER, Chas. MILLER, Andy CAMPBELL.

Wayne - 1st ward, Sim RICHARDS, Robert PERRIN, Fred VOLPP, William MEARS; 2d ward, I.W. ALTER, J.W. BARTLETT, D.A. DANILSON, Wm. BENSCHOOF; 3d ward, Nelson GRIMSLEY, W.O. GAMBLE, Abernon JETT, John LARISON.

The following claims were examined and allowed and warrants ordered drawn for same:

Albert KRUGER, road work	$1.25
Aug. ULRICH, road work	3.50
Thos. VINSANT, road work	2.50
Omaha Printing Co., supplies, claimed $28.45, allowed	26.80
Met GOODYEAR, oil	3.00
E. HUNTER, Co. Judge, costs State vs. ROTTER	4.60
Wayne Herald, supplies	16.51
J.M. CHERRY, jailor's fees	23.70
P.L. RANSDELL, sal. and boarding paupers, claimed $20.17, allowed	16.04

Upon motion the depository bond of the Carroll State bank was approved.

The matter of settlement between S.R. RUSSELL and Wayne county was discussed at some length, defendant being represented by his bondsmen, A.L. TUCKER and T.J. STEELE. No

agreement was reached.
On motion board adjourned until March 19, 1898.

The Wayne Republican
March 30, 1898 (Vol. 5, No. 7)

BIRTH: Mr. and Mrs. NELSON are the proud parents of a bouncing baby boy. (Plum Creek)

BIRTH: Jack BARBOUR was looking uncommonly happy along the first of the week and inquiry developed that the arrival of a new girl at his home on Sunday was the cause.

LICENSED TO WED: Fred SLAHN and Lena BUCK.

LICENSED TO WED: Erek VERTERGEN and Anna ANDERSON.

LICENSED TO WED: Edward MITCHELL and Mrs. Sarah E. MILLER.

MARRIED: HEFTI - GRIM. On Tuesday evening March 29, Rev. GRABER spoke the magic words that bound for life Rudolph HEFTI and Mata GRIM. The young people start out on the journey of life with the best of wishes of a host of friends for a successful and happy future.

DIED: MYERS. At his home in South Omaha, Friday, March 25, 1898, A.O. MYERS, aged 68 years. The immediate cause of death was cancer of the stomach from which he had been a sufferer for some time. The deceased was well and favorably known in our city having resided here for a number of years. The sympathies of our people will be with the bereaved wife and family in their sore afflication.

DIED: Another has been added to the number of diptheria victims who have died near Hoskins this winter. Sam G. BRAUN, a young man 22 years of age, is the last he having died about midnight Thursday evening at his home four miles northeast of Hoskins, and the funeral will take place at the church this side of Hoskins. Mr. BRAUN was a school teacher and taught the school in the WOLLSCHLAGER district this winter. He formerly taught the school in the village, which is now presided over by John BARNES of this city. The father of the deceased is a minister, Rev. J.B. BRAUN, residing at Duncan, and has been with his boy since he was taken with the disease. This disease seems to be gaining quite a foothold in that neighborhood and fears are entertained that it will become malignant and epidemic. There appears to be no way of handling it as there is no local authority to exercise quarantine regulations and the state is provided with no board of health with such powers; but in the name of humanity there should be some means at hand or provided to keep this contagion within bounds. The state has no arrangement of this kind, however and how to keep the disease from taking more lives is the question that is bothering the people. The family where the disease started are free in the use of their liberty and circulate at large with no more care to keep from spreading the disease than though it was a case of cold or some other harmless ailment. (Norfolk News)

Real Estate Transfers.

Real estate transfers for the week ending March 15, 1898, reported by I. ALTER, bonded abstractor, Wayne, Nebraska.

J.C. DRAKE to H.E. CORBIT,
 e 1/2 ne 1/4 18 and 6 in se corner of 7-26-4 $3,320.00
L.C. MITTELSTADT & Co. to J.R. MUNDY,
 quit claim, w 1/2 nw 1/4 23-25-2   5.00
J.R. MUNDY to John KAUFL,
 w 1/2 nw 1/4, 23-25-2   1,900.00
C.C. MERRIMAN to J.H. CLAUSEN,
 nw 1/4, 27-26-4   3,300.00
Rhode Island Hospital & Trust Co. to C.I.G. DANIELSON,
 n 1/2 nw 1/4 3-25-4   100.00
Sheriff of Wayne county to L.C. MITTELSTADT & Co.,
 w 1/2 nw 1/4 23-25-2   600.00
Geo. SCOTT to Lottie CHAON,
 lot 12, blk. 5, e add to Wayne   300.00
Eliza SEDWICH to F. WESTERHOLD,
 quit claim, ne 1/4, 34-25-5   1.00
Madison County Building & Loan Association to J.F. CROSBY,
 lot 2, blk. 5, B&P's add to Winside   525.00
B.W. GUE to A.B. CLARK,
 lot 12, blk. 3, B&P's first add to Winside   20.00
C.A. GROTHE to J.H. PRESCOTT,
 lot 11, blk. 2, B&P's first add to Winside   1,400.00
Wm. MOYER to J.C. BENDER,
 lot 4, blk. 6 and lot 8 outlot 2, B&P's
 first add to Winside   40.00

The Woodmen of the World effected an organization here Saturday evening with a charter membership of 36. Guy WILBUR is Consul Commander, R.C. OSBORN, Adviser Lieut.; H.C. WRIGHT, Secy.; J.R. COYLE, Banker; H.B. SKEEN, Escort; J.J. WILLIAMS, Physician; Mel NORTON, Watchman; J.W. WILLIAMS, Sentry; J.R. MANNING, D.A. JONES and W.E. WALLACE, managers. The organization expects to obtain a membership of 70 within a month.

Election Board.

The election board in the coming municipal election is composed of the following named persons as the same appears on record in this office:

First Ward - Peter MEARS, G.P. HITCHCOCK, Ira C. RICHARDS, judges. Frank GAERTNER, Fred VOLPP, clerks.

Second Ward - J.W. BARTLETT, C.D. MARTIN, Henry MERRIMAN, judges. W.S. GOLDIE, Arthur MERRIMAN, clerks.

Third Ward - James BARBOUR, Henry WRIGHT, J. LOVE, judges. Harry B. JONES, Chas. GROTHE, clerks.

E. HUNTER,
Co. Judge.

The Wayne Republican
April 6, 1898 (Vol. 5, No. 8)

BIRTH: Simon FOLTZ and his good wife rejoice over the birth of a brand new baby girl that arrived at their home Monday morning.

BIRTH: Born to Mr. and Mrs. R. TEMPLIN, April 4, a girl. Mr. T. steps high as this is his first. (Hoskins)

BIRTH: The home of W.C. JASTRAM was brightened by the birth of a son.

DIED: RENNICK. At the M.E. hospital at Omaha on April 5th, Mrs. E.T. RENNICK died from the effects of an operation performed about two weeks prior to her death. The deceased was 47 years of age and leaves to mourn her departure, a husband and eight children the youngest being about two years old, also father, mother and brother besides a large circle of friends and acquaintances who had learned to love and respect her as a friend and neighbor. At this writing we are not informed as to when the funeral will occur.

Advertised List.

Of letters, etc., remaining at the post office, Wayne, Nebraska, for the week ending April 4, 1898.

J.D. ADAMS, L.A. BEAR, G. ANDERSON, Jas HEIGH, Pet. JOHNSON.

Parties calling for the above please give date when advertised.

W.H. McNEAL, P.M.

The Wayne Republican
April 13, 1898 (Vol. 5, No. 9)

BIRTH: Dr. WILLIAMS reports a girl baby born to Mr. and Mrs. John BARRETT Monday morning.

LICENSED TO WED: W.H. THIES of Cuming county and Miss A.L. DORING of Wayne county.

LICENSED TO WED: Henry DAUM and Miss Lena REMHARDT both of Wayne county.

MARRIED: HOOD - WADSWORTH. At noon on Tuesday April 12, at the Presbyterian parsonage in this city. Rev. MONTGOMERY pronounced the words that forever join in marriage Samuel HOOD of Red Oak, Iowa, and Bertha WADSWORTH of our city. Both the high contracting parties are well known in our city having been residents here for many years and both are held in high esteem, and will start on life's journey accompanied by the well wishes of a host of friends in which the Republican most heartily joins. They will reside at Red Oak for which place they left on the afternoon train on the day of their marriage.

DIED: At the home of her daughter, Mrs. Elizabeth JONES, after a long and lingering illness, Grandma HARRIS passed quietly away Sunday afternoon and was laid to rest Tuesday morning in Bethany cemetry. (Welsh neighborhood)

Obituary.

RENNICK - Roxa Olive PINGREY was born Feb. 7, 1850, at Mt. Holly, Vt., and died in the M.E. Hospital at Omaha, Neb., April 5, 1898. At the age of three years she removed with her parents from Vermont to Muscatine Co., Iowa. October 27, 1867, she was married to John H. PRESCOTT, at Durant, Ia., and three years later they removed to Pottowattomie Co., Ia. Of this union five children were born, four of whom are still living. She became a widow in 1878 and soon after removed to Wilton, Ia. Here April 16, 1885 she was married to E.T. RENNICK of Wayne county, Neb., and they immediately took up their residence in that place. To them four children were born, all of whom survive. In 1879 she united with the Congregational church at Wilton, Ia., in which she became an earnest christian worker, rendering efficient service in the choir and teaching in the Sabbath school. When the Grace M.E. church, now a part of the Winside charge, was organized in 1889, she at once transferred her church membership to this class, and not only did she give her name to the church, but also her heart and her hand to the work. She was an earnest, sincere christian, a devoted wife, a kind and loving mother, an affectionate daughter, and a true friend. She was a woman with a clear, christian experience and a faith in Jesus Christ which gave to her whole life a noble purpose. In her character were combined the elements of strength and beauty. Firm in her convictions and principles, always cheerful, even admist the storms of adversity, and hopeful even for the unpromising. Her friends were many being limited only by her acquaintances. Her enemies were none. She possessed the sweet gift of song, which she used to sing her Master's praise. In this, as well as in many other ways, will she be missed by us. She was taken to the M.E. Hospital at Omaha Mch. 15, 1898, where she underwent a surgical operation a few days later. This seemed to give the needed relief, and it was hoped that she would soon be returned to her home and friends, but on the morning of the 5th of April, as the sun mounted the sky, the angel of the Lord crept over pillow and gave her the summons to depart. Great was the sorrow that settled upon many hearts when the sad and startling news reached her home community that she was gone. All felt that a foundation stone in the community was removed, that a pillar in the church had fallen, and that a life upon which many lives leaned was taken away. Yet amid this sorrow and gloom there shines the blooming hope of immortality and eternal life, for truly do we feel that "she is not dead but sleepeth." How gladly would loved ones have ministered to her in her last earthly hours but they were not permitted so to do; she passed away in the hands of strangers.

The funeral services were held at the M.E. church in Wayne, Neb., April 7th, conducted by her pastor, Rev. F.M. WRIGHT, who used as a text I Kings 7-22, and Rev. 3-12. Interment was made in the Wayne cemetery. She leaves a husband, eight children, an aged father and mother, and one brother, who deeply feel their great loss. A host of loving friends sympathize with the bereaved.

Court Proceedings.
WIGHTMAN vs LAUMAN, continued.
HARRISON vs PERRY, continued.
SMITH & ELLIS vs AGLER, continued.
COLLARD vs PATE, continued.
STUART vs CLARK, continued.
FOSTER vs RUBECK, continued.
BRESSLER, et al., vs HURLBERT, et al., dismissed.
Co of Wayne vs RUSSELL four cases, dismissed.
CLAUDE Horse Co. vs BOSTEDER, dismissed.
RUSSELL vs. Wayne Co., dismissed.
PHILLEO, et al., vs WAGNER, dismissed.
GERARD vs LEWIS, foreclosure ordered.
McCLUSKY & N. vs HURLBERT, deed ordered.
FRENCH vs MILLER, demurrer overruled, deft given 10 days to answer.

State of Neb vs S. Walter SASSMAN, was a case where deft was charged with selling mortgaged property without written consent of mortgagee. Defendant plead guilty and was fined $100.

SOHRN vs SOHRN, temporary alimony of $25 and an attorney fee of $25 allowed defendant.

WEBSTER vs HULBERT, pltff required to give bond for cost.
State of Neb vs Mike MOORE, defendant discharged.
EVANS vs MOHLKE, default against all defendants.
Caldonia Dep Bank vs REICHERT, cause to be shown in 20 days why judgment should not be revived against deft.

First Nat Bk of Wayne vs F. BROWN, et al., receiver ordered to pay all taxes and assessments out of funds in his hands so far as same will reach and to continue receivership.

BARTLETT vs HEISTER, conf'd deed ordered.
TALBOT vs RUSH, conf'd deed ordered.
MITTLESTADT vs KAUFLE, conf'd deed ordered.
ELTING vs W.A. LOVE, conf'd deed ordered.
KINGMAN & Co. vs OLMSTED & Co., judgment for pltff $331.

J.J. TRACY vs R.J. TRACY, judgment for pltff $1,936.69.
MIDDLESTADT vs FARRAN, default against deft.
BURR vs WEATHERHOLT, f'closure as prayed.
Occid'l B & L Ass'n vs TWEED, foreclosure as prayed.
GARNER vs GLASSON, f'closure as prayed.
LINDELL vs STROMBERG, f'closure as prayed.

Equitable Mfg Co vs HANSEN, settled and dismissed at defendants cost.

FULLER vs POND, judgment for pltff $1,197.75.

Real Estate Transfers.

Real estate transfers for the week ending April 4, 1898, reported by I. ALTER, bonded abstractor, Wayne, Nebraska.

J.A. ELLIOTT to C. and Geo. HARRIGFELDT, se 1/4, 14-25-1	$4,500.00
D.R. ROBINSON to C.D. HANCOCK, lots 1, 2 and 3, blk. 3, and lot 9, blk. 5, Carroll	100.00
Battain AGLER to Mary E. HUNTER, ne 1/4, 26-26-4	3,113.00
H.I. MILLER to Minette CLARK, lot 10, Out lot 2, B&P's add to Winside	600.00
L. NUERNBERGER to A. NUERNBERGER, e 1/2 se 1/4 and s 1/2 of se 1/2 of ne 1/4, 26-26-2	- - -
Otillie E. SEBALD to S.Q. HOGUE, lot 8, blk. 9, C&B's add to Wayne	1,500.00
Frank P. WILBUR to F.A. DEARBORN, sw 1/4, 23-27-3	3,700.00
Wm. H. LINN to S.H. ALEXANDER, lot 18, blk. 5, N add to Wayne	1,000.00
H.B. BOYD to Steven O'BRIEN, n 100 ft lot 29, T&W's add and lot 8, blk. 21 all in Wayne	1,500.00
W.M. WRIGHT to Fred ALTSTADT, s 1/2, 17-26-1	7,400.00
Herman BENTHIEN to A.W. CROSS, nw 1/4, 24-25-2	2,565.00
Gustav BORCHERT to Anton SWENSEN, n 1/2, 6-27-1	4,600.00
Security State Bank to J.G. BUOL, sw 1/4, 17-27-1	3,200.00
Logan Valley Land Co. to Mrs. A. MAAS, lots 14, 15, 16, 17 and 18, blk. 12, Hoskins	125.00
L. NUERNBERGER to D. McQUINSTON, ne 10-25-2	4,150.00
F.A. DEARBORN to A.M. JACOBS, sw 1/4, 23-27-3	4,000.00
Simon LESSMAN to H.W. LESSMAN, lots 5 and 6, blk. 27, College Hill, Wayne	190.00

J.M. LLOYD to Ezera SKINNER,	
sw 1/4, 28-27-3	$3,000.00
Ezera SKINNER to J.M. LLOYD,	
sw 1/4, 28-27-3	3,000.00
John T. BRESSLER to Geo. L. COLBERT,	
lot 11 of outlot 2 in B&P's add to Winside	22.00
Aug. REHLING to Herman REHLING,	
n 1/2 se 1/4, 22-25-5	2,000.00
Geo. B. & C.R. AISTROPE to Mary AISTROPE,	
e 1/2 ne 1/4, 28-26-5	2,800.00
Geo. B. AISTROPE, et al., to C.R. AISTROPE,	
w 1/2 ne 1/4, 28-26-5	2,800.00

Advertised List.

Of letters, etc., remaining at the post office, Wayne, Nebraska, for the week ending April 12, 1898.

Chas. G. BRAGG, Frank CROWLEY, Miss Lizzie CLINE, H.J. GOLD, Chase KELLEY.

Parties calling for the above please give date when advertised.

W.H. McNEAL, P.M.

**The Wayne Republican
April 20, 1898 (Vol. 5, No. 10)**

BIRTH: George YARYAN is setting up the cigars over the arrival of a new girl at his home. (Carroll)

BIRTH: Born to Mr. and Mrs. August BEHMER a son of standard weight. (Hoskins)

DIED: STINROD. At her home in this city on Sunday morning April 17, the dreaded messenger entered the home of D. STINROD and removed therefrom the wife and mother. The cause of death was consumption. Mrs. STINROD was born in Canada thirty-nine years ago and leaves to mourn her taking away a husband, seven children and many friends. The funeral services were held at the Presbyterian church on Monday afternoon and were conducted by Rev. MONTGOMERY after which all that was mortal of the deceased was laid to rest in our silent city there to await the call of the master on the resurrection morn.

Public Sale.

The undersigned will sell at his home 4 miles east and

seven miles south of Wayne - just east of Dan McMANIGAL's at 12 o'clock Monday April 25, 1898, one span of 9 year old mules weight 2300, one span of draft horses 5 years old weight 2000 and one pair of drivers, three milch cows and one calf, 10 sows safe in pig and 24 shoats. Farm implements of all kinds also the house, barn, sheds and fence on farm. The house has three rooms and is 14x22, 9 foot posts and the barn is 16x30 with granary room for 600 bushels of grain.

Carl HERZBERG.
E. CUNNINGHAM, Auctioneer.

The Wayne Republican
April 27, 1898 (Vol. 5, No. 11)

LICENSED TO WED: Clinton LAING and Stena THOMPSON.

LICENSED TO WED: William KANT and Amelia REHMUS.

MARRIED: SAUNDERS - BARRETT. At Carroll, Justice BAKER officiating, Warren SAUNDERS and Etta BARRETT.

Real Estate Transfers.

Real estate transfers for the past three weeks, as reported by I.W. ALTER, bonded abstractor, Wayne, Nebraska.

C.D. BROWN to D.H. SULLIVAN,	
lot 6, blk. 5, n ad Wayne	$100.00
Wm. STOBER to Sarah E. STOBER,	
n 1/2 sw 1/4, 40-26-1	2,000.00
State of Neb to P. ULRICH,	
s 1/2, 36-26-1	2,240.00
MELLOR & NORTHROP to S.B. RUSSELL,	
w 1/2 lots 7, 8 and 9, blk. 7, n ad Wayne	120.00
S.B. RUSSELL to C.O. FISHER, trustee,	
lots 5, 6, 7 and 8, blk. 25, Wayne &	
w 1/2 lots 7, 8 and 9, blk. 7, n ad Wayne &	
lots 7, 8, 9, 10, 11 and 12, blk. 4 &	
lot 12, blk. 3, all in College Hill, ad Wayne	4,200.00
Wm. ZUTZ to H. ZEIMER,	
lots 1, 3 and 4, blk. 4, Hoskins	650.00
Alvin NICHOLS to E.J. TADLOCK,	
n 1/2 ne 1/4, 18-27-1	1,200.00
Sheriff of Wayne Co to L.C. MITTELSTADT & Co.,	
ne 1/4, 18-27-1	438.00

Same to Alvin NICHOLS,	
ne 1/4, 18-27-1	$1,500.00
Same to Jonathan BRUGGER,	
sw 1/4, 11-26-2	3,500.00
Same to McCLUSKY & NEEDHAM,	
w 1/2, 36-26-2	3,300.00
A.T. CHAPIN to Sarah K. SMITH,	
lots 1 and 2, blk. 5, B&P ad Winside	40.00
Sheriff of Wayne Co to M.M. ELTING,	
e 1/2 lots 1, 2 and 3, blk. 11, C&B ad Wayne	400.00
TYLER, M.D. to Aug. WEICH,	
n 1/2 sw 19-25-1	575.00
James BRITTON to F.A. DEARBORN,	
und 1/2 of e 28 ft of 2 50 ft, lots 7 and 8, blk. 12, Wayne	1,500.00
Emma MOFFATT to W.M. GUE,	
lot 25, blk. 2, Winside	111.00
Jacob FUOSS to Silas DILLON,	
w 1/4 nw 1/4, 16-26-5	320.00

The Wayne Republican
May 4, 1898 (Vol. 5, No. 12)

BIRTH: Born to Mr. and Mrs. Ralph WADDELL Thursday of last week a boy of standard weight. (Hoskins)

Real Estate Transfers.

Sallie DODGE to Florence J. PARSONS,	
lots 4, 5 and 6, blk. 8, Hoskins	$300.00
A.C. CROCKET to D.E. NEWTON,	
e 1/2 lots 1, 2 and 3, blk. 15, Wayne	500.00
Rosa and Frank KRUGER to Omaha Brewing Co.,	
e 25 ft lot 2, blk. 7, Winside	600.00
Henrietta ZEIMER to W. TRENN,	
lot 15, blk. 1, Winside	100.00
L.J. HANSEN to H. HILKE,	
w 1/2 se 1/4 13 and nw of ne 1/4, 24-26-4	3,300.00
H. BOCK to F. GRAPMEYER,	
se 1/2, 6-27-2	3,900.00
U.S. to Minerva BALDWIN,	
ne 1/4, 30-27-3. Patent	- - -
Same to same,	
e 1/2 ne 1/4 and e 1/2 of se 1/4, 19-27-3. Patent	- - -
Same to same, all of section 29-27-3. Patent	- - -

The Wayne Republican
May 11, 1898 (Vol. 5, No. 13)

BIRTH: Henry FREVERT and wife are the proud parents of a fine baby boy.

DIED: On last Tuesday the grim messenger entered the home of Frank LONG of Leslie precinct and called hence the mother Mrs. Augusta LONG, aged 63 years, 4 months and 10 days. Mrs. LONG was the mother of ten children eight of whom survive her. The deceased was a devout Christian and has been a member of the German Lutheran church from youth and passed to the other land full of hope and faith in a glorious life beyond. The deceased had been ill several weeks but of late seemed to be improving so that on the day of her death she was up and around the house until in the afternoon she suddenly grew worse and in a few hours passed away, with heart disease. The funeral was on Thursday conducted by Rev. SCHULZ when all that was mortal of the loved one was quietly laid to rest in the Leslie cemetery.

The Wayne Republican
May 18, 1898 (Vol. 5, No. 14)

DIED: THARP. On Tuesday, May 10, at Pueblo, Colorado, R.F. THARP aged 37 years. The deceased was a son of our townsman, L.R. THARP and to him and his family the sympathy of our people will be extended in their bereavement. The father has not yet learned the exact cause of death.

Too Much Booze.

On Sunday afternoon the people living within a block of the post office were entertained by songs, shouts and various other sounds that originated in the neighborhood mentioned. Someone rang up Sheriff CHERRY and informed him of what was in progress and in a little while he and Marshal MINER proceeded to investigate and soon found that the rooms over DANIELSON's jewelry store contained the source of the different unearthly sounds and on going up there found George GRANT, D.A. DANIELSON and several others among whom was a young lad, having a first class blowout around a keg of beer. The sheriff undertook to gather in some of the hilarious ones when DANIELSON got mixed up with the marshal in a way that resulted in the latter paralyzing him with an open handed slap that caused him to strike the floor in such a way as to split his nose and otherwise mar the beauty of his phiz. GRANT and DANIELSON were finally locked up in jail and on Monday morning Judge HUNTER fined GRANT $10 and costs for intoxication; DANIELSON was not ready for trial and his hearing is set for Saturday.

The Wayne Republican
May 25, 1898 (Vol. 5, No. 15)

LICENSED TO WED: August H. THUN and Miss Catharine C.M. JACOBSON.

MARRIED: LANGE - HARRIGFELD. At the home of the bride's parents near Emerson, Nebraska, Monday, May 23. David LANGE, of Wayne county and Caroline HARRIGFELD of Dakota county. The newly married couple will go to housekeeping on the groom's farm in the southeast part of the county and start on their journey of double blessedness with the hearty congratulations of a host of friends.

DIED: BROWN. On Saturday evening the angel of death entered the home of Mr. and Mrs. Bert BROWN and called to the great beyond their 6-months-old child. The funeral was held on Monday. In their sad bereavement the stricken parents have the heartfelt sympathy of a wide circle of friends.

DIED: LLOYD. On Monday, May 23, 1898, Mrs. Julia, wife of J.M. LLOYD, aged 45 years. The cause of death was a tumor from which deceased has suffered for quite a length of time. Mrs. LLOYD was born in Shelby county, Indiana, and is a sister of the SERBER brothers, she was married to Mr. LLOYD December 20, 1874, and with him has made our county her home for a number of years, respected and beloved by all her neighbors and acquaintances. She leaves a husband, one son, father, brothers and sisters, and a wide circle of acquaintances who deeply mourn her death. Funeral services were held at the M.E. church at 4 o'clock Tuesday afternoon, the sermon being delivered by Rev. BITHEL after which all that was mortal of deceased was laid to rest in our silent city.

Obituary.

In memory of R.F. THARP, who departed this life in Pueblo, May 10, 1898: Another life has gone out; death has again made sad the hearts of the wife and children, parents, brothers and sisters. Frank, the oldest son of Mr. and Mrs. R.L. THARP of Wayne, Neb., was born August 2, 1861, in LaSalle county, Illinois. He was married to Miss Nora CROUCH of Hale City, Mo., April 19, 1899, coming directly to Pueblo, where they have made their home. He leaves a faithful, devoted wife and children. His mother and brother of Wayne, Nebraska, were present during his last illness. He was a dutiful son and brother, a dear father and a loving husband. (Pueblo Daily Chieftain, Saturday, May 14.)

The Wayne Republican
June 1, 1898 (Vol. 5, No. 16)

LICENSED TO WED: On Saturday Judge HUNTER issued a license to wed to Martin SCHONEBAUM and Rosa RICE.

MARRIED: It is reported that Hugo LENZER and a Miss MORTY were married at the bride's home east of town last Sunday. (Hoskins)

DIED: JOHANSEN. On Tuesday May 31, Mrs. Mary JOHANSEN aged 73 years. The deceased was the mother of our townsman L.J. HANSEN, and leaves to mourn her death four sons and one daughter. The funeral will be at Wakefield tomorrow.

The Wayne Republican
June 8, 1898 (Vol. 5, No. 17)

BIRTH: Chas. BEEBE is now the tather of another daughter which arrived this a.m. This makes six girls in the Herald family. It now remains for Goldie and Fred STOCKWELL to settle the boy question. (the Herald)

Wayne County Soldiers.

Here is a list of the Wayne county boys in Co. G., the Wakefield company.

R.E. BENSER, F. MEADE, H.E. HIATT, R.F. MALLORY, F.H. OVERTURF, H. TAYLOR, C.B. HADLEY, L.H. CURRIER, F.H. BURNETT, L. MOORE, W. VAUGHT, R.E. FARLEY, F. CARLSON, W.F. BAINSTER, I.C. ARVOLD, J.C. HAYES, O.L. TAYLOR, O. HAYES, M.D. COLEMAN, J.W. GILDERSLEEVE, L. ACREN, F. BROWER, A.W. LARSON, H.M. PICKARD, W.F. LUTH, H.H. NETTLETON, Frank DIX, C. DIX, D.M. BROWER, M.P. MADSEN, Tim CASEY, E.W. CARTER, B.J. BUCK, F. WHIPPERMAN, W.A. NELSON, John P. HYATT; 36.

This shows up well for Wayne county and these taken with those already in the service makes over 40 of our county's sons that have offered their services to their country and certainly puts us in the front rank when population is considered and if the same ratio prevailed all over the United States Uncle Sam would have a pretty respectable sized army.

Commencement.
The Wayne High School Class of '98 Graduates.
Nine Members Receive Their Diplomas.

Again commencement day of the High school has come and gone. The weary hours of toil in the school room for the class of '98 are over, at least insomuch as the Wayne High school is concerned, but in reality the door is only open to the schoolroom of life where so much is to be learned as the days and years roll by. The class of '98 is as good one as ever finished the course in our schools and we believe we are not putting it too strongly when we say their work has been as well done as the best and in a manner that ought to be satisfactory to their instructors and that leaves no room for regret on the part of any member of the class. That some of the members may have suffered disappointment in some particular is to be expected and where such has been the case it should only serve as a greater stimulus in the future to overcome all obstacles and lead to greater achievments in the future. We cannot go into a detailed account of the entire program as rendered during the evening, or give a write-up of the work of individual members of the class as it would require greater space than we have at command and in order to do justice to each one a better pen than ours should attempt the task. The members of the class were

James R. WRIGHT, Alice M. RUNDELL, Laura E. HOLTZ, Ethel P. TUCKER, Harry B. CRAVEN, Reba D. NANGLE, Rena B. OLMSTED, Mary E. PAWELSKI, Julia ANDRESS.

The first named being the salutatorian and the latter the valedictorian and while to them the honors were accorded yet to the casual observer or to one listening to the addresses of the different members of the class it would be a difficult task to place the award as there seemed to be so very little difference. Following the delivery of the addresses of the class came the presentation of diplomas by the president of the school board, A.F. BRENNER. The music and exercises were entertaining and the immense audience that filled every available inch in the opera house were dismissed at a late hour feeling that they had been well repaid for coming out to see and hear and by their presence cheer the class in launching their boat upon life's sea of real life.

The Wayne Republican
June 15, 1898 (Vol. 5, No. 18)

County Officers.
John R. COYLE . . . . Clerk
Phil H. KOHL . . . . Treasurer
J.M. CHERRY . . . . Sheriff
Enoch HUNTER . . . . County Judge
Bert BROWN . . . . Clerk of Courts
Charlotte M. WHITE . . . . Superintendent
Anson A. WELCH . . . . County Attorney

Commissioners.
Geo. HARRIGFELD
Richard RUSSELL
J.W. ZEIGLER

City Officials.
Henry LEY . . . . Mayor
Everett LAUGHLIN . . . . Clerk
Lambert ROE . . . . Treasurer
G.L. MINER . . . . Marshal
F.C. LARGEN . . . . Water Commissioner
Chas. GROVES . . . . Street Commissioner

Councilmen.
First Ward
S.P. GAERTNER
J.H. GOLL
Second Ward
F.E. STRAHAN
Ran FRAZIER
Third Ward
D.C. MAIN
John SHERBAHN

Church Directory.
First Presbyterian - Services each Sabbath at 11 a.m. and 8 p.m.
D.C. MONTGOMERY, Pastor.
Methodist - Services each Sabbath 11 a.m. and 8 p.m.
Thos. BITHEL, Pastor.

Baptist - Services each Sabbath at 11 a.m. and 8 p.m.
C.A. LEMON, Pastor.
German Evangelical - Services each Sabbath alternately at
11 a.m. and 2:30 p.m.
Otto GRABER, Pastor.
St. Mary's Catholic - Services alternate Sundays at 10:30 a.m.
J.D. FITZGERALD, Father in Charge.

BIRTH: It's a girl and arrived at the home of Mr. and Mrs. L.F. HOLTZ Friday last.

A.F. and A.M. Elects Officers.

At the regular meeting of Wayne Lodge No. 120 A.F. and A.M. on Friday evening June 10, the following officers were elected for the ensuing year. J.M. CHERRY, W.M.; F.L. NEELY, S.W.; E.P. OLMSTED, J.W.; A.T. WITTER, Sec'y; Henry LEY, Treas. The installation of the new officers will occur on St. John's Day, Friday June 24, 1898.

Real Estate Transfers.

For the week ending June 6, 1898, reported by I.W. ALTER, bonded abstracter, Wayne, Nebraska:

Sheriff of Wayne co to Geo. A. VAIL,	
se 1/4, 31-26-2	$2,010.00
Fred GLASER to G.H. GLASER,	
e 1/2 ne 1/4 22-26-2	1,200.00
John M. SCARR to Ed CULLEN,	
sw 1/4, 22-26-2	3,520.00
Ed CULLEN to Lucius WELLS,	
qc, sw 22-26-2	1.00
A.W. CROSS to Herman BENTHIEN,	
nw 1/4, 24-25-2	2,746.00
Jas. BLAIR to W.M. WRIGHT,	
e 1/2 nw 1/4 23-36-4	2,800.00
W.M. WRIGHT to Jas. BLAIR,	
se 1/4 & s 1/2 of ne 1/4 18-26-1	5,400.00

• • •

MARK STRINGER & SON
General Blacksmithing
Wayne, Neb.

The Wayne Republican
June 22, 1898 (Vol. 5, No. 19)

BIRTH: To Mr. and Mrs. H.C. CLINE on Saturday the 18th, a son that tipped the beam at nine pounds, both mother and babe are doing well.

COMMISSIONER PROCEEDINGS, Wayne, Neb., June 20, 1898.
  Board met pursuant to adjournment, members all present. The following claims were examined and allowed:

J.L. CLINE, Assessor, Hoskins	$63.50
W.C. LOWRY, Assessor, Chapin	84.00
A.T. WITTER, Assessor, Wayne	130.00
G.F. WRIGHT, Assessor, Winside	45.00
H. REHMUS, Assessor, Hancock	88.00
Levi DILTZ, Assessor, Logan	59.90
Neal NYE, Assessor, Leslie	56.00
Daniel DAVIS, Assessor, Sherman	78.00
H.E. HANSEN, Assessor, Wilbur	68.20
Pat COLEMAN, Assessor, Plum Creek	90.00
N.B. CULLEN, Assessor, Strahan	98.90
C. ECKMAN, Assessor, Garfield	76.60
J.J.W. FOX, Assessor, Hunter	92.00
L. SIMMERMAN, Assessor, Deer Creek	102.00
P. BENSHOOF, Assessor, Brenna	90.00
PERKINS Bros., supplies	54.50
Ed STEPHENS, road work	33.50
B.W. McKEEN, printing	6.31
Chas. GREEN, road work	5.00
A.T. WADDELL, road work	25.00
John SHANNON, coal	4.98
Chas. BAGGART, labor	7.50
J.M. CHERRY, jailor fees	22.52
R. RUSSELL, Com. fees	17.80
Geo. HARRIGFELD, Com. fees	16.20
J.W. ZEIGLER, Com. fees	13.50

Adjourned to July 6th, 1898.

The Wayne Republican
June 29, 1898 (Vol. 5, No. 20)

BIRTH: A boy was born to Wm. WATSON and wife Sunday.

MARRIED: STRINGER - CHAPIN. At 8 o'clock last evening at the home of the father of the bride, A.T. CHAPIN, in Winside, Rev. F.M. WRIGHT pronounced the words that bind the lives of Mark STRINGER, Jr., of our city and Edith CHAPIN of Winside. The high contracting parties are well known young people who have grown to manhood and womanhood in our county and are very highly respected by a large circle of friends both in Wayne and Winside. The groom is a son of ex-Mayor STRINGER of this city and is one of Wayne's best and most respected young men while the bride is the daughter of Art. T. CHAPIN, president of Merchants State Bank of Winside, she is a highly accomplished young lady and one worthy of the best. The Republican desires to extend with numberless friends its heartiest congratulations and most earnest hopes for the future of the young couple who embark under the most favorable skies.

DIED: WHITE. At the home of her daughter in our city on Monday evening June 27, Mrs. Margaret Ann WHITE in the fullness of years quietly passed from life. The funeral was held in our city June 28.

Margaret Ann MORRISON was born Nov. 8, 1808 near Tarentum, Allegany county, Pa. She was married July 18, 1838 to John G. WHITE, who died Jan. 18, 1889 in Rock county this state.

Born to religious parents, she early in life united with the Bull Creek Presbyterian church then under the ministry of Abram BOYD, who had baptized her in infancy. She was a woman of the strongest convictions and always with the courage of them. When every one furnished liquor to harvest hands, she was open in her denunciations of the traffic and all drinking customs, and no one ever partook of liquor in her home or at her hands. Among a proslavery people she was always an Abolitionist. Every oppressed people of whatever race or color had in her a personal friend, an earnest advocate. She was charitable in both word and deed. Every beggar, every tramp, every disconsolate mourner, came to her and found relief. Her Bible was her constant companion. Even as her mind has been failing as it has since that terrible disease softening of the brain came to her, she never forgot to pray, almost whole days she spent in prayer. She leaves five children all that were ever born to her, twelve grand children, and two great grand children, to miss one of the most unselfish of mothers.

A Pioneer Nebraskan at Rest.

At Wakefield, Nebraska, on Saturday June 25th, Jacob HEIKES one of the states pioneers after months of suffering peacefully passed from the care of life to that other and better world on high. Jacob HEIKES was born in Milford township, Juniata county, Pa., May 5, 1837, and there grew to manhood and at his country's call in the great civil war answered the summons to arms and served his country well and faithfully. In the same township he was married to Mary J. AUGHEY Feb. 16, 1858, she and nine children survive him. With his wife and some of the older children he came to Nebraska in 1868 and settled in Dakota county where they remained until about 12 years ago when the parents and some of the younger members of the family moved to this county and settled on a farm just south of the town of Wakefield.

The funeral was held at Wakefield Monday June 27, and was conducted by the G.A.R. Post of this city, twenty-three members of the post and quite a goodly number of veterans followed the remains of their comrade to their last resting place. The wife in her advanced years has lost a good husband the family a kind father, the community a respected member and the state a citizen who was law abiding and ready to do his duty at all times.

The Wayne Republican
July 6, 1898 (Vol. 5, No. 21)

BIRTH: It is a girl that came to make her home with Mort McMANIGAL and wife on last Thursday.

MARRIED: RICHMOND - LEWMAN. At the county Judge's office on June 30, Ernest A. RICHMOND and Hester LEWMAN.

MARRIED: MARSH - MORT. On June 30, Judge HUNTER officiating, T.A. MARSH and Julianna MORT, both of Wayne county.

DIED: A.B. CHARDE died last night about 10:30 at the hospital for the insane, he having been brought there several months ago. The remains were brought to the undertaking rooms of SESSIONS & BELL where they were prepared for interment. Mrs. CHARDE was here and accompanied the corpse to Oakland on the one o'clock train over the C. St. P. M. & O., where it will be interred. Mr. CHARDE was formely a member of the Odd Fellows lodge at O'Neill and that order will take charge of the funeral at Oakland.

Norfolk Odd Fellows formed an escort and conducted the remains and the widow to the train. The deceased was formerly very prominent in democratic state politics and served a term of four years as register of the land office at O'Neill. He formerly resided in Wayne county and was very highly respected by all who knew him. He was 45 years of age at the time of his death. (Norfolk News)

Real Estate Transfers.

For the week ending June 30, 1898, reported by I.W. ALTER, bonded abstracter, Wayne, Nebraska:

J.T. ROBERTS to Elizabeth ROBERTS,	
s 1/2 n 1/2 se 1/4 19-27-1	$1,000.00
A.W. and E.E. CULVER to J.D. KING & W.H. EHRED,	
ne 1/4, 1-25-3	4,500.00
A. STEWART to L. NUERNBERGER,	
sw 1/4 ne 1/4 & se 1/4 nw 1/4, e 1/2 sw 1/4 & w 1/2 se 1/4 29-26-5	6,960.00
Mrs. L.A. PLUMB to R. PHILLEO,	
lot 1, blk. 5, n add Wayne	135.00
A.M. AVERILL to Geo. MATSON,	
lot 15, blk. 4, Winside	25.00
J.T. BRESSLER to George MATSON,	
lot 13, blk. 4, Winside	30.00
F.M. NORTHROP, trustee, to John & Mary PRICE,	
lot 12 & n 1/2 lot 11, blk. 3, Wayne	400.00
M.S. MERRILL to R.D. MERRILL,	
lot 9, blk. 8, Carroll	100.00
W.H. McCLUSKY to L.S. NEEDHAM,	
und 1/2 lot 23, blk. 2, Winside	100.00
O.O. WHITED to R.D. MERRILL,	
lots 1, 2 & 3, blk. 1, 1st add Carroll	75.00
A.C. GOLTZ to Andrew HUPP,	
lot 4, blk. 5, B&P's add Winside	35.00
A. HUPP to W.I. LOWREY,	
lot 4, blk. 5, B&P's add Winside	555.00
E.W. ZUTZ to Wm. ZUTZ,	
lots 1, 2 and 3, blk. 5, Hoskins, and 13 acres in nw 27-25-1	1.00
Chas. W. KING to J.D. KING,	
lot 2, blk. 8, Lakes add Wayne	400.00
J.D. KING to E.D. MITCHELL,	
lots 4, 5 and 6, blk. 6, C&B's add city	800.00

J.H. MILLARD, trustee, to South Omaha Nat'l Bank,
nw 1/4 24, se 1/4 sw 1/4 13, ne 1/4 23, also
63 acres in s 1/2 nw 1/4 13, all in 26-3; also
all north of railroad in nw 1/4 se 1/4 and all
of ne 1/4 ne 1/4 1/4 south of railroad in
8-26-4, also s 1/2 nw 1/4 24-27-2, and all of
Sec. 36-27-2 $100.00

John PRICE to Chas. FISHER,
lot 12 & n 1/2 lot 11, blk. 3, city   600.00

The Wayne Republican
July 13, 1898 (Vol. 5, No. 22)

BIRTH: Henry GOLL told us it was a boy, but parties in attendance say it is a girl, but it don't do to say much about it to Henry.

BIRTH: Last week notes the arrival of a fine baby at the home of Harry HUGHES, mother and child doing well. (Welsh neighborhood)

BIRTH: A new baby took up its residence with Frank VICK and wife last week. (Hoskins)

DIED: JEFFREY. On Tuesday, July 12, Mary, the 16-months-old daughter of Mark JEFFREY, died of cholera infantum. The funeral is to be held from the family home east of the city at 11 o'clock today.

DIED: KNEBEL. Miss Matilda KNEBEL, at the home of her parents near Winside, passed to the great beyond June 8. Deceased was a sister of Mrs. Bert BROWN of our city and has been ill for a long time.

Found Dead in His Chair.

O.H. SELBERG, a swede about 66 years of age living about ten miles southeast of this city, was found sitting at a table in his home on Saturday afternoon dead. He was a widower without a family and for sometime has been living entirely alone in a house on his farm which was farmed by John JOHNSON. On Saturday forenoon JOHNSON's hired man was at SELBERG's house and noticed the old gentlemen was not looking well and on his return home told his employer so. As soon as they had dinner JOHNSON and his man repaired to SELBERG's house where they found him as stated above. The neighbors were summoned and Coroner GAERTNER notified who after making inquiry was satisfied that death resulted from natural causes and didn't deem it necessary to hold an inquest. The funeral was held on Sunday. Deceased was possessed of a fine quarter section of land free from all incumbrance and had some other means, and after his death a will was found disposing of his effects.

County Central Committee Called to Meet.

A meeting of the members of the republican county central committee has been called for Saturday afternoon July 16th, in this city to fix time for holding county convention and transacting any other business that may come before it. The committee will probably determine at this meeting as to whether to hold one or two conventions this fall and if you have any suggestions to make in all probability the committeeman from your precinct would be pleased to hear from you. The following is a list of the committeemen.

Archie LINDSAY, Brenna; Geo. LEWIS, Chapin; J.R. MANNING, Deer Creek; E.C. BROOKS, Garfield; H. ULRICH, Hancock; Geo. HARRIGFELD, Hoskins; Grant MEARS, Hunter; George BUSKIRK, Leslie; Eph. ANDERSON, Logan; S.K. WEST, Plum Creek; M.S. MOATS, Sherman; George PORTER, Strahan; C. SHULTHEIS, Wilbur; R.R. SMITH, Winside; H.L. KIMBALL, 1st ward, Wayne; A.T. WITTER, 2nd ward, Wayne; J.J. WILLIAMS, 3rd ward, Wayne.

The Wayne Republican
July 20, 1898 (Vol. 5, No. 23)

Real Estate Transfers.

As reported by I.W. ALTER, bonded abstracter, Wayne, Nebraska:

State of Neb to O.M. HURLBERT, se 1/4 sw 1/4 21-27-2	$280.00
L.C. BLACK to John R. MORRIS, sw 1/4, 28-27-1	2,000.00
D.R. ROBINSON to Alex FOLK, lots 2 and 3, blk. 7, Carroll	75.00
F.A. DEARBORN to Minnie WILL, a lot 75x246 ft in nw corner of the e 5 cares of e 1/2 of nw 1/4 18-26-4 n of rr track	1,000.00
W.H. McNEAL to Minnie WILL, lots 1, 2 and 3, blk. 3, e ad Wayne	500.00

R.W. WILKINS to Minnie WILL, lot 3, blk. 2, S&S's ad Wayne	$500.00
SMITH & ELLIS Co to A.H. ELLIS, sw 1/4, 12-25-5	1,900.00
Minnie WILL to F.A. DEARBORN, lot 12, blk. 8, Carroll	1,000.00

The Wayne Republican
July 27, 1898 (Vol. 5, No. 24)

BIRTH: A new baby girl arrived at the home of John S. LEWIS, jr. on Saturday.

BIRTH: To Mr. and Mrs. Geo. WESTROPE Monday, July 24, a daughter.

MARRIED: Mrs. Jennie ADSIT and Mr. L.P. ORTH were married last evening at Mrs. ADSIT's residence on Washington St., which was charmingly decorated with summer flowers for the occasion. The ceremony was performed by Rev. J.C. CARMAN, who came from Northport to be present. The wedding was a very pretty and quiet one, only the immediate relatives being present, and Mr. and Mrs. ORTH and her family will leave at once for Wayne, Nebraska, where Mr. ORTH has a flourishing drug business.

Both Mr. and Mrs. ORTH have a wide circle of acquaintances here who will extend hearty congratulations and best wishes to them. Mr. ORTH was for some years a resident of Traverse City and an active member of the Baptist church, where Mrs. ORTH has also been one of the earnest workers for many years. She will be much missed in her church connections here. (Traverse City Eagle, July 20)

DIED: ALEXANDER. On Friday, July 22, Mrs. J.F. ALEXANDER at the family home in Dixon county. The deceased was well known in the city having been a resident for some time a few years ago. The funeral occurred Saturday afternoon, the interment being made in the Wayne cemetery.

DIED: JONES. On Sunday morning at the family home in this city, Jared W. JONES quietly passed from earth into the great beyond. Mr. JONES was born in Paulet, Rutland county, Vermont, Nov. 14, 1815. When 22 years of age he left his native state and settled in Marshal county, Ill., where he bought land and settled down to the hard life of the pioneers of those days, living in a log house until 1854 when he moved into Putnam county, built a comfortable house and lived there until 1885 when he sold his Illinois farm and moved to our own county where he owned considerable land and where he made a host of friends whose sympathies are with the stricken family in their time of sorrow. He was married March 1st, 1847 to Mary J. POOL, to them seven children were born three of whom survive their father, his wife died in 1866, and January 19, 1871, he was married to Mary E. BAKER, to them one child Harry B. was born. His surviving children, three sons Maurice W. of Miles City, Montana, Eugene L. of Duluth, Harry B. of this city and his daughter Mrs. HANSOM of Chicago, with the loving wife ministered to him in his last days. While his death had been expected for some time by his friends yet when the announcement came all were shocked. He was a sturdy American, of a strong personality and one that believed in living and doing right and by so doing has in his going left behind a memory not soon to be forgotten. His remains were taken to his old home at Henry, Illinois, on Monday morning for interment and were accompanied there by his son Harry and daughter Mrs. HANSOM.

The Wayne Republican
August 3, 1898 (Vol. 5, No. 25)

MARRIED: At the home of L.E. HUNTER in this city Tuesday evening, Aug. 2nd, Miss Sarah T. KNAGGS and Mr. Wm. POFF both of Wakefield. Rev. Thos. BITHEL officiating.

MARRIED: John H. NIEMAN, of Petersburg, and Miss Hannah B. WHITTEN of Whitten Valley, were married at the residence of the bride's parents Tuesday morning, July 26, 1898, by Rev. L. HEDDIN of Petersburg. This was a quiet wedding, there being no one present but the bride's parents and the family and one brother of the groom. After the ceremony the company partook of a luxurious feast, then the happy couple started for Albion to take the train for Omaha where they expect to take in the sights of the exposition. They were accompanied by the bride's sister, Miss Mae WHITTEN. The groom is a popular druggist of Petersburg, his father is a physician in Wayne, this state, and the bride is one of Boone county's most popular school teachers and has taught for the last four or five years in the public school of Petersburg to the satisfaction of all, and both will be heartily welcomed upon their return as citizens of Petersburg. (Albion News)

The Wayne Republican
August 10, 1898 (Vol. 5, No. 26)

BIRTH: Bob OSBORNE told us not to say anything about the fine new boy that came to his home on Thursday and we are going to be "mum."

BIRTH: Born, August 5, 1898, to Mr. and Mrs. Chas. E. JAMES, of Wayne, Neb., a son.

BIRTH: A bouncing boy came to Geo. KAUTZ' on the 5th inst. George is elated. (Hoskins)

BIRTH: A bonny lass took up its residence at E.E. BEHMER's on the 4th. Mother and babe are doing well. (Hoskins)

MARRIED: Judge HUNTER succeeded in settling the difficulty between William MILLER and Bertha REDMER, both of Hancock precinct, by performing the marriage ceremony for them last Saturday.

Normal College Commencement.
That is what the Present Week is at the Wayne Normal College.
Nineteen Students Complete the Teachers Course.
Four Finish in Music.

Again has come about the ending of another year's work of the Nebraska Normal College. Twenty three persons will receive their diplomas that have been well earned by close application to the work assigned them. The exercises of commencement week really began Friday evening when the Philomathean Society rendered an excellent program at the opera house this was followed on Saturday evening by the exercises of the Cresent's. On Sunday Rev. BITHEL, pastor of the M.E. church of this place delivered the bacalaureate sermon that was listened to by an immense audience and who were repaid for going by a most excellent sermon. Monday evening the elocution department gave an entertainment and the real work of commencement was on Tuesday evening in the graduating exercises of the Conservatory class composed of

    Minnie BROWN
    Minnie GAERTNER
    Prudence BUSH
    Ross CUNNINGHAM.

The teachers class composed of nineteen members as follows:
  Myrtle A. MILLS
  Smith E. WINCHEL
  Celia WILKINSON
  Annie LUND
  Joseph CARROLL
  Ione D. LEMONDS
  Mamie V. WEBSTER
  Chas. E. HILL
  Minnie Maude BURSON
  L.H. CURRIER
occupied Wednesday evening with their exercises and on Thursday evening the balance of the class,
  Mary E. AHERN
  Lewis OMEY
  Mary COX
  Emma KLINTWORT
  Samuel V. MARTIN
  Lena C. NELSON
  H. Henry SCHULTIE
  Emmie E. SHINBUR
  Will F. MOGAREIDGE
finished the program. It is utterly impossible to give the personal credit due different members of the graduating classes for the manner in which they delivered their finals and should we undertake it we feel that our efforts would be a failure. The Alumni Association will hold its feast of reason and flow of soul Friday evening and finish the work of the year with a banquet where all the trials and tribulations of the year will vanish as mists before a summer sun. It is not putting it too strong to say that the year just ended has been one of grand success for the institution of which we are all so justly proud and in which every person is so deeply interested. It grows stronger as the years roll by and demonstrates the wisdom of those instrumental in securing it for our city. The old bell will be silent now for two short weeks and then its tongue will ring out the glad notes of the opening of a new year, calling to work some of the old and scores of new students. To the retiring students the Republican on behalf of the people of Wayne desires to bid you Godspeed on the course you have mapped out for your life's work and hopes that unbounded success may crown your efforts wherever your lot may be cast and that each of you will always retain a warm place for the North Nebraska Normal College and our little city.

Real Estate Transfers.

As reported by I.W. ALTER, bonded abstracter, Wayne, Nebraska:

Peter ULRICH, sr., to Peter ULRICH, jr., sw 1/4, 36-26-1	$1.00
Same to Henry ULRICH, ne 1/4, 5-25-2	1.00
Henry ULRICH to Peter ULRICH, sr., lot 9, blk. 2, B&P's ad to Winside	1.00
O.O. WHITED to Nettie BAKER, lot 2, blk. 1, Carroll	1.00
C.B. FRENCH, jr., to Ole ANDERSON, sw 1/4, 1-25-2	2,000.00
Mary E. SEERY to Carl F. LENZ, se 1/4, 17-25-1	1,350.00
P.P. GOREHAM to Lucinda GOREHAM, nw 1/4, 22-25-5	4,800.00

The Wayne Republican
August 17, 1898 (Vol. 5, No. 27)

BIRTH: A new girl baby is reported at the home of F.O. MARTIN on the 10.

LICENSED TO WED: Licensed to wed Aug. 15, 1898, Geo. C.I. ANDERSON of Wayne, Nebraska, and Mrs. August MEYER of Iowa.

The Year Is Ended.

The work of the classes at the college is completed, finished with the meeting of the Alumni Association at Chapel Hall on Friday evening where with music, addresses and responses the early hours of the evening quickly passed. The following was the program.

Trio - Grace LUDEKE, Theo SCACE and Pearl REYNOLDS.
Piano Solo - Prudence BUSH.
Address of Welcome - President Fred FRENCH.
Response by teachers class - W.F. MORGARIEDGE.
Vocal Solo - Nellie W. STEWART.
Response by music class - Ross CUNNINGHAM.
Response by Scientific's - Mary E. AHERN.
Piano Solo - Minnie BURSON.
Recitation - Grace NEIHART.
Recitation - Jennie METTLEN.
Piano Duet - Theo SCACE, Pearl REYNOLDS.

The music and addresses were all very entertaining and gave additional evidence if any were needed of how well the work of the college has and is being done. After the exercises came the Banquet Board and here an ample preparation had been made in the beautifully decorated dining hall of the college to fittingly complete the year's labors. We append the menu to show that the physical as well as the intellectual receives careful attention at this grand school.

MENU

Punch

Celery Olives Pickels

Chicken Salad Ham Pickled Lambs Tongue

Rolls Saratoga Chips

Gold Cake Angel Food Fruit Cake

Coffee

Kisses Macaroons Neopolitan Ice Cream

Assorted Fruit Bon Bons

TOASTS.

"The Old Oaken Bucket,"	Mrs. J.M. PILE.
"Demand and Supply,"	Mr. F. FULLER.
"Our Fair Classmates,"	Mr. CURRIER.
"Our Stalwarts,"	Miss KLINTWORK.
"How Well I Remember,"	L.M. POWERS.
"My Relations,"	Mr. C. BEEBE.
"The Same Thing Over Again,"	H.E. MASON.
"The Spinster,"	Mrs. WALLIS.
"University Life,"	H. THEOBALD.
"Liberty,"	Mr. WINCHELL.
"Our Boys at the Front,"	Clement THEOBALD.

The toasts were responded to by the different ones assigned and it was past the hour of midnight when the final farewell was given by that leader among educators of the Northwest, President J.M. PILE.

Here are the names and yields of a few of our farmer's wheat fields: Geo. CULLER, 18 3/4 bushels; W.B. STAMBAUGH, 21 1/2; C.S. ASH, 19; T.E. HILL, 20; R.E.K. MELLOR, 25; Otto FREDERICKSON, 24; Fred KAY, 17 1/2; H.C. WOLF, 20; John LEUCKE, 20; and E.J. VAUGHN, 15 1/2 to the acre. These are only a few of the many that have threshed and are fair samples of the general condition of the crop in the county.

The Wayne Republican
August 24, 1898 (Vol. 5, No. 28)

BIRTH: Alex SUHR says: "It is a 14-pound girl and I am worth a million."

BIRTH: Sunday, to Ed WILLIAMS and wife, a girl.

BIRTH: A baby girl was born at the home of Mr. BERGT.

MARRIED: On last Thursday at Columbus Walter TAYLOR of this place and Lucy A. CROSS of the former place were united in the holy bonds of matrimony. The Republican desires to extend its best wishes for the future happiness of the newly married couple.

DIED: The 7-year-old son of Henry SMITH southwest of the city died Monday morning of inflamation of the bowels and was buried yesterday.

DIED: On last Thursday death entered the home of Oscar MUNSON northeast of the city and removed from earth their seven year old daughter. It was their only child and around her life all their hopes were centered. The funeral occurred on Friday.

The Wayne Republican
August 31, 1898 (Vol. 5, No. 29)

LICENSED TO WED: Judge HUNTER issued a license to wed to R.G. ROHRKE and Martha E. ZUTZ both of Hoskins.

DIED: The wife of John M. CASSELL living southwest of the city a dozen miles died last Wednesday and was interred at this place Friday the 26.

DIED: Frank ANDERSON, a young man 19 years of age, was found dead in his bed Sunday morning, at the residence of Nels ERICKSON north ot town, where he had been working. ANDERSON had just recovered from a hard tussle with dephtheria under the skillful care of Dr. LEISENRING. The doctor cautioned him to be very careful about returning to work or over-exerting himself. Saturday afternoon the threshers arrived at the ERICKSON place, and at three o'clock, despite warnings of Mr. ERICKSON, ANDERSON went to work. Later he became sick and Sunday morning, hearing a slight noise in his bedroom, he was found to have passed away. The funeral was held yesterday. (Democrat)

Real Estate Transfers.

As reported by I.W. ALTER, bonded abstracter, Wayne, Nebraska:

Henry LEY, agt, to GOOP & ELLIS, part of ne 1/4 se 1/4 13-26-3	$1,898.00
Martin REDMER to John DIMMEL, part of lot 1, blk. 9, Winside	3,575.00
Anna E. HACKET to Elizabeth KIMKEL, quit claim, se 1/4 9-27-2, also sw 1/4 of 21 & ne 1/4 of 27-27-3	- - -
E.M. SMITH to Clara E. SMITH, se 1/4, 31-37-2	500.00
Peter ULRICH, sr., to Aug. ULRICH, se 1/4, 36-26-1	1.00
Jacob BACKER to Nick M. LAKAS, n 1/2 sw 1/4 7-26-2	700.00

The Wayne Republican
September 7, 1898 (Vol. 5, No. 30)

BIRTH: Charley GILDERSLEEVE's are happy over the arrival of a new girl at their home last Friday.

LICENSED TO WED: On September 6, Judge HUNTER issued a license to wed to Johannes HATTIG and Annie M. JAEGER, both of Wayne county.

MARRIED: Aug. 31, 1898, at Hoskins Mr. R.G. ROHRKE and Miss Martha ZUTZ, both of Hoskins.

Wind and Fire Brings the Gospel Meetings to a very Abrupt Close Monday Evening.
The Big Tent Collapses and is Quickly Consumed by Fire.
Wild Scenes and Several Persons Injured.

Monday witnessed a wild scene at the tent where the gospel meetings were being held. The tent was pretty well filled with people and the services progressing nicely when all of a sudden the wind came roaring down from the north with the force of an incipient hurricane and the tent began to sway under the pressure. The audience showed indications of fear and some began to leave when the evangelist assured them there was no danger and in rather forcible language expressed his opinion of those who were leaving and while he was exhorting them to remain and be quiet, the guy ropes gave way and the vast canvass came down about the lamps that immediately set it on fire and then followed a scene that almost beggars description. The people became panic stricken and rushed wildly for the open air regardless of their neighbors, everyone apparently believing that self preservation was the first law of nature and the weak found themselves knocked down and tramped under foot by the stronger and it seems almost marvelous that there was no loss of life. All succeeded in getting out from the hell of flame, but many will carry bruises and cuts as reminders of those moments of peril. The entire city was for a time thrown into a condition bordering on a panic until its people learned that their dear ones and neighbors had not fallen victims to the flames. The tent was entirely consumed and quite a number of chairs and benches were burned up and for a time it looked as though Wayne county was going to be short a court house as the burning tent was located between it and the opera house and the wind was blowing a terrific gale from the north. The fire boys, however, were quick to respond to the alarm and in a very short time had two streams of water turned onto the flames and soon dispelled all fear of the fire gaining any further headway. Our people have had an object lesson that in all probability will give them a pretty wholesome fear of tents and tent meetings in the future and had the tent been seated with elevated seats we would now be mourning the loss of friends and neighbors but as it is each one feels like offering up thanks that it was no worse.

The pecuniary loss will be something like $650, the following being the approximate losses:

Tent, $350; Lumber, $40; Lutherans, chairs, $75; Methodists, chairs, lamps and seats, $50; Baptists, pulpit, chairs, lamps and seats, $70; Presbyterians, chairs and lamps, $35; Wayne county, chairs, $15; Y.M.C.A., chairs, $5 to $10; R.E.K. MELLOR, chairs, $7 to $10; Song books, $10.

The tent was rented by Rev. CORDNER and we have not learned whether the loss will fall on him or on the owner.

Notes of the Fire.

A great many wild and exaggerated stories are afloat as to what the evangelist said in his efforts to stop the audience from leaving the tent before the fire occurred and investigation proves that most of the things attributed to him are untrue.

Charley MARTIN is a philospher of the old school and says that "if they hadn't any lights in the tent there would have been no fire."

The fire boys are made of the kind of stuff that comes to the front in an emergency. In less than five minutes after the first alarm was given they had two streams of water turned on the fire.

The school board was in session in the county judge's office and didn't even go through the formality of putting a motion to ajdourn.

Clerk COYLE remembered that the incompleted tax list and the assessors' books were in the upper part of the court house and he didn't go through the formality of getting a key but opened the door with a brick.

F.M. SKEEN had his head quite badly bruised and cut by a falling pole and it will be several days before he fully recovers from the shock.

John JUHLIN carried a black eye as the result of a collision with someone else's head in the rush.

There were some wicked enough to express sorrow that the court house escaped.

The Wayne Republican
September 14, 1898 (Vol. 5, No. 31)

BIRTH: There is an arc of light at the home of F.C. LARGEN; its a boy born September 9.

LICENSED TO WED: Judge HUNTER issued on yesterday a license to wed to John BOSE of Dixon county and Nora SYDOW of Wayne county.

LICENSED TO WED: On Saturday Judge HUNTER issued a license to wed to Hugo LENSER and Anna MAROTZ, both of Hoskins.

LICENSED TO WED: On Saturday Judge HUNTER issued a license to wed to Emil MAROTZ and Bertha HARGENS, both of Hoskins.

MARRIED: GEARHART - CUNNINGHAM. At high noon today at the home of the bride's parents, Mr. and Mrs. David CUNNINGHAM, their daughter Ellen R. will be married to Charles D. GEARHART. The ceremony will be performed by Rev. D.C. MONTGOMERY in the presence of the immediate relatives and a few of the friends of the high contracting parties. After the ceremony lunch will be served and the bridal pair will take the afternoon train for the east. The groom is the pastor of the Congregational church at Pierce and is well spoken of by those acquainted with him. The bride is one of Wayne county's best known young ladies and for a number of years was one of its prominent teachers. Her friends are only numbered by the extent of her acquaintances and the couple in their new relationship have the best wishes of all for their future happiness.

Wayne of Today.
Rich, Natural, and Social Advantages - - - Picture of Prosperity, Industrial Possibilities and Prominent Business Men.

Wayne is wonderful in the brevity of its history; wonderful in the rapidity of its growth. Only a few years ago but a few families, today a growing little city of nearly 3,000 souls. Majestically located upon one of the most prolific garden spots of the great state of Nebraska, whose equable climate, generous soils, clear streams, beautiful woodlands, beautiful orchards, green hedge rows, splendid farms, noble herds and happy homes are the glory of the state. Ascend to the roof of any of the business blocks in the city and look on scenes beneath and stretching far around you, lofty buildings, palatial residences, beautiful churches and the hustle and bustle of the busy streets meet the sight. Industry affluence and enjoyment are evidenced in every quarter. There seems no merchandise but what has its mort, no interest without its representation. The history of the city is one of continuous struggles against great obstacles and strong competition, but her growth has been exceedingly rapid and permanent, and today Wayne is financially in a strong position, the principal educational center of the county which both socially as well as in various other respects she offers valuable inducements both for business and residence that are fully demonstrated by her remarkable development and prosperity. In determining the value of a city or country whether it is to secure educational greatness or individual wealth and happiness, the character of the soil is of the first importance, as the largest portion of wealth of individuals and the powers of nations depends principally upon the products of the earth and indeed without a good soil no nation can hope to enjoy any permanent prosperity and greatness. It is doubtless true that the soil of Wayne county surpasses that of any other equal portion of our state in fertility and variety and in adaptation to the varied wants of our enlightened people. The country around Wayne is noted for its extraordinary productiveness, yielding always substantial returns for the labor of the husbandman and equally substantial inducements for investment in farm lands, wheat, corn, barley, oats and other grain never fail and give a yeild far above the general average. Vegetables find the soil and climate congenial as well as fruits of many varieties yield large returns. The health of Wayne has long been exceptionally good, its death rate has always been among the lowest in the country. This is, in part owing, doubtless to the nature of the subsoil which is a coarse sand and which furnishes a natural filter, still another condition is the adaptability of the soil to the growth of lawns and shade trees and their productiveness, both of which tends to coolness and salubrity of the air during the summer season. Wayne has every facility for educating its rising population that could be desired in a place of residence. The public school system is ably conducted upon a broad and liberal basis, indicating the appreciation by our people at large of the great benefits of society which follows the education of the masses. There are two public school buildings which belong to the city and are equipped and arranged with all the necessary facilities. The members of the board of education are gentlemen of the very highest prominence and influence who strain every effort to further and foster the educational interest of Wayne. Wayne has two railroads, she has a rolling surface, broad streets abundantly shaded, four banks, water works costing $22,000 and a volunteer fire department, two first class hotels, three grain elevators, a Fair ground, fourteen civic societies, opera house with seating capacity of 800, six organized churches property of which is worth about $40,000, two public schools, one normal school, three newspapers, flour mill, brick kiln, electric light plant under construction, and supplementing this is a thrifty little population whose concentrated energy and effort coupled with a reasonable show of public spirit is equal to the building of a great city. These are some of Wayne's strong features and to the thoughtful investigator here is a chapter worthy of consideration and confidence. There may be more dashing and pretentious towns and cities than Wayne but that there are more delightful or safely prosperous vicinities than Wayne of today is a question which will find hundreds of enthusiastic disputants in citizens who have lived here, and a studious perusal of these pages will prove that we have a magnificent citizenship and abundance of room for people who want to make the most of life by living in a healthy, sociable, conservative community of good schools, good society and good opportunities for financial success.

FURCHNER, DUERIG & Co. - One of the enterprising establishments which it is our province to mention in connection with the best interest of the city is that of FURCHNER, DUERIG & Co. This firm has been established here in Wayne for the past eight years and by their energy and peculiar adaptation to their business has built up an extensive trade which extends throughout the entire county. They handle a full line of clothing and dry goods, hats, caps, boots and shoes and a general line of staple and fancy groceries. The house occupied is especially arranged for the large stock of goods carried being 25x80 feet in dimensions and five assistants are employed to wait on the trade. They are thoroughly conversant with every detail of the business and have an excellent reputation as men of upright character always interested in any project to advance the city.

S.R. THEOBALD & Co. "The Racket" - Among the leading concerns which have come to the front within the past few years and have attained a well deserved prominence in the city's circles. We know of none more deserving of special mention in these pages than that of S.R. THEOBALD & Co. proprietors of the famous Racket store. They fill a very important position in the ranks of the trade and their operations annually reach a very high figure. They conduct a general store, handling shoes, dry goods, notions, etc. The building occupied is handsomely arranged and thoroughly equipped for the proper display of the immense stock carried and no effort is spared in putting before the people the very best goods in each department at such prices as are noted for their moderation. They are both prominent business men and thoroughly in touch with the best interest of the city and are highly esteemed by everyone.

Joseph T. BRESSLER. - Mr. BRESSLER has been in active operation for the past thirty years in Wayne county and from the first has steadily won his way to public favor and patronage, his business today being at once large, permanent and prosperous, many prominent deals have been transacted successfully by him. In addition to a general real estate and loan business, he makes a speciality of investing money and the settlement of estates, paying taxes, etc., with the greatest care only the most approved security being taken rendering him always a desirable agent to transact business with. Mr. BRESSLER was the first president of the Logan Valley Bank which was moved to Wayne in 1885 and nationalized as First National Bank of Wayne. Since Mr. BRESSLER has made himself prominent in the interest of the city of Wayne, being always a man of integrity and known as an upright, public spirited citizen.

D.H. SULLIVAN, Main Street Grocery. - The grocery business is one which requires a degree of enterprise that makes it the most important of all our trades and the success of the Main Street Grocery which was established here four years ago is a conspicuous example of the highest degree of enterprise which may be credited to D.H. SULLIVAN the well known proprietor. The up-to-date and select stock to be found here is too well known to require a very close description, suffice to say the purest and best goods in all departments, comprising staple and fancy groceries, flour, etc. Mr. SULLIVAN also makes a specialty of fruits and vegetables as well as a complete line of glassware, queensware, etc. His store is elegantly arranged being 25x80 feet in dimensions and the customers include some of our best people. No little effort is spared by Mr. SULLIVAN to please all and that he has succeeded is evidence by the large trade he commands.

First National Bank. - As is natural in a growing community there is a strong healthy demand for money with which to develop and enrich the country and carry on the ever increasing business which concentrates here. The condition of banks is, perhaps as good a barometer as any to indicate the public temperature and in this special edition we are impelled to give more than a passing glance at the strong banking institution of the First National Bank of Wayne. This bank was organized in 1885 and has at present a capital stock of $75,000. The business premises owned by the bank are most centrally located and present a metropolitan appearance. They transact a general banking business in all the word implies, discounting paper, selling exchange and collecting in all parts of the country. The officers are thoroughly progressive and prominent business man and are as follows: J.M. STRAHAN, President; Frank E. STRAHAN, Vice President; H.F. WILSON, Cashier; Nathan CHACE, Asst. Cashier. Directors, J.M. STRAHAN, Frank E. STRAHAN, Geo. BOGART, James PAUL, John T. BRESSLER, Frank FULLER, H.F. WILSON and the last statement shows the following gratifying state of affairs:

Resources,

Loans and discounts	$144,957.61
Overdrafts, secured and unsecured	3,398.51
U.S. Bonds to secure circulation	18,750.00
Stocks, securities, etc.	200.00
Banking house, furniture and fixtures	13,800.00
Other real estate and mortgages owned	7,565.27
Due from National Banks (not Reserve Agents)	$ 4,805.42
Due from approved reserve agents	21,479.03
Checks and other cash items	45.57

Notes of other National Banks	$ 4,535.00
Fractional paper currency, nickels & cents	12.20
Lawful Money Reserve in Bank, viz:	
Specie	4,987.25
Legal Tender Notes	<u>2,000.00</u>
	37,864.47
Redemption fund with U.S. Treasurer (5 per cent of circulation)	<u>843.75</u>
Total,	$227,319.61

Liabilities,

Capital stock paid in	75,000.00
Surplus fund	15,000.00
Undivided profits, less expenses and taxes paid	12,843.13
National Bank notes outstanding	16,875.00
Individual deposits subject to check	$34,294.99
Demand certificates of deposit	<u>53,306.49</u>
	<u>107,601.48</u>
Total,	227,319.61

The Wayne National Bank. - The history of Wayne discloses no business institution which can advance and favor as that of the Wayne National Bank. This bank was organized in 1890 and today has a capital stock of $50,000. From its inception its career has been marked by steady progress achieved by confining its operations to the legitimate fields of banking and winning the confidence of all who have business relations with it by fair dealings. The persons of the executive management being as follows: W.E. BROWN, President; B.F. SWAN, Cashier; P.L. MILLER, Vice President. These names represent some of the most substantial and thoroughly progressive business men in the city and their connections gives it a foremost position throughout the commercial world. The last statement is as follows:

Resources,

Loans and discounts	$74,717.57
Overdrafts, secured and unsecured	469.77
U.S. Bonds to secure circulation	12,500.00
Stocks, securities, etc.	252.00
Banking house, furniture and fixtures	13,087.00
Other real estate and mortgages owned	5,714.75
Due from state Banks and Bankers	566.70
Due from approved Reserve Agents	690.43
Checks and other cash items	289.88
Notes of other National Banks	500.00
Fractional paper currency, nickels & cents	36.60

Specie	$4,791.50	
Legal Tender Notes	<u>1,010.00</u>	
		5,801.50
Redemption fund with U.S. Treasurer		
(5 per cent of circulation)		<u>262.50</u>
Total,		$114,888.70

Liabilities,

Capital stock paid in	50,000.00
Surplus fund	4,302.19
Undivided profits, less expenses and taxes paid	22.33
National Bank notes outstanding	11,250.00
Individual deposits subject to check	21,267.51
Demand certificates of deposit	200.75
Time certificates of deposit	22,551.92
Bills Payable	<u>5,000.00</u>
Total,	$114,888.70

HARRINGTON & ROBBINS. - Much has been said in the last few years concerning the actual advantages of the above concern and in speaking of this firm we cannot add anything to their already established reputation. The business was begun here four years ago and reviewing its career we find that it has always maintained the front rank, handling a very superior class of goods, prompt and reliable in making sales, courteous to the trade, and with all exceptionally moderate in prices. The world of fashion it is admitted in Wayne is governed by the styles which compose the general stock of this institution in gentlemens, youths, and childrens dress, such as fine clothing, furnishings, hats, caps, etc. The premises occupied consist of a building 25x80 feet in dimensions two floors. Under a separate department Messrs. HARRINGTON & ROBBINS make a prominent speciality of a very extensive line of carpets of the latest designs, mattings, window shades and draperies. This department is well stocked, the selection of which indicates the most excellent taste and judgment and the large trade at their command is the honest effort to please which is evidenced by the large trade enjoyed.

J.P. GAERTNER. - This is a house that lives up to its profession and is a house whose announcements may be taken for facts. Those who want the latest and best designs at reasonable prices can find no better place than that of Mr. J.P. GAERTNER who is the occupant of a house with an area of 68x90 feet, four floors, situated in the heart of the city forming one of the most complete furniture houses in the city. He has been established for the last sixteen years and every department is well stocked, the selection of which indicates the most excellent taste and judgment. The stock embraces all the latest in furniture as to variety and quality as well as carpets of the latest design, mattings, window shades and draperies. Mr. GAERTNER is also a graduate embalmer and makes it a speciality in connection with the furniture trade. He is thoroughly progressive and generally well thought of.

Eli JONES. - This gentleman is widely and favorably known in business circles here. The premises occupied for the immense business transacted by him necessitates the use of a building 30x60 feet in dimensions which gives ample accommodation for the storage manipulation and display of the comprehensive lines of goods carried which include farm machinery, implements, wagons, buggies, etc. Mr. JONES is also agent for the Hartman four ton scales. He also conducts one of the largest livery stables in the city as well as boards and sells stock and does some real estate business. Mr. JONES has been established for the last thirteen years and will always be found an enterprising and progressive business man and a keen competitor for legitimate trade. He has built an excellent trade and is a man who takes interest in the welfare of the city.

CHACE & NEELY. - Among the institutions which have contributed materially to the up building of Wayne we can refer our readers to no better firm than that of CHACE & NEELY whose immense establishment is the scene of constant activity and where can be found what is elsewhere regarded to be a complete stock of heavy and shelf hardware occupying a building thoroughly arranged and equipped being 24x80 feet in dimensions also ware room 24x60 feet. They have been established for the last fifteen years and no firm in the city can offer better inducements while their honorable career has won success and a proud position among the business men of the county and are considered as thoroughly progressive business men as we have, public spirited as well.

ANDRESEN The Tailor. - Necessary to every stylish and modern city is the tailor who can furnish neat and up-to-date attires for its male population for nothing can so embrace a man as well fitting and stylish apparel while cheap "hand me down" clothing often destroys the appearance of a perfect physique. ANDRESEN The Tailor established in Wayne for sometime is prepared to supply all necessary requirements to a successful tailoring house at any time. He carries a complete stock of suitings at all times and at prices ranging from $18 upwards. Mr. ANDRESEN enjoys the confidence of the people at large and is one of our worthy citizens.

L.F. HOLTZ, Merchant Tailor. - There is in every city tailors who command the very best trade. Such an establishment in the city of Wayne is that of L.F. HOLTZ, merchant tailor, who has been located in Wayne for the last fourteen years. The stock comprises the finest fabrics to be found anywhere, including the latest importations, in quality and finish, in artistic workmanship and in all that goes to make perfect tailoring, the garments turned out here is perfection itself, and the name of the firm is the highest guarantee. He employees three men and supplying the demand for low prices in this line is a success in gaining the best patronage in the city.

W.E. BROOKINGS. - This establishment is one of the most popular and well managed stores in the city of Wayne and since it was established here seven years ago has been a decided and deserved success. The stock of fine family groceries is always large, fresh and pure, while no little effort is spared in attending to the trade. The management is in charge of an active business man who gives every detail of the business his courteous and constant direction. The store is well arranged and two men are employed to wait on the trade.

Guy R. WILBUR, Attorney at Law. - Wayne county is indeed fortunate in the class of its attorneys which are not excelled by any in the state and prominent among the number is our efficient counsellor and attorney at law, Mr. Guy R. WILBUR, who is among our early settlers having been raised in the state coming to Wayne from Hartington twenty years ago, and locating in the city of Wayne. Not only does he possess an extensive friendship here at home, but few men can claim as general acquaintance and established popularity throughout the state as he. Mr. WILBUR also does some real estate and abstracting as well, he deals extensively in farm loans, etc. He has always been foremost in promoting the best interest of the city and county which is due to a great extent to his most honorable reputation and standing with the people at large.

WEBER Bros. - Wayne has enjoyed peculiar and important advantages as a milling center and one of the most prominent in the state is the Wayne Roller mills conducted under the management of the WEBER Bros. This time honored concern dates its commercial existence as far back as 1885. The premises occupied consist of two buildings, the machinery of the entire plant is of the best pattern, the output at the mills aggregate 65 barrels per day. The best obtainable grades of grain only are used and as a result the flour produced is absolutely unexcelled in all desirable qualities and is always popular with all competent judges that give them a fair trial. The leading brands are the "Superlative" which they make a speciality of, and the "Snow Flake" both brands meet with a ready sale throughout the entire country. Messrs. WEBER Bros. have always been enterprising and progressive business men possessed with public spirit.

I.W. ALTER. - Among the leading area estate agents of Wayne is Mr. I.W. ALTER whose business was established six years ago. He is a general real estate and insurance agent as well as being a bonded abstractor which is a speciality, and his connection with our non-resident property owners is of the most superior character. He has likewise secured a high reputation for the care and management of estates and possesses every facility for renting and maintaining estates at the highest standard of productive efficiency. Mr. ALTER does some collecting and has ever sustained an untarnished reputation for square and honorable dealings.

J.F. SHERBAHN. - Sixteen years of uninterrupted prosperity sums up in brief the history of this widely known and representative business institution, it having been founded by the well known proprietor Mr. J.F. SHERBAHN who has always been indefatigable in working to the city's interest as well as his own to which position will be accorded him by all the prominent business men throughout Wayne county. An idea as to the magnitude of his plant will be given in the fact that the space utilized for its operation covers an area of ten acres, fifteen people being constantly employed, the capacity being 30,000 brick per day which are shipped to all parts of the state and parts of the adjoining states. Mr. SHERBAHN is a native of Pennsylvania, he has been here for the past sixteen years during which period he has closely identified himself with the commercial advancement of the city of his adoption and deserves the high esteem and consideration in which he is held by this community.

Robert UTTER. - One of the distinctive industries of every commercial, manufacturing and agricultural center is that of the book and stationery business and which contributes not a little to its material prosperity. The only house engaged in this industry in the city of Wayne is that of Mr. Robert UTTER's established here four years ago and during this period has gained a wide reputation for good and fair dealings. Mr. UTTER occupies a house especially arranged and convenient for meeting the requirements of the trade at his command. The stock includes books, stationery of all kinds, wall paper, dolls, toys, and novelties and a complete news stand. Besides he handles a very select line of musical merchandise making a prominent speciality of the following makes of organs. The Chicago Cottage, Western Cottage, Camp & Co's goods and the Baldwin, also the world's famous Estey Piano. Through his honorable methods he has pursued is wherein his success lies in becoming our leader in this branch.

Otto VOGET. - In the course of our survey of the concerns which give to Wayne her commercial backing, it becomes our duty to accord a sketch to the business of the above mentioned gentleman. He established here six years ago and since has given to the city of Wayne a prominence in this branch of activity. He does everything in the line of plumbing, steam and gas fitting and carries a large stock of steam and gas fitting supplies, being sole agent for the famous Buffington Acetyline gas company. Mr. VOGET occupies a house suitable for his business, using only the best material and guaranteeing first class work in every particular.

Aug. PIEPENSTOCK. - The question of food is one with which every man has to grapple, and in all communities that have attained to any degree of civilization the business of supplying food material in all its branches becomes a very extensive industry. In this connection it is a pleasure to note the establishment of Mr. Aug. PIEPENSTOCK. Such a business as this has not been built up in a day, it is the legitimate results of careful industry, a thorough knowledge of the wants of the trade, enterprise in procuring supplies from first hands and handling them at a small margin and energy to preserve for thirteen years a high standard of excellence on all goods offered. Mr. PIEPENSTOCK's store is located in a very desirable portion of the city and he carries a most complete line of staple and fancy groceries and in connection runs a first class bakery. He has also purchased the HANSON stock of goods and has moved them in his present store which is thoroughly arranged for successfully conducting an immense business.

Prof. R. DURRIN. - The sculptured marble and graceful granite monuments which mark the resting place of the dead are mute but touching evidences of a love that cherished their memory and testify the noblest sentiments which finds expression in human action. The desire to embellish sometimes with art works has been one of the most marked evidence of a higher civilization and word the beautiful poems into which these lasting monuments are made, bearing record of our love for lost ones, call for an artist of the highest skill and we can truthfully say none rank higher in the country than Prof. R. DURRIN who for the last thirty years has made it a profession, having located in Wayne just six years ago and by a close application to business has built up a trade that many others can well envy. He does all kinds of sarcophagus and monumental works as well as being patentee and owner of a process of making portraits on marble. Prof. DURRIN has also placed on exhibition at the exposition an elegant piece of work which is of very rare merit and proves conclusively that he is a strictly up-to-date and thoroughly deserves a widespread patronage.

Phil. H. KOHL. - In going to press with a general review of Wayne's representative business men we only refer to those who are today connected with her best interests and those who take special pride in promoting her advancement. In this connection we make due reference to our thoroughly efficient county treasurer, Mr. Phil H. KOHL, now serving his second term as treasurer. Mr. KOHL located in Wayne in 1891, and since has ever sustained a reputable name as thoroughly abreast of times in promoting the general prosperity of the city of his adoption, and it can be said that no man in the city stands better with the people at large, and his actions has always been characterized by fair, square and honorable dealings.

J.S. LEWIS, jr. - This progressive house was established in Wayne fourteen years ago by the above gentleman and by strict attention to business with a thorough practical knowledge of its every feature has deservedly succeeded in reaching a large trade which is distributed throughout the county. He carries the largest line of harness and saddles in the city of Wayne and is also sole agent for the celebrated Cooper Wagons and Buggies of Davenport, Ia., and makes a prominent specialty of all kinds of repairing. The house occupied is thoroughly arranged and no little effort is spared in meeting the requirements of the first class patronage built up. Mr. LEWIS is as well one of our leading business men and thoroughly progressive.

E. HUNTER, County Judge. - A business and official career of nineteen years has made E. HUNTER one of our conspicuous and widely known men of Wayne county. His reputation as a business man has extended far and wide and there are many doubtless whom that reputation has reached who not having seen him personally will be gratified with a view of the excellent likeness which we publish. Beginning in a small way, attending to his own business with a clear head and unswerving integrity we find him what he is today, one of our leading and representative citizens. He has held many positions of trust and confidence imposed upon him by his fellow citizens being county clerk for four years and now serving his first term as county Judge. Mr. HUNTER has always labored earnestly in the welfare of the city and it can truthfully be said that it would be difficult to find in Wayne county a more public spirited citizen or more highly esteemed gentleman, always foremost to advance the interest of the county at large.

J.W. EPLER & Co. - Among the wide awake business firms of Wayne that deserves special mention in this commercial review is that of Messrs. J.W. EPLER & Co. This business was established one year ago and the building occupied is elegantly arranged and equipped for conducting the business already built up. They keep at all times a heavy line of staple and fancy groceries, teas, coffees, provisions, etc., also glass and queensware which are offered to customers at rock bottom prices. Only the best goods in each line are handled and they give their very best attention to providing every convenience for their many customers and are among our leading citizens.

TOWER & BENSHOOF. - We deem that we are doing only simple justice in giving special prominence in this issue to so important a concern as that of TOWER & BENSHOOF. In the special line to which they devote their energies they represent the leading house in the city. They are dealers in farming implements, wagons, buggies, etc., representing such firms as the Fish Wagon Co., Racine, Wis., Henney buggy, The Moline Plow Co. and the John Deere Plow Co., and also do some grain and real estate business. For the business they occupy a house 50x150 feet in dimensions and their trade covers the county. Seven years of business in the city has demonstrated the wisdom of their plan of operation, placing them at the head of the trade with a promising future.

John HARRINGTON & Co. - No line of business is better represented in the county than the lumber and coal business and we can safely say that no establishment is better fitted to well and thoroughly represent this important industry than that of Messrs. John HARRINGTON & Co. They have been in operation here for sometime and deals extensively in these lines. They carry at all times an immense line of lumber of all descriptions as well as a large stock of coal. They have established already a reputation of the highest kind as honorable for public patronage and appreciation and our readers will find at their hand every want in these different lines fully supplied and at such fair and liberal treatment as will invite a continuance of business relations.

D.E. NEWTON. - In this review we make special mention of the Wayne Feed Mills conducted by Mr. D.E. NEWTON who has been established for the last twelve years and from the start has enjoyed the distinction of being among our leading industries from the fact that his sales amount to as much almost as any firm in the city. He handles everything in the feed line besides carries a large supply of windmills, pumps, pipes, round tanks, etc., and also has charge of the Wayne ice house which has a capacity of 300 tons. Mr. NEWTON has the fullest confidence of his patrons and his standing in commerical circles has been such as entitles him to the consideration of all who may enter into business relations with him. He is closely identified with the best interest of the city.

R.W. WILKINS & Co. - When a person needs the service of a druggist he desires to feel that the most absolute care is given to his order and that there is no haste in filling it, but clean, careful deliberation. Messrs. R.W. WILKINS & Co. conduct one of the most reliable drug stores in the city and one where particular attention is given to orders. The store has been located here since 1882, R.W. WILKINS taking charge in 1891, and H.D. BLANCHARD who forms the company coming in 1893, and the premises occupied are large and elegantly arranged and fitted up in a way that makes it one of the most desirable places in the city to deal. The stock embraces a full line of pure, fresh drugs, chemicals, patent medicines, toilet articles, paints, oils, tobaccos, cigars, books, stationery, etc., and in connection a most elegant soda fountain where the latest beverages are dispensed with the utmost care. It may be said the general qualities of these gentlemen command for them the esteem of all who come in contact with them.

Citizens Bank. - To portray the commercial importance of any business center necessity gives a position of prominence to its leading banking institutions. They hold the great medium of exchange between trade centers and occupy the position of arbiters between debtors and creditors. The success and ability displayed in their management forms an important gauge by which to estimate the commercial standing of the business community, where their influence is felt and an inspection of their standing and resources gives a valuable index to the condition of all business interest. The Citizens Bank stands first among the banks of Wayne in the amount of capital and aggregate of business transacted. The present officers are as follows: A.L. TUCKER, President; E.D. MITCHELL, Vice Pres.; D.C. MAIN, Cashier; G.E. FRENCH, Asst. Cashier. Directors - E.D. MITCHELL, A.A. WELCH, D.C. MAIN, G.E. FRENCH, J.S. FRENCH, A.L. TUCKER and James PAUL. These names are all representative citizens bringing to bear their business experience and ability in the upbuilding of the bank. They confine the business to the legitimate fields of banking, discounting, etc., while advantageous connections are maintained with the best banks all over the country which affords excellent facilities for transacting business with promptness.

C.M. CRAVEN. - Mr. CRAVEN is endowed with an education in his line of business such as few have taken the trouble to acquire and when locating here ten years ago he took that initial step which could lead to one position, that of doing good work, prompt and at a moderate cost. His studio is well arranged and his work in Wayne county is eloquent with testimony. He is thoroughly familiar with all the details of the photographic business and that his aim is nothing short of the highest attainments is the conviction of all who have given him work, as he spares no little effort in giving satisfaction and is one of our prominent business men.

J.R. COYLE. - There is nothing that exerts a more powerful influence upon the new comer in forming an opinion of a city than the character and standing of its public men and leading citizens. In this connection we make special reference to our able and efficient county clerk, Mr. John R. COYLE, who has been a resident of Wayne county for the past fifteen years. Mr. COYLE came from the state of Iowa and the most of his time since in Nebraska has been devoted to railroading up until Jan., 1898, when elected to the office of county clerk. He is an office-holder of recognized ability throughout the county and as a result enjoys and extensive friendship. He is a gentleman of sound character and unquestioned integrity and no man in the county stands better than he with the people always lending a helping hand to any cause calculated to advance the public interest as well as his own.

E.P. OLMSTED & Co. - This progressive house was established in Wayne eight years ago by the above gentleman and by strict attention to business with a thorough practical knowledge of its every feature has succeeded in securing a large trade which is distributed throughout the county and which makes it the leading hardware institution. The premises occupied are 25x100 feet in dimensions, two floors and basement and a general line of shelf and heavy hardware is carried also farming machinery, being agent for the Deering binders of Chicago. The Cresent bicycles are also carried and the world's famous Household sewing machine. The Majestic wrought iron ranges and the Beckwith round oak stoves. E.P. OLMSTED and R.E.K. MELLOR compose the firm and no effort is spared in promoting the city's best interest as well as their own which has met with a decided appreciation.

EDWARDS & BRADFORD Lumber Co. - The progress and development made in production, capacity and character of business transacted in the lumber business within recent years are marked and varied, and a most important department in Wayne's trade is the business of supplying the demand in lumber. The heading of this article directs attention to one of the leading lumber companies of the entire west, having yards in almost every town in this part of the state of Nebraska, the headquarters being at Sioux City, Iowa. The office and yards at this point cover three lots and are under the able and efficient management of Mr. T.A. BERRY who is a gentleman with superior business qualifications and thoroughly conversant with every detail of the business and has had charge for one year.

The Wayne Republican
September 21, 1898 (Vol. 5, No. 32)

BIRTH: Born to Mr. and Mrs. Charles KIRCHMER, September 19, a daughter of standard weight and beauty. (Hoskins)

MARRIED: At the Lutheran church on Sunday, September 18, 1898, Emil MAROTZ and Miss Bertha GARGENS. (Hoskins)

MARRIED: BOSE - SYDOW. At the Plum Creek German church on last Friday afternoon at 5:30, Rev. SCHULTZ pronounced the words that bind for life John BOSE of Dixon county and Nora SYDOW of Wayne county. The ceremony was performed in the presence of fourteen families, friends of the high contracting parties. The groom is one of Dixon county's most industrious and energetic young farmers and the bride is the daughter of Chris SYDOW of Plum Creek. She is in every way worthy of the best of husbands and will be a helpmate in every sense of the word. The young couple were the recipients of many presents from their friends. After the wedding a reception was held at the bride's home where the guests were elegantly entertained. The young couple will begin life on a farm in Dixon county where the best wishes of a large circle of friends will be with them.

MARRIED: A very pretty home wedding occurred Wednesday noon at the home of the bride when Miss Ellen CUNNINGHAM, daughter of Mr. and Mrs. David CUNNINGHAM, was united in marriage to Charles D. GEARHART of Pierce. The rooms were beautifully decorated with asparagus, ferns, asters and roses. An arch of white asters and asparagus formed the nook where the young people were joined for life by Rev. MONTGOMERY. Ross CUNINGHAM played the "Wedding March." Miss Mattie CUNNINGHAM of Madison, cousin of the bride, was maid of honor and Lloyd CUNNINGHAM, brother of the bride, best man. The bride looked charming in a white silk dress trimmed in chiffon and ribbon. The ceremony was witnessed by relatives and a few friends. The whole company sat down to an elaborate luncheon. Mr. and Mrs. GEARHART left on the evening train for a two weeks' trip in Norfolk, Lincoln, Omaha and places in Iowa back to Wayne, then to their future home in Pierce, where the groom is pastor of the Congregational church.

DIED: On Sunday afternoon the spirit took its flight from the earthly tenement of Ora BIBLER the 8-year-old son of E.E. BIBLER and wife. The little fellow was at school on Wednesday and on Thursday complained of not feeling well and on Saturday the attending physician pronounced the case of diptheria from which he died at the time stated. The funeral occured on Monday morning.

Real Estate Tranfers.

Reported by I.W. ALTER, bonded abstracter, Wayne, Nebraska:

J.H. SHERE to Martin REDMER,	
lots 10, 11 and 12, blk. 1, Winside	$450.00
O.O. WHITED to George W. PONCE,	
w 1/2 blk. 2, 1st ad Carroll	1.00
Clause RASMUSEN to school dist.,	
no. 6 plat 18x12 rods in ne corner of 11-26-4	50.00
L.C. MITTELSTADT to A.C. GOLTZ,	
ne 1/4, 23-25-2	1.00
RICHARDS & KEENE to Alex HINES,	
se 1/4 ne 1/4 10-27-1	680.00
Wm. M. WRIGHT to Carl C. THOMSEN,	
s 1/4 nw 1/4 & n 1/2 sw 1/4 34-26-4	3,000.00
Wm. PIEPENSTOCK to Aug. PIEPENSTOCK,	
und 1/2 lots 15, 16, 17, 18, 19 and 20,	
blk. 21, Coll hill ad Wayne	90.00
Chas. SHIPLEY to Helfrich GETTMAN,	
pt ne 1/4 se 1/4 13-26-3	115.00

The Wayne Republican
September 28, 1898 (Vol. 5, No. 33)

LICENSED TO WED: Licensed to wed, September 24, Julius CHAON and Clara CLASMAN, both of Dixon county.

MARRIED: MYERS - SPIKE. Monday afternoon, September 26, Judge HUNTER united in marriage J.B. MYERS and Anna SPIKE, both of Wayne county.

MARRIED: There is to be a double wedding at the SHORTEN home down in Brenna precinct at noon today. At that hour Rev. LEMON of the Baptist church will pronounce the words that bind for life Will T. SHORTEN and Sarah COWLEY and Charles E. TRUMBULL and Dora J. SHORTEN. The newly wedded couples expect to take the afternoon train for Omaha and the exposition. The Repbulican extends best wishes for the future of these young people.

DIED: The infant child of Wilbur SPAHR and wife died at the family home north of this city Monday morning. The funeral occured yesterday.

The Wayne Republican
October 5, 1898 (Vol. 5, No. 34)

BIRTH: Born on Monday to Mr. and Mrs. Geo. WEATHERHOLT a son. (Hoskins)

BIRTH: Born to Mr. and Mrs. Aamyal MORTZ on last Saturday a son. (Hoskins)

MARRIED: On September 28, Julius CHAON and Clara CLASSMAN were united in marriage by Rev. Father FITZGERALD at the Cathlic church in the city of Wayne. After the ceremony the happy couple repaired to the home of the bride's parents, Henry CLASSMAN and wife, west of Wakefield where in company with a host of friends they found a splendid dinner and grand reception awaiting them. The groom is a well know young farmer of Dixon county and the bride is one of the best of our young ladies, loved and respected by all. When the shades of evening had fallen there began an entertainment for the lovers of dancing that lasted several hours and that was heartily enjoyed by the many young folks and others that desired to participate. The boys of the neighborhood didn't propose that they should be forgotten as the big charivari demonstrated. It is the universal wish of the friends of the young couple that their's may be a peaceful, prosperus and happy voyage through life. The presents were very numerous and we append as nearly as possible a list of same with names of donors.

Cups, Sidonia CHAON and May CHENAUER; Plates, P.L. MILLER; Silver knives and forks, H. CLASSMAN, Jr.; Pickle dish, Anna CHAON; Lamp, Mr. and Mrs. John LUTT; Glass set, Mrs. M.W. and J.J.W. FOX; Water pitcher, Amelia CHAON; Tea set, Ella MINER; Towels, table and teaspoons, Mr. and Mrs. PACKER; Chair, Mr. and Mrs. A.F. CHAON; Potato dish, Clara CHAON; Clock, Mr. and Mrs. Henry CLASSMAN; Lamp, Geo. JOHN and Joseph CLASSMAN; Water set, Leo CHAPMAN; Table cloth, Mrs. S. BROWN of Sioux City; Lamp, fruit dish and tooth pick holder, Mr. and Mrs. Wm. BROWN of Sioux City; Fruit dish, Mrs. V. CONLIN of Sioux City; Silver spoons, Mr. and Mrs. R.H. SKILES and Lydia CHAON; Bed stead, Mr. and Mrs. Joseph CLASSMAN of Dixon; Water set and tea spoons, Mr. and Mrs. Frank JOHNSON; Glass cup, Blanche and Grace JOHNSON.

DIED: WILSON. On Tuesday forenoon, October 4th, 1898, Mrs. Mercena WILSON passed quietly away, at the home of her son S.T. WILSON in our city. The deceased was born in Pennsylvania over 76 years ago and for a number of years has been a resident of Nebraska and for a year or more our city has been her home. Two or more years ago she was stricken with paralysis and has been an invalid from that time until her death. Four sons and quite a number of other relatives and an extended circle of friends who had learned to love and respect her mourn her death. The funeral will be at Ponca Thursday afternoon at 3 o'clock.

Real Estate Transfers.

Reported by I.W. ALTER, bonded abstracter, Wayne, Nebraska:

BANISTER, John W. to Robert MICK,
    sw 1/4, 4-26-3 $4,550.00
August PIEPENSTOCK to L.J. HANSEN,
    lot 5, blk. 13, Wayne, lots 1, 2, 3 and 12,
    blk. 6, e add Wayne, also lots 15, 16, 17,
    18, 19 and 20, blk. 21, College hill add
    to Wayne   4,500.00
Chas. ROBBINS to C.F. BARNES,
    lot 12, blk. 4, Lakes add to Wayne   650.00

Solomon SLAUGHTER to Gertrude E. GRAVES, nw 1/4, 21-25-5	$5,500.00
Sarah and M. STOBER to W.W. BLACK, n 1/2 of sw 1/4 and sw 1/4 of nw 1/4, 30-27-1	944.00
A.A. BARNARD to Willis HOWARD, n 1/2 of sw 1/4, 32-26-3	1,500.00
Leslie BAKER to Antonio SCHLACK, lot 14, blk. 8, Hoskins	150.00
A.W. TAYLOR to Henry HANSEN, lot 9, blk. 5, east add to Wayne	700.00

The Wayne Republican
October 12, 1898 (Vol. 5, No. 35)

BIRTH: A new son arrived at the home of Mr. and Mrs. Chas. DOBBIN, of near Hoskins, Monday.

BIRTH: Dr. LEISENRING reports a fine boy baby as arriving at the home of Ned LLOYD last Saturday.

MARRIED: ANDERSON - MATHSON. His honor Judge HUNTER on the 7th married L.O. ANDERSON and Anna MATHSON.

MARRIED: GREER - HITCHCOCK. The home of Mr. and Mrs. G.P. HITCHCOCK was the scene of a very pretty wedding on Tuesday at high noon, their daughter Miss Lena, being united in marriage to Ralph GREER of Blunt, S.D. The couple entered the room precisely at 12 m. to the strains of the wedding march played by Miss Clara PHILLEO and took their places in a beautiful bower of green and immediately under a white dove suspended from the arch. Rev. BITHEL then pronounced the magic words that made them man and wife. The bride was attired in a beautiful tailor made traveling gown of blue and looked charming. Mr. GREER has taken from Wayne one of the first girls of the place and one that will be missed in musical circles. Having filled the position of organist at the M.E. church for so long, that organization remembered her by sending her a beautiful case of silver. Mr. GREER has been known here for years and there never was a young man went from out midst who was more beloved by young and old alike. He is at present cashier of the bank at Blunt, S.D., to which place he takes his bride, having purchased a pretty and comfortable home there. The young couple departed for Omaha on the 2:50 train amid a shower of rice and kind wishes. They will return to this place the last of the week before going to their home. Mr. and Mrs. GREER were the recipients of many beautiful gifts. The friends from abroad were Mr. and Mrs. BAKER of Marshalltown, Ia.; Mrs. HOFFMAN of Randolph, Neb.; Mrs. CAMERON, son and daughter of Blair, Neb.; Mr. DRAKE of S.D.; and Mr. and Mrs. CHAPIN and son of Winside, Neb.

COMMISSIONER PROCEEDINGS, Wayne, Neb., Oct. 5, 1898.
Board met pursuant to adjournment all members present.
On motion the following claims were examined and allowed:

EDWARDS & BRADFORD Co., lumber	$66.09
M.S. ENGLERT, road work	27.50
HAMMOND Bros & STEPHENS, supplies, claimed $20.50, allowed	2.50

Comes now Bert BROWN, clerk of the district court, and submits his report of fees, not reported prior hereto, showing the sum of $13 received as trial fees and turned into the county treasury receipt for which is attached to report. Report approved.

The county judge fee book for third quarter showing fees received $212.90. Approved.

Comes now Robt. FENSKE, et al., and presents a petition praying that the voting place of Hancock precinct will be changed from school district 53 (WITTLER schoolhouse) to school district 31 (Herman RHEMUS school house). On motion change is granted.

The following is a list of names selected from which to draw jurors for the November term of district court:

Brenna - C.F. SEASTRAND, J.G. HAAS, T.B. COBB, J.C. RITCHEY.

Strahan - John BEAL, A.G. METTLEN, Andrew SHINN, June CONGER.

Wilbur - John HARDER, Chas. SCHULTHIES, Fred HOFELDT.

Wayne - 1st ward, Jas. PORTERFIELD, C.A. CHACE, Fred VOLPP, C.B. OWENS. 2d ward, R.C. OSBORN, W.D. HAMMOND, S.D. RELYEA, F.E. STRAHAN. 3d ward, G.W. RILEY, M. STRINGER, Eli JONES, M.P. AHERN.

Plum Creek - John LEUCK, Mort McMANIGAL, John FINN, Eugene SULLIVAN.

Leslie - Neal NYE, Frank LONG.

Logan - Thos. FITZSIMMONS, R.B. LEONARD.

Hunter - Ray AGLER, Rome HUNTER, John OLSON, Otis STRINGER, Grant MEARS.

Hoskins - Wm. ZUTZ, Wm. SHELLENBERG, Simon

STROTE, Geo. MEISKE.
    Garfield - John KNOUSE, Hayden HUTCHINSON, John BRUSE.
    Sherman - Joel HANCOCK, W.H. BURNHAM, Andrew HARPER.
    Hancock - Herman REHMUS, Aug. DECK, Ernest MILLER.
    Chapin - John PRINCE, Paul HEYER, William WORTHING.
    Deer Creek - C.J. NARIN, W.W. GARWOOD, Guy MANNING, John AHERN, S.W. WILLIAMSON.
    Winside - A.H. CARTER, Wm. HART, D.J. CAVANAUGH.
    On motion board adjourned to Oct. 6, 1898, at 9 a.m.

The Wayne Republican
October 19, 1898 (Vol. 5, No. 36)

LICENSED TO WED: Licensed to wed by Judge HUNTER, October 18, E.B. DOWLING of Coleridge and Caroline EBY of Carroll.

DIED: The youngest child of Mr. and Mrs. FLING, a little girl aged about two and one half years died Wednesday afternoon from diphtheria. The child had not been well for sometime previous and soon succumbed to the dreaded disease. The little one was buried Thursday morning. The eldest child is fast improving and is thought to be out of danger.

John HYATT is Dead.

    The last roll call has been answered and another of the boys of the Third Nebraska who answered to his country's call for volunteers has passed the picket line between life and death and joined the great army in that land toward which we are all traveling at a rapid rate. Only a few short months ago John HYATT was one of the best specimens of a vigorous young manhood that walked the streets of our city, but the southern climate and army life proved too much for him and on Monday the announcement of his death came in the form of a brief telegram to his father; typhoid fever was the cause of his death. His remains are on the way to this place and will be laid to rest in our cemetery to await the final call to arms of the Great Commander. His parents, brothers and sisters have the heartfelt sympathy of the entire community in their great bereavement, but this we know is at best poor consolation for the stricken ones and only the Great Commander can bring peace to the stricken at times like this and may that peace be given unto these at this time.

The Wayne Republican
October 26, 1898 (Vol. 5, No. 37)

BIRTH: Dr. LEISENRING reports the arrival of a very nice girl baby at the home of W.S. GOLDIE and wife yesterday.

MARRIED: Today at the home of his mother in Leslie precinct Arthur NURNBERGER will be married to Tillie VOLDENBERG. The young couple will leave immediately after their marriage for Omaha where they expect to make their future home. The Republican extends congratulations and hopes for their success in life.

MARRIED: This is a world of surprises and the latest and most startling to us was the following received one day after the event occurred: "Frank MILLS and Ethel TOLLES were married Wednesday, October 19, 1898. At home November 19, 1898. Laurel, Neb." We supposed Frank MILLS was a confirmed "old batch," but it seems when Dorr CARROLL, Walt GOLDIE and Fred STOCKWELL broke down the fence and got out of the corral Frank went along and has been an estray ever since until the excellent lady that now bears the name of Mrs. MILLS lariated him and brought him into the fold. The Republican extends its heartiest congratulations to Mr. and Mrs. Frank MILLS.

FUNERAL: On Thursday evening the remains of Private John HYATT arrived in the city from Jacksonville, Florida. They were taken to the home of William BENSHOOF and on Friday at 11 o'clock the funeral took place from the M.E. church where the sermon was delivered by Rev. BITHEL. The G.A.R. Post acted as an escort of honor to the remains of the young soldier and at the cemetery fired the usual military salute over his grave. The pall bearers were Abram GILDERSLEEVE and Geo. BIGLEY both members of his regiment home on sick leave and four members of the G.A.R. Post. The church was well filled with those who had gone to pay their last respects to the soldier boy and to extend their sympathy to the stricken parents, brothers and sisters.

Real Estate Transfers.

R.B. CRAWFORD to John T. BRESSLER,
    n 1/2 nw 1/4 12-26-3 $3,200.00
Geo. BUSKIRK to Detlef KAI,
    e 1/2 se 1/4 30-25-5   2,800.00
Detlef KAI to August KAI,
    w 20 a ne & se 1/4 30-25-5   700.00

Vaughn DAVIS to Emos DAVIS, e 1/2 se 1/4 35-27-1	$3,000.00
A. SHINN to G. HALLER, w 1/4 n 1/2 se 1/4 31-26-3	1,200.00
W. COLLARD, et al., to Geo. F. THIES, nw 1/4, 31-25-4	3,918.25
E.B. MASON to P.H. KOHL, e 1/4, 29-27-1	7,000.00
Enos DAVIS to Robt. JONES, se 1/4 ne 1/4 2-26-1	800.00
Martin ZUTZ to Anna JOHNSON, lots 4 & 5, blk. 5, Hoskins	50.00
Neal H. NYE to R.H. LENTON, sw 1/4, 7-27-1	3,200.00
Sheriff to State B'k of Crawford, lot 15, blk. 2, Winside	670.00
State B'k of Crawford to H. WOHLERS, lot 15, blk. 2, Winside	408.00
J.H. EHLERS to Walter WEBER, w 1/2 se 1/4 31-27-1	1,200.00
F. EHLERS to Walter WEBER, sw 1/4, 31-27-1	2,220.00
O.O. WHITED to Cordelia A. McKAY, w 1/4 of blk. 3, Carroll	1.00

The Wayne Republican
November 2, 1898 (Vol. 5, No. 38)

Probable Death.

A sad case was that of the probably fatal burning of the eight months old child of Mr. and Mrs. Charles SCHMIDT on Saturday. The family was in the field digging potatoes, and the child was placed on a bunch of hay. In looking up from their work soon after the hay pile was seen to be all ablaze. The child was rescued from the fiery fiend as soon as possible but not until it was so badly burned that its recovery is very doubtful. It is not known just how the fire originated. Mr. and Mrs. SCHMIDT will have the sympathy of all in their misfortune. (Winside Tribune)

The Wayne Republican
November 9, 1898 (Vol. 5, No. 39)

BIRTH: A daughter was born to J.G. MINES and wife Tuesday morning.

LICENSED TO WED: On Monday Judge HUNTER licensed to wed George MIELKE and Grace CHRISTENSON both of Winside.

Real Estate Transfers.

Reported by I.W. ALTER, bonded abstracter, Wayne, Nebraska.

Fred EHLERS to Walter WEBER, sw 1/4 & w 1/2 se 1/4 31-27-1	$3,425.00
C.M. YOKUM to Ellis KENRICK, w 1/2 nw 1/4 10-26-1	800.00
Vaughn DAVIS to Enos O. DAVIS, e 1/2 se 1/4 35-27-1	3,000.00
F. BOWDEN and W. COLLARD to Geo. F. THEIS, nw 1/4, 31-25-4	3,918.00
State Bk of Crawford to Wm. WOHLER, lot 15, blk. 2, Winside	418.00
Sheriff of Wayne county to State Bk of Crawford, lot 15, blk. 2, Winside	668.00
N.H. NYE to R.H. LENTON, sw 1/4, 17-27-1	3,200.00
E.O. DAVIS to Robert H. JONES, se 1/4 ne 1/4 2-26-1	800.00
John C. LUDEKE to John W. GIBSON, n 1/2 lot 4, blk. 8 B&B's ad Wayne	1,200.00
Ed B. MASON to Phil H. KOHL, e 1/2, 29-27-1	7,000.00
M.E. ZUTZ to Anna JOHNSON, lots 4 & 5, blk. 5, Hoskins	50.00
M.L. GOREHAM to Sam SABENSON, lot 12, blk. 22, Wayne	1,200.00
C.F. GRAHAM to A.L. TUCKER, sw 1/4, 7-27-3	4,000.00
Matilda LINN to E.S. BLAIR, lot 1 and n 1/4 lot 2, blk. 11, N ad Wayne	1,157.00
John WINGERT to Citizens' Bk, a lt 50x150 s cf, blk. 28, Wayne	350.00
John DREVSEN to Maria C. GOTTSCH, s 1/2 sw 1/4 34-26-1	- - -

The Wayne Republican
November 16, 1898 (Vol. 5, No. 40)

BIRTH: Dr. WIGHTMAN and wife are rejoicing over the arrival of a girl baby at their home Monday.

DIED: MORAN. On Saturday night the angel of death entered the home of our townsman, T.W. MORAN and called from earth to the great beyond, Mildred, the 3-year-old daughter. The cause of death was the much dreaded diptheria. In their great bereavement the family have the deepest sympathy of the entire community.

Court in Session.

Court convened Monday afternoon Judge John S. ROBINSON presiding up to this morning the following cases have been disposes of:

WIGHTMAN vs LAUMAN, continued.
HILDRE vs HILDRE, continued.
SMITH & ELLIS vs ALGER, continued.
SASSMAN vs HURLBERT, continued.
WILSON vs BOYD, continued.
WIGHTMAN vs BOYD, continued.
MIDDLESTADT vs KRUGER, off docket.
W.A. WOOD vs TALLMAN, judg't revived.
W.A. WOOD vs OLMSTED, settled.
State vs WHITMAN, settled.
SAVIDGE vs WILCOX, not at issue.
Anthony L&T Co vs MUELLER, foreclosure granted.
GUSTINE vs CHERRY, pltf given leave to file amended answer, deft excepts.
SCRANTON vs SCRANTON, divorce granted.
CROSS vs CROSS, divorce granted.
WEBSTER vs HURLBERT, pltf given until next term of court to furnish security for costs.
State vs Henry ANDERSON. This is known as the harness-stealing case and the defendant is generally known as Klondyke. It was given to the jury in the afternoon yesterday and up to the hour of going to press no decision has been reached as to his guilt or innocence.
Nat'l Bank Commerce vs Geo. GYLES, et al., verdict for deft.

The Wayne Republican
November 23, 1898 (Vol. 5, No. 41)

BIRTH: Born to Mr. and Mrs. Sam LANE a son on November 18th.

BIRTH: Born to Mr. and Mrs. Mell CASE, November 2, bouncing boy of standard weight.

BIRTH: Born last week to T.A. BERRY and wife, a boy.

BIRTH: Born last week to Will RICKABAUGH and wife, a boy.

Hoskins Business Directory
W.C. PARSONS, general merchandise; R.G. RHORKE, general merchandise; Carl F. LEENZE, blacksmith and farm machinery; Nels NELSON, blacksmith; H.C. MANK, harnessmaker; CLINE & TEMPLIN, contractors and builders; John SHANNON, live stock, grain and coal; EDWARDS & BRADFORD, lumber, lime and coal; Knute ERICKSON, shoemaker; KAUTZ Bros., saloon; Charles GREEN, hotel; L. ZIEMER, postmaster; John DONNER, liveryman; Wm. LALK, plasterer and brick mason; Mr. HARDING, separator; Andrew JOHNSON, house mover.

Klondike the harness thief got a sentence of one year in the penitentiary, the two fellows who were arrested at Winside a few weeks ago charged with the theft of a lot of clothing, shoes, etc., from the store of Frank WEIBLE plead guilty and got a dose of a year. Mike MOORE of Sherman precinct charged with the theft of eight bushels of wheat from Roy SELLEN was after an all days trial and 42 hours of deliberation by a jury of twelve men found guilty and received a fine of $20 and costs and is committed to jail until paid.

The Wayne Republican
November 30, 1898 (Vol. 5, No. 42)

BIRTH: Ben ROBINSON and wife are rejoicing over the arrival of a boy at their home. (Carroll)

BIRTH: John KOEFOED and wife are rejoicing over the birth of a fine boy at their home. (Carroll)

MARRIED: At noon today Rev. McCOOL of West Point will at the home of the bride's parents, Mr. and Mrs. T.J. CAFFEE, in our city pronounce the words that bind in the marital tie for life the lives of Edgar A. WADE and Elnora May CAFFEE. The young people will have the best wishes of their friends for a safe and prosperous journey through life.

DIED: At her home in Hancock precinct on Sunday, November 27th, 1898, Mrs. R.G. SINES, aged 70 years. The lady leaves an aged husband, five children and a large circle of friends to mourn her departure from this world.

DIED: HUFF. At the family home northwest of Carroll on Wednesday, November 23, William HUFF was called from life to the land beyond. The deceased was born in Henderson county, Illinois, in April 56 years ago and for several years has been a resident of our county. His death was the result of kidney complications that eventually called him away after months of suffering. He leaves to mourn his departure a wife, four daughters, four sons and a large circle of acquaintances. The funeral services were held at the Baptist church in Wayne Friday afternoon and his remains laid to rest in our silent city.

The Wayne Republican
December 7, 1898 (Vol. 5, No. 43)

BIRTH: Alex FALK is the happiest man in town at present over the advent of a fine baby at his home. (Carroll)

LICENSED TO WED: Judge HUNTER issued a license to wed to William C. THIES and Edith THIES on last Thursday.

MARRIED: On Monday evening Dec. 5, at the home of George W. JONES in Wilbur precinct his daughter Roxie and Will EVANS were married in the presence of the family and a few invited guests.

DIED: Mrs. Gus BERGESON, residing near La Porte, died Tuesday, Nov. 29, the funeral was from the Swedish Lutheran church today.

DIED: Death has again invaded one of the homes of our village and called to the great beyond L.F. ROBINSON on Thursday, December 1, 1898. The deceased was born in Huron county, Ohio, in August, 1845, and moved to Iowa in 1870, was married to M.E. GRANT in 1876 and the couple came to Nebraska where they resided until 1890 when they moved to Missouri, returning to Coleridge, Nebraska, in 1894 and coming from there to this place the following year where they have resided since. The deceased leaves to mourn his going, his wife, two daughters and three sons.

At a regular meeting of CaseyPost, No. 5, G.A.R., the following officers were elected for the following year: J.D. KING, commander; Wm. F. RAMSEY, senior vice; Ami LEWIS, junior vice; A.J.

FERGUSON, chaplain; Enoch HUNTER, quarter-master; J.W. BARTLETT, officer of the day; G.W. CULLER, inside guard; C.A. BAGERT, surgeon.

The Daughters of Rebekah held their election of officers Friday evening resulting as follows: Mrs. I.W. ALTER, N.G.; Mrs. Charles WARNER, V.G.; Mrs. H.E. FOOTE, Sec'y; Mrs. S.B. RUSSELL, Treas.

At a regular meeting of Wayne Lodge, 108, A.O.U.W., Thursday, December 1, the following officers were elected: Guy R. WILBUR, M.W.; R.M. FARR, Overseer; I.W. ALTER, recorder; E. HUNTER, financier; S.B. RUSSELL, receiver; A.W. CHAFFEE, guide; R.Q. WARNOCK, I.W.; J.H. GOLL, O.W.; Mark STRINGER, trustee; Dr.'s E.S. BLAIR and G. NEIMAN, medical examiners. There was a good attendance. Everything was lively and four new applications were favorably acted upon, so that next meeting will no doubt be still more lively. If you are a member don't forget to be present at the next meeting, December 15.

Real Estate Transfers.

Reported by I.W. ALTER, Bonded Abstracter, Wayne, Nebraska.

J.D. KING to E.D. MITCHELL, und 1/2 ne 1/4 20-27-1	$1,200.00
Elizabeth SINES to Amra FOSTER, e 1/2 sw 1/4 7-25-2	1,600.00
Elizabeth SINES to Frank SINES, w 1/2 sw 1/4 7-25-2	1,600.00
Elizabeth SINES to Grant SINES, w 1/2 se 1/4 7-25-2	1,600.00
J. WEATHERHOLT to Carl JOCKINS, n 1/2 & sw 1/4 and w 1/2 of se 1/4, all in 15-25-2	18,000.00
G.G. WESTROPE to Sarah SMITH, lots 11 and 12, blk. 8, B&P's 1st ad to Winside	825.00
C. ROUNDY to Fred MUHLMEIER, ne 1/4, 15-25-1	3,200.00
Sheriff of Wayne county to Seth TALBOT, Jr., w 1/2 sw 1/4 and w 1/2 ne 1/4 10-25-1	2,319.00
L. ZIEMER to Louis LONGENBURG, sw 1/4, 24-25-1	4,000.00
Wm. NAGEL to Alfred HAGLUND, ne 1/4 nw 1/4 25-26-4	1,200.00

Allen C. FULLER to J.A. PINGREY, e 1/2, 31-25-3	$1,200.00
John CONNOR to First National Bank of Wayne, und 2/3 lot 12, blk. 13, Wayne, quit claim	1.00
John F. CROSBY to H.E. POCKRANDT, lot 2, blk. 5, B&P's 2nd ad Winside	550.00
Edwin BOWERS to Chas. S. ASH, e 1/2 nw 1/4 19-26-4	2,800.00
Edwin BOWERS to Eva ASH, n 1/2 sw 1/4 19-26-4	2,800.00
Henry GREEN to KANTZ Bros., lot 9, blk. 3, Hoskins	50.00
A.B. & Jennie SLATER to E.T. RENNICK, w 1/2, 24-25-3	3,300.00

Program Teacher's Association.
Presbyterian Church, Wayne, Dec. 10, 1898; 10 A.M.

Opening Exercises	Rev. BITHELL
How to Awaken an Interest and Secure Good Government	Jennie METTLEN
Discussion	Gertie BAYES, Winside
Country Schools, Elementary Science	E. Roy SURBER
Discussion	Nellie CAREY
Drawing	Mrs. Ella PILE

NOON.

Orthography	Paper
Discussion	Geo. PHILLEO
Should we do any 9th Grade Work in the Rural Schools	Jos. CULLEN
Reading	W.C. BONHAM

No grades were endorsed for those who do not attend association.

President, C.M. WHITE.
Secretary, Nellie MILLER.

The Wayne Republican
December 14, 1898 (Vol. 5, No. 44)

LICENSED TO WED: On Friday Judge HUNTER licensed to wed Frank LANG of Leslie precinct and Louise ERXLEBEN of Plum Creek.

LICENSED TO WED: Judge HUNTER issued a license to wed on Monday to Charles S. LARSON and Emily J. TELL, both of

Wakefield.

MARRIED: LaCROIX - MILLER. In Winside, Thursday, Dec. 8, 1898, W.R. LaCROIX and Blanche MILLER were married. The young couple are receiving the hearty congratulations of their friends.

Real Estate Transfers.

As reported by I.W. ALTER, bonded abstracter, Wayne, Nebraska:

M.P. SAVIDGE to Geo. J. SAVIDGE, an irregular tract of about 18 acres near the center of sec 18-26-4	$3,300.00
Same to same, s. 35 ft of lot 5, blk. 28, Wayne	1,200.00
F.O. JOHNSON to Carrie ANDERSON, und 1/2 of e 1/2 se 1/4 5-25-1	1,000.00
Rosa and Frank KRUGER to L.S. NEEDHAM, lot 25, blk. 5, B&P ad Winside	1.00
Elias HAIN to M. BLENKIRON, et al., lot 4, blk. 9, Carroll	400.00
Frank A. DEARBORN to F.W. BLOTZ, se 1/4, 5-27-1	3,000.00
A.S. MINER to Chas. NEISS, s 1/2 of nw 1/4 and n 1/2 of sw 1/4 10-26-4	3,920.00
Gertrude and Guy GRAVES to I.G. SLOCUM, nw 1/4 of 21-25-5	5,000.00
Clara H. BURSON to Frank KRUGER, that part of 13-26-3 lying s of lot 7, blk. 27, Wayne and n of RR right of way	- - -
John C. BENDER to Frank A. DEARBORN, s 77 ft of lot 22, blk. 4, and lot 26, blk. 3, Winside	1,500.00
Joseph GLASSON to A.L. HOWSER, lot 9, blk. 22, Wayne	1,600.00
Geo. W. and W.J. WEATHERHOLT to Ludwig ZIEMER, about 9 acres adjoining Hoskins	50.00

The Wayne Republican
December 21, 1898 (Vol. 5, No. 45)

LICENSED TO WED: On Friday Judge HUNTER licensed Fred W. BOSCHEN and Amelia H.E. TOLL to wed.

MARRIED: THARP - COX. At the home of the bride's parents Mr. and Mrs. Carter COX living 2 1/4 miles southwest of Carroll at noon today, Rev. TYSON will speak the words that join in the holy bonds of matrimony George L. THARP and Minnie COX. The groom is a son of our townsmen L.R. THARP and is a young man highly respected by all and the bride is one of Carroll's best young ladies. They begin life's voyage with the best wishes of their friends for a happy journey and amidst the hearty congratulations of all in which the Republican desires to be considered as one.

MARRIED: LANG - ERXLEBEN. At the home of the bride's father Charles ERXLEBEN, in Plum Creek, on last Wednesday evening. Frank LANG and Louise ERXLEBEN were married in the presence of an assemblage of invited guests. The young couple are well and favorably known in the southwest part of the county and their numerous friends will all join in wishing them a happy voyage n life.

At the meeting of the Camp of Modern Woodmen last evening the following officers were elected for the ensuing year: T.W. MORAN, V.C.; G.W. CROSSLAND, W.A.; T.B. HECKERT, banker; E. HUNTER, clerk; Simon FOLTZ, escort; H. LAYMAN, I.W.; J.P. HOGELAND, O.W.; Drs. WILLIAMS and BLAIR, physicians; A.H. ELLIS, manager; Dr. BLAIR, W.H. HOGUEWOOD, Phil KOHL, delegates to county convention that meets in Wayne January 10, 1899, for the purpose of choosing delegates to state convention.

The Woodmen of the World held their election of officers Saturday evening resulting as follows: Guy R. WILBUR, C.C.; F.M. HOOPER, A.L.; R.C. OSBORN, clerk; Homer SKEEN, banker; J.M. COLEMAN, escort; Mel NORTON, watchman; Dan LEGAN, sentry; Sam DAVIES, organist.

COMMISSIONER PROCEEDINGS, Wayne, Neb., Dec. 17, 1898.
Board met pursuant to adjournment. All members present.
On motion the petition of M.S. MOATS, et al., dated Sep. 26, 1898, for a public road along the north side of the right of way of the Northeast Neb. R.R. in Deer Creek and Sherman precincts is rejected.
On motion the Clerk is instructed to advertise for bids for county physician and county poor house for the year 1899; bids to be in by January 10, 1899.
On motion the following official bonds were approved:

C.M. SUNDAHL, road overseer, Dist 35.
C.C. BOSTEDER, road overseer, Dist. 3.
Aug. ZIEMER, assessor, Hoskins prec't.
John OLSON, road overseer, Dist. 11.
Perry BENSHOOF, assessor, Brenna.
Chris Hansen BLACO, road overseer, Dist. 27.
J.W. AGLER, assessor, Hunter precinct.
D.H. SURBER, road overseer, Dist. No. 9.
Jenkin DAVIS, road overseer, Dist. No. 25.
J.W. MURPHY, road overseer, Dist. No. 20.
P. COLEMAN, road overseer, Dist. No. 30.
C.W. REED, road overseer, Dist. No. 46.
T.J. THOMAS, road overseer, Dist. No. 44.
Jacob REICHERT, road overseer, Dist. No. 33.
Robt. FENSKI, assessor, Hancock prec't.
P. COLEMAN, assessor, Plum Creek.
Board adjourned to Dec. 26, 1898, at 9 o'clock a.m.
J.R. COYLE, Clerk.

The Wayne Republican
December 28, 1898 (Vol. 5, No. 46)

LICENSED TO WED: Judge HUNTER on Saturday licensed A. MARSH and Lovena CASTANETTE to wed.

LICENSED TO WED: Judge HUNTER has licensed Bert OMAN and Mary TEDRICK to wed.

DIED: The wife of T.N. ARMACOST who lives in the RENNICK neighborhood died at her home on Saturday and was interred at this place on Monday.

The City of Wayne
Improves During the Year to the
Tune of over $50,000.00.
Next Year Will Surpass It.

When the people of Wayne count up the building improvements of their city for the year 1898, they have just cause for gratification at the result. It shows a marked improvement over the conditions that prevailed for a few years previous and indicates that the city is again on the forward movement and all indications at the present time point to a greater showing for the next year. By the courtesy of the Herald we are enabled to present a detailed statement of the building operations:
Presbyterian Church $10,000

Electric light system	$4,500
Brick engine house	1,000
Robt. MELLOR, residence	4,500
Chas. LUND, residence and barn	3,500
F.L. NEELY, residence	1,300
M.P. AHERN, add residence	800
J.F. SHERBAHN, brick yards	1,600
Ward school addition	2,200
PHILLEO & Son, machine house and improvements	1,500
A. McINTOSH, cottage	750
C.A. GROTHE, elevator, etc.	1,200
A.J. FERGUSON, add. residence	700
F.W. BURDICK, add. residence	350
J.O. MILLIGAN, imp. store	500
E.P. OLMSTED & Co., additions	500
DEPLER & WILLIAMS, wagon shop	275
L.S. WINSOR, improvements	150
E. HUNTER, add. residence	150
Will WEBER, addition	600
WEBER Bros., Roller Mill imp.	500
C.M. WHITE, cottage	450
H. MILDNER, add. residence	400
H. MILDNER, add. saloon	100
Mrs. H. MYERS, improvements	75
P.L. MILLER, add. residence	1,000
F. STRAHAN, add. residence	500
MILLER & SWAN, Store bldg.	3,000
College dormitory	3,500
Wm. PIEPENSTOCK, add. store	500
A.F. BRENNER, add elevator	1,000
Omaha Brew'g Co., cold storage	500
Electric light fixtures in bldgs	500
F.M. SKEEN, add. to ten. house	500
Miscellaneous improvements	3,000
	$51,395

The Wayne Republican
January 4, 1899 (Vol. 5, No. 47)

BIRTH: C.G. NIEMAN and wife are rejoicing over the birth of a daughter.

MARRIED: CLARK - MINER. At the county Judge's office Saturday evening December 31, 1898, Frank A. CLARK and Della MINER, both of Wakefield.

MARRIED: LYON - PERDUE. At the home of the bride's parents, Mr. and Mrs. James T. PERDUE, residing just east of the city, occurred on Sunday afternoon, January 1, 1899, the marriage of their daughter Sadie to O.D. LYON of Madison county. The ceremony was performed by Rev. LEMON of the Baptist church of this city in the presence of the immediate friends, relatives and a few invited guests. The home was beautifully decorated for the occasion and an excellent repast served following the ceremony and congratulations. The bride is well known in the city and vicinity and while we are unacquainted with the groom yet we are certain that he must be worthy of the very estimable lady that he has won as his companion for life's battles. The heartiest congratulations of the Republican are herewith extended.

Crystal Wedding

About sixty of the friends of Mr. and Mrs. E.A. SURBER met at the pleasant home Tuesday evening, December 27, to help celebrate the fifteenth anniversary of their marriage. After a sociable time and a bountiful supper the guests departed for their homes wishing "mine host" many happy returns of the day and hoping they might celebrate another anniversary tinged with silver. The presents received were as follows: Berry and sauce dishes, E. VAUGHN and wife; Fruit dish, Miss Lizzie BROWN; China dish, D. SULLIVAN and wife; Water set, fruit dish and salt and pepper holders, Messrs. FORBES, MELLICK, ATKINS and wives; Pair linen towels and berry dish, C. SHULTHIES and wife; Tea set, J. CULLEN; Water set, Messrs. LAURIE, GOSS, PORTER and wives; Fruit dish, Alice BROWN; Cracker dish, Maude SPAHR; Berry and sauce dishes, J.M. LLOYD and family; Fancy dish, Howard PORTER and wife; Cream and sugar holder, Florence and Maude SERBER.

Real Estate Transfers.

J.T. BRESSLER to W.C. WIGHTMAN, lot 4, blk. 10, B&B's ad to Wayne	$500.00
S.Q. HOGUE to W.M. WRIGHT, se 1/4, 18-26-2	3,600.00
J.R. MANNING to R.D. MERRILL, lot 7, blk. 8, Carroll	1,741.00
B.F. SWAN to Aug WESTERHAUS, e 1/2 ne 1/4 6-25-3 and se 1/4 se 1/4 36-26-3	1,900.00
Henry C. HOPE to Robert R. SMITH, lot 18, blk. 4, Winside	25.00

Mary J. BARBER to Gilbert E. FRENCH, ne 1/4, 20-27-3	$2,880.00
C.E. PERKINS to Jos. GLASSON, se 1/4, 11-25-1	1,000.00
DEARBORN & BURR to John BENDER, nw 1/4 nw 1/4 and s 1/2 nw 1/4 6-25-1	1,500.00
Merchants State Bank to J.R. COOKUS, lot 1, blk. 6, Winside	2,740.00
C.B. FRENCH to Miles R. LIVINGSTON, sw 1/4 of 19 and nw 1/4 of nw 1/4 of 30-27-1	3,834.00
Geo. A. RICHARDS to Marie S. WATERBURY, 1/8 interest in se 1/4 1-25-2	340.00
Wm. ZUTZ to Henry GREEN, pt se 1/4 nw 1/4 27-25-1	40.00
Fred WICHMAN to Fred MEIERHENRICH, nw 1/4, 35-25-1	4,000.00

The Wayne Republican
January 11, 1899 (Vol. 5, No. 48)

MARRIED: It is rumored that Rudolph LANGE and Millie KAY are to be married Wednesday, February 15, 1899. While we may be a little premature in our congratulations yet they are freely offered.

MARRIED: JONES - GLASS. In the city of Wayne, Judge HUNTER officiating, William E. JONES of Carroll and Elsie GLASS of Norfolk. The young couple have the congratulations of the Republican and a large circle of friends.

DIED: Last night, January 10, at 6:20, death entered the home of our townsman Frank E. STRAHAN and took therefrom very unexpectedly the youngest child a little boy less than one year old. The parents are sadly bereaved and have the sympathy of a host of sincere friends in their bereavement.

DIED: Last evening, January 10, at 6:20, death entered our city and called from life to the great beyond our beloved and much respected citizen James BARBOUR. The deceased was born in Renfrewshire, Scotland, in 1828 and came to American in 1854. On August 21, 1856, he was married to Mary YOUNG in Cook county, Illinois, where the couple lived for two years and then moved to Will county, remaining there until February, 1884, when they moved to our county and have been among our best and most respected citizens until the present time. Four children came to bless the union, three of whom, Mrs. Adam GRIER, Mrs. Brown PALMER and J.A. BARBOUR with the aged wife and mother, are left to mourn the death of one of the best husbands and fathers that ever lived. In his death our county loses one of its most valuable citizens and the stricken family will have the sympathy of all in their great loss. The funeral will take place from the Presbyterian church Friday afternoon at 2 o'clock.

Death of Mrs. Lydia MARSHALL MEARS.

Mrs. Lydia MARSHALL MEARS died at the home of her daughter, Mrs. STALLSMITH, Tuesday, January 3, 1899 at 8:15 p.m. aged 74 years, 5 months, 8 days.

Lydia MARSHALL was born in Guernsey county, Ohio, July 26, 1824, and was married to Peter MEARS May 23, 1844. Soon after the marriage she united with the Washington township Baptist church of Muskingum county, Ohio. In September, 1855, she with her husband moved to Iowa, living at Mt. Pleasant, Brooklyn and later at Grinnell. In the spring of 1879 she moved to Wayne county, Nebraska, where she has since resided. There was born to her three sons and six daughters, all of whom survive her except one. They are Mrs. Hettie HOGUE of Kansas City, Kansas, Mrs. Jennie STALLSMITH, Mrs. Lydia BENSON, William MEARS, Wayne county, Nebraska, Mrs. Sadie MILLS of Nekoma, Kansas, Mrs. Mary CROSS, Grant S. MEARS and Mrs. Edith CHERRY, Wayne, Neb.

She lived to see 24 grandchildren, 23 of whom are still living, and one great grandchild.

The funeral services were conducted at the Baptist church, in Wayne, by Rev. LEMON, on Tuesday, Jan. 5, 1899, assisted by Rev. BITHELL, of the M.E. church.

Thus another earthly life is run, but not in vain for her influence still lives in the lives of those with whom she loved to mingle,

>Death has been here and born away,
>Our darling from our fold;
>He took dear mother up to Heaven
>To walk the streets of gold.
>
>We are grieved to part with Mother
>Who was light and life of home,
>We will see her over yonder
>When we meet no more to roam.

She has gone to be with Jesus,
One more tie beckons us on
To the land that knows no sorrow,
Knows no clouds nor setting sun.

We will praise our dear Redeemer
For we know she is secure
From the trials and the pain
Which all mankind must endure.

Then let us not weep for our loved one
All spotless and robed in white,
But live so we'll meet in Heaven
When our spirits take their flight.

-- A.B.

A tribute to the memory of little Maggie, daughter of Mr. and Mrs. G. DAVIS, who died at their home southwest of Carroll, November 20, 1898 age one year and four days:

There's another home that's darkened
By the chilling hand of Death;
There's a little one that's missing
From the home around the hearth.

You will miss your little darling
In the coming weary years.
You will miss her, you will miss her
Traveling in this vale of tears.

But today she knows no sorrow;
Pain nor grief can't mar her face,
For she's with the happy angels
Singing the Redeemer's praise.

Then cease weeping, loving parents
For the one that knows no pain
For the Living God has promised
The pure in heart shall meet again.

-- Mrs. Evan JENKINS
Carroll, Neb.

One of the most pleasant social events in Lodge circles took place Monday evening, the occasion being a public installation of officers of the I.O.O.F. and Rebekah lodges.

After installing the officers of the I.O.O.F. lodge, Miss Lulu COOK sang a very pretty solo which was heartily appreciated by all present. The officers of the Rebekah lodge were then installed, after which Mrs. HARRISON sang one of her solos in a very charming manner being accompanied by Miss ARMSTRONG.

The Rebekah's then gave their floor drill in such an "a la militarie" way that it made the members of the subordinate lodge feel rather insignificant.

Then came the even of the evening, the supper, and a more jolly crowd never sat down to do justice to a repast than they. The tables were then cleared from the room and the brothers thought they might even up matters by showing the ladies how they could march. After retiring from the room, their captain, Mark JEFFREY, announced the working team of the lodge and in they came attired in their robes. They made a very pretty showing and were vigorously applauded, although their drill was not equal to the ladies', considering they have drilled over eight years and the Rebekah's only three evenings.

Then came the good of the order, the audience having the privilege of listening to some very interesting remarks by several of those present, after which all departed for their homes feeling that they had spend an enjoyable evening as well as a profitable one.

District Deputy J.J.W. FOX installed the following officers of Wayne lodge No. 118: N.G., N.I. JUHLIN, V.G., Ira C. RICHARDS; Sec., Chas WARNER; Treas., Henry LEY; W.G., A. BENSON; C., Jas. PORTERFIELD; R.S.N.G., A.B. JEFFREY; L.S.N.G., Chas. HOLTGREN; Chaplain, S.B. RUSSELL; I.G.J.M., G. HARRISON; O.G., Chas. HOSTETTER; R.S.S., Will RICKABAUGH; L.S.S., John RILEY; R.S.V.G., Geo. J. SAVIDGE; L.S.V.G., Ed SHULTHEIS.

Mrs. Cora A. BEELS of Norfolk installed the following officers of Protection Rebekah lodge No. 122: N.G., Mrs. I.W. ALTER; V.G., Mrs. Chas. WARNER; Sec., Mrs. Lulu FOOTE; Treas., Mrs. S.B. RUSSELL; W., Miss Ethel WILLIAMS; C., Mrs. Will RICKABAUGH; I.G., Mrs. G.A. BENSON; O.G., Mrs. N.I. JUHLIN; R.S.N.G., Mrs. Chas. SHULTHEIS; L.S.N.G., Mrs. B. CUNNINGHAM; Chap., Mrs. John KREITLE; R.S.V.G., Mrs. Wm. VINCENT; L.S.V.G., Mrs. A. GOULD.

The Wayne Republican
January 18, 1899 (Vol. 5, No. 49)

LICENSED TO WED: This morning Judge HUNTER issued a license to wed to Wm. KOCH and Elsie WESTERHAUS.

LICENSED TO WED: Yesterday Judge HUNTER issued license to wed to E.L. CHICHESTER of Walnut, Kansas, and Bethia NORTON of Wayne.

MARRIED: PRINCE - PULLEN. At the home of the county judge on Saturday evening, January 16, Herbert C. PRINCE and Maggie PULLEN were married.

MARRIED: CLARK - TAYLOR. At the home of the bride's parents Mr. and Mrs. Joseph TAYLOR near Carroll Rev. BITHEL will this evening unite in marriage George CLARK and Miss Amy TAYLOR. The groom is the son of S.M. CLARK, one of the well known and highly respected farmers of Wilbur precinct, and the bride is as we have stated above, the daughter of Mr. and Mrs. TAYLOR and is one that is very highly respected and much beloved by all. The Republican extends congratulations.

Last night was the Woodmen's and Royal Neighbors' night for a glorious old time and from all that we can learn they had it. The Woodmen installed T.W. MORAN, V.C.; G.W. CROSSLAND, W.A.; T.B. HECKERT, banker; E. HUNTER, clerk; Simon FOLTZ, Escort; Henry LAYMAN, I.W.; and J.P. HOGELAND, O.W. The Royal Neighbors which as our readers are aware is the ladies auxiliary of the Woodmen installed Mrs. A.H. ELLIS, oracle; Mrs. G.W. CROSSLAND, recorder; Mrs. BRENNER, chancellor; Mrs. W.L. JONES, marshal; Mrs. LAUMAN and HOGUEWOOD as sentinels. The exercises at the camps were such as to be highly entertaining to all and the banquet at the Little Delmonico was heartily enjoyed by all.

COMMISSIONER PROCEEDINGS, Wayne, Neb., Jan. 10, 1899.
    Board of county commissioners met in regular session. Present Commissioners RUSSELL, ZIEGLER and Carroll and Clerk COYLE.
    On motion the following official bonds were approved.
    Chas. MILLER, road overseer Dist. No. 7.
    W.A.K. NEELY, road overseer Dist. No. 39.
    T.E. HILL, road overseer Dist. No. 12.
    Geo. WHIPPERMAN, road overseer Dist. No. 10.

John BEALE, road overseer Dist. No. 22.
P. PRYOR, road overseer Dist. No. 48.
W.A. JONES, road overseer Dist. No. 29.
Adam GRIER, road overseer Dist. No. 40.
A. LOHBERG, road overseer Dist. No. 43.
G.W. SCHWERGALD, road overseer Dist. No. 48.
Jas BAYDERS, road overseer Dist. No. 16.
Cal RITCHEY, road overseer Dist. No. 31.
Anton JENSEN, road overseer Dist. No. 32.
Levi DILTZ, road overseer Dist. No. 16.
Herman DECK, road overseer Dist. No. 51.
W.B. GROAT, road overseer Dist. No. 36.
Thos. CASSON, road overseer Dist. No. 38.
Jay E. WILSON, road overseer Dist. No. 4.
P.L. RANSDELL, road overseer Dist. No. 52.
John H. COOK, road overseer Dist. No. 17.
Fred UTECT, road overseer Dist. No. 1.
J.P. MARVIN, assessor, Winside precinct.
H.E. HANSON, assessor, Wilbur precinct.
Levi DILTZ, assessor, Logan precinct.
J.R. WASHBURN, assessor, Chapin precinct.
J.S. BAKER, assessor, Sherman precinct.
F.E. FRANCES, assessor, Garfield precinct.
Aug. WITTLER, assessor, Strahan precinct.

Bids for county physician for the year 1899 were opened as advertised. The bid for Dr. A.L. MUIRHEAD being the lowest, on motion the said A.L. MUIRHEAD was appointed physician for the year beginning Jan. 10, 1899, at a salary of $118.99 per year, payable quarterly.

Bids for stationery for the year 1899 were opened and the matter laid over until the next day.

On motion the county attorney's salary was fixed at $800 per year.

On motion the county superintendent's salary was fixed at $800 per year.

On motion Adam GRIER was appointed road overseer for district 40 and bond approved.

On motion board adjourned to Jan. 11, 1899, at 9 a.m.

J.R. COYLE, Clerk.

COMMISSIONER PROCEEDINGS, Wayne, Neb., Jan. 11, 1899.

Board met pursuant to adjournment all members present.

Comes now E. CUNNINGHAM of the Wayne Republican and withdraws his bid for county attorney for the ensuing year.

Comes now W.H. McNEAL of the Wayne Herald and

withdraws his bid for county stationery for the ensuing year.

Comes now W.S. GOLDIE of the Nebraska Democrat and withdraws his bid for county stationery for the ensuing year.

On motion the contracts for stationery and blanks for the year 1899 was let to the Wayne Herald and Nebraska Democrat, the work to be equally distributed between the two papers.

On motion the contract for supplies was awarded to the State Journal Co., Lincoln, Neb.

The following is a list of names selected from which to draw jurors for the Feb. 1899 term of district court.

Plum Creek - W.T. POWELL, F.C. KEENAN, Phil THOMPSON.

Hunter - Nels NELSON, Mark JEFFREY, Wm. VINCENT, Homer GRAVES.

Leslie - Frank HILL, Jake CHILCUTT.

Logan - John HARRISON, Eph ANDERSON.

Wayne 2nd ward - W. SKADDEN, Wm. HOUSE, Henry MERRIMAN, Geo. HEADY.

Hoskins - Charley DOBBIN, A.T. WADDELL, Chas. GREEN, John WEATHERHOLT, Chas. MOSS.

Garfield - Wm. JENKINS, Joe DOBBIN, Frank JAMES.

Sherman - D.M. DAVIS, J.T. KENNY, H. BURNHAM.

Hancock - Wm. FLETCHER, Perrin LONG, Sam LANE.

Chapin - C.M. SUNDALL, B.P. PETERSON, Jacob BRUGGER.

Winside - Thos LOUND, Frank BROWER, E.W. CULLEN.

Deer Creek - James STEPHENS, Henry BILLETER, Fred BARTELLS, T.M. WOODS, August LOHBERG.

Brenna - Albert TIDRICK, Wm. McMILLIN, Perry BENSHOOF, Mat THIES.

Strahan - H. KLOPPING, John OWENS, G.G. HALLER, F.M. HOSTETTER, J.B. STALLSMITH.

Wilber - John HARDER, Andy CAMPBELL, Geo. JONES.

Wayne 1st ward - Peter COYLE, G.A. BENSON, G.P. HITCHCOCK.

Wayne 3d ward - W.F. RAMSEY, Theo DUERIG, J.A. LOVE, A.J. FERGUSON, Robt MELLOR.

State of Nebraska, Wayne county, ss. I, J.R. COYLE, county clerk in and for said county, hereby certify that the foregoing is a true and correct list of the names selected by the board of commissioners from which to draw petit Jurors for the February, 1899, term of the district court of Wayne county, Nebraska.

Witness my hand and official seal this 11th day of January, A D 1899.   J.R. COYLE, County Clerk.

The following claims were allowed:

F.M. HOOPER, settlement	$39.75
S.K. BRUNER, settlement	37.50
John FERRIS, settlement	34.50
D.H. SURBER, settlement	30.00
T.J. THOMAS, settlement	30.00
Andrew F. JOHNSON, settlement	27.00
John KEOFOED, settlement	30.00
L. SIMMERMAN, settlement	30.00
S.C. BRESSLER, settlement	30.00
Geo. H. SNELL, settlement	30.00
W.W. BURNHAM, settlement	31.50
Jacob REICHERT, settlement	30.00
Edward MILLER, settlement	36.00
J.J. MOORE, settlement	43.50
C.D. JONES, settlement	31.25
J.W. AGLER, settlement	37.50
August LOHBERG, settlement	37.50
Henry HODSON, settlement	40.65
W.H. EASTBURN, settlement	35.00
G.W. SCHWEIGARD, settlement	24.00
John OLESON, settlement	18.00
Anton JENSEN, settlement	30.75
C.O. SELLAR, settlement	34.75
James STEPHENS, settlement	32.25
W.C. LOWRY, settlement	28.00
Peter BRUMMELS, settlement	49.00
J.H. ATKINS, settlement	30.00
Herman DECK, settlement	37.50
C. SCHNEIDER, settlement	35.00
Jenkin DAVIS, settlement	30.00
Wm. PRINCE, settlement	30.00
E.O. BEHMER, settlement	42.00
Wm. SPITTGARBER, settlement	22.00
Fred UTECT, settlement	30.00
Levi DILTZ, settlement	30.00
John HARDER, settlement	31.50
T.E. HILL, settlement	30.00
Pat COLEMAN, settlement	30.00
W.A.K. NEELY, settlement	30.00
Geo. OMAN, settlement	30.00
Alex CAMPBELL, settlement	30.00

The Wayne Republican
January 25, 1899 (Vol. 5, No. 50)

MARRIED: CHICHESTER - NORTON. On Wednesday evening, Jan. 18, 1898, the marriage of E.L. CHICHESTER of Walnut, Kansas, and Bethia NORTON of our city was solemized at the home of the bride's parents Mr. and Mrs. Mel. NORTON in our city, Rev. LEMON of the Baptist church officiating. The groom is the son of E. CHICHESTER of Walnut, Kansas, a former resident of our city and a young man very well known and highly respected by many of our residents. The bride is one of Wayne's best and fairest daughters, a graduate of the schools in our county. We understand the young couple will make their future home in Kansas and wherever they go the best wishes of a host of friends will follow them and hope that their's may be a pleasant voyage through life.

MARRIED: That was a very neat surprise that Ed OWENS so successfully carried out in quietly taking a trip a couple of weeks ago and informing or allowing the impression to go out among his friends that he was going to Rushville to look after some cattle interests of the firm and instead of doing this he met Miss Anna RUSH at Norfolk and they proceeded to Omaha where they were married and are now at home on the farm west of the city. The numerous friends of Ed are offering their congratulations and he accepts the same very gracefully.

MARRIED: Mr. Sherman WEATHERHOLT, of Wayne county, and Miss Lena STENNER of Pierce were united in marriage by Rev. G.M. COUFFER on Wednesday, the 18th inst. The bride has been a resident of Pierce since her girlhood and has a warm circle of friends who will wish her joy and happiness in her new life. The groom is highly spoken of as an energetic and well to do young man. The couple left the same evening for their home at Hoskins.

DIED: BEHRES. On Sunday, January 22, the dreaded messenger of death entered the home of George BEHRES living south of the city and claimed two victims, a boy of about six and a girl of eight or nine years. Both children died of inflamation of the brain. The boy had been sick for about a week, but the girl went to bed Saturday evening in good health as usual and along in the night awoke very ill and shortly became unconscious and died Sunday afternoon, the brother passing away during the early morning hours. It is a terrible affliction and the heartbroken parents have the sympathy of the entire community.

DIED: STRAHAN. On Saturday night, Don, the 22-months-old son of Mr. and Mrs. Frank STRAHAN, was summoned to the great beyond by the angel of death. The cause of the little one's demise was lagrippe and, as our readers are aware, this is the second one to be called away from this home within the past three weeks. The bereaved family have all the sympathy that earthly friends can give in their time of extreme sorrow.

The Wayne Republican
February 1, 1899 (Vol. 5, No. 51)

BIRTH: Mr. and Mrs. B.F. SWAN are rejoicing over the birth of a boy at their home yesterday.

LICENSED TO WED: Licensed to wed January 27, Rudolph LONG and Amelia KAY, both of Leslie precinct.

MARRIED: The marriage of Wm. SHANNAHAN of North Bend, Neb., to Miss Kate HEALEY of Wayne was solemonized at St. Mary's church in this city at 8 a.m. last Wednesday, Father FITZGERALD officiating, Peter HEALEY from Beemer brother of the bride, and Miss CAULEY were best man and lady. The bride has a host of friends in Wayne county and elsewhere who will wish her a happy wedded life. Mr. SHANNAHAN is a well-to-do citizen of North Bend. (Democrat)

DIED: J.W. HAINES was born at Mt. Pleasant, Iowa on Feb. 23, 1860, and died near Carroll, Neb., on Jan. 23, 1899. He was united in marriage with Melissa McPHERRON at Mt. Pleasant in 1882, and became a member of the Methodist church during the same year. He later removed to Pottawatamie county where he resided for three years and then with his family came to Wayne county which has sine been his home until his death which was caused by liver and kidney complaint. He leaves to mourn his death, a mother, several sisters and brothers, a wife and five young daughters, the oldest sixteen and the youngest six. Deceased was well and favorably known throughout Wayne county and leaves a host of friends who sympathize with the stricken family in this sad bereavement. The funeral services were conducted by Rev. BITHEL of Wayne at the Methodist church in Carroll on Tuesday at eleven o'clock and the remains were laid to rest in the Carroll cemetery.

> O thou who mournest on the way,
> With longings for the close of day -
> He walks with thee, that angel kind,

And gently whispers, "be resigned."
Bear up, bear on, the end shall tell
The dear Lord orderth all things well.

FUNERAL: The funeral of the child of Mr. and Mrs. GRANT occurred on Monday. The remains of the dear one were taken to Wayne and there laid to rest. (Carroll)

FUNERAL: The funeral services of J.W. HAINES who passed away on Saturday evening were held in the M.E. church of this place yesterday and was largely attended by friends and neighbors of the deceased. (Carroll)

Sales.

Feb. 8, Nels SWANSON sells horses, cattle, hogs and farm implements, on Wm. PARK's farm 3 miles west and 1 1/2 miles north of Wakefield.

Victor CARLSON living on the LEISENRING farm 11 miles west of Wayne will sell Tuesday, February 21, at 12 o'clock 12 cows and heifers, 5 work horses, 20 sows in pig, some hay and all his farm implements.

J.A. BARBOUR will sell at his home 3 miles northeast of Wayne at 12 o'clock, Friday, February 17, horses, cattle, hogs, machinery and household furniture.

Feb. 3, N.H. PETERSON 1 mile south and 1 mile east of Wakefield will sell cattle, horses, hogs and farm implements.

Feb. 14, Charles SHULTHEIS northwest of Wayne 7 miles will sell horses, cattle, hogs and farm implements.

February 6 Levi DILTS will sell at his farm south of Wakefield a lot of Herefords and Jerseys.

February 10, Benjamin PORTER, 2 miles east and 2 miles south of La Porte will sell hogs, cattle and farm implements.

Lillie F. ROBINSON will sell at her home 1 1/2 miles south of Carroll on Feb. 13, 43 head of cows, heifers and calves, several head of horses and a lot of implements.

Real Estate Transfers.

Reported by I.W. ALTER, bonded abstractor, Wayne, Neb.

J.H. PINGREY to Wm. MELLOR, w 1/2, 20-26-3	$8,000.00
E.D. MITCHELL to D.C. MAIN, und 1/3 sw 1/4 32-26-2	1,000.00
Chas. M. CRAVEN to M. CRAVEN, e 1/2 of lot 3, blk. 7, B&B's ad to Wayne	100.00

Wm. ZUTZ to Wm. PFIEL,
    nw 1/4, 16-26-1 — $1,800.00

W.M. WRIGHT to C.M. HURLBERT,
    lot 18, T&W's ad to Wayne — 520.00

Frank KRUGER, et al., to Hans HOLM,
    w 1/2 of se 1/4, 26-25-2 — 1,800.00

Henry C. McCREADY to Sarah A. McCREADY,
    pt of 13-26-3 and out lot 7 C&B's ad to Wayne — 150.00

Frances J. & Geo. P. ARTLEY to Geo. B. BUSH,
    pt nw 1/4 of ne 1/4, 18-26-4, about 11 acres — 3,000.00

Catherine CHAFFEE to Mary E. JONES,
    lots 4, 5 and 6, blk. 10, College hill ad to Wayne — 110.00

Melissa SWEIGART, et al., to W.M. WRIGHT,
    sw 1/4, 12-26-3 — 4,900.00

Elizabeth CHILDS to Ella J.I. WILBUR,
    lot 15, blk. 4 — 1,200.00

Rosa KRUGER to G.H. GLASER,
    e 25 ft of lot 2, blk. 7, Winside — 900.00

P.H. SHUMWAY to Levi DILTZ,
    s 1/2 nw 1/4 9-26-5 — 2,500.00

Carl STARMM to R.D. MERRILL,
    lot 4, blk. 1, Carroll — 200.00

O.O. WHITED to Carl STARMM,
    lot 4, blk. 1, Carroll — 1.00

Stella CHERRY to Allen B. CHERRY,
    lot 4, blk. 6, B&P's ad to Winside — 100.00

J.J. HAYES to Lena REICHERT,
    lot 7, blk. 4, Winside — 400.00

Mary TITSWORTH to L.C. TITSWORTH,
    sw 1/4 of se 1/4 and the se of se 1/4 and ne 1/4 of nw 1/4 and nw 1/4 of ne 1/4 8-25-3 — 1.00

Emily CHAPMAN to Chas. FISHER,
    lots 1 and 2, blk. 2, S&S's ad to Wayne — 200.00

State of Nebraska to C.S. KNIGHT,
    section 16-27-3 — 4,480.00

S.B. RUSSELL to John C. BENDER,
    lot 7, blk. 5, B&P's 2nd ad to Winside — 25.00

The Wayne Republican
February 8, 1899 (Vol. 5, No. 52)

BIRTH: James McINTOSH and wife have a fine boy baby at their home.

Wayne County, Nebraska, Newspaper Abstracts, 1876 - 1899

BIRTH: Herbert WORTH is the papa of a fine baby girl, which arrived at his home last Monday. (Wakefield Journal)

LICENSED TO WED: Herbert PHILLIPS and Edith O. DARNELL.

MARRIED: Judge HUNTER married C. Henry ALBERS and Maggie JENSEN on Friday.

DIED: RUSSELL. At the family home in Leslie precinct, Tuesday, February 7, 1899, Margaret, wife of Richard RUSSELL was called from this to the great beyond. In the deceased our readers will recognize the wife of the chairman of the board of commissioners of Wayne county. It has been impossible up to time of going to press to get any particulars as all that is known is the information contained in a brief telegram yesterday to John T. BRESSLER conveying the sad intelligence. It is learned, however, that the lady was recently afflicted with measles which is supposed to be the cause of death. The people of the county sympathize with husband and children in the loss of wife and mother.

Fifty-Fifth Wedding Anniversary.

That is what our townsman J.H. PINGREY and his estimable wife did at their home in our city on February 1st, 1899. It is seldom that man and wife are allowed to travel life's path hand in hand for that number of years and we are happy to be able to congratulate our venerable friends in being among the fortunate ones. In their home on that day surrounded by children, grand and great grand children they passed the day in a fitting manner and but for the place made vacant by the death of their only daughter during the past year the circle would have been complete. In their declining days the aged couple can look back on the years of their past life with no regrets for having allowed precious moments to pass without improving them and their labors have been most abundantly blessed and the word is better for their being among its sons and daughters. We trust that year after year as the anniversary of their wedding comes and goes they and their friends may have an unbroken circle until the diamond anniversary may be passed.

The Wayne Republican
February 15, 1899 (Vol. 6, No. 1)

BIRTH: A fine boy arrived at the home of J.T. KENNY on Thursday last.

BIRTH: Born, on Monday to Lawrence BROWN and wife, south of Wayne, a nice baby boy.

DIED: STINROD. On Friday night, Feb. 10, 1899, Dan STINROD died at his home in this city of lockjaw arising from injuries to one of his hands received about two weeks prior to his death. The deceased was born in Virginia almost 57 years ago and for a number of years has been a resident of our city. By his death seven children are left without a parents care, the wife and mother having preceded him to the grave less than a year ago. Mr. STINROD was an old soldier, having served in the navy during the great civil war. The sympathy of the entire community will go out to the orphaned children in their great bereavement.

DIED: WHITNEY. On Tuesday morning, Mamie, the four year old daughter of A.D. WHITNEY, of congestion of the lungs. The deceased had only been sick a few days and not considered seriously ill until a few hours before her death. The Republican extends to the parents, brother and sisters the sympathy of the community in this their dark hour.

To the memory of Freddie, son of Mr. and Mrs. T.D. JONES, who died at Red Oak, Iowa, where he had been on a visit with them and was taken sick there with lung fever and died January 18, 1899, aged 11 months, and was buried in the Welsh cemetery south of Carroll.

We are called once more together,
Round the grave of one we love,
One we cherished so with gladness,
One that is gone to his home above.

How we miss you little Freddie,
How we miss your smiling face,
How we miss you little prattle
All the long and weary days.

There's a little empty cradle,
There's a little vacant chair,
There are hearts that are almost breaking,
There are souls filled with despair.

For this little flower was blooming
Like a flower on a summer's day,
But in the few short hours of sickness,
Death's cold hand swept it away.

Weep not then dear parents,
For your Freddie bright and fair,
For he is fairer now than ever,
Up above the golden stair.

- - Mrs. Eva JENKINS

Court Proceedings.

WIGHTMAN vs LAUMAN, continued.
SASSMAN vs HURLBERT, continued.
McCormick H. Co. vs John GUSTAFSON, judgment for plaintiff.
BURR vs KIEPKE, et al., sale confirmed.
LINDELL vs STROMSBURG, sale confirmed.
WEBSTER vs HURLBERT, dismissed at plaintiffs cost.
STEWART vs CLARK, dismissed at plaintiffs cost.
JOHNSON vs JORDEN, settled and dismissed.
State of Nebraska vs. CHAPMAN, settled and dismissed.
State of Nebraska vs HARRIGFELDT, dismissed. This is the case in which defendant was charged with an assault.
State of Nebraska vs HARRIGFELDT, defendant plead guilty to carrying concealed weapons and was fined $50 and costs.
LEATHERBY vs LEATHERBY, divorce granted to plaintiff and she given custody of minor child.
BAER vs Dakota Mtg and Loan Co., foreclosure ordered.
MELLOR vs HOFELDT, foreclosure ordered.
MELLOR vs CONLEY, foreclosure ordered.
FOX vs EDSON, et al., foreclosure ordered.

Sales.

Bion PORTER will sell horses and machinery on his farm 5 miles northwest of Wayne on Feb. 24th.
On Thursday March 2, 1899, D.L. HUGHES will sell at his farm 4 miles southwest of Carroll and 9 miles northwest of Winside, 18 head of cows, yearlings and calves, a lot of high bred hogs and horses, implements and household goods. Sale to commence at 12 o'clock.
On Tuesday Feb. 28, 1899, N.E. LARSEN 2 miles east and 5 miles north of Wayne will sell cattle, hogs, horses and implements.
Victor CARLSON living on the LEISENRING farm 11 miles

west of Wayne will sell Tuesday, February 21, at 12 o'clock 12 cows and heifers, 5 work horses, 20 sows in pig, some hay and all his farm implements.

J.A. BARBOUR will sell at his home 3 miles northeast of Wayne at 12 o'clock, Friday, February 17, horses, cattle, hogs, machinery and household furniture.

Chester SLAUGHTER living in Leslie precinct will on Monday, February 20, sell cattle, hogs and implements. He is going to quit the farm.

Bur CUNNINGHAM will sell on his farm three miles south of Wayne at 12 o'clock February 23, all his cattle, horses, hogs, and implements. Free lunch at noon.

On account of the severity of the weather on last Wednesday the Public Sale of Nels SWANSON living on Park Hill in Dixon county was postponed until Wednesday, February 22, when it will come off without fail.

Don't fail to attend Victor CARLSON's sale 11 miles west of Wayne next Tuesday, February 21, at 12 o'clock.

The Wayne Republican
February 22, 1899 (Vol. 6, No. 2)

BIRTH: Born to Mr. and Mrs. C.E. VAUGHN Monday, February 13, a fine boy baby and Grandpa LONGNECKER feels awful proud of the lad.

MARRIED: CUNNINGHAM - BROWN. At the home of the bride's mother, Mrs. M.S. MERRILL in Vermillion, S.D., on Wednesday, February 15, M.O. CUNNINGHAM and Dottie BROWN were married. To many in the city and county surrounding this event was not altogether unexpected and yet it came as a surprise to most of us. The groom is a young man that is very widely known in this county, being a son of B. CUNNINGHAM one of the county's best farmers, and having been for a number of years a teacher in the schools of the county. He is a graduate of the law department of the Nebraska State University and is at present having a very successful practice in his chosen profession in the city of Omaha. He is a young man of sterling qualities and one fully deserving of the excellent wife obtained in the person of Miss BROWN, who is a daughter of the late J.H. BROWN for a number of years the efficient deputy clerk of the county. She is a graduate of our high school and we believe also of the Nebraska Normal College and for several terms was a very successful teacher in the city schools. The newly married couple arrived in the city Friday evening where they received the hearty congratulations of friends and the Republican feels safe in extending the best wishes of numberless others who have been unable to tender them personally. They will make their home in Omaha.

DIED: Joe KELLEY died on pneumonia at the home of his father Michael KELLEY in Brenna precinct Sunday evening. He had been sick but a short time and it was thought nothing serious. His aged parents have the sympathy of the entire community.

Real Estate Transfers.

Reported by I.W. ALTER, bonded abstracter, Wayne, Nebraska.

W.D. MEAD, jr., to D.H. BREWER, lot 11, T&W's add Wayne	$83.00
GAMMELL, et al., to H.J. NUERNBERGER, w d w 1/2 nw 1/4 6-25-5	2,049.00
Chas. NEISS to S.E. AUKER, nw 1/4 sw 1/4 & sw 1/4 nw 1/4 10-26-4	2,700.00
R. RANTONBERG to Peter ERICKSON, s 1/2 nw 1/4 28-26-1	1,800.00
J.S. FRENCH to Jane WILKINSON, n 100 ft lot 24, T&W's add	125.00
O.D. BROWN to R. & F.G. PHILLEO, lot 2, blk. 5, n add to Wayne	200.00
Fred JENSEN to Frank LEAHY, s 1/2 sw 34-25-4	2,800.00
J.W. GIBSON to Chas. ROBBINS, n 1/2 lot 4, blk. 8, B&B's add city	1,265.00
E.J. TADLOCK to Louie SCHMIDT, n 1/4, 18-27-1	4,000.00
J.P. STROMSBERG to F.M. SKEEN, lots 7 and 8, blk. 28, Wayne	1,000.00
L.J. JORDAN to J.W. MASON, QC s 1/2 sw 1/4 4-27-3	1,550.00

The Wayne Republican
March 1, 1899 (Vol. 6, No. 3)

BIRTH: Dr. LEISENRING reports the birth of a nice girl baby at the home of John GUSTAFSON northeast of town last Thursday.

DIED: Mr. and Mrs. Jos. OVERMAN mourn the death of their infant babe which was called to its home above on Saturday morning. The little one was in the best of health on Friday night and on awakening Saturday morning the parents found it dead.

The suddenness of the death makes the sad event seem even more sorrowful. The remains will be laid to rest in the Carroll cemetery on Tuesday.

The Wayne Republican
March 8, 1899 (Vol. 6, No. 4)

BIRTH: A new baby put in an appearance at Mr. MEISKY's last week. (Hoskins)

BIRTH: George MINER and wife are rejoicing over the arrival of a boy at their home Sunday.

BIRTH: A girl baby of standard weight arrived at the home of Mr. and Mrs. T.E. SPENCER Monday.

The Wayne Republican
March 15, 1899 (Vol. 6, No. 5)

BIRTH: A girl baby was born to Mr. and Mrs. Rudolph HEFTI on Thursday of last week.

BIRTH: Magnus WESTLUND is stepping pretty high since the arrival of the fine boy baby at his home last Thursday.

The Wayne Republican
March 22, 1899 (Vol. 6, No. 6)

BIRTH: Born to Mr. and Mrs. Dow WOOLEY on Thursday, a nine pound boy.

LICENSED TO WED: Judge HUNTER issued a license to wed on Saturday to Eugene BLAKESLEY and Della WINELAND, both of Carroll.

MARRIED: Judge HUNTER one day last week married John T. HAAS and Jennie MILLER, both of Laurel.

MARRIED: Married, February 15, 1899 at Verdon, Richardson county, Nebraska, at 5 p.m., L.O. EVANS and Mary ISAACS. The bride is the oldest daughter of Daniel ISAACS living west of Carroll and is a very highly esteemed young lady and dearly loved by all who chance to maker her acquaintance. The groom is a young man from Gallia county, Ohio. The young couple arrived here Friday evening and drove out to the bride's home where a reception had been prepared for them. About forty guests were invited and although it was a very stormy night none thought of staying at home on such an occasion as this. The supper was simply immense, so we town folks thought, for we don't often get a chance like this to test our capacity in this line. After supper a short time was spent in general conversation and amusement after which the crowd left for home, leaving behind them many good wishes for the happy pair. They will soon be at home to their many friends on one Mr. ISAAC's farms where they will go to housekeeping as soon as they get their house built and other necessary arrangements can be made. Below we will give a list of the presents received by them at the reception. They received many other presents of which we did not get the list.

Parlor lamp, Enos DAVIS and wife; Set glass dishes, J.R. HAINES and wife; Sugar bowl, cream pitcher, syrup jug, S. JONES and wife; Water pitcher, Will THOMAS and wife; Silver dessert spoons, J.R. MORRIS and wife; Set of goblets, Mrs. EDWARDS; Set of silver tea spoons, Evan JENKINS and wife; Linen table cloth, T.D. JONES and wife; Set of silver knives and forks, Wm. JENKINS and wife; Set of cups and saucers, J. DAVIS and wife; Silver knives and forks, F. WEBER; Set of silver tea spoons, T.E. EVANS and wife; Berry dish, Howell REES and wife; Set plates, T.C. MORRIS and wife; Silver fruit dish, J.A. JONES and wife; Jewel basket, Sarah JENKINS.

DIED: The infant daughter of John FOLK died at the family home in this city Sunday and the funeral was held Monday afternoon, Rev. MONTGOMERY, pastor of the Presbyterian church, conducting the services.

FUNERAL: Mr. BLAZE who lived two miles south of town was buried at Hoskins Friday aged 88 years.

Fair Association Meets.

In accordance with the call quite a number of the stockholders of the Fair Association met at the office of STRAHAN, GRIMSLEY & Co. Saturday afternoon and elected a new directorate as follows: F.E. MOSES, C.J. LUND, Ran FRAZIER, W.H. BUETOW, J.S. LEWIS, F.E. STRAHAN, D.L. STRICKLAND, F.M. GRIFFITH, A.H. CARTER and C.H. WOLF. The treasurer's report showed that the receipts of the association in 1897 were $1,064.34 and the expenditures $910.10, leaving a balance on hand of $154.24. The prevailing opinion of those present at the meeting seemed to favor the holding of a fair this fall, though that is a matter for the consideration of the new directors and in order that the matter might be decided soon they were called to meet at the same place on Saturday afternoon, April 1, when they will also elect a new president, secretary and treasurer. If there is to be a Fair held a decision ought to be arrived at immediately, because in order to make it a success in keeping with the county and its people there is no time to spare.

The Wayne Republican
March 29, 1899 (Vol. 6, No. 7)

BIRTH: A girl of the standard weight arrived at the home of A.A. HALE on Monday.

MARRIAGE: On Tuesday the marriage of H.S. WELCH of our city and Miss Harriet A. HENDERSON took place at Oceola, Ia., the home of the bride. Mr. WELCH has been a resident of Wayne for nearly a year and can number his friends by the score and the bride is one of Oceola's most prominent young ladies. They are expected to arrive in Wayne sometime this week. The Republican extends congratulations.

MARRIED: Wednesday, at noon, at the residence of the bride's parents, in Carroll, by Rev. BITHEL of Wayne, Mr. Eugene BLAKESLEY and Miss Della WINELAND. Mr. BLAKESLEY is one of Wayne county's best teachers. The bride has grown to womanhood in our midst and numbers her friends by the score. Their many friends extend congratulations.

The Wayne Republican
April 5, 1899 (Vol. 6, No. 8)

MARRIED: Mr. Bernard H. VON SEGGERN and Miss Maggie REIBOLD, both residing northwest of town in the edge of Wayne county, were married last Tuesday. The Chronicle tenders best wishes and congratulations. (Wisner Chronicle)

MARRIED: Yesterday afternoon at the home of Mr. and Mrs. Eph ANDERSON southeast of town, Rev. P. SJOBLOM united in marriage Nathan SACKERSON and Miss Ida JOHNSON, both of Wakefield. The groom is an industrious young man in the employ of Rawlings Bros. and the bride is well and favorably known. They will go to housekeeping in the eastern part of town. Their many friends wish them a happy and contented life. (Wakefield Republican)

City Election.

Yesterday was city election and a large vote was polled resulting as follows:

For Mayor - GAERTNER 135, Henry LEY, 217.
For Clerk - Everett LAUGHLIN, no opposition.
For Treasurer - L.W. ROE 176, Fred VOLPP, 171.
For Police Judge - A.T. WITTER 154, James BRITTON 190.
For City Engineer - A.L. HOWSER, no opposition.
Members of School Board - WARNOCH 257, BENSON 116, WELSH 183.

COUNCILMEN.

First ward - GOLL 44, PIPENSTOCK 56.
Second ward - HOLTZ 51, FRAZIER 76.
Third ward - C.M. CRAVEN, no opposition.

Making the city officers elected, mayor, Henry LEY; clerk, Everett LAUGHLIN; treasurer, L.W. ROE; police judge, James BRITTON; engineer, A.L. HOWSER; members of school board, R.Q. WARNOCH, A.A. WELSH; councilman, 1st ward, William PIEPENSTOCK; 2nd ward, Randal FRAZIER; 3rd ward, C.M. CRAVEN.

At the regular meeting of the Royal Highlanders Friday, March 31st, the following officers were elected for the ensuing year: P.I.P., J.M. CHERRY; I.P., Bert BROWN; C.C., H.L. KIMBALL; W.E., Chas. BEEBE; Sec., E. LAUGHLIN; Treas., H.B. JONES; Physician, H.G. LEISENRING; W., Jas. BUSH; S., O. GRAVES; H., L.F. HOLTZ; G., Joe CULLEN; 1st W.C., R.W. WILKINS; 2nd W.C., John SHERBAHN; C.S., E.D. MITCHELL; C.A., U.S. CONN; P.C. 1 yr., A.F. BRENNER; 2 yrs., Jas. BUSH; 3 yrs., R.W. WILKINS.

Election is over and L.S. NEEHAM, E.W. CULLEN, F. WEIBLE, John ELLIOTT, W.H. McCLUSKY will take all the abuse for the coming year. There was considerable work done by all parties, especially by Mr. McCLUSKY, who had a man carrying a banner on one side of which was the appeal, "Vote for McCLUSKY," on the other side he consigned "Ten-foot Sidewalk" to the place where they don't shovel snow. (Winside)

Real Estate Transfers.

O.O. WHITED to Lena STAARM,
    lots 10, 11 and 12, blk. 6, Carroll $40.00
A.H. BURCH to P.C. ANDREWS,
    s 1/2 sw 1/4 33-25-3   1,800.00

C.N. BIRKLAND to C.G. SWARD,
    e 1/2 nw 1/4 5-27-3 and lands in Cedar Co $4,000.00
O.O. WHITED to G.A. BAILEY,
    lots 4, 5 and 6, blk. 3, Carroll   45.00
A.B. SLATER to R. PERRIN,
    qc pt sw 1/4 18-26-4   1.00
Daniel OLESON to G.J. NEWHAM,
    ne 1/4, 26-27-2   3,810.00
A.R. FINLAYSON to Mary FINLAYSON,
    ne 1/4 9-26-5 1/3 int   600.00
C.H. WATTS to W.F. NORRIS,
    und 1/2 pt sw 1/4 18-26-4   100.00
Ira DAVENPORT to C.B. FRENCH, jr.,
    nw 1/4 se 1/4 8-26-2   560.00
Same to same,
    sw 1/4, 9-26-2   3,000.00
Curt BENSHOOF to W.H. GILLIAND,
    lot 39, blk. 4, Coll Hill add Wayne   30.00
G.A. BAILEY to E.D. ACTON,
    lots 5 and 6, blk. 3, Carroll   50.00
F.M. McELRATH to Carrie JOHNSON,
    lots 7, 8 and 9, blk. 7, Winside   1,400.00
Maggie GORDON to P. PRYOR,
    sw 1/4, 21-26-2   3,200.00
J.O. MILLIGAN to Theodore LONG,
    n 1/2 n 1/2 31-26-5   4,000.00
W.H. McCLUSKY to G.L. COLBERT,
    lot 2, blk. 6, B&P add Winside   15.00
James W. BUSH to Eph ANDERSON,
    w 1/2 sw 1/4 17-26-4   2,400.00
M.C. LIVINGSTONE to D. McCARTHY,
    sw 1/4 19 & nw 1/4 nw 1/4 30-27-1   4,540.00
Jas EVANS to Wm. BAYES,
    lot 5, blk. 1, Winside   50.00
E & B lbr Co to Wm. SONNEKEN,
    lot 6, blk. 20, Wayne   1,000.00
Sarah REAM to Aug BRUNE,
    ne 1/4, 20-26-3   4,640.00
J.A. JONES to T.E. EVANS,
    nw 1/4 of se 1/4 26-27-1   1,000.00
J.M. BEALE to J.D. KING,
    lots 19, 20, 21, 22, 23 and 24, blk. 8, Col Hill   30.00
Curt BENSHOOF to H.M. FRAZIER,
    lot 20, blk. 14, Col Hill Wayne   30.00

Theo LONG to Max BRUDIGAN,	
nw 1/4 nw 1/4 & ne 1/4 nw 1/4 25-26-4	$2,400.00
W.F. NORRIS to Otto VOGET,	
w 50 ft lt 4, 5, 6, blk. 3, E add Wayne	500.00
Rosa KRUGER to F.M. McELRATH,	
lots 4, 5, 6, 7, 8 and 9, blk. 9, Winside	2,000.00
B. CUNNINGHAM to J.L. STINER,	
ne 1/4, 36-26-3	5,600.00
J.L. STINER to A. LINDSAY,	
s 1/2 nw 1/4 9-26-4	2,800.00
Carrie M. CHAPIN to John G. SCHUSTER,	
lots 9 and 10, blk. 4, N add Wayne	500.00
A.T. CHAPIN to A.B. CHERRY,	
lots 7, 8, 9 and 10, blk. 5, B&P ad Winside	400.00

The Wayne Republican
April 12, 1899 (Vol. 6, No. 9)

FUNERAL: The funeral of Herman FISHER of Leslie precinct who dropped dead of heart disease in one of PEAVEY's coal sheds at Wakefield last Monday, was very largely attended at the German church in that precinct on Wednesday afternoon. Mr. FISHER was born in Kiel, Holstein, a little over 44 years ago and has been in this country for a good many years and was a man very much beloved and respected by his friends and neighbors. By careful methods and close attention to business he succeeded in acquiring quite a competence. He has been in poor health for a number of months and yet so sudden an ending was scarcely anticipated. He leaves a wife and two sons to mourn the loss of husband and father.

Real Estate Transfers.

C.B. FRENCH, jr., to Adaline H. MILLER,	
se 36-26-2	$1,300.00
C.W. LAWVER to O.W. GUDGELL,	
s 1/2 sw 1/2 & n 1/2 ne 10-27-1	2,900.00
H.B. MILLER to C.B. FRENCH, jr.,	
ne 36-26-2, quit claim	1.00
John G. O'ROURKE to E.E. REED,	
n 1/2 se, & n 1/2 sw 2-27-1, & sw 2-26-1	5,025.00
E.E. REED to Alex HINES,	
n 1/2 se 1/4 10-27-1	1,500.00
Alex HINES to J.L. BEATON,	
s 1/2 ne 1/4 10-27-1	1,837.00

J.W. BARTLETT to Caroline BARTLETT, lot 10, blk. 26, Wayne	$450.00
Frank VICK to Katherine KNEBEL, nw 1/4, 10-25-1	3,760.00
Malissa SWEGART to W.M. WRIGHT, sw 1/4, 12-26-3	1.00
L.M. SQUIRES to M.D. CHILSON, ne 1/4, 4-27-3	3,360.00
J.P. BUTLER to H. KELLOGG, s 1/2 sw 1/4 15-26-4	2,600.00
B. CUNNINGHAM to J.T. BRESSLER, lots 21 and 22, blk. 23, Coll Hill	80.00
J.W. MASON to H.E. MASON, s 1/2 sw 1/4 4-27-3	1,800.00
F.A. McCORNACK to W.W. GARWOOD, n 1/2 sw 1/4 11-27-2	1,600.00
J.T. BRESSLER to S.G. FUOSS, s 1/2 ne 1/4 4-25-5	2,500.00
C.V. THURSTON to J.W. MASON, n 1/2 sw 1/4 4-27-5	2,000.00
F. LESSMAN, et al., to J.P. BUTLER, s 1/2 sw 1/4 15-26-4, qc	50.00
A.C. GOLTZ to W.P. GABLER, lot 6, blk. 5, B&P 2nd add Winside	60.00
Ira DAVENPORT to John T. DAVIS, e 1/2 nw 1/4 26-26-2	1,360.00
State of Nebraska to A.M. MILLER, se 1/4, 36-26-2	1,120.00
H.C. WRIGHT to J.R. MANNING, qc, n 1/2 lot 5, all of 6, blk. 7, Wayne	1,700.00
Jos. DOBBIN to H. HOOVER, ne 1/4, 28-16-1	3,200.00
Elizabeth SHEPARD to P. COLEMAN, w 1/2 se 1/4 18-25-4	2,500.00
J.P. MORRISON to A.H. CARTER, lot 7 out blk. 1 B&P add Winside	15.00

The Wayne Republican
April 19, 1899 (Vol. 6, No. 10)

MARRIED: RICHARDS - McGRAIL. At the home of W.R. KING six miles southwest of this city on Monday April 17, Judge HUNTER performed the ceremony that made S.H. RICHARDS and Miss Katie McGRAIL husband and wife. The Republican joins the wide circle of friends in wishing the newly married couple a life filled with happiness prosperity and trusts that their's may be a path strewn with good things.

DIED: PRATT. On Thursday evening April 13 in this city the two year old daughter of F.J. PRATT died of spinal meningitis. The funeral occurred on Saturday.

DIED: WILLIAMS. The boy baby of Neal WILLIAMS and wife died at the family home in this city Saturday night. The funeral was held on Monday.

DIED: FRY. On Friday, April 14th, the year old child of Mr. and Mrs. Clint FRY died at their home northwest of the city.

DIED: PULS. On Sunday, April 16th, the youngest child of Henry PULS died at the home south of Winside.

Real Estate Transfers.
As reported by I.W. ALTER, abstractor, Wayne, Nebraska.

O.D. BROWN to M.E. Church of Wayne,	
lots 14, 15 and 16, blk. 1, C&B's add Wayne	$330.00
Sarah K. SMITH to F.M. McELRATH,	
lots 11 and 12, blk. 18, B&P's add Winside	840.00
Wm. R. DRISKELL to E.E. DRISKELL,	
und int in w 1/2 22 & e 1/2 27-26-5	2,500.00
M.A. MOFFAT to J.H. KRIMMINGER,	
lot 11, blk. 4, Winside	100.00
D.H. BREWER to Susan M. HUNTER,	
lot 11, T&W's add Wayne	700.00
Citizen's Bank to Amelia NIEMAN,	
lot 1, C&B's add to Wayne except the s 150 feet	300.00
J.H. BOWMAN to Chas. E. JONES,	
lots 1, 2 and 3, blk. 5, Carroll	100.00
Claus SCHROEDER to Ludwig BAUER,	
ne 1/4, 31-27-1	4,500.00
W.H. GILILAND to Richards Bros.,	
lot 39, blk. 4, College hill add Wayne	125.00
Elmer SWARTZ to Sadie A. YOUNG,	
lots 1, 2 and 3, blk. 6, Carroll	275.00
W.F. NORRIS to Clara A. FARRAND,	
pt sw 1/4, 18-26-4	250.00
Mrs. E.F. TRAVIS to F.M. SKEEN,	
lots 5 & 6, TAYLOR and WACHOB's add to Wayne	1,200.00

The Wayne Republican
April 26, 1899 (Vol. 6, No. 11)

BIRTH: Born, on Sunday, to Mr. and Mrs. GREEBER, a son. (Hoskins)

BIRTH: Born, on Saturday, to Mr. and Mrs. Art. ZIEGLER, a son. (Hoskins)

BIRTH: Born, on Friday, to Mr. and Mrs. John WENDT, a son of standard weight. (Hoskins)

DIED: WILKINS. At his home at University place, Lincoln, Nebraska, Saturday morning April 22, 1899, Charles WILKINS in the 66th year of his age. Deceased was born in Pittsburg, Pa., July 2, 1833, was married to Sarah J. BELL at New Albany, Ind., March 31, 1861, lived after marriage in Indiana, Ohio, Kentucky and Illinois until 1882, when he came to Nebraska and became a resident of our city and remained here during the years 1882, '83 and '84 and has made this state his home ever since. He joined the Presbyterian church when a young man and always remained steadfast in his faith. The funeral occurred from his home in the city of Lincoln Monday, April 24th at 10 a.m. His death was very sudden and unexpected having retired on Friday evening in his usual health and gave no indication of the approaching end until about 3 a.m. Saturday and in a few minutes was silent forever. He leaves a devoted wife, two sons and two daughters to mourn his death, the oldest son Robert W., is the senior member of the drug firm of R.W. WILKINS & Co. of this city. The deceased and his family are well known to many of the older residents of our city who join as one in their expressions of sympathy.

The Wayne Republican
May 3, 1899 (Vol. 6, No. 12)

BIRTH: Dr. NIEMAN reports a boy baby at Carl THOMPSON's on Sunday.

BIRTH: Dr. NIEMAN reports a fine girl at Frank TILLMAN's on May 1.

DIED: SKAHILL. At the family home south of Wayne on Thursday evening April 27, Gertrude the 10 year old daughter of Thomas SKAHILL and wife died of inflamation of the bowels. The funeral was held from the Catholic church in this city Saturday forenoon.

DIED: MARTIN. On Monday evening, May 1, at the family home southeast of the city, the 9-months-old daughter of Frank MARTIN and wife was called to the great beyond. The little one was sick but a few hours and her death was very unexpected. The funeral was held from the Baptist church on Tuesday afternoon. The bereaved parents have the sympathy of all in their affliction.

Teachers' Association.
High School Building, 10:00 A.M.,
May 13, 1899.

Geography by Outline	Elmer LUNDBURG.
Value of Special Day Program	May SCACE,
	Maud REYNOLDS.
Bad Effects of High Grading	H.E. GARWOOD,
	Jos. CULLEN.
A New Scheme for High School	Frank SKEEN.

NOON.

Solo by,	Clara PHILLEO.
Patriotism in Our Schools	H.B. MILLER.
Ancient History	W.E. HOWARD.
School Library, Selection and Use	E. Roy SURBER,
	Ella WILLIAMS.

Invite all the patrons.

Nellie MILLER, Sec'y.

The Wayne Republican
May 10, 1899 (Vol. 6, No. 13)

MARRIED: On Saturday Judge HUNTER united in matrimony, Eric COOK of Winside and Sarah PETERSON of Omaha.

DIED: ANDERSON. The eleven months old boy of A.G. ANDERSON who lives eight miles north of Wayne died on Wednesday afternoon, May 3, of measles. The funeral was held at Concord Friday, May 5.

DIED: The seven year old daughter of Mr. and Mrs. H.D. FRISBY two miles northeast of Winside died Friday of lung fever. The funeral was held at the house Saturday at 3 p.m., and the remains were taken to Cass county for burial.

Real Estate Transfers.

As reported by I.W. ALTER, abstractor, Wayne, Nebraska.

Frank DALY to F.C. KEENAN,	
s 1/2 of sw 1/4, 34-25-4	$2,800.00
R.E.K. MELLOR to Wm. MELLOR,	
nw 1/4, 12-25-3	2,500.00
State of Nebraska to W.H. BELETER,	
ne 1/4, 9-27-2	1,129.00
Henry J. SEIVERS to John C. CARSTENS,	
nw 1/4, 15-27-3	3,600.00
Nellie AMENT to Wm. PIEPENSTOCK,	
not 7, blk. 22, Wayne	500.00
D.S. ESTABROOK to Robt. FENSKE,	
nw 1/4, 30-25-2	1,400.00
Helwig NINDEL to Paul NINDEL,	
e 1/2 lots 4, 5 and 6, blk. 23, Wayne	1.00
Geo. C. WILBUR to John A. WILBUR,	
e 1/2 nw 1/4 26-27-3	1.00
WILBUR, Guy R. and F.P., to Jno. A. WILBUR,	
e 1/2 nw 1/4 26-27-3	1.00
EVERETT & WAITE to L.C. TOLLERS,	
lots 1 and 2, blk. 12, College Hill add Wayne	200.00
Matthias JONES to J.A. JONES,	
lot 10, blk. 4, Carroll	50.00
Henry R. BECK to Abbie S. KINGSTON,	
sw 1/4 of ne 1/4 and nw 1/4 of 15-27-1	6,000.00
J. JEANPERT to F.E. EVANS,	
sw 1/4 of 22-25-4	4,400.00
State of Nebraska to John H. JONES,	
s 1/2 se 1/4 of 14-26-1	660.00
M.M. ELTING to Rebecca J. RAMSEY,	
e 1/2 lots 1, 2 and 3, blk. 7, Wayne, and	
e 1/2 lot 4, blk. 11, C&B's add to Wayne	700.00
Albertina MAAS to Ludwig ZIEMER,	
lots 13 to 18, blk. 12, Hoskins	150.00
Helen C. CRAWFORD to E.E. REED,	
lot 9, TAYLOR's add to Wayne	1,500.00
J.T. BRESSLER to Margaret E. and A.J. LAUGHLIN,	
lot 10, TAYLOR's add to Wayne	800.00
Erasmus E. REED to Fred DRUHE,	
n 1/2 sw 1/4 2-27-1	1,600.00
C.W. REED to Albert H. CARTER,	
lot 9, outlot 1, B&P's add to Winside	20.00
Winside Mill Co. to C.W. REED,	
lot 9, outlot 1, B&P's add to Winside	80.00

The Wayne Republican
May 24, 1899 (Vol. 6, No. 15)

BIRTH: M.T. HEALY and wife have a brand new boy baby at their home.

BIRTH: Born to Mr. and Mrs. George BOSTARD last Thursday a son of standard weight and beauty.

MARRIAGE: The marriage of Mr. E.J. GALLAGHER to Miss Estella SHIVELY was consumated at the Catholic church in this city at 7:30 Tuesday morning. The bride is a daughter of Captain and Mrs. W.T. SHIVELY of this city and has many friends here. She has been identified with the educational interests of the county for some time past. The groom is quite well known in O'Neil, having been engaged in business here a few years ago, and is a brother of the GALLAGHER boys who used to reside on a farm northeast of here. They will be remembered as James and Will, the former of whom is station agent at Laurel, the latter being dead. The bride was dressed in pink, trimmed in cream, and wore pink roses. Miss Mae METZ, niece of the groom, was bridesmaid. The groom was dressed in black. G.E. SHIVELY, brother of the bride, was groomsman. At the conclusion of the ceremony the wedding party repaired to the home of the bride's parents, where breakfast was served. Many beautiful gifts were received. The young couple departed the same morning for Wayne, where Mr. GALLAGHER has resided the past two years and where they will make their home. The Frontier extends congratulations and wishes them continued joy. Those who attended the wedding from out of town were: James GALLAGHER and wife, Mrs. Charles METZ and daughter May of Laurel, Mrs. T. SHIVELY of Norfolk and Mrs. ANDERSON and Miss Bertha SHIVELY of Council Bluffs. (O'Niel Frontier)

DIED: At the family home in this place on Monday morning, May 22, after a very short illness, Mrs. M.S. LINN. The remains were taken to Ashland for interment. The lady leaves a husband, five little children and a very large circle of friends who will deeply sympathize with the bereaved ones in their great loss.

DIED: Mack RICE and old resident of Wayne county departed this life Monday by the concentrated lye route. He was living with his sister Mrs. E. EDDY in Wakefield and Monday morning he got up about 5 o'clock built a fire and then left the house. When breakfast was ready he did not return and when they went to look for him he was found in the barn suffering terribly from the effect of the lye he had drank. A doctor was quickly summoned but could render no relief and he died in an our or two in great agony. He was 44 years old and unmarried.

Teachers Elected.

The school board at its meeting last Wednesday and Thursday evening elected part of the corps of teachers for the ensuing year and fixed salaries to be paid which in several instances is an advance over what has been paid. The reelections and salaries are as follows:

Mrs. CONN, Salary $50. Miss SKILES, Salary $45.00. Miss BRITTON, Salary $45.00. Miss SHULTZ, Salary $50.00. W.E. HOWARD, Salary $55.00.

The new teacher elected is Miss STOCKING for Primary, salary $55.

The places yet to be filled are those recently occupied by Misses FRAZIER, METTLIN and WEAVER and assistant principalship at the high school as Mr. HOWARD is to be taken from there and placed in charge of the 6th and 7th grades at the Ward schools; this move being necessitated by the crowded condition of those grades at the high school.

The Wayne Republican
May 31, 1899 (Vol. 6, No. 16)

BIRTH: A new boy came on Sunday to cheer the home of L.C. TITSWORTH and wife.

MARRIED: SHULTHEIS - BARKLEY. At the home of the bride's parents, 309 16th avenue, Detroit, Michigan, Wednesday evening, May 24, Edward SHULTHEIS of Wayne county, Neb., and Miss Margaret BARKLEY were united in marriage. The following day the newly wedded couple went to the former home of Mr. S. at Three Rivers, Michigan, and visited there until they started for this place arriving here yesterday. they were handsomely entertained last evening at the pleasant home of his brother Charles northwest of the city. The Republican desires to extend to Mr. and Mrs. SHULTHEIS the best wishes of itself and readers for a happy and prosperous future.

The Masonic Lodge of this city held its regular annual election of officers Friday evening with the following result: F.L. NELY, W.M.; F.A. DEARBORN, S.W.; G.E. FRENCH, J.W.; H. LEY, Treas., A.T. WITTER, Secy.

On Monday night the Odd Fellows elected as N.G., Ira RICHARDS; V.G., Chas. SHULTHIES; Representative to Grand Lodge, G.A. BENSON.

Real Estate Transfers.

E.M. SMITH to F.H. JONES, lot 4 and n 25 ft lot 5, blk. 5, C&B's ad and n 1/2 outlot 12, C&B's ad to Wayne	$3,500.00
F.A. DEARBORN to Mary MULLER, sw 1/4, 23-26-1	3,000.00
H. LEISENRING to E.M. SMITH, n 1/2 outlot 12, C&B's ad	1.00
John H. GOLL to John LOBSACK, lots 15, 16 and 17, blk. 5, east ad to Wayne	25.00
P.H. KOHL to M.C. LIVINGSTON, e 1/2, 29-27-1	640.00
W.H. ELDRED to J.D. KING, und 1/2 ne 1/4 1-25-3	2,500.00
Geo. BUSKIRK to G.H. ALBERS, w 1/2 ne 1/4 31-25-5	2,468.00
1st National Bank, Wyoming, Ia., to P.G. JAMES, n 1/2, 30-26-4	9,500.00
O.O. WHITED to Mary ZIELKE, lots 1, 2, 3 and 4, blk. 2, Carroll	300.00

The Wayne Republican
June 7, 1899 (Vol. 6, No. 17)

Obituary.

The following is taken from the Park Hill, (Ont.) Review and has reference to the father of Alex LAURIE and Mrs. James McINTOSH.

Obituary. - We regret to record the death of the last Alex. LAURIE, which occurred at his residence on the 11th inst. He was born near Maxeltown, Dumfries, Scotland, in 1830, and emigrated to Canada in 1852. He first settled in the township of Whitby where he resided for upwards of 25 years. In the fall of 1878 he came to McGillivray with his family, having purchased the farm on which he has resided since that time.

He was one of the first promoters of the Corbett Presbyterian church and gave liberally of his means both for its erection and its support. When the congregation was organized he was chosen elder, which position he filled until the time of his death. Mr. LAURIE was a good neighbor, a kind husband and an indulgent father. In politics he was always a Reform. About the middle of February he was stricken with la grippe and kept constantly growing weaker until the end came, but his sickness was borne with wonderful patience and courage and he anticipated death with a cheerfulness that impressed all who saw him. His wife, three sons and four daughters survive him. The children are: Mrs. William LEASK of Oshawa, James, John and Mrs. George JONES of McGillivray, Alexander and Mrs. James McINTOSH of Wayne, Nebraska, and Mrs. Freeman TALBOT of Dorchester.

Teacher's Institute.

The regular yearly session of the Teachers institute of this county is being held at the Presbyterian church this week. The lecturers are Prof. SAYLOR of Lancaster, and PILE and CONN of our own county. The attendance is good, the enrollment at noon yesterday being 104, as follows:

Fred R. WRIGHT	Mary MASON
Ida HEYER	Eva VERNON
Olga JOHNSON	Angie WADSWORTH
Carrie HUPP	Mary HOWARTH
Lelia OLMSTED	Mrs. Lizzie MITCHELL
Lena LUSH	Lizzie WILLIAMS
Mattie PORTER	Marguerite DILTZ
Edna SEWELL	Retta PERDUE
Pearl SEWELL	Lila JOHNSON
Maude JOHNSON	Mary RICHARDSON
Maude BENSHOOF	Emma RICHARDSON
Rena OLMSTED	Nettie KILLION
Mrs. W.I. LOWRY	Pearl KILLION
Laurette PRYOR	Mary PRESTON
G.W. HUSTED	Seth BRAUN
Reba NANGLE	E.C. ARMACOST
Abram GILDERSLEEVE	Anna BRIGHT
Lulu STEPHENS	C.H. BRIGHT
Nellie BLAKESLEY	Edwin MILLER
E.A. LUNDBERG	Marie BROWN
Elmer LUNDBERG	Etta OLMSTEAD
Myrtle BENSON	W.L. CUNNINGHAM
Nora LARSON	Fannie SKILES
Lucy FAHNESTOCK	Anna HANSON
Minta LEWIS	Jessie PALMER
Mame HUGHES	Lizzie BROWN
Hattie JEFFREY	Mae CUNNINGHAM
Winnie CLAYBAUGH	Roy SURBER
Nellie MILLER	Edna BRITTON

Tessie HANSON
Wilma ANDERSON
Mary CLAYBAUGH
Louise SULLIVAN
John NEIHART
Minnie BENEDICT
Josie NETTLETON
Jennie LOWDER
Marguerite DIXON
Anna WEAVER
Jennie METTLEN
Laura HOLTZ
Etta BECKENHAUER
Lizzie HAYES
Claude WRIGHT
A.G. STAGE
Mary PAWELSKI
Alice RUNDELL
Lillie PHILLEN
Halsey S. MOSES
Nellie JOHNSON
H.V. GARWOOD
W.H. WOLF

Pearl REYNOLDS
Chas. REYNOLDS
Theo SCACE
Geo. BLAKESLEY
Eugene BLAKESLEY
Hallie CAFFEE
Minnie WRIGHT
Clara THOMPSON
Ella SHELLINGTON
Louise McKINZIE
Emma REICHERT
Lide WRIGHT
Jennie CARTER
Mamie ELLIOTT
Caroline TAYLOR
Clara BURSON
Mrs. Marie WOLF
Mary CHILDS
Tillie ANDERBERY
Blanche SHAW
C.E. MORGAN
Gertrude BAYES
Blanche WEAVER

The Wayne Republican
June 14, 1899 (Vol. 6, No. 18)

DIED: William RAGO living eight miles north of Hoskins had the sad misfortune to lose their 18-months-old baby by its falling head first into a large pail of water and drowning before it was discovered. They have the sympathy of the entire community.

Report of Wayne Public Schools.

The following is a synopsis of U.S. CONN's report to the Board of Education at its meeting Monday evening:

Total enrollment for the year, 538; average attendance, 375; pupils enrolled between 8 and 14 years of aged, 409; average enrollment for each room, 59; average attendance for each room 42.

The average attendance has been materially lowered by the epidemic of diphtheria. Many pupils went out of school at that time and did not re-enter afterwards. The irregular attendance caused many pupils to do poor work, and more than usual have failed to make their grades. Those, however, who have been regular in attendance have progressed very satisfactorily, and have made up nearly all of the time lost by the enforced vacation. The teachers have been earnest and as a whole have done as good work as could be desired.

High School

The good results of the change in the course of study from a single course of three years to two courses, of three and four years respectively is beginning to show itself. Before the present course of study went into effect the enrollment of the high school was less than 40, while during the year just closed the enrollment was 73, being fifty per cent higher than has ever before been in the high school. Next year present indications point to an enrollment of at least 90.

The former course of study did not provide for any very definite work in grammar and arithmetic and the pupils so graduating were usually found to be deficient in these subject. Now a full year is given to the fundamental principles of arithmetic and six months of technical grammar. As a consequence the pupils are not only thoroughly grounded in the fundamentals of mathematics and language, but they are much stronger in all the rest of their work.

Since the public schools are for the public they best serve it when the largest percentage of the school population is in school. This is the policy which we are attempting to carry out.

The three years' course of study has no Latin in it, but the four years' course has all the Latin necessary for entrance to the freshmen work of the state university, besides additional mathematics and literature.

The school equipment is very deficient in reference books. At the main building there are but few reference books and at the ward building there are none whatever. An investment could be made in this direction very much to the advantage of the school.

Estimated Expenses.

Teachers and janitors	$5,900.00
Text books and stationery	350.00
Fuel	300.00
Water closets	200.00
Windows and door	25.00
Stove and miscellaneous	125.00
Organ and microscope, library, maps, globe, etc.	125.00

Real Estate Transfers.

Mrs. H. TITSWORTH to Leonard TITSWORTH,
se 1/4 sw 1/4 & sw 1/4 se 1/4 5 &
nw 1/4 ne 1/4 & ne 1/4 nw 1/4 8-25-2 $1.00

Leonard TITSWORTH to C.O. FISHER & J.S. FRENCH, 3/5 int in above land	$500.00
FURCHNER, DUERIG & Co. to Chas. MEYER, e 1/2 sw 1/4 9-27-3	1,300.00
J.V. HINCHMAN to Wm. MELLOR, all the e 1/2 & s 1/2 nw 1/4 & n 1/2 sw 1/4 & se 1/4 sw 1/4 1-27-3	13,000.00
Matilda MARTIN to J.H. WRIGHT, lots 10, 11 and 12, blk. 2, Lake's add Wayne	250.00
Albert REDMER to Herman BRENDERICK, se 1/4 29 & se 1/4 sw 1/4 28-25-2	4,800.00
P.J. SAMUELSON to Frank W. UTECHT, ne 1/4, 19-25-5	6,000.00
Frank W. UTECHT to P.J. SAMUELSON, e 1/2 of nw 1/4 19-26-5	2,800.00

The Wayne Republican
June 21, 1899 (Vol. 6, No. 19)

BIRTH: Born to Mr. and Mrs. R.G. RHORKE a fine girl on Saturday, both mother and baby are doing well.

BIRTH: Fred SCHRADER and wife are rejoicing over the arrival of a baby girl in their home. (Carroll)

Real Estate Transfers.

M.E. and R. PERRIN to C.F. BARNES, lots 11 and 12, blk. 19, College Hill	$50.00
J.T. BRESSLER to L. LOWERY, 2 acres in sw 1/2 35-26-2	150.00
Wm. MOYER to G.M. NEEDHAM, lots 27 and 28, blk. 22, College Hill	40.00
Peter ERICKSON to Andrew FRID, s 1/2 nw 1/4 18-26-1	1,800.00
Emma BORCHERT to Gust BORCHERT, n 1/2 of 6-27-1	1,500.00
Anton SORENSON to Emma BORCHERT, n 1/2 of 6-27-1	4,700.00
Chas. E. MILLER to Jesse A. MILLIGAN, s 1/2 of se 1/4, 16-27-1	1,640.00
H.A. PASSEWALK to John McKENIGAN, se 1/4 of 19-25-1	2,700.00
Henry A. MOORE to W.C. KELLEY and A.N. GOODWIN, se 1/4 of 25-27-3	1,609.00

The Wayne Republican
June 28, 1899 (Vol. 6, No. 20)

Wayne Lodge No. 120 A.F. & A.M. installed the following officers Saturday evening June 24. F.L. NEELY, W.M.; Gilbert FRENCH, J.W.; Henry LEY, Treas.; A.T. WITTER, Sec.; and Louis EDSON, S.W. The Senior Warden elect was out of the city and will be installed at a future meeting.

Real Estate Transfers.

For the two weeks ending June 26, 1899, reported by I.W. ALTER, bonded abstracter, Wayne, Nebraska:

F.A. DEARBORN to B.W. McKEAN, s 75 ft lot 22, blk. 4, Winside	$400.00
State of Nebraska to Peter ULRICH, n 1/2 36-26-1	2,240.00
H.J. COLE to Gustav MAROTZ, ne 1/4 25-25-1	2,450.00
L.S. NEEDHAM to W.I. LOWRY, lot 3, blk. 5, B&P's 1st add Winside	35.00
Chas. H. BURR to E. CUNNINGHAM, tr., e 1/2 ne 1/4 34-25-2	1,725.00
Henrietta ZIEMER to Ludwig ZIEMER, lot 16, blk. 1, Winside	200.00
August MILLER to Ernest MILLER, se 1/4, 33-35-2	1.00
E.T. JUDKINS to W.M. WRIGHT, se 1/4 23, sw 1/4 & s 1/2 se 1/4 24-26-1	- - -

The Wayne Republican
July 12, 1899 (Vol. 6, No. 22)

BIRTH: Born, to Mr. and Mrs. W.F. ROBERTS, on July 4, a boy.

BIRTH: Charley JEFFREY and wife are rejoicing over the birth of a fine boy at their home in this city Tuesday afternoon.

MARRIED: The News understands that Thressa BAUMANN was married to a gentleman of Wayne by the name of Alfred MILLER on the 3d inst. They will reside in Wayne. (Allen News)

MARRIED: On Wednesday evening, July 5, 1899, occurred the marriage of Mr. Jesse A. CLAYTON and Miss Eureka SCHULTZ, at the Presbyterian parsonage in Wayne, Rev. MONTGOMERY officiating. Both parties are highly esteemed young people of

Winside, who are too well and favorably known to need any words of introduction from us. They, in company with Mr. and Mrs. W.I. LOWRY, drove to Wayne last evening, where the marriage ceremony was performed, as stated above. After the ceremony the party returned to Winside. Mr. and Mrs. CLAYTON will make their home in Winside, and will take up their abode in the pleasant rooms at the rear of LOWRY's barber shop, which the groom has had fitted and furnished, but will for a brief time at least abide with Mr. and Mrs. W.I. LOWRY. May long life, success and happiness be theirs. (Winside Tribune)

Real Estate Transfers.

Real Estate transfers as reported by I.W. ALTER, bonded Abstracter, Wayne.

Sarah KING to Almeda MERRILL, se 1/4, 21-27-1	$3,000.00
E. CUNNINGHAM (tr) to D. MEYER, n 1/2 sw 1/4 28-26-4	2,800.00
Walter COLLARD to Chas. A. COLLARD, nw 1/4, 32-25-3	1.00
A.L. HOWSER to Ludwig ZIEMER, lots 4, 5 and 6, blk. 11, Hoskins	330.00
Mrs. Carrie JOHNSON to C.E. BENSHOOF, sw 1/4, 34-26-2	4,445.00
C.D. LARSED to G.L. DEVINE, und 1/2 ne 34 and w 1/2 of nw 35-26-4	2,000.00
Adelbert FRENCH to Geo. C. MERRILL, se 11-27-1	3,000.00
C.B. FRENCH, jr., to McCLUSKY & NEEDHAM, lot 4, blk. 3, B&P's addition to Winside	1.00
Frank WEIBLE to McCLUSKY & NEEDHAM, lot 2, blk. 12, Winside	75.00
A. SCHLACK to Hanna KRAUS, lot 14, blk. 8, Hoskins	150.00

The Wayne Republican
July 19, 1899 (Vol. 6, No. 23)

DIED: Died, July 11, Roy R., only son of J.W. and M.E. TAYLOR, aged 10 years, 10 months and 7 days. Rev. DAVIDSON preached the funeral sermon Wednesday in the Methodist church and the interment took place in the Carroll cemetery. Roy was an exceedingly bright boy and the pride of his parents and will be greatly missed by them and all who knew him. (Carroll Cor. Randolph Reporter)

The Odd Fellows of the city installed Ira RICHARDS, N.G.; Chas. SHULTHEIS, V.G.; Henry LEY, P.S.; Chas. WARNER, R. Sec.; Henry LEY, Treas.; Mark STRINGER, G.A. BENSON and I.W. ALTER trustees; G.A. BENSON, representative to Grand Lodge; W. RICKABAUGH, Con.; Chas. HOSTETTER, W.; J. PORTERFIELD, R.S.N.G.; Mark STRINGER, L.S.N.G.; J. RILEY, R.S.S.; Phil KOHL, L.S.S.; R.T. CARPENTER, I.G.; J.G. MINES, O.G.; R.H. SKILES, R.S.V.G.; Otis STRINGER, L.S.V.G.

The Wayne Republican
July 26, 1899 (Vol. 6, No. 24)

BIRTH: The home of Fred WEBER across the creek south of town is happy because of the arrival of a girl baby lately.

Obituary.

McINTOSH. At his home near Park Hill, Ontario, July 8, 1899, A.R. McINTOSH, aged 72 years. Deceased was born in Iverness, Scotland, June 24, 1827, came to Canada with his parents where he was married and has since made his home. His wife and seven children survive him, two of his sons, James and Archie, and a daughter, Mrs. Alex LAURIE, are residents of this county. Mr. McINTOSH had been a consistent member of the Presbyterian church for many years; the funeral services were conducted by his pastor, Rev. AILWARD, and his remains laid to rest in the Park Hill cemetery.

Real Estate Transfers.

Reported by I.W. ALTER, abstracter, Wayne, Nebraska.

Wm. HEYER to May E. GRIGGS,	
lot 5, blk. 4, Wayne	$500.00
Emilie HAAS admx to John WESTERHAUS,	
s 1/2 sw 32-26-3	2,050.00
A.F. BRENNER to E. CUNNINGHAM, tr.,	
nw 33-27-3	4,000.00
McCLUSKY & NEEDHAM to Frank WEIBLE,	
lot 12, blk. 6, B&P add Winside	28.00
Henry SAMUEL to A.A. WELCH,	
lot 10, SKEEN's add Wayne	10.00
Nels UTTER to Olai NELSON,	
w 1/2 sw 32-28-3 also w 1/2 nw 5-27-3	3,300.00
Wm. WINTER to Johanna WINTER, love and affection,	
nw & w 1/2 sw 30 & s 1/2 of sw 19, all in 35-1	- - -
A.W. CHAPIN to L.D. METCALF,	
w 1/2 nw 19-26-5	2,800.00

The Wayne Republican
August 2, 1899 (Vol. 6, No. 25)

LICENSED TO WED: Licensed to wed August 1, Joachim F. DEUCKER, of Waterloo, Neb., and Katie HENDRICKS, of Wayne county.

MARRIED: BAILEY - LORE. In the town of DuBois, Nebraska, at high noon today, at the home of the bride's parents, Mr. and Mrs. J.P. LORE, the marriage of their daughter Nellie to Geo. A. BAILEY will occur. It is a pleasure to make the above announcement, because in the person of the groom our readers will recognize one of Wayne county's best young men, one honored and respected by his fellows because of the upright life he has led and who by his gentlemanly bearing is enabled to count his friends by the hundred. He is the Carroll agent for the PEAVEY Elevator Company in whose employ he has been for several years and where he has built himself an enviable reputation as a business man entitled to the respect and confidence of his fellows. The bride is a most estimable young lady well known to the people of Carroll where for several terms she was a teacher in the public schools, in which capacity she gained the love and respect of parents, pupils and all with whom she was brought in contact. The young couple will be at home in Carroll in a few days in their own home that has just been completed and is one in which their friends will always receive a cordial welcome. We know that we but echo the sentiment of all the acquaintances of Mr. and Mrs. George BAILEY in hoping that theirs may be a voyage of happiness through life.

DIED: M.S. LINN's little boy died last Sunday. Mr. LINN seems to have more than his share of trouble in the past few months and his many friends sympathize with him in this sad hour. (Carroll)

The Wayne Republican
August 9, 1899 (Vol. 6, No. 26)

Laying of the Corner Stone.

The ceremony of laying the corner stone of the Wayne county court house was successfully carried out by the Grand Lodge of Masons of Nebraska in an emergent convocation on last Thursday. Grand Master W.W. KEYSOR of Omaha had charge of the ceremonies and was ably assisted by Judge R.E. EVANS, Grand Senior Warden, and Morris H. EVANS of Emerson, acting as Grand Junior Warden; John A. EHRHARDT, Stanton, as

Deputy Grand Master; C.E. HUNTER, Wakefield, as Grand Treasurer; A.T. WITTER, Wayne, as Grand Secretary; Enoch HUNTER, Wayne, as Grand Orator; John F. POUCHER, Grand Chaplain; A.P. CHILDS, Norfolk, Grand Marshal; Z.M. BAIRD, Hartington, Grand Senior Deacon; A.B. CHERRY, Winside, Grand Junior Deacon; A.A. WELCH, Wayne, Grand Tyler.

Owing to a wait in getting the contents of the stone in readiness it was just 12 o'clock when the procession formed on Main St., and, headed by Wayne's Corn Palace Band, marched to the courthouse square where the ceremony was performed in the presence of a considerable number of spectators, citizens of the city and county. The ceremony consisted of music by the band, prayer by the Grand Chaplain, address by Grand Master explanatory of the reasons why the laying of corner stones was peculiarly fitting to be performed by speculative Masons and also congratulating the county and its people for their thrift and enterprise in the erection of the present edifice. After this came the lowering of the corner stone into position which was done by three depressions; then the stone was tried by the different implements of the craft and it was declared that the "craftsmen" had performed their work well; corn, wine and oil were then poured upon the stone, being emblematic of Plenty, Health and Peace. Frank M. NORTHROP in behalf of the county commissioners, who were present, stepped forward and in a few well chosen words thanked the Masonic brethren for the ceremony they were about concluding and congratulated the people of the county on their general prosperity and commended them for their love of law and order and the respect of the rights of their fellows. Enoch HUNTER, Grand Orator, gave quite a history of Wayne county, the Grand Chaplain pronounced the benediction, when the procession was again formed and marched back to the hall of the local lodge where the closing exercises were had and from there all the visiting brethren and many of the home lodge, with the band and county officers repaired to the Boyd and enjoyed a very nice banquet given by the Wayne Masonic Lodge. Several of the Lodges of North Nebraska sent delegations to assist in the ceremonies, Winside, Norfolk, Stanton, Lyons, Emerson, Dakota City, Hartington and Wakefield being among the number. the contents of the corner stone are: Copies of each of the Wayne papers, and the Norfolk Times-Tribune, edited by A.P. CHILDS, a bible, short history of Wayne county up to the present, proceedings of last Grand lodge of the state, copy of constitution and by-laws of Wayne lodge, list of its officers and members, list of county officials and copy of program of laying of corner stone.

The following is a copy of the history of the county as

prepared by the commissioners and deposited in the corner stone of the new court house:

"Wayne county lies in the northeast portion of the state, is bounded by Cedar and Dixon counties on the north, Thurston on the east, Cuming and Stanton on the south and Pierce on the west. It contains 13 townships and 258,582 7-10 acres.

The county was first settled by a few farmers, mostly from Illinois, in the year 1869, who located in the eastern part of the county and by a few German settlers located in the extreme southwestern part of the county in the same year. The county was organized as a county in 1870, by a proclamation issued by Gov. David BUTLER, and an election held on September 5th, 1870, at which time the following officers were chosen: County commissioners, Martin T. SPERRY, W.E. DURIN, Isaac MINER; County clerk, Cyrus E. HUNTER; Treasurer, B.F. WHITTEN; Sheriff, A.D. ALLEN; Probate judge, A. FLETCHER; Surveyor, Wm. G. VROMAN; Supt. of public instruction, Ralph B. CRAWFORD; Coroner, Nathaniel ALLEN. Mr. WHITTEN failed to qualify as treasurer and George SCOTT was appointed to fill vacancy.

The first settler in the county was B.F. WHITTEN, located in township 26, range 5, east, near the Logan in the summer of 1868. Wm. JONES soon followed, and in the spring of 1869 WHITTEN and JONES returned with their families and made a permanent settlement. The first post office was established September 8, 1870, near the Logan bridge, and called Taffee after the Hon. John TAFFEE of Dakota county who was the representative delegate in congress with Wm. P. AGLER as postmaster. The first child born in the county was Patience E., daughter of Mr. and Mrs. Enoch HUNTER, on December 16, 1870, and who died at La Porte in September, 1881. Some claim is made, however, that the first child was born to Mr. and Mrs. Wm. G. VROMAN, but to the best of our knowledge the credit is due as above. The first marriage was that of M.T. SPERRY, county commissioner, to Sarah Ann EAYRS, on May 14, 1871, and the first death that of a child of Mr. and Mrs. Wm. G. VROMAN, on August 6, 1870. The first sermon preached in the county was by Rev. Van DUSER, of the Methodist church, at the home of Albert S. MINER, near the Logan bridge in October, 1870. Prof. Samuel AUGHEY, afterwards state geologist, preached at the house of Wm. AGLER in December, 1870, and Mrs. M.B. RICHARDSON, who is still living, Second Day Adventists, preached her first sermon at the funeral of C.E. HUNTER's little son in February, 1871, and afterwards held regular services at the home of Alexander SCOTT. The first school district organized in the county embraced the whole county, and the first school was at

La Porte in the summer of 1871.

With the organization of the county the county seat was established at La Porte which was laid out as a town on May 22, 1874, and Solon BEVINS built the first house and the first store in the town the following summer. The court house was erected in the fall of 1874, the county having voted bonds to the amount of $15,000 for its erection. These bonds run 20 years and bore 10 per cent interest and the credit of the county at that time was so poor that the bonds only brought 85 1/2 cents on the dollar.

From its first settlement in 1869 up to the summer of 1880 the growth of the county was very small. One reason being that there was so little of government land open to homestead entry, and it is doubtful if at that time 1869, there were to exceed twenty-five sections of unentered land in the entire county. Speculators had entered large tracts of land, amounting in some instances to nearly whole townships, while the B. & M. railway had been allowed to take up thousands of acres under their contract with the government. And other large tracts had been entered by the state under the Agricultural College act. These facts had tended to retard immigration, so that when the county was organized in 1870 there was not to exceed twenty-five families in the entire county. In 1879 the growth had been so slow that there were but 140 voters in the county at the election that fall, while the population in the following year had increased to only 817.

January 18, 1876, the county voted bonds in the sum of $88,000 to aid in the construction of the Covington, Columbus & Black Hills railroad, but these bonds were never issued, the railroad company failed to build, although they graded a narrow gauge road as far as La Porte. In 1880 the C., St. P., M. and O. railroad bought up this grade and proceeded to build, passing through the county during the summer of 1880 and winter of 1881 and building the road to Norfolk.

With the advent of the iron horse all was changed, and immigrants began to pour into the county be the hundreds. These immigrants were mostly well-to-do farmers who bought large tracts of land at from 90 cents to $3.50 per acre, and have built fine residences and developed the same until now the same land which went begging in 1879 and brought from 90 cents upwards is worth from $25 to $60 an acre. It was this class of immigrants that has done so much to build up the county and is one reason why Wayne county today contains more comfortable farm houses and a better class of buildings throughout than any of the older counties in this section of the state.

At the time the county was bonded for the court house 47

votes were cast, for the bonds 26, against them 21. These bonds were afterwards refunded at 6 per cent interest and have all been paid with the exception of one bond of $500. Another bond issue was voted December 23, 1878, in the sum of $2,000 to aid in the erection of a flour mill on the Logan about two miles below the present site of Wakefield in 1880, but they were never certified to by the state auditor and have never been presented for payment, although they were sold January 1, 1880. There was no other issue of bonds by the county until the election in November, 1898, an issued of $25,000 in 5 per cent bonds were issued to build a court house. The vote stood 757 for to 363 against, and the bonds were issued on January 12, 1899, and sold for $27,450, quite a change from the financial standing of the county from the time when 10 per cent bonds were sold at a discount of 15 per cent in 1874.

As previously stated the first school district, embracing the entire county, was organized in 1870. In 1882 there had been organized 18 school districts with 16 school houses and 17 qualified school teachers and 341 children of school age. There are now in the county 79 organized school districts, 150 qualified teachers and 3,282 children of school age. The population of the county has grown from 182 in 1870 until there are now 9,280 inhabitants.

Sometime in 1871 a post office was established at La Porte by the removal of the post office at Taffee with Cyrus E. HUNTER as postmaster, and this was the only post office in the county until the fall of 1881 when a post office was established at Wayne with James BRITTON as postmaster. Later post offices were established at Hoskins and Northside (now Winside). The post office was discontinued at La Porte some two yeas after the establishment at Wayne. There are now seven post offices in Wayne county, as follows: Wayne, Winside, Hoskins, Carroll, Altona, Bird and Meliven.

The city of Wayne was platted in June, 1881, and the first load of lumber hauled to the present site of the town on July 4 of that year. It is situated on a plateau and low hillside and is most substantially built, showing that its people came here to found homes, and not merely temporary abiding places. The citizenship is composed very largely of wide-awake, hustling, representative American born people who take great pride in their city and are not afraid to stand up for it at all times and under all circumstances.

The city now contains six church organizations as follows: Presbyterian, Rev. D. C. MONTGOMERY, pastor; Methodist, Rev. Thos. BITHEL, pastor; Catholic, Rev. Father FITZGERALD; German

Lutheran, A. GRABER; English Lutheran; Baptist, Rev. C.R. WELDEN. These all own substantial buildings. The Presbyterian congregation erected during the present year a handsome church building costing in the neighborhood of $12,000. The oldest fraternal organization in the city is Casey Post, No. 5., G.A.R., which was organized at La Porte in the year 1881. The next in point of age is Wayne Lodge No. 120, A.F. & A.M., organized in 1882. There are also lodges of I.O.O.F., K. of P., M.W.A., Sons of Herman, A.O.U.W., Royal Highlanders, Royal Mystic Legion, Ladies Auxiliary to A.O.U.W., and M.W.A., and Degree of Honor and Royal Neighbors and others.

The present city officers are: Mayor, Henry LEY; Clerk, Everett LAUGHLIN; Treasurer, Lambert ROE; Police Judge, I.W. ALTER; Marshal, Geo. L. MINER; Supt. of Water Works and Electric Lights, F.C. LARGEN; Councilmen, Randal FRAZIER, Frank STRAHAN, C.M. CRAVEN, John SHERBAHN, Wm. PIEPENSTOCK, John GEARTNER.

The very efficient system of water works was built in 1891 at a cost of about $20,000 and last year the city put in one of the most efficient systems of electric lighting to be found in the state of Nebraska.

There are now four newspapers published in the county as follows: Wayne Herald, Nebraska Democrat, Wayne Republican and Winside Tribune.

Wayne has two public school buildings located on very sightly eminences and able to accommodate all the pupils of the district. They are under the management of the Board of Education of which F.L. NEELY is president and Enoch HUNTER secretary. The present superintendent is U.S. CONN. The city also has one of the leading educational institutions of the state in the Nebraska Normal College which was built in 1891 and of which Prof. James M. PILE, A.M., is president.

The present county officials are as follows: County commissioners, R. RUSSELL, J.W. ZIEGLER, E.H. CARROLL; Clerk, J.R. COYLE; Treasurer, Phil H. KOHL; Sheriff, J.M. CHERRY; Judge, Enoch HUNTER; Supt. of Public Instruction, Miss Charlotte M. WHITE; Clerk of the District Court, Bert BROWN; Coroner, John P. GEARTNER; Surveyor, A.L. HOWSER.

On February 7, 1899, after fully advertising for plans and specifications the plans of ORFF & GILBERT were accepted. The board then advertised for bids for the construction of the building and on May 2 the contract was entered into with Messrs. ROWLES & MOORE to erect the building at a cost of $25,600 which contract was approved May 20, 1899. The contract for the plumbing and heating of the building was awarded to the MOORE

Heating Company at $2,860 and the contract signed July 3, 1899. Ground was broken for the erection of the present building early in May of this year and this corner stone was laid August 3, 1899, by the Grand Master of Masons of the state of Nebraska, Judge W.W. KEYSOR of Omaha, with the assistance of the brethren of Wayne Lodge, No. 120, A.F. & A.M., and there deposited with this sketch copies of each of the several town papers and the Holy Bible."

        E.H. CARROLL }
        J.W. ZIEGLER } Co. Com's.
        R. RUSSELL }

The Wayne Republican
August 16, 1899 (Vol. 6, No. 27)

BIRTH: A boy was born to Mr. and Mrs. T.J. THOMAS, August 9.

One of the Big Events.

The G.A.R. reunion of Wayne county veterans and their friends on Wednesday, September 6, 1899, at GRIMSLEY's grove, two miles west of the city. This is the annual reunion and picnic of the Veteran's Association of Wayne county and everybody is invited to come. Bring along your own dinner and the old soldiers will provide the coffee, seats and entertainment. The following are the committees: music, J.D. KING; grounds, Mark STRINGER; finances, A.J. FERGUSON, B. CUNNINGHAM; coffee, R.P. WILLIAMS and Charles BAGGERT. The speakers will be Revs. BITHEL and MONTGOMERY; after dinner talks by J.D. KING and Miss WHITE. It is not to be understood that the above is the entire program, as you will find when you get there. Let everybody prepare for a day off on Sept. 6, and spend it with the veterans.

Real Estate Transfers.

  Reported by I.W. ALTER, bonded abstracter, Wayne, Nebraska:

W.H. McCLUSKY to Anna LEUCK,	
lot 1, blk. 4, B&P's 2nd add to Winside	$25.00
Arthur ZIEGLER to Ant. SCHLACK,	
lot 4, blk. 5, Hoskins	250.00
B.W. & W.M. GUE to J.A. ELLIOTT,	
lot 2, blk. 3, B&P's 2nd add to Winside	15.00
Aug. & Ed KRAUSE to J.A. ELLIOTT,	
lot 4, blk. 3, B&P's add Winside	20.00
State of Nebraska to H.C. BARTELS,	
sw 12-27-3	1,120.00

State of Nebraska to J.R. MORRIS, nw 36-27-1	$1,120.00
O.O. WHITED to D.B. ROBINSON, lot 17, blk. 9, Carroll	20.00
State of Nebraska to Pat COLEMAN, e 1/2, 19-25-4	2,240.00
O.O. WHITED to Geo. C. MERRILL, lots 7, 8 and 9, blk. 6, 1st add Carroll	40.00
McCLUSKY & NEEDHAM to C.B. French, jr., lot 24, blk. 2, Winside	1,086.00
Eliza & N.F. BENNETT to Frank KRUGER, lots 1, 2 and 3, blk. 12, Wayne	3,000.00
Anton LERNER to Anton BIEGLER, lot 4, T&W's add Wayne	325.00
Lewis ROMAN to E.W. MILLER, sw 5-27-3	3,680.00
Mrs. L.A. PLUMB to W.S. GOLDIE, lot 1, blk. 4, n add Wayne	100.00
J.T. BRESSLER to Chris BARTELLS, se 12-27-2	1.00
State of Nebraska to Christ BARTELS, se 12-27-2	- - -
State of Nebraska to Chas. O. SELLON, s 1/2 ne, 4, ne of se 16-27-1	840.00

The Wayne Republican
August 23, 1899 (Vol. 6, No. 28)

BIRTH: Prof. and Mrs. GREGG are rejoicing over the birth of a nice girl baby Monday morning.

BIRTH: Born to Mr. and Mrs. George KAUTZ, a fine daughter of standard weight and beauty. (Hoskins)

DIED: John YENTER and wife had the misfortune to lose their twin babies. They buried one on Friday and the other on Monday. They have the sympathy of the entire community. (Hoskins)

COMMISSIONER PROCEEDINGS, Wayne, Neb., Aug. 14, 1899.
Board met pursuant to adjournment; all members present.
The quarterly report of Justice of the Peace FEATHER, showing no fees, was on motion approved.
The following is a list of names selected by the board from which to draw jurors for the September, 1899, term of the district court:

Hoskins - Wm. ZUTZ, Frank VICK, P. BRUMELS, A.T. WADDEL, And. JOHNSON.

Garfield - Geo. F. DREVESON, G.W. SWEIGARD, W.H. EASTBURN.

Sherman - C.O. SELLON, Jas. EVANS, Alex HINES.

Hancock - Wm. BRICKNER, Herman DECK, W.E. DECK.

Chapin - E.E. OLDS, P. PRYOR, J.R. WASHBURN.

Winside - C.E. MILLER, Harry PRESCOTT, John AGLER.

Deer Creek - Ben ROBINSON, James STEPHENS, Fred BARTEL, T.M. WOOD, C.H. WOLF.

Brenna - Andrew FOLK, E.W. DARNELL, A.B. TIDRICK, John BARRETT.

Strahan - Wm. ALLBERRY, Chas. FISK, F.M. HOSTETTER, O. FRANKS, E.H. WRIGHT.

Wilbur - Geo. JONES, D. SHAY, Al STONE.

Wayne, 1st ward - J.W. TURNER, Frank GAERTNER, C.J. RUNDELL.

3rd ward - C.M. CRAVEN, C.H. JEFFREY, J.W. MASON, Fred PHILLEO, Byron PRESTON.

2nd ward - Jas. BUSH, Met GOODYEAR, L.F. HOLTZ, W.M. HOUSE.

Leslie - Herman LONGE, L. WADE.

Hunter - H.J. WORTH, George FOX, Joseph AGLER, Chris JENSEN.

Logan - E.E. DRISKELL, Fred UTECHT.

Plum Creek - Mort McMANIGAL, Jas. FINN, R.J. SHAWGO.

On motion Board adjourned to Sept. 1, 1899, at 9 o'clock a.m.

J.R. COYLE, County Clerk.

The Wayne Republican
August 30, 1899 (Vol. 6, No. 29)

BIRTH: Born to Mr. and Mrs. John ZIEMER on Thursday last a fine baby girl. All parties doing well. (Hoskins)

BIRTH: Born to Mr. and Mrs. Isaac CARR on Sunday last, a son. (Hoskins)

BIRTH: Mr. and Mrs. Robert GEMMELL are rejoicing over the arrival of a fine baby boy at their home. (Carroll)

The Wayne Republican
September 6, 1899 (Vol. 6, No. 30)

MARRIED: There was a quite wedding at the home of Wm. LOVETT in our city on August 30 at which time and place Rev. C.A. LEMON pronounced Alex HINES and Sina STAMBLOCK man and wife.

MARRIED: HARMES - BRUNE. At the German church southwest of the city on last Thursday afternoon in the presence of a large assemblage occurred the wedding of George HARMES of Manley, Nebraska, and Minnie BRUEN, Rev. GRABER officiating. The groom is engaged in the general merchandise business at Manley and is highly spoken of by those acquainted with him. The bride is well known to many of our readers as a young lady of estimable qualities. After the ceremony at the church the guests repaired to the home of the bride's parents William BRUNE and wife where an elegant repast was served and where hospitality was dispensed with a lavish hand for a time. The young couple have gone to their home at Manley, whether the best wishes of a large circle of friends will be with them bidding them God speed in their journey as man and wife.

MARRIED: AGLER - LONGNECKER. Miss Sadie AGLER and Jerry LONGNECKER were united in marriage at the home of the bride Wednesday, August 30. The young couple have the kindest wishes of a host of friends.

DIED: Died, September 3, George TIDRICK, aged 47 years. Deceased had been in poor health for some time and although every human help was given death claimed its own. He leaves a wife and three children. The burial took place Monday afternoon.

The Wayne Republican
September 13, 1899 (Vol. 6, No. 31)

The G.A.R. picnic at GRIMSLEY's grove on Wednesday was not as well attended as usually. The day was the worst known in years the hot wind being unbearable and the air filled with dust. A few of the bravest, however, went out and tried to think they were enjoying themselves. Rev. BITHEL made the address before dinner after which Miss WHITE, Rev. MONTGOMERY, Rev. DODGE and others spoke. The following officers were elected for the coming year: E.J. NANGLE, Pres.; Levi DILTZ, V.P.; B.F. FEATHER, Sec'y.; Ed. REYNOLDS, Treas.

Wayne County Schools.

A report of the schools of Wayne county for the year beginning July 12, 1898, and ending June 27, 1899.

There are now in the county, seventy-eight districts employing ninety-two teachers. There are 3,435 children between the ages of five and twenty-one. Of these there were 2,645 enrolled in the schools, with an average attendance of 1500. There was expended in the county for all school purposes $43,421.48. Deducting from this $1283 spent for house-building, leaving a balance of $42,138.48, and dividing by 1500, the average attendance, we find it cost us almost $29 per pupil for tuition during the year. There were three new school houses built.

We had five teacher's meetings during the year; twice we had to withdraw our appointments owing to contagious disease in the town. I have not the Secretary's book so can not give the average attendance at these meetings but I know the coldest day last winter there were thirty-five teachers present. Forty-three of the schools, a little over 50 per cent, employed the same teacher during the year.

We had one week of Institute work with an attendance of 117, and for the first time in the history of the county the teachers paid no institute fee, nor was there any money received from the county. The county superintendent made 127 visits to schools during the year.

C.M. WHITE, Sup't.

Republican Committeemen Meet.

At a meeting of the Republican county central committee held at the office of A.A. WELCH the following business was transacted. Meeting called to order by the chairman F.L. NEELY chairman, and roll call found the following precincts represented, Brenna, Chapin, Hoskins, Leslie, Garfield, Sherman, Strahan, Wilbur, Winside, Wayne 1st and 2nd wards. Absent and not represented, Deer Creek, Hancock, Logan and Plum Creek. B. WELBAUM was appointed to fill vacancy in Hunter precinct and F.M. NORTHROP to fill vacancy in 3rd ward of Wayne. The Republican county convention will be held on Saturday, Sept. 30, 1899 at 2:00 p.m. The following delegates were selected for the judicial and state conventions.

Judicial: B.W. McKEEN, J.R. MANNING, F.M. NORTHROP, J.H. PORTER, Louis ZIEMER, A.H. CARTER, J.D. KING, J.T. BRESSLER and Geo. LEWIS.

State: F.M. NORTHROP, E.C. BROOKS, A.A. WELCH, J.T. BRESSLER, J. GOLL, W.H. McNEAL, W.M. GUE, E. CUNNINGHAM and M.S. MOATS.

Real Estate Transfers.
Reported by I.W. ALTER, Wayne, Neb.

North Nebr L & Ipm Co. to O.O. WHITED, lots 10, 11 and 12, blk. 3, Carroll	$25.00
Eunice L. OCONNER to E.A. SURBER, e 1/2 se 3-26-3	1.00
R.H.I. GODDARD to Henry A. FREVERT, w 1/2 nw 15-25-4	2,700.00
R.H.I. GODDARD to Conrad FREVERT, s 1/2 se 11-25-4	2,620.00
B.W. ASHLEY to Frank MOORE, lot 7, blk. 5, college hill Wayne	15.00
Aug. BOCKEMUEHL to Aug WESTERHAUS, s 1/2 sw 32-26-3	1.00
R.W. WILKINS to Frank MOORE, lot 8, blk. 5, college hill Wayne	12.00
Geo. L. DEVINE to Christ THOMPSON, 1/2 int ne 34 & w 1/2 nw 35-26-4	3,250.00
O.O. WHITED to R.D. MERRILL, lots 15, 16, 17 and 18, blk. 1, 1st ad Carroll	350.00
A.M. MAXWELL to Geo. L. DEVINE, ne 14-26-2	4,200.00
W.C. WIGHTMAN to F.L. NEELY, und 1/2 of w 1/2 23-26-2	1.00
X. LAMM to Wm. MELLOR, n 1/2, 30-25-3	9,000.00
Johan BORK to Fannie E. SHAW, lot 6, blk. 1, Winside	37.00
McCLUSKY & NEEDHAM to G. SHABRAM, lot 28, blk. 1, Winside	200.00
A.K. ELLIS to Fred VanNORMAN, sw 12-25-3	5,000.00
Chas. E. MILLER to school dist 67, 1 acre se corner 16-27-1	25.00
Chas. ROLAND to Fred NIEMAN, nw 31-26-3	5,000.00
A.W. BOOECKHOFF to Barbara ROTTER, lot 4, blk. 9, B&B's ad Wayne	700.00
John R. COOKUS to Ida COOKUS, lot 1, blk. 6, Winside	1,000.00

The Wayne Republican
September 27, 1899 (Vol. 6, No. 33)

Real Estate Transfers.
As reported by I.W. ALTER, abstractor, Wayne, Nebraska.

A.W. BOECKHOFF to Barbara ROTTER, lot 4, blk. 9, B&B's addition to Wayne	$700.00
Jno R. COOKUS to Ida COOKUS, lot 1, blk. 6, Winside	1,000.00
Edward PERRY to Clarence CORBIT, pt ne 8-26-4	1.00
Ira RICHARDS to S.H. RICHARDS, pt e 1/2 se 13-26-3	165.00
B.H.I. GADDARD to Hans JORGENSEN, se 1/4 of se 1/4 26-26-4	1,350.00
B.H. GIVINS to C.B. FRENCH, jr., pt lot 1, blk. 9, Winside	400.00
Fannie LOUND to Fred GLASER, lot 5, blk. 5, B&P's 2nd ad Winside	60.00
Bruce SIRES to R.J. WILLIAMS, sw 1/4, 5-26-1	4,270.00
Levi RODOCKER to Bruce SIRES, sw 1/4, 5-26-1	4,000.00
Miles C. LIVINGSTONE to J.R. REESE, east 1/2 29-27-1	7,000.00
Wilhelm ROGGOW to Fred ROGGOW, nw 1/4, 21-26-1	1,800.00
Wm. THOMAS to W.M. WRIGHT, sw 1/4, 15-27-1	4,000.00
Peter MEARS to German Ev. Lutheran church, lots 1, 2 and 3, blk. 25	225.00
Winside Mill Co. to J.R. MUNDY, lots 2 and 4, blk. 1, lots 7 and 13, blk. 2, lots 5 and 6, blk. 6, B&P's 2nd ad, lot 6, outlot 1 1st ad to Winside	1.00
E.E. ADAMS to D.C. MAIN, lot 9, blk. 13, Wayne	2,200.00
J.T. BRESSLER to E. CLAYTON, lot 7, blk. 1, B&P's 1st ad Winside	40.00
Gilbert E. FRENCH to School Dis. 62, 1 acre in ne corner ne 7-27-3	25.00

The Wayne Republican
October 11, 1899 (Vol. 6, No. 35)

BIRTH: Mr. and Mrs. Dennis KELLEHER rejoice over the arrival of a girl baby October 1.

BIRTH: A new girl baby came to the home of Chas. NEISE a few days ago. This makes a baker's dozen for Mr. and Mrs. NEISE.

LICENSED TO WED: Yesterday license to wed was issued E.A. MORIKE and Charlotte McLAUGHLIN and it is expected the parties will be married at Randolph today.

DIED: August NIELE had the misfortune to loose their babe Saturday, the funeral occurred Sunday.

The Wayne Republican
October 18, 1899 (Vol. 6, No. 36)

BIRTH: The home of Fred PETERSON was made happy on Thursday by the birth of a fine boy.

BURIAL: The body of Danial CHENAUR, who died at Fonda, Iowa, a few days ago of typhoid fever was shipped to this place for burial on Monday. This is the oldest son of Ed CHENAUR who recently lived south of the city, but at the present time is somewhere on the Pacific Coast. The young man for a time was in the employ of Robt. UTTER in his bookstore.

The Wayne Republican
October 25, 1899 (Vol. 6, No. 37)

BURIAL: The infant child of Charles PFEIL was interred in the cemetery on Saturday afternoon.

The Wayne Republican
November 1, 1899 (Vol. 6, No. 38)

BIRTH: Born to Mr. and Mrs. Ray GLEASON a find daughter. (Hoskins)

BIRTH: Born to Mr. and Mrs. Ralf WADDELL on Monday last a fine daughter. (Hoskins)

MARRIED: At high noon today at the home of the bride's parents in Lincoln, Nebraska, Rev. C.R. WELDEN, pastor of the Baptist church of this city, and Miss CUSHMAN will be married. It is the intention of the newly wedded couple to go from Lincoln to the home of Mr. WELDEN's parents at Coffeeville, Missouri, for a short visit. They will arrive in this city during next week and expect to go to housekeeping in the residence now occupied by Mrs. NEIHART in the east part of the city. The Republican in its own and on behalf of the citizens of Wayne extends the heartiest congratulations to Mr. and Mrs. WELDEN.

The Wayne Republican
November 29, 1899 (Vol. 6, No. 42)

LICENSED TO WED: J.H. SHEETS AND Maude TIDRICK.

MARRIED: Wednesday evening the wedding bells will ring in behalf of Miss Ida MARTIN and James PORTERFIELD.

MARRIED: Frank DAVEY and Miss Pearl SKEEN are to be married at the home of the young lady's parents Mr. and Mrs. F.M. SKEEN in this city at high noon tomorrow, Thursday November 30.

MARRIED: BAKER - BRUDIGAM. At 2 o'clock today Rev. SCHULTZ will pronounce the words that will bind as husband and wife the lives of Henry BAKER and Rosa BRUDIGAM. The ceremony is to take place at the German Lutheran Church in Leslie precinct and will be in the presence of a large assembly of friends and neighbors of the high contracting parties. The groom is the eldest son of John BAKER one of the thrifty German farmers of Plum Creek and the bride is the daughter of Max BRUDIGAM one of Logan's best known farmers. Tonight a reception will be held at the home of the bride's parents and we know that we are not anticipating too much in saying the event will be a memorable one. The young couple will start out in life with the very best wishes of a large circle of friends among whom the Republican is glad to be classed.

FUNERAL: The funeral of little Wilbur McVICKERS took place at the M.E. Church on Friday afternoon and was quite largely attended. Rev. Thos. BITTEL preached the funeral sermon.

"Tinhorns" Pulled.
Sheriff CHERRY and Marshal MINER
Pull Two Gambling Hells.

For a long time complaints have been coming to the peace

officers of the county and city that gambling hells were being run in the city and while the officers have been anxious to put a stop to the operation of these places, it has proven to be quite a difficult thing to definitely fix their locations, because every time they thought they had the game spotted someone has notified the gangs and they have quietly moved their quarters elsewhere. Like everything else of this kind however there came a day of reckoning and last Thursday night the officers succeeded in locating one of these hells down in the old BUTLER nursery building just north of TURNER & BRENNER's elevator office and another in the back room of the building until lately occupied by KRUGER for saloon purposes. In the first named place were found Gilbert HARRISON, L.C. TITSWORTH, John HAYS, W.O. HARMON and James HEARST. The other place, in the old saloon building, was occupied by Chas. SEASTRAND, "Scotty" MARTIN, Robert CARR, Elmer FULLER, C.B. OWENS, H. SEIK and Dick WILLIAMS. The places were pretty well stocked with the paraphernalia necessary to carry on the business and the games were in full blast when the officers entered and placed proprietors and all others under arrest. Early Friday morning all parties appeared in Judge HUNTER's court and asked for a continuance until the afternoon, which was granted until 1:30 at which time the case of HARRISON and TITSWORTH, charged as keepers of the first place, was called and after hearing the testimony in the case the Judge deemed it sufficient to hold the parties to District court and their bonds were fixed at $500 each which they furnished.

On Saturday the county attorney substituted a complaint for misdemeanor against TITSWORTH and dismissed the case against HARRISON. TITSWORTH plead guilty and was fined $30 and costs. SEASTRAND and MARTIN were charged in the original complaint with being proprietors of the place in the back of the old saloon building and in their case on the same day a complaint for misdemeanor was substituted for the original, and SEASTRAND was named in the substitute as the offender and MARTIN dismissed. SEASTRAND received the same dose as TITSWORTH. The other parties were only held as witnesses.

RASH is at Large.
The Norfolk Asylum Authorities do not
Believe Him Insane and Turn Him Loose.

The News of November 24 brings to us the not unlooked for news that C.K. RASH, the demon in human form that killed his wife and three babies in this county on January 27, 1897, is at liberty. The paper does not give the exact date of his release, saying that he "was given his freedom the other day." It states further that "on his release he took passage for Missouri where he will reside. There is no one sorry that he has chosen Missouri for his home unless it be the people of that state, as Nebraska is glad enough to get rid of him." Most of our readers are fully acquainted with the horrible details of the fiends crime and for which he only escaped the hangman's noose by the jurors being in doubt as to the sanity of anyone who could commit such a terrible deed. It is well that he has gone to Missouri, because had he returned to this country there is room for doubt as to whether his old neighbors would have been as merciful to him as was the Pierce county jury that declared him insane instead of sending him to the gallows to have paid the penalty of his awful deed by going up his own miserable life. It is to be hoped that he will remain in Missouri or at least that he will never again show up in Nebraska or Wayne county, until the Judge of the Universe shall be called upon to pass on him the penalty deserved for his crimes.

Real Estate Transfers.

Reported by I.W. ALTER, Bonded Abstracter, Wayne, Neb.

McCLUSKY & NEEDHAM to TURNER & BRENNER,	
lot 1, blk. 15, Winside	$3,500.00
C.F. BARNES to Julia RICHARDSON,	
lot 12, blk. 4, Lake's add Wayne	600.00
Wm. H. LINN to Chas. S. BEEBE,	
lot 17, blk. 5, north add Wayne	1,000.00
Claud HANCOCK to J.A. KREBS,	
lots 1, 2 and 3, blk. 3, Carroll	76.00
T.W. MORAN to Samuel BARLEY,	
lot 9, blk. 26, Wayne	435.0
South Omaha National Bank to Guy C. BARTON,	
n 1/2 & sw 1/4 & w 1/2 se 1/4 Sec. 18; &	
s 1/2 se 1/4 of 14, & ne 1/4 of 23, &	
s 1/4 of 14, & sw 1/4 of 13 except R R right	
of way, & 63 acres in s 1/2 nw 1/4 of 13,	
all in 26 3; also s 1/2 of nw 1/4 of 24, &	
all of Sec. 26, in 27-2	56,000.00
A.W. CROSS to Wm. VIERGUTG,	
ne 1/4 of 31-26-1	3,200.00
Dewitt D. FORWARD to Charlotte A. HOGUE,	
75 feet off w side lot 14, T&W's add to Wayne	800.00
Clara K. MOORE to A.W. CROSS,	
ne 1/4 of 31-26-1	3,036.00
P.N. PETERSON to R.M. WADDELL,	
lots 1 & 2, blk. 9, and all block 2, Hoskins	450.00

Sarah A. ELDER to A.J. DURLAND,
    e 1/2 sw 1/4 31, and w 1/2 sw 1/4, 31 all in 25-1 $- - -
E.C. McDOWELL to Minnie MUIRHEAD,
    lot 15, blk. 2, Winside   800.00
Mrs. E.A. SLATER to Maud E. SLATER,
    n 72 feet outlot 5, C&B's add to Wayne   350.00
L. PRESTON to Jas. DONAHUE,
    lots 7, 8, 9, 10, 11 and 12, blk. 2,
    college hill, Wayne   70.00
O.L. BRIGGS to Fred VERGES,
    n 1/2 Sec. 22-26-1   8,000.00
E.F. BARTLETT to J.W. BARTLETT,
    lots 3 & 4, blk. 11, college add   2.00
Plumer CRIST to Frank WEIBLE,
    nw 1/4, 33-26-2   3,360.00
S.O. REESE, et al., to Jas M. REESE,
    ne 1/4, 12-27-1   3,600.00
S.O. REESE, et al., to Fred W. COLE,
    nw 1/4, 7-27-1   <u>5,117.00</u>
                TOTAL TRANSFERS $90,396.00

The Wayne Republican
December 13, 1899 (Vol. 6, No. 44)

DIED: On Monday afternoon December 11, the angel of death entered our city and summoned to his final rest E. MARTIN aged 79 years 7 months and 23 days. The immediate cause of death was bladder troubles from which the deceased has been a sufferer for a long time. Judge MARTIN, for by that name he is best known to most of our readers, was born in Bristol, Conn., in 1820, came into Wayne county, Nebraska from Council Bluffs, Iowa, sometime during the fall of 1881 and has been a resident thereof from that date until death called him hence. He was an earnest christian, a loving husband and kind father; a man respected by his fellows and one in whom they placed implicit confidence. For 14 years prior to January 1, 1898, he held the office of County Judge and so administered its affairs as to gain for himself the regard of all having business relations with him. Before coming to this state he held the office Justice of the Peace in the city of Council Bluffs and for several years was Sheriff at Baraboo, Wis. He leaves to mourn his departure an aged wife and three children, Mrs. HARTPENCE of New Jersey, Mrs. Will SEARS and Charles MARTIN of this county. Three brothers John H. of California, C.D. of this city and Thos. M. of Minnesota survive him. He is one that will be missed and mourned by a large circle of friends and acquaintances whose tears will be mingled in sympathy with the afflicted family. The funeral takes place from the Baptist church of this city at 2:30 to-day December 13, 1899.

The Wayne Republican
December 20, 1899 (Vol. 6, No. 45)

BIRTH: Twin boys were born to Fred SLAHN and wife yesterday, so Dr. NIEMAN reports.

LICENSED TO WED: Milo KREMKE and Mary KRACHT.

MARRIED: HASTINGS - RUSSELL. On Tuesday evening December 19 at the home of S.B. RUSSELL in this city occurred the marriage of his daughter Ida Elnora to Harry HASTINGS of Washington, Pa. Rev. Thos. BITHEL performed the ceremony in the presence of the immediate relatives and friends of the bride. On Thursday the newly married couple will take their departure for Washington, Pa., where the groom is engaged in the hardware business and where they will make their home in the future.

DIED: FARRAND. On Thursday morning December 14 Clara A. wife of Thos. FARRAND, passed from life to the great beyond. The deceased was 46 years of age and was a native of Pennsylvania. The cause of death was lung fever. Mrs. FARRAND was a lady beloved by her friends and neighbors who will sympathize with the husband so sadly stricken by her death. The funeral occurred on Sunday afternoon and was very largely attended.

The Wayne Republican
December 27, 1899 (Vol. 6, No. 46)

MARRIED: MORGAN - CAFFEE. At the home of the bride's parents Mr. and Mrs. T.J. CAFFEE of this city at nine o'clock Xmas morning Rev. JOHNSON of Wakefield pronounced the words that bind for all time the lives of Charles E. MORGAN and Hallie C. CAFFEE. The ceremony was performed in the presence of a number of invited guests. The groom is not unknown to many of our readers, as for several terms he was a student in our Normal College and if we mistake not has taught in schools of the county. At present he is Principal of Pilger schools, this being his second year in that position. The bride is the daughter of our well known citizen T.J. CAFFEE, and is a young lady highly respected in the community and one beloved by her friends. After January 4, the newly married couple will be home to their friends at Pilger, Neb.

DIED: Death has again entered our city and called away from our midst Mrs. Vaughn DAVIS, on Thursday, December 21. The deceased has been ill for several months, but her illness had not been of the nature that led most of us to expect that the end was so near and the announcement was much of a surprise. The sympathy of the community will be extended to the bereaved husband, children and other relatives in their day of great sorrow.

Improvements in the City.
The Building Operations for the Year 1899.
Foot up over $81,000.00

The building operations in our city during the year 1899 have been much greater than most people imagine without giving the matter careful thought. The figures we herewith present are not given as covering all that has been done during the year, because in all probability we have overlooked some. In some instances the figures are estimates and may not be exactly correct, but as a whole we believe they will be found approximately correct. These figures do not take into account the thousands of dollars that have been expended in painting, building sidewalks and beautifying the homes of the city which it taken into the account would swell the grand total above the $100,000 mark. Here is the list of improvements as gathered by us.

Wayne county court house	$30,000
Presbyterian church	10,000
German church	2,500
J.H. GOLL, new residence	3,000
E.M. SMITH, new residence	2,500
Thos. FARRAND, new residence	1,300
J.H. WRIGHT, new residence	600
SWAN & MILLER, new storeroom	3,500
F. KRUGERS, new residence	2,500
Dr. NIEMAN, new residence	2,300
L.J. HANSEN, new residence	1,000
A.E. CHAFFEE, new residence	1,800
F.L. NEELY, new residence	1,500
F. HOOD, new residence	1,000
Geo. LEOBSACK, new residence	600
A.J. FERGUSON, ad to residence	800
J.D. KING, ad to residence	250
H. GETMAN, ad to residence	450
A.A. WELCH, ad to residence	250
A. GOULD, ad to residence	250
C. WARNER, ad to residence	400
G.C. TERWILLIGER, ad to residence	200

H.F. WILSON, ad to residence	$200
Phil LUNDBERG, ad to residence	600
F.M. NORTHROP, ad to residence	50
Mrs. BIRLENMEYER, ad to residence	500
W.H. McNEAL, ad to residence	250
I.W. ALTER, ad to residence	250
L. PRESTON, ad to residence	400
F.M. SKEEN, ad to residence	1,000
T. FARRAND, ad to residence	250
Sam BARLEY, ad to residence	200
KRUGERS, new saloon	1,800
SONNEKEN, storeroom	1,200
GRIMSLEY, barn	1,000
Eli JONES, livery barn	5,000
Ad to B. ROOSA's store	400
J. SHERBAHN's brick yard	1,000
Mrs. H.C. CUNNINGHAM, barn	75
R.H. JOHANSEN, barn	150
Barn at fair grounds	300
School buildings	350
J.W. CHAFFEE, imp. residence	100
TOTAL	81.025

Surname Index

AARON, 251
ABBOTT, 215
ACKLEY, 189
ACKLIN, 189
ACREN, 395
ACTON, 93 101 470
ADAMS, 70 89 135 299 349 386 499
ADAMSON, 67 71 138 142 285
ADSIT, 405
AGLER, 1 2 5 6 8 19 31 33 65 70 94 154 187 197 214 233 234 238 244 245 246 251 252 259 261 263 265 274 297 298 321 389 434 446 456 489 495 496
AHERN, 23 38 62 73 94 160 184 272 274 331 352 368 382 388 408 409 434 435 447
AILWARD, 486
AIRN, 342
AISTROPE, 390
AITKEN, 97
ALBEE, 74
ALBERS, 189 461 479
ALBERT, 88
ALDEN, 128 130
ALEXANDER, 23 73 170 201 271 318 366 389 405
ALGER, 133 255 265 320 439
ALLBERRY, 495
ALLEN, 2 8 22 56 71 72 112 352 489
ALSTADT, 254 296
ALTER, 161 165 185 213 224 276 339 340 342 349 355 373 380 382 384 389 391 398 402 404 409 412 423 430 432 438 442 444 452 459 465 473 476 484 485 486 492 493 498 499 503 507
ALTERS, 203
ALTSTADT, 389
AMADON, 148
AMENT, 62 75 231 476
ANDERBERRY, 481
ANDERSEN, 128
ANDERSON, 28 30 36 70 78 91 94 113 114 119 120 130 137 138 144 148 164 165 169 174 178 182 187 189 195 203 210 213 215 235 236 250 255 262 264 267 272 309 310 323 382 383 386 404 409 411 433 439

ANDERSON (Cont.), 444 455 468 470 475 477 481
ANDREAS, 303
ANDRESEN, 420
ANDRESS, 160 287 366 396
ANDREWS, 55 178 263 274 275 469
ANDVENS, 120
ANSON, 270 321 324
ANTHONY, 150
APPLETON, 16
ARCHER, 146 324
ARMACOST, 446 480
ARMSTRONG, 34 49 53 69 73 74 75 76 106 144 154 181 187 191 200 203 233 251 266 272 318 342 367 452
ARNOLD, 113 119
ARTLEY, 318 460
ARVOLD, 395
ASH, 160 295 333 334 336 337 338 410 443
ASHLEY, 202 214 498
ASMUS, 171 378
ATKINS, 159 255 265 333 448 456
ATLES, 290
AUGHEY, 401 489
AUKER, 465
AUSENHEIMER 189
AVERHILL, 227
AVERILL, 214 283 285
BACKER, 130 412
BAER, 463
BAGERT, 442
BAGGART, 292 399
BAGGERT, 181 203 238 259 287 321 331 493
BAILEY, 64 153 168 177 178 247 256 265 348 374 470 487
BAINSTER, 395
BAIRD, 71 138 142 203 236 246 256 264 265 342 382 488
BAKER, 29 128 131 134 145 149 156 158 165 168 177 178 186 198 207 290 293 296 323 325 340 382 391 406 409 433 434 454 501
BALDWIN, 149 392
BALLARD, 130
BANISTER, 191 432
BANNON, 215
BARBER, 321 449
BARBOUR, 54 138 160 165 186

Surname Index

BARBOUR (Cont.), 194 226 231 233 234 250 251 258 263 274 285 324 331 333 337 383 385 449 450 459 464
BARCKLEY, 33
BARD, 255
BARGER, 270 355
BARGHOLZ, 254 296 354
BARKLEY, 478
BARLEY, 503 507
BARNARD, 433
BARNES, 30 134 159 171 204 247 256 257 264 383 432 483 503
BARNHARDT, 307
BARRET, 161
BARRETT, 218 349 386 391 495
BARRON, 285
BARTEL, 495
BARTELLS, 455
BARTELS, 219 493 494
BARTLETT, 8 17 20 23 66 109 115 116 117 167 182 204 249 264 267 270 287 292 299 321 337 355 372 382 385 388 442 472 504
BARTON, 503
BASSFORD, 290 293
BASTIAN, 113 119 138 255 265
BATEMAN, 290
BATTAM, 277
BAUER, 473
BAUMANN, 484
BAUMGARDNER, 184
BAUSE, 342
BAWDEN, 120
BAXTER, 16
BAYDERS, 454
BAYES, 110 128 150 172 221 355 443 470 481
BEACH, 97 215
BEALE, 169 172 219 220 254 333 336 338 349 353 434 454 470
BEALS, 219
BEAM, 152
BEAR, 386
BEARDSHEAR, 9 10 14 31 34 49 52 53 54 74
BEARDSLEY, 254 349
BEATON, 471
BECK, 476
BECKENHAUER, 94 161 185

BECKENHAUER (Cont.), 223 230 303 481
BECKENHAUR, 91 334
BECKMAN, 199
BEEBE, 69 72 73 74 165 169 181 187 194 203 217 221 236 246 255 257 264 361 366 395 410 469 503
BEELS, 112 452
BEEMER, 263
BEHMER, 11 17 18 21 124 165 191 226 255 277 304 341 342 381 390 407 456
BEHNER, 169
BEHRES, 457
BEHRNIDE, 166
BEIRMAN, 111
BELDEN, 290 293
BELDON, 220
BELETER, 476
BELFORD, 168 178 192 215 290
BELL, 31 165 174 190 265 323 401 474
BENDER, 214 216 217 356 384 444 449 460
BENEDICT, 157 277 481
BENN, 87 101
BENNER, 272 321
BENNET, 137
BENNETT, 36 49 52 72 74 76 82 95 104 105 125 132 133 139 142 143 144 149 494
BENNING, 106 277
BENRHARDT, 29 71 78
BENSCHOFF, 71
BENSEN, 181
BENSER, 124 162 232 238 250 323 342 355 380 382 395
BENSHOOF, 160 187 197 216 232 236 238 259 262 270 274 275 340 342 382 399 426 436 446 455 470 480 485
BENSON, 34 49 52 165 191 233 450 452 455 469 479 480 486
BENT, 75 245
BENTH, 113 119
BENTHEIR, 296
BENTHEIRE, 288 289
BENTHIAN, 220
BENTHIEN, 389 398
BENTHIER, 257 290
BENTLEY, 111

Surname Index

BENTLY, 255 264
BENTON, 349
BENU, 61
BENUTH, 200
BERGESON, 441
BERGT, 411
BERGUSON, 159
BERKHEIMER, 256
BERKLEY, 181 198
BERRIS, 187
BERRY, 70 86 97 179 223 265 284 334 340 362 368 429 440
BEUTHEIN, 187
BEVINS, 3 4 6 490
BIBLER, 334 430
BIEGLER, 494
BIERMAN, 71
BIGLER, 271 274
BIGLEY, 436
BILLETER, 455
BILLITER, 240
BILLMAN, 215
BILLS, 76
BINDERUP, 31
BINGER, 263
BINNEY, 328
BIRKHEIMER, 265
BIRKLAND, 470
BIRLENMEYER, 507
BISHOP, 155 206
BISSELL, 290
BITHEL, 356 374 394 397 406 407 433 436 450 458 468 491 493 496 501 505
BITHELL, 361 367 443
BJORKLAND, 166
BLACK, 31 64 65 122 202 370 404 433
BLACO, 446
BLAGG, 177
BLAIR, 169 184 191 197 233 271 339 349 354 398 438 442 445
BLAKE, 172 289
BLAKESLEY, 262 269 271 373 466 468 480 481
BLANCHARD, 250 257 272 274
BLAZE, 467
BLEICH, 355
BLENKIRON, 171 444
BLOODHART, 39
BLOTCKY, 215
BLOTZ, 444

BLUE, 91
BOCK, 161 340 392
BOCKEMUEHL, 297 498
BOCKEMULE, 150
BOECKHOFF, 499
BOEKENHAUER, 1 7 17 44 76
BOETEL, 378
BOGART, 154 220 296 299 302 418
BOKELOH, 144
BOLIN, 137
BOLING, 341
BOMERMASTER, 291
BON, 146
BONAWITZ, 125 279 309 310 367
BONER, 230 261 269 301 350
BONESTEDT, 374
BONHAM, 233 382 443
BONNAWITZ, 79
BOOCK, 260 262 296
BOOCKE, 235
BOOECKHOFF, 498
BOOK, 120 287
BOOKE, 331
BOOTH, 343
BORCHERT, 389 483
BORDERS, 174
BORGENHAGEN, 79
BORK, 498
BORKENHAGEN, 52
BOSCHEN, 444
BOSE, 414 429
BOSTARD, 477
BOSTEDER, 132 194 446
BOSTETTER, 321
BOSTROM, 171 218 253 257 296 380
BOTHWELL, 212
BOUCHER, 219 228
BOUCK, 372
BOUGHN, 350
BOVEE, 153
BOWDEN, 185 438
BOWER, 329
BOWERS, 39 443
BOWMAN, 187 473
BOYD, 65 211 221 240 247 285 299 389 400 439
BOYER, 81 82
BRAASCH, 65 210 252 303
BRADFORD, 150 156 164 165 171 175 185 187 203 221 234

BRADFORD (Cont.), 267 292 297 330 429 434 440
BRADY, 219 239 254 257 299
BRAGG, 390
BRAMHALL, 134
BRANDT, 281 296
BRANMER, 120
BRANT, 143
BRASCH, 31 323
BRASSFIELD, 8 10
BRAUN, 383 480
BRECKENRIDGE, 189
BRENDERICK, 483
BRENNER, 160 169 200 217 287 292 335 336 339 362 396 447 453 469 486 502 503
BRESSLER, 1 15 34 37 50 62 65 75 76 80 94 102 106 108 110 130 132 146 147 157 160 168 171 172 173 179 183 211 219 221 222 227 240 245 246 254 255 265 266 271 283 290 291 295 296 299 349 355 368 369 388 390 402 417 418 436 448 456 461 472 476 483 494 497 499
BREWER, 296 299 465 473
BRICKNER, 495
BRIDAL, 120
BRIGGS, 86 90 106 151 285 504
BRIGHT, 480
BRITTON, 4 8 10 11 12 13 21 25 27 29 36 38 50 55 62 67 73 76 80 88 94 95 102 103 110 111 115 116 117 124 130 132 134 144 200 240 249 261 262 269 295 299 392 469 478 480 491
BROD, 9 14 34 75
BROKS, 258
BROLINE, 176
BROME, 31
BROMMELL, 329
BRONSYNSKI, 288 289
BROOKINGS, 422
BROOKS, 165 404 497
BROWER, 157 215 297 349 369 395 455
BROWN, 25 36 37 42 49 53 69 70 73 76 82 90 97 121 128 133 134 135 148 153 158 165 168 172 174 175 178 179 180 192 200 213 214 221 226 231
BROWN (Cont.), 232 239 249 251 252 256 257 259 261 262 269 270 271 274 283 285 303 305 334 342 356 360 369 373 376 388 391 394 397 403 407 419 432 434 448 462 464 465 469 473 480 492
BRUCKNER, 264
BRUDIGAM, 501
BRUDIGAN, 471
BRUECHNER, 295
BRUECKNER, 172
BRUGER, 159 160 262 325 336 338 392 455
BRUGGEMAN, 166
BRUGGERMAN, 200 291
BRUGGERMON, 180
BRUMELS, 495
BRUMMELS, 277 456
BRUNE, 159 175 470 496
BRUNER, 31 194 230 231 456
BRUSE, 186 235 238 381 435
BRYAN, 101 223
BRYANT, 30 32 61 81 94 107 172 219 259
BUCHANAN, 123 134 136 149
BUCHOLTZ, 220
BUCHOLZ, 224 240 243
BUCK, 383 395
BUCKER, 149
BUCKNER, 199
BUCKS, 75
BUETOW, 467
BUFFINGTON, 255 366
BUOL, 214 251 389
BURCH, 156 469
BURCHART, 192
BURDICK, 160 231 447
BURGERSON, 166
BURK, 207
BURKS, 171
BURNETT, 395
BURNHAM, 37 196 198 235 250 262 331 435 455 456
BURR, 172 219 254 295 296 353 355 388 449 463 484
BURSON, 50 226 262 321 328 408 409 444 481
BURTON, 81
BUSBEE, 54
BUSBY, 92
BUSH, 34 56 135 146 161 202 207 210 214 236 237 287 407

Surname Index

BUSH (Cont.), 409 460 469 470 495
BUSKIRK, 169 294 341 404 436 479
BUSS, 291 374
BUTLER, 2 79 215 472 502
BYRD, 174
BYRNE, 304 305
CADWELL, 299 305 342
CAFFEE, 440 481 505
CAGLY, 182
CAHOON, 220 254 256 299
CAMERON, 434
CAMPBELL, 35 159 160 161 275 325 334 337 382 455 456
CANANAUGH, 215
CANN, 364
CAREY, 443
CARLIN, 77
CARLSON, 148 210 230 296 395 459 463 464
CARMAN, 305
CARNELL, 9 31 34
CARNS, 202
CARPENTER, 38 49 73 276 343 486
CARR, 106 253 258 320 495 502
CARRO, 368
CARROLL, 100 168 169 173 174 203 215 233 238 247 251 253 255 259 262 266 287 294 408 436 453 492 493
CARSTENS, 299 476
CARTER, 162 169 178 180 181 188 192 236 247 297 323 342 382 395 435 467 472 476 481 497
CARTWRIGHT, 77
CARVER, 177 348
CARY, 215
CASE, 64 133 134 180 196 222 246 323 342 381 439
CASEY, 375 395
CASS, 126
CASSEL, 162
CASSELL, 195 411
CASSON, 454
CASTANETTE, 446
CATTNACH, 113 119 120
CAULEY, 458
CAVANAUGH, 77 80 186 297 435
CAVENAUGH, 343
CAVENOUGH, 211
CHACE, 20 31 39 54 73 77 87 94 96 134 139 147 165 168 173 187 235 236 237 252 272 280 295 342 366 367 418 420 434
CHAFFE, 120
CHAFFEE, 9 10 20 26 110 133 134 257 274 380 442 460 506 507
CHAFFIE, 243
CHAMBERS, 183 255 265
CHANCE, 257 274 291 331
CHAON, 78 109 384 431 432
CHAPIN, 8 44 50 76 95 109 113 124 125 128 129 138 162 168 184 222 240 323 392 400 434 471 486
CHAPMAN, 78 432 460 463
CHARD, 225
CHARDE, 170 214 401
CHEERY, 192
CHENAUER, 299 349 432
CHENAUR, 109 325 500
CHERRY, 94 127 160 162 214 229 244 297 318 340 343 344 345 346 347 350 351 360 369 382 393 397 398 399 439 460 469 471 488 492 501
CHICHESTER, 166 234 240 260 453 457
CHILCUTT, 455
CHILDS, 11 23 34 37 40 50 60 62 67 72 94 102 104 108 120 124 134 136 138 139 140 149 152 155 164 166 178 189 196 198 200 206 209 225 231 234 239 241 244 248 252 263 270 287 290 292 321 368 460 481 488
CHILSON, 472
CHOAN, 160 161
CHRISTENSON, 438
CHRISTIANSON, 160
CLARK, 31 54 65 106 125 144 162 200 206 211 213 241 287 291 342 365 368 377 384 388 389 447 453 463
CLARKE, 208
CLASMAN, 431
CLASSMAN, 431 432
CLAUDE, 388

Surname Index

CLAUSEN, 328 384
CLAYBAUGH, 199 236 250 290 325 375 480 481
CLAYTON, 325 381 484 485 499
CLINE, 77 136 192 204 232 262 298 323 332 367 390 399 440
CLINGMAN, 180 211
COABOSE, 120
COATES, 16
COBB, 434
COCHRAN, 160 161
COEN, 233
COFFIN, 185
COLBERT, 163 390 470
COLE, 200 484 504
COLEBURN, 48
COLEMAN, 98 135 160 186 195 232 235 262 263 265 275 382 395 399 445 446 456 472 494
COLLARD, 303 388 437 438 485
COLLINS, 114 119 162 251 331
COLLINSON, 157 170
COMPTON, 364
COMSTOCK, 76
CONE, 9 22 76 111 365
CONES, 307
CONET, 80
CONGER, 255 265 434
CONKLIN, 230
CONLEY, 463
CONLIN, 432
CONN, 206 242 253 261 303 305 362 469 478 480 481 492
CONNOR, 92 109 124 128 129 136 142 150 326 443
CONOVER, 83
CONRAD, 101
COOK, 34 48 73 74 81 101 104 107 137 143 144 152 160 161 185 201 206 216 228 236 248 271 292 303 318 322 367 370 372 452 454 475
COOKSIE, 133
COOKUS, 498 499
COON, 250
COONEY, 339
COONS, 157 240 254 349
COOPER, 44 130
COPPLE, 212
CORBIT, 122 160 186 200 231 280 308 309 384 499
CORDNER, 413
COREY, 9 92

COTTERELL, 241
COTTRELL, 178
COUFFER, 304 457
COVIE, 300
COWLEY, 431
COX, 181 220 250 408 445
COYLE, 9 10 15 34 48 50 54 68 69 72 73 74 75 80 82 96 105 184 225 233 244 318 322 343 344 345 346 347 360 362 385 397 414 428 446 453 454 455 492 495
CRAMER, 120 125 215
CRANE, 6 8 11 12 13 17 18 19 20 24 50 95 102 115 116 117 155 221
CRAVEN, 160 167 235 318 366 396 428 459 469 492 495
CRAWFORD, 1 2 4 5 9 24 29 30 31 32 35 36 38 48 53 56 62 64 65 66 75 94 95 97 104 110 138 143 350 436 476 489
CREAMER, 122
CREWS, 112
CRISSWELL, 114 119
CRIST, 90 504
CROCKET, 166 392
CROFFER, 200
CROSBY, 65 67 353 384 443
CROSS, 76 109 250 257 274 389 398 411 439 450 503
CROSSLAND, 160 243 271 334 336 337 338 445 453
CROUCH, 395
CROWLEY, 390
CULLEN, 156 179 180 192 194 206 214 223 233 234 238 251 255 262 267 269 369 398 399 443 448 455 469 475
CULLER, 160 182 194 246 249 250 258 261 262 270 322 367 410 442
CULVER, 20 50 112 140 14 212 402
CUMMINGS, 126
CUMMINS, 69
CUNNINGHAM, 48 80 120 130 132 153 165 168 169 171 172 173 182 191 200 202 203 206 210 213 224 228 229 233 237 238 242 248 250 252 258 259 261 262 266 269 272 273 284 287 289 292 295 297 298 303

CUNNINGHAM (Cont.), 321 322 325 342 350 361 366 367 370 372 380 391 407 409 414 429 430 452 454 464 471 472 480 484 485 486 493 497 507
CURRAN, 144
CURRIER, 395 408 410
CURTIS, 33 113 119
CUSHMAN, 501
CUTLER, 10 106
CUTTER, 113 119
DAESS, 343
DAHLBERE, 105
DAHLBERG, 290
DALL, 286
DALY, 476
DAMME, 153 160 187 215 246 257
DANBERG, 159
DANBURG, 80 202
DANIELS, 78 216 394
DANIELSON, 384 393
DANILSON, 382
DANN, 328
DARNELL, 201 461 495
DARNER, 148
DART, 185
DAUM, 341 386
DAVENPORT, 27 76 239 470 472
DAVEY, 501
DAVIDSON, 114 119 485
DAVIES, 11 17 23 27 30 37 47 49 52 53 54 56 58 64 67 69 73 74 75 80 81 88 96 112 115 118 136 139 140 144 149 167 168 177 224 235 236 253 255 264 272 336 445
DAVIS, 49 99 105 113 119 134 191 192 211 227 235 253 258 262 264 266 267 275 399 437 438 446 455 456 467 472 506
DAWIDAT, 319
DEAN, 137
DEARING, 320
DEARBORN, 10 34 37 38 50 60 61 66 77 79 87 91 94 97 100 101 114 115 116 117 119 120 125 126 128 129 130 131 138 143 144 145 146 148 149 152 153 166 179 202 216 240 250 257 264 271 274 290 319 342 380 389 392 404 405 444 449

DEARBORN (Cont.), 478 479 484
DEARBOW, 157
DECK, 195 239 262 271 297 435 454 456 495
DECKER, 23 113 119
DEDLA, 353
DELAHOYDE, 124 125 134 147
DELAPLAIN, 339
DELEVAN, 16
DELFS, 219
De LONG, 100 323
DEMAREE, 104
De MASSE, 245 246
DeMOSS, 320
DEPLER, 177 447
DERICK, 96
DEUCKER, 487
DEVIDAT, 379
DEVINE, 130 485 498
DEVLIN, 149
DICKERSON, 246
DICKEY, 261 269 303 305
DICKSON, 114 119
DILLARD, 152
DILLON, 392
DILTS, 135 232 234 255 459
DILTZ, 160 192 258 263 264 274 323 369 382 399 454 456 460 480 496
DIMMEL, 184 412
DINKLANG, 380
DITTLE, 200
DIX, 395
DIXON, 481
DOBBIN, 186 220 228 232 254 299 433 455 472
DOBBINS, 157
DOCK, 37
DODGE, 137 175 215 220 286 295 392 496
DOFFINY, 155
DOLAN, 379
DONAHUE, 504
DONNER, 165 179 214 222 236 440
DORAN, 382
DORAW, 341
DORING, 386
DORMAN, 261 269 270
DORN, 32
DORNICE, 166
DOTY, 215

Surname Index

DOUGLASS, 166 322
DOVEDAT, 375
DOVEE, 155
DOWLING, 435
DRAKE, 61 101 384 434
DREVESON, 495
DREVSEN, 438
DREW, 376
DRIER, 340
DRISCOLL, 342 382
DRISKELL, 323 473 495
DRUHE, 476
DUERIG, 160 175 187 220 296 416 417 455 483
DUFF, 76
DUGAN, 31 64 65 124
DUKE, 65
DUMM, 113
DUNCAN, 343
DUNLAP, 286
DURHAM, 211
DURIN, 2 489
DURKE, 133
DURLAND, 504
DURRIN, 334 335 424 425
DUTCHER, 89 102
DYE, 16
DYER, 64 199
DYSART, 382
EASTBURN, 196 233 235 238 258 262 275 456 495
EATON, 202
EAYRS, 5
EBERSOLE, 215
EBY, 435
ECHARDT, 78
ECHART, 274
ECKHARDT, 277
ECKHART, 242 250 257 272
ECKMAN, 214 218 296 399
ECKMANN, 262
ECKROTH, 296
EDDY, 477
EDSON, 463 484
EDWARDS, 128 144 150 156 171 175 187 200 203 212 221 234 267 297 331 429 434 440 467
EGELER, 164
EHLERS, 437 438
EHLUS, 290
EHRED, 402
EHRHARDT, 487

EICH, 186 235 258 342 368
EICHE, 178
EICHOFF, 236
EISENHEUER, 367
ELDER, 504
ELDRED, 175 479
ELLIOT, 160
ELLIOTT, 28 78 80 106 115 116 117 135 183 184 251 255 264 389 469 481 493
ELLIS, 53 87 94 160 181 186 200 215 219 232 234 239 244 252 267 331 336 340 375 388 405 412 439 445 453 498
ELLISON, 128
ELLSWORTH, 34 53 56 57 74 99
ELTING, 295 388 392 476
EMCH, 367
EMERICK, 106
EMERSON, 17 37 40 50 62 77 80 95
EMERY, 89
EMGLERT, 368
ENDERS, 155
ENGLERT, 133 255 258 434
ENGLISCH, 10 34 52 65 76 79
ENGLISH, 127 133
EOUGHN, 255
EPLER, 426
ERICKSON, 272 299 342 411 440 465 483
ERKSHIRE, 295
ERXLEBEN, 1 71 187 255 265 267 287 443 445
ESTABROOK, 47
EVANS, 111 155 192 200 208 240 253 287 288 326 369 388 441 466 467 470 476 487 495
EVERT, 144 186
EVERETT, 219 254 257 299 476
EVERINGHAM, 238
EWING, 190
FAHNESTOCK, 480
FAIRBAIN, 214
FALK, 441
FARIS, 164
FARLEY, 395
FARR, 132 246 250 257 274 331 442
FARRAN, 388
FARRAND, 322 473 505 506 507
FAVAR, 137
FEATHER, 10 21 37 62 67 95

FEATHER (Cont.), 107 109 132 152 182 186 238 248 255 259 264 270 287 300 319 322 355 367 373 494 496
FELDENHEIMER, 134
FELKER, 254
FENSKE, 223 434 476
FENSKI, 446
FENTON, 125 144
FERGUSON, 23 127 149 164 248 292 322 372 373 442 447 455 493 506
FERMAN, 11
FERRIS, 456
FEUCHS, 156
FEUSKE, 382
FIGGINS, 70
FILKNER, 200
FINLAYSON, 31 47 64 470
FINN, 190 263 434 495
FINNELL, 8 10
FISHER, 49 53 62 73 74 96 109 110 123 160 174 212 217 225 244 246 250 255 264 265 289 292 301 318 322 328 340 362 366 381 391 403 460 471 483
FISK, 495
FITCH, 307
FITZGERALD, 329 361 375 379 398 431 458 491
FITZSIMMONS, 266 327 354 434
FLEMING, 134
FLETCHER, 2 5 6 120 168 186 200 237 238 249 252 261 267 269 298 331 455 489
FLICKINGER, 10 11 13 31 65 75
FLING, 435
FLOHR, 54 77 80 96
FLYNN, 253
FOGG, 94 255
FOLCK, 240 376
FOLEY, 128
FOLK, 404 467 495
FOLTZ, 215 335 385 445 453
FOOTE, 159 291 442 452
FORBES, 185 448
FORD, 81 111 118 120
FORDYCE, 73 74 81
FORMAN, 37
FORTNER, 160 173 186 342 368
FORWARD, 503

FOSTER, 137 165 211 255 263 302 388 442
FOUSS, 212
FOWLER, 273
FOX, 8 11 12 17 18 19 20 24 26 70 80 115 124 160 165 169 170 182 186 191 224 232 236 250 262 276 331 399 432 452 463 495
FRANCES, 454
FRANCIS, 169 174 256 262 268 275 374
FRANKS, 495
FRASER, 304
FRAYER, 200
FRAZIER, 41 42 95 111 124 125 128 130 135 136 138 139 159 160 161 170 182 185 201 202 210 212 213 219 226 255 292 301 305 318 319 320 333 334 344 345 346 347 348 362 397 467 469 470 478 492
FREBERG, 182
FREDERICKSON, 201 410
FREED, 211
FREELAND, 64 133
FREEMAN, 57 58
FREESE, 164
FREITLE, 173
FRENCH, 126 131 155 171 172 173 175 183 202 216 219 221 271 285 286 299 300 328 340 349 350 355 356 388 409 427 449 465 470 471 478 483 484 485 494 499
FREVERT, 393 498
FREVORT, 304
FREWIER, 120
FREY, 232 245
FRID, 483
FRIDOLPH, 156 165
FRIEDRICH, 307
FRIENDS, 254
FRINK, 61 71 98 120
FRISBY, 475
FRUECHTE, 299
FRY, 17 188 473
FULLER, 9 11 13 21 37 50 55 62 64 67 70 95 97 130 136 154 168 169 200 211 221 222 235 272 301 306 307 321 389 410 418 443 502
FUOSS, 380 392 472

Surname Index

FURCHINER, 183
FURCHNER, 161 175 182 185 187 220 229 296 416 417 483
GAADY, 216
GABLER, 20 472
GADDARD, 499
GAEBLER, 223 252 264 295 354 356
GAERTNER, 21 34 49 52 57 68 69 72 74 76 114 136 161 168 169 185 186 193 238 255 264 280 292 297 298 309 343 348 360 385 397 404 407 420 421 469 492 495
GAINES, 173 339
GALBRAITH, 251 258 318
GALBRATH, 251
GALLAGER, 42 130
GALLAGHER, 477
GAMBLE, 11 22 24 32 40 53 65 69 73 74 75 80 81 88 133 145 176 208 236 246 250 255 264 271 272 280 303 322 382
GAMMEL, 75 465
GANDT, 220
GANDY, 215
GANTT, 30 171
GARDILE, 155
GARDNER, 133
GARGENS, 429
GARMEN, 250 254
GARNER, 388
GARRETTSON, 133
GARRISON, 177
GARTNER, 178
GARWOOD, 97 147 191 213 262 342 382 435 472 475 481
GATES, 179
GAYLORD, 121
GEARHARD, 36
GEARHART, 104 112 414 429 430
GEHRKE, 354
GEISE, 120
GEISS, 380
GELDER, 161 182 224 255 276 289 337 363
GEMMELL, 289 495
GERARD, 299 388
GETMAN, 506
GETTMAN, 430
GIBSON, 39 65 74 130 136 159 161 172 249 253 299 349 350

GIBSON (Cont.), 354 382 438 465
GIDDINGS, 62 83 109 113
GILBERT, 148
GILCHREST, 109
GILDER, 264
GILDERSLEEVE, 48 71 96 160 162 164 165 192 208 209 219 236 239 246 276 283 295 310 311 312 395 412 436 480
GILES, 112
GILFERT, 187 232
GILILAND, 473
GILL, 76
GILLETTE, 130 146
GILLIAND, 470
GILSON, 224
GIRTEN, 265
GIRTON, 159 161 255
GIVENS, 499
GLANDT, 283
GLASENAP, 331
GLASER, 295 398 460 499
GLASS, 53 72 113 449
GLASSON, 388 444 449
GLEASON, 78 155 214 221 226 250 299 323 500
GODDARD, 75 76 133 300 498
GODRICH, 172
GOELDER, 186
GOFMAN, 126
GOLD, 390
GOLDIE, 144 154 240 252 342 349 361 385 436 455 494
GOLDSTIEN, 189
GOLL, 127 132 186 235 236 273 281 287 292 301 362 381 397 403 442 469 479 497 506
GOLTZ, 214 216 219 283 299 355 402 472
GOODRICH, 16 219
GOODWIN, 483
GOODYEAR, 160 184 185 216 252 261 324 382 495
GOOLD, 380
GOOP, 412
GORDON, 470
GOREHAM, 274 285 409 438
GORST, 129 132 140 145 147
GOSHORN, 95 100 136 139 144 218 254 349 365
GOSS, 41 56 160 247 257 321 322 344 347 448

GOSTICK, 342
GOTTSCH, 438
GOULD, 31 64 222 247 370 452 506
GOURGHAN, 26
GRABER, 263 361 383 398 492 496
GRACE, 276 285
GRAHAM, 438
GRANFIELD, 62
GRANGER, 48
GRANT, 393 394 441 459
GRAPMEYER, 392
GRAVES, 5 157 159 208 287 322 333 341 353 382 433 444 455 469
GRAY, 65 71 124 142 246
GRAYSON, 31
GREAR, 180
GREEBER, 474
GREEK, 166
GREEN, 31 148 191 220 262 298 317 368 399 440 443 449 455
GREENWALD, 25 198 246 257 354
GREENWOALD, 170
GREENWOOD, 368
GREER, 433 434
GREGG, 494
GREGORY, 147 150 161 164 185 334
GRIER, 159 160 187 195 233 235 247 250 255 265 266 271 287 324 337 342 450 454
GRIFFITH, 159 160 176 188 246 318 321 333 467
GRIFFITHS, 74
GRIGGS, 160 276 330 331 334 486
GRIM, 383
GRIMSLEY, 126 159 165 168 169 174 208 221 222 235 236 321 322 341 362 368 382 467 493 496 507
GROAT, 174 195 196 233 235 238 454
GROESBECK, 114 119
GROH, 10
GRONER, 56
GROST, 150
GROTHE, 106 138 173 216 384 385 446

GROVER, 225
GROVES, 397
GUARD, 37
GUDGEL, 179
GUDGELL, 471
GUDGLE, 176
GUE, 181 186 196 215 233 259 264 384 392 493 497
GUERNSEY, 94
GULDBERG, 164
GUNSOLLY, 164
GUSTAFSON, 159 160 463 465
GUSS, 326
GUSTINE, 439
GUTHRIDGE, 309
GUTKNECHT, 177
GUY, 171 172
GYLES, 439
HAAS, 147 226 434 466 486
HAASE, 332
HACKET, 412
HADLEY, 395
HAGELAND, 250
HAGELIN, 40 53 77 80
HAGLUND, 442
HAIN, 277 444
HAINES, 186 202 247 341 370 371 372 458 459 467
HAINING, 48
HAKE, 8 14 19 71 72 81 96 97 102 107 112 113
HALBERT, 299
HALE, 97 468
HALL, 16 97 181 187 252 266 375
HALLER, 301 437 455
HALLETT, 231 341 342
HAM, 219
HAMER, 186 256 264 380
HAMILTON, 10 25 63 128 152 157 166 172
HAMLIN, 145
HAMLOTH, 290
HAMMON, 61
HAMMOND, 31 101 159 160 162 165 335 434
HANARTH, 207
HANCOCK, 9 253 323 342 368 382 389 435 503
HANKE, 91
HANKINS, 343
HANLY, 81 82
HANSEN, 165 167 177 185 215

HANSEN (Cont.), 219 246 249 255 258 261 266 269 295 296 299 324 327 334 337 354 367 376 378 389 392 395 399 432 433 506
HANSOM, 406
HANSON, 16 44 105 148 160 263 265 342 424 454 480 481
HAPEMAN, 294
HARDENBAUGH, 214 254
HARDENBERG, 295 299
HARDENBERGH, 285
HARDENBURG, 64 219
HARDENBURGH, 31
HARDER, 180 186 194 234 253 258 263 274 434 455 456
HARDING, 240 440
HARDY, 17 18 115 370
HARGENS, 340 414
HARLAN, 220
HARMAN, 133
HARMES, 496
HARMON, 4 20 37 38 50 70 502
HARMSEN, 48 49 51 52
HARPER, 203 435
HARRIGFELD, 252 257 259 297 298 300 360 369 394 397 399 404
HARRIGFELDT, 156 169 193 196 197 204 216 221 222 234 236 263 267 325 332 389 463
HARRINGTON, 128 139 142 173 181 186 219 271 295 420 426
HARRIS, 8 22 23 49 52 62 88 147 386
HARRISON, 16 79 147 160 180 183 200 254 289 342 388 452 455 502
HART, 32 203 254 259 382 435
HARTPENCE, 106 111 504
HARVEY, 133 155
HASKELL, 350
HASSIN, 125
HASTINGS, 505
HATCH, 88 95 101 112
HATHERALL, 225 229
HATTIG, 412
HAVEMEYER, 75 226 277 342
HAVILAND, 81
HAYE, 236
HAYES, 49 53 62 69 73 127 214 232 254 322 323 329 349 373 395 460 481

HAYS, 216 502
HEADY, 455
HEALD, 364
HEALEY, 188 379 458
HEALY, 477
HEARST, 502
HEATH, 254
HECKERT, 160 200 272 445 453
HECKT, 293
HEDDIN, 406
HEFNER, 294
HEFFNER, 181
HEFMER, 148
HEFT, 130
HEFTI, 73 272 277 378 383 466
HEIGH, 386
HEIKES, 160 401
HEILNER, 10 23 44
HEILSEN, 218
HEISTER, 299 388
HELVA, 91
HENCH, 160
HENDERSON, 468
HENDRICKS, 487
HENRIQUE, 295
HENRY, 34 55 65 66 171 172 200 211 253 254 299
HENSCHKE, 212
HENSON, 177
HEREN, 224
HERNER, 18 31 64 94 174 352
HERRICK, 134 143
HERRINGTON, 61 215 292
HERRON, 212
HERZBERG, 258 391
HESS, 296
HESTEN, 86
HETTINGER, 76
HEWER, 226
HEWINS, 171
HEYER, 213 215 255 256 264 295 331 369 382 435 480 486 480 486
HEYL, 215
HIATT, 395
HICK, 58
HICKERT, 70
HICKMAN, 314
HICKS, 94 189 261
HIESTER, 167 272
HIGGENBOTHAM, 50
HIGMAN, 133

HILBREDS, 177
HILDER, 172 253 296 349
HILDRE, 439
HILDRETH, 343
HILGIT, 125
HILKE, 392
HILL, 159 160 180 194 322 369 371 372 408 410 453 455 456
HILLE, 340
HINCHMAN, 182 483
HIND, 133
HINDES, 147
HINDS, 114 119
HINES, 41 114 119 430 471 495 496
HINMAN, 16 106
HINRICHS, 86 127
HITCHCOCK, 160 161 270 271 288 301 302 385 433 455
HODGETTS, 273
HODSON, 194 322 331 333 337 338 354 456
HOFELDT, 274 434 463
HOFFMAN, 291 434
HOGAN, 175 243
HOGELAND, 445 453
HOGUE, 286 331 389 448 450 503
HOGUEWOOD, 133 167 184 222 235 271 272 276 445 453
HOHNEKE, 78
HOHNQUIST, 240
HOILE, 222 270
HOLLINGSWORTH, 81
HOLM, 460
HOLMAN, 32
HOLMES, 125 210 214
HOLST, 202
HOLTGREEN, 224 276
HOLTGREN, 452
HOLTGRENEVE, 125
HOLTZ, 101 156 182 185 216 225 226 236 291 295 303 350 366 368 396 398 422 469 481 495
HOLZ, 9 54 90
HONEY, 172 217 243 254 323 340
HOOD, 52 70 138 185 192 226 386 506
HOOPER, 382 445 456
HOOVER, 170 191 224 260 276 334 472
HOPE, 448
HORN, 254
HORNBY, 106 236 340 341
HORNICK, 133 296
HORST, 370
HOSTETTER, 160 242 266 382 452 455 486 495
HOUSE, 77 187 225 285 286 299 302 325 353 455 495
HOUSER, 33 88 225 353 360 374
HOWARD, 9 64 77 96 104 107 124 128 134 136 139 144 145 165 208 242 243 249 261 269 270 287 294 295 301 302 303 305 344 345 346 347 348 366 433 475 478
HOWARTH, 323 480
HOWE, 30 299
HOWORTH, 153
HOWSER, 39 71 78 115 116 117 118 323 444 469 485 492
HOYLE, 298
HUDSON, 37 246
HUFF, 74 231 441
HUFFER, 164
HUGHES, 75 118 121 122 142 150 153 185 186 212 246 257 326 349 354 403 463 480
HUGLIN, 125 144
HULT, 176 376
HUNGERFORD, 324
HUNT, 8 9 33 36 63 155 180 186 194 212 214 220 255 264
HUNTER, 2 3 4 5 6 7 8 11 12 13 17 18 33 54 71 97 99 102 107 152 160 166 175 186 196 204 221 222 229 233 235 238 244 246 255 257 258 264 267 272 276 280 295 310 322 341 343 344 345 346 347 348 349 360 368 372 375 376 380 381 382 389 394 395 397 401 406 407 411 412 414 425 431 433 434 435 438 441 442 443 444 445 446 447 449 453 466 472 473 475 488 489 491 492 502
HUPP, 215 233 255 265 402 480
HURD, 150
HURLBERT, 153 254 256 293 388 404 439 460 463
HURLBURT, 172 177 221 290

HURLBURT (Cont.), 295 349
HUSTED, 480
HUTCHINS, 213
HUTCHINSON, 170 192 235 381 435
HUTCHISON, 262
HUTH, 219 228 239
HYATT, 182 323 395 435 436
INGALLS, 186 200 332
INGHAM, 17
INGLES, 218
INGRAHAM, 69
IRELAND, 254
ISAAC, 211
ISAACS, 253 288 466 467
IVANSON, 302
IVORY, 105 131 240 242 243 271 287
JACKSON, 177 374
JACOBS, 160 165 178 180 181 188 195 196 197 203 234 239 252 257 259 263 267 297 300 331 369 389
JACOBSEN, 160
JACOBSON, 394
JAEGER, 244 412
JAMES, 90 135 187 219 220 256 262 264 277 286 288 354 366 407 455 479
JANS, 376
JANSAN, 144
JANSEN, 146
JASPERSON, 145
JASTRAM, 294 385
JASZKOYIACK, 215
JEANPERT, 476
JEFFERSON, 202
JEFFREY, 165 168 169 178 188 191 192 193 194 196 197 201 204 215 222 234 235 238 250 252 255 257 258 259 263 265 266 267 272 284 319 403 452 455 480 484 495
JENKINS, 74 165 169 214 218 288 350 451 455 463 467
JENNINGS, 368 370 375
JENSEN, 19 20 27 74 106 198 203 215 256 264 324 331 380 454 456 461 465 495
JENSON, 262 382
JENSTENS, 147
JENTON, 130
JEPPSON, 120

JETT, 184 272 368 382
JOCKINS, 442
JOHANSEN, 304 395 507
JOHNSON, 9 13 26 31 34 36 37 38 62 64 65 67 76 77 78 80 81 87 94 95 102 104 110 111 114 115 116 117 119 120 124 130 135 137 143 145 148 151 154 171 179 180 198 210 215 233 246 254 255 295 323 337 373 376 386 403 432 437 438 440 444 456 463 468 470 480 481 485 495 505
JOHNSTON, 64 97 120
JONES, 35 76 77 79 100 108 120 125 130 137 140 143 154 160 165 170 171 180 181 192 195 197 200 203 206 214 215 218 223 229 232 235 240 241 246 247 250 251 252 253 254 255 257 263 264 266 275 276 286 288 291 299 323 328 335 336 341 349 354 367 368 385 386 405 420 434 437 438 441 449 454 455 456 460 462 467 469 470 473 476 479 480 489 495 507
JONSEN, 263
JOOST, 263 274 331
JORDAN, 133 465
JORDEN, 463
JORGENSEN, 263 268 274 326 499
JOSLYN, 187 263
JOUST, 135
JOYNER, 138 152
JUDKINS, 164 484
JUHLIN, 89 100 185 191 224 270 283 414 452
KAI, 436
KAISER, 166
KAMPE, 155
KANT, 391
KANTZ, 443
KARNES, 277
KARO, 186 219
KASS, 127 296
KAUFL, 247 257 296 384
KAUFLE, 377
KAUFMAN, 218
KAUFFMAN, 171
KAUFLE, 212 354 388
KAUTZ, 285 343 407 440 494

Surname Index

KAY, 67 165 173 201 206 215 233 251 368 410 449 458
KEARNEY, 62
KEATING, 254 276 353
KEEFER, 174
KEEFOOT, 37
KEENAN, 455 476
KEENE, 430
KEGIR, 207
KEIPER, 227
KELLEHER, 500
KELLER, 70 108 126 319
KELLEY, 71 76 148 171 390 465 483
KELLOGG, 16 19 246 255 257 265 472
KELLY, 124 253 295 341
KEMP, 171 248
KENNEDY, 54
KENNY, 455 461
KENRICK, 438
KENYON, 130
KEOFOED, 456
KEPE, 130
KERCHEUR, 120
KETCHUM, 110
KETTLER, 118
KEYS, 152
KEYSOR, 487 493
KIEFER, 160
KIEPER, 341
KIEPKE, 463
KIESAU, 252
KILLIAN, 234 246 255 258 260 263 265 274
KILLION, 196 341 480
KILPATRICK, 172
KIMBALL, 271 287 404 469
KIMKEL, 412
KING, 76 121 127 128 132 139 149 201 219 247 248 252 287 292 295 322 349 355 366 373 402 441 442 470 472 479 485 493 497 506
KINGMAN, 388
KINGSLEY, 16
KINGSTON, 181 476
KINKAID, 164
KIPKE, 239 240
KIRCHMER, 429
KITE, 134 188
KLANAN, 297
KLAPMEIR, 171 256
KLAWAN, 88 319
KLAWOON, 254 353
KLEINE, 290
KLEUVER, 40 41
KLEVER, 109 110 123 149
KLINTWORK, 410
KLINTWORT, 364 408
KLOPPING, 159 162 265 455
KLOPTON, 163
KLOSTERMAN, 31
KLOTH, 268
KLUEVER, 77 80
KLUG, 319
KNAGGS, 71 406
KNAPP, 178 187 241 300 356
KNEBEL, 403 472
KNEBLE, 270 271
KNEEDLER, 157
KNIGHT, 460
KNOUSE, 174 196 296 342 435
KNOX, 339
KNUTSON, 256
KOCH, 159 172 453
KOEBKE, 180
KOEFOED, 74 109 188 204 217 235 238 254 258 260 263 276 440
KOEHLER, 341
KOENTY, 121
KOHL, 160 184 193 224 232 234 244 251 259 266 275 285 343 344 345 346 347 360 397 425 437 438 445 479 486 492
KOHLER, 341
KOMMER, 137
KORTH, 174 245
KORTRIGHT, 92 111 132 133 147 246 257 259 266 270 274
KOUNSE, 381
KRACHT, 505
KRAUS, 301 485
KRAUSE, 34 192 203 256 493
KREBBE, 250
KREBBS, 191
KREBS, 133 225 503
KREMKE, 505
KREITLE, 276 452
KRETTLE, 226
KRIE, 376
KRIMMINGER, 473
KRISTENSEN, 144
KROGER, 264
KROW, 50

Surname Index

KRUEGER, 250 257
KRUEGLER, 114 119
KRUGER, 154 157 160 172 175 180 220 224 226 263 291 295 296 305 349 353 373 377 381 382 392 439 444 460 471 494 502
KRUGERS, 506 507
KRUITGER, 209
KRUSE, 235 274 275
KUGLER, 130
KUHL, 307
KUHN, 88
KUNKELMAN, 190
LAASE, 212
LaCROIX, 137 199 444
LAGE, 144
LAING, 391
LAKAS, 412
LAKE, 64 75 112 144 369
LALK, 40 71 120 173 240 342 368 440
LAMB, 31 64
LAMBERT, 349
LAMM, 498
LANE, 25 439 455
LANG, 380 443 445
LANGE, 394 449
LANGENBURG, 377
LANSON, 120
LAPSELY, 54
LAPSLEY, 109
LARGEN, 397 414 492
LARIMER, 160
LARISON, 89 250 321 382
LARRISON, 246 255
LARSED, 485
LARSEN, 32 245 251 258 266 287 463
LARSON, 109 114 119 211 373 376 395 443 480
LASE, 166
LATHAM, 77
LAUGHLIN, 160 271 285 292 339 362 397 469 476 492
LAUMAN, 133 171 218 253 296 324 349 388 439 453 463
LAURIE, 448 479 486
LAWRENCE, 10 14 22 34 40 53 93 94
LAWVER, 471
LAYMAN, 246 277 445 453
LAYTON, 215

LEACH, 2
LEAGON, 274
LEAHY, 465
LEAMON, 16
LEAMY, 307
LEARNER, 182
LEASE, 374
LEASKE, 480
LEATHERBY, 201 349 463
LeCROIX, 148
LEDER, 114 119
LEE, 258 298 332 377
LEEDON, 28
LEENZE, 440
LEGAN, 445
LEHMAN, 130
LEHRER, 170
LEIBFRIED, 34 61
LEISENRING, 38 136 157 163 171 266 297 301 311 317 323 411 433 436 459 463 465 469 479
LEJEUNE, 133
LeMAY, 215
LEMHKUHL, 320
LEMMON, 207
LEMOBARD, 126
LEMON, 375 398 431 448 450 457 496
LEMONDS, 408
LENN, 328
LENSER, 217 414
LENTON, 437 438
LENZ, 187 233 236 238 251 273 324 342 368 409
LENZER, 395
LEOBSACK, 506
LEONARD, 250 342 434
LERNER, 160 494
LESSMAN, 160 208 212 217 287 389 472
LEUCK, 368 434 493
LEUCKE, 268 410
LEVERINGHOUSE, 166
LEVIN, 66
LEWIS, 55 80 91 92 96 125 137 142 146 152 65 172 173 175 180 185 186 202 203 229 232 234 236 247 253 256 265 266 287 296 299 338 341 368 388 404 405 425 441 467 480 497
LEWMAN, 401
LEY, 10 15 23 24 34 37 65 77

LEY (Cont.), 108 130 138 142 160 182 191 200 224 229 238 240 255 276 292 299 301 362 397 398 412 452 469 478 484 486 492
LICHTY, 298
LIEBERSTEIN, 126
LIEF, 235 238 267 289
LIKES, 147
LILLEY, 137
LILLARD, 201
LILLEJEBERG, 245
LILLIGEBERT, 295
LILLJEBERG, 126
LINDELL, 388 463
LINDLEY, 350
LINDLY, 22 35 40 67 119 122 149
LINDSAY, 138 165 287 322 342 368 404 471
LINN, 10 15 20 76 81 86 136 138 143 174 215 271 438 477 487 503
LIVERINGHOUSE, 341 368
LIVINGSTON, 177 449 479
LIVINGSTONE, 470 499
LLOYD, 367 390 394 433 448
LOBERY, 195
LOBSACK, 479
LOCKE, 153
LODGE, 10 17 35 45 49 50 53 55 57 58 67 69 71 73 75 76 81 89 91 92 95 104 105
LOHAER, 298
LOHBERG, 180 219 235 454 455 456
LONG, 28 71 133 138 165 170 181 196 215 222 232 236 247 257 262 300 393 434 455 458 470 471
LONGE, 211 495
LONGENBURG, 442
LONGNECKER, 135 188 203 219 239 250 257 333 336 337 338 349 367 464 496
LONND, 239
LORD, 120
LORE, 487
LORGE, 165
LOTSPIECH, 104 108
LOUND, 62 65 66 254 354 455 499
LOVE, 15 37 48 57 58 85 102

LOVE (Cont.), 138 165 214 265 295 299 355 368 385 388 455
LOVELACE, 144 149
LOVETT, 496
LOWDER, 215 481
LOWENBERG, 152
LOWER, 160 210
LOWERY, 483
LOWREY, 402
LOWRIE, 72
LOWRY, 165 214 215 236 323 399 456 480 484 485
LUDEKE, 270 272 409 438
LUDERS, 274 381
LUECK, 307
LUMSDEN, 256
LUND, 150 160 165 284 321 326 374 380 408 447 467
LUNDBERG, 158 255 264 299 322 480 507
LUNDBURG, 223 475
LUNDINS, 293
LUNDSEN, 264
LUS, 120
LUSH, 480
LUTH, 28 212 395
LUTT, 105 432
LUTZ, 90 184 226
LYON, 448
MAAS, 179 253 301 389 476
MacCONNELL, 247
MACK, 76 255 265
MACKAY, 317
MACKEN, 178
MADSEN, 146 395
MAHER, 175 179 219 228 257
MAHIKE, 219
MAHLKE, 299
MAHOLM, 7 135 160 277
MAIN, 126 150 151 171 225 257 271 277 292 301 362 397 427 459 499
MAKIN, 54
MALLORY, 395
MALONE, 62
MAMMEN, 376
MANGAN, 138
MANK, 246 440
MANNING, 17 57 70 130 135 136 138 139 153 165 168 177 178 214 247 256 257 265 344 345 346 347 382 385 404 435 448 472 497

Surname Index

MARKLEY, 145 287
MAROTZ, 414 429 484
MARQUARDT, 134
MARQUETTE, 112 144
MARRIOTT, 48
MARSH, 114 119 401 446
MARSHALL, 450
MARTEN, 351
MARTIN, 8 10 11 12 14 23 27 30 31 48 57 67 70 86 87 91 93 94 96 105 106 107 108 109 110 111 112 113 114 115 116 117 119 124 128 136 139 145 147 149 153 154 160 161 162 163 16? 168 176 178 179 180 181 182 185 186 187 198 203 212 213 217 230 232 234 238 239 251 252 255 258 264 266 268 272 276 277 281 289 290 293 301 307 334 337 338 356 385 408 409 413 475 483 501 502 504
MARUE, 221
MARVIN, 203 214 232 233 454
MASON, 79 160 240 241 242 251 271 277 410 437 438 465 472 480 495
MASS, 78
MAST, 240
MATHSON, 433
MATRAN, 240 277
MATSEN, 341 380
MATSON, 149 402
MATTHEWS, 242 248 269 270 285 292 318 319 322 335
MATTHEWSON, 350
MATTSON, 272
MAUDE, 343
MAUK, 81
MAURER, 31 49 53 62 69 73 81
MAXFIELD, 112 113
MAXWELL, 309 498
MAY, 189
McALEN, 190
McANNICK, 125
McBRIDE, 155 220
McBURNEY, 126
McCAFFREY, 178
McCANDISH, 55
McCANDLISS, 133
McCARTHY, 470
McCAULEY, 297
McCLINTOC, 263

McCLOUD, 163
McCLURE, 177
McCLUSKY, 157 162 173 183 227 254 255 257 285 295 299 373 388 392 402 469 470 485 486 493 494 498 503
McCOLLOUGH, 114 119 150 156
McCONAGHEY, 251
McCONNELL, 173 175 200
McCONOUGHEY, 234 255 264 266
McCONOUGHY, 165 194 222 287
McCOOL, 145 146 378 440
McCORKENDALE, 254
McCORKINDALE, 342
McCORNACK, 472
McCOY, 49 53 54 69 73 75 96 134 144
McCRARY, 225
McCREADY, 460
McDONALD, 120
McDONNELL, 268
McDOWELL, 504
McELRATH, 470 471 473
McELROY, 150
McFARLAND, 123 134 144 148
McFEE, 97 128
McGILL, 254 268
McGINNIS, 54
McGRAIL, 201 472
McGRATH, 189 190 253
McGREGOR, 230
McGUIRE, 211 230
McHENEKY, 120
McINSTOSH, 159 216 271 355 447 460 479 480 486
McINTYRE, 380
McKAY, 114 119 437
McKEAN, 484
McKEEN, 399 497
McKENIGAN, 483
McKENZIE, 276 277
McKINLEY, 222
McKINZIE, 481
McLAUGHLIN, 182 226 271 500
McLEOD, 54 101
McLOOD, 23
McMACKEN, 165
McMAKIN, 42 97 192 214 248 322 331 336 369
McMANIGAL, 214 236 255 256

Surname Index

McMANIGAL (Cont.), 265 268 300 322 341 379 391 401 434 495
McMILLAN, 214
McMILLIN, 455
McMIVAGAL, 368
McNEAL, 61 89 94 95 100 101 136 139 168 181 187 194 200 201 203 222 235 272 343 361 386 390 404 454 497 507
McNIGHT, 310
McNISH, 133
McNUTT, 16
McPHERRON, 370 458
McPHERSON, 256
McQUINN, 65
McQUINSTON, 389
McUMBER, 144
McVAY, 178 180 194 203 225
McVEY, 232
McVICKER, 166 272
McVICKERS, 160 236 248 501
MEAD, 465
MEADE, 395
MEAHAN, 41
MEAN, 178
MEARS, 54 55 62 74 94 97 109 167 246 250 254 382 385 404 434 450 499
MEHUS, 348
MEIERHENRICH, 449
MEIRE, 202
MEIRMAN, 53
MEISKE, 435
MEISKY, 466
MELICK, 149 448
MELLOR, 185 200 211 219 221 274 285 289 291 299 302 305 342 391 410 413 428 447 455 459 463 476 483 498
MELTON, 199
MENTIS, 27
MERCER, 120
MERRIAM, 24 65 77 107
MERRILL, 155 165 168 169 170 177 178 191 215 222 227 252 256 274 286 323 340 341 342 369 382 402 448 460 464 485 494 498
MERRIMAN, 9 22 33 42 184 219 228 239 240 246 384 385 455
MERTEN, 255 265
MERTON, 341

MESTHALER, 26
METCALF, 133 486
METON, 148
METTLEN, 34 70 94 115 116 117 124 125 128 135 136 138 139 158 159 203 215 225 231 234 247 251 256 261 263 269 270 275 292 295 322 324 326 409 434 443 481
METTLIN, 478
MEYER, 219 254 287 483 485
MEYERS, 299
MICHELS, 146
MICK, 161 173 207 263 380 432
MIDDLESTADT, 219 220 254 296 388 439
MIDDLETON, 99 202 221
MIDTGAADT, 145
MIELKE, 438
MIESKY, 212
MILDNER, 274 447
MILES, 159
MILLARD, 165 176 179 189 199 210 212 215 224 228 230 246 256 257 272 289 293 300 332 340 370 373 403
MILLER, 41 48 52 54 57 67 77 80 86 104 105 109 110 114 115 116 117 120 122 124 125 128 134 135 136 138 139 142 146 163 172 175 181 186 200 212 219 235 250 255 256 262 264 265 285 289 291 297 299 326 333 334 336 342 343 349 368 375 380 382 383 388 389 407 419 432 435 443 444 447 453 456 466 471 472 475 480 483 484 494 495 498 506
MILLIGAN, 10 15 64 111 133 134 150 152 160 161 300 447 470 483
MILLIKEN, 234 246 263
MILLNER, 226 267
MILLS, 75 408 436 450
MINER, 2 5 6 8 9 10 11 20 26 37 38 40 49 52 53 55 73 80 94 99 107 115 116 117 120 124 128 133 136 139 143 160 179 225 251 266 301 356 362 368 393 397 432 444 447 466 489 492 501
MINES, 165 295 365 437 486
MINIHAN, 202

MISKIMMENS, 185
MISKIMMONS, 237
MITCHELL, 20 70 109 111 120 165 169 217 222 225 246 251 257 263 277 295 341 350 383 402 427 442 459 469 480
MITTELSTADT, 234 239 384 391 430
MITTLESTADT, 181 252 353 354 388
MOATS, 156 247 253 257 404 445 497
MOCK, 131
MODING, 172
MOFFAT, 473
MOFFATT, 392
MOELLER, 376
MOGAREIDGE, 408
MOGARIEDGE, 409
MOIR, 332
MOHKE, 154
MOHLKE, 388
MONICLE, 200
MONK, 299
MONROE, 31 64
MONSON, 93
MONTGOMERY, 215 361 378 386 390 397 414 430 467 484 491 493 496
MOORE, 10 22 23 30 32 51 53 65 75 76 77 81 112 125 133 184 206 273 296 323 324 388 395 440 456 483 492 498 503
MORAN, 34 41 101 105 184 276 439 445 453 503
MOREY, 74
MORGAN, 23 53 61 62 80 132 261 481 505
MORGANSON, 109
MORIARITY, 105
MORIKE, 500
MORIN, 215
MORNE, 144
MORNS, 192
MORRILL, 171
MORRIS, 120 135 173 195 211 214 233 235 255 266 288 324 342 382 404 467 494
MORRISON, 166 212 248 400 472
MORROW, 305
MORT, 162 180 196 262 381 401

MORTON, 9 49 50 52 53 58 68 69 72 73 74
MORTY, 395
MORTZ, 431
MOSES, 37 77 115 116 117 118 130 139 142 161 287 467 481
MOSS, 455
MOSSMAN, 198 199 340
MOTTER, 145
MOUK, 173
MOUR, 173
MOWRY, 240
MOYER, 202 384 483
MUELLER, 144 148 190 214 296 299 349 439
MUHLER, 374
MUHLMEIER, 442
MUIRHEAD, 454 504
MULKEY, 175
MULLER, 155 179 187 204 220 479
MULM, 125
MULVANEY, 177 195 196 226 235 247 250 253 287 342 368
MUNDHENKE, 161
MUNSON, 411
MUNDY, 323 351 373 384 499
MURPHY, 446
MURRILL, 270 322
MURRY, 114
MUSTIFER, 163
MUTH, 263 275 333
MYERS, 10 20 24 34 50 63 74 80 104 111 124 128 149 208 255 287 289 305 383 431 447
NAFZINER, 31
NAGEL, 442
NAIRN, 382
NANGLE, 37 48 49 53 72 77 80 110 124 130 144 145 160 184 200 255 261 265 269 271 295 303 322 335 396 480 496
NARIN, 435
NEASHET, 67
NEEDHAM, 157 173 183 227 254 273 295 299 373 380 392 402 444 483 484 485 486 494 498 503
NEEHAM, 469
NEEL, 86
NEELY, 20 31 34 37 39 77 106 110 111 138 139 160 187 200 235 236 252 258 265 271 292

Surname Index

NEELY (Cont.), 295 318 329 330 334 344 345 346 347 348 381 382 398 420 447 453 456 478 484 492 497 498 506
NEFF, 149 219 272 284 343
NEHRING, 240
NEIBUHR, 23
NEIGENFIND, 133 138
NEIHART, 158 160 242 409 481
NEILAN, 97
NEIMAN, 159 231 304 381 406 442
NEISE, 500
NEISS, 262 321 444 465
NEITZKE, 301
NELSON, 30 92 94 106 114 119 133 147 155 177 182 191 196 198 210 218 226 246 251 257 268 276 277 282 283 284 303 304 333 355 374 383 395 408 440 455 486
NENNSON, 183
NETTLETON, 160 375 395 481
NEWHAM, 470
NEWMAN, 128 144
NEWTON, 76 107 109 110 127 132 143 246 259 266 334 392 426 427
NICHOLS, 31 211 214 391 392
NIELE, 500
NIELSEN, 27
NIELSON, 27 54
NIEMAN, 299 324 447 473 474 498 505 506
NINDEL, 159 476
NINDELL, 268
NOBLE, 133
NORLING, 13 14
NORRIS, 49 50 145 372 470 471 473
NORTHROP, 8 11 13 21 24 77 87 103 118 119 130 136 154 159 161 162 165 169 208 213 218 219 222 231 245 290 291 299 321 335 336 337 349 366 374 391 402 488 497 507
NORTON, 257 274 340 385 445 453 457
NUERENBERGER, 231
NUERNBERGER, 266 326 389 402 465
NUREMBERGER, 194
NURENBERGER, 111 120 187

NURENBERGER (Cont.), 191 231 291 337
NURNBERGER, 380 436
NURNBURGER, 110 115 116 117
NUSBAUM, 69 82 111 150
NYDAHL, 213
NYE, 66 88 94 112 192 232 262 399 434 437 438
NYEBERG, 259
NYEGREN, 254
O'BRIEN, 189 389
O'CONNOR, 498
O'FLAHERTY, 206
O'HARA, 61 106 363
O'NEAL, 152
O'ROURKE, 471
OAK, 291
OBERY, 93
OBST, 322 333
ODEEN, 31
OGDEN, 213
OLDS, 495
OLESON, 89 218 456 470
OLIN, 6
OLINGER, 112 113
OLIVER, 163 206 323 354
OLK, 215
OLMSTEAD, 143 160 161 175 331 480
OLMSTED, 172 185 217 221 225 250 257 259 272 274 297 301 303 318 334 362 388 396 398 428 439 447 480
OLSEN, 226
OLSON, 114 119 124 373 434 446
OMAN, 41 130 140 153 170 254 285 382 446 456
OMEY, 408
ORCUTT, 76 342
ORR, 352
ORTH, 405
OSBORN, 68 106 124 185 191 192 194 232 235 236 260 322 362 385 434 445
OSBORNE, 407
OTT, 194 215 322 372
OTTE, 180 186 195 235 258 263
OTTO, 202
OVERTURF, 395
OVERMAN, 341 465
OWEN, 16 165 342

OWENS, 131 170 287 434 455 457 502
OXFORD, 10 69 72 74 82 99 104 108 218 221 296
PACKER, 432
PACKRANDT, 215
PADEN, 369
PALMER, 159 239 333 334 450 480
PANABAKER, 96
PANKOW, 90
PANKRATZ, 274 335
PANKRAUTZ, 244
PARISH, 64
PARK, 208 249 261 262 269 270 289 356 459
PARKER, 80 112
PARKS, 249
PARRISH, 30
PARSON, 187 298
PARSONS, 165 232 236 297 368 373 392 440
PASSEWALK, 483
PASSON, 144
PATCH, 61 101
PATE, 303 388
PATES, 208
PATRICK, 133
PATTERSON, 11 13 15 32 33 42 51 58 62 76 108 130 133 218 379
PAUL, 76 126 271 298 427
PAULSKI, 161
PAULSEN, 244 263
PAULSON, 247 258 276
PAWELSKI, 196 481
PAWLSKI, 303
PAYNE, 155 331
PEARSON, 293 319
PEAVEY, 90 93 267 283 285 471 487
PECK, 108
PECKARD, 196
PEIPENSTOCK, 186
PEIPER, 88
PELLEREN, 41
PENDLETON, 16
PERDUE, 160 251 448 480
PERFECT, 161 191 217 220
PERINS, 259
PERKINS, 17 187 188 203 204 214 233 252 266 350 399 449
PERRIN, 91 140 142 150 215

PERRIN (Cont.), 322 337 350 382 470 483
PERRINE, 122 134
PERRY, 23 34 40 70 94 95 96 109 138 142 154 172 354 388 499
PETER, 27
PETERS, 85 165 167 170 210 380
PETERSON, 31 64 89 105 130 160 180 184 186 187 194 195 212 215 234 237 249 250 258 267 269 274 331 455 459 475 500 503
PETTY, 176
PETTYS, 172 175
PFEIL, 275 500
PFELL, 246
PFIEL, 262 291 341 368
PFLUGER, 187 203
PHEIL, 120
PHIEL, 91 460
PHILLEN, 481
PHILLEO, 81 127 134 144 149 160 186 221 222 228 235 261 262 266 267 269 285 295 334 335 336 339 380 388 402 433 443 447 465 475 495
PHILLIPS, 5 9 34 52 87 146 179 293 298 461
PHILPOT, 237
PICKARD, 195 235 262 395
PIEPENSTOCK, 125 182 225 233 272 287 334 381 424 430 432 447 469 476 492
PIEPGRASS, 215
PIERCE, 16
PILE, 174 250 257 274 340 363 364 373 410 443 480 492
PINGERY, 77
PINGREY, 90 151 219 283 342 350 386 443 459 461
PIOFESEL, 138
PITKINS, 99
PITTENGER, 51 57 112 118 135 142 170
PITTINGER, 67
PLATNER, 76
PLIMPTON, 249
PLUMB, 402 494
POCKRANDT, 318 443
PODDOLL, 301
POFF, 377 406

Surname Index

POLLEY, 120
PONCE, 430
POND, 202 274 389
POPE, 91
PORTER, 9 49 53 69 73 80 81 82 94 130 145 160 161 162 165 171 192 253 264 333 335 336 337 338 404 448 459 463 480 497
PORTERFIELD, 182 191 224 276 318 434 452 486 501
POTE, 137
POTTER, 327
POUCHER, 488
POUTY, 240
POWELL, 71 139 165 187 323 455
POWERS, 32 410
PRATT, 64 473
PRESCOTT, 90 145 151 163 262 266 331 384 386 495
PRESTON, 75 183 231 249 269 273 277 322 355 480 495 504 507
PRICE, 71 137 402 403
PRIEST, 112
PRINCE, 159 171 180 194 195 247 285 287 382 435 453 456
PRITCHARD, 176
PROUTY, 277
PRYOR, 454 470 480 495
PULLEN, 77 453
PULS, 40 473
PUTZIER, 268
QUINLIN, 65
QUINN, 49 52
RABER, 112
RAGO, 481
RAHDER, 283
RAINBOLT, 240 302
RALPH, 253
RAMSEY, 322 355 368 372 373 441 455 476
RAND, 137
RANNOW, 39
RANSDALL, 377
RANSDELL, 382 454
RANTENBERG, 157
RANTENBURG, 170
RANTONBERG, 286 465
RASH, 278 279 280 281 282 283 292 293 295 296 297 298 301 304 305 306 308

RASH (Cont.), 309 310 311 312 314 315 317 321 331 502
RASHMAN, 173
RASMENSEN, 27
RASMUSEN, 430
RAWHOUSER, 202 218
RAWLINGS, 178 215
RAWSON, 76
RAYBURN, 124 178 181 197 259
RAYMER, 16
RAYMOND, 23 48 54 88
REAL, 252 256
REALE, 120
REAM, 470
REAUGH, 242
RECEIVER, 133
REDMER, 19 20 154 155 240 256 264 318 407 412 430 483
REDOUTY, 69
REECE, 354
REED, 23 48 92 137 239 256 264 446 471 476
REES, 29 30 33 39 40 75 467
REESE, 9 166 229 245 499 504
REHLING, 390
REHMUS, 266 267 287 291 391 399 435
REIBOLD, 296 341 468
REICHERT, 170 181 225 233 235 256 258 262 264 267 326 369 388 446 456 460 481
REINHART, 66 233
REINKING, 76
RELG, 144
RELYEA, 132 215 434
REMHARDT, 386
RENICK, 165 170
RENNETT, 115
RENNICK, 90 106 122 142 145 148 256 265 310 311 342 350 379 385 386 387 443 446
RESACKER, 376
RETHWISCH, 213
REYNOLDS, 161 174 178 179 181 183 185 186 187 200 203 208 209 214 226 228 239 259 266 289 293 295 299 301 311 314 318 319 320 322 331 340 355 369 409 475 481 496
RHEA, 61
RHEMUS, 310 434
RHODES, 307

RHORKE, 440 483
RICE, 10 48 114 119 165 395 477
RICHARDS, 76 140 183 217 238 240 276 280 301 381 382 385 430 449 452 472 479 486 499
RICHARDSON, 1 5 21 48 80 136 171 176 192 208 233 234 248 250 258 321 362 480 489 503
RICHEY, 106 262
RICHIE, 70
RICHMOND, 114 118 119 120 401
RICKABAUGH, 89 118 160 255 264 292 340 363 381 440 452 486
RICKARDSON, 130
RIDDLER, 106
RIDGE, 40
RIDWELL, 137
RIECHART, 203
RIED, 249
RIGGS, 185
RILEY, 123 132 171 174 303 304 331 337 338 434 452 486
RITCHEY, 170 198 199 210 238 249 251 272 285 368 434 454
RITCHIE, 37 195 262
RITZE, 187
ROACKER, 328
ROBB, 96
ROBBINS, 186 219 322 342 366 420 432 465
ROBERTS, 144 214 241 256 261 264 402 484
ROBERTSON, 337
ROBINSON, 9 49 52 68 72 87 92 115 120 169 215 229 247 253 323 374 389 404 440 441 459 494 495
ROBITAILLE, 14 34 69
ROBSIN, 343
ROCK 34 94 105 110
RODOCKER, 499
ROE, 118 123 148 159 160 164 166 173 186 217 292 341 362 368 397 469 492
ROEBER, 106
ROGERS, 130
ROGGOW, 170 499
ROHDE, 177 290
ROHLFS, 221

ROHMUS, 234
ROHRKE, 411 412
ROHWER, 207
ROLAND, 286 291 498
ROMAN, 152 161 166 494
ROMJINE, 180
ROOSA, 305 507
ROOT, 17 20 70 125 133 142 176 185 215
ROOTH, 9
ROSE, 166
ROSEKA, 237
ROSLMAN, 166
ROTEMAN, 244
ROTTER, 382 498 499
ROUNDY, 442
ROUSE, 181
ROUSH, 186 240 241 323
ROUSS, 215
ROWE, 97
ROWLES, 492
ROWSE, 215
ROYER, 332
RUBECK, 211 375 388
RUDAT, 172 219
RUFF, 289
RUNDELL, 171 303 322 396 481 495
RUNYON, 224
RUSH, 325 388 457
RUSS, 375
RUSSEL, 31 94 111 115 222
RUSSELL, 9 34 36 142 153 154 178 180 181 188 189 192 196 197 203 206 221 235 238 239 244 252 257 260 263 267 275 296 299 318 332 337 342 349 354 360 369 382 388 397 399 442 452 453 460 461 492 493 505
RYTHER, 37 93 98 99
SABENSON, 438
SACKERS, 468
SAHO, 161
SAHS, 350
SAID, 147
SALTER, 120 236 283
SALTERS, 169
SALTZWEDEL, 73
SAMSON, 236
SAMUEL, 486
SAMUELSON, 90 165 195 258 483

Surname Index

SAND, 158
SANDAHL, 160 207
SANDERS, 148 248
SASSMAN, 388 439 463
SAUNDERS, 120 133 138 253 296 391
SAUTTER, 377
SAVIDGE, 184 187 272 282 439 444 452
SAWYER, 136 221 296
SAWYERS, 2
SAYLOR, 480
SCACE, 181 200 228 261 269 333 409 475 481
SCANNELL, 155 188
SCARR, 398
SCHEEL, 198
SCHLACK, 485 493
SCHLOTFELDT, 158
SCHLUNS, 300
SCHMIDT, 437 465
SCHMILL, 299
SCHNEIDER, 86 456
SCHNIEDER, 219
SCHNUR, 23 37 57 67 77 106 109
SCHOENFELDT, 307
SCHONEBAUM, 395
SCHRADER, 483
SCHREIBER, 223
SCHRIEBER, 155
SCHRODER, 76 180
SCHROEDER, 174 184 191 194 195 215 255 265 266 275 281 473
SCHROER, 180
SCHUHARDT, 28
SCHULTHEIS, 265
SCHULTHIES, 255 434
SCHULTIE, 408
SCHULTZ, 429 484 501
SCHULZ, 203 217 235 251 340 393
SCHUMACHER, 216 226
SCHUSTER, 471
SCHUTT, 202
SCHWAERZEL, 173
SCHWEARZEL, 338
SCHWEIGARD, 456
SCHWERGALD, 454
SCOFIELD, 380
SCOTT, 2 5 6 75 85 89 92 104 134 198 238 307 384 489

SCRANTON, 439
SEARIGHT, 331
SEARS, 504
SEASTRAND, 434 502
SEARS, 23 34 106 134 160 221 222
SEBALD, 89 166 194 204 389
SECHLER, 65 133
SEDWICH, 384
SEDGEWICK, 155 200
SEERY, 409
SEIBER, 48
SEIFKEN, 219
SEIK, 502
SEIVERS, 476
SELBERG, 403
SELLAR, 456
SELLEN, 440
SELLON, 320 494 495
SERANTON, 182
SERBER, 215 394 448
SESSIONS, 401
SESSUP, 170
SEVERNS, 220
SEWALL, 72
SEWELL, 10 49 68 74 77 108 228 261 269 480
SHABRAM, 498
SHAFEE, 177
SHAFER, 272 285 325
SHANNAHAN, 458
SHANNON, 165 215 221 236 240 255 263 285 303 381 399 440
SHARP, 114 119 144 158 289 340 350
SHATTO, 339
SHAW, 44 110 111 124 125 128 133 136 142 149 156 170 203 215 372 481 498
SHAWGO, 189 196 234 250 263 274 341 348 382 495
SHAY, 193 232 262 495
SHEA, 181
SHEETS, 501
SHEHAN, 137
SHELDON, 254
SHELLENBERG, 214 263 287 434
SHELLINGTON, 183 380 481
SHEPARD, 31 350 472
SHEPHARD, 300
SHEPHERD, 77

SHERBAHN, 34 55 56 106 185 206 235 236 349 355 364 397 423 447 469 492 507
SHERBIN, 94
SHERE, 184 430
SHERMAN, 42 54 106 141 142
SHERO, 216
SHEULTHEIS, 165
SHIELDS, 106 110 170
SHINBUR, 408
SHINKLE, 227
SHINN, 138 223 434 437
SHIPLEY, 430
SHIPPEY, 342
SHIPPY, 343
SHIRTS, 127 134
SHIVELY, 477
SHOEMAKER, 218
SHOENHOLZ, 120
SHORT, 91 251 266
SHORTEN, 302 325 328 431
SHOWGO, 146
SHRADER, 78
SHUEL, 220
SHUFELT, 107
SHULTHEIS, 171 404 452 459 478 486
SHULTHIES, 448 479
SHULTZ, 287 303 478
SHULZ, 269 305
SHUMWAY, 61 64 101 186 219 221 254 257 460
SIEFKEN, 180
SIGLER, 119
SIGWORTH, 335 336 338 339
SIMERMAN, 180
SIMMERMAN, 168 178 180 195 196 232 235 262 399 456
SIMMONS, 69 75 94 139
SIMON, 285
SIMONS, 215
SIMONSON, 269
SIMONTON, 269 325 332
SIMPSON, 215
SINES, 28 33 137 266 287 440 442
SINGER, 172 175
SIRES, 499
SJOBLOM, 468
SKADDEN, 455
SKAHILL, 474
SKEEN, 18 25 29 40 49 65 72 74 108 152 174 179 222

SKEEN (Cont.), 227 240 271 385 414 445 447 465 473 475 501 507
SKEENS, 138
SKIFF, 273
SKILES, 80 158 180 322 432 478 480 486
SKINNER, 390
SLAHN, 383 505
SLATER, 9 10 22 29 31 37 42 49 53 62 65 69 75 77 80 82 83 86 87 105 109 110 123 130 134 443 470 504
SLAUGHTER, 165 179 180 258 287 296 368 433 464
SLOAN, 171 259
SLOCUM, 444
SMITH, 10 16 17 26 34 37 38 61 72 73 75 76 77 79 80 81 92 94 95 106 111 157 160 163 173 176 177 181 186 200 206 19 227 232 234 239 252 255 256 258 262 265 267 294 299 331 338 339 388 392 404 405 411 412 439 442 448 473 479 506
SNEATH, 109 160 182 219 323 349
SNELL, 213 456
SNODDY, 246
SNOWDEN, 37
SNYDER, 173 219
SODERBERG, 251
SOENNEKEN, 39 90 147 342
SOHNSON, 148
SOHRN, 388
SOLEMELL, 376
SONNEKEN, 160 470 507
SORENBERGER, 160 219
SORENSON, 285 483
SORRENSON, 252
SOUDERS, 375
SOULES, 160
SOWERS, 289
SPAHR, 109 165 230 231 246 247 255 262 265 325 431 448
SPANNAN, 125
SPARMAN, 137
SPEARS, 126
SPEER, 97
SPENCE, 211
SPENCER, 32 207 254 295 466
SPERRY, 2 5 352 489

Surname Index

SPHAR, 77 80
SPIKE, 250 272 431
SPITTGARBER, 456
SPRAGUE, 134 144 369
SPRAT, 227
SPRING, 141
SPRINGER, 243 244
SQUIRES, 472
STAARM, 374 469
STAGE, 481
STAHN, 274
STALLCUP, 8
STALLSMITH, 149 292 322 342 355 450 455
STALSMITH, 165 247 248
STAMBAUGH, 86 287 378 410
STAMBLOCK, 496
STAMM, 214 251
STANLEY, 91
STANN, 267
STARKS, 175
STARMM, 460
STARR, 28 58 71 76
STEECE, 114 119
STEEL, 215
STEELE, 8 9 11 12 18 19 20 21 24 37 42 67 76 91 94 95 103 104 106 130 133 138 165 169 174 226 238 382
STEFFEN, 332
STENNER, 457
STEPHENS, 171 183 202 204 217 235 250 283 348 399 434 455 456 480 495
STERRETT, 70 109 110
STETSON, 175 349
STEVENS, 163 218 268 325
STEWART, 26 146 154 184 215 219 235 250 349 364 402 409 463
STILES, 128
STINER, 277 471
STINROD, 390 462
STOBER, 391 433
STOCKING, 478
STOCKWELL, 376 395 436
STOLTENBERG, 213 214
STONE, 9 112 143 147 156 171 217 218 257 258 272 296 342 376 495
STONER, 93
STONKE, 237
STORTZ, 298

STOWE, 76
STRACHAN, 34
STRAHAN, 36 41 42 76 318 379 381 397 418 434 447 449 458 467 492
STRAHN, 154 254 299 321
STRAINE, 256
STRANE, 252
STRATE, 20 246
STRATES, 375
STRAW, 99
STRICKLAND, 37 63 76 94 99 132 159 297 321 333 378 467
STRINGER, 164 182 191 217 225 231 246 263 269 275 276 280 292 322 355 373 398 400 434 442 486 493
STROHN, 176
STROMBERG, 202 388
STROMSBERG, 465
STROMSBURG, 463
STROTE, 435
STUART, 388
STUBBS, 219 257 274
STUCKEY, 81
STUMP, 250
STUMPF, 263
STYRES, 275
SUHR, 182 276 411
SUING, 90
SULLEN, 162
SULLIVAN, 160 161 162 185 200 206 246 270 391 417 418 434 448 480
SUNDAHL, 262 349 369 373 446
SUNDALL, 134 172 221 256 266 455
SURBER, 261 269 303 325 382 443 446 448 456 475 480 498
SUSSENHAM, 94
SVAGERSON, 138
SWAN, 160 202 305 335 336 419 447 448 458 506
SWANSON, 179 210 258 272 323 459 464
SWARD, 470
SWARTZ, 160 290 342 368 473
SWEET, 122
SWEGART, 472
SWEIGARD, 495
SWEIGART, 460
SWENSON, 215 355 389

Surname Index

SYDOW, 187 203 414 429
TACKERBERRY, 218
TADLOCK, 391 465
TALBERT, 32 42
TALBOT, 220 299 388 443 480
TALBOTT, 163 219
TALLMAN, 137 220 223 253 299 439
TAMBEAGE, 114 119
TAYLOR, 37 49 52 58 72 74 76 80 86 87 92 96 98 106 108 110 114 119 133 134 137 145 148 152 157 164 167 182 183 215 222 226 248 265 270 274 292 322 350 355 372 373 395 411 433 453 473 481 485
TEDRICK, 446
TELL, 443
TEMPLIN, 25 62 125 157 253 323 385 440
TERWILLIGER, 334 506
THARP, 393 394 395 445
THAYER, 99
THEIS, 290 328 438
THEOBALD, 163 188 206 225 227 242 243 271 285 286 289 292 293 294 318 329 330 354 410 417
THIELMAN, 343
THIES, 386 437 441 455
THOMAS, 173 212 258 446 456 467 493 499
THOMPSON, 1 4 22 25 67 68 76 92 137 148 179 184 187 188 200 201 208 213 214 228 250 261 262 269 277 293 341 372 391 455 474 481 498
THOMSEN, 258 430
THORPE, 165 202 243 322
THUN, 394
THURSTON, 472
TIDRICK, 163 273 455 495 496 501
TILLMAN, 474
TILLSON, 172 216 220 254 256 323
TIMMONS, 138
TIRRILL, 75
TITSWORTH, 216 243 460 478 482 483 502
TOFT, 198
TOLANDER, 74 114 119
TOLERTON, 349

TOLL, 444
TOLLERS, 476
TOLLERTON, 175
TOLLES, 133 436
TOLLINGER, 61 63 87 101 104 108
TOLLMAN, 121 122 129 296
TOMLINSON, 155
TOMPSON, 381
TONLINSON, 255
TOWER, 160 216 217 229 236 249 259 344 345 346 347 381 426
TOWL, 134 143
TOWNS, 54 65 66
TOWNSEND, 164
TRACEY, 296
TRACY, 73 75 110 165 200 214 219 226 254 285 296 318 349 388
TRAIN, 134
TRAVER, 217
TRAVIS, 57 58 67 69 74 88 89 95 97 100 109 473
TRENN, 392
TREVERT, 285
TRIPP, 96 352
TROTTER, 24 25 166 241 258 300 349
TRUEDLER, 233
TRUMBULL, 431
TRYON, 120
TUCKER, 172 270 289 303 382
TURNER, 495 502 503
TYLER, 171 184 392
TUCKER, 126 129 134 160 174 219 228 271 290 295 341 349 355 396 427 438
TUHN, 174
TWEED, 388
TYSON, 445
ULRICH, 137 145 155 247 258 301 307 323 341 342 368 382 391 404 409 412 484
ULRICK, 179
UTECHT, 154 340 342 483 495
UTECT, 454 456
UTRECHT, 120
UTTER, 165 167 222 245 246 259 291 295 331 334 423 486 500
VAASE, 162
VAFFKAMP, 368

Surname Index

VAHLKAMP, 144 290
VAIL, 215 254 256 299 398
VAL KAMP, 259
VAN CAMP, 122 126 173 212 219
VAN DER SHULE, 61
VAN DUSER, 489
VAN NOONAN, 198
VAN NORMAN, 498
VAN PELT, 202
VAN SHUR, 254 296 353
VAN VELSOR, 10
VAUGHN, 202 219 305 367 410 448 464
VAUGHT, 395
VENERBERRY, 155
VENNERBEY, 335
VENNERBURG, 295
VERNON, 480
VERGES, 504
VERTERGEN, 383
VICK, 403 472 495
VIERGUTG, 503
VINCENT, 180 188 191 194 224 323 341 452 455
VINSANT, 382
VOGET, 233 274 424 471
VOLDENBERG, 436
VOLPP, 153 155 181 223 225 238 244 274 276 354 381 382 385 434 469
VON SEGGERN, 468
VOORMAN, 352
VOSE, 200
VOSK, 130
VOSTEEN, 144
VRENDENBERG, 277
VROMAN, 2 5 6 9 50 489
WACHOB, 52 53 72 74 75 80 81 144 237 473
WADDEL, 170 495
WADDELL, 192 233 235 238 250 251 262 266 298 331 369 392 399 455 500 503
WADE, 16 17 350 440 495
WADSWORTH, 161 165 168 170 187 189 190 235 334 386 480
WAECHTER, 198
WAFFLE, 254
WAGNER, 120 145 388
WAIT, 219
WAITE, 299 476
WAITT, 42

WAKEFIELD, 94 340
WALDEN, 165 215 254
WALDREF, 220
WALKER, 87 243 307 360
WALKINS, 146
WALL, 2
WALLACE, 10 34 49 52 53 73 74 75 86 89 94 111 114 119 120 291 382 385
WALLIS, 410
WALLOR, 221
WALTER, 299
WALTERS, 42 52 72 88 92 104 119 135 145
WALTON, 54
WANTOCH, 179
WARD, 166
WARDDRIP, 171
WARNER, 10 15 23 50 91 104 137 191 224 276 442 452 486 506
WARNOCH, 276 469
WARNOCK, 16 70 114 119 125 155 261 269 274 442
WARREN, 96
WASHBURN, 104 159 256 262 264 454 495
WATERBURY, 449
WATKINS, 173 175
WATSON, 210 225 227 291 300 303 304 399
WATTERS, 94
WATTS, 171 173 220 470
WEATHERALL, 314
WEATHERHOLD, 274
WEATHERHOLDT, 144 155
WEATHERHOLT, 71 76 106 170 192 202 234 238 239 243 246 254 255 298 299 328 331 341 368 388 431 442 444 455 457
WEATHERILL, 355
WEAVER, 36 149 191 255 261 262 264 269 293 478 481
WEBBER, 238
WEBER, 115 116 117 128 131 161 179 184 185 189 200 212 248 274 364 422 423 437 438 447 467 486
WEBSTER, 388 408 439 463
WEDNT, 165
WEIBLE, 440 469 485 486
WEICH, 219 392
WEIGLE, 331

Surname Index

WEIR, 75
WEISEMANN, 298
WELBAUM, 162 219 497
WELCH, 11 12 21 27 30 31 37
  58 67 82 95 97 115 116 117
  118 119 126 134 162 168 171
  174 178 182 191 193 208 219
  220 224 228 238 252 254 276
  290 307 318 355 360 397 427
  468 486 488 497 506
WELDEN, 492 501
WELDON, 120
WELKER, 250 274 324
WELLBAUM, 251
WELLS, 173 179 398
WELSCHLAGER, 179 340
WELSH, 469
WELTY, 234 238 259 367
WENDT, 78 120 232 331 342
  368 474
WENT, 219 241
WENTT, 332
WERNICK, 126 211 240
WERT, 259
WESSELSCHMIDT, 220
WEST, 165 187 194 236 404
WESTERHAUS, 448 453 486
  498
WESTERHOLD, 384
WESTLUND, 270 466
WESTON, 184
WESTROPE, 215 217 370 405
  442
WETHERBY, 148
WHEATON, 9 87 91 334 337
WHEELER, 54 215
WHIPPERMAN, 223 382 395 453
WHIPPLE, 237
WHITAKER, 123
WHITE, 70 77 81 86 160 178
  191 192 200 210 213 249 294
  323 324 344 345 346 347 350
  360 369 397 400 443 447 492
  493 496 497
WHITED, 227 350 402 409 430
  437 460 469 470 479 494 498
WHITHAM, 75
WHITING, 9 63
WHITMAN, 439
WHITNEY, 114 119 341 381 462
WHITTAKER, 31 64
WHITTEN, 2 3 406 489
WHITTON, 10 63 77 296 352

WICHMAN, 246 449
WICKE, 215
WIDLEY, 137
WIER, 368
WIFFEN, 329
WIGHT, 158 228 230 239 244
  245
WIGHTMAN, 35 37 38 49 86 140
  163 166 171 173 204 218 237
  253 266 296 317 341 349 369
  388 438 439 448 463 498
WILBER, 164
WILBUR, 35 50 158 160 212
  219 225 244 254 259 268 295
  340 385 389 422 442 445 460
  476
WILCOX, 168 178 192 212 255
  439
WILCUT, 86 107 112
WILHELM, 165 254
WILKERSON, 158
WILKINS, 21 26 34 37 65 78 94
  120 169 233 318 331 405 427
  469 474 498
WILKINSON, 5 32 40 114 322
  408 465
WILL, 240 290 293 325 328 404
  405
WILLIAMS, 155 159 161 182
  184 191 200 222 233 235 236
  251 259 264 266 292 317 339
  343 362 368 380 385 386 404
  411 445 447 452 473 475 480
  493 499 502
WILLIAMSON, 323 435
WILLS, 121
WILSON, 154 169 170 177 187
  194 225 231 234 250 251 253
  255 265 350 365 418 432 439
  454 507
WINCHEL, 408
WINCHELL, 410
WINEBRENNER, 350
WINELAND, 215 265 466 468
WINGERT, 214 274 438
WINSOR, 145 175 182 447
WINSTON, 29
WINTER, 71 120 203 246 258
  296 298 299 486
WINTERBURN, 160 161 216 335
  337
WISCHOFF, 287 365
WISE, 49 53 54 72 74 75 89 97

Surname Index

WISE (Cont.), 114 115 130
WISHMAN, 258
WITLER, 287
WITMAN, 120
WITSAMUN, 293
WITT, 88
WITTER, 68 69 73 74 80 82 98 102 134 191 208 209 252 259 262 268 292 304 318 362 398 399 404 469 478 484 488
WITTIE, 349
WITTLER, 105 153 165 181 382 434 454
WJEESE, 114 119
WOEHLER, 243 315 355
WOELER, 256
WOELLER, 254
WOHLER, 172 438
WOHLERS, 437
WOLF, 152 153 161 170 172 175 219 228 254 261 269 290 293 410 467 481 495
WOLFSHIGHER, 375
WOLFSLAGER, 379
WOLLSCHLAGER, 383
WOLVERTON, 223 239
WOODALL, 10 41 75
WOOD, 81 171 219 343 439 495
WOODMEN, 216
WOODROW, 104
WOODS, 32 34 81 176 207 455
WOODWARD, 114 119 155 215 241 247 258
WOODWORTH, 307
WOOLEY, 78 147 169 248 466
WOOLSTON, 63 162 168 236 262 269
WORDLEY, 64
WORKING, 175
WORKINGS, 219 226
WORKMAN, 125 150 265
WORTH, 165 211 215 382 461 495
WORTHING, 149 224 382 435
WRIGHT, 34 40 55 65 68 70 78 79 114 115 120 125 134 144 147 179 215 219 248 253 262 287 289 291 296 303 306 310 311 312 315 316 322 327 341 379 381 385 387 389 396 398 399 400 430 448 460 472 480 481 483 484 495 499 506
WROBEL, 172 175 338

WYDAHL, 148
YALE, 133
YARYAN, 168 178 186 256 265 390
YENTER, 494
YOCUM, 277
YOKUM, 438
YOUNG, 327 449 473
YOUTZ, 130
YUNGDAHL, 250
ZEIGLER, 24 223 224 397 399
ZEILKE, 253
ZEIMER, 168 180 193 223 233 238 239 240 254 255 266 297 298 391 392
ZEINER, 200
ZELKIE, 162
ZEMAN, 255
ZENAN, 181
ZIEGLER, 246 344 347 360 453 474 492 493
ZIELKE, 479
ZIEMER, 28 33 39 78 121 133 134 136 147 178 250 251 259 263 331 343 348 380 440 442 446 476 484 485 495 497
ZIMMERMAN, 23
ZOOK, 36
ZUTZ, 153 277 298 381 391 402 411 412 434 437 438 449 460 495
ZWALD, 44 66 70 72 73 77 83
ZWIGHT, 224 240

www.ingramcontent.com/pod-product-compliance
Ingram Content Group UK Ltd.
Pitfield, Milton Keynes, MK11 3LW, UK
UKHW021301180426
11947UKWH00015B/953